JOIN THE
ARMY AIR SERVICE
BE AN AMERICAN EAGLE!
CONSULT YOUR LOCAL DRAFT BOARD. READ THE ILLUSTRATED
BOOKLET AT ANY RECRUITING OFFICE, OR WRITE TO THE CHIEF
SIGNAL OFFICER OF THE ARMY, WASHINGTON, D.C.

LORDS OF THE SKY

ALSO BY DAN HAMPTON

NONFICTION

Viper Pilot

FICTION

The Mercenary

LORDS OF THE SKY

Fighter Pilots and Air Combat, from the Red Baron to the F-16

DAN HAMPTON

wm

WILLIAM MORROW
An Imprint of Harper Collins*Publishers*

HarperCollins books may be purchased for educational, business, or sales promotional use. For information please e-mail the Special Markets Department at SPsales@harpercollins.com.

FIRST EDITION

Designed by Jamie Lynn Kerner

Library of Congress Cataloging-in-Publication Data has been applied for.

ISBN 978-0-06-226201-1

14 15 16 17 18 OV/RRD 10 9 8 7 6 5 4 3 2 1

YOU SHOULD LIVE GLORIOUSLY, GENEROUSLY, DANGEROUSLY. SAFETY LAST . . . WE WHO FLY DO SO FOR THE LOVE OF FLYING. WE ARE ALIVE IN THE AIR WITH THIS MIRACLE THAT LIES IN OUR HANDS . . . YOU CAN'T GET THAT FEELING IN ANYTHING ELSE.

—CECIL LEWIS, *SAGITTARIUS RISING*

CONTENTS

PART IV

DAWN OF THE JET AGE

AUTHOR'S NOTE

LORDS OF THE SKY is about the fighter pilot.

There is no way to study him without knowing something of the great conflicts that created him. Each of these subjects could be the work of a lifetime, and this is certainly true for some scholars. There is simply no way to mention everyone who deserves recognition in the past century of aircraft and weapons development, tactical innovation, and war. Nor is this the format to describe the immense dedication and sacrifices by all those who put aviators in the air to fight—you have my thanks and my hope that some author does your service justice as well. My intent in this book is to provide snapshots into key people, important technological innovations, and the places in which these aviators fought in order to better understand the impact that this past century has had upon us all.

The book begins with the Great War, as World War I was originally known, and in particular the Western Front. This is no reflection on the other vast battlefields of this war; I chose this as a starting point simply because the sky over the trenches was the birthplace of the fighter pilot. There were many fine pilots in other theaters who fought brilliantly, but the main event was here. Also, the development of fighter aircraft and the combat pilot was more closely tied to ground actions during the Great War than was the case in subsequent conflicts. Aviation services were a fledging military branch and closely attached to their parent armies. So the ground situation is explained in some detail to give the reader an explanation of *why* fighter development occurred as it did. The immense scale and relatively independent air campaigns of the future were just that—in the future. Everything that came later will reveal the debt we owe to a very few pilots, the Lords of the Sky, who shaped history and largely gave us the world we live in today.

LORDS OF THE SKY

PART ONE

THE WAR TO END ALL WARS: 1914–1918

Lo! thy dread Empire, Chaos! is restor'd;
Light dies before thy uncreating word;
Thy hand, great Anarch! lets the curtain fall;
And universal Darkness buries All . . .

—Alexander Pope

CHAPTER 1

"FROM FLIGHT TO FIGHT"

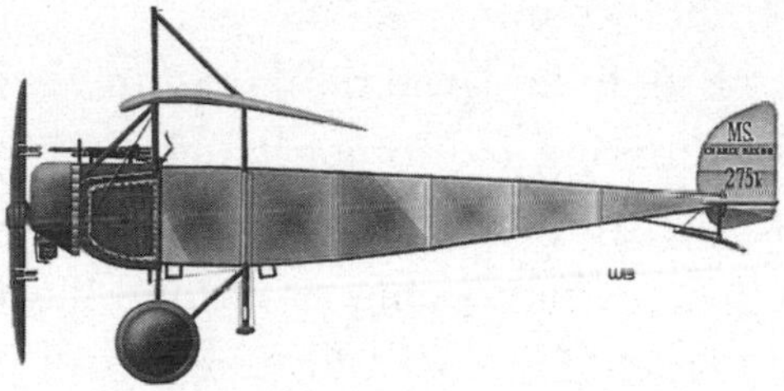

MORANE SAULNIER L

APRIL 1, 1915
DIXMUDE, BELGIUM

COLD.

It was cold. And wet.

The French pilot shivered in his sodden leather flying jacket, his shoulders hunched against the damp, chill air. Wriggling his icy toes against the rudder bar to restore a little blood flow, he decided the goggles were nearly useless. They were fogged over on the inside and fuzzy with rain on the outside, so he shoved them up and squinted through the wet air.

He opened the narrow throttle lever, and the 80-horsepower Gnome rotary engine roared. As he eased the stick back, the big tail surfaces bit into the thick air and the aircraft's nose came up. Wiping his streaming face, the pilot tugged the goggles down and stared through the spinning propeller, willing the clouds to disappear. Gray tendrils slipped over the wings as the little monoplane slowly climbed, motor straining to push it through the opaque clouds.

Roland Garros muttered, blinking against the blowing rain. Normally the French aviator could hunch down behind the windscreen and at least have a dry face, but not today. Smiling a bit, he reached up and touched the wooden grip of the machine gun bolted in front of him.

No rifle or pistol today. And no flare gun . . . *that* had been funny. Imagine, shooting at another flying machine with a flare pistol. He'd even heard that another pilot had trailed a grapnel behind an aircraft, trying to snag a German. Last week two of the *boche* had taunted Garros, and he was still infuriated; the observer had actually stood up in the backseat and grabbed his crotch before they'd flown away laughing.

But not today.

Teeth gleaming against his dark, wet skin, the pilot smiled. Today he had a surprise for them. He patted the weapon again, then tucked his hand back inside to keep warm. The Hotchkiss model 1907 was a French infantry machine gun, heavy and short-barreled, but he'd managed to fasten it on his machine in such a way that the Germans would never suspect a thing. He hoped.

As his Morane-Saulnier passed 1,500 meters, Garros broke into the brilliant April sunlight over Belgium. Off to the west, he could see darker gray patches of water through breaks in the clouds. He'd flown over the English Channel before the war, and the Mediterranean also. He shivered and hunched down deeper into the leather coat. *Why not fight in a warm place?*

This war had been going on for eight months now and showed no sign of ending soon. Christmas, they'd said; it would be finished by Christmas. Here it was April already, freezing and wet . . . and the food! Absolute shit. Not a decent cup of coffee since New Year's Eve.

Leveling off at 2,000 meters, he leaned out the fuel-oil mixture, shoved the goggles up once more, and felt cold rain seep in under his collar. Nudging the stick left, he pushed against the left rudder bar, and his boot slipped on the metal. The aircraft lurched to the left. Glancing at his watch, Garros did the math in his head and figured on another forty-five minutes of flying. He'd been working on a gauge that would show how many liters of fuel remained. It was a needle on a round dial, like a clock face, attached to a float in the fuel tank, but he couldn't get it to work right. Yet.

Squinting against the wind, Garros checked the machine gun. His mechanic had fashioned several metal straps and bolted them on the fuselage perpendicular to the cockpit. Then he'd welded two horseshoe-shaped brackets to the straps and mounted the gun. The gas-operated Hotchkiss fired twenty-four rounds from a metal strip inserted in the breech, and Garros had four such strips shoved into his boot tops, two in each leg. He'd have to load, aim, fly, and shoot, but he knew this would work. The attack would be unexpected, and this time he'd be the one laughing.

A flicker of movement caught his eye off to the southeast and he peered out over the wing. Nothing . . . then he saw it again. Blinking rapidly, he squinted through the wet mist.

There!

A dark dot crawling along just above the horizon where the clouds broke. The Frenchman smiled slowly. Just where he'd expect to find an observation plane. Shifting a bit in the seat,

Garros pulled his goggles down and leaned forward. Going to full rich on the fuel mixture, he pulled the lever slowly aft and opened the throttle. Staring intently at the other aircraft, he figured it to be at least five kilometers away. As he eased the stick back slightly, the Moraine began a gentle climb, and Garros angled it at a cloud well in front of the German.

Well, he didn't know for certain it was a *boche*, but he'd put himself in a good position anyway. With that thought, he reached down and yanked one of the ammo strips from his left boot. Both came out, and the second one clattered down to the floorboard. He groped around for a moment, causing the plane to porpoise a bit. *Forget it* . . . there were two other ammo strips in his right boot. Laying one in his lap, Roland eyeballed the other airplane, banking up slightly left and carefully feeling along the gun breech. *There it was*. . . . Letting go of the stick, he used both hands to insert the ammo strip, and it clicked in place.

Heart thumping, he grabbed the stick again and gazed ahead. Suddenly white puffs appeared against the darker clouds, and his smile widened. Anti-aircraft fire. Again, that didn't necessarily mean it was an enemy aircraft, since infantry tended to shoot at anything that flew. He stared ahead for a few moments, then grunted with satisfaction. Torpedo-shaped nose, swept-back tail . . . it was a German Albatros reconnaissance plane. Leaving the power up, he pointed the plane directly at it and pushed the stick forward slightly. The German began to turn away in a big, lazy circle.

Banking up to follow, Garros saw that the ammo strip was bobbling in the slipstream, so he eased the turn and frowned. He hadn't thought of that; it could cause a jam. *Careful* . . . The Morane-Saulnier was vibrating and rapidly gaining on the Albatros, so he closed the throttle an inch to slow down. At

100 meters he could see both Germans leaning out and looking down to the right. Easing the throttle another inch, Garros reached up to grasp the cocking bar on the gun's left side. He'd left his glove off, and the metal was cold. As he pulled back, the slick bar slipped from his fingers, and he rapped his knuckles against the stock.

He snarled, and pulled again. This time it slid all the way back and locked. Nodding, he added power and began closing again on the other plane. They'd seen him by this time, and the observer raised a pair of binoculars. Garros knew he was looking for a gun mount above the wing or an observer who might have a weapon. Lifting a hand, the Frenchman waved to put the German at ease. If Garros was lucky, the man wouldn't be able to see anything dangerous through the spinning blade and he'd go back to watching the ground.

And that was the real surprise here, wasn't it? Garros chuckled, pointing the nose of his Morane-Saulnier directly at the German plane's cockpit. His mechanic and armorer had screwed wedge-shaped metal plates onto each blade so he could fire directly through the blades now, using the wedges to protect his propeller, instead of an unwieldy and highly visible over-wing mount. It had worked well enough on the ground, with maybe three in ten bullets getting through. But he'd have to get close.

Now at 50 meters, Garros saw the observer shrug and turn back to the side. It often happened over a battlefield that several observation planes ended up in the same piece of sky, all looking at the same thing. Once in a while someone took a shot, but mostly they simply ignored each other.

Not today.

At about 30 meters out he could plainly see the details of the German plane. It was relatively clean save for the dark oil streaks down the cowling and was painted a nondescript brown, with a black Maltese cross on the fuselage. The Albatros was unarmed, though either German was likely to have a weapon. Tugging the cocking bar one more time, he nudged the throttle, then let go, grabbing the machine gun's stock with his left hand. It was awkward, but he needed his right hand to fly—and hence aim.

Taking a deep breath, he exhaled and, nearly on top of the German plane, squeezed the trigger. The noise was a surprise, and Garros flinched as shell casings flew back into his face. Shuddering from the recoil, the little monoplane bounced, and the stick jolted in his hand. Swallowing hard, he let go of the gun, closed the throttle, then fired again. Smoke blew back in his face, and he was glad his goggles were down. The gun chattered loudly, then stopped abruptly as the ammo strip ran out. Pulling back and rolling left, Garros skidded the Morane-Saulnier sideways away from the German plane, reaching for another clip.

He needn't bother.

As his eyes cleared, Roland saw the Albatros nose over, wings waggling back and forth. The German pilot was hunched over the stick, unmoving, and shreds of fabric flapped wildly around the cockpit. The Frenchman blinked rapidly. His bursts had gone straight into the other pilot's back.

The observer was still very much alive, however, and struggling. It looked like the man was trying to climb into the front cockpit, but the dead weight on the controls forced the Albatros further down, and it began spinning. Garros arced around to keep it in sight, and the last image he had of the Albatros was a flash of blue from the observer's scarf. Then the German plane slipped into the heavy gray clouds and vanished.*

---

*Gefreiter Spacholz and Leutnant Grosskopf were reported killed in action on April 1, 1915, south of Dixmude.

ON THAT extraordinary Thursday in April 1915, fighter aviation and the fighter pilot were born. Aviation has advanced more quickly, with wider-ranging impacts, than any other field of human endeavor, yet flying itself—that is, controlled, manned, motorized flight—had begun less than a dozen years before Roland Garros's 1915 encounter. Although the Wright brothers were not the first men into the air, they did pioneer controlled flight in an aircraft operating under its own power.

Ballooning, at least with humans attached, had been around since Etienne Montgolfier ascended in October 1783.* The value of aerial reconnaissance was recognized by the militaries of the day and was used whenever possible to spy out enemy movements. By the 1880s, most of the great powers (Britain, France, Germany, and Russia) had a balloon corps of some type. But unpowered ballooning involves floating around at the mercy of the wind or being tethered to a big winch for observation purposes—it's not flying.

Gliding had been around much longer. Abbas Ibn Firnas, a Berber living in Moorish Spain, made the first known systematic attempt at flight. In a specially constructed glider, he launched himself from a mountainside and floated for more than ten minutes before gliding safely back to earth. Four centuries later, the English philosopher-scientist Roger Bacon provided the first written technical details of an aircraft in his *Secrets of Art and Nature*. Called an ornithopter, it was a machine that flew by flapping its wings like birds and bats. Incidentally, there have been several successful motorized ornithopters, but human muscles have never proven a sufficient means of power. The magnificent and multitalented Leonardo da Vinci added control surfaces to his ornithopter design, demonstrating that

*Interestingly, the Montgolfiers had sent aloft a rooster, a duck, and a sheep named Montauciel the month before.

he understood the basic properties of airflow and how it might be manipulated.

In 1633 an extremely brave (or completely crazy) Turk named Lagari Hasan Çelebi launched himself from the grounds of the Topkapi Palace in Istanbul on a seven-winged rocket. Using 140 pounds of gunpowder to get airborne, he fell into the sea, survived, and swam ashore. No one ever recorded how high he ascended.

One hundred sixty years later, a Spaniard with no formal education or scientific training built a flying machine from wood, cloth, and feathers plucked from angry vultures that had been trapped with rotten meat. On May 15, 1793, accompanied by his sister and the village blacksmith who'd helped with the construction, Diego Marin Aguilera leapt from the castle of Coruña del Conde. Under a brilliant full moon he flapped the mechanical wings of his glider and, according to the American Institute of Aeronautics and Astronautics, flew "about 360 meters."

Marin crossed the river Arandilla but crashed when one of the glider's metal joints fractured under the stress of flight. Unfortunately, the inhabitants of the nearby town thought him a heretic and burned his glider, which they considered an affront to God. Though he never flew again, Marin is widely regarded (by the Spanish at least) as the father of aviation.

In 1843 it fell to William Henson, an English lace maker, to make the initial leap to powered flight. Along with John Stringfellow, another engineer, he patented the Henson Aerial Steam Carriage. Though it never truly got airborne, his scale model did manage to hop a bit under its own power. Henson and others were so excited by this that they incorporated the grandly named Aerial Transit Company in order to build a passenger-carrying monoplane. Eventually Henson and Stringfellow discovered that steam engines are impractical aircraft power sources, as they weigh more than any lift generated, so five years later Henson dissolved the company and immigrated to the United States. Though he never succeeded in aviation, anyone who shaves owes him a debt of gratitude for inventing, among other things, the modern safety razor.

So it was left to two self-educated bicycle makers to make the first successful powered and controlled flight in December 1903. Despite their undoubted vision and mechanical skill, Orville and Wilbur were a strange pair: extremely secretive, legally combative, both lifelong bachelors. Wilbur once stated that he "did not have time for both a wife and an airplane."

Following their flight, aviation became a new sport, a fad, and an exciting expression of man's possibilities. This arrived during an age where fascination with new technologies—and they were sprouting regularly—was commonplace. To conquer the air, though, was special.

The Wrights' first American patent (no. 821,393) made no reference to a flying machine. Rather, it was a patent for an aerodynamic control system that adjusted the outer portion of a machine's wings to achieve lateral control. The technique was called wing warping, as the surfaces were physically twisted, or "warped," to produce lift from one wingtip while dumping lift from the other.

To circumvent the Wrights' patent, another American pioneer, Glenn Curtiss, developed the aileron system, which accomplishes the same result but in a much more effective manner. The Wrights promptly sued him, and the resulting legal battle continued for more than a decade. During the process it emerged that in 1868 a British inventor named Matthew P. W. Boulton had patented the first aileron-type device for lateral control, thus likely negating the Wrights' claim of infringement. Curtiss couldn't have cared less, however, and he continued selling aircraft even after a U.S. Circuit Court of Appeals upheld the verdict against him. A much better businessman than the Wrights, Curtiss cashed out in 1920 for over $30 million and moved to Florida. Ironically, in 1929 Wright Aeronautical and the Curtiss Aeroplane and Motor Company merged into the Curtiss-Wright Corporation, which still exists today.

During the years immediately following the Wrights' experiments at Kitty Hawk, the principles of aerodynamics were still being worked out. There was an imperfect understanding of basic concepts such as lift, drag, weight, and thrust. *Lift* occurs when airflow splits over a surface. As it moves more quickly across the top than the bottom, a lower pressure is created above the wing; the higher pressure under the wing pushes upward, creating lift and allowing the wing and anything attached to it to fly. Next time you're in a car, stick your hand out the window, parallel to the road, then angle it up slightly and you'll feel the lift that's generated.

Drag is basically anything that counteracts lift. It's helpful to visualize air like water and then imagine being towed through the water with your shoes and clothes slowing you down. This is drag. Imagine also how the position of your body, streamlined or spread-eagled, would impact your ride through the water; this also is drag. From an aerodynamic standpoint, the struts, wires, fixed landing gear, and exposed structural components on early aircraft all caused drag and worsened the plane's performance. So did the shape of the fuselage and wings, the areas where these joined together, the placement of the cockpit, and so on. All of this had to be worked out by trial and error until engineering and experience caught up with design.

Drag has to be overcome by lift for an aircraft to fly. This had been done before 1903 with gliders, either launched from a height or towed behind a vehicle traveling on the ground. The Wright brothers are famous for successfully using an engine to move a craft through the air, creating airflow over a wing and thereby generating lift. This sounds simple enough to modern ears, but engines of the day were rudimentary and had been designed for automobiles, not aircraft. Charlie Taylor's motor for the Wright Flyer, although custom made, was a basic inline design without spark plugs or a carburetor, and only produced 12 horsepower. *Weight* for a car motor wasn't as critical as for a plane, and at the time more power (to generate more thrust) meant a bigger, heavier engine. *Thrust* is the forward movement that results when an aircraft is propelled through the air. Enough extra thrust, or excess thrust, had to be produced to overcome the aircraft weight, otherwise the two would simply cancel each other out. In the early days of flight this excess thrust occupied a razor-thin margin, so while engine technology improved, designers sought ways to maximize lift with whatever power they had available.

Early wing design was crucial to utilize the available lift—which wasn't much. Most of the early flying machines were biplanes, with two sets of wings braced by struts and wires. Wing loading, which is the weight a wing must support for the aircraft to fly, is overcome by lift. This can be done by flying much faster (which wasn't yet possible) or by using two wings. Having two wings spread the load, thus permitting a stronger design, which permitted heavier, more powerful engines, and the eventual addition of armament.

But in the years leading up to World War I no one really gave serious thought to armed aircraft. In fact, the U.S. War Department turned the Wright brothers down on three occasions for a military version of their contraption, and the British secretary of war stated in 1910, "We do not consider that aeroplanes will be of any possible use for war purposes."

No, it was in the fields of reconnaissance and scouting that the first military applications of airpower debuted. But the gradual and peaceful progression of aviation was about to change meteorically. During the brief Italian-Turkish War in Libya, the Italians took several balloons and nine aircraft along for reconnaissance and on November 1, 1911, they claimed the first bombing mission from the air. In 1912 the French used aircraft in Morocco, and several Morane monoplanes were lent to Rumania during the Balkan Wars of 1912–13. Flown by foreigners, these apparently weren't used offensively; still, the Turks declared that captured airmen would be executed.

IN LATE JUNE 1914, a man pulled out a pistol and shot another man in Sarajevo. Unfortunately for the millions who would subsequently die, the assailant with the pistol was a radical Yugoslav named Gavrilo Princip. He was a member of Mlada Bosna (Young Bosnia), a secret society dedicated to Slavic liberation, and the man assassinated was Archduke Franz Ferdinand, heir to the Hapsburg emperor of Austria-Hungary. Though this event is often cited as the *casus belli*, in truth no single event provoked the Great War. Four years later, with 10 million dead and some 20 million scarred for life, certainly no one was thinking about Sarajevo.

The four decades following the 1871 Franco-Prussian War had been known for technological developments and relatively peaceful coexistence. The telegraph, telephone, and railroad expansion brought people together as never before, leading to increased trade, education, and, in some cases, true cultural enlightenment. This long period of peace and prosperity also yielded a population explosion, and between 1850 and 1900 Europe's population grew more than 50 percent.

One way to control such a surge of young males was

through compulsory military service, which became commonplace. Cheap, high-grade steel and weaponry advancements, including bolt action rifles, gas artillery shells, and machine guns, exponentially bolstered the lethality of armies. There was also a groundswell of fervent nationalism to encourage the use of these armies. Europe in 1914 was a collection of fiercely prideful countries with large standing militaries armed with new and exciting weapons—a perfect storm waiting for the spark that came along with Gavrilo Princip and his pistol.

None of the great powers tried too hard to avoid the war, and in fact they had already chosen sides. Britain and France, two imperial powers that had fought each other for centuries, decided in 1904 that cooperation better served their national interests. London wished to deal with Egypt without interference, and Paris wanted to expand in North Africa, specifically Morocco, so the Entente Cordiale was established. Furthermore, the French had become alarmed at Germany's militancy and figured an alliance with the British was prudent. England had a similar motive, calculating that a large standing French army placed squarely between Germany and the Channel was a wise strategic move.

In response, Germany joined with Austria-Hungary and Italy to form the Triple Alliance. There were minor players, too, which continued to complicate matters. The Ottoman Empire, a moldering, disparate collection of territories, sought German protection against Russia. Tributaries such as Arabia angled for British or French help in gaining their freedom from the Turks, while Egypt and Libya wanted independence from their colonial masters. In short, it was a tangled mess.

Then the dominoes began to fall.

On July 28, 1914, one month to the day after Franz Ferdinand's assassination, the Austro-Hungarians declared war on

Serbia. Russia, still smarting from a defeat by Japan and the 1909 loss of Bosnia-Herzegovina, began mobilizing to defend her Slavic "brethren." Germany retaliated with her own mobilization, belligerently demanding French neutrality and, for good measure, the capitulation of two fortresses on their shared border.

Germany then declared war on Russia, invaded Luxembourg, and demanded the right of transit through neutral Belgium. On August 3, following Paris's rejection of neutrality and surrender, the Germans declared war on France and invaded Belgium. Britain answered the next day with her own declaration against the Kaiser, and four days later, on August 7, 1914, the first English troops landed in France.

FLYING SIX DIFFERENT types of motley, unarmed aircraft, four squadrons of the British Royal Flying Corps (RFC) left Dover on August 13 and landed in Amiens, France. Little more than mechanized kites, their canvas wings lacquered with varnish and wired together, these Parasols, Blériots, Avros, and Farmans were leftovers from the post–Kitty Hawk world of experimental aviation. The first RFC casualty in the combat zone occurred on August 16 when 2nd Lt. E. W. C. Perry stalled his plane on takeoff and was killed.

The Royal Naval Air Service (RNAS) was initially given the job of patrolling England's eastern coastline. However, the Eastchurch Squadron (later No. 3 Squadron, RNAS) was sent to Ostend, Belgium, with a few Blériots, Farmans, and assorted biplanes.

Such was the infancy of the RFC, and the dire need across the Channel, that City of London vans, still advertising Peek Frean biscuits and Lazenby's Sauce, had to carry the flying equipment, ground personnel, and baggage. Within months there would be more than sixty British aircraft and a hundred pilots in France, supported by eight hundred mechanics.

The early pilots either were self-taught or had completed widely varying courses at civilian flying schools. They knew very little theory, only the most basic flight maneuvers, and certainly no gunnery. Observers were officers who were already expected to know how to read a map, so they were simply tossed in the rear cockpit. Later, if a gun was added, they might be shown how to shoot it and clear a jam, but there was no formal training. In any event, both sides expected a short war and figured they could make do with the personnel they had.

Now, as early as 1905, the Imperial German Staff had anticipated a two-front war, and Count Alfred von Schlieffen devised a strategy to fight it. In accordance with his plan, the German army would make an end run through Luxembourg and Belgium, avoiding the fixed fortresses along the French border. Reaching the open land of northern France, they would seize the Channel ports and prevent reinforcements from England. This done, they could then encircle Paris and cut apart the French from behind. With France out of the way, the Germans would be free to deal with Russia.

But several assumptions had been made that turned the plan into a house of cards. First, the Germans counted on six weeks for a slow, disorganized Russia to mobilize. Second, they calculated a continuously successful westward advance of about 20 miles per day even with ongoing combat against the Belgians and the French. Third, to paraphrase Napoleon, an army marches on its stomach, and the Germans grossly underestimated the logistical difficulties in keeping such a fast-moving mass of men resupplied.

In fact, the Russians mobilized in about ten days rather

than six weeks and the Belgians fought much harder than anticipated, effectively using natural chokepoints to slow the onslaught. Britain also reacted very quickly and landed troops before the Channel ports could be seized. Logistically, the Germans had no special units to repair railroads and bridges, nor did they possess an effective transportation corps. Most units ceased receiving supplies once they crossed the German border, and thus had to rely on foraging.

Even so, by August 23 the German First Army had advanced as far as Mons, on the Belgian-French border, where it first made contact with the British Expeditionary Force, forcing it into a 200-mile southward retreat. On the twenty-fourth, Capt. G. S. Shephard and Lt. I. M. Bonham-Carter of No. 4 Squadron discovered that the Germans would outflank the BEF unless the retreat was continued. This news undoubtedly saved the British Army from being cut off and destroyed.

Nevertheless the Germans, despite their problems, advanced to within 10 miles of Paris. The French Fifth Army and the BEF then counterattacked, pressing into service some six hundred Parisian taxicabs to bring up reinforcements. By September 9, 1914, the exhausted Germans began a withdrawal north back across the Marne and Aisne rivers.

From late September through October, both sides moved northwest, trying to get around each other to the coast during the "race to the sea." On October 18, the British V Corps and remnants of some French cavalry ran smack into the German Fourth Army outside the western Belgian town of Ypres. In October's final days the German Sixth Army approached from the south, so the Belgians opened the sluice gates built to hold back the sea. This flooded the area east of the Yser River and brought the offensive to a halt for the winter.

There were some smaller battles that finally ended on October 22 as surviving BEF units were replaced by the French. Mobile operations effectively ended and trench warfare took their place. The Germans, having thrown vast numbers of raw recruits into the battle, suffered enormous losses and were in no mood to pull back, and the Allies also refused to withdraw. More than 250,000 men lost their lives during the First Battle of Ypres, and each side realized the prospects of a short war had disappeared. They dug in for the winter to lick their wounds, take stock, and resupply.

The resulting stalemate hardened the lines into the Western Front with massive armies facing each other across a network of trenches stretching from Switzerland to the North Sea. Both sides were led by generals from another era, fighting on a scale they'd never imagined, with weapons they didn't truly understand. In point of fact, no commanding general in 1914 had experience leading anything larger than a division into battle. As mobility on the ground ended, new means had to be found to scout enemy positions, gather intelligence, and take the fight to the enemy. This had always been a cavalry role, but there was no way to deploy cavalry in the spiderweb of trenches, hidden machine gun nests, and minefields.

Once the fortifications became fixed, balloons rose from tethers over the trenches of the Western Front and the German soldiers nicknamed the huge phallus-shaped balloons *das Mädchens Traum*, or "the maiden's dream." From such a vantage point, often as high as 5,000 feet, an observer might see 15 miles on a clear day. With a field telephone, he could immediately describe what he was seeing and, in a limited way, direct the artillery fire that was becoming so vital to trench warfare. The balloons were a threat, but reconnaissance aircraft became a worse danger to miserable infantry huddled in their holes.

With initial ceilings up to 12,000 feet, aircraft had what

the mobility balloons lacked. The tactical implications for directing artillery fire were obvious, and the army that controlled the sky had the edge on the ground. Throughout the winter, pilots and observers on both sides fired flare guns and pistols, and sometimes even threw bricks at each other. Grenades and grapnels were towed behind aircraft in absurd attempts to bring the enemy down. Sometimes they laughed so hard that no one even came close. Sometimes they did. Planes were lost to rifles and shotguns, bad weather, poor flying, and anti-aircraft fire. As the importance of reconnaissance grew, so did the need to deny it to the other side. Everyone knew that the times were changing.

As losses mounted and friends perished the initial camaraderie of flyers lessened somewhat. It was not, after all, a game between gentlemen and those in the other planes were still the enemy. This fundamentally changed how aviation was viewed, both by those who flew and by those who needed aircraft to make war. So it was here, caught between the cavalry lance and the machine gun, that the age of the fighter pilot dawned.

CHAPTER 2

KILLER SCOUTS: 1914–1916

FOKKER EINDECKER

TO KILL IN the air from an aircraft . . . how to do it and survive to kill again?

Lt. Jacob Fickel, an American army officer, fired the first shot from the air in 1910, hitting a three-by-five-foot target with a rifle from an altitude of 100 feet. Two years later another American, Capt. Charles deForest Chandler, fired the first machine gun from an airplane. The following day, from 500 feet, he fired forty-four bullets and scored fourteen hits. Despite the possibilities, an Army staff officer declared that "airplanes were suitable only for reconnaissance and that thoughts of air battles were purely the product of the young flyers' fertile imaginations."

Yet two years later, in October 1914, a French observer downed a German reconnaissance aircraft using a Hotchkiss machine gun.* The next day the Germans claimed to have knocked off a French plane by throwing a brick through its propeller. Weaponry and how to employ it with lethality were the immediate problems. Early aircraft were frail, lightweight contraptions; not very maneuverable and relatively underpowered. Any extra weight had to be considered carefully, and guns weighed a great deal. The main weapons available for aircraft in the Great War were the Browning, Maxim, Hotchkiss, and Lewis machine guns—all designed by Americans.

Benjamin Hotchkiss, from Connecticut, went to France for financial backing, since the U.S. War Department showed no interest in his weapon. By the end of World War I, some forty-seven thousand had been delivered, and it had become a staple of the French army. The Hotchkiss gun was an *open-bolt* design, like an automatic rifle, meaning that the bolt was pulled back to cock it and firing would chamber a round. Using gas from the discharge, the bolt would cycle back after each shot, ejecting the case and self-loading another cartridge.

A simple gun with only thirty-two moving parts, the Hotchkiss fired a twenty-five-round strip of 8 mm ammunition. It was also air-cooled and weighed much less than water-cooled systems with their tanks and hoses. Unfortunately, an open-bolt system was very difficult to synchronize for firing through the propeller arc (which is why Roland Garros employed his wedges).

Maxim Ltd. teamed up with Vickers and Sons to produce the Vickers medium machine gun. The British Vickers was a belt-fed, .303-caliber (7.7 mm) gun using a *closed-bolt* system, which made synchronization much easier. Extremely reliable and very tough, one ground unit continuously fired off a million rounds from their ten Vickers during a single twelve-hour fight.

---

*Either an Aviatik or Albatros—reports disagree.

The infantry version was water cooled via a bronze jacket surrounding the barrel. Water cooling was unnecessary when the gun was mounted on an aircraft, but the jacket was still required for the recoil mechanism, so slots were cut for air cooling and the jacket remained in place. There were also problems with the original 250-round belt, as the canvas would constrict when wet and often jam the gun. This was solved by using an aluminum link system, which would feed any length of belt an aircraft could carry.

Ironically, as business knows no borders, Germany's Spandau machine gun was actually a Vickers-Maxim design built under license in Berlin. The Spandau, especially the twin-mounted type common on German single-seat fighters, sent hundreds of Allied aircrews to their deaths. The aircraft variant was the Maschinengewehr 08 (IMG 08), a lightened water-cooled adaptation of the standard German infantry gun. Incidentally, it was Manfred von Richthofen, the air ace who later became known as the "Red Baron," who suggested the use of a trigger instead of a thumbpiece to fire the weapon. He said it was "more natural for a marksman to fire a gun with his trigger finger rather than with his thumb." He was right.

The Lewis gun was extensively used by the Allies after 1915, and with the heavy cooling jacket removed it became relatively lightweight.* More important was the self-contained, drum-style ammunition feed system. The Lewis had a forty-seven-round (later a ninety-seven-round) capacity, with a drum that could be replaced in flight. Some aircraft, such as the SE-5a, had a wooden tray added to the pilot's console so he could quickly switch drums when needed.

---

*The Lewis with the jacket removed weighed 17 pounds, versus the 33-pound Vickers and the 50-pound Hotchkiss.

There were also rockets. Yves Paul Gaston Le Prieur, a French naval officer, tackled the knotty problem of bringing down observation balloons.* He filled a cardboard tube with 200 grams of black powder, fitted a knife blade into the conical head, attached the assembly to the wing struts, and wired it to the cockpit. The rockets were fired consecutively at a range of about 100 yards and always against the wind. Interestingly, the weapons were inclined to 45 degrees so that the pilot could fire from a dive and not get caught in the balloon's explosion. Carried by the Allies on the Nieuport, SPAD, and Sopwith fighters, Le Prieur rockets were successful against balloons (but not Zeppelins) and were widely used until the development of incendiary bullets.

Mounting weapons, preferably a machine gun, wasn't a new idea. But to do this effectively, one also had to be able to aim the gun while engaged in a wild, corkscrewing dogfight. Furthermore, the pilot was better situated to fire the weapon, as observers were at the mercy of the pilot's maneuvering. There was no intercom or headset, and communication between two men in an open-cockpit aircraft was problematic at best. So single-seat fighters with the gun or guns aimed along the aircraft axis was the natural progression.

Unfortunately, the propeller was in the way. This was a problem that had to be solved, and quickly. Roland Garros, as noted in Chapter 1, devised the deflector plate solution. The way he figured it, a prop rotating at 2,000 rpm would allow at least 10 percent of the gun's bullets through, which would be sufficient if the pilot got close enough. His armed Morane-Saulnier Type L was a battlefield shock, though it would not be long before the

---

*In 1934 the industrious Le Prieur also was granted French patent #768083 for the SCUBA (Self Contained Underwater Breathing Apparatus) system.

Germans figured out what Garros had done. After he disposed of his sixth victim, engine failure forced the French flyer down behind enemy lines. He tried setting fire to his aircraft, but the wet wood and fabric wouldn't burn, and searching German soldiers found him in a ditch.* They took possession of the French "secret weapon" and sent it to Berlin for aviation pioneer Anthony Fokker's evaluation.

Wedges were impractical, and Fokker knew it immediately. They were aerodynamically unpredictable and could throw the propeller out of balance. Then there was the very real danger of ricochets, not to mention the inefficient use of a gun's very limited ammunition supply. Also, French bullets were sheathed in copper, so deflection via wedges *was* possible for a while, but German shells were steel-jacketed and would splinter the propeller in no time.

In any event, Fokker instinctively knew that a better, less French, solution was possible. Perhaps his childhood in Holland throwing rocks through the arms of windmills inspired his answer. Or perhaps he simply borrowed the idea, as both August Euler and Franz Schneider had designed similar mechanical solutions. In any event, it was only a matter of days before he had a simple, workable interrupter gear installed and tested. Fokker wrote:

> *I attached a small knob to the propeller, which struck a cam as it revolved. This cam was hooked up with the hammer of the machine gun, which automatically loaded itself. Thus as I slowly revolved the propeller, I found that the gun shot between the blades.*
>
> *During the night I found out the basic operation,*

*They were paid a 100-mark bonus for Garros (about six months' pay).

> *and began next morning to perfect the device. One blade was enough to strike the cam, because the gun could shoot only 600 times a minute, while the blades passed a given point 2,400 times a minute. To the cam was fastened a simple knee lever, which operated a rod, held back by a spring. In order that the pilot could control the shooting, a piece of the rod which struck the hammer was hinged to hit or miss as the operator required. That was the entire device.*

The Fokker A-III and M-5K scouts were shoulder-wing monoplanes and nearly identical in appearance to Garros's Moraine-Saulnier. Modified with a 7.92 mm Parabellum light machine gun (LMG) and the new interrupter gear, the upgraded plane was called the Fokker E-1. The Eindecker (meaning "one wing") would change aviation history.

The Germans insisted Fokker prove his invention by shooting down an enemy aircraft. However, as he was Dutch, and the Netherlands was a neutral country, the designer demurred, only to be told that if he refused he'd be drafted and sent to the trenches. His mind made up for him, Fokker was forcibly dressed in an *oberleutnant*'s uniform, with the proper ID in his pocket, and sent up over Douai to shoot something down. Like many savants, he'd never really considered the practical consequences of his inventions, and was now face-to-face with a very real problem. Despite putting himself in a perfect position to kill a vulnerable Farman two-seater, Fokker just couldn't pull the trigger.

Who actually did score the first shoot-down with this new weapon system is debatable. Max Immelmann, Kurt Wintgens, and Oswald Boelcke have all been credited, but the records are ambiguous. On July 1, 1915, the fifth production Fokker E-1, flown by Lieutenant Wintgens, engaged a Moraine-Saulnier L near Luneville. Wintgens claimed a kill, but the enemy aircraft disappeared too far behind French lines for verification. A French squadron, MS 48, subsequently reported that one of their aircraft had been forced down.* Immelmann, who'd only managed to pass his last set of flying tests in March, didn't score his first victory until the first of August. When Anthony Fokker departed from the Douai aerodrome in May he left his Eindecker behind. Oswald Boelcke was there and took a keen interest in the test work, so he might have been the first line pilot to fly the monoplane yet he was still officially listed as a two-seater pilot until July 4, three days after Wintgens's victory.

In the end, it doesn't really matter who was first. With the combination of a maneuverable aircraft, a lethal machine gun, and aggressive flyers, the age of the fighter pilot had begun in earnest. As Boelcke himself wrote, "I believe in the saying that 'the strong man is mightiest alone.' I have attained my ideal with this single-seater; now I can be pilot, observer and fighter all in one."

So who were these men who weren't content to be just aviators and scouts, these men who made themselves into fighter pilots? What did they have in common beyond the very high likelihood of dying young and dying soon? The stereotypical World War I flyer cut a dashing, heroic figure, and he was viewed as honorable and brave; a knight of the air, and the last of a chivalric breed of gentleman warriors. For men caught in the transition between the old ways and modern, industrialized mass warfare, there was some truth in this perception. Remember, once the armies dug into their trenches, aircraft took over from cavalry and in any army, the cavalry was an elite force of

*Flown by Capt. Paul du Peuty with Lt. Louis de Boutiny as observer.

fast-moving shock troops. As such, it attracted many adventorous young men from the upper classes and nobility.

Transitioning to their various air services was a logical move for hundreds of these officers once the need for cavalry faded. Flying was a new profession, inspiring awe and admiration among a public that really didn't understand it. So the attraction for these men was the danger, the unique skill involved, and the chance for inclusion in a very selective brotherhood. They also shared a love of flying and a genuine desire to serve their country. As flyers, they were generally free of the hidebound traditions permeating their respective militaries, and being pilots, they had unique control over their fate, unlike the "poor bloody infantry," as the Brits called foot soldiers.

In 1914, Britain placed most of the responsibility for her security on the Royal Navy and maintained only a small volunteer army. Before the war, officers in all branches were overwhelmingly from the upper classes. A career as an officer was an honorable and acceptable profession for such men, many of them younger sons who would not inherit family estates. They possessed important family connections, often came from military families, and were graduates of the public school system (roughly equivalent to American prep schools). Through a classical education, sports, and an emphasis on proper conduct this produced educated, socially responsible leaders with a sense of obligation to the nation and the Crown. Combining these attributes with the English ideal of extreme (perhaps even suicidal) courage produced the typical British officer. It was said that "the Battle of Waterloo was won on the playing fields of Eton," and there was truth in this. In 1914, nearly all of Britain's 28,000 army officers fit this mold. On the Western Front they formed the British Expeditionary Force, which was deemed so insignificant by Kaiser Wilhelm that he called it "contemptible." With perverse English pride, the BEF took on the nickname "The Old Contemptibles."

The original Royal Flying Corps pilots and observers were seconded from regular military and naval units. Initially, many of the pilots were sergeants and regarded as mere "drivers." The officers took the role of observer and aircraft commander, as they had been trained to read maps, navigate, and spot for artillery.

But a month after fighting began in France, it was apparent that the rapid military expansion required more officers, so commissions were offered to veteran sergeants of the prewar regular army and qualified volunteers within the ranks. Many of the soldiers who had answered the call to duty in August 1914 had been university or public school students before signing up. Because they all believed the war would be over by Christmas and didn't want to incur the commitment of a commission, they'd simply enlisted as private soldiers. However, some 13,000 of them had been enrolled in their school's Officers' Training Corps (rather like the American ROTC system) and most of these men were directly commissioned—even those who didn't apply.

By contrast, the typical German officer of 1914 was a member of a caste, rather than a member of a social class. While social classes were present, of course, German society and government were much more autocratic than the English system. Industrialization had arrived somewhat later, and as a result, democratic thinking and liberalism had been slower to take root. When they did, these progressive ideas ran squarely into opposition from the landed gentry and the military-based aristocracy, who opposed any change that threatened their status.

Germany was also intensely segregated; the north was generally Protestant, while the south was predominantly Catholic.

Most of the industry lay in the west, as opposed to immense agrarian interests in the east. Only in 1871 had the four kingdoms of Prussia, Saxony, Bavaria, and Wurttemberg been united into the Deutsches Reich by Otto von Bismarck. Also called the Zweites (Second) Reich, it was ruled by the noble Prussian House of Hohenzollern.*

The Kaiser was subsequently more of a warlord than a sovereign monarch, with each of the four kingdoms maintaining its unique identity and a separate military. However, within the new German confederation, Prussia reigned supreme and was itself ruled by landowners, called Junkers (the word derives from *Juncherre*, "young lord"), who exerted tremendous influence on Prussian politics and Germany.

As in England, younger sons who could not inherit frequently became career soldiers, and men from this background undoubtedly colored the German officer corps. However, things were changing, and by 1914 many officers hailed from the middle class. The Imperial German Air Service attracted many such bourgeois men, perhaps due to its technical nature or because it offered advancement in a new branch of the military. Family connections can't help you fly and being a pilot is an unforgiving equalizer; either you can do it or you cannot.

BOTH THE BRITISH and German militaries realized that just because a man could be an officer didn't mean he could be a *flying* officer. What, officials wondered, were the traits that made the difference?

"Guts," "fitness," and the ability to "make quick decisions" were the most frequently listed traits from a 1918 *Lancet* study

---

*Their motto, somewhat ironically, was *Nihil sine deo*—nothing without God.

titled "The Essential Characteristics of Successful and Unsuccessful Aviators." Sixty-one pilots turned in questionnaires that sought to identify commonalities. The pilots came from all walks of life and, by 1918, also from the middle "artisan" classes of society. The results, correlated by an RAF medical doctor (T. S. Rippon) and an experienced pilot (E. G. Manuel), were illuminating but not surprising.

The picture that emerges is of a young man under twenty-five (the average age was twenty-three), high-spirited, and in excellent health, with superb eyesight and coordination. Only a third were married—thirty-six of the sixty-one pilots considered marriage a handicap! Occupations had generally been technical (engineers, architects, and accountants) but there were also farmers, students, and lawyers. Nearly all enjoyed "motoring," and the majority surveyed listed "horseback riding" as a favored pastime. "Sports" and "women" were also frequent amusements, and "it appears necessary for the well-being of the average pilot that he should indulge in a really riotous evening at least once or twice a month."* Natural history, the theater, and music were listed as pastimes as well, while one pilot mentioned "killing Huns and dancing" as his primary interests. Having good "hands" was another recurring requirement. This quality goes beyond the ability to simply fly in the mechanical sense. Gifted pilots can truly feel their aircraft, and they control it through a light, supremely confident touch. You're thinking ahead of the plane, and your desires are almost unconsciously transmitted through your hands to the controls.

"Hands appear to be congenital and cannot be acquired, although they may be improved," Rippon and Manuel concluded, adding that a man with good hands is "invariably a graceful

* Everything changes and yet nothing changes. Thankfully.

flyer, and never unconsciously throws an undue strain on the machine, just as a good riding man will never make a horse's mouth bleed." People can be taught to fly, but you can't teach "hands," and having that gift is a defining characteristic of a fighter pilot over other types of aviators. It would become strikingly obvious when men began shooting at each other in the air. Flying is one thing; fighting while flying is something altogether different.

The other fundamental trait, a "fighting spirit," was more elusive to isolate. It is a combination of aggressiveness, confidence, and attitude that transcends one's background or training. Crossing nationalities and enduring, as we shall see, down through the generations, this fighting spirit also cannot be taught. But it *can* be developed and, above all, encouraged. According to the report, "Anyone who has lived with pilots for any length of time cannot fail to notice that they possess in a very high degree a fund of animal spirits and excessive vitality." Fighter pilots *are* different, truly a breed apart.

The life expectancy of a frontline pilot during the Great War was about two weeks, and anywhere from 15 to 25 percent of Allied and German pilots were killed during the war. This casualty rate was generally higher than that seen in infantry units. Added to the daily stress of possibly dying in flames or a crash was the normal pressure of flying. It was, and remains, an extremely taxing combination of physical and mental strains.

Aircraft flown during the Great War all had open cockpits, exposing the pilots and observers to all types of weather; wind, rain, and sleet were normal and the air temperatures usually below freezing. There were no autopilots, and trim tabs, if they existed at all, were primitive. So the pilot had to be constantly focused on flying the aircraft from takeoff to landing, without a break. Rotary engines were particularly fatiguing, as the motor itself was spinning and considerable strength was required to counter this force.

The transition from unarmed reconnaissance pilot to fighter pilot or armed scout is best personified by Germany's Oswald Boelcke. Called the "Father of Fighter Aviation," Boelcke was brave, chivalrous, and admired equally by both friend and foe. His star pupil, Manfred von Richthofen, said of him, "It is remarkable that everyone who knew Boelcke imagined himself to be his one and only friend. . . . He was equally amiable to everyone and neither more nor less to anyone."

Boelcke was twenty-three years old when the war began, the son of a middle-class schoolmaster, and had always been expected to follow his father's path. Yet in addition to his natural studiousness with a talent for physics and mathematics, the boy loved sports and adventure. Short but very strong, Boelcke was a superb gymnast and an accomplished swimmer. Utterly determined to succeed but short on funds, he wrote a letter to the Kaiser in 1911 asking for an appointment to the cadet corps. The appointment arrived with the amused reply, "You will, of course, complete your grammar school subjects before you report."

Finishing his officer's courses at the War School in Metz, Boelcke was accepted into flight training and was a certified pilot by October 1914. Initially posted to Fliegerabteilungen (FA) 32 as a reconnaissance pilot, he was flying LVG C-1s with FA 62 by early 1915. The "C machine," as it was called, was an armed two-seater LVG biplane.

On July 4, 1915, near Valenciennes, Boelcke and his observer engaged a French Parasol that had been spotting for the artillery. Their victim hit the trees near Marchiennes, and Boelcke landed to arrange for the funeral of the two Frenchmen.

Ironically, the dead pilot happened to be Comte de Beauvicourt, who owned the very estate upon which the Parasol crashed. This was also Boelcke's last combat mission in a two-seater, since Anthony Fokker had left his armed Eindecker, complete with the new interrupter gear, for the young flyer's use.

The period immediately following the introduction of the monoplane and its line-of-sight-aimed, forward-firing machine gun was called the "Fokker Scourge." Early Fokkers could manage about 90 knots and climb to nearly 12,000 feet. This gave advantages in both speed and ceiling over most of the Allied opposition. Nieuports, Avros, Voisins, and BE-2s ranged from 65 to 97 knots and had a variety of combat ceilings. In any event, the Fokker's forward-firing Spandau overcame any shortfall in performance.

During this time the relative air superiority enjoyed by the British and French had been overturned by this new weapon, yet the Germans were cautious in exploiting it. Scout missions had been one of escort and close protection until now, and there were standing orders forbidding flights beyond the German lines. It would take men such as Boelcke, Wintgens, and Immelmann to demonstrate the lethality of the new aircraft and devise suitable tactics for its employment. All told, the Germans destroyed one hundred Allied planes in air combat during the year of the Scourge, and so the technical advance could hardly be ignored.

Oswald Boelcke was in the thick of things. Despite abysmal weather and mechanical growing pains with aircraft and weapons, he'd scored eight more kills by January 1916. Sitting down for dinner on the night of January 15, Boelcke was told that he'd been awarded the Pour le Mérite by the Kaiser himself.* Nick-

*Actually, it was a Prussian award adopted for all of Germany and could also be awarded for significant civil achievements.

named the "Blue Max," it was Germany's highest combat award, and he and Immelmann were the first aviators to receive it.

On March 13, Boelcke attacked a formation of French Voisins, putting a long burst into a straggler. The plane stalled, then spun into a cloud deck. Following it down, Boelcke was astonished to see that the gunner had climbed out onto the wing to try to keep the aircraft level. It would have been an easy kill, but Boelcke was close enough to see the terror in the man's eyes and didn't fire. Suddenly the Voisin's left wing cracked apart and the plane flipped over, tossing the gunner out into space, his arms and legs flailing.*

By the time Max Immelmann died in June, Boelcke had increased his score to eighteen and was the top-scoring *kanone*, or German ace. Like the French, the Germans had seen the propaganda value associated with the new breed of warriors—readymade heroes fighting a "noble" war. Somehow an air war seemed cleaner and more honorable than machine-gunning each other in muddy, rat-infested trenches. The French called a man who scored five aerial victories *un as* (an ace; a term used for sportsmen, or for any spectacular feat of skill). The Germans eventually settled on ten victories as the initial requirement to be a *kanone*, and twenty kills to earn the Blue Max.

With Immelmann gone, both the chief of the air service and the Kaiser feared losing Boelcke, too. So he was ordered to the rear, ostensibly to form a special *Staffel* (squadron) of Fokkers at Charleville. Being involuntarily removed from combat provoked a typical response from a fighting man such as Boelcke, who said, "I cursed the adjutant and other pen pushers in a most offensive fashion."

Unable to get the decision reversed, he personally telephoned the Kaiser and asked to do an inspection tour of the Eastern

*At this stage of the war no one but balloonists wore parachutes.

Front. Happy to oblige a national hero, Wilhelm officially ordered him to Turkey. While the details for his trip were being arranged, Boelcke spent some days with the Air Service staff formally compiling the very first principles of aerial combat. These were hard-won truths distilled from the initial year of air fighting. They became known as the "Dicta Boelcke."

1. Try to secure advantages before attacking. If possible, keep the sun behind you.
2. Always carry through an attack when you have started it.
3. Fire only at close range and only when your opponent is properly in your sights.
4. Always keep your eyes on your opponent, and never let yourself be deceived by ruses.
5. In any form of attack it is essential to assail your opponent from behind.
6. If your opponent dives on you, do not try to avoid his onslaught, but fly to meet it.
7. When over the enemy's lines, never forget your own line of retreat.
8. For the *Staffel:* Attack on principle in groups of four or six. When the fight breaks up into a series of single combats, take care that several do not go for one opponent.

Simple though they may be, Boelcke's dicta were remarkable in that they represented the first codified thoughts on an emerging tactical subject. By formalizing these basic principles, the Germans were also acknowledging the seriousness with which they viewed this form of fighting. In this they were well ahead of their opponents, and this mind-set paid enormous dividends in the months to come.

Boelcke departed for the east on July 10, 1916, and for the next six weeks he got his first and last opportunity to live as a young man should. Traveling through Vienna, he was wined and dined while surveying the Austrian front. Then from Budapest he took a mail steamer to Constantinople. Entertained by diplomats and royalty of all types, Boelcke even wrangled a trip onto another of Germany's technologically advanced weapons, U-38 (a U-boat—*Unterseeboot* or submarine).

After boating on the Dardanelles, he traveled south, ending up on the beach in Smyrna. Hans-Joachim Buddecke, another German flyer from the Western Front, had been assigned to Turkey and was traveling with Boelcke. Much of the strain slipped away as they went yachting during the day (always in the company of ladies) and entertained nightly.

But the news from home wasn't good. At 6:50 a.m. on July 1, a British engineer detonated 40,000 pounds of high explosives under Hawthorne Ridge on the German front lines. This heralded the beginning of the Somme Offensive, an enormous Allied push to recapture occupied territories east of the Somme River. It forever prevented the Germans from reaching the Channel coast.

Eleven divisions of the French Sixth Army and thirteen British divisions went "over the top" across no-man's-land and straight into the German guns. The British alone suffered 60,000 casualties on the first day and, all told, more than a million men would die during the next four months.

In the air, Britain's Royal Flying Corps conducted line patrols and offensive sweeps to destroy reconnaissance aircraft or spot for artillery. They went into the battle with numerical superiority (185 RFC aircraft vs. 129 German planes) and a technological advantage with Sopwith 1½ Strutters and the Nieuport 11. Losing the air superiority they'd enjoyed since

April 1915, the Germans were now hard-pressed on the ground and in the air. Col. Hermann von der Leith-Thomsen, chief of the Imperial Air Service, cut Boelcke's trip short with a request that he return as soon as possible.

Departing Constantinople on August 1, Boelcke was visiting his brother Wilhelm, also a fighter pilot, near Kovel in occupied Russia. He received a telegram from Thomsen that ended with, "Return to west front as quickly as possible to organize and lead Jagdstaffel 2 on the Somme front."

During Boelcke's absence the old Imperial German Aviation Service had been reorganized, on paper at least. Aircraft would no longer be grouped into small special units, or *Feldfliegerabteilungen*, and subordinated to army units. Brought about largely by Boelcke's theories and his combat successes, the new Deutschen Luftstreitkräfte (German Air Force) became official on October 8, 1916. This very significantly grouped fighter aircraft into specially formed *Jagdstaffeln*, or "hunting squadrons," called *Jastas* for short. Boelcke was to command the first operational fighter squadron, and he was allowed to select the pilots. Right there in Kovel, with his brother's help, he picked Erwin Böhme and a young cavalry officer turned flyer named Manfred von Richthofen. Jagdstaffel 2 was formally assembled by August 27 at the Bertincourt aerodrome outside Calais in northern France.

Jasta 2 had four officers, sixty-four men, and no aircraft initially. Five days later the first planes arrived: a single Albatros D-I and two Fokker D-IIIs. For the first few weeks in September Boelcke used his own victories as case studies and taught his men to be fighter pilots. Without radio communications, signals were vital, so they worked out a simple system using hands or wings. Boelcke briefed his pilots on prearranged rejoin points all along the front, so that if they became separated they might find each other again. He conducted organized flight briefings and insisted upon the postflight analytical debriefings that survive to this day.

The machine gun was thoroughly studied and understood. Individual rounds were examined, and pilots did their own loading to ensure quality and reduce jams. They broke apart the plane's engine, learned its components, and became proficient at field repairs in case they were forced down with mechanical issues. His "cubs," as he called them, also analyzed their opponents, scrupulously committing to memory rates of climb, armament, endurance, and maneuverability. Strong points and weaknesses of both sides were carefully studied so basic plans of attack could be discussed. An example reads:

> *Vickers single seater. Very agile, somewhat slower than the Albatros, generally loses fight in steep turns. Generally armed with only one machine gun. Defenseless in the rear, where the pilot's view is obstructed. Best attacked from behind; can also be very effectively attacked from behind and below by means of a zoom.*

On September 2, Boelcke forced down a British DH-2 fighter near Thiepval and used the plane as a training aid. The pilot, Captain Robert Wilson of 32 Squadron, was courteously given lunch, coffee, and a tour of the aerodrome before being sent off to prison camp.

Having practiced formation flying, gunnery, and teamwork, Jasta 2 was deemed ready for combat on September 17, 1916. At 1:00 p.m. that Sunday, they got airborne in their new Albatros D-I fighters and bounced eight British BE-2 bombers with six FE-2 escorts bound for the railway station at Marcoing. The

Germans shot down four of the fighters and two bombers with no losses. Boelcke's pilots learned his lessons well and would end the year with eighty-five confirmed kills.* As always in flying units, the cost was high. Starting with twelve pilots in September, by the end of October Jagdstaffel 2 had lost two pilots to complete physical collapse, another was badly wounded, and six were dead—including Oswald Boelcke.

On Saturday morning, October 28, he'd departed from Lagnicourt for the first of five sorties.† About 4:30 that afternoon Jasta 2 received a call from a unit at the front asking for air support. Boelcke was exhausted but took off nonetheless and headed west with von Richthofen, Erwin Böhme, and three other pilots.

Finding two de Havilland Scouts over Flers, the Germans attacked. In the ensuing *kurvenkampf*, or dogfight, six more German fighters appeared in the swirling melee. Böhme and his leader were chasing one of the Scouts when the other Englishman, closely pursued by von Richthofen, sliced across in front of them. In Böhme's words: "How am I to describe my sensations from the moment when Boelcke suddenly loomed up a few meters away on my right! He put his machine down and I pulled mine up, but we touched as we passed, and we both fell earthwards."

Böhme's undercarriage apparently only lightly grazed the other aircraft's upper wing, but it was enough. Boelcke went into a long glide down through the clouds, his damaged right wing pulling him over. Scorning a helmet and rarely strapping himself in tightly, Oswald Boelcke crashed near an artillery battery and died on impact.

---

*By the end of the war in November 1918, Jasta 2 had 336 confirmed victories.
†Jasta 2 had relocated due to a September 22 attack on Bertincourt by the RFC.

Princes and generals attended his funeral on October 31 in the great Cambrai cathedral. On foot, holding a cushion displaying Boelcke's decorations, walked Manfred von Richthofen. Six immense black horses pulled the carriage and its shining coffin while fighter pilots circled slowly overhead. After the ceremony, Boelcke's body began the long journey home and was finally laid to rest on November 2 at St. John's Church in Dessau. With royalty and family in attendance, pilots again arced above the town until the coffin emerged. They then cut their engines and glided silently down over the graveyard in tribute to the man they'd admired above all others.

Oswald Boelcke died a warrior's death, in the middle of a fight and undefeated. His impact on fighter aviation was enormous, yet more often it is his famous pupil, the future Red Baron, who is remembered today. Had he lived longer, Boelcke certainly would have killed more Allied airmen—it was his profession and his duty. This, in addition to his skill and leadership, is at the heart of Boelcke's spirit. He certainly didn't love war and he personally disliked killing. It was not a sport to him, as it was with others, nor was it a game. It was something he had to do, so he did it well. Boelcke's British enemies recognized this and dropped a wreath behind the German lines with a simple but poignant, message: "To the memory of Captain Boelcke, our brave and chivalrous opponent. From the English Royal Flying Corps." French, Italian, and British airmen also sent messages and wreaths from various prisoner-of-war camps. But the most fitting tribute came from a man who would come to embody many of the traits of a successful fighter pilot. Ruthless, a born leader, and a true killer, Manfred von Richthofen had this to say of his teacher: "I am only a fighting airman, but Boelcke was a hero."

"STANDING ORDER OF the Day: Attack Everything."

On June 30, 1916, Maj. Lanoe George Hawker posted this notice for his pilots in No. 24 Squadron, RFC.

Called the "British Boelcke," Hawker had joined the RFC from the Royal Engineers and began the war as a pilot. He'd been part of the initial deployment in October 1914, flying across the Channel with No. 6 Squadron. On April 18, 1915, Hawker took his BE-2c and single-handedly attacked the Zeppelin base at Gontrode with a bag full of hand grenades and three melinite bombs.* To defeat the German anti-aircraft gunners, Hawker actually spiraled down around the tethered Zeppelin, throwing hand grenades at it finally. He blew a hole in the skin and the blimp waffled to the ground. Through the ensuing hail of ground fire, Hawker then destroyed a new hangar with his last melinite bomb. Managing to escape and land back at Abeele Aerodrome, he found thirty-eight holes in the aircraft. Largely as a result of his spectacular lone attack, the Zeppelins—the bogeymen of the early air war, attacking targets in England, killing civilians, and generally scaring the hell out of people—were removed from Gontrode.

Hawker's feat earned him the Distinguished Service Order and the beginning of a fearsome reputation.† Like Boelcke, he was a superb flyer, but also a thinker and an innovator. By the summer of 1915, about the time Fokker was testing his interrupter gear, Hawker had fixed a Lewis gun to the top wing of his Bristol Scout. This eventually led to his perfection of a double drum magazine arrangement that permitted a pilot to

---

*The name is from the French *melon*. Melinite is a high explosive made with picric acid, a pharmaceutical used for treating herpes, among other things.

†The DSO ranks above the Military Cross and was only awarded to officers. Usually for actions under fire, the DSO was considered a decoration for majors or above unless the circumstances were extreme.

fire ninety-seven rounds before reloading. He fine-tuned the existing gunsight design and invented a new ammo belt, based on disposable links, that nearly eliminated jamming. Hawker also set up a forward intelligence system with field telephones at strategic points along the front lines to alert him to incoming enemy aircraft.

On July 25, Hawker took off to hunt in the skies above Flanders. A new weapon, the flamethrower, had been used with devastating effect by German infantry to breach the lines along the Menin Road, about two miles east of Ypres. Ground fighting was heavy, so reconnaissance patrols were everywhere. Late in the afternoon, Lanoe Hawker attacked a two-seat Aviatik over Passchendaele so fiercely that the German dove into the ground. At dusk, he found an Albatros C and sent it spinning into the Houthulst Forest, behind the British lines. With the light fading over cheering British troops, Hawker put a thirty-round burst into the belly of another Albatros C and sent it down in flames over the front lines at Hooge.

He would go on shooting down planes until called back to England for a rest, to receive a promotion to major, and to be awarded Great Britain's highest decoration for bravery—the Victoria Cross. Major Hawker also took command of the newly formed 24 Squadron, equipped with DH-2 single-seat fighters.

Combat had taught him priceless lessons. As Boelcke was doing, Hawker formalized these lifesaving jewels and passed them along to his pilots. A full five months of formation flying, gunnery, navigation, and squadron-level tactics went into 24 Squadron's preparations before the new commanding officer was satisfied. Hawker returned to France in February 1916 and immediately went to work killing Germans, despite the limitations of the DH-2.

Bug-like in appearance, this was a "pusher" aircraft with

the propeller *behind* the pilot. Without workable interrupter gear, this at least solved the problem of a clear field of view for firing, but that was about all it did. Faster than the Albatros and Eindecker planes, the DH-2 was also extremely maneuverable. However, the 100-horsepower French Gnome engines were often rebuilt pieces of secondhand junk that fell apart in flight. With a pusher engine there was nothing shielding the pilot from the icy air so Hawker also invented hip-high, fleece-lined "lug" boots in an attempt to stay warm enough to work the rudder bar. Nicknamed the "Spinning Incinerator," the DH-2 was hardly an ideal solution, but it was the best available single-seat aircraft for the moment.

From June to October 1916, 24 Squadron destroyed eighty German aircraft. In all likelihood, Hawker accounted for more than twenty of these, although his confirmed total stands at nine. The RFC attitude toward counting personal victories was fundamentally different from that of the Germans or even fellow allies. The British high command believed that singling out fighter pilots was unfair to bomber and reconnaissance crews, who flew equally dangerous missions. In fact, it wasn't until the latter part of 1915 that records were officially compiled, and even then the totals weren't published.* Everyone else, Americans included, believed it unfair *not* to recognize such exploits. This was no reflection on the courage and skill of other types of pilots, just an illustration of the difference. Other air forces also concluded that such a status might encourage greater efforts by fighter pilots, and since war is about killing, then special recognition seemed warranted.

---

*The main sources of pre-1916 British claims are from decoration citations. Eventually, these were all compiled with combat and casualty reports in Trevor Henshaw's excellent reference book *The Sky Their Battlefield*.

But there was a practical side to the British thinking as well. Due to the essentially defensive nature of German strategy and the prevailing westerly winds, most of the air combat occurred over the German lines. It was often difficult for the Allies to verify kill claims, as many aircraft that appeared doomed were recovered and flown again. The end result was a rather informal tally that was much less stringent than the German system.

But the damage done to the German flying corps was real. Their previous control of the air was disappearing and the blow to morale, both for soldiers and pilots, was severe. This was the situation that led to the formation of the *Jagdstaffeln* and the ascendency of both Boelcke and Hawker.

On a cold twenty-third of November, 1916, Major Hawker was prowling alone over the Western Front when he saw five Albatros fighters near Bapaume. Without hesitation, he attacked, concentrating on the leader. For over thirty minutes Hawker and his opponent fought a twisting, looping, gut-wrenching dogfight. The Albatros was more powerful and armed with twin Spandau guns, while the British DH-2 was lighter and more maneuverable.

At around 2,000 feet, the two aircraft continued turning into each other in what would later be called a "one-circle" fight. Round and round they went, each trying to outturn the other and get into firing position. Often close enough to see each other, the British pilot even waved once, undoubtedly surprised that he couldn't gain an advantage. Neither could his opponent.

Keenly aware that the winds had pushed the fight deeper over the German lines, Hawker was also running out of fuel. Passing the Albatros, he pulled into the vertical, attempting to use altitude for a tighter turn and get behind the German. Coming down out of the loop, he fired off a long burst from his Lewis gun and dove for the ground.

The pilot of the Albatros wasn't rattled, nor did he break off the attack. With ten victories behind him, Manfred von Richthofen was confident, dangerous, and he clearly realized that he was fighting no ordinary pilot. The Baron wasn't the gifted flyer that Hawker was, but his calm, cold nature and superb marksmanship made him an extremely lethal fighter pilot. The superior performance of the Albatros also helped as he followed the DH-2 around and down, his faster machine rapidly closing the gap. Just above the trees, a bare 100 feet behind, the German cleared a gun jam and fired a double burst with the last of his nine hundred rounds of ammunition.

Whether or not the Englishman was killed outright or grazed and knocked unconscious, his plane went down. Bouncing end over end across shell holes, the shattered debris finally came to rest in the muddy filth of no-man's-land. Major Lanoe George Hawker, VC, DSO, was buried south of Ligny, off the Flers Road, by a squad of German grenadiers.

Upon learning whom he had killed, von Richthofen said, "My eleventh Britisher was Major Hawker, twenty-six years old and the commander of an English squadron. According to prisoners' accounts, he was the English Boelcke. He gave me the hardest fight I have experienced so far."

THE FALL OF 1916 changed World War I.

If we need a date to mark the end of one era and the beginning of the next, this will suffice. Nearly a million men were lost during the Somme Offensive for a total eastward gain of about a mile. Even then, the Germans were able to hold their secondary defenses, and the armies once again were pulped together in a stinking morass of rotting corpses, rats, and mud. On December 12, the British Army Council officially approved an unprecedented expansion of the Royal Flying Corps. More than two hundred squadrons were to be added, including fighter units equipped with the new Sopwith Pup. Additionally, four Royal Naval Air Service (RNAS) squadrons were created.

Obscene losses at Verdun and on the Somme ended any hopes for a negotiated peace, and both sides were now fully aware that the war would not end soon. The month also brought changes to the governments of Britain, France, and Germany—all promised new thinking, new strategies, and an end to the stalemate. Germany and Austria were collapsing internally due to the naval blockade of their ports. Food prices in Berlin jumped 600 percent in two years, and in Vienna people were eating their dogs. Neither empire had anticipated a protracted war, and they were ill prepared for it when it happened. Any available rubber and copper went to the war effort, with spoons, church bells, and door latches melted down for their metal. Germany's sources of fertilizer, grain, and animal fodder dried up, and agricultural production fell by 50 percent. Germans were drinking coffee made from tree bark and surviving on turnips augmented by a weekly allowance of two ounces of butter with a single egg. The wet, cold fall of 1916 yielded a miserable harvest, so by Christmas the people were starving on 1,200 calories a day.* Ten thousand Viennese women had become part-time prostitutes.

Great Britain was nearly as badly off. More than 60 percent of prewar foodstuffs had been imports, which now were severely curtailed. Malnutrition, infant mortality, and a critical shortage of doctors all contributed to the misery. Following the death of his son on the Somme, Prime Minister H. H. Asquith lost his motivation and was replaced by David Lloyd George.

*Prewar adults had a daily average of around 3,400 calories.

A fiery Liberal reformer, Lloyd George had swayed with the political breeze in 1914 and joined those who wanted England to fight. He'd solved the munitions shortage of 1915 and now instituted mandatory rationing, with compulsory conscription soon to follow. He was strong-willed, decisive, and politically astute.

France had also replaced the commander-in-chief of her army, Joseph Joffre. Blamed for the disaster at Verdun, he was first promoted to Marshal of France and then fired. Despite several very competent choices, his replacement was the cosmopolitan, bilingual, and inexperienced General Robert Nivelle.

The Russians had always produced enough food to feed themselves, but a decrepit infrastructure and corrupt, inefficient government left food rotting in the fields. A million tons of grain was piled up on ships and wharves in Black Sea ports because the Ottoman Turks, a Central Power ally of Germany, had closed the Dardanelles passage. Fuel was scarce; wages, when they were paid at all, couldn't begin to keep up with the price of necessities. Riots had erupted and Russian troops were siding with the people. The Tsar, never very capable, was living in a state of detached, vacillating fear.

This, then, was the big picture in the fall of 1916 as the old ways and the old leaders were replaced. In these grim days, after the deaths of Oswald Boelcke and Lanoe Hawker, the time of the scout aircraft passed and the era of the true fighter pilot began its ascent. The men who came next possessed little of the idealism of prewar flyers. That high-mindedness was long forgotten amid the reality of freezing air, burning death, and the loss of so many friends to a war dragging on into 1917.

CHAPTER 3

THE CRUCIBLE

ROYAL AIRCRAFT FACTORY SE-5

ON BOTH SIDES of the Western Front men stared at each other, bloody, cold, and exhausted. Heavy rain-filled clouds sagged down from a flat, pewter-colored sky. The soft rolling fields of Flanders had been turned into a pockmarked, sticky mess by millions of pounds of high explosives. Ice gleamed from barbed wire strung across no-man's-land between the trenches, and water-filled shell holes had hardened into jagged brown death traps. Rats gnawed on limbs from thousands of frozen corpses splayed across the mud.

Germany's military leaders had been replaced by two men who knew they couldn't win a war of attrition. Paul von Hindenburg and Erich Ludendorff also realized that time was running out as the United States would soon enter the conflict. Victory, or some type of negotiated peace, had to be won—now.

Germany's only hope against the Royal Navy blockade was the U-boats prowling the Atlantic. Many of the ships bringing supplies to England were neutral; in fact, most were American. As they began sinking, there was enormous political pressure on Washington to respond. Woodrow Wilson had won the November election with the slogan, "He kept us out of war," but now he had a free hand to act. Germany now had a narrow window of opportunity to force a conclusion before being overwhelmed by Yankee troops, planes, and industrial might.

Through the winter of 1917, under atrocious weather, von Hindenburg and Ludendorff quietly constructed new defensive fortifications 20 miles behind the current central section of the front. More than 350,000 Russian prisoners and German reservists made concrete, hauled steel, dug trenches, and erected pillboxes—all in secret. During a gueling four-month period they shortened the line by 25 miles between Arras and St. Quentin. Then, on February 9, Operation Alberich, a strategic pull-back, was activated.*

The withdrawal caught the Allies completely by surprise. Aerial reconnaissance had failed to detect either the movement or the construction of the new defenses. In fact, the first real awareness came from British patrols encountering empty German positions. Later, German artillery opened up on their former front lines to destroy anything left behind, and the entire area became a wasteland, devoid of life or usefulness. The new Siegfried-Stellung Line (called the Hindenburg Line by the Allies) was designed to preserve German resources, to be impregnable, and therefore to give the Entente powers a problem they could not solve but by negotiated peace.

To the men on the lines and in the aerodromes, this was

*Named for a malicious dwarf king from German mythology.

quite beside the point. They all lived day to day, trying to stay alive in their trench or cockpit. Despite the cold, lice were everywhere. A bluish haze hung over the Allied lines from countless braziers, and curved sheets of rusting corrugated tin covered the trenches wherever possible. Field kitchens churned out meals, but food had to be carried forward and arrived cold. One particular favorite of British soldiers was Maconochie's, a vegetable and beef stew, though they usually settled for corned beef. French soldiers suffered less acutely from food shortages, benefiting from short supply lines and local connections—they always seemed to have their essential chocolate and alcohol rations.

British trenches were built in a series of "firebay" sections that ran continuously but were never straight. There were front, support, and reserve lines all running parallel to each other and intersected by communications trenches. The whole arrangement was about 500 to 800 yards deep, and many ran through low ground that flooded easily. "Dead Man's Road," "Ale Alley," "Bond Street"—prosaic names for a thoroughly miserable existence where a man had a 50 percent chance of being wounded or killed.

The Germans built better fortifications, using reinforced concrete to construct deep, ventilated redoubts, or fortified emplacements. These were drier and easier to heat. Since they'd been able to choose the terrain, many of their positions were on high ground or even in caves. Germans generally utilized the three-line system as well, but it was much, much deeper, often with three miles between the front and the reserve area.

On both sides the pilots lived better. Aerodromes among all the air services were fairly similar and had the same basic needs. Typically at least five miles behind the lines, an airfield was usually located near a town and constructed around a flat, smoothed-out field about a half mile square. Repair shops, junk piles, and fueling areas were all necessities. In the beginning these were relatively haphazard arrangements given the fluidity of the ground situation and lack of experience with aviation operations. This changed rapidly, as huts and shacks were replaced by dugouts, wooden buildings, and canvas hangars whenever possible.

There could be up to four squadrons per airfield, which meant approximately eighty planes. British units listed about twenty-four pilots each and needed two hundred enlisted men to service, repair, and load the aircraft. Then there were cooks, anti-aircraft gunners, and radio and administrative personnel. In total, upwards of a thousand people, with a variety of specialties, lived and worked on each little self-contained airfield. This uniqueness remains the same today.

British flyers typically lived on the aerodrome with separate quarters for living, socializing, and eating. Each had an orderly—a "batman"—to look after his personal needs. French and German pilots were usually quartered in private homes or a commandeered hotel in the nearby town.* Meals were often taken in local restaurants, though large airfields such as Douai had their own messes. Food also varied widely. British pilots seemed to dress the best but eat the worst. One Frenchman, naturally, remembered English food as "everything boiled to death in live steam, then covered with a white sauce made of wall paper paste." The Germans purloined their food from the French whenever possible. They favored soup, sausage, and lots of pork when available. In fact, many soldiers and pilots ate better at the front than their families did back in Germany.

*Early in the war the Germans experimented with a sort of mobile squadron that was billeted on a train.

French food was the best. Supplies from the Mediterranean were unhindered by the U-boat threat, and locals were obviously sympathetic to their own countrymen. Fresh fish was often available, along with soup, mutton, and real coffee.

Aerodromes always had some type of officers' lounge. The décor was heavy on propellers, captured machine guns, and other war souvenirs. Pictures of women, nude if at all possible, festooned the walls. Blackboards were scattered about for notices, weather sheets, and rhyming verses. In British lounges there was likely to be a piano or at least a gramophone. They all had bars stocked with whiskey, cognac, brandy, and whatever else could be found. Brits were the hardest drinkers, a tendency that would continue in the wars to come. Many Germans, contrary to the stereotype of the martinet with a shaved head, drank and sang a good deal. Canadians, ANZAC pilots,* and the late-arriving Americans all knew how to throw a party when they weren't flying. Singing and drinking helped take the edge off, something that continuously offended the rear-echelon types. What really angered them was that they couldn't do a thing about it—something else that hasn't changed.

Keep the home fires burning
While your hearts are yearning,
Though your lads are far away
They dream of home,
There's a silver lining
Through the dark clouds shining,
Turn the dark clouds inside out,
Till the boys come home.

---

*ANZAC: the Australia and New Zealand Army Corps.

And why drink, sing, and chase women? Typically, the pilots were young men with a testosterone-charged warrior spirit who had an excellent chance of dying horribly within weeks. They *knew* this, yet they continued to fly into the bullets every day. Their discipline was in the air, where it counted, and they had little use for it on the ground or for the institutional trappings of military life beloved by noncombatants. Gambling in its various forms was always popular, as, of course, were girls. Frederick Libby, an American who flew with the RFC, summed it up neatly: "Girls weren't expensive, all of them trying to do their bit for King and Country. What more could a fellow ask?"

But by early 1917 the pilots themselves were changing. The war had lost its glamour, and the survivors were battered, cynical, and much more businesslike. Flight training schools had been established, and veterans at least attempted to create a curriculum that would give a young pilot a chance. At this point, the Royal Flying Corps course included a ground school for both prospective pilots and observers. The two-month school taught basic military indoctrination, useless close-order drill, and rudimentary navigation, with practical mechanics related to engines and machine guns. Qualified pilot candidates then went off to preliminary flight training at smaller airfields such as Waddington, outside London.

A student pilot was expected to solo after a few hours of dual instruction. If he couldn't solo, he was sent to observer school or back to the regular army. Following about five hours of post-solo flight, he would take a flight check and go on to advanced training at fields such as Upavon or Lincoln. A demonstrated ability to handle faster aircraft, more solo time, and training in aerobatics were all required before earning the coveted wings of a pilot. In 1914, pilots went into action with less than ten hours of solo flight time; in British schools this was a result of the resistance to a formal flying curriculum, as initially it was believed that any sort of rigid training would inhibit pilots. By 1917, flyers had about twenty-five hours when they went off to war, ideally including some time in the plane they'd use in combat. Toward the end of the war, a man usually had nearer to fifty hours before he first crossed the Channel.

German training was predictably much more structured. Prewar training was at bases such as Halberstadt and accomplished in slow, steady aircraft such as a Bristol-Taube. Underpowered and generally forgiving, it was a fairly good trainer. It also had dual controls, and a student typically took three to four hours of instruction prior to his solo. The entire course lasted about two months and was very, very basic. But again, in 1914, aircraft were used for reconnaissance and artillery spotting, so no one really gave much thought to flying that wasn't straight, level, non-maneuvering, and during the day—yet.

At the beginning of the war the French Air Service had been the most progressive in both aircraft design and organizational thinking. It was the first to group aircraft together by specialized types, and by March 1915 there were four such groups: Bombing, Infantry and Artillery Cooperation, Reconnaissance, and Fighting.

However, the French training system was unique in that no dual instruction was used for prospective fighter pilots. Their philosophy was that a man best learned to fly through a self-paced increase in his comfort level, based on gradual exposure. In the *rouler* phase, a student was placed, by himself, in a scaled-down Blériot with an underpowered 25-horsepower engine and half wings. This contraption couldn't fly, but it could, theoretically, familiarize a student with controlling a machine.* If the

*Also called a "penguin" or "grass cutter."

machine was run at full throttle, the tail would actually lift and the student could "fly" across the field on the rollers—the wheels.

Then came the *décoller* class, where a student, again with no real instruction, could get a few feet off the ground.* This was usually accomplished using a field with a hump in it, followed by a slight depression, so the plane could get airborne. The *pique* class still involved flying in a straight line, with no maneuvering. Then finally came several *tour de piste* flights. In this phase, a student was permitted to fly around the field about 600 feet up. The future pilot next did a "high-altitude" flight, then spirals (spins), and after that was ready for his *brevet* tests if he had the total hours required. This number varied throughout the war, but by 1917 a student needed fourteen hours before being allowed to take his tests. Then he began a series of *petits voyages*—cross-country adventures to unfamiliar aerodromes. Upon completing this he was now *un aviateur,* a pilot. This system took a great deal of time and produced wildly inconsistent results.

Not surprisingly, as combat losses increased, pilots were needed much faster, and so was some type of minimum standard. By the end of the war, the French had adopted the British method, and the Americans did the same.

AFTER LOSING AIR superiority to the Germans over the Somme, the Allies were well aware of what they had to do in order to deal with the Fokker Eindecker and its biplane cousins. Increased understanding of aerodynamics and the construction process resulted in several significant changes. Biplanes, with their in-

***Décoller* means "to take off." Interestingly, the word can also mean "to behead."

creased lift and wing loading, were now the standard design. Wings became thicker as the principle of lift was better understood, and this allowed greater strength for violent maneuvering. Monocoque fuselage construction also became commonplace: the external skin supported loads and was no longer merely a covering, thus streamlining the aircraft and making it much, much stronger. A stronger airframe permitted more powerful engines and heavier armament, and it could also now withstand the stress of dogfighting. The true fighter aircraft was born.

Engine design also drastically improved. Prior to the war, aircraft and automobile engines had shared the stage, but this changed rapidly. Cars only ran for limited periods, didn't need much power, and had to be inexpensive to manufacture. Aircraft engines had to run continuously with great power, and they had to withstand drastic atmospheric changes, primitive maintenance conditions, abuse from pilots, and battle damage. They had to be powerful, tough, and reliable, and as governments were the customer, cost ceased to be a limiting factor.

There were two basic types of piston-driven combustion engines for military aircraft at the start of the Great War. In a *rotary* configuration, the entire engine spins around the crankshaft. This has several advantages. First, it is a very smooth, practically vibration-free engine, so this means less wear and a more stable gun platform. Though a rotary produces significant torque, this can be overcome by the rudder.* Rotary motors are easy to air-cool, so no extra fluid is needed and the system is much lighter. Less weight usually results in excess lift, which can be exchanged for better performance and maneuvering.

But since it's spinning around in the airstream, a rotary engine produces a great deal of drag. Hence 200 horsepower

*Torque is a twisting movement in the direction of rotation.

was about the maximum power you could give a rotary engine before it became impractical. It was also a fuel guzzler, consuming 20 to 30 percent more fuel than stationary motors, thus effectively negating the weight saved from air cooling as it required more gas. Or you settled for an aircraft that carried less fuel with a correspondingly shorter flying time.

Stationary engines, which remain fixed while the crankshaft spins, became the norm after 1916. One way to produce more power was to increase the displacement in an engine. This is basically the volume of air in each cylinder that is moved, or displaced, by the piston. More air displaced means greater pressure inside the combustion chamber, which generates more horsepower. You can create displacement by making bigger pistons or by adding more of them. Larger pistons mean more frontal area, greater weight, problems fitting them into an airframe—or all of these. So designers began adding cylinders, all the way up to the Liberty V-12 in 1918, as a way to increase displacement.

Also key in producing engine power is the compression ratio. Think of a big can (the cylinder) with a smaller can inside (the piston). As the piston moves up and down it pushes, or compresses, the air in the cylinder. This "packed" air, when mixed with fuel and ignited, generates the energy to operate the engine. Greater compression results in a more powerful explosion, which can mean more horsepower. In 1914 the typical ratio was about 4:1, and this increased to 6:1 by the end of war through improvements in design and fuels.

The arrangement of the cylinders was also important and directly affected performance. *Inline* engines placed them down both sides of the crankshaft, while a *radial* configuration made a star shape. "V" motors angled the cylinders up and away from the shaft. Lubrication was a challenge, since castor oil was the only available fluid that could be mixed with fuel and remain effective at high engine operating temperatures. A vegetable oil derived from the castor bean, it was ideal for engines that were taken apart and rebuilt regularly, like aircraft motors. During the war a rotary engine needed a complete overhaul for each twenty-five flying hours, while inlines were rebuilt at around the three-hundred-hour point.*

Improving fuel also resulted in power gains. Aircraft engines of 1914 were operating on low-octane fuels (40–70 octane) of dubious quality. Fuel with higher ratings can be compressed more before detonating, thus producing more power, and by the end of the war aviation fuel was up to about 80 octane. As a result of shortages caused by the naval blockade, Germany led the world in developing chemical additives and synthetic replacements for necessities such as oil and rubber. This chemical research carried over into fuels, but there was still never enough to meet demand.

Engines and airframes could be improved and refined, but literally at the end of everything lay the propeller. If it was primitive or inefficient, then any improvements in engine power and performance would matter very little. Props that attached directly to the crankshaft were fine in early aircraft, but as engine speed increased above 1,500 rpm the propeller simply couldn't spin fast enough to keep up. So a reduction mechanism was added whereby a series of gears transmitted the motor's energy without the speed. This gave a propeller power, but at a manageable number of revolutions per minute.

However, the best-designed fighter aircraft in the world is just for show without weaponry, and aerial gunnery was fast evolving into an art. The guns themselves were good by this

*Modern piston engines go for 2,000–3,000 hours between overhauls.

time, though ammunition was often a problem. Badly fitted rounds in canvas belts could cause a jam or even explode. The metallic belt-and-link system had been added, which was a great improvement, but really good pilots still armed their own planes whenever possible.

Tracer shells had a chemical (usually phosphorus or magnesium) in a hollow base that would ignite and leave a visible trail, which allowed the shooter to correct his aim instantly. Unfortunately, the weight of the tracer shells was different from that of ordinary ball bullets, so the trajectory was different. Also, the chemical sometimes burned out early. Both factors could make aiming corrections problematic, but tracer shells were better than nothing at all.

Gunsights were similarly being continuously refined. Unless you happened to be directly behind or in front of a target, there were *deflection* angles involved in getting a bullet to hit. Compensating for these angles required "leading the target" as it moves across your line of sight. Think of playing dodgeball and aiming your throw *ahead* of where the target is frantically running.

Visualize a big half circle, a 180-degree arc, extending out 200 yards in front of your cockpit. Any target within this arc is something that you can turn, point, and shoot at fairly easily. One degree of this arc (referred to as a *mil*) equals 1 foot at 1,000 feet.* If you then extend your 1-degree cone out to 2,000 feet, the same mil is 2 feet wide.

If you have a known reference, such as the size of your gunsight, then you can estimate the range to your enemy by how much of him fills up the sight. For instance, the Albatros D-I had a 28-foot wingspan. Understanding mils now, we know

---

*Short for *milliradian*.

that at 1,000 feet an aircraft with a 28-foot span would fill a 28-mil aiming reticule. Of course, 1,000 feet is much too far to shoot with your Vickers gun, so we double the aiming reticle to 56 mils, and the target's wingspan would fill it at 500 feet. (See Appendix A, "Anatomy of a Dogfight.")

One of the first aerial sights was called a *frame* or *gate sight.* This was a little metal rectangle just like a picture frame, and the idea was to put the target within the frame and shoot away. Adapted from a naval gun-laying system, it worked well enough against non-maneuvering aircraft such as bombers and reconnaissance planes. The early Fokkers flown by Boelcke and Immelmann had gate sights because there was no alternative. But it only really accounted for deflection if the target was moving horizontally across your line of sight, and once aerial fighting evolved to aggressive, three-dimensional maneuvering, another solution was needed.

A *ring sight* was constructed of concentric metal circles and was mounted on the back of the gun. Up near the muzzle was a vertical post with a small red painted bead on the tip. If you lined up the tip of the post within the inner circle of the ring, then the bullets would go where you aimed them at zero degrees of deflection. However, by using a ring instead of a frame, you could now also judge lead angles for deflection shots no matter how your target was maneuvering. Guns were typically bore-sighted for 200 yards and the rings were sized to assume an enemy traveling at 100 mph was crossing perpendicular to you at a full 90-degree deflection angle. This meant a bullet time of flight of two and a half seconds against an enemy who would travel about 38 feet during that time. Another part of the mental gymnastics you had to do while flying and fighting was to compensate for the bullet drop (against gravity), since none of the sights did. However, it was known that a Mark VII shell fell 14.4 inches over 200 yards, so the pilot just had to wing it and aim a bit high. It took a lot of practice.

Single-seat pilots had to do this alone and rarely had the time that gunners and observers enjoyed in multiseat aircraft. They needed some way to accurately and immediately point and fire without aligning rings and beads. In 1915 an optical sight was proposed by the Aldis brothers of Birmingham, England. Like a modern rifle scope, the lenses provided several key advantages. It showed a prealigned aiming point that appeared over the target image. Unlike iron sights, the viewer's eye distance from the sight makes no difference, since the lenses are collimated, or focused on infinity; as a result, the pilot doesn't have to hunch forward to shoot.

The prototype had a 3X magnification, which would be fine for a stationary rifleman but proved extremely disorienting to a pilot moving at 100 mph, so the magnification feature was discontinued. The outer ring was sized to provide a full deflection shot against a 100-mph target at a range of 200 yards. All four lenses were hermetically sealed, and the tube was filled with an inert gas to prevent fogging. Because it was mounted on the cowling, the sight could be obscured by leaking engine oil, so an anti-fouling flap was installed that the pilot could close or open as needed. Later production sights protruded through a hole cut in the windscreen.

British fighters began flying with operational Aldis sights by mid-1916, and they became standard equipment for the last two years of the war. Both the French and the Germans copied the Aldis sight but didn't get them fielded until 1918.*

---

*Chrétien and Oigee sights were plagued by fogging issues. Surprisingly, the Germans never realized that inert gases would solve the problem.

WERNER VOSS OF Jasta 2 saw the ungainly, slow-moving FE-2 reconnaissance plane and immediately pounced. It wasn't much of a fight.*

Not only did he have an altitude advantage, but Voss was also flying a new Albatros D-I fighter. Designed from the beginning as a fighter, the plane was unique in several ways. The fuselage was a plywood shell, not fabric over wood framing, so it was strong and light. The Benz Bz.III engine was a 150-horsepower, six-cylinder, water-cooled inline that gave the Albatros a maximum speed of 110 mph, a 30-mph advantage over the British plane.

Voss also had twin Spandau machine guns, firing through the prop at 500 rounds per minute. His first bursts tore through the other aircraft's wings, and the plane dove toward the ground, streaming flames. Following it down, the German saw the plane flop into no-man's-land very near the British trenches and fall to pieces. As one of the crew carried the other to safety, Voss wheeled overhead, pounding his knee in frustration. Procedures for claiming kills were very strict and required another flyer as a witness or corroboration from the German army.† He had neither.

Shoving his goggles up to see better, Voss pulled the power and glided down. Skidding to a sloppy stop amid the barbed wire and shell holes, he jumped from the cockpit and sprinted toward the wrecked British plane. Yanking the quick-release pin, he pulled the rear machine gun out. As he stumbled back to the Albatros, bullets whined past his head and smacked wetly into the stinking mud. Wedging his trophy next to the bulkhead, Voss firewalled the throttle, bounced back into the air,

*Voss mistakenly identified this as an FB 5 "Gunbus"—a common error.
†FE-2b, tail #4915, 18 Squadron RFC. Near Ginchy.

and waved a cocky goodbye to the angry British infantry. Later that night, amid the beer and noise, the .303 Lewis gun was mounted in the Officers' Mess of Jasta 2, giving the young pilot his first verified kill. It was the twenty-seventh of November, 1916.

Son of a wealthy dye factory owner, Werner Voss began his military career with the 11th Westphalian Hussars, subsequently fighting in the last big cavalry battle of the war.* Then, hearing that Hussars were being converted into infantry units, he applied for a transfer to the air service and became an observer. But Voss wanted to fly and fight, not ride in the backseat and spot for the artillery. Trying again this time he was accepted for pilot training during the summer of 1916. Then as now, aptitude and instructor evaluations were critical if one wished to fly fighters, and Voss was impressive. By the fall of 1916, he'd been commissioned a *Leutnant* and assigned to Oswald Boelcke's famous Jasta 2 along with von Richthofen and Erwin Boehme.

In stark contrast to his more reserved friend Manfred "The Red Baron" von Richthofen, Werner loved women, wine, and life. Surprisingly, Richthofen and Voss got on very well. Voss was one of the few pilots who were actually close to the Baron, and the two pilots even spent a leave together at Voss's family home. Voss was a very skilled flyer and superb marksman who only wished to fight. He had no interest in administration or command, and though he embraced Boelcke's principles, Voss showed no inclination toward the scientific side of air combat.

Nor was Richthofen the thinker his mentor had been. He was a killer. The von Richthofens were landowners and hunters, and Manfred regarded fighting as his duty and saw killing

---

*Hussars were a type of light, fast cavalry used mainly for scouting.

as an extension of blood sport. He didn't appear to hate his enemies, nor did he suffer from a romantic view of war. It was simply his business, his true vocation. Once, as a young cavalry officer on the Eastern Front, he'd locked a village priest in a church and politely informed him: "At the first sign of hostility from your villagers you will be executed."

The Baron was methodical and always had a plan. If he encountered an unknown situation, he sometimes became confused, disengaged, or both. Conversely, Voss would improvise, adapt, and overcome. He was an instinctive flyer who exhibited what would later be called excellent "situational awareness." Both men were deadly serious about their work; they simply approached it differently. Werner Voss, however, was by far a better natural pilot and was held in very high regard by his enemies. After twenty-four kills he was awarded the Pour le Mérite in April 1917.

"Bloody April," it was called by the British, and April 1917 was exactly that. Bloody *and* a turning point in the war—both on the ground and in the air. The new Allied leadership had promised results, and now they had to deliver. French general Robert Nivelle won approval for a plan that he vowed would break the stalemate and end the war. The British (meaning Colonial and Dominion troops, such as Canadians, Indians, and the ANZAC) would attack east of Arras and capture Vimy Ridge. This, they hoped, would attract German attention and troops away from Nivelle's assault. The French would go over the top near the river Aisne and punch a hole in the German lines above the Chemin des Dames.* The armies would drive north and east, respectively, and link up behind the German rear.

*Named for the daughters of Louis XV, who used it as a bridle path.

British and French generals alike had no confidence in the plan. It hadn't accounted for the German withdrawal to the Hindenburg Line, nor would there be any real cooperation between the BEF on the northern flank and the French to the south. The biggest reason that waiting made sense was the imminent involvement of the Americans.

Failing to defeat the Royal Navy at Jutland the previous year, the German High Seas Fleet had no real way to fight at sea except with its U-boats. To break the naval blockade and force the Allies to the bargaining table, Germany had resumed unrestricted submarine warfare in January 1917, and by the end of March seven American merchant ships had been sunk. Additionally, the Americans had decoded the infamous Zimmermann Telegram, which offered German support to Mexico against the United States if Washington declared war against the Central Powers.

April's weather was also horrible, with rain, sleet, and even snow accompanied by gale-force westerly winds. There was no urgent strategic reason to attack the German positions and every incentive to wait. But Nivelle had a reputation from the Battle of Verdun and was intent on furthering his military and political ambitions. With his Gallic charm, unaccented English, and self-confidence, he'd persuaded the new British prime minister, David Lloyd George, that his plan would succeed. Lloyd George overrode the objections from his generals and placed the BEF under French command for the offensive. Understandably, the British, especially the Royal Flying Corps and Royal Naval Air Service, were incensed.

The attack was to commence on April 8 following days of concentrated artillery bombardments, extensive photo reconnaissance, and scores of army cooperation (close-air-support) missions to destroy ammo dumps, railroads, communications, and airfields. The RFC had a clear superiority in numbers with its 754 aircraft, of which about 350 were single-seat scouts. The Germans possessed 250 single-seat scouts out of 480 operational planes. Ironically, just as the Royal Navy had proven at the Battle of Jutland that quality defeats quantity, so now the Luftstreitkräfte would prove the same lesson with their superior aircraft.

Every hostile machine completely outmanoeuvred us and were capable of beating us in climbing, turning and speed.

—2ND LT. GEOFFREY COCK, 45 SQUADRON RFC

Though numerically larger, the forty-one squadrons of the RFC and RNAS generally flew obsolete aircraft such as the BE-2, FE-2, and DH-2. All had performed well enough during the battles of 1916, but German aviation had made tremendous strides since then. The imperative to regain air superiority that brought Boelcke back to the front and would permit von Richthofen to create the unit known as the "Flying Circus" was very much in force. The Albatros series of fighters, now at the D-III variant, was proof of this. If, the Germans reasoned, the Allies could be swept from the sky, then whatever they planned on the ground was unlikely to succeed. Such was the rise in importance of airpower in only two years.

To further complicate matters, the RFC commander, Hugh Trenchard, had decided to withhold his latest and most advanced aircraft until the offensive began. His logic was that if the planes were fielded too soon, the Germans would devise countertactics and the effectiveness of his new fighters would be minimized when it was most needed. The flip side was that if fielded early, the superior aircraft could clear the skies of enemy aircraft. It was a calculated risk; Trenchard, unlike most generals, was a very hands-on commander who knew his people and the environment in which they fought. He simply made the wrong decision and was so sick during the opening days of April that he couldn't reverse it.

Photo reconnaissance was still a priority for the RFC so that it could ascertain exact enemy troop concentrations and carry out the absolutely critical task of artillery spotting. Aerial photography was not a new idea and had been around since the previous century. A Russian military engineer had developed the first semiautomatic aerial camera and the Germans perfected the technology. By the end of 1918 enlarged photos taken from above 15,000 feet would be good enough to reveal footprints. Over the course of the war, the British alone would process half a million photographs.

So they fought the winds, lousy weather, and German line patrols in an attempt to gather intelligence. Recon aircraft had to be unmolested, which meant a close escort of fighters to keep the Germans away. Even so, 60 percent of RFC casualties during the first four days of April occurred during photo recon missions. These dismal numbers led Hugh Trenchard to unleash the new Bristol F-2 fighter—what he hoped would be an answer to the Albatros.

The Bristol was built around a 275-horsepower, inline V-12 Rolls-Royce Falcon engine giving a maximum speed of 120 mph with a service ceiling of 18,000 feet. It had a forward-firing, synchronized Lewis machine gun and another in the rear, with a third gun mount over the wing. Relatively maneuverable and very tough, it was expected to be a big success. Inexplicably, however, a decision was made to equip an entirely new unit (48 Squadron) with both new planes *and* new pilots. Capt. William Leefe Robinson, who'd won a Victoria Cross for shooting down the SL 11 airship over London in 1916, was to lead.

Though a fine pilot and a brave man, Leefe-Robinson had never flown on the Western Front, nor had he ever flown against other fighters. At the beginning of the formal air offensive, six of the Bristols, flown by rookie pilots with an inexperienced combat leader, took off on the morning of April 5 to patrol over Douai—the lair of Jasta 11 and the Red Baron. Unfortunately for the RFC, Hugh Trenchard, and 48 Squadron, Leefe-Robinson flew directly into an offensive patrol of Albatros D-IIIs led by Manfred von Richthofen himself. The Baron's subsequent combat report read:

> *It was foggy and altogether very bad weather when I attacked an enemy squad while it was flying between Douai and Valenciennes. I attacked with four planes of my Staffel. It was a new type of plane, which we had not known before, and it appears to be quick and rather handy, with a powerful motor, V-shaped and twelve cylindered. Its name could not be recognized. The D-III Albatros was, both in speed and ability to climb, undoubtedly superior.*

Four of the six Bristols were lost, two of them to the Baron personally—a stunning blow for RFC morale and Hugh Trenchard. But the British still had teeth. Lt. Gordon Taylor was flying a Sopwith Pup and came across six Albatros fighters strafing British trenches. Without hesitation he dove into the middle of them, breaking apart their attack. He then managed to escape by diving for the dirt and running full throttle for the British side of the front.

The Pup was a definite success story for the time. It had been flying operationally, though in limited numbers, with the RNAS since October 1916 and would become the first aircraft to land on a moving ship.* Formally called the Sopwith Scout,

*Squadron Cmdr. Edwin Dunning aboard HMS *Furious* in August 1917.

the story goes that during testing a pilot looked at the Scout next to the larger Sopwith 1½ Strutter and said, "Looks as though your machine has had a pup."

Fabric over a wood frame, the Pup was only 1,225 pounds fully loaded (the Albatros D-III weighed 1,949 pounds). This lightweight construction combined with large, staggered wings and low wing loading meant it climbed very well. The Pup also had ailerons fitted to the outboard, trailing edges of the wings. When moved, the ailerons altered the lift over the wingtips, making the aircraft maneuverable enough to outturn any German fighter. In the quickly developing world of air combat, this was critical for several reasons. First, single-seat fighters only had forward-firing guns, so you aimed and attacked by pointing the plane at the enemy. Second, if you were reacting defensively to someone firing at you, then with a quick turning aircraft you could spoil the shot and, you hoped, stay alive a bit longer.

It had problems, though. The 80-horsepower Le Rhône motor was woefully underpowered and only worked because the aircraft was so light. By comparison, the Albatros D-III had a 170-horsepower Mercedes engine, permitting the German fighter to outclimb the Pup or run it down. The Albatros also mounted twin 7.92 mm, synchronized Spandau machine guns, versus one .303 Lewis gun for the Pup. So again we have the classic trade-offs of agility against speed and firepower.

The Pup had been developed independently by Tommy Sopwith in response to British Admiralty requirements (the Royal Naval Air Service was controlled by the Admiralty, while the Royal Flying Corps was run by the War Office). So it's hardly surprising that the centuries-old rivalry between the army and the navy would manifest itself in this new technical arena. Perhaps it was the inherent unpredictability of the sea or the fluidity of naval engagements that made the Admiralty the more flexible of the pair. Or maybe naval officers were initially more inclined to think "beyond the box."

In any event, the Admiralty purchased directly from various aircraft manufacturers and didn't attempt to interfere with design and production. Private companies were free to think creatively and use efficient business practices to get their planes into the field. This resulted in superb aircraft such as the Sopwith Pup, Triplane, and Camel. Because of this, at the beginning of Bloody April, Hugh Trenchard had three squadrons of Pups (54 and 66 Squadrons, and 3 Squadron RNAS) and two RNAS squadrons equipped with the new Sopwith Triplane.

Conversely, the War Office kept the Royal Aircraft Factory's designs in-house and subcontracted out the work it couldn't do itself. This placed production under the control of government officials and military officers who didn't always understand manufacturing practices. "If God had intended aeroplanes to turn then he would have given them the means from the start": this sad philosophy was indicative of the slow-changing War Office attitude concerning aviation.

Long seen as a mere extension of the cavalry scouting arm, the aircraft's primary role, as the War Office saw it, was observation, reconnaissance, and spotting for artillery. The whole business of an armed scout, or fighter aircraft, was at odds with their view of aviation, so entire lines of pusher aircraft such as the RE-8, BE-12, and FE-8 were obsolete by the time they reached the front. Technical advances such as interrupter gears, ailerons, and better engines also took longer than they should to enter RFC service. This was largely due to bureaucratic inefficiency and politics, not indifference, as the Royal Aircraft Factory *did* lead the way in applied research.

Following the loss of Allied air superiority during the

Fokker Scourge, the War Office belatedly realized that victory on the ground was more likely if success could be achieved in the air. With ample government funds, the factory devoted its efforts to design improvements, especially vital research into better engines.

The Sopwith Triplane was a perfect example. Though the fuselage and empennage came from the Pup, there were significant differences. The three narrow-chord wings were staggered, each with its own set of ailerons.* This improved the visibility and lowered wing loading, so the Triplane was highly maneuverable. A Clerget 130-horsepower rotary engine gave a top speed of 117 mph at 5,000 feet. Because the Triplane weighed only 1,400 pounds fully loaded, this meant plenty of excess power, giving it the ability to outclimb the Albatros. In short, it was an aircraft that could change the tide of the air war.

Unfortunately, even the Admiralty was hamstrung by the War Office's larger budget and political support when it came to actually fielding aircraft. Sopwith had two Admiralty contracts for ninety-five aircraft; subcontracts went to Clayton & Shuttleworth for forty-six Triplanes and Oakley & Co. for an additional twenty-five.† The War Office had also placed an order with Clayton & Shuttleworth for 106 aircraft but later, inexplicably, canceled it instead of simply transferring the contract to the RNAS. In the end, only 147 of these superb fighters were built. Nicknamed "Tripehound" or just "Tripe," the Triplane had shortcomings, with the single .303 Lewis gun being one of them. The plane was also difficult to maintain in the field

*The width of the wing's surface. Not to be confused with the chord line.

†Oakley & Co. had no experience building aircraft and only delivered three Triplanes.

since the wings had to be disassembled to access the fuel tanks, and spare parts were a perennial problem.

No. 1 Squadron (RNAS) was operational in December 1916, followed by No. 8 (RNAS) in February 1917 and also a French naval squadron based from Dunkirk. A month later 8 Squadron was attached to aid the hard-pressed Royal Flying Corps. In April a British Triplane pilot came across eleven or twelve enemy fighters and immediately attacked. Following a whirling, nasty dogfight, he managed to outperform and outmaneuver the astonished Germans; though not able to shoot any down, he did escape unharmed.

But with dogfights between roughly equivalent aircraft, it usually came down to the pilot. Lanoe Hawker's death was a glaring illustration that skill alone is insufficient when the technological gap is too wide. All things being relatively equal, skill and experience win, and the Germans had plenty of both on their side. The average German pilot at the time started out as an observer, so he already had some practical flying experience before undergoing formal pilot training. Being observers, they also knew the basics of aerial gunnery. After training, new pilots passed through a special fighter transition school at Valenciennes on their way to the front.

The British lagged badly in both training methods and practice. Some pilots were showing up at line units with as little as four hours of solo flight. And that time likely had been in an outdated aircraft with an exhausted instructor who'd been posted in a training unit for a rest. Inexperience combined with outclassed aircraft such as the BE-2, RE-8, and Strutters rapidly created German aces. During the initial RFC offensive between April 4 and 8, more than seventy aircraft were lost in four days; seventeen pilots were missing, thirteen had been wounded, and nineteen killed. Casualty rates of 30 to 50 percent were normal, with new pilots often lasting only one mission—a matter of hours. For example, 43 Squadron began Bloody April with thirty-two pilots and observers and lost thirty-five—a casualty rate over 100 percent—by the end of the month.

ON THE NIGHT of April 8, 1917, the Canadian and British infantry near Arras began moving east. Using sewers, tunnels, and cellars beneath the city, they slowly made their way up through the cold rain to assault positions within 150 yards of the German lines. At 5:30 a.m. on Easter Monday the big guns opened fire and howitzers bombarded the German support trenches behind the lines. The flashes were fuzzy through the rain, but the 18-pound field artillery began a perfectly timed rolling barrage. Shot screamed down through the overcast, detonating pillars of mud, while once again the infantry went over the top and across no-man's-land.

Caught by surprise, the Germans on Vimy Ridge were blown apart by the shelling. Dazed survivors were easy targets for Canadian bayonets thrusting through the murky dawn haze. South on the ridge, the 51st Highlanders, famed for their ferociousness, came over the trench lips looking for Germans.

> *Up the steps came four Jerries with their hands up. "Kamarad, kamarad!" they wailed. Never mind the fucking "kamarad," let's be having you bastards now.*
>
> —PRIVATE WILLIAM HAY, 1/9TH BATTALION, ROYAL SCOTS, 154TH BRIGADE, 51ST DIVISION

Less than two hours later, Vimy Ridge and the high ground east of Arras were in Allied hands. The bulk of the British Third Army, advancing through the Scarpe River valley, was able to drive past the north end of the Hindenburg Line toward Monchy le Preux. Accurate counterbattery operations, made possible by the RFC, were a tremendous success, and the advancing infantry suffered none of the heinous losses they had in 1916.

During the first few days the Allies advanced up to six miles, huge gains compared with what had been accomplished in the past three years. Fourteen thousand Germans were captured with 180 pieces of artillery, but once the infantry had moved about a mile forward they were beyond artillery support. Rain changed the earth to sticky, grasping mud that prevented the heavy guns from moving forward, and low clouds made flying nearly impossible.

Tactically, at least in the north, the attack was a modest success. Strategically it was not. Three days of fighting had cost 150,000 British casualties, and no link-up would be possible with French forces in the south. This happened for several reasons. General Nivelle had delayed his attack three times, and the French finally went over the top with fifty-three divisions, some 1.2 million men, on the morning of April 16—a week after the British assault.

Unfortunately, in his haste to become the savior of France, Nivelle had made several calamitous planning errors. The German positions in the south were dug in on the ridge above the Chemin des Dames road. They'd been there since August 1914, they knew the terrain, and had made significant improvements. Also, the German trenches were on the back side of the ridge, so nearly all the carefully massed French artillery barrage passed harmlessly overhead, leaving the barbed wire and machine gun nests untouched.

By the time the exhausted French troops forded the river and climbed the hill, they encountered fortified, well-rested enemy infantry. The Germans were also commanded by Crown Prince

Wilhelm, son of the Kaiser, who, unlike his father, was a competent military commander. Expecting the attack, the Germans had quietly added twelve divisions, with an additional twenty-seven divisions held back in reserve for counterattack. In the south they followed the plan and fell back in the face of overwhelming numbers. This left empty trenches and a kill zone that would be shredded by counterartillery fire. Fresh reserve troops would then counterattack the surviving but battered Frenchmen. And that's exactly what happened. In the early afternoon German artillery and reserve troops moved forward, assaulted the French, and drove them back. Their net gain for the day was 600 yards—well short of the six miles General Nivelle had predicted.

It was also revealed that the German Sixth Army commander who faced the British in the north disregarded the new defensive strategy. He'd resisted the Canadian advance by trying to hold rather than relocating to the blockhouses. His second and third lines were too close to the front, so they were wiped out by artillery. Even worse, his reserves were 15 miles to the rear, much too far to be brought up quickly.

Inevitably the northern attack ground to a halt. In the south, Nivelle tried again and continued to fail miserably—to the point where the French minister of war begged him to halt. It was not until April 25 that the president of France ordered the offensive to cease. Nivelle reacted childishly by blaming his subordinates for the failure. One of them, Somme veteran Gen. Alfred Micheler, replied contemptuously, "What, you try to make me responsible for the mistake when I never ceased to warn you? Do you know what such an action is called? It is called cowardice."

The RFC bravely continued to fly whenever possible in an attempt to gather crucial intelligence about the battle. Six RE-8s of 59 Squadron took off at 8:15 a.m. on April 13 for a photo reconnaissance mission of the line between Quiery-la-Motte and Etaing. Two had cameras, and four were acting as escorts. It wasn't enough.

A morning patrol of Jasta 11 Albatros fighters, including Manfred von Richthofen, his brother Lothar, and Kurt Wolff, shot down all six. Ten out of the twelve crewmembers were killed outright, with only Lieutenants Watson and Law surviving, though both wounded, to become prisoners of war.

Werner Voss was gone on leave in April, and Manfred von Richthofen had a busy month without him. It was a rare day that he didn't have "his customary Englishman for dinner," and April 13 wasn't one of them. In fact, it was on this date that he surpassed Boelcke's record of forty kills. His forty-first victim was part of the ill-fated flight of six RE-8s from 59 Squadron. Capt. Jimmy Stuart and Capt. M. H. Wood were escorts and lasted only a minute or so before burning to death between Vitry and Brebières.

Richthofen returned to Douai, calmly ate breakfast, and took off again shortly after noon for his forty-second kill. Later that evening the Baron found an archaic FE-2b and sent it spinning down into the village of Noyelles-Godault. Lt. Allan Harold Bates, a brilliant young engineer turned pilot, had lasted just ten days in combat.

The Officers' Mess at Douai was exuberant that night as the Jasta 11 fighter pilots drank to their leader's victories. Captured flyers were also there. This happened whenever possible, a sort of a professional courtesy between men who knew they were different from the rest. So after trying to kill each other, they would sit together to eat and then drink to their respective health and flying skills. Sometimes letters or personal belongings were passed to be mailed home.

Richthofen later wrote, "Of course the prisoner inquired

after my red airplane. In the squadron to which the prisoner belonged, there was a rumor that the red machine was occupied by a girl—a kind of Jeanne d'Arc. He was intensely surprised when I assured him that the supposed girl was standing in front of him." Humor wasn't a big part of von Richthofen's personality, and English humor evidently was quite beyond him. He was never aware that the British flyer, surrounded by enemies and on his way to a prison camp, was bravely making a joke.

April 13 also saw the baptism by fire of the man who would become the highest-scoring British ace of the war. Edward "Mick" Mannock had joined 40 Squadron at Aire during the previous week and flew his first combat mission in a Nieuport Scout. Escorting FE-2 bombers, he encountered heavy anti-aircraft artillery fire and managed to lose sight of his flight lead. Even on his first combat sortie, Mannock showed signs of situational awareness by sighting hostile aircraft, avoiding ground fire, and surviving to return to base alone.

The son of a hard-drinking British Army corporal who deserted his wife and children, Mannock grew up scrabbling simply to stay alive. Dropping out of school to help support his mother and siblings, he worked as a barber's assistant, a grocery delivery boy, and whatever other odd jobs would pay a bit of money. Despite his upbringing, Mannock was a very intelligent and curious man. Leaving Britain at twenty, he worked his way through the Middle East and ended up in Turkey installing telephones. After seeing something of the world's poverty and deprivation, he decided England wasn't such a bad place after all, and in 1914 Mannock enlisted in the Medical Corps following his release from a Turkish prison.

Not content in a support role, he transferred to the Royal Engineers and was commissioned an officer during Lord Kitchener's big army reorganization of 1915. Still not close enough to the action, he applied for the Royal Flying Corps and was sent to Joyce Green aerodrome for flight training. Once there, Mick was extremely lucky to have Capt. James "Mac" McCudden, home from the front, as an instructor. McCudden had been in France as a pilot since July 1916 with 29 Squadron, logging more than four hundred flying hours and tallying several victories. Like Boelcke and Hawker, McCudden took a very professional, technical view of flying and the development of fighter tactics. He worked incessantly on his own engine, tuning it for every bit of horsepower, and meticulously inspected his gun belts. This deliberate approach, rather than the slashing style of Ball or Voss, was what Mannock absorbed. It would serve him well—eventually.

Mannock had a rough start in France. He inadvertently sat in a dead pilot's chair during his first night at dinner, and his quiet manner was at odds with the boisterous habits of the other flyers. Cautious and a bit unsure of himself, Mick initially hung back from the swirling dogfights that sent so many pilots down in flames. Truth be known, his biggest fear was burning to death, and for the rest of his flying career, he readily admitted this and struggled to overcome the terror. This was another marked contrast to the average fighter pilot who projected a cheerful, if often affected, nonchalance about death.

Any doubts about Mick Mannock disappeared when he started killing Germans in May 1916. By the end of July he had four confirmed victories, a Military Cross, and had been promoted to flight commander.

He'd learned stalking and ambush from McCudden, then gradually perfected his own techniques. If possible, he'd attack from above or from behind (or both) and use "environmentals" such as the sun and clouds whenever they provided an advantage. A perfectionist and a thinker, Mannock devoted himself to aerial combat. Like Boelcke before him, his hard-won techniques were codified and passed on to younger, less experienced pilots.*

1. Pilots must dive to attack with zest, and must hold their fire until they get within 100 yards of their target.
2. Achieve surprise by approaching from the East. *(From the German side of the front.)*
3. Utilize the sun's glare and clouds to achieve surprise.
4. Pilots must keep physically fit by exercise and the moderate use of stimulants.
5. Pilots must sight their guns and practice as much as possible as targets are normally fleeting.
6. Pilots must practice spotting machines in the air and recognizing them at long range, and every aeroplane is to be treated as an enemy until it is certain it is not.
7. Pilots must learn where the enemy's blind spots are.
8. Scouts must be attacked from above and two-seaters from beneath their tails.
9. Pilots must practice quick turns, as this maneuver is more used than any other in a fight.
10. Pilots must practice judging distances in the air as these are very deceptive.
11. Decoys must be guarded against—a single enemy is often a decoy—therefore the air above should be searched before attacking.
12. If the day is sunny, machines should be turned with as little bank as possible, otherwise the sun glistening on the wings will give away their presence at a long range.

*Also to the generation of pilots who would come after him. World War II RAF aces Jimmy Johnson and Douglas Bader both acknowledged the debt they owed to Mannock.

13. Pilots must keep turning in a dogfight and never fly straight except when firing.
14. Pilots must never, under any circumstances, dive away from an enemy, as he gives his opponent a non-deflection shot—bullets are faster than aeroplanes.
15. Pilots must keep their eye on their watches during patrols, and on the direction and strength of the wind.

There was no standardized gunnery practice nor ongoing combat training requirements for pilots in 1917, but Mannock constantly worked on marksmanship. And it paid off, as he later wrote:

> *I was only ten yards away from him—on top so I couldn't miss. A beautifully colored insect he was—red, blue, green and yellow. I let him have 60 rounds, so there wasn't much left of him.*

A born leader, he began fostering his own collection of wingmen, patiently teaching them all he'd learned. Like the predator he was, Mick had a very "hands-on" approach to teaching. "Sight your own guns," he would say, "the armorer doesn't have to do the fighting." His approach even extended to letting his young pilots finish off enemy aircraft he'd damaged.*

In a fight he was merciless. The old-world notion of chivalry was utterly foreign to him, and—perhaps due to his incarceration by the Turks—he loathed the Germans. Like most fighter pilots, Mannock was a complicated man and a study in contradictions. His ruthlessness was always at odds with the conviction that he was, in his own words, "just like a murderer."

---

*It can never be proven, but because of this Mannock likely had more than seventy-three credited kills.

This was a man who would also later say, "The journey to the trenches was rather nauseating—dead men's legs sticking through the sides with puttees and boots still on—bits of bones and skulls with the hair peeling off, and tons of equipment and clothing lying about. This sort of thing, together with the strong graveyard stench and the dead and mangled body of the pilot combined to upset me for a few days."

But once he forced down a German reconnaissance plane, then strafed the crew. When asked about it, he replied hotly, "The swines are better dead—no prisoners." Intelligent and sensitive, Mick was always high-strung and often unable to hide his fear of death. It never stopped him from fighting, though, and by October 1917 he'd been promoted to captain with a second Military Cross. Shortly thereafter, with sixteen victories to his credit, he returned to England for a well-deserved rest.

Death, it seemed, would have to wait.

"IF IT'S THERE, kill it!"

1917 saw the return to action of Albert Ball from his posting as a fighting instructor. He'd come back to France in April as part of 56 Squadron. Newly equipped with SE-5s and a bevy of combat-proven pilots including McCudden and Arthur Rhys-Davies, the "Fighting Fifty-Sixth" was to be unleashed in concert with the Arras offensive. Hugh Trenchard believed that the SE-5 was a game changer and that when flown by veterans leading specially selected new pilots it would turn the tide of the air war.

Designed at the Royal Aircraft Factory, the airplane was powerful, fast, and well armed.* With its 200-horsepower

*Specifically designed by Maj. Frank Gooden, Henry Folland, and John Kenworthy.

Hispano-Suiza 8B engine, the SE-5a topped out at 135 mph at sea level and could climb to 10,000 feet in about eleven minutes. The 8B engine had a high compression ratio, producing greater power than any previous engine.

Unfortunately, the Hispo, as it was known, had a serious defect. The reduction gear, fitted to keep the prop turning slower than the engine, had a nasty tendency to come apart in flight, taking the driving gear with it. The airframe also had a few bugs, including the oversized windscreen. Nicknamed "the greenhouse" by pilots, it generated excess drag and interfered with the top Lewis gun. But the big broad-chord ailerons on both wings gave the SE-5 a superior roll rate compared to the Albatros. Unlike other Allied single-seat fighters, it mounted two .303 Lewis guns; one gun was fuselage-mounted to the left of the cockpit and synchronized with the prop, and the other was on an upper-wing Foster mount.

The synchronization gear, such as the Constantinescu-Colley (CC), actually permits a gun to fire by passing sonic impulses, through fluid, to the firing pin. A pilot engages the system by pulling a handle in the cockpit that raises or lowers the cam follower onto the cam disk. In the case of the CC gear in the SE-5, this was done with oil through a series of reservoirs using high pressure from the engine. By employing hydraulic pressure, which could be constantly maintained once the engine was started, gun firing was independent of the engine revolutions. Higher sustained rates of fire were possible, and the gun could be "tuned" to shoot more accurately, thus saving ammunition.

This obviously wasn't the case with interrupter systems. When the throttle was back, the engine was revolving slower, so the gun had a lower rate of fire—certainly not ideal in a dogfight. The interrupter gear was also functioning whenever the engine was turning, so it wore out more quickly than a synchronization system, which the pilot could engage or disengage.

As with any hydraulic system, however, with the CC there were more moving parts that needed to be maintained and repaired—and which could malfunction in flight. The CC gear was susceptible to high-altitude flight limitations and extreme cold.

But the SE-5 had two guns, and that alone was a great improvement. The pilot also sat aft of the wings and had good all-around visibility. When combined with a powerful (albeit finicky) engine, you had a stable gun platform that could outrun and outmaneuver most of its opponents. Then it just came down to fate and the pilot—the Brits again had a fighting chance.

Albert Ball had begun flying in France in 1916 and had started his combat career in 13 Squadron with the old BE-2. Called a "Quirk," it was heavy, slow, and, worst of all for him, had an observer. Back then each squadron had a few single-seat scouts attached, and Ball flew them as much as possible. Always an individualist, he continually chafed under rules and discipline. As Ball saw it, he was there to kill Huns for God and Country, not to have room inspections and fill out paperwork. Eventually his commanding officer sent him over to No. 11 Squadron with a note that read: "This young man can be entrusted with the best single-seater on the front. Please give him something to do." Smack in the middle of the Somme battles of July 1916, Alfred Ball did army cooperation work, trench attacks, and air-to-air combat whenever he could pick a fight.

As his skills developed he was often at odds with conventional air combat wisdom. When every other pilot was preaching that "height was life," meaning always attack from above, Ball preferred just the opposite. He'd either attack from below or dive under a formation, then pull up to fire into the enemy's belly at close range.* His specialty was slashing into large German formations, sometimes at twelve-to-one odds, then picking off the surprised survivors. And he was known for the captured red nose spinner that one of his mechanics had fitted to the propeller hub of his Nieuport.

He continued his furious, impetuous solo attacks until October 1916, when he was suddenly sent back to England. It seemed by now that the RFC and the government had begun to realize the propaganda value of pilots such as Albert Ball, and they sent him on a lecture tour. "Of all the fool's games," he complained. "I shall pass away if I don't get a different job soon. Why must they be such fools?"

Eventually he found himself back in France as a flight commander, fighting a war very different from the one he'd left in 1916. The Germans had recaptured air superiority with the dominating Albatros, which forced a change in British tactics. The days of the lone hunter seemed past, as now patrols were carried out by flights of two or more aircraft—one to lead and the others to protect the leader's tail.

Albert Ball was supposed to lead, teach, and keep alive other pilots rather than simply kill Germans—and he hated it. He also disliked the SE-5 and preferred fighting in his Nieuport 17. Amazingly, Hugh Trenchard permitted a compromise: during scheduled squadron patrols Ball would use the SE, but when out alone he could continue to fly the little French fighter. Lone-wolfing it one day, he attacked a pair of Germans. Running out of ammunition, he chased them back to their airfield, firing his pistol all the way. After they landed, he tossed down a note

*He once followed his commander all the way back to base directly below and behind him just to prove how vulnerable a plane was to such an attack.

challenging the same pilots to meet him over their field the following day at the same time.

And they did . . . but not alone.

Three other enemy fighters were orbiting well above him and attacked as soon as he did. Facing odds of five to one, behind the German lines, Ball had no choice but to attack. Fortunately, everything in front of him was a target and, unlike the Germans, he had no one to watch out for. Running out of ammunition again, Ball spun down and landed in a field nearby. Slumping sideways across the cockpit, he played dead and watched three of the enemy fly away while the other two landed to claim his corpse or take him prisoner. As the two Germans scrambled out of their cockpits and ran toward him, he came to life, gunned the engine, and lurched back into the air.

His days were filled with missions like that. His tactics were simple: attack. Not a thinker like Mannock or McCudden, nor a scavenger like the Baron, he was more akin to Werner Voss in flying technique.* But as was true for so many on both sides, the incomparable strain of daily air combat was wearing him down. He'd always lived off by himself in a hut, keeping a small garden and a hutch of rabbits. On some nights, his fellow pilots would see the red glow from a signal flare stuck in the ground and Ball's dark silhouette as he played the violin in his pajamas.†

One of the reasons for his introspection was a woman. He'd fallen in love during his time off in England, but he refused to marry the girl until the war ended. It appears he didn't believe he'd survive; he once said to his father, Sir Albert Ball, that "no

* As we would say in later years, "all balls and no forehead."
† Schubert's Unfinished Symphony was his favorite.

fighter pilot who fought seriously could hope to escape from the war alive."

MAY 7, 1917, dawned wet and blurry, with Ball leading a flight of eleven SE-5s over the Bourlon Wood area. Destroying Jasta 11 was a priority, and the RFC had been conducting offensive patrols around the Douai sector hoping to lure the Germans into combat. The Baron had gone home on leave, and his brother Lothar was rumored to hold temporary command, so the timing was good.

On the other side of a line of clouds, they ran straight into von Richthofen's Flying Circus. Cecil Lewis, a 56 Squadron SE-5 pilot, would later write:

> *The May evening is heavy with threatening masses of cumulus cloud, majestic skyscapes, solid-looking as snow mountains, fraught with caves and valleys, rifts and ravines. . . .*
>
> *Steadily the body of scouts rises higher and higher, threading its way between the cloud precipices. . . .*
>
> *A red light curls up from the leader's cockpit and falls away. Action! He alters direction slightly and the patrol, shifting throttle and rudder, keep close like a pack of hounds on the scent. He has seen, and they see soon, six scouts three thousand feet below. Black crosses! It seems interminable till the eleven come within diving distance. The pilots nurse their engines, hard-minded and set, test their guns and watch their indicators. At last the leader sways sideways, as a signal that each should take his man, and suddenly drops.*

The British formation and whatever tactical plan they'd had disintegrated immediately, as it usually does in a fight. Planes dove and turned, machine guns barked, and white tracer smoke crisscrossed the sky. As it began to rain, Ball was joined by a lone SPAD and another SE-5 flight commander, so together they continued to hunt.

Ball spotted a red and yellow Fokker triplane low off the nose and dove to attack. The German disappeared into a cloud, Ball followed, and that was the last time his pilots saw him. Rumors abounded, including Lothar von Richthofen's claim that he'd shot down Albert Ball.* But there were several problems with this. First of all, Lothar (or someone writing up a combat report) claimed that Ball was flying a Sopwith Triplane, not an SE-5 (#A4850). The report had the correct engine number, which would have been recovered from the wreckage, but not the right aircraft tail number. There was also the inconvenient fact that Lothar von Richthofen was actually in a Berlin hospital on May 7, 1917.

Another explanation was given later by French civilians in the village of Annoeullin, 11 miles northwest of Douai. Whenever possible, on the way back to his base at Estrée-Blanche, Ball had been in the habit of dropping down over the town and buzzing the Eglise St. Martin clock tower to check the time. As Ball's legend grew, the Germans had become aware of him and were just as eager to kill him as the RFC was to get von Richthofen. So they'd mounted a machine gun in the pretty white bell tower and waited patiently for the British scout with the red nose spinner to appear. On that afternoon in May, one theory holds, he came.

Yet another possibility comes from Leutnant Hailer, a

---

*Lothar von Richthofen had been known to exaggerate combat claims; however, it's more likely that German propaganda created the false report.

German infantry officer, who said he watched Ball come down through the clouds, nearly upside down. If he'd chased the Albatros into the cloud and became disoriented, then this makes sense. The German officer said the SE-5 was barely 200 feet above the ground when it appeared, and that left no altitude to regain control. A French woman swore that she pulled the young man from his shattered plane, still alive, and held him while he died. No one will ever know for certain.

Less than a month after his death, on June 3, Capt. Albert Ball was awarded a medal rarely seen on the living. For his forty-four victories, the Victoria Cross reads:

> *Lt. (temp. Capt.) Albert Ball, D.S.O., M.C., late Notts, and Derby. R., and R.F.C. For most conspicuous and consistent bravery from the 25th of April to the 6th of May, 1917, during which period Capt. Ball took part in twenty-six combats in the air and destroyed eleven hostile aeroplanes, drove down two out of control, and forced several others to land. In these combats Capt. Ball, flying alone, on one occasion fought six hostile machines, twice he fought five and once four. When leading two other British aeroplanes he attacked an enemy formation of eight. On each of these occasions he brought down at least one enemy. Several times his aeroplane was badly damaged, once so seriously that but for the most delicate handling his machine would have collapsed, as nearly all the control wires had been shot away. On returning with a damaged machine he had always to be restrained from immediately going out on another. In all, Capt. Ball has destroyed forty-three German aeroplanes and one balloon, and has always displayed most exceptional courage, determination, and skill.*

He rests now less than 1,000 feet from the crash site in a little cemetery near Annoeullin. The gray headstone, shaped like a Victoria Cross, is sheltered by trees and cool grass. Sir Albert Ball bought the field where his son died and erected a monument on the spot where the plane fell.

The night of Ball's death, after hearing the sad news, the 56 Squadron officers gathered around the piano to pay tribute. Cecil Lewis, with his fine tenor voice, sang Stevenson's "Requiem":

Under the wide and starry sky,
Dig the grave and let me lie
Glad did I live and gladly die,
And I laid me down with a will.
These be the words you grave for me,
Here he lies where he longed to be;
Home is the sailor, home from the sea
And the hunter home from the hill.

Albert Ball was typical of the sort of man who became a pilot. He was a paradox—or perhaps he was just a young man trying to find himself during the surreal experience of war. Self-confident, highly lethal, and just a bit strange, he was a man who would unhesitatingly put fifty .303 rounds into an enemy pilot but could beautifully sing "Thank God for a Garden" to his girlfriend. A man who could have chosen and succeeded at anything in life had the war not interfered. Had he lived, Albert likely would have been a husband and a father; perhaps he would have been a musician, scholar, or businessman.

It *is* certain that he was a fighter pilot.

BY THE END of Bloody April the French had suffered the loss of 275,000 men against 163,000 casualties for the Germans, and had nothing to show for it. Nivelle was fired (a decision he initially refused to accept) and sent to Africa.

The new British planes hadn't arrived in time nor in sufficient numbers to make a decisive difference. During January and February only 250 were delivered, followed by 612 over the next two months. However, losses for April alone were 249 aircraft, with more than 400 men killed or wounded, and the average RFC pilot had an eighteen-hour combat life expectancy.

But despite being a tactical victory, April was a tremendous strategic failure for the Luftstreitkräfte. Germany had the technical advantage with the Albatros and had dominated air combat for nine months, yet hadn't swept the skies of Allied fighters. Sticking to their defensive mentality, they lost the only chance they'd have to win the war—both in the air and on the ground. This would be the first graphic illustration of a new reality: while one couldn't win a war solely from the air, losing a war was nearly certain without control of the skies.

By now the shortage of raw materials, oil, rubber, and men was beyond recovery. Though Allied technology had caught up to the Germans, Anthony Fokker was about to field the best single-seat fighter of the war. Russia's revolution and its separate peace with the Kaiser freed close to a million German soldiers from the Eastern Front. The French army had also mutinied, so there was no better chance for a final, desperate German gamble. It was hoped that this would get them to the negotiating table from a position of strength and end the war—but they were quickly running out of time.

The Americans were coming.

CHAPTER 4

THE YEAR OF THE FIGHTER: APRIL 1917–APRIL 1918

FOKKER DR I

GERMANY WAS STARVING. Flour, heating oil, and all other staples—even potatoes—were in critically short supply. Paper underwear was issued to soldiers because there was no cotton. Kaiser Wilhelm, impotent and vacillating, had no answers, and Chancellor Theobold von Bethmann Hollweg resigned. This left Ludendorff and von Hindenburg exactly where they wished to be—in total control. They essentially took over the Empire, transforming it into a military dictatorship. Baghdad had fallen to the British, and T. E. Lawrence's guerilla war against the Turks had turned Arabia upside down. Austria-Hungary was on the verge of collapse. The young emperor Karl I had attempted a separate peace with the Entente and offered the Alsace-Lorraine region to France.

But the Allies had their problems as well. Within the French Army the mutiny had rendered nearly half its frontline divisions ineffective, and the new commander, Henri Philippe Pétain, had only just started to restore order and discipline. The leaders of the mutiny had been arrested and condemned to death while Pétain personally addressed the soldiers' grievances. Leaves were granted, food improved, and new clothing and equipment delivered. Most of all, he used his reputation as a soldier's general to promise his men that there would be no more futile offensives—and they believed him. The mutiny had been a protest, not a revolution, and France had both the resources and the governmental will to resolve such a problem.

Russia did not. Tsar Nicholas II abdicated in March, and Moscow was in turmoil. Whole units of Russian soldiers declared an impromptu Easter truce, sometimes shooting officers and sergeants who tried to stop them. By mid-April, Lenin had returned from Switzerland and the Bolsheviks were on the rise against the provisional government. Yet Russian forces would still mount an offensive along a 30-mile front in Galicia during July. When the combined German and Austrian army counterattacked, tens of thousands of soldiers simply quit. The writing was on the wall: Russian participation in the Great War was ending.

Douglas Haig, the BEF commander, apparently saw none of this. Or if he did, he didn't care. He was more concerned with finishing the Arras offensive and he would do so without the French, whom he openly despised. Before dawn on May 3, the British First, Third, and Fifth Armies clambered out of their trenches and headed east. Along a 16-mile stretch between Vimy Ridge and Bullecourt the tired British, Canadians, and ANZACs once again walked into the German guns. Their covering artillery barrage had been insufficient to tear holes in the German wire or destroy the machine guns now pointing at them.

It was a disaster from the beginning and was halted the following day. With the exception of the spectacular (for World War I) gains during the opening forty-eight hours, the Allies didn't have much to show for several hundred thousand dead, wounded, or missing men.

It was clear to the British that specialized equipment, including tanks and aircraft, attacking with infantry and artillery could breach the strongest defenses before them. But at the moment the exhausted, overextended infantry was vulnerable. As they fought back, the RFC came to the rescue with "counter-attack" patrols, a newly conceived solution to an old problem.

> *Only two days before we had received orders that were specially designed for such an event, and which, new in conception, were known as counter-attack patrols. . . . I was given instructions that my squadron should make very low-level machine and bomb attack on the enemy positions. We flew at heights varying from 50 to 300 feet, shooting up and bombing scattered parties of the enemy troops, trench positions and transport . . . the Sopwith 1½ Stutter came into its own in this work.*
>
> —MAJOR SHOLTO DOUGLAS, 43 SQUADRON, RFC

Out of necessity, the first seeds of combined warfare and dedicated close air support were born. All of this in just over two years since Roland Garros, with his frail monoplane and bolted-on gun, graphically illustrated the military potential of the aircraft.

IMMEDIATELY FOLLOWING ARRAS, the British had begun moving men and equipment into the Ypres area of Belgium on an unprecedented scale. Douglas Haig, never one to change his mind, had decided to launch his long-awaited amphibious assault behind the German lines in conjunction with an attack near Ypres. He felt that if a breakthrough was made here, along the coast, then the Belgian ports harboring U-boats could be retaken and the far end of the German line turned. If this was done, then the BEF could attack the enemy flank, roll up the Hindenburg Line, and force the Germans back.

Estimating that meaningful American intervention was at least a year away, Ludendorff was very secure in the effectiveness of the Hindenburg Line. It had been proven during the April offensives, and he was counting on this strength, added to French military weakness and English political issues, to give him time. But he miscalculated.

The Royal Flying Corps had not only caught up in technology but in training, too. Between 1914 and 1916, British flight schools were abysmal; pilots were given little or no instruction in aerobatics, they were taught no aerial gunnery, and nothing in the way of tactics had been formulated well enough to pass on. Pilots generally had two hours of dual instruction followed by another few of solo flight. If they passed their half-hour flight check, then they were granted a certificate from the Royal Aeronautical Club and went on to the Central Flying School at Upavon.

There, the students received little in the way of ground schooling or lecturing, and they would spend about six weeks flying the BE-2. Anywhere from fifteen to twenty flying hours was normal to complete the course (weather depending), concluding with another check ride examination. Given the situation in France, graduating pilots were usually sent immediately to their line squadrons and often with no time at all in the type of aircraft they'd take into combat. Most squadrons tried to give a new arrival at least a "joy ride" to look at the airfield, learn a few landmarks, and make a landing or two. Sometimes this wasn't possible and the new man simply had to "cut it." Even so, with loss rates as high as 100 percent in some units, numerical superiority was the only thing keeping the Allies in the sky. This had to change.

And it did. By early 1917, Lt. Col. Robert Smith-Barry had been ordered to form a Special School of Aerial Fighting, which he established at Gosport. In France from the beginning, he'd flown BE-8s with 5 Squadron, then joined 60 Squadron in April 1916. Taking command during July, Smith-Barry was taught to recover from a spin by Capt. Rainsford Balcombe-Brown, a New Zealander, who'd mastered the technique.* Spinning wasn't understood until then and was nearly always fatal. Of course, nothing of the kind was taught in flying schools, and if anyone was aware of the shortfalls of the British training system, it was Smith-Barry. So for his new school he had to design a curriculum from the ground up.

At Gosport, lectures on engines, weapons, and aeronautics were combined with the latest tactical lessons from the front. Speaking tubes were put into the aircraft so that an instructor could talk to his student, not merely whack him on the skull and scream.

Smith-Barry chose the Avro 504 for his primary trainer, as it was a docile, forgiving type of aircraft with dual controls. In the field since the beginning of the war, the Avro also had the dubious honor of being the first British aircraft shot down in France.† Nevertheless, it was perfect for Smith-Barry's pur-

---

*By the end of the war 60 Squadron had claimed 320 victories. It would produce twenty-six aces, including Billy Bishop and Albert Ball.

†Tail #390, 5 Squadron RFC on August 22, 1914. Interestingly, this was actually the first real proof accepted by the German High Command that the British had arrived in France.

poses, since he required that students be placed in dangerous situations in order to learn how to recover from them. Aerobatics, spins, and simulated engine difficulties were all accomplished under controlled situations. This, he felt, built confidence and *really* taught a man to fly—two essential characteristics of fighter pilots. It also meant that a pilot went into combat thoroughly familiar with his aircraft and didn't have to master the machine while learning to fight and trying to survive.

The Gosport system became the model that all future training courses emulated in some fashion.* Hugh Trenchard said that Smith-Barry was the man who "taught the air forces of the world how to fly." Consequently, pilots arriving in France later in 1917 had the benefit of much better training than those who had come before. This was occurring simultaneously with the introduction of the latest SE-5s and the tremendously successful Sopwith Camel. As survival rates increased, so did the effectiveness of the Royal Flying Corps.

In many ways, the Camel represented the pinnacle of British fighter development during the Great War. Roughly the same size as the Pup, it was heavier and could climb higher. Definitely more powerful, the Camel used a variety of engines, predominantly the Bentley or Clerget, and had the great virtue of mounting twin guns. It was from the hump caused by a metal fairing over these two synchronized .303 Vickers guns that the Sopwith F1 was nicknamed the "Camel."

This also admirably described its temperament. Described as a "beast" to fly, the Camel had an aerodynamically unstable design that made it extremely maneuverable, but difficult to handle. In order to simplify production and get the plane

*The Americans copied it exactly, and it still forms the basis of our flying training programs today.

fielded, Tommy Sopwith used a straight, horizontal upper wing with no dihedral.* By way of compensating, Sopwith merely doubled the lower wing's dihedral. This can (and did) cause all sorts of issues with the aircraft's roll stability, especially when coupled with a powerful motor generating tremendous torque. If a pilot didn't hold full right rudder throughout the takeoff roll, the Camel would ground-loop, giving it a well-deserved reputation for killing pilots.† However, in the hands of the correct pilot, instability becomes lethal maneuverability, and the Camel could outturn any German aircraft in the sky.

Combined with greater numbers and the long-awaited twin guns, the Camel terrorized the Luftstreitkräfte. But the Germans were far from finished. Their aircraft designs may have hit a plateau (with several notable exceptions yet to come), but their surviving experienced pilots were still unmatched. During the close of the Arras offensive, the Red Baron was on leave, and shortly after he left his brother Lothar was badly wounded. But Voss was around, as were Kurt Wolff, Josef Jacobs, and scores of others. The Allies didn't yet have an equivalent of von Richthofen, and the average experience level of British and French squadrons was less than that of the Germans. This was changing, but it would take some time.

Werner Voss, the "Flying Hussar," had come back from Germany with a vengeance. Probably the best German fighter pilot of the war, he was an excellent marksman and a superb flyer. A naturally skilled mechanic, Voss worked on his own engines and machine guns, tuning and adjusting both for maximum effectiveness. Born to wealth, he had a casual indolence common to his social class, yet he always went into combat in

*A dihedral forms a slightly upward angle on a wing.

†A total of 385 Camel pilots died from accidents; 413 died in combat.

full uniform in case he was forced down. Barely twenty years old, he had over a year of frontline experience, and had begun shooting down Englishmen at the age of eighteen. By the end of May 1917, Voss had 31 kills, the Blue Max, and command of Jasta 5.

By this time, flyers on both sides understood the practical and theoretical aspects of dogfighting. They understood deflection shooting, though not many could do it well before the advent of lead-computing sights. They understood the turn circle. (See Appendix A, "Anatomy of a Dogfight.") In a time of short-range, forward-firing machine guns, the turn circle was vital. Not that you had to get behind an aircraft to kill him—you did not—but if you could get behind his wing line, then the single-seat type of fighter couldn't shoot back as his guns were pointed forward.

Pilots like Voss also grasped the use of the "vertical." This involves maneuvering up, down, and diagonally, not only sideways in the "horizontal." There are many advantages to this. First, a vertical fight requires more flying finesse, which many inexperienced flyers didn't have. Second, the tendency is for most pilots to look about horizontally and directly behind their own tail (the latter is called "checking six").* It takes conscious effort and training to cross-check the vertical, both up and down. Many men didn't do it and so would never see the enemy that killed them. Third, using the vertical drastically changes the maneuvering potential of an aircraft. For example, if you're descending or diving, your airspeed is much greater. Combine that with being unobserved because no one is looking up, and you're set up for a slashing kill. If you're coming up from below,

*From the position on a watch face if you're looking down on it. Six o'clock is to the rear.

then you're also likely undetected and aiming for the vulnerable belly. This was Albert Ball's favored method of attack, and few could emulate him.

The turn circle of an ascending aircraft will be much smaller, as you've got gravity working for you at the top of your turn. Think of an egg viewed from the side, with the vertical aircraft on the much smaller, rounded tip and the horizontal aircraft flying along the wider middle section. Your smaller circle fits inside his bigger one, allowing you to turn, point, and shoot. This gets you inside the enemy circle while keeping your aircraft "out of plane" and, you hope, beyond his guns. Environmental factors, such as the sun, are extremely lethal when used with this type of out-of-plane maneuvering. Most combat pilots who survive use combinations of these techniques to slash through a fight, shooting what they can, then extending away from the mess of swirling aircraft. Alternately called a "fur ball," or "knife fight," getting caught up in one was a fast way home in a box. Processing that much information and keeping accurate situational awareness on multiple fast-moving aircraft is extremely difficult. No matter how good you are, someone is likely to get you before you kill all of them or get away.

Voss took off early one Sunday morning from his aerodrome at Markebeke, near the Belgian-French border. Just back from Berlin, he'd been traveling all night and was still hungover. Tony Fokker loved throwing parties and had hosted a big one at the Bristol Hotel on Berlin's famous Unter den Linden.

At about half past eight, a 57 Squadron DH-4 piloted by Lt. S. L. J. Bramley was over Roulers in western Belgium heading back for the British lines. Quick, strong, and well armed as it was, the single-engine British bomber was no match for the Fokker Triplane. Bramley and his observer, Lt. J. M. de Lacey, likely never saw Voss's black skull-and-crossbones insignia before a burst from his guns sent them crashing down in flames.

Coming back with engine trouble, Voss landed, ate breakfast, and took a long nap. Later that afternoon he took off again in a spare Triplane, this one sporting a silver-blue finish and red nose spinner. Heading west for the front lines, he spotted a lone SE-5 and immediately attacked, not seeing a British flight of fighters a little farther west and a bit higher.

These were six SE-5s from 56 Squadron, led by Capt. James McCudden, and they'd crossed the front at Bikschote at 6,000 feet, heading northeast. McCudden spotted the SE-5 jinking and half spinning with a blue triplane stuck to its tail. Rolling inverted over Poelcappelle, the six Brits attacked, McCudden and Lt. Arthur Rhys-Davies bracketing right and left, respectively.

But Voss was too experienced to be caught that way. Even while lining up on his target he was still checking six and immediately picked up the threats swooping down from above. With himself now the target and with no way to run, Voss flipped the wonderfully maneuverable triplane around and attacked. Watching the vulnerable tail turn into twin Spandau machine guns broke up the British formation. McCudden later recalled, "The German pilot saw us and turned in a most disconcertingly quick manner, not a climbing nor Immelmann turn, but a sort of half spin. . . . As soon as I fired up came his nose at me, and I heard clack-clack-clack-clack as his bullets passed close to me."

Having survived the initial pass, Voss now had the advantage. His opponents were either level or descending, building up speed *away* from him. His triplane could easily outturn any SE-5 and he was now on top of the fight, slower but with altitude and more maneuverability. Maybe he could've disengaged by heading back into the clouds, then sprinting for home. For a half second there was probably that option, but Voss was a fighter pilot and his blood was up. He certainly showed no signs of hesitation and stayed where he was, turning and shooting at any target of opportunity.

> *By now the German triplane was in the middle of our formation, and its handling was wonderful to behold. The pilot seemed to be firing at all of us simultaneously, and although I got behind him a second time, I could hardly stay there for a second. His movements were so quick and uncertain that none of us could hold him in sight at all for any decisive time. . . . I noted the triplane in the apex of a cone of tracer bullets from at least five machines simultaneously, and each machine had two guns.*
>
> —CAPT. JAMES MCCUDDEN, 56 SQUADRON RFC

Voss was fighting for his life and, at those odds, was flying instinctively—there would be no other way to fight at that point. Everything was a target. A lucky bullet hitting a British pilot or engine, one of the British planes running out of fuel or ammunition—it was all still possible, as was the chance that a comrade would come to help. In fact, Lt. Karl Menckhoff, flying a red-nosed Albatros from Jasta 3, did just that. Ignoring the odds and his poor position, he dove straight into the fight and tried to protect the triplane's tail. Voss instantly switched from purely defensive flying and began attacking again. Menckhoff was also a superb pilot, but in covering Voss he got himself shot down by Rhys-Davies.

By now, however, the fight had drifted southeast and fallen much lower against the darkening ground. Arthur Rhys-Davies was still knife-fighting with the triplane. Slow from all the turning, Voss had no more altitude to trade and was forced into a purely horizontal fight. Rhys-Davies was firing both guns when the triplane passed off his right wing, began flying erratically, then dove straight down into the ground. Whether he was already dead by the time his plane went into a dive or had just been wounded, the German and his plane disappeared into a thousand pieces just north of Frezenburg behind the British lines.

The 56 Squadron pilots knew they'd battled one of the best and no one else could've survived against all of them. The British pilots in that dogfight had accounted for more than eighty German planes, yet Werner Voss had fought them for ten minutes, so badly damaging five aircraft that three made forced landings and two were written off completely.

His body was identified by papers in his pockets and the Blue Max around his neck. Upon hearing the news, Arthur Rhys-Davies said, "Oh, if I could only have brought him down alive."

McCudden agreed and later wrote:

> *As long as I live I shall never forget my admiration for that German pilot, who single-handed fought seven of us for ten minutes, and also put some bullets through all of our machines. His flying was wonderful, his courage magnificent.*

There is no finer epitaph for a fighter pilot.

AMONG THE OTHER German miscalculations in 1917 was the resumption of unrestricted submarine warfare, which they regarded as the only way to strangle England and end the blockade of Germany. The U-boat attacks provided ample argument for those in England and the United States who wanted America to openly join the fighting. So America's declaration of war on April 6, 1917, was no real surprise. Unlike today, where a declaration is followed immediately by an attack from the other side of the world, nothing of the sort could happen in 1917. The United States had no tanks, no aircraft to speak of, and an army so small that its largest unit was a regiment. There was also no recent combat experience—Cuba and Mexico hardly counted.

Individually, Americans had been in it from the beginning. Three different volunteer ambulance groups provided men and vehicles to French line divisions.* Others, who wanted to fight and not drive a truck, joined the British or French military directly. Norman Prince and William Thaw were Americans living in France, and they had the notion of forming a separate flying unit of American volunteers. Both men became pilots with the French Air Service and went to different combat squadrons at the front. Elliot Cowdin was another American pilot serving with the French; he joined them in December 1915.

Paris hosted a colony of American expatriates. Usually wealthy, they counted businessmen, entertainers, literary figures, and students among their numbers. The American Hospital of Paris had been founded by Dr. Edmund Gros to tend to their needs, so when war broke out, he created a transportation unit that would eventually become the American Field Service.

> *There were Americans fighting in the Foreign Legion, but their identity was lost in this body; they were simply units in a tremendous group. Dr. Gros and his associates dreamed of some other form of service in which Americans might participate as Ameri-*

---

*Ernest Hemingway, E. E. Cummings, John Dos Passos, and Dashiell Hammett were all ambulance drivers.

cans, even though the flag of the United States might not officially be carried into the war. The idea was constantly before them, and, when they found that among the Americans already in France and already anxious to help as best they might, were men who had learned the art of flying in this country, the plan for a special American flying corps was conceived and developed.

On April 18, 1916, Nieuport 124, a squadron of seven Americans under the command of a French *capitaine*, Georges Thenault, was officially designated as the Escadrille Américaine. In response to German protests, the name was changed in November to the Escadrille des Volontaires and finally to the Escadrille Lafayette by December 1916.

Volunteers from the American expat community included college students looking for adventure, mercenaries, and a few criminals. The volunteers were mostly patriotic young men who felt that America belonged in the war. Many of them started out in one of the ambulance services but decided that shooting back was preferable to dying driving a truck. Others had joined the French Foreign Legion directly, defending Champagne and Navarin Farm during the opening battles of 1914.*

A committee, including the prominent financiers William Vanderbilt and J. P. Morgan, was appointed to oversee recruitment and provide private funding for the aviators. There was tremendous propaganda value in the involvement of the volunteers, as America was still officially undecided about a commitment. It was hoped that the Escadrille Américaine would fire

*Enlisting in the Foreign Legion did not mean a loss of citizenship. On the other hand, those fighting for the British usually came by way of Canada and forfeited their citizenship.

imaginations. Coincidentally, most of the committee members owned extensive property in France and had significant business ties to French government and industry.* A less cynical motivation would be the development of a trained, combat-experienced cadre of pilots who could be used by the American military once the United States actually declared war.

These young men, whatever their reasons, did not have to serve. Of the 269 volunteers, 169 of them were college men of good family and various levels of wealth. Thirty-five were from Harvard, and another forty-two came from Yale, Princeton, or Dartmouth. Norman Prince was a graduate of Harvard Law School and a practicing attorney in Chicago. His father was a financier and investment banker who'd made an enormous fortune in railroads and stockyards. Others had similar stories—in short, they could've led a life of ease and safety, but they chose not to. There was something in all of them that made them fly.

To cope with the influx of men, the Franco-American Flying Corps was formed by mid-1916 to spread the volunteers among French units.† Eventually 179 of these pilots would go to more than ninety different French squadrons. The Aviation Section of the U.S. Army Signal Corps would retrieve 128 of them when America entered the conflict in 1917. Sixty-three of these men, including Norman Prince, would die in combat during the war.

By the late summer of 1917, the Germans were steadily losing the war of spare parts and aircraft. The Luftstreitkräfte had been unofficially combining their *Jagdstaffeln* to meet the waves of allied aircraft and now decided to organize its fighter

---

*J. P. Morgan had loaned the French government $50 million (at an interest rate of 5 percent) in 1915. Vanderbilt was heavily invested in France, owning a château and a famous horse-breeding farm near Deauville in Normandy.

†This would later become the Lafayette Flying Corps.

units into *Jagdgeschwader* (JG), with four *Jastas* per group; command of JG 1 went to Manfred von Richthofen.

He immediately began making changes. A long and vocal opponent of camouflage, the Baron had taken to painting his own plane bright red. This was partially to help his pilots identify him and partially as a challenge to his enemies. Pilots were permitted individual color schemes, though each *Jasta* had something unique about it, such as Jasta 10's yellow cowlings. JG 1 also occasionally traveled by train to wherever the fighting was, setting up in tents on makeshift airfields. Both the brightly colored aircraft and the trains were the reasons for the "Flying Circus" nickname.

They fought in a swarm. The sky would be empty one moment, then filled with swooping multicolored planes. Tactically, the Circus would overwhelm whatever enemy formation was encountered, breaking it apart by sheer numbers. Protected by their wingmen, the leaders would then attack the stragglers. This was fine up to a point, but visual signals from a flight leader only worked temporarily. Tight formations of fighters meant that wingmen were really only watching their leader, not the enemy—and dogfights happen *fast*. Without radio communications, there was then no way to coordinate a fight, and mutual support disappeared quickly. Yet the steadily increasing Allied numbers and technical superiority were able to counter the Circus's tactics, costing the Luftstreitkräfte nine of its top aces by the end of 1917.*

On June 24 a DH-4 from 57 Squadron was shot down by a red Albatros D-V over the Polygon Wood area of southwestern Belgium. It was a bit past 9 a.m., and Manfred von Richthofen, back in action after a long leave, pulled away from the

*Voss, Karl Allmenröder, Gontermann, and Kurt Wolff, among others.

smoke trail satisfied with his fifty-fifth victory. The next day a 53 Squadron RE-8 was bounced by the Flying Circus near Le Bizet, south of the Messines Ridge. The Baron shot it down, but his patrol was in turn attacked by a formation of all-black Sopwith Triplanes.

This was the infamous "Black Flight" from 10 (Naval) Squadron, commanded by Raymond "Collie" Collishaw. During June and July they would shoot down more than eighty Germans with the loss of only one pilot—and that was today. Flight Sub-Lt. G. E. Nash was flying Triplane N5376, called *Black Sheep*, when he went down east of the ridge late that afternoon. Karl Allmenröder of JG 1, former medical student and the Baron's good friend, claimed the kill.*

Stung by the loss, two days later the Black Flight went hunting and caught the Circus over Courtai. Like angry wasps, both groups of fighters shot each other up as the dogfight drifted over Polygon Wood. White tracers arced across the afternoon sky, and Collishaw, flying *Black Maria*, picked out Allmenröder's green and red striped Albatros. Collie made a slashing pass and fired one burst, after which the thirty-victory German ace nosed over to crash near Zillebeke. The rest of the Circus, including von Richthofen, had scattered for the day.

A few weeks later more than a hundred aircraft met up together over Polygon Wood. From the surface to about 18,000 feet, Sopwith Pups, Camels, and Triplanes fought the new Pfalz D-III and Albatros fighters. Down lower, two-seaters traded shots as planes dove, twisted, and came apart in the darkening sky. Surprisingly, there were very few confirmed shoot-downs—possibly because everyone involved was more concerned about avoiding midair collisions.

The French-built Nieuport 24 began rolling off production

---

*Nash actually survived to become a POW.

lines that summer to replace the very successful Nieuport 17. Also designed by Gustave Delage, the N-24 had rather unique rounded wingtips and a larger 130-horsepower Le Rhône engine. Not much faster than the Nieuport 17, it was widely used by the British Royal Flying Corps and RNAS as an interim fighter until their own domestic aircraft production caught up.

The SPAD VII had been introduced in late 1916 and was also used to replace aging Nieuports. Louis Béchereau had been with SPAD (by 1917 this was an acronym for Société pour l'Aviation et Ses Dérivés) since the prewar years. His early refinement of the monocoque technique and its outer, load-bearing shell produced a strong, streamlined fuselage better able to withstand the strain of dogfighting than its predecessors. The SPAD VII was a well-made, relatively agile dogfighter. Though downward visibility was poor and radiator issues caused cooling problems throughout its service life, the SPAD VII combined many of the lessons learned to date and was a successful trade-off between strength, speed, and versatility.

ON JUNE 7 at 3:10 a.m., the Messines Ridge south of Ypres disappeared in an explosion so powerful that it was felt across the English Channel in London. Despite groundwater and blue clay, the British had managed to pack nineteen tunnels under the ridge with high explosives. Preceded by a weeklong bombardment using more than 3.5 million artillery shells, the II ANZACs with the British 9th and 10th Corps attacked.

Gen. Sir Herbert Plumer, the very able commander of the British Second Army, had large-scale maps and, using engineers with RFC aerial photography, had plotted more than 90 percent of the German gun positions. He'd also calibrated his own guns (one for every seven yards of line) and accomplished surveys of forward positions his guns would move to following the attack.

This, combined with army cooperation flights (close air support), would mean his infantry would never be without artillery cover. The RFC conducted trench-strafing missions, counterair against German observation aircraft and fighters, and daylight bombing against the airfields around Courtrai.

Results were ambiguous. Both sides broke even on casualties: about 25,000 to 28,000 Germans and 24,562 British, ANZACs, and Canadians. What it did accomplish was the capture of some critical ground, permitting the British to extend their supply lines. It also allowed General Plumer and others to see the weaknesses of the German defensive strategy, thus making the Third Battle of Ypres possible.

The RFC blooded its new pilots and worked out bugs from aircraft such as the SE-5, Triplane, and Camel. It further refined army cooperation missions and trench strafing—both vital to continued Allied success on the ground. Signaling systems were refined using a combination of colored cloth and Very lights. Two-seat aircraft had the inestimable benefit of wireless sets and could communicate directly with ground units. So many generals on both sides had become accustomed to the Western Front mentality of mindless mass attacks that the idea of concentrated, combined arms assaults hadn't quite caught on.

Except to Sir Herbert Plumer. A skilled general and open-minded in his tactical thinking, Plumer had found the big weakness in the German defensive system. The premise behind the Hindenburg Line was a semimobile defense in depth; rather than resist to the last man, defenders would fall back, pulling the attackers into the meat grinder of artillery and fresh reserve troops. The trick, Plumer realized, was not to penetrate far enough through the German lines to trigger a counterattack.

During the dry weeks of September he amassed enough artillery to place a gun every five yards along the trenches. The barrage itself would be different as well. Planned as five zones, 200 yards each, the initial attack would begin with shrapnel followed by high explosives. Third came indirect machine gun fire, then two more zones of high explosive.* This created a pattern of destruction a half mile deep that consumed more than 3.5 million artillery rounds during his September 20 assault. Known as the Battle of Menin Road, it was wildly successful and caught the Germans flatfooted. Plumer's men halted at their initial objectives, then set about digging in and improving their positions as their artillery was moved up. The Germans never countered, and six days later the Allies attacked again.

Through this and the short battles that followed, the French Air Service and the RFC spotted for artillery, bombed German positions, and strafed supply lines. They were opposed by Albatros or Pfalz fighters with the unwelcome addition of Fokker Dr 1 triplanes. Copied from a captured Sopwith, the new machine had all the same qualities: it was light and very maneuverable, and Fokker had added two synchronized Spandaus with centrally mounted triggers on a stick in the cockpit, letting the pilot aim the plane like he would a rifle. Unfortunately, he also installed a nine-cylinder, 110-horsepower rotary engine. The triplane had a top speed of only about 100 miles per hour, some 30 mph slower than the SE-5, but with its low wing loading and low weight, it had superb climbing capabilities.

They'd appeared over the front with Jastas 10 and 11 in late September and immediately began killing. Werner Voss shot down eleven aircraft in September, during the last twenty days of his life. Manfred von Richthofen was also part of the combat evaluation, shooting down a Sopwith Pup and an RE-8 early in the month.

---

*Indirect fire is aimed upward so the bullets come down from above, just like rain.

But the triplane was also prone to wing failures. As a lack of varnish on the wing spars weakened them when wet—a common occurrence on the Western Front. Lt. Heinrich Gontermann, a thirty-nine-victory ace and commander of Jasta 15, was killed after his triplane came apart in flight. By the time the modified and strengthened production aircraft began appearing in German squadrons, 1917 was drawing to a close.

It began raining on October 3, turning Flanders into a large, shell-pocked puddle of mud. Plumer wanted to stop the offensive, knowing full well that with the drainage system destroyed, the entire region was impassable. The weather would hamper air support, and without photo reconnaissance or artillery-spotting missions, any further assaults were doomed. Nevertheless Haig, the BEF commander, ordered a further attack to capitalize on his gains. Knowing Lloyd George's reaction to the casualties already incurred, he continued to gamble with the lives of his soldiers by assaulting Passchendaele on the north flank.

Valley of the Passion indeed.

It was impossible from the start. The muck meant that infantry could barely move, not to mention the heavy artillery. Even if guns were fired, the shells often disappeared into the saturated earth and never detonated. The ANZACs fought their way up to the entrenched German machine guns and then were driven back, leaving wounded comrades literally drowning in mud. The Canadians tried on October 26 and again four days later. After suffering nearly 16,000 casualties, they would eventually take Passchendaele Ridge in early November, finally bringing an end to the Third Battle of Ypres.

Three hundred sixty-two thousand Entente troops had been killed on the Western Front in 1917. Nearly a million more were wounded, missing, or captured, all for a net gain of about five miles—and no end in sight.

IT WAS READILY apparent that the dawning of 1918 marked *the* year of the Great War. Much had changed. Germany now stood alone, as Austria-Hungary was a shambles and Ottoman Turkey had become an empty shell. But the Entente was also different from what it had been in 1914. Tsar Nicholas and his family were captives and the Bolsheviks controlled a Russia that was essentially out of the fight. Italy was impotent and undependable.

The United States had entered the conflict but was months away from effective contribution, so from a practical standpoint Britain and France remained the Entente. France, due to the installment of Georges Clemenceau as premier, was recovering some motivation. German leadership knew that the time to act was *now;* when the weather permitted, there had to be an assault in the west, one successful enough to drive the Allies to negotiate before the Americans rolled over everything. In late November 1917, the new Bolshevik chief of staff communicated Moscow's desire for a separate peace, and by Christmas a thirty-day armistice had been agreed. With the Russians nullified, Ludendorff was now free to put his plans in motion for the last great German western offensive and thus end the war.

Operation Michael, named for the patron archangel of Germany, was massive. Three and a half million men in 191 divisions were poised to attack. Forty-four of these were storm troopers trained in the new Hutier method to move fast, following a concentrated artillery barrage, through a shattered enemy line. Their job was to penetrate deep into the enemy rear, bypassing fortified positions and cutting them off to be destroyed piecemeal by slower, heavy infantry.

At five in the morning of March 21, 6,473 guns opened up on the British and French lines. Gas, high explosives, and shrapnel pummeled the first line of trenches, then switched to the rear. The guns, like the arriving troops, hadn't been detected by Allied photo reconnaissance because they'd moved by night. Some ten thousand trains, also traveling by night, had brought the shells, food, and equipment forward. The assault troops didn't even move into place until several days prior to the offensive. No one knew. And the surprise was complete.

For over five hours the German guns destroyed barbed wire, blew holes in the British line, collapsed trenches, and shredded men. Then came five minutes of shocking silence before the field artillery and howitzers opened up again with a precisely timed, creeping barrage. Storm troopers appeared at close range out of the mist, overrunning emplacements and avoiding strong points. Within a few hours the British had lost nearly fifty battalions, scores of gun batteries, and their Fifth Army was routed.

Heavy ground fog initially prevented both sides from using aircraft, and for the attacking Germans this was particularly galling, since they'd created special army cooperation aircraft and squadrons. Close air support was so successful that the old *Schutzstaffeln*, or escort squadron, arrangement had been reorganized into *Schlachstaffeln*, or battle squadrons. And they were just that. By the opening of Operation Michael, also known as the Kaiserschlach,* the Germans had twenty-seven of their thirty-eight *Schlachstaffeln* deployed against the British. But the fog covering the ground assault also prevented the Hannovers and Halberstadts from flying. The Junkers J-1, a startling new aircraft, carried more than 1,000 pounds of armor, two machine guns, and a wireless set. It could be broken down into four main components to be transported anywhere needed. A ground team of about eight men could then put the whole plane back together again in six hours. Nicknamed the

*The name translates as "Kaiser's Battle."

Blechesel, or "Metal Donkey," and weighing a massive 4,700 pounds, this first all-metal mass-produced aircraft was nearly impossible to shoot down.

By late morning the weather had lifted, and both sides got airborne. The Germans were well aware that the shock, surprise, and effectiveness of their assault would have to quickly overcome the Allied numerical and logistical advantage. The Luftstreitkräfte could muster about 1,350 aircraft between all three Western Front sectors, but they were opposed by at least 3,500 Allied planes.

The British response was to simply counterattack with everything. Scouting aircraft that had never strafed were suddenly thrown into close air support missions. Most of the pilots had no real training nor experience for this role, but the situation was desperate so the Camels and SE-5s loaded up and dove into the battle. Cooper bombs, with their small 25-pound warheads, were carried in racks under the wings. The RFC would shoot more than 28,000 rounds of ammunition and drop 15 tons of bombs on that first day alone.

But no one had worked out the bombing "wires," or complex delivery and release parameters that would come in later years, so the pilots just eyeballed it. They figured if they got close enough to the huge concentrations of troops and transport vehicles, they just couldn't miss. The British often flew so low that German anti-aircraft guns couldn't depress their barrels enough to shoot.

> *RFC planes seemed to be everywhere and tried to stop the advance. Most of the time they were too low for us, diving down with machine guns going full blast, and never high enough to become safe targets. The chances of hitting such fast moving targets*

were practically nil, while the danger of hitting our own soldiers and showering them with splinters was great . . . these RFC flyers continued to dive in regardless of the risk.

—LT. FRITZ NAGEL, NR 82 K-FLAK*

As in so many Western Front offensives, Operation Michael made enormous initial gains. The combination of heavy ground fog, a well-coordinated artillery *feuerwaltz* (fire dance), and storm troopers was devastating to the defenders. The thinly stretched British line, which Haig was warned about, gave way. The Germans were shocked to discover beef, bacon, and Woodbine cigarettes in great supply. Also woolen clothes, real rubber raincoats, cocoa, and liquor—all the things they didn't have and had been told the Entente lacked as well.

All along the southern section of the line, the British fell back toward the Somme. Germans crossed the river at the Crozat Canal, and Saturday morning, March 23, found the Allies in a precarious situation after a German penetration of nearly 20 miles. The French had sent a total of thirteen divisions north but were expecting an attack on their lines as well and wouldn't send more. The British were also retreating faster than the French could advance, so no link-up between forces was made.

The real danger was losing the city of Amiens. Viewed from the air, it was the center of an enormous wheel with spokes of rail lines and roads radiating in every direction. If the Germans took it, then the entire front would be paralyzed. It was also the de facto juncture of the British and French lines and like the

---

*Fliegerabwehrkanone. Alternately Flugabwehrkanone.

weak link in a chain: if it was captured, the Allied front would split.

But Ludendorff did not attack.

Before judging him too harshly, it's useful to remember that accurate battlefield intelligence is always an issue. With limited communications and no clear picture of the remaining Entente order of battle, he probably didn't realize the opportunity that lay before him. He might have kept his right anchored in Flanders and advanced straight into Amiens, splitting the British and French. If the Seventh and First Armies on his left flank had driven directly at Paris, the French would've abandoned everything but the defense of their capital. Ludendorff then might have headed for the coast with his center and encircled the entire BEF. With Paris threatened and the British with their backs against the sea, this would've been an ideal bargaining position for a negotiated peace—and the end of the war.

Fortunately, just as in 1914, they had no way of exploiting the breakthrough. The armored blitzkrieg thrust that would characterize the German army in the next war did not exist. Most equipment was packed on horses, which were in short supply. Germany had long since run out of rubber, and the pitifully few vehicles it had were balanced on steel rims. Even so, the unbelievable political machinations between the British and French leaders nearly won the battle for Ludendorff.

But it wasn't enough, and by March 26 Operation Michael was grinding to a halt. The British had thrown twenty-seven squadrons into close air support missions, and the results were showing. The following day they'd drop 50 tons of bombs and shoot 300,000 machine gun rounds at the Germans. The German Air Service suffered from the same supply issues that plagued the army. Fuel, ammunition, spare parts—all had to be brought forward, and it was a logistical nightmare. Fuel, in particular, was becoming a critical problem.

April was tumultuous for both sides. Even though Kaiserschlacht hadn't ended completely, the British War Council went ahead with its plans to merge the Royal Flying Corps and the Royal Naval Air Service on April 1, 1918. This had been proposed back in the fall of 1916 and made sense in many ways. One service would simplify planning, equipment requirements, training, and the command structure. The resulting independent Royal Air Force would also be free of overriding army and navy priorities to focus solely on the emerging business of airpower.

But the timing was ridiculous.* The appointment of Harold Harmsworth as air minister was guaranteed to cause problems with Hugh Trenchard. Harmsworth was also Baron Rothermere, the founder of the London *Daily Mail* and *Daily Mirror*—a superb businessman who'd never served in the military.† Trenchard, who'd never wanted to be chief of staff for the new Royal Air Force, resigned in protest. A few weeks later so did Rothermere.

As so often happens, those at the tactical level simply "make it happen," regardless of the stupidity or shortsightedness of those appointed over them. The men of the Royal Air Force kept flying and fighting, and France's Marshal Foch, the new supreme commander of the Allied armies, made it clear that regardless of whatever happened in London, "the first duty of fighting aeroplanes is to assist the troops on the ground by incessant attacks, with bombs and machine guns."

---

*April 1, 1918—somewhat ironically, "All Fools' Day."

†All three of his sons fought in the Great War. The elder two were killed in action.

By the first week of April the last big German offensive was over, and with it ended Ludendorff's chance to negotiate from a position of strength. On April 9 at 4:15 a.m. the German guns erupted again, but this time the attack came exactly where Field Marshal Haig had expected it the first time—Flanders. Operation Georgette was supposed to be a lightning assault by the German Fourth and Sixth Armies in the Ypres area. The goal was to drive the British back and capture the Channel ports of Dunkirk and Calais. Not only would this cripple the supply chain from England, but the loss of repair and logistics depots, training bases, and crucial rail junctions would paralyze the BEF.

If the resources for this assault had been committed in conjunction with Operation Michael, the Germans might have bagged the entire British Army in France and fractured the Entente. The Portuguese were entrenched in the Aubers sector and broke immediately, running for the rear. A general rout followed, as the few tattered British divisions were unable to slow the German advance. Fog again prevented the RAF from getting airborne, and the Germans gained several miles.

By April 12 the weather had cleared, so the RAF was flying and Mick Mannock had returned to the battlefront. In England since January, he'd been chomping at the bit to get back in action. A squadron had been converted from trainers to SE-5s in March, and Mannock arrived back as a flight commander. Fresh from the fighter tactics school in Ayr, Scotland, 74 Squadron was heavily engaged in the April battles. Mannock would shoot down a pair of Albatros D-Vs this day, followed by three more Germans before the end of the month.

April 21 dawned cold with a wind out of the east. Manfred von Richthofen, eleven days short of his twenty-sixth birthday, took off from Cappy leading two flights of five aircraft each.

They found a flight of old RE-8 reconnaissance planes near the little town of Hamel and pounced. Australian observers opened fire at the Germans, as did British anti-aircraft guns. This got the attention of Capt. Roy Brown from 209 Squadron out of Bertangles. He was leading the second of three flights of five Camels when they ran into the Flying Circus.

It was a swirling knife fight from the beginning. Tumbling wildly from 12,000 feet down to the surface, Fokker Dr 1's and Albatros D-Vs were twisting and spinning with the Camels. During the melee, Brown saw a red triplane latch on to the tail of Lt. Wilfred May. Nosing over, the Canadian fired a long burst at the Baron, then pulled up and away. Richthofen went vertical toward the ground, and that was the last Brown saw of him.

What happened next has fueled a ninety-year controversy. Lieutenant May dropped down to treetop level in the Somme River valley near Corbie, running flat-out for the British lines, and inexplicably Richthofen followed. He knew it was nearly certain death to fly low over trenches with their thousands of guns, but the Baron went on alone, ignoring the winds blowing him deeper behind the enemy lines.

May, whose only thought was surviving the next few minutes, later wrote, "I ran out of sky and had to hedge hop over the ground. Richthofen was firing at me continually, the only thing that saved me was my poor flying. I didn't know what I was doing myself and I do not suppose that Richthofen could figure out what I was going to do."

Richthofen's triplane crashed several minutes later a few miles west of the main dogfight. He came down in a field just south of the St. Collette brickworks on the Bray-Corbie road, north of the Somme. His body was recovered and examined by everyone nearby, including several junior medical officers who concluded that the wound could only have come from the air. However, these were doctors, not pilots or forensic experts, so how did they arrive at this conclusion? No one knows. Another doctor, an Australian colonel named G. W. Barber, later stated for the official record that the wound was "just as would be sustained as a result of a bullet from the ground whilst the machine was banking." The wound itself has been well documented. The Baron was killed by a single bullet that entered below his right armpit, hit the spine, was deflected through the heart, and exited near his left nipple. Two aspects of this argue against an aerial kill. First of all, Brown was firing from above, so there is no viable explanation of how a bullet could've entered beneath Richthofen's right arm. Even if it somehow had, the bullet hit his spine, then exploded through his heart, so death would've been nearly instantaneous, precluding a low-altitude pursuit through the Somme Valley over thousands of witnesses.

This leaves us with ground fire as the only alternative— but which ground fire? The entire area was occupied by the 3rd Australian Division, specifically the high ground of Morlancourt Ridge running north of the Somme to the Ancre River. When the two aircraft—and all the witnesses say there were only two—came down the river, the red triplane was about 20 yards behind the Camel and firing controlled, short bursts. Hardly the action of a man with a mortal wound.

May was flying around the curve in the Somme near Corbie, and Richthofen cut the corner by hopping the ridge. It was here that two machine gun posts of the 53rd Battery opened fire. Gunner Robert Buie reported:

> *I began firing with steady bursts. His plane was bearing frontal and just a little to the right of me and after 20 rounds I knew that the bullets were striking the*

right side and front of the machine for I clearly saw fragments flying. Still Richthofen came on firing at Lieutenant May with both guns blazing. Then, just before my last shots finished at a range of 40 yards Richthofen's guns stopped abruptly.

The Australians were firing at the front quarter of the triplane and clearly saw hits on the aircraft—not surprising given that they'd fired an entire magazine at less than 200 yards. But it would be virtually impossible for a fatal right-side wound to come from this position. However, it is almost certain that the gunners hit the engine, which was shielding the Baron, and forced him to break off the combat. What happened next, according to Buie's account, nearly guarantees it:

Immediately I noticed a sharp change in engine sound as the red triplane passed over our gun position at less than 50 feet and still a little to my right. It slackened speed considerably and the propeller slowed down although the machine still appeared to be under control. Then it veered a bit to the right and then back to the left and lost height gradually coming down near an abandoned brick kiln 400 yards away on the Bray-Corbie road.

If the Baron had been wounded earlier, from the air or the ground, he would've died within a minute or so. If the triplane had been hit sooner, Richthofen would certainly have broken off and tried to get back toward his own lines. Indeed, it appears that's exactly what he tried to do as he cleared the ridge. He would've turned right toward the east and safety, as his own aerodrome at Cappy was less than 10 miles away. However, at such a low altitude with an obviously damaged engine, he knew immediately that it wouldn't work. Turning back a little left, he cleared the trees and aimed to land in the fields close to the east-west road.

In Buie's account, the machine still appeared to be under control. Of course, he could have stated this to make his own claim stronger, but witnesses say the red triplane made a decent landing—it didn't crash. So it's very possible that Richthofen was alive and unwounded when he landed near the brickworks. The following account is from an original letter written by Maj. L. E. Beavis, the former commanding officer of the 53rd Field Artillery Battery, Australian Imperial Force, who was on Morlancourt Ridge that morning in 1918:

> *As an officer commanding the 53rd Battery, 5th Division, I am intimately associated with the claim that one of the two anti-aircraft Lewis guns of the Battery was responsible for the destruction of Richthofen. I was a close eye witness of the circumstances and as I had Richthofen's body brought from the aeroplane to my dugout before it was called for by an R.A.F. tender, there is no question of the identity of the airman.*

So who killed him?

Peter Hart, in his excellent book *Aces Falling*, says, "In the absence of any real evidence to the contrary, I have always sentimentally preferred to believe that it was indeed Brown and that Richthofen spent his last dying minute, as he would surely have wished, trying to get his eighty-first kill. No one will ever know and one cannot be dogmatic at this distance in time."

Maybe so. It's possible that Brown hit him with his long-range single burst. It is also possible that one or several gunners on the ground hit him, too. Cedric Popkin was a gunner with the 24th Machine Gun Company. He and R. F. Weston also opened fire on the red triplane as it cleared the ridge and began to turn back toward the German lines. Recalled Popkin:*

> *As it came towards me, I opened fire a second time and observed at once that my fire took effect. The machine swerved, attempted to bank and make for the ground, and immediately crashed. The distance from the spot where the plane crashed and my gun was about 600 yards.*

Popkin made it clear in subsequent interviews that he was fairly sure his fire caused the crash, but he would not claim to have killed von Richthofen. A low-altitude deflection shot against a maneuvering target 600 yards away would be either very, very good or extremely lucky. But it could happen.

The author's opinion, backed by the stated evidence in conjunction with the Beavis letter, is that the Baron was killed after he landed. The ground near Sailly-le-Sec and Corbie was a no-man's-land, and any pilot coming down would be fired upon by both sides. The natural thing for any pilot in that situation would be to get away from the aircraft attracting all the attention. In this case, there were German positions about a quarter of a mile to the east. The Baron would've raised both arms, grasping the struts to pull himself out of the cockpit. This would have clearly exposed his right armpit to ground fire, aimed or otherwise. The slight upward entry angle is also consistent given that the cockpit was a few feet in the air and above a shooter on lower ground. It might also have been a ricochet. No one knows. But

* "As soon as an event has taken place, it becomes as many events as it had witnesses, for they all tell different versions" (Tolstoy).

however it happened, Manfred von Richthofen, Germany's Red Knight and premier ace, was dead.

Amid as much ceremony as they could manage, the Royal Air Force buried their greatest foe at Bertangles. Later his remains were exhumed and reburied at Fricourt with 18,000 other Germans. Bolko von Richthofen, the Baron's youngest brother, dug him up again in 1925 and had the remains shipped to Berlin, where they remain.

There were those who hated him and those who loved him. His enemies, whatever their personal feelings, respected and feared his abilities—as well they should. He became a yardstick by whom all others would be measured. Aloof, somewhat formal and cold, the Baron was a product of his heritage and the times in which he lived. As Napoleon once said, "Prussia was hatched by a cannonball." This certainly applies to Manfred von Richthofen, as he was, above all else, a fighter pilot.

In one sense his death was also the death of the German Air Service. Had events been going their way, they could have recovered and an Ernst Udet or Josef Jacobs might have filled the leadership void. But at this point in the Great War, Richthofen was more than just a superb combat flyer. He was a national hero, a symbol desperately needed by war-weary Germans—and a symbol that the Entente was equally desperate to destroy.

CHAPTER 5

DARKNESS CRUMBLES

Sopwith Snipe

"I HOPE HE roasted all the way down."

Mick Mannock grumbled loudly and turned away from the circle of RAF officers in the mess. They had all learned about Richthofen's death and were drinking to the memory of their enemy. Mannock would have none of it. By late April, as Operation Georgette continued, he'd shot down twenty-one Germans and was fanatical about killing more.

Over the next five weeks, he would claim twenty-three more, including four in one day. The Luftstreitkräfte was taking a beating, losing some of its finest pilots, but was in no way defeated. However, its fate, like that of all the air services, was closely tied to events on the ground.

The offensive ended by April 29, and the Channel ports remained in Allied hands. Ludendorff's plan was to attack up and down the line, wearing out the Allied reserves. He could then launch a major offensive against Paris followed by another in the north against the British. While the situation was hardly ideal, the Germans were far from finished. The Hindenburg Line was still intact and sat directly between any Allied force and the German border. All the fighting had taken place outside Germany, and as long as the line held, then the Fatherland would be safe. The High Command thought of it as a breakwater that the Allied armies would smash against and thus destroy themselves.

Perhaps that would have been true in 1916, but by the spring of 1918 many things were different. Tanks, though still primitive, were playing an increasingly active role in frontline fighting. Aviation had grown from a curious sideshow into a decisive force multiplier. No attack would even be considered now without photo reconnaissance and close air support, which meant fighting scouts were needed to sweep the skies clear. The latest British and French assortment of aircraft were proving themselves daily in multiple roles to support ground forces.

On May 27 at 0100 hours, more than 3,500 German guns opened up along a 30-mile front in the Champagne region near Reims. In nearly the same place where Nivelle's 1917 offensive collapsed, the German Seventh Army now came over the top. A textbook artillery barrage hammered the line, and close air support aircraft strafed the trenches, so the storm troopers met very little resistance.

In a stroke of incredibly bad luck, the Allies had chosen Reims as an ideal place to rest five battered British divisions after the fighting in Flanders. The 50th Division had been part of Gough's Fifth Army and had borne the brunt of Operation Michael. What was left of it was pulled out and sent north to Lys to recover—just in time to catch the opening of Operation

Georgette. The Germans punched through the line and made it to the Marne in three days. Less than 40 miles from Paris, they were stopped by French reserves and the first American infantry to fight in France.

The Royal Air Force and French Air Service were also confronted by a new threat. Often labeled as the best fighter of the war, the Fokker D-VII arrived on the Western Front in May. Operating from Puisieux-et-Clanlieu, Jasta 10 was the first unit to receive the winner of the January 1918 fighter competition—the plane that was the first choice of both Manfred von Richthofen and Ernst Udet.

Capable of speeds between 115 and 125 mph and a service ceiling of 20,000 feet, the D-VII was armed with standard twin Spandau guns. Initial production motors were water-cooled six-cylinder Mercedes models. This was much preferred over the vibrating, air-cooled rotary of the triplane. After lagging considerably in engine development, the Germans were finally back on track and quickly modified the Fokker with a stunning 185-horsepower BMW IIIa engine. This gave the fighter a climb rate exceeding 1,500 feet per minute and unparalleled performance above 12,000 feet. Suddenly the Sopwith Camel had a very serious problem.

In addition to the engine, the new fighter used cantilever wings with steel tubing for the struts and ailerons. This made it extremely strong yet very lightweight relative to all-wooden aircraft. The wings were thick, with rounded ends, so the plane was easy to fly and hard to spin, thus allowing the pilot to concentrate on fighting. It was so easy to fly, in fact, that Rudolf Berthold, the irrepressible one-armed German ace, loved it. He'd suffered wounds to his pelvis, thigh, and skull and had been hurt badly enough in the fall of 1917 to lose the use of his right arm. Teaching himself to fly left-handed, Berthold was soon back in the air, and by March 1918 he was commanding JG 2. A very tough man, he was one of those who stepped up to fill von Richthofen's boots.

> *My arm has got worse. It is rather swollen and infected underneath the still open wound. I believe the bone splinters are forcibly pushing themselves out because the swollen area is very hard. The pain is incredible. During my air battle yesterday, in which I shot down in flames two English single-seaters, I screamed out loud from the pain.*
>
> —HPTM. RUDOLF BERTHOLD, JG 2

But the Fokker wasn't perfect. The 7.92 mm incendiary ammunition drums were placed too close to the engine and would sometimes cook off from the heat. This was solved by adding vents in the cowling. Despite the teething issues, the Fokker D-VII fast became *the* threat in the skies over the Western Front. The biggest problem for the Germans was that there weren't enough of them, and by June 3 the advance against Paris had run out of steam. French reserves with the 3rd American Infantry Division had held the line and destroyed the bridge over the Marne near Château-Thierry. The U.S. 2nd Infantry Division would move into Belleau Wood and eventually take some 5,000 casualties. Accompanying them were the first Air Service squadrons of the U.S. Army to fight in France.

The 1st Pursuit Group consisted of the 27th, 94th, 95th, and 147th Aero Squadrons from the United States Air Service. Originally based at Toul and flying Nieuport 28s, the group followed the American advances up from the south. They would move to Torquin, east of Paris, and eventually finish the war based from Rembercourt.

The original Nieuports supplied to the Americans in March were not armed. Luckily for Lt. Douglas Campbell and Lt. Alan Winslow, both of the 94th Aero Squadron, the guns had been installed by the middle of April. On the morning of the fourteenth, Campbell shot down a Pfalz D-IIIa, the first kill by a USAS pilot, and Winslow followed a minute later by bringing down an Albatros.* Both Germans were from Jasta 64, attached to the Fifth Army and operating out of Mars-la-Tour, west of Metz in the Lorraine region.

In its brief combat history, the 1st Pursuit Group would fight in 1,413 engagements, creating nineteen aces in the process, while claiming more than 150 enemy aircraft and 50 balloons. Transitioning to the SPAD XIII, they would be joined by the 2nd, 3rd, and 4th Pursuit Groups and increasingly devote themselves to close air support as the air war diminished.

The SPAD was tough and rugged but difficult to fly for inexperienced pilots. Its V-8 Hispano-Suiza engine produced a top speed of 138 mph and the twin, synchronized Vickers guns gave it a powerful punch. But it was particularly hard to land given its poor slow-speed flight characteristics, and was much more difficult to master than its Fokker adversary. By summertime SPADs were rolling off the production line, and eventually more than eight thousand would be fielded. By comparison, only three thousand or so Fokker D-VIIs would find their way into frontline units.

The three main spring offensives (Michael, Georgette, and Blücher-Yorck) cost the Germans more than 350,000 men. Due to the tactical reorganization concentrating their elite troops,

---

*In February 1918, U.S. observer Lt. Steven Thompson shot down an Albatros D-IIIa while flying as a guest during a French raid on Saarbrucken. He was subsequently shot down during May 1918 by Erich Löwenhardt.

most of these casualties were the best remaining soldiers in the German army. Infrastructure was tattered, hundreds of bridges were knocked out, and more than three hundred locomotives were destroyed.

Also, as Ludendorff had predicted, by June there were 600,000 fresh American fighting men in France, with more arriving all the time. In its combat debut, the U.S. 1st Infantry Division had recaptured the village of Cantigny. The Germans would lash out with two more ill-planned and ineffective offensives (Gneisenau and Marne-Reims) that would leave them exhausted by the end of June.

At home nearly 700,000 Germans were dead from malnutrition, and scientists had developed ersatz foods to offset the severe shortages. "Meat" made from mushrooms and barley, dandelion root "coffee," and paper clothes were commonplace. Fuel and soap shortages left ordinary people cold, dirty, and susceptible to disease. Spanish influenza was particularly virulent and left whole units incapable of combat.* Soldiers deserted in record numbers, raiding military supply depots on their way home.

As the Allies began counterattacking in July, they found a surprised, often sick, and frequently demoralized enemy. On July 18, five U.S. divisions and three French armies caught the Germans off guard and reached the Marne River in two days. In less than two weeks they would advance 30 miles and take more than 20,000 prisoners.

But they didn't have it all their way.

Now a major, James McCudden had lobbied to return to the fighting, and he finally prevailed. On his way to command

*Spanish flu would kill over 60,000 American troops—more than were lost on the battlefield.

60 Squadron, he was ferrying SE-5 C1126 and stopped in Kent to visit his sister. On July 9 he took off for France. Well aware of the fast-shifting ground battle, he decided to stop at Auxi-le-Château to get directions. Directly after takeoff, McCudden lost his engine and, breaking his own rule, tried to turn back for the field. The plane stalled at low altitude and spun in. He was tossed from the aircraft, sustaining a severe skull fracture, and died two hours later without regaining consciousness. Tragically, he was just five miles short of his intended airfield. James McCudden, with fifty-seven credited kills, had been awarded the Victoria Cross, the DSO with bar, and the Military Cross with bar, among others. He was just twenty-three years old.

July found Mick Mannock also back in France and commanding 85 Squadron. Always high-strung, he'd now become somewhat preoccupied with the prospect of his own death and carried a revolver with him, vowing to shoot himself if he ever started to burn. Never a tidy man, he'd also become obsessed with neatness and was carefully shaved and dressed for each flight. However, his fears didn't keep him from the cockpit. He was a superb instructor and combat leader, and in his brief time as commander Mannock created a cohesive squadron that fought as a team. One of his pilots would later write of him, "He wasn't interested in just killing them himself. He wanted a lot of them killed, and he trained us how to do it."

On the morning of the twenty-sixth, he took off with Lt. David Inglis, a new arrival, to introduce him to combat. They happened upon an LVG two-seater, and Mannock attacked. Again, like McCudden, he broke one of his cardinal rules and followed his victim down. A nearby German machine gun post opened fire, and Mannock was hit. His aircraft caught fire, as he'd foreseen. The burning SE-5 made two descending circles, then hit the ground.

Interestingly, it took the British government over a year to posthumously award Edward Mannock, with sixty-one kills, the Victoria Cross. This was a man who'd won two Military Crosses and three Distinguished Service Orders. Like McCudden, he'd risen from humble origins, and even in the thick of the Great War old prejudices died hard, it seemed.

In the span of two weeks the RAF had lost its two greatest fighter pilots. These were men who went well beyond being great flyers and deadly marksmen. They could teach as well, effectively passing on lessons only learned in combat. Both were thinkers, both developed fighting systems, and both were more interested in keeping their men alive than in running up a personal score. They would be sorely missed.

NEWLY DERIVED TACTICS of coordinated artillery used in conjunction with tanks and aircraft had driven the Germans back. Big gains were made east of Amiens along a 15-mile section of the front. The British shattered six German divisions, driving up to seven miles deep and capturing more than four hundred guns. And while the growth of military aviation had been tied directly to the ground war in the waning days of the war, as the armies fell back, the Luftstreitkräfte was fighting its own war.

Hampered by a lack of supplies, especially fuel, and forced to relocate to remain behind the lines, German fighter pilots continued to interdict troop movements, strafe trenches, and challenge the Allies in the air. Their losses had been severe, but so were those of the French and British, and with the Fokker D-VII the Germans still had a fighter that could hold its own. They also had a hardened cadre of battle-tested veterans to lead the *Jastas*, including Lothar von Richthofen, Josef Jacobs, Ernst Udet, and Eduard von Schleich, the "Black Knight."

Yet by late September the Germans had lost another 290,000 men, Austria-Hungary was seeking a separate peace, and Bulgaria signed its own armistice. Turkey, all but finished, had lost the Battle of Megiddo and Ludendorff collapsed with a seizure. Finally, on October 4, a request for formal negotiations was sent to Woodrow Wilson.

Smelling blood, the Allies continued pressing hard. From the Argonne to St. Quentin, Germans fell back toward the Belgian and Luxembourg borders. The decisive fighting was in the center, near Cambrai, where the First and Third Armies succeeded in punching through the Hindenburg Line during the last days of September. The French and Americans, slogging through the Meuse-Argonne, had been bogged down in a costly diversionary campaign that finally reached Sedan on Armistice Day. To the north, the British and Belgians secured the coast, and with the line breached the Germans had no choice but to fall back even further.

DURING THE CLOSING days of October an incident occurred that could be regarded as the zenith or apex of air combat during the Great War. Technology, tactics, skill, and fighting spirit—all came together on one extraordinary morning.

Major Billy Barker had been in France with the Royal Canadian Mounted Rifles since the beginning of the war. Commissioned an officer in April 1915, he served first as an observer and then as a pilot. Transferring to fighters, Barker began his killing career during October 1917 and was an ace by the end of the year. Ordered to the Italian Front, he remained there till the following September. Known for pranks against the enemy, he once took his squadron down low into San Vito al Tagliamento to attack a headquarters building. Shooting up windows and doors, they then pulled up into a wheel over the town and dropped Cooper bombs on the roofs. Later, trying to provoke the Austrians to fight, he dropped a note over the Godega aerodrome that read:

> *Major Barker, DSO, MC and the Officers under his Command present their compliments to Captain Bronmoski, 41 Recon. Portobouffole, Ritter von Fiala, 51 Pursuit, Gajarine, Captain Navratil, 3rd Company, and the Pilots under their command, and request the pleasure and honour of meeting in the air. In order to save Captain Bronmoski, Ritter von Fiala and Captain Navratil and gentlemen of his party the inconvenience of searching for them, Major Barker and his Officers will bomb Godigo aerodrome at 10 a.m. daily, weather permitting, for the ensuing two weeks.*

When ordered to take command of the RAF Training School at Hounslow, Barker promptly made the argument that he couldn't very well teach young pilots about the Western Front if he wasn't up to date himself. So he was given a Sopwith Snipe and ten days to roam about and reacquaint himself with the war in the west.

Developed as a Sopwith 7F-1, the Snipe was the first fighter delivered to the newly formed Royal Air Force. It was to British aircraft design what the Fokker D-VII was to the Germans: a culmination of all the hard lessons learned from the previous years. Designed in 1917 as a replacement for the Camel, the new aircraft was powered by a 230-horsepower Bentley B.R.2 air-cooled rotary engine. The cockpit was also planned to include an electrically heated flying suit and oxygen system for higher-altitude operations. The engine, like the aircraft, represented the pinnacle of design for the time, and it was the last rotary engine to be ordered for the RAF.

The center section of the upper wing was left open and the pilot sat higher than in the Camel; both features markedly improved visibility. Twin synchronized Vickers .303 machine guns with an Aldis sight gave it a respectable punch. Heavier than the Camel, it also had a two-bay wingspan for increased strength. Combined with its maneuverability and powerful performance at higher altitudes, the Snipe was a winner.

Billy Barker could now get at German reconnaissance aircraft that were operating with near impunity above 20,000 feet. By the end of October his score was up to forty-six aircraft and nine balloons. However, the rear echelon eventually caught up with him, and he was ordered directly to return and assume command of the Hounslow school. Barker packed up, took off from Beugnatre, France, and headed northeast along the front. Passing St. Quentin at 24,000 feet, he spotted a big German two-seater over the Mormal Forest and promptly attacked. Though the gunner fought back, Barker shot the wings off and watched the shattered plane make its long, final fall.

Suddenly the Snipe lurched, Barker's right leg went numb, and he instinctively rolled off to the left. Snapping his head around, he saw the Fokker D-VIII behind him and immediately began a vertical one-circle fight. The numbness eventually wore off, but he was unable to use his right leg. Gritting his teeth against the searing pain, Barker finally brought his guns to bear and fired a burst into the Germans' tank, sending it spinning down in flames.

Gasping for breath, he realized that the surrounding sky was full of airplanes. His brief dogfight had landed him in the middle of an entire German circus* and, like enraged wasps, the Fokkers and Triplanes swarmed around, shooting furi-

*Jagdgruppe 12, consisting of Jastas 12 and 44.

ously. Flying reflexively, Barker shot down two fighters but was wounded again, this time in the left leg. As he passed out and the Snipe went into a spin, the Germans assumed he was finished.

But the cold, rushing air revived him so he booted opposite rudder, pumped the stick forward, and recovered from the spin. One of the Fokkers had followed him down, but the abrupt recovery caught the German off guard. Overshooting, he flashed in front of the Snipe, the surprised pilot twisting around in his seat. Barker pulled the nose up and squeezed off a short burst into the other cockpit. The Fokker simply rolled over and dove into the ground. But as the swarm caught up and attacked, tracers shot past him and Barker ducked, jinking back and forth to spoil their aim. Nevertheless, another bullet shattered his elbow, and he fainted again from blood loss and pain.

Coming around again only a few thousand feet up, Barker found himself in the middle of the last *Jasta*. He shot down another Fokker, then flipped the Snipe over and raced toward the British lines. Incensed, the Germans followed, so the Canadian pitched back into the fight, shooting the last of his ammunition and scattering his pursuers. Dizzy and in tremendous pain, Billy Barker managed to crash just behind the British lines. Rescued by a regiment of Highlanders, he woke up days later at Number 8 Hospital in Rouen. The entire dogfight had taken place over the startled heads of thousands of British soldiers and at least one astonished general.

Credited with five German fighters shot down plus the two-seater, Billy Barker was awarded the Victoria Cross for his actions that day. In addition to three Military Crosses, two Distinguished Service Orders, the French Croix de Guerre, and two Italian Silver Medals for Military Valor, Billy Barker became the most-decorated fighting man in the history of Canada, the

British Empire, and the Commonwealth of Nations. The other two most-decorated flyers were James McCudden and Mick Mannock.

While Billy Barker was lying in a hospital room, the heaviest day of air fighting in the war took place. As their army withdrew, German fighters concentrated over the chokepoints of Namur, Charleroi, and Mons. Big de Havilland bombers were attacking roads, troops, and railways but they were easy targets, and sixty-three were lost in October alone. This last desperate fight would finally drain the Luftstreitkräfte, and even the strength and skill of individual German aces couldn't stem the Allied tide. One Snipe squadron shot down thirty-six German aircraft in four days.

Real dogfighting ended on November 4 as the German retreat became a complete rout in most places. Valenciennes had fallen on November 2, and Le Quesnoy, Landrecies, and the Mormal Wood were now all in Allied hands. Riots had broken out in earnest in Berlin, and the flu epidemic continued.* The German High Seas Fleet had even mutinied after being ordered out to fight.

The next several days saw back-and-forth confusion exacerbated by bad communications and poor leadership on both sides. Kaiser Wilhelm officially abdicated and fled for the Netherlands on November 10, so a German delegation asked for terms. The reply stated that the Germans had to evacuate Belgium, Luxembourg, Alsace-Lorraine, and France within fifteen days. Additionally, the initial armistice terms demanded the withdrawal of all troops inside Germany to a point 25 miles east of the Rhine, and all Allied prisoners were to be repatriated.

---

*There would be more than 400,000 deaths from influenza in Germany during 1918.

Artillery, tanks, machine guns, and nearly all other weapons of war were to be handed over to the Allies. The Luftstreitkräfte would assemble at Strasbourg, and all aircraft were to be surrendered to a French commission. As of 11:00 a.m. on Monday, November 11, 1918, the war was over.

Haggard German regiments began marching west over the Rhine bridges on November 14, bound for home. Sometimes a band would play "Fridericus Rex" or the "Torgauer Marsch," and by December 11, the Döberitz Guards were stomping down the Unter den Linden in Berlin. Friedrich Ebert, who would serve as the new president of Germany, presented a "victory" to the people. After all, it was an armistice, not a surrender. "We welcome you home," he shouted from a flower-covered podium under a clear blue sky. "No enemy has defeated you."

Nevertheless, the armistice terms were harsh, and those coming from the 1919 Treaty of Versailles would be worse. The victors wanted Germany to suffer—understandable, given that the war had cost some 30 million dead, wounded, and missing.* Some cities in America banned Beethoven and the Strauss waltzes; others forbade speaking in German, and in Cincinnati a priest was beaten because he'd prayed for the Kaiser's soul. The French spit on passing Germans.

In the meantime, the survivors came home and picked up the pieces as best they could. The old order of things was gone, and they tried to make their way in the new. England and France both persevered and recovered, but the empires of Austria-Hungary, tsarist Russia, and Ottoman Turkey vanished forever. Germany, like its allies, descended into chaos for a time, yet would eventually emerge bitter and vengeful.

---

*France, 6 million; Great Britain, 3 million; Russia, 9 million; Germany and Austria-Hungary, 14 million.

For the pilots it was now a world that included aviation on a scale unimagined five years before. Ernst Udet and many others would become barnstormers and stunt flyers. Lothar von Richthofen and Eddie Rickenbacker were among those who joined fledging air carrier operations. Other pilots, disillusioned or simply bored, would follow the war drums into lesser-known but equally deadly conflicts in Russia, Poland, and Spain.

A terrible price had been paid by all. Men had burned, bled, and fallen to horrible deaths. The Royal Air Force alone suffered a 15 percent casualty rate, with some 16,500 airmen killed, wounded, or missing. Despite such horrifying losses, by 1918 the RAF was 114,000 strong and could field more than four thousand combat aircraft—this after a start of barely 2,000 men with a few dozen mismatched, unarmed machines in 1914. Other nations had seen similar explosive growth.

The end of the war brought a widespread desire to put away the weapons and cut back the armies. After all, it had been the "war to end all wars," and the enemy was vanquished, so the victors wanted to live and celebrate. Unfortunately, as with most illusions, this one was dangerous and would have dire consequences for the future.

PART TWO

IN THE LAP OF THE GODS: 1919–1939

It is finished, and, as no one is satisfied, it makes me hope we have made a just peace; but it is all in the lap of the gods.

—President Woodrow Wilson, June 1919

CHAPTER 6

RISE OF THE MERCENARIES

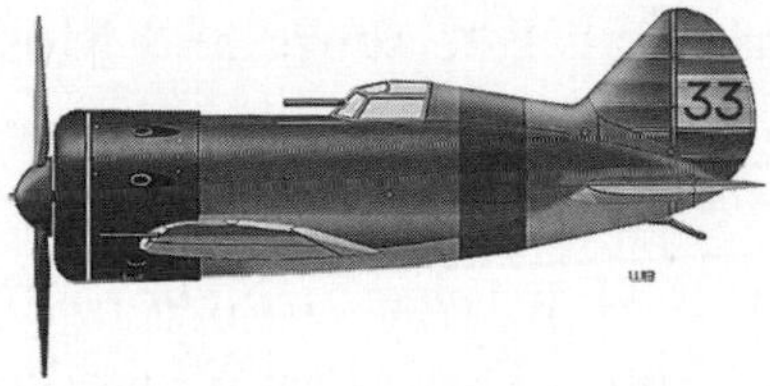

POLIKARPOV I-16

These, in the day when heaven was falling,
The hour when earth's foundations fled,
Followed their mercenary calling,
And took their wages, and are dead.

Their shoulders held the sky suspended;
They stood, and earth's foundations stay;
What God abandoned, these defended,
And saved the sum of things for pay.

—A. E. HOUSMAN, "EPITAPH ON AN ARMY OF MERCENARIES"

THE GREAT WAR was over, but the world was far from peaceful.

Russia was convulsed in a desperate struggle that would

have extreme consequences for the next seven decades. The provisional government replacing the tsar had collapsed in early 1918, leaving two main factions vying for control. The "Reds" were Bolsheviks, led by Lenin, and they controlled much of the populated areas as well as most of the industrial centers—a key advantage in a civil war, where popular support was critical. They were opposed by the "Whites," remnants of the monarchists, aristocratic upper classes, and many former military officers.

By 1919 White Russian forces controlled a great deal of the agricultural territory in the middle of the country with the notable exceptions of St. Petersburg and Moscow. With much better leadership, they also enjoyed widespread support from Japan, the United States, and Great Britain.* In April of that year, 47 Squadron RAF arrived at Novorossiysk on the Black Sea to assist Gen. Anton Denikin's White Volunteer Army. A combat corps commander from World War I and former chief of staff, Denikin was advancing north along the Volga toward Moscow.

The RAF squadron was commanded by none other than Raymond Collishaw (see Chapter 4), whose Black Flight of Sopwith triplanes had caused so much mayhem over the Western Front in 1917. Now a lieutenant colonel, Collishaw had been sent to augment the official RAF training mission in Russia. They were supposed to be merely instructors, teaching Russian pilots to fly the RE-8, but that changed rapidly.

As the British Empire's third-ranked ace, having finished the war with sixty victories, Collishaw took command of a squadron containing DH-9s and Sopwith Camels. Collie, a fighter

---

*France, perhaps the most vocal supporter, had already come and gone by April 1919, without any real fighting.

pilot to the core, had an incentive program for his pilots that went like this: The first pilot to shoot down a "Bolshie" plane was entitled to the first Russian princess they found, while the man who received the first medal (of any type) got the first duchess. Additional kills and medals entitled the winners to additional princesses and duchesses. There was also a liquor ration, since there was enough "ale, beer, Scotch, brandy, rye and vodka for a regiment of the Royal Irish." Caviar, vodka, beautiful girls, and a war—what fighter pilot could want more?

By late June, Collie was back in combat, bombing boats and railroads and, above all, strafing Red troops. The steppes were ideally suited to fast-moving horsemen, so—unlike on the Western Front—cavalry played a tremendous role in the Russian campaign. They were opposed by a Red air force of Nieuports, SPADs, and Fokkers flown largely by a mixed bag of mercenaries left over from the Great War.

During the crucial battle for Tsaritsyn, Red cavalry under Boris Dumenko was attacked and shredded by 47 Squadron's B Flight and its Camels.* Routed and disoriented, the survivors were then cut to pieces by White Cossacks. Led by a South African named Samuel "Kink" Kinkead, a thirty-two-victory ace of the Great War, the four Camels killed more than a thousand Bolsheviks with their twin Vickers guns.

This would become a viable and effective tactic: a shocking, surprise air attack followed by the coup de grâce of a charge and flashing sabers. A curious blending of ancient horse-borne weaponry with the devastation of aircraft, it worked largely because the steppes were wide, flat, and offered little cover.

Interestingly, one of the B Flight Camel pilots was an Amer-

*Renamed Stalingrad in April 1925. The city would be at the center of another epic battle seventeen years later.

ican. Son of a Texas Ranger, Marion Aten had made his way to England and joined the Royal Flying Corps in 1917. Finishing flight training the day after the armistice was signed, Aten would stay with 47 Squadron for the duration of the conflict, then go on to fight in Iraq. There were other Yankees who had fought during the previous year at Arkhangelsk. The American Expeditionary Force Siberia was also active, protecting U.S.-supplied equipment in the east, but in both cases there was little air involvement.

For his assault on Moscow, General Denikin decided to use a three-pronged attack. This had the advantage of tying up large concentrations of Red troops, but it also left his own lines dangerously extended. The Red Army needed reorganizing, and had been reformed with Leon Trotsky as war commissar. Unfortunately, the Bolsheviks had bolstered their numbers with tens of thousands of dispossessed peasants and returning soldiers. Thousands of ex-tsarist officers rejoined the army, reacting with a typical Russian xenophobia toward foreigners that Trotsky quickly exploited. The Bolsheviks had also been joined by the Black Army (Revolutionary Insurrectionary Army of Ukraine), and their combined forces soundly defeated the Whites at Orel in October 1919.

If Denikin had won at Orel, the White Army would have marched on Moscow. If the city had fallen in 1919, the Bolsheviks might well have been defeated and the Soviet Union would never have existed. How different would the rest of the century have been with no Russian Communist threat to work against?

But Denikin was forced to fall back, and the pilots went with him. Collishaw himself had contracted typhus and didn't get back in action until the end of November 1919. Part of the fighting retreat to Rostov, 47 Squadron flew close air support missions against Red cavalry, railroads, and boats on the Volga

River. Collie's DH-9s made it to the Crimea in January 1920 and began flying from an aerodrome near Djankoi. During one such sortie, he was hit by ground fire and made an emergency landing in enemy territory. The engine was still gasping and wheezing, so, rather than walk, Collie taxied the wounded bird some 20 miles through the snow to safety.

B Flight eventually made it back to Novorossiysk but had to destroy their battered Camels in the face of the advancing Bolsheviks. Using a tank, they flattened the planes, and then did the same to forty new DH-9 two-seaters still crated on the docks. Late in March they sailed for Constantinople, and Marion Aten wrote later that:

> *the waterfront was black with human beings. A solid mass of people covered the shore, the quay, the piers, the mole and the breakwater. As we left the train and started towards the ship the refugees pressed around us, shrieking, begging, imploring . . . a mob of desperate refugees suddenly rushed the steamer gangplank and machine guns on the deck cut loose. Ten men and women fell, twenty, thirty, and I could watch no more.*

Collie and the rest of his squadron also escaped to Turkey. He would go on to command 84 Squadron in Egypt, then be sent on to Persia. Knighted in 1921, Raymond Collishaw commanded Number 5 Wing during the Second Italo-Abyssinian War in 1936 and remained in the RAF through World War II. Marion Aten would also continue flying and traveled to Iraq after Russia. He survived and in 1927 retired to the family ranch in California. General Denikin relinquished command to Baron Wrangel and fled to Paris, where he lived as a writer until the city fell in 1940. Denikin died in Ann Arbor, Michigan, in 1947.

ATROCITIES ON BOTH sides of the civil war were widespread and horrific. The Red Army carried out anti-Jewish pogroms, and the White Cossacks were infamous for their rapine and plunder. In the end, popular support swung to the Bolsheviks, and this turned the tide. The old tsarist regime represented by the Whites was hardly a stirring memory for most Russians, and Red propaganda was particularly effective in exploiting this.

Lenin and the Bolsheviks also exploited the escalating hostilities with the newly created Polish Second Republic. Poland had been broken apart a century before and pieces absorbed into Russia, Germany, and Austria-Hungary. As those three nations hemorrhaged following the Great War, the time seemed ideal for a new Poland to rise.

Borders were a problem, as was the economy, the disparate cultures, the military, the infrastructure . . . the list was long. But the border issue was a top priority for Jozef Pilsudski, the ex-soldier turned chief of state. The British had proposed the so-called Curzon Line, based on ethnicity and language, to define Poland. Most Poles, Pilsudski included, were anxious that their nation extend to the farthest borders they'd enjoyed during the sixteenth century.* This meant Lithuania, the Ukraine, and big slices of Germany and Austria. Pilsudski wanted this not only for security but also to foster nationalism—and for economic reasons as well. He needed a seaport on the Baltic and the extensive mineral resources produced by Silesian mines.

---

*The Polish-Lithuanian Commonwealth from 1569 to 1795.

Taking advantage of Russia's own civil war, the Poles crossed the Nieman River during March 1919, moving toward Pinsk in southwestern Russia. Pilsudski initially had the campaign his way and stopped advancing as Denikin threatened Moscow. But by late 1919 the writing was on the wall that the Bolsheviks would be victorious, and Pilsudski found himself facing most of the Red Army.

As the Russians transferred troops to their European border, Pilsudski launched a surprise offensive of his own deep into the Ukraine. In two weeks he'd made it to the Dnieper River and captured Kiev, but by late May Gen. Semyon Budyonny's First Red Cavalry broke through the Polish lines, forcing them to abandon the city. Trotsky sent five armies, totaling about 160,000 men, through Lithuania and Belarus under the command of Mikhail Tukhachevsky, a former tsarist officer. Threatened by his fast-moving cavalry, the Poles were outflanked and driven back toward Warsaw.

But now it was the Russians' turn for miscalculation. Lenin had a dream of spreading Communism into Europe by uniting with pro-Communist Poles and Germans. He'd been warned that there wasn't enough indigenous support for this and that nationalistic pride was stronger than ideology. Lenin also grossly underestimated the profound distrust of all things Russian by the Germans and especially by the Poles. Regardless, Tukhachevsky's armies crossed the Bug River on July 22, headed for Warsaw. Tukhachevsky planned to split and encircle the city, attacking from the northwest to avoid the heavily fortified northern defenses.

Pilsudski, now a marshal, began the defense of Warsaw, which, to nearly everyone's mind, *was* Poland. He now had more than 300,000 men at his disposal; some were badly armed and poorly trained, but there were others, including a Polish legion that had seen line service on the Western Front. He also had the fledgling Polish Air Force and a hodgepodge mix of SPADs, Fokkers, Albatros fighters, and Italian-made Ansaldos A-1 Balillas. The Balilla was the only indigenously produced Italian fighter of the Great War and received mixed reviews. Compared to its Nieuport, Sopwith, and Fokker counterparts, the A-1 was mediocre at best. But the Polish war was primarily a ground conflict, and agility in air-to-air combat took second place to bombing and strafing. The Balilla was relatively sturdy and mounted twin Vickers machine guns. The British Bristol F2B was the most numerous scout/reconnaissance aircraft.

The Poles also had the Kosciuszko Squadron. Named for Tadeusz Kosciuszko, a Polish soldier who fought against Poland's partition in 1792, the squadron was composed of mainly American volunteers.* These included Maj. Cedric Fauntleroy and Capt. Merian Cooper.†

On August 12 the Red Army attacked the Vistula bridgehead at Praga, east of Warsaw. Heavy fighting occurred north of the city, and the lines of the Polish Fifth Army were broken on August 14. By calling in reserves and cracking the Russian ciphers, Pilsudski bought enough time for his own counterattack. The Bolsheviks also failed to coordinate their breakthrough and lost the advantage that might have won the battle. General Budyonny's vicious 1st Cavalry might have made a difference, but it missed the fight altogether.

Polish air support around Warsaw, including the Kosciusko Squadron, dropped nine tons of bombs during nearly two hundred combat sorties. This slowed the enemy advance, giving the

---

*Kosciuszko also fought as a colonel during the American Revolution.

†Cooper would survive to found Pan American Airways and to head production at RKO Pictures in Hollywood. He also co-authored *King Kong*, among other stories.

ground units time to move, and on August 16 Pilsudski began a bold assault. Stabbing northward through the Russian lines, covered by aircraft and tanks, he penetrated some 75 miles in three days. This cut off the entire Sixteenth Red Army, threw the Russians into confusion, and took the pressure off Warsaw.

General Puchucki of the 13th Polish Infantry Division wrote:

> *The American pilots, though exhausted, fight tenaciously. During the last offensive, their commander attacked enemy formations from the rear, training machine-gun bullets down on their heads. Without the American pilots' help, we would long ago have been done for.*

The Russians quickly realized they'd been split, outflanked, and outfought, so by August 18 many Red units had fled for the border. Others were trapped and forced to fight, their tattered survivors eventually limping into Prussia or back east across the Bug River. Tukhachevsky's entire Fourth Army was trapped and had to surrender. All told, the Russians lost nearly 100,000 men, more than 200 artillery pieces, and 10,000 vehicles.

From an aviation standpoint, the Russian Civil War and the Polish-Soviet War were purely tactical fights, albeit with immense strategic consequences. There were very few fixed fortifications, and much of the fighting was done with cavalry and fast armored vehicles. Close air support and combined warfare assaults were used in the Great War, but it was still a comparatively new science. So bombing triangles, fragmentation patterns, and strafe mechanics (see Appendix B, "Anatomy of a Surface Attack") were all being worked out to take advantage of the increasing effectiveness of airpower.

The salient fact in both of these cases was that aircraft were essential from the very beginning, with no paradigms or prejudices to overcome. True, there were constant disagreements about *how* aircraft were to be used, but no one suggested fighting without them. As on the Western Front, fighter aircraft were decisive, but whether they were *crucial* is a point of debate. The Russian Civil War was not won or lost in the air, and the Reds would likely have been victorious anyway—the vastness of Russia and geopolitical realities would have seen to that. The war for Polish independence is another matter, and it certainly would have ended differently without tactical air support. If Warsaw had fallen, then Soviet Communism would have spread west a generation earlier than it did, and how far would it have extended? Likely straight through the Slavic lands, and maybe to Paris itself.

Yet it didn't. And Europe would never again be the same.

"MISERY ACQUAINTS A man with strange bedfellows." So said the shipwrecked sailor upon awakening in a monster's cave.*

The truth of this line certainly applies to one of the strangest alliances in military aviation. As we've seen, Germany was denied all aircraft manufacturing following the Great War. Thousands of fighters were confiscated or destroyed by the victors, leaving, it was hoped, no possibility of a future air threat. Without an indigenous industry, there would be no need for research and development, nor for large training schools. All pilots in Germany were members of sports flying clubs or enrolled in the Civil Aviation Pilot Training Center. This environment, plus the supervision of the Allied Control Commission, made training military flyers impossible—which was the point.

*Trinculo to Caliban in Shakespeare's *The Tempest*.

Already humiliated, feeling defenseless and betrayed, the Weimar Republic reached out to the newly created Russian Soviet Federative Socialist Republic. Another pariah, distrusted and without allies or official recognition, the Soviet government eagerly accepted the invitation to cooperate.

Signed in 1922, the Treaty of Rapallo between Germany and the postwar Russian government repudiated any claims, territorial or financial, imposed by the 1918 Treaty of Brest-Litovsk, the separate peace the Bolsheviks had concluded with the Central Powers, giving Lenin time to finish his revolution and releasing millions of German soldiers to fight on the Western Front.

A secret protocol of the Rapallo treaty also provided for the establishment of German training and testing facilities within Russia. Lipetsk Air Base, south of Moscow, was selected, and housing, hangars, and maintenance facilities were discreetly constructed. In June 1925 the *Hugo Stinnes IV*, a German steamship, left Stettin bound for Leningrad carrying fifty carefully crated Fokker D XIII aircraft. Anthony Fokker had no qualms about supplying the planes, though the sale was run through dummy corporations and was ostensibly intended for the Argentinean air force.

The Fokker was a good choice. A typical design of fabric-covered steel tubing, it had wooden wings and fixed gear. Powered by a twelve-cylinder British Napier Lion engine, the plane could manage 160 mph with a service ceiling of 24,000 feet. It handled well and made a good advanced fighter trainer, especially with Great War combat vets as instructors. Major Walter Schtaar was just such a pilot, and he became the first commander of the Lipetsk Flying School. Known to the Germans as Wivupal, the Scientific Experimental and Test Establishment for Aircraft was supposed to train Soviets as well and provide them with all test results.* This was the price for conducting whatever business the Reichswehr deemed necessary beyond the prying eyes of the Allies. In truth, it was a one-sided arrangement, and the Soviets received very little useful information or technology.

The school operated for eight years and only trained some two hundred pilots and observers. The real value was derived from testing new airframes, engines, and weaponry. The Arado 64, Germany's first postwar fighter, was evaluated here to circumvent the Versailles restrictions. Also of note was Dissimilar Air Combat Training (DACT), which brought the Soviets and Germans together for practice combat and provided invaluable experience for both sides. Training against your own pilots and platforms is fine, but DACT gives pilots a taste of fighting the unknown—something and someone different. Consequently, a pilot will not encounter a different aircraft for the first time in a real battle. This offers a split-second advantage in reaction time, which in an air battle can mean life over death.

The new German air force, the Luftwaffe, took this training seriously. They even discovered the inestimable value of using gun cameras for debriefing and evaluation purposes, just as the RAF had been doing since 1917. Modern machine guns, aerial photography, and bombs were tested on a range the Soviets provided. Ominously, both air forces also collaborated on airborne poison gas delivery. But despite the initial military benefits, such cooperation could never last—the ideological chasm between the two nations was too great.

By a joint declaration between Soviet Russia and her various satellites, the USSR had been formed. Lenin died in 1924

**Wissenschaftliche Versuchs und Prufanstalt fur Luftfahrzeuge*, in German jaw-cracking style.

and Trotsky resigned as War Commissar after failing to contain the General Secretary of the Soviet Union, Josef Besarionus Jugashvili—known to the world as Joseph Stalin.

While Stalin consolidated his power in the newly formed Soviet Union, far to the west another man sat in a prison cell writing a book. Adolf Hitler would eventually be released, of course, and would become chancellor of Germany in 1933, ending the Weimar Republic, and his book, *Mein Kampf*, became a bestselling blueprint for his intentions. Stalin and Hitler hated and feared each other, so relations naturally deteriorated to a point where the Lipetsk school shut down in 1933.

Aside from research and development, there was another significant consequence of this ill-fated joint effort. Scores of military officers would be executed during Stalin's purges in the 1930s, among them many of the most talented Soviet pilots produced at Lipetsk. These were pilots whose skills and knowledge of the Germans would have saved thousands of Russian lives in the conflict yet to come, and perhaps changed the course of history.

EARLY ON AUGUST 7, 1936, the SS *Usaramo* docked in Cadiz harbor. Sailing from the Petersen Dock in Hamburg at midnight a week before, she was a cargo ship owned by the Woermann Line, a German company. Ninety-one men disembarked that morning and quietly boarded a train bound for Seville and the Cristina Hotel. Their papers said they were journalists, photographers, artists, and even a few salesmen; all tourists belonging to the Reisegesellschaft Union, a travel association. But they were not.

They were mercenaries.

General Francisco Franco, ex-commander of the Spanish

Foreign Legion and former chief of staff of the Spanish army, had landed the month prior at the head of the rebel Nationalist Army. As a lieutenant colonel, he had saved the remnants of a defeated Spanish army during the Rif War of 1923 and now, at thirty-one, Franco was the youngest general in Europe. Nationalism in Spain, like Italian Fascism and German National Socialism, was born from democratic failure, in this case the Spanish Second Republic. Signed in 1930, the Pact of San Sebastián consolidated revolutionary groups in their effort to remove the monarchy. The resulting constitution provided for women's suffrage, guaranteed the right of free speech and assembly, legalized divorce, and emasculated the Spanish nobility. The Nationalists were generally opposed to all of that and while they included some fanatics, they were also monarchists, clerics, anti-anarchists, and other right-wingers; they were neither National Socialists like the Germans nor Fascists like the Italians.

Franco himself was a conservative monarchist and so viewed the Republic as a conspiracy of anarchists and Communists.* A left-wing revolt broke out in 1934, but Franco suppressed it, labeling the insurrection as "a frontier war and its fronts are socialism, communism and whatever attacks civilization in order to replace it with barbarism." Alarmed by Franco, the Republican government made him military commander of the Canary Islands—sending him into professional oblivion.

On July 15, 1936, a plane touched down on Las Palmas in the Canary Islands. The flight plan had originated from Casablanca, on the Atlantic coast of French Morocco, and given the events unfolding in Spain, if it hadn't been a British aircraft there would've been questions. As it was, no one paid much attention to the white de Havilland Dragon Rapide, and if they

*King Alfonso XIII of Spain had been best man at Franco's wedding in 1923.

had, they would've been satisfied with the Olley Air Service livery. The captain was W. H. "Cecil" Bebb and the "navigator" was named Pollard. There was also an immaculately dressed Mediterranean-looking man accompanied by two stunning young girls. This same dark-skinned man had remained behind in Morocco while the plane departed for the Canary Islands. Eyebrows were raised knowingly at the sight of middle-aged men flying around with blond eye candy, but no questions were asked.

Which was precisely the point. In fact, Pollard was an intelligence officer, and the girls were his daughter Diana and her good friend Dorothy Watson.* The young women had agreed to come along as cover and were enjoying themselves immensely.

The dark-skinned man was Luis Bolin, a London-based journalist who would later become Franco's press advisor. Bolin had chartered the plane to fly to the Canaries by way of Casablanca and pick up Franco—which they did. On July 18, the Dragon Rapide landed back in Casablanca and collected Bolin. From there, they flew to Tétuan, on the Mediterranean coast of Spanish Morocco.

Once there, Franco took command of the Spanish Army of Africa and rapidly pacified northern Morocco. He also began negotiations with Germany, Italy, and Great Britain for military support. Using mostly German-supplied transport aircraft, he was able to create an air bridge from Morocco to the southern Spanish city of Seville. By flying in about 120 soldiers per day, he had more than a thousand men in place by the first week in August. Franco was then able to defeat a Republican naval blockade and begin convoying his troops across in strength.

On August 7 the *Usaramo* began offloading her "agricul-

---

*Hugh Pollard would eventually become the MI6 station chief in Madrid.

tural equipment," which was moved 50 miles up the road to Seville's Tablada airfield. No one should've been surprised at the aircraft fuselages, wings, and other "farm machinery" that appeared. On August 9 six Heinkel He 51B single-seat fighters were rapidly assembled and made ready for action.*

Hannes Trautloft, a young German fighter pilot, would later write:

> *The next morning we found ourselves at Seville airfield. . . . On 9 August we started the job of rebuilding our six He 51s, a real piece of teamwork involving pilots and ground personnel. The Spanish personnel were quite surprised to witness us work with such energy, but we really were getting quite impatient and wanted to get our machines into the air as soon as possible.*

By the summer of 1936 the Heinkel had become the Luftwaffe's primary fighter. Powered by a twelve-cylinder, liquid-cooled BMW engine, it topped out at 200 mph with a ceiling of 25,000 feet. Tough and fast, the He 51 was armed with two MG-17 7.9 mm machine guns and could also carry bombs for ground attack.

But it really wasn't much of a dogfighter. There were also no radios, and the guns had to be manually charged each time they were used. During a fight over Zaragoza on October 19, a flight of three Germans was attacked by thirteen Republicans. Shooting down five and losing none, the German pilots proved

---

*Smith and Hall say twelve fighters were delivered, while Forsyth lists six. The original complement of pilots was only six, and Germany was still tentative in her support, so the smaller number is more likely.

that their skill and training could overcome most technical difficulties. Augmented by Italian pilots from the Escuadrilla de Caza flying Fiat CR.2s, the Nationalist Air Force controlled the sky over Spain—more or less.

This would rapidly change when the Republicans began receiving arms shipments and pilots from the Soviet Union. On September 9, 1936, the freighter *Neva* docked in Alicante. Among the equipment offloaded were the disassembled fuselages of Soviet-built Polikarpov I-15 and I-16 fighters, plus engines, guns, and other equipment. The I-15 was an indigenous Russian biplane fighter, powered by a 500-horsepower Wright Cyclone engine and armed with four Nadashkevich PV-1 7.62 mm machine guns.

Arranged about the engine, the guns were synchronized to fire through the prop at over 750 rounds per minute. The top pair were bore-sighted to 400 yards and the lower guns to 600 yards. The I-15 held over 1,200 rounds and the combined damage potential of this arrangement was considerable. The back and bottom of the pilot's seat were sheathed in 9 mm armor. To the Russians, the I-15 was a "Seagull"; the Spanish nicknamed it "Chato" (Snub-nose), while German pilots often called it a "Curtiss" because it resembled the F-9C Sparrowhawk.

The Chato was fairly forgiving and easy to fly, and with a relatively low wing loading, it landed like a big kite. Like most Russian weapons, it was overdesigned on purpose to withstand abuse from rough pilots, primitive mechanics, and poor operating conditions.

The other Soviet fighter in Spain was the I-16 Mosca. Nicknamed the "Rata" by the Germans, this was arguably the world's finest fielded fighter in 1936. Though the cockpit was basic, the I-16 was extremely nimble, and its 300 mph speed was very fast for the time. Most dangerous to the Germans were the two 7.62 mm ShKAS machine guns mounted in the wings. This avoided synchronization issues and permitted a much higher firing rate of 1,800 rounds per minute, compared to 1,200 rounds per minute from the Heinkel. There was also more room to store ammunition and the Mosca carried 650 rounds per weapon versus 500 for the He 51. Though the gas-operated gun fired quicker, it was also prone to jamming. Still, with a heavier caliber and the ability to deliver 300 rounds on target from a five-second burst, the I-16 was a deadly threat. Subsequent versions carried an extra pair of guns on the cowling that were eventually replaced with cannons.

A low-winged monoplane with stressed aluminum skin, the Mosca had retractable landing gear, a controllable-pitch propeller, and an enclosed cockpit. With the wheels up, the little fighter and its short wings rolled extremely well. This came at the cost of high wing loading, however, so the I-16 couldn't turn tightly in any dimension.* As in most cases, pilot training and skill would make the difference.

On November 13, eight Moscas with sixteen I-15s pounced on a flight of Heinkels over Madrid. The Germans shot down five of them, but it was obvious that the He 51 was badly outclassed. They also lost Oblt. Kraft Eberhardt, their leader, to a midair collision with a Russian.† Tactically, the Republican I-16 pilots would quickly learn not to get into a turning fight with the Heinkels and Fiats. It was better to drop down from altitude, using the speed advantage, and slash through formations delivering deadly, short bursts from their heavier guns.

Even so, encounters like this demonstrated the need for both

---

*The Mosca had a 29-foot wingspan with a wing loading of 27 pounds per square foot. The He 51 had a 36-foot span with a wing loading of 14 pounds per square foot.

†The Soviet pilot was kicked to death by a mob who believed him to be a German.

experienced pilots and better planes. As one can only compensate for the other for so long. Almost all of the active flying officers in the old Republican Air Force had promptly switched sides and joined Franco. In fact, the Republican military was generally split along class lines, with the conservative, monarchist officers joining the rebels and most of the lower ranks remaining with the Madrid government. When the Republican Air Force reorganized itself into the Fuerzas Aéreas de la República Española (FARE), there wasn't much left: flying sergeants, whom the Spanish used for reconnaissance or transport flying, and older pilots who were serving on staffs and teaching at schools.

Most of the Spanish Air Force pilots had defected to Franco, so to augment their squadrons the Republicans turned to mercenaries and volunteers. Some of these, like the American volunteers Frank Tinker and Albert Baumler, were former military aviators and were well trained, particularly in instrument flying.

Frank Tinker was a 1933 graduate of the U.S. Naval Academy so how did he wind up in air combat over Spain? In a typically poorly thought-out and embarrassingly pointless move, the White House attempted to reduce its 1933 budget by *not* commissioning Naval Academy cadets who graduated that year. These men, with their expensive elite education, would be simply dumped back into the civilian world. Some sanity prevailed, however, and the resulting compromise was to only commission the top half of the class and give reserve commissions to the rest. One cadet complained to his congressman, Lister Hill of Alabama, who persuaded the Army Air Corps to accept seven naval cadets for flight training. One hundred applied for those seven spots and forty of them failed the flight physical. Luckily, Frank Tinker passed, and in October 1933 he showed up at Randolph Field in San Antonio, Texas, for training.

By the spring of 1934, ready to pass into advanced training, Tinker learned that the Air Corps also now had a surplus of officers itself, and so he would likely not be commissioned into the Army either, even after graduating from flight school. Fortunately, by this time the Navy had regained a bit of common sense and invited the Class of '33 back into service. This brought Tinker and his surviving classmates to Pensacola in July, and there he was finally commissioned an ensign in the U.S. Navy. Awarded his wings in January 1935, Frank Tinker was assigned to the cruiser *San Francisco,* flying Vought Corsair floatplanes.

It was a short, turbulent career. In less than six months he'd been court-martialed once and had a string of professional and private mishaps to his credit. Recommended for a second court-martial, he chose to resign and began searching for aviation work. Through the Spanish embassy in Mexico City, Tinker was given a contract of $1,500 per month to fly for the Republicans plus a bonus of $1,000 for every enemy plane destroyed. A death benefit would be paid to his next of kin, and he was free to terminate the arrangement with thirty days' notice. This was during the Great Depression, and the money was a major inducement—that $1,500 was equivalent to about $25,000 per month in 2013 dollars.* By comparison, the American foot soldiers fighting in the Abraham Lincoln Brigade were being paid about ten cents per day for a three-year contract.

For Spain, the civil war was national life and death. For the other nations who supplied men and equipment, it was certainly less drastic, though no less important. Spain was as much a proving ground for new weapons and aircraft as it was an ideological conflict between Communism and everything else.

*A modern mercenary is paid between $500 and $5,500 per day, based on his particular skills.

Also, and perhaps more important, it was a tactical bridge between World War I and what was to come. Hitler decided that Spain was too good an opportunity to pass up, so he ordered increased aid for Franco to counter Stalin's involvement. Sixty more crated He 51 biplanes arrived in Seville by the middle of November, and twenty-five freighters loaded with other weapons and equipment left Stettin for Cadiz by the end of the month.

The single Jagdstaffel Eberhardt would be reorganized into three fighter squadrons as Jagdgruppe/88. There would also be a Kampfgruppe (bomber) group, K/88, and similar groups for reconnaissance, signals, and maritime reconnaissance. A full complement of support organizations for maintenance, supply, and medical needs was also sent along. Initially labeled the Eiserne Legion (Iron Legion), its name was changed to the Condor Legion, and it was ready for action by the second week in December.

Commanded by Generalmajor Hugo Sperrle, the Germans fought back hard. Everything was under review—men, machines, and tactics. Hannes Trautloft, Werner Mölders, and eventually Adolf Galland, all gifted aviators and tacticians, went to work slaying the ghosts of World War I. The most obvious change would come from an offensive doctrine instead of a defensive one. The new Luftwaffe would be supporting ground units and gaining air superiority by attacking, rather than defending the sky over a stagnant land battle.

This meant multipurpose aircraft with radios for effective communications and sufficient firepower to destroy all types of targets. The Germans ceased flying Great War tight formations and experimented with new methods suited to the weapons, aircraft, and the current situation. Mölders created the *Rotte*, the basic fighting pair that survives to this day. Two *Rotte* then combine to form a *Schwarm* of four aircraft. Wider spacing was also used, making a wingman truly useful. Now he wasn't just staring at a wingtip; he was scanning the sky for enemy planes, protecting his leader from threats, and attacking when necessary.

Technology had always been key to German success. From the early days of the synchronized gun on the Eindecker through the advanced Fokkers, they'd acknowledged the need to maintain technical superiority. Madrid in December 1936 was a slap of reality in the face. The skill of individual German pilots couldn't overcome the true technological advantage of the I-16 any more than they had been able to do so against the Sopwiths and SPADs eighteen years earlier. A new plane was needed, one that could be paired with well-trained, experienced pilots and achieve total air superiority.

Fortunately for the Germans, there was such an aircraft. In July 1933 the Luftwaffe's Technical Office for Development had issued an official "Tactical Requirement for Fighter Aircraft (Land)." This stated the need for a single-seat day fighter that was armed with a minimum of two fixed machine guns and 500 rounds per gun, a radio, an oxygen system with heat, a parachute, and the ability to reach 19,500 feet in seventeen minutes and maintain this altitude for twenty minutes at 250 mph.

Enter the Bf 109.*

By January 1937 the commander of J/88 reported to Sperrle that the Heinkel was ineffective against the I-16 and that he would no longer sacrifice his men by flying an inferior aircraft. Astonishingly, Sperrle and Berlin agreed, so the He 51

* After July 1938, the Bayerische Flugzeugwerke (Bavarian Aircraft Factory) was renamed Messerschmitt AG. Any aircraft that originated prior to this change bore the prefix "Bf," and any after were designated with the "Me" prefix. For simplicity, I have elected to use the "Bf" designation throughout the book.

was immediately relegated to ground attack missions. Now the Condor Legion also included a *Versuchsjadgstaffel*—an experimental fighter squadron—formed specifically to test the Bf 109. At least three prototypes had arrived in Spain in late December 1936, and this may well have been the impetus for replacing the aging Heinkels.

The brainchild of Willy Messerschmitt, the 109 was the next generation of fighter aircraft. It featured an enclosed cockpit, cantilever wings, a stressed skin, and a semi-monocoque fuselage. The retractable undercarriage was hydraulic, not hand cranked like in the I-16, and incorporated leading-edge slats for unequaled slow-speed maneuvering.* Because fighter weapons of the period were forward-facing, the nose position of the aircraft meant everything in a fight, since you could only shoot where the plane was pointing. Thus the ability to turn and point quite literally meant the difference between life and death. As you turn and try to point, the angle at which air hits the wings, called the angle of attack, constantly changes. If you imagine airflow as parallel to the horizon, a wing usually tilts further up and away from this airflow as it slows. This angle can only increase so far before the air separates completely and the wing stalls. Messerschmitt's automatic *leading-edge slats* were designed to alleviate this condition and expand the 109's ability to fight at these higher angles of attack.† This meant the new fighter could turn and point more effectively at the slow speeds and wild vertical maneuvering common in dogfights.

Slats work like this. As the speed slows and the air resistance lessens, they slide out from the front edge of the wing. This

---

* It took about forty cranks to raise the I-16's gear, and this resulted in some truly interesting one-handed takeoffs.

†Actually developed by Frederick Handley-Page, a British designer; more or less in concert with Gustav Lachmann, a German aerodynamicist.

physically, but temporarily, changes the camber or curvature of the wing. By making the wing bigger, the slats increase the wing's surface area and delay the eventual separation of airflow over the wing. If the separation is delayed, then the wing takes longer to stall and can fly at lower speeds. Furthermore, when the slats extended, a gap was created between the slats and the wing. Now air was flowing directly from under the wing to the upper surface, which also aided slow-speed handling characteristics.

Messerschmitt believed in low weight, low drag, and simple designs. Fuel tanks were aft of the 109's cockpit, and its seat was armored to protect the pilot from bullets and burning aviation gas. The landing gear was attached to the fuselage, so the wings could be removed with no extra support equipment. The wings themselves had a single off-center spar, making them very strong and much lighter than two-spar wings. Stronger construction meant that a small surface area was possible, which increased wing loading to an astounding 40 pounds per square foot.* Vast improvements in engine technology were the only way this trade-off was possible.

Ironically, due to manufacturing shortfalls, the first Bf 109 prototype was powered by a British Rolls-Royce Kestrel engine. Junkers Motorenwerke then built the Jumo 210 series, which would power most of the remaining early Messerschmitt fighters. It was a 600-horsepower, twelve-cylinder engine constructed in an inverted V arrangement. This meant a very streamlined fuselage was possible with an engine less susceptible to damage from ground fire. It also boasted a direct injection fuel system instead of a carburetor, making it more fuel efficient; this also

*The World War I–era Fokker Triplane had a wing loading of 6.5 pounds per square foot, and the Spitfire would have a load of about 27 pounds per square foot.

made the engine more powerful and permitted negative-g flight. This capability would become *very* significant in future dogfights.

In effect, the entire design overcame the old trade-offs between speed and lift by utilizing better engines and advanced, high-lift devices such as the slats. Both factors enabled the aircraft's performance to match the phase of flight: slower and easier for takeoffs and landings, efficient for cruising, and more versatile during the rapid changes necessary in a fight. As intended, the simple design lent itself to the inevitable improvements and modifications that Willy Messerschmitt knew would occur as a result of combat experience.

The three prototypes sent to Spain in December 1936 were perfect examples of this flexible mind-set. One of them added a 20 mm Oerlikon cannon to the engine mount that fired through the propeller hub. The other two aircraft had variable-pitch metal propellers rather than the older fixed-pitch wooden Schwarz props. Germans were big proponents of operational test and evaluation, so Hannes Trautloft went to work immediately. He quickly realized that the new plane was more than a match for the Russian fighters, and his initial assessment was very favorable. Range, ceiling, and speed combined with superb handling characteristics to make the Bf 109 an immediate combat necessity.

This was good, since the Legion suffered a 20 percent loss rate in January 1937 and the Heinkels shot down just three Republican aircraft. Soviet involvement meant that the Nationalist Air Force was now outnumbered and outgunned, so J/88 had dispersed somewhat until the production 109s could arrive. The He 51 was given over almost entirely to close air support, mainly in the north of Spain, away from the Chatos and Ratas.

Fighting Bolshevism, testing new weapons, and gaining priceless combat experience, the Condor Legion received twelve

Bf 109B-1 fighters in March 1937. About this time, Franco decided to shift his attacks from Madrid to a small pocket of resistance in the north, along the Bay of Biscay. This province held most of the coal and iron deposits, and if it could be captured, Franco would also have a secure northern flank against any French reinforcement. The Republican Army of the North contained some 150,000 men, outnumbering Franco nearly three to one, but there was little unity among the Asturians, Santaderinos, and Basques fighting for the Republic. The Nationalists also had a pronounced numerical superiority in aircraft.

Franco's troops had advanced as far as Ochandiano by April 4, encircling it and conducting heavy close air support attacks on the Republican positions. The Bf 109 opened its combat score on April 6 when Oblt. Günther Lützow of 2 Staffel shot down an I-15 over the town. A few days later Capt. Felipe del Rio Crespo, a leading Republican ace, was shot down by Lt. Günther Radusch. Republican air superiority was waning, and as April ended, the Nationalists trapped the retreating Republicans by destroying the Rentaria bridge over the Oca River near Guernica.

On April 26 a reconnaissance aircraft reported large numbers of troops in and around the town. Twenty-six Condor Legion bombers and sixteen fighters were dispatched, and they attacked the bridge and targets of opportunity within Guernica. Unfortunately, they missed the bridge, a weapons factory, and generally anything of military significance. The "troops" also turned out to be civilians on their way to the daily market. The ensuing media frenzy over the fifteen hundred reported dead handed Franco a tactical failure and the Republicans a propaganda victory.

Undeterred, the Nationalists pushed ahead and captured Bilbao, the capital of the northern Basque region, in mid-June.

In an effort to relieve the pressure, Republicans countered by renewing the offensive around the Madrid area. This resulted in a salient, or bulge, west of the city around the village of Brunete, and Franco personally requested the Legion's Bf 109s be committed at once. Sperrle transferred two fighter squadrons from Burgos to several airfields near Madrid, and they immediately began flying combat sweeps.

Launching for at least three missions per day, plus sitting alert, the German pilots were also flying without oxygen.* With summer heat well over 100° F, the mechanics wore swim trunks with sombreros, while the pilots flew in shorts and tennis clothes. Even with their new fighter, the Germans were outnumbered about four to one and were hard-pressed for a few weeks.

On July 7, Frank Tinker was trolling for targets over the vast Guadarrama plain when he spotted three Messerschmitts chasing a Republican I-15. He dove into the middle of it with his new Russian wingmen, but the I-15 went down in flames even as Tinker pulled the "Mayser-Schmidt," as he called it, into his sights. Some 300 rounds of 7.62 mm shells chewed up the 109's fuselage and sent it down flaming for his sixth confirmed kill.

The air battles over Brunete, sometimes with several hundred aircraft involved, were really the first use of the new fighter in the south. Tinker and his fellow pilots weren't particularly worried about the maneuverability compared to their own I-16's, but the three tracer trails streaming from the 109 made them cautious.

As the Germans quickly discovered, below 10,000 feet the Mosca was basically an even match for the Bf 109, except in fire-

---

*The Republicans had oxygen masks and hoses in their I-16s—but someone in the Soviet Union had forgotten to ship the regulators that manage and control the system, so it was useless.

power. But above 10,000 feet the Bf 109, with its supercharged or direct injection engine, thoroughly owned the sky. Without air superiority there was no way for the Republic to halt the Savoia-Marchetti and Ju 52 bombers. Coming in above 15,000 feet, they'd pull the power back to glide down fast and silent at their targets—roads, railroads, troops, and especially airfields. Tinker and the other Republican fighters would usually only get airborne at the last minute during the bomb run, if at all.

The Republicans lost 25,000 men and more than one hundred aircraft versus twenty-three aircraft and 10,000 men from the Nationalist side. Desperate to reassure the French and Soviets that they were winning, the Republic declared a victory. No one believed it, and as the offensive spluttered out, Franco resumed his northern operations, capturing Santander in August. By the end of October the Nationalists had occupied the ports of Aviles and Gijon, effectively eliminating the Cantabrian Pocket.

Men like Adolf Galland and Werner Mölders would continue refining tactics and suggesting improvements for the Luftwaffe. Aside from the four-ship formations that would become standard, they identified the critical need for radios—not just on fighters but on all aircraft. Close escort of bomber or reconnaissance planes without radios was fatiguing and often impossible except under ideal conditions. Radios would allow plans to be changed in flight and combat to be coordinated. Night operations were also a key developmental point. If you could operate at night but your enemy could not, this became a tactical exclusion zone that could be exploited.

The year 1938 began with Nationalist offensives that eventually drove through the Ebro River valley and threatened Barcelona. With the Biscay ports closed, France opened its borders to resupply the Republic, but it was too late. The Soviet Union had already bled the Republic of over $500 million in gold reserves, and support was thinning out.*

The Republicans counterattacked, pitting their 176 serviceable Republican fighters against 168 Nationalist Bf 109s and Fiats. Constant ground attacks on Republican supply lines, communications, and chokepoints resulted in massive losses, and by July Franco was pushing his forces back across the Ebro River.

During the ground war seesaw, Willy Messerschmitt hadn't been idle. In early summer the Bf 109D arrived in Spain. With a more powerful engine, the D model also boasted four MG-17 guns, a pair in the nose and one each for the wings. However, the real improvements, taking into account all that had been learned the hard way in Spain, would manifest themselves in the Bf 109E model, the venerable "Emil." Production had been delayed because the new Daimler-Benz 600A engine necessitated design changes to the aircraft's structure, cooling system, and landing gear, but it was now ready.

Rated at an astounding (for the time) 1,175 horsepower, the new engine maxed out around 330 mph and utilized fuel injection for a performance envelope unmatched by any other fighter in the world.† The two 7.62 mm fuselage guns carried 1,000 rounds apiece, with a further 500 rounds each for the wing guns. It even had a radio. During the last few days of 1938 the Legion shot down sixteen Republican aircraft.

But the end was approaching. On March 5, 1939, the remaining leaders of the Republic boarded a plane at Alicante and ran for France. On the twenty-eighth of March, Franco marched tri-

*Ironically, much of this gold had been pillaged by the Spanish conquests of Mexico and Peru. In mid-1937 Soviet aid totaled nearly $120 million, compared to $1.5 million in early 1939.

†The Fokker D-VII had a 160-horsepower Mercedes engine in 1918.

umphantly into Madrid without firing a shot, and on April 1, 1939, the Spanish Civil War officially came to an end.

Condor Legion personnel had been rotating back to Germany at regular intervals to pass on their hard-won experience.* Lessons learned about tactics, field maintenance, and logistics would be invaluable in the coming months and years. Though combined operations had begun in World War I, new technology such as radios and improved weaponry now had to be incorporated in battle planning. On a tactical level, the Spanish conflict provided an ideal testing ground, and some two hundred German pilots had become combat veterans.

Many enduring legacies from the Great War had been revised, modernized, and in some cases thrown out altogether. From this standpoint Spain gave the Luftwaffe a leg up on those who would enter the next conflict using outdated tactics and techniques. However, other flawed lessons were derived from the Spanish experience. First, it was a tactical war, and so it didn't provide much useful material for larger-scale operations. Second, because the value of strategic bombing was largely overlooked, the limited range of the Bf 109, though fine for a small theater like Spain, would prove a critical shortcoming in the near future. As Adolf Galland would later say, "Whatever may have been the importance of the tests of German arms in the Spanish Civil War from tactical, technical and operational points of view, they did not provide the experience that was needed nor lead to the formulation of sound strategic concepts."

In any event, the veterans were dispersed widely so that they could pass along what they'd learned. This was indeed fortunate for the Luftwaffe, as September 1939 was fast approaching and the world, as it was known, was about to change forever.

---

*Pilots left after a year or after shooting down five aircraft.

PART THREE

CATACLYSM: 1939–1945

HE WHO GIVES BACK AT THE FIRST REPULSE,
AND WITHOUT STRIKING THE SECOND BLOW,
DESPAIRS OF SUCCESS, HAS NEVER BEEN, IS NOT,
AND NEVER WILL BE A HERO IN WAR, LOVE OR BUSINESS.
—FREDERIC TUDOR

CHAPTER 7

COLORS

PZL P.11

A PENETRATING, UNEARTHLY wail instantly jarred the men awake from a sound sleep. It was the kind of sound that made teeth ache and turned the heart cold; a steadily rising scream that made skin itch and hair stand on end. Eyes wide, the soldiers rolled from their bunks and tumbled toward the doors, grabbing rifles in the predawn gloom. Some covered their ears, and some fell to the ground. Others lifted their rifles and stared at the sky, trying to see the threat—an enemy that was out of reach up beyond the mist.

All they saw was death.

As the ground erupted in explosions, a bicycle flew into the air, followed by boots and several pots. Even the braver sort of man dropped his weapon and ran for the trees or the river. The concrete blockhouses guarding the bridge disappeared, and most of those inside were vaporized in an instant. Pieces of the others were flung high into the air before thudding back to earth in bloody, charred fragments. The horrible banshee screaming gave way to roaring engines and the rushing noise of wind over metal. If anyone had been left alive, he would've seen the three gull-winged aircraft level off, vapor streaming from thick wing tips, then duck lower just above the trees before turning west and disappearing. It was nearly 4:45 a.m. in the morning of September 1, 1939—and the Second World War had just begun.

Twenty-year-old political bandages of Versailles fell away, exposing the festering wounds remaining from the Great War. A treaty that was both too shortsighted and too visionary had finally unraveled in a spectacularly bad manner. The Soviet Union, enormous, unpredictable, and tenacious, was determined to forge a place in the world, while Germany, bitter and proud, was fanatical about regaining its status.

Case White, the German plan for the invasion and destruction of Poland, was the first link in this chain. The pretext given was the Polish Corridor created at Versailles and its threat to Germany. Backed by President Wilson's Fourteen Points, the corridor gave Poland "free and secure access to the sea" by cutting a large swath of territory through Germany to the Baltic port of Danzig. There were issues with this that Hitler exploited as justification for going to war. Danzig, like most of the cities along the Baltic shore, was predominantly German, with infrastructure, port facilities, and shipping industries heavily financed by German investors. Nearly two million Germans lived in the area, and the corridor also severed East Prussia from Germany itself.

Part of the solution had been a railway connecting Berlin to its eastern province. This crossed the Vistula River at Dirschau (modern Tczew) just below Danzig (modern Gdansk) and was a linchpin for any German advance into the area. Both sides knew this, and the Poles had carefully prepared the bridge for demolition in the event of a German attack. Blockhouses adjoining the bridge contained troops who would blow the structure if ordered. These blockhouses were the first, critical targets of the war and had to destroyed on time, with precision and surprise.

Enter the Stuka.

Flown in Spain with the Condor Legion, the Ju 87 was capable of highly accurate surface attacks using 250 and 50 kilogram bombs or its 20 mm cannon. The inverted gull-wing design both improved the pilot's visibility and permitted the shorter, sturdier landing gear necessary for rough fields. The wing was also constructed in sections, allowing for easy disassembly and transport by rail to a combat operations area. In keeping with the forward operating base concept, the fuselage was constructed in large removable sections for engine maintenance. Interchangeable parts were common, as was the avoidance of welded fittings whenever possible.

The Stuka's diving technique was unique. A more vertical dive angle made for less aiming error, so the pilot acquired the target through a window in the floor, then set a dive lever. This limited the movement of his control column and automatically popped dive brakes, which would keep the aircraft at 350 mph during the attack. Rolling in around 15,000 feet, the pilot set the dive angle at 60°, 75°, or 90° by using red lines painted on the cockpit window. He would then aim with his cannon sight at the target and release the bomb manually at a preplanned altitude.

The pilot could also initiate a sequence that began a 6 g dive recovery at 1,500 feet. This would automatically pull the aircraft back through the horizon, set the propeller for full throttle, climb, and retract the dive brakes. In those days, 6 g's was considered excessive so the auto system saved many a Stuka crew from the barely understood g-forces of high-performance aircraft.* Bombing accuracy was very good, and the addition of the Jericho-Trompete dive siren was initially devastating to the defenders on the ground. It was precisely this combination of surprise, tight accuracy, and devastation that Oberleutnant Bruno Dilley delivered to the Polish defenders of the Dirschau bridge early on that Friday morning in September 1939.

In the minutes following the attack, four German army groups lunged across the borders into Poland from Pomerania, East Prussia, and Slovakia. Warsaw, though expecting such an attack, was hopeful that Britain and France would honor their pledges to defend against any German aggression. Those pledges had been made with the naive understanding that the Soviet Union, much closer and with strategic interests in mind, would also move to defend Poland should it become necessary.

What London, Paris, and Warsaw didn't know was that Germany and the USSR had concluded a secret nonaggression pact on August 22. This gave Stalin eastern Poland all the way to the Vistula River plus Lithuania, Latvia, and Estonia all in return for noninterference with any German attack, should it become necessary. And Hitler made certain that it was necessary. On August 30, a German border post near Gleiwitz was "attacked" by the Poles—or at least by men wearing Polish uniforms.†

So Poland was on her own. Hitler had rightly calculated

---

*Modern jet fighters routinely pull 9 g's. But this is with advanced equipment, including g suits, and a much, much higher level of pilot physical fitness.
†Prisoners and condemned criminals dressed in Polish uniforms.

that France and Britain would not move fast enough to stop him, and if he could win quickly, then there was little for his adversaries to gain by a declaration of war. With the Polish Corridor absorbed back into Germany, then there was no port available to reinforce Poland, so aid could come only from the Soviet Union—and that had been dealt with.

Checkmate.

And it worked.

Despite the betrayal, the Poles fought back hard. Their victories in the air were visible reminders of what fighting spirit can accomplish, and they were a shock to the Luftwaffe. The Poles were flying Pzl P.7 and Pzl P.11 fighters—at one point fairly advanced but now hopelessly outclassed by the Bf 109. The Pzl P.11 was an all-metal open-cockpit monoplane with decent range and a maximum speed of 240 mph. The gull wing gave some improved visibility, good turning performance, and an easy recovery from stalls. It generally mounted two 7.92 mm machine guns, but with nonretractable landing gear, a fixed propeller, and very few radios, it was severely disadvantaged. This makes the 110 acknowledged German losses to this monument of a bygone era even more astounding. The first Polish combat loss probably occurred on September 1 at 5:30 a.m. near Krakow in southern Poland. Capt. Mieczyslaw Medwecki and his wingman Wladyslaw Gnys scrambled out of Balice and were attacked by two Stukas. Medwecki, the group commander, was immediately shot down and killed. Gnys turned on the Stukas, damaging one of them. He then found two Do 17 bombers, and German sources confirm they both came down near the village of Zurada (though not necessarily shot down by Gnys).

September 3 found the German Fourth Army advancing east from Pomerania to link up with the Third Army moving west from Prussia. Four days later Warsaw was in danger of encirclement from two enemy armies, and by September 19, 100,000 Polish troops had surrendered. Contrary to the myth that the Polish air force was destroyed on the ground, the fighters, particularly the Pursuit Brigade's five squadrons near Warsaw, battled the Germans every day.

Fighting on to the inevitable conclusion, the Poles eventually lost more than 100 of their 130 aircraft before combat ended on October 6, 1939. However, many of the pilots escaped and, as we shall see, continued flying in France or England. As for the Germans, though they claimed a tactical victory, the campaign was a strategic defeat. The Soviet Union gained eastern Poland, including the oil basins of Lublin and Krasno, without shedding a drop of blood. More important, the Red Army was closer to Berlin and the Wehrmacht some 75 miles farther from Moscow.

The Polish campaign gave the Luftwaffe valuable lessons concerning supply, logistics, and, above all, surface attack. Five *Schlachtgruppen* had been created by Adolf Galland, adding power to the combined-arms blitzkrieg ground assault tactics. Three of these groups would be equipped with Stukas and one with Do 17 bombers. The last one, Fliegergruppe 10, became part of a test and evaluation unit dedicated to the development of new tactics. Everything learned in Poland was passed back for dissection and consideration.

Many technical innovations had been affirmed, such as radio communication, the accuracy of the dive-bomber, and the vital component of close air support. Other lessons were not so straightforward. How, for instance, had the numerically and technically inferior Poles inflicted such damage on the best air force in the world? Other scenarios were lost in the euphoria surrounding victory, but Galland wondered what would occur when they faced an enemy who fought back on even terms.

THE FACT THAT Hitler's next moves were against Denmark and Norway pushed this very real consideration even further to the rear. In February, Norway's territorial waters had been used by the Royal Navy to capture the *Altmark*, a German resupply ship, and Hitler decided to take this as an excuse to implement Case Green, the invasion of Denmark. This would seal off the Baltic and give him a secure land route for desperately needed Swedish iron ore. Denmark surrendered immediately, so the Germans then drove through Oslo, Norway, and north toward Trondheim to link up with their troops at Narvik. In mid-April the British and French countered by sending some 12,000 men into Norway, but they were forced to evacuate in early May.

On May 10, 1940, following many postponements, Hitler executed Case Yellow. Only the fall of France, he reasoned, would force Britain to sue for peace. Both Paris and London had been expecting an attack, but they'd assumed it would come the previous fall, so by now the edge had been dulled somewhat. And the French felt secure: on their northern flank were twenty-one divisions of the Belgian army and a network of fortified positions along the Meuse River. To the south lay the seemingly impassable Ardennes Forest and the Maginot Line. Besides, the French army was one of the largest in the world, augmented by British Expeditionary Force ground troops and the Royal Air Force.

Initially there were nine RAF fighter squadrons on the continent, all flying Hawker Hurricanes. Accompanied by Blenheims, Lysanders, and Fairey Battles, they were part of the British Air Force (BAF) in France. This augmented the BEF Air Component, with six Hurricane squadrons, supporting Lord Gort and the army.* Three more fighter squadrons were

*These were the 85 (Lille), 87 (Senon), 607 (Vitry-en-Artois), 615 (Le Touquet), 3, and 79 (Merville) Fighter Squadrons.

attached to the Advanced Air Striking Force (AASF) and answered to RAF Bomber Command in England.*

The Hurricane had been developed in response to Air Ministry specification F.7/30 during the 1930's, when Germany began rearming and war looked likely. Sydney Camm, Hawker's chief designer, insisted on conventional technology that could be assembled using existing jigs and tooling. The plane used a box-girder-type construction with no welds for ease of maintenance and field repairs. Wood and fabric were utilized over hollow steel tubing, which again made the Hurricane easier to service. It was found in early fights that German shells would often pass through the fabric without exploding. Powered by a 1,030-horsepower Rolls-Royce Merlin II engine, the fighter maxed out at around 330 mph. Initial aircraft carried eight .303 Browning machine guns and enough ammunition for fifteen seconds of continuous firing. Production began in June 1936, and when the war began there were some five hundred Hurricanes in service with eighteen RAF fighter squadrons.

By the spring of 1940 it had proven itself in combat. On October 21, 1939, a flight of six Hurricanes from 46 Squadron shot down four of nine Heinkel 115 floatplanes over the North Sea. A few days later in France, Pilot Officer "Boy" Mould from 1 Squadron sent a Dornier Do 17 spinning down in flames near Toul.

Several months later, on the morning of May 10, the Führer's personal train stopped at Euskirchen on the German-Belgian border.† A new bunker called Felsennest had been built there expressly for Hitler so he could watch his invasion begin. At

---

*These were the 1 (Wassincourt), 73 (Rouve), and 501 (Bethenville) Fighter Squadrons.

†Hitler's train was named *Amerika*.

5:30 a.m. Heinz Guderian's 1st Panzer Division rumbled across the Luxembourg border and headed west into the trees, eventually emerging from the forest on the French border. It was part of *Generaloberst* Gerd von Rundstedt's Army Group A, which was the largest group, with forty-five divisions. Guderian had seven panzer divisions, three of which would be used to shatter the French defenses at Sedan. Nose to tail, the tanks crept through ditches, along paths and railway lines, always to the west.

Farther north, Army Group B rolled through the Low Countries of Holland and Belgium, thrusting toward Flanders. Accompanied by more than 1,500 dive-bombers and medium bombers, Group B also included Luftwaffe paratroopers.* In reality, this was a colossal feint designed to draw the Allies toward the center—and it worked.

General Maurice Gamelin, the commander in chief of all French and British forces in France, took the bait. He'd never expected the Germans to attack the Maginot Line, but he also didn't believe that tanks could penetrate the Ardennes. Given the well-known and purposely well-publicized German fondness for armor, Gamelin naturally assumed the attack would come across the Low Countries. In fact, a German plane had made a forced landing in January near the Belgian town of Mechelen. The Luftwaffe officer on board had all the latest plans detailing an offensive through Belgium. The plans were real at the time and actually turned out to be a very effective subterfuge.

The scale of German air operations over the Low Countries was equally convincing. A key weak point in the Allied de-

*Unlike their Allied counterparts, *Fallschirmjäger* (paratroopers) were not army units—they belonged to the Luftwaffe.

fenses, and therefore a critical German objective, was the town of Maastricht. Straddling the Dutch-Belgian border, the town sat at the junction of the Meuse River and the Albert Canal. It was protected by the Belgian 7th Infantry Division and a tear-drop shaped fortress called Eben-Emael just south of the town.

Fallschirmjäger from the 1st Parachute Regiment were formed into a glider assault force to subdue the fortress and capture the bridges intact. At 4:30 on the morning Case Yellow began, 493 paratroopers were towed in fifty gliders to a point 20 miles from the target and released from 7,000 feet. Group Concrete, 96 men in eleven gliders, landed at the Vroenhaven bridge; Group Steel's 92 men in nine gliders were to take the Veldswezel bridge just west of Maastricht; the 96 men of Group Iron landed near the Kanne bridge; and last, all eleven gliders holding Group Granite's 85 men came down on Eben-Emael itself.

By 12:30 p.m. two of the three bridges had been captured intact and the fortress garrison had surrendered. A carefully timed and precisely executed airborne operation, though common today, had never been attempted before and would have been unthinkable a few decades earlier. Using a combination of logistics, airpower, and specially trained troops to take a key objective meant that the German Eighteenth Army could bypass heavy border defenses and charge straight into Belgium.*

Reacting exactly as they'd done in 1914, the French lunged forward to meet the visible threat of Field Marshal Fedor von Bock's Army Group B with their First Army and the British Expeditionary Force. Ironically, they were marching directly over the old Great War battlefields of Flanders and the Somme,

---

*Not without heavy cost, though—the German assault force suffered nearly 30 percent casualties.

where their fathers (and some of them) had fought. The French Seventh Army also swept up the Channel coast to reinforce the Belgians and the Dutch. Germans were nothing if not predictable, and this was simply a beefed-up version of the old Schlieffen Plan . . . or so they thought.

Not that there wasn't evidence to the contrary. The RAF immediately began reconnaissance flights, and those that survived reported multiple columns of German vehicles moving through the Ardennes. This was duly reported to the intelligence section of the French Ninth Army opposite Sedan—and promptly ridiculed. Despite prepositioned supply depots and trucks carrying fuel for the panzers, there were delays. Within days traffic jams formed, some of them over 150 miles long. If the RAF had been believed, Army Group A could've been halted or at least delayed long enough to stall the entire offensive.

The British flyers in France hadn't been idle but were in an extremely poor position. They should've been able to count on the French, but the Armée de l'Air was divided piecemeal into zones of operations, and each commander was independent of any overall command or control. Even so, the French could field 4,300 aircraft, of which 3,800 were modern types. This was arrayed against a Luftwaffe that could put 2,500 aircraft maximum into action during May 1940.

France had emerged from the Great War with a powerful air force and a considerable lead in technology. The Dewoitine 510 reached the magic airspeed of 250 mph before any other operational fighter, and it was the first to fire a cannon through its propeller hub. Eleven of twenty-two world speed records were held by the French, but politics and interservice animosity bred a dysfunctional, myopic mess that surpassed even their fear of the Germans. Even after creating an Air Ministry, the French army and navy retained operational control of most air force squadrons. Each army group fought tooth and nail to retain its own air units, for the primary mission of aviation, they steadfastly maintained, was to support ground forces. It was defensive thinking based on a generally static, infantry-dominated war—it was the Great War all over again.

The army won the catfight, even to the point of controlling air force procurement until 1936. In yet another twist of fate, the government decided to buy many of its fighters and engines from the United States rather than produce them indigenously. Curtiss built a nimble monoplane fighter, mostly metal and powered by a 1,200-horsepower air-cooled radial engine. Armed with either four or six 7.5 mm machine guns, the Americans called it a P-36 Hawk; to the French it was the H75A, and they took delivery of about three hundred. In climb performance, the Hawk was comparable to the Bf 109 below 10,000 feet. But at higher altitudes the Curtiss could barely manage 275 knots, while the Messerschmitt loafed along at 350 knots.

The other front-line fighter was the Dewoitine D-520. Another low-winged monoplane, it had much sleeker lines than the bulkier Curtiss and much better performance. A sliding canopy gave good visibility, and the pilot's seat was armored in the back. The cockpit was fully instrumented and well set up, barring the typical French throttle mechanization.* Easy to maintain and rearm, a 20 mm cannon fired through the propeller hub. It could be reloaded in about five minutes, as could the four MAC 39 7.5 mm wing guns. The D-520 was quirky, though, and not easy to fly. The Hispano-Suiza 12Y-45/49 engine was underpowered, even with a supercharger. Deliveries

*Unlike the rest of the world, full power with a French throttle was all the way aft. Full forward was idle.

of the plane were delayed until April and by May 1940, only seventy-five had been fielded.

But numbers are only part of the equation, and they rank lower in importance than technology, experience, and training. However, we saw higher levels of training and experience long maintain Luftstreitkräfte air superiority during World War I against a numerically superior but hastily trained Royal Flying Corps. France had fine pilots who fought well as individuals, but the French air force was never a cohesive fighting unit.

During the critical years leading up to the war, infighting and politicking caused serious morale ramifications—as did several air ministers. One of them was a bomber enthusiast, and he turned the air force upside down, reorganizing along those lines. When the generals didn't support him, he pushed through a law lowering the retirement age and forced many of them out. It also retired about 40 percent of the serving officers, a group that, unfortunately, included those with any combat experience from the Great War. His successor then reversed the bomber prioritization and backed close air support instead. Lack of focus from the top meant that facilities and infrastructure were neglected, while effective control simply didn't exist.

This was very apparent in the hours and days following the German attack. Even so, fighter squadrons reacted as you'd expect during an invasion and attacked on their own initiative. More than 190 Luftwaffe aircraft were lost on May 10, though this includes losses from ground fire as well. All told, in the first four days, more than 450 German planes were shot down—heavy losses for an air force that was producing only 600 fighters and bombers per month.*

*This doesn't include gliders but does include losses to the Belgian and Dutch air forces as well as the RAF.

Unfortunately, the defensive nature of French thinking negated any advantage they had in numbers. You see, they'd never really gotten over the horrors of the Great War and were determined that it should never happen to them again. This mindset prompted construction of the Maginot Line and extensive defensive systems along rivers and canals that could block any westward advance. The key to the whole assault was Allied ignorance of the German southern thrust, and the key to the whole southern thrust was Sedan. James Holland, in his excellent book *The Battle of Britain*, summed it up neatly:

> *The town effectively formed the hinge between the top of the Maginot Line . . . and the mobile northeast part of the line that had swung up into Belgium at the start of the offensive. Clearly, if this hinge could be broken, the two halves of the French line would be critically severed in two.*

This is exactly what occurred on the evening of May 12 as Rommel's 7th Panzer Division appeared from the Ardennes near Houx, north of Sedan. They found an intact dam with a footpath big enough to cross, so a reconnaissance in force did just that. Remarkably, it was the same dam that had been used by German troops in 1914, and it was *still* undefended. It also happened to be on the border between two French corps who couldn't decide who should take the defensive responsibility—so neither did.

Despite the surprise and confusion on the French side, the Germans also had their issues. Fuel was ingeniously brought alongside the panzers in jerry cans, and the crews refueled on the move. Field kitchens put out tens of thousands of bread loaves, sausages, dried fruit, and coffee. But engines failed and tank tracks broke down, so a huge logistical chain was constantly working. The tanks themselves were another cause of concern, and a majority of early German models carried light armor and were only armed with machine guns.

May 12 was historic for another reason as well. Adolf Galland, frustrated warrior and fighter pilot, had finally gotten back into the air and opened his account. Flying some three hundred close air support missions with the Condor Legion, he'd emerged from Spain as the Luftwaffe's expert on ground attack. This meant he'd been relegated to planning during Poland, and "Dolfo," as he was known, had had enough. Somehow he'd convinced a doctor to pronounce him unfit to fly open-cockpit aircraft (the air would affect his ears!) and he'd finally gotten back into fighters.

Now, as the adjutant for Jagdgeschwader 27, he was closer to the action but still not in it. Knowing that his skill and experience were wasted behind a desk, on May 12 he simply took off on his own authority and joined a patrol over Belgium in the Maastricht area. Just west of Liege Dolfo found eight Belgian Hurricanes and immediately pounced from above. Using proven Bf 109 tactics, he slashed into them from behind and shot down two. Later that same day he added another Hurricane to his score. Galland would become the highest-scoring German ace during the upcoming Battle of Britain and the youngest general officer in the German military. But that was yet to come.

In any event, by the following morning Rommel's engineers were laying pontoon bridges, and the first tanks crossed the Meuse into France on the evening of May 13. Caught in the past, the French had always planned on the response that had saved them in 1914. They'd counted on mobilizing their reserves and bringing them ponderously forward to wherever in Flanders the front stabilized. But in 1940 there was no front;

the invaders had moved too fast for that. The ten to fourteen days the French had planned on having to prepare just hadn't happened.

And the Germans weren't going to give it to them.

THE BATTLE FOR France was lost by the morning of May 14, 1940. Astonishingly, the French High Command still hadn't grasped the significance of the German panzers and mechanized infantry near Sedan. Not until 3:00 a.m. on May 14 did Gen. Alphonse Joseph Georges, commander of the French North East Front, piece it all together. André Beaufre, a junior officer in 1940, later wrote, "Georges was terribly pale. He flung himself into a chair and burst into tears. He was the first man I had seen weep in this campaign."

The British were too busy fighting to cry.

Their BEF was the only coherent fighting force left to oppose the Germans, but with its flanks left unprotected by French surrender fever, it had no option other than falling back to the coast. Churchill made the correct call in committing his RAF *only* to protect the withdrawal of ground forces to the Channel ports. After all, every fighter lost in France was one less available to protect Britain.

Guderian himself had crossed the Meuse on May 13 in a dinghy with his infantry. Disobeying orders to halt and consolidate, he pressed forward with his exhausted men and captured Hill 301 southwest of Sedan. The 1st and 10th Panzers began moving across in force early on the fourteenth, headed for Bulson Ridge, south of town. French armor had been ordered forward to take the Bulson Ridge at 4 p.m. the *previous* afternoon but, inexplicably, took more than seventeen hours to travel 12 miles. By the time they finally arrived the Germans were waiting in ambush. A short, bloody fight ensued, and the French remnants fled, joining most of the French field artillery and Gen. Pierre Lafontaine, commander of the 55th Infantry Division. Shortly thereafter, Guderian learned that the bridge over the Ardennes Canal west of Sedan had been taken intact and the way for his panzers was open—due west into the heart of France.

Failing to capitalize on German vulnerability in the Ardennes, the Belgians and Dutch were now shattered and the French army was collapsing. The French notion of suddenly beefing up their fighter squadrons with new planes and transitioning pilots simply wouldn't work because, again, there wasn't time. Same thing with their infantry reserves. In a strange practice, infantry units were rotated periodically between line service, construction, and agricultural duties, of all things. This may have allowed men to rest during the Great War, but had no usefulness in 1940. Bad communications were also a French trademark. There were few, if any, radios connecting Gamelin's headquarters with line units. In fact, it took up to forty-eight hours for messages from headquarters to reach combat outfits.

The Germans had radios and their generals led from the front, wasting no time appraising the situation, since they were there on the spot. German commanders and even NCOs followed the principle of *Aufstragstaktik*, meaning they were given an objective, then left alone to accomplish it. This promoted independent thinking, tactical innovation, and an offensive mentality that overwhelmed the defensive French.

The defensive mind-set is also why the French kept just a quarter of their operational aircraft close enough for immediate tactical intervention. Like artillery and armor, aircraft were only really viewed as infantry support. Everything the French had done was simply intended to buy enough time to gather their massive reserves, plus the British, Belgians, and Dutch, for a counterattack.

By the morning of the fifteenth it was obvious this wasn't going to happen. The traffic jams in the Ardennes had been cleared, so all three German bridgeheads at Dinant, Monthermé, and Sedan had been expanded and reinforced. The French 1 Division Cuirassée (1st Armored Division) was finally ordered across the Belgian border at Charleroi but had been caught refueling by Rommel's panzers. The 1st Armored had advanced with 170 tanks and ended the day with less than 40—it was completely routed.

Panzer Corps Reinhardt punched through at Monthermé and advanced some 30 miles in one day. At Sedan, Guderian left the 10th Panzer back as a reserve to guard the bridgehead and sprinted west with the 1st and 2nd Panzer Divisions. As the Meuse Front collapsed, the French military began surrendering faster than the Germans could take them prisoner. Accompanying the 6th Panzer Division, war correspondent Karl von Stackelberg would write:

> *There finally 20,000 men here . . . in this one sector and on this one day were heading backward as prisoners. It was inexplicable. How was it possible that, after this first major battle on French territory . . . this gigantic consequence should follow? How was it possible these French soldiers with their officers, so completely downcast, so completely demoralized, would allow themselves to go more or less voluntarily into imprisonment?*

Winston Churchill received a call on the morning of the fifteenth from Paul Reynaud, the French president, who simply said, "We have been defeated. We are beaten; we have lost the battle." The next day the British Expeditionary Force was ordered to fall back along the Escaut River to avoid being outflanked, since the Belgians had collapsed to the north and the French had surrendered to the south. By May 20 Guderian's tanks had captured Abbeville and reached the sea, cutting the Allied front in two. The following day, as the RAF ramped up to cover the impending evacuation, one of its future top aces got into the fight.

"Sailor" Malan, known to his close friends as John, got airborne at 5:37 p.m. from the RAF satellite field at Rochford and headed east.* Breaking out of the clouds at 15,000 feet, his two sections of three Supermarine Spitfire Mk I's continued climbing out over the Channel to 20,000 feet, heading toward the French coast. Malan was a product of extensive peacetime RAF training and was a disciplined, aggressive pilot. However, unlike the Luftwaffe in Spain, Poland, and France, the RAF had no recent combat experience. British fighter pilots flew the outdated "welded wing" close formation of the Great War and also employed a three-aircraft fighting unit called a "Vic."

In the Vic, both wingmen flew very close and stayed on their respective sides regardless of how the leader maneuvered. This was flawed for several reasons. First, combat is fluid and doesn't permit cookbook-type solutions. This is especially true of air combat, which moves fast in three dimensions and demands split-second reactions. Confining two-thirds of the available fighting power to staring at a wingtip was foolish and dangerous. The RAF also had set-piece tactics and specific, numbered attacks that were supposed to deliver maximum firepower against flights of enemy bombers:

---

*Actually he was born Adolph Gysbert Malan in Wellington, South Africa.

1. An attack from Dead Astern and from Above Cloud
2. From Directly Below
3. From Dead Astern (a) Approach Pursuit (b) Approach Turning, Above Cloud
4. From Directly Below, Two Types of Approach
5. From Dead Astern, Two Types of Approach
6. Two Types of Attack

These were complicated formation assaults that assumed (1) the targets were nonmaneuvering bombers that would just fly straight ahead and die and (2) there was no fighter escort. Both assumptions were dead wrong and very costly. These attacks were identical in mind-set to the British military infantry tactics of the previous century, which marched men into lines for massed firepower. It didn't work unless your opponent did precisely as you expected and relying on enemy cooperation for *any* tactical success is extremely risky.

The Germans certainly did not oblige.

Another problem that had to be quickly overcome was one of mentality. "Johnnie" Johnson, who would become Britain's top ace, wrote that the pre–World War II RAF was "the best flying club in the world."* Many of the lessons of the Great War had been forgotten and flying outfits, particularly fighter squadrons, had reverted somewhat into extensions of upper-class public schools. It was an idyllic world of gentlemanly flying hours (the hangar doors were usually shut by teatime) with plenty of time for leisurely strolls through manicured gardens near the mess. Flying consisted of aerobatics and the perfection of those beautifully useless formation attacks. There were few, if any,

*Johnson would survive the war with thirty-four confirmed kills—all either Bf 109 or FW 190 fighters.

tactical lectures, and only one annual trip to Sutton Bridge for live firing at towed targets. But behind this carefully cultivated facade RAF fighter pilots then, and now, are absolutely ferocious in the air. Unfortunately, this laissez-faire attitude had seeped into tactics, aircraft procurement, and the upper command structure. It would be corrected quickly enough, but not before many fine and desperately needed fighter pilots were lost.

The other mentality issue was with the "Never Land" crowd. These are the people who periodically emerge throughout history claiming something will *never* occur again. We'll read more about them later, but in this case they said that dogfighting was over forever—it would never happen again. Bombers were the way of the future, and so who needed fighter pilots? Besides, it was argued, the speeds involved produced g-forces that would be fatal to pilots. This point of view was rapidly shattered during the Battle for France, when RAF bomber units suffered 80 to 95 percent casualty rates.*

In the event, RAF fighters did the best they could to cover the BEF retreat. However, the political need to support the Allies lost out to the survival of Britain itself. If the French had held on, then British support would have followed, as a German threat contained on French soil was preferable to repelling an invasion of England. That strategy had stopped the kaiser in Flanders during the Great War but wouldn't work against the blitzkrieg—the French were surrendering too fast.

Lord Gort, the BEF commander, had very few options open to him and increasingly looked west toward the English Channel. He couldn't get far enough to the north to make Oostende, nor could he go south to Calais. There was really only one port

---

*Not all from fighters, but the myth of bomber invincibility was buried.

that might offer an escape for the entire British regular army and England's only chance for continuing the war.

Dunkirk.

By the twenty-fourth of May, what remained of the Allied armies had their backs to the sea. The French First Army was squeezed into a pocket around Lille, and the surviving Belgians occupied a shrinking pocket between Bruges and the coast. The BEF was generally west of Lille in a line north toward Dunkirk, and Lord Gort was trying to pull in the widely scattered survivors. Calais had been overrun by the 1st and 10th Panzers, which were now driving hard along the Channel shoreline. Nine panzer divisions, three motorized infantry divisions, and the rest of the German Sixth and Fourth Armies were converging from three sides on the Allied pocket.

Here the Allies got their first real break from Adolf Hitler himself. Worried about the reported tank losses, the great risk taker had an attack of caution. He ordered the panzers to stay east of the Gravelines–Saint Omer canal 10 miles from Dunkirk—the Luftwaffe and the infantry would deal with the British. This "halt order" would remain in effect for two days and would go down retroactively as one of Hitler's biggest blunders.

Rallying to fight, the Royal Air Force began appearing over the French coast to cover the retreat and impending evacuation. Robert "Bob" Stanford Tuck of 92 Squadron had gotten into action the day before. More than two hundred Hurricanes had been lost during the Battle for France, and Tuck's squadron was fortunate to have the new Spitfire Mk I fighter. Taught to fly the Spit by Supermarine's chief test pilot, Bob Tuck was a 700-hour pilot by the time he saw combat. As he appeared over Dunkirk, leading six fighters from Hornchurch, his flight was bounced by a gaggle of Bf 109's.

Diving through the Brits at high speed, the 109's sent a Spitfire down in flames. Immediately rolling after the leader, Tuck jammed the black throttle forward and the 1,175-horsepower Merlin engine surged. The German didn't see him and pitched back toward the fight, which helped the Spitfire close the distance. As the 109 filled his GM-2 gunsight, Bob Tuck pressed down hard on the firing button. With all eight .303 Brownings spitting out over 100 rounds per second, the recoil made the plane vibrate. Aiming at the vulnerable wing root, the British pilot saw pieces fly off the German fighter. First an aileron tore loose, then the entire right wing broke off, spinning the 109 crazily toward the earth.

Then the sky was empty.

One second it had been full of flashing fighters, shooting, burning, turning, and then . . . nothing. Elated by his victory, Tuck also realized his very serious predicament. He'd been airborne for over ninety minutes and was low on fuel and ammunition, plus he was now alone. Climbing away from the French coast, he turned northwest toward England, swiveling his head constantly and searching for Germans—but there were none in sight.

Landing at Hornchurch after lunch, he stepped back while the riggers and armorers swarmed over the Spitfire. Debriefing at the operations hut, Tuck described the combat in detail for the squadron intelligence officer, then joined the other pilots for lunch. He didn't know it at the time, but they'd be back over Dunkirk by 5:45 p.m. This time he'd hammer an Me 110 fighter to bits over the beaches. Eschewing the slash-and-run tactics of the 109, the twin-engine Zerstörers would actually try to turn and engage in a dogfight with the Spitfires. The British fighter's heavy, bulletproof windscreen would save Bob Tuck and allow him to attack a third German. After a wild twenty-minute fight, the second Me 110 crashed, but the pilot crawled free. In an echo of Great War chivalry—and carelessness—the British pilot slid back his canopy, flew down low, and waved.

Suddenly several thumps startled him and a small hole appeared in the bulkhead below his canopy. Flushing with anger, he raised the flaps, firewalled the throttle, and stood the fighter on its wingtip, turning rapidly back around. Snapping level, Tuck steadied his gunsight on the burning German plane and the man beside it who was again lifting his pistol. As he pressed the firing button, the Spitfire shuddered, and hundreds of de Wilde shells churned the earth and chewed up the plane. The German pilot also disappeared.

Again low on fuel and over enemy territory, Tuck headed west and carefully climbed. His heart was pumping and his skin was prickly with the adrenaline-laced edge that only combat gives. Three kills in one day . . . but now he had to survive. Scanning his gauges as well as the sky, Tuck noticed that the Merlin was running hot. One of the 110 gunners had hit his cooling system, and the glycol was draining out. Flying smooth and easy, Tuck nursed the stricken fighter back over the chalky English coastline, limping toward Hornchurch. The field was in sight when his engine finally seized. Delaying to the last possible second, he lowered the flaps and gear to bounce down, just short of the landing area but safe enough.

The squadron would fight continuously to cover the evacuation and lose 45 percent of its pilots. Bob Tuck would close out 1940 with eighteen kills, and over the next year he'd become a squadron leader, then wing commander at Biggin Hill. In January 1942, while strafing targets near Boulogne, he'd be shot down and captured. Tuck spent three years as a POW but eventually escaped from a camp in Poland and got to Moscow, then to Odessa on the Black Sea, and finally safely back to England.

But in May 1940 all of that was still ahead of him, and for the moment Tuck had all he needed: a great plane to fly, an enemy to fight, and a country to defend.

WHILE BOB TUCK and the RAF tore through the skies overhead, Lord Gort, the BEF commander, made a pivotal decision. Early on May 25, on his own initiative, Gort ignored orders to launch a southern attack supporting the French. He pulled two divisions north, reinforced II Corps, and began his breakout to the sea. At this point, if Hitler had permitted the 1st, 6th, and 8th Panzers to press their attacks, it's very likely the entire Allied army would've been destroyed. As it was, the British and remnants of the French First Army caught their breath and dug in around a much-reduced defensive perimeter along the canals connecting Gravelines, Bergues, Furnes, and Nieuport.

Stukas had destroyed the inner harbor, but by the afternoon of the twenty-sixth, scores of smaller ships sent from England entered the outer harbor. At 7:00 p.m. Operation Dynamo, the evacuation of Allied troops from Dunkirk, officially began. Thousands of small boats took men off the Malo, Bray, and La Penne beaches to larger ships offshore. Tens of thousands of men would eventually be rescued by Royal Navy destroyers that entered the outer harbor and docked alongside the east breakwater. Dutch *schuyts*, broad-beamed canal boats, ran continuously across the Channel and would safely deliver 22,000 soldiers.

But on the first full day of evacuation, May 27, Sailor Malan and the 74 Squadron "Tigers" were in the thick of it. Arriving over Dunkirk in the morning, they spotted roving flights of Messerschmitts and immediately attacked. Having learned the futility of the Vic, Malan split his flight into two pairs and pulled straight up toward a 109's belly. The German rolled away and dove, a now-standard defensive maneuver, and Sailor followed. Getting in four bursts from 300 yards, he saw the German plane begin smoking before it disappeared into the clouds. Banking away to the west, he picked up eight Dornier 17's heading toward the harbor to bomb ships and strafe the beaches. Low on fuel, he and his wingman attacked anyway, shooting down one and scattering the rest. His wingman, Pilot Officer Stevenson, suffered damage to his plane and glided down toward Dunkirk, vanishing beneath the clouds. Malan managed to land back at Rochford with two gallons of fuel remaining in his tanks. Over the harbor again that afternoon the Tigers attacked another bomber formation, chasing the Germans away from the beaches and following them inland as far as St. Omer. By sunset his squadron had accounted for eight aircraft destroyed, with three more probables.

But this day also saw the Germans on the move again. The halt order had been lifted, and if Berlin was hesitant, the German field commanders knew a priceless opportunity when they saw it and weren't about to let soldiers escape that would one day fight back. So the panzers advanced, bringing Dunkirk within artillery range, and they shelled the town every day. But the destruction had an unintended benefit, as a heavy pall of smoke hung over the entire area and made accurate German air attacks nearly impossible. The low-lying ground around the port was also flooded, and that, combined with a stubborn defense, kept the Germans at bay.

However, on May 28 the Belgians surrendered unconditionally, opening up the entire Allied left flank. The commander of the French First Army, Georges Blanchard, finally realized that the British had no intention of dying for France and were planning to evacuate. According to Gort's chief of staff, General

Pownall, the Frenchman went "completely off the deep end" and adamantly refused to cooperate, adding to the confusion of an already complicated defense. However, despite assaults from the panzers and the French general's petulance, tens of thousands of British soldiers reached the defensive perimeter by the day's end.

Others did not.

Hauptsturmführer Fritz Knochlein, a company commander of the Brandenburg Regiment of the Waffen SS Totenkopf Division, ordered ninety-seven British prisoners to be executed. These men were part of the 2nd Royal Norfolks and were machine-gunned in the northern French village of Paradis.* A further eighty French and British captives were murdered by soldiers of the 1st SS Division Leibstandarte Adolf Hitler in a barn near Wormhoudt.

But then there was Hans-Ekkehard Bob.

Flying a Bf 109E, the young lieutenant was escorting Stukas over Dunkirk when his flight was attacked by seventeen French fighters. Splitting off, he latched onto a Curtiss Hawk and had a wild twenty-minute dogfight that ended in a treetop-level stalemate. The German pilot was surprised. With three victories and thirty missions under his belt, Bob was no novice, *and* he was flying an Emil. Low on fuel, he decided to separate and pulled around to the east. Glancing behind him, he saw the Hawk turn back toward the Allied lines. Immediately pitching back, Hans opened the throttle and the faster 109 rapidly closed the distance. Maybe tired but certainly unaware, the Frenchman didn't react, and Hans opened fire with both guns and cannon.

Mortally damaged, the other fighter glided down into a field behind the German lines, burning and smoking. Pulling up, the

---

*Knochlein was hanged on January 28, 1949, for war crimes.

German throttled back and circled as the French pilot tumbled out and lay still. Unhesitatingly, Hans lowered his gear, cobbed the throttle, and bounced in for a landing. Coasting to a stop beside the shattered Hawk, he shut down the engine and jumped out, grabbing his first-aid kit. Bandaging the Frenchman's wounds, he got the pilot's name and parents' address, promising to let them know that their son was alive. He then climbed back into his fighter and took off, heading for home. Despite his excellent record and ace status, Hans could've been court-martialed and shot for aiding the enemy. But right is right, and he was a fighter pilot—a killer, not a butcher.

May 29 was a bad day in many respects. With Belgium's collapse, the German Fourth and Sixth Armies had gotten around Lille to encircle the Allied forces not already on the beaches. Most of the French First Army, though fighting savagely, was cut off, and they surrendered. Four divisions of the BEF made it to the coast before the net closed. This did nothing to assuage the bitterness felt by French leadership that the English had deserted them. The British point of view was that the fall of France was inevitable and the destruction of the BEF would do nothing to prevent it. So the only sensible choice, and indeed the only way to continue fighting the Nazis, was to withdraw. A tough decision, but many Brits felt that France's predicament was of her own making. After all, if the Germans had been stopped at the Meuse, the Allies wouldn't be in the sand now.

On the twenty-ninth some 47,300 men were evacuated from the harbor by small civilian boats and the Royal Navy. Not without loss, though, as two destroyers were sunk. HMS *Wakeful* was torpedoed by a German E-boat off the Belgian coast, losing 85 of her 110-man crew. She was also carrying over 650 soldiers—of whom only one was rescued. HMS *Grafton* came to her aid and was subsequently torpedoed by a U-62, losing her captain and a dozen men before sinking. Stukas caught a third destroyer, HMS *Grenade*, on the east pier in Dunkirk harbor, and she went down later that afternoon.

Though the RAF had more than twenty Chain Home radar stations for early warning, they were for Britain's protection, not the French Channel ports. The indomitable Air Vice Marshal Keith Park's 11 Fighter Group was responsible for southeast England and the French coast near Dunkirk. Park, a New Zealander, had enlisted during the Great War and fought his way ashore at Gallipoli. Earning a battlefield commission, he transferred to the British regular army as an artillery lieutenant. After being wounded during the Battle of the Somme, Park joined the Royal Flying Corps. A fighter pilot now, he'd been posted to 48 Squadron in France and had shot down five Germans to finish the war as a major and commanding officer. Park was definitely a "lead from the front" sort and often took his own Hurricane over the coast to evaluate the situation for himself.

Yet with just sixteen of thirty-six squadrons remaining, the only effective British response was to keep Hurricanes and Spitfires in the air over the beaches—high over the beaches. This left some of the infantry below feeling abandoned by the RAF. Ignorant of air combat, they didn't realize what was happening above them and rarely saw the savage fighting taking place. Also, in true infantry fashion, anything flying was a threat, and they shot at whatever they could see, so RAF fighter pilots understandably avoided the beaches unless engaged in hot pursuit. Not that it mattered to the men on the ground; there were numerous accounts of fighters being damaged or downed by friendly troops.

Aviation losses were proportionately heavy, and nearly a quarter of the RAF fighters sent to the Battle for France and to cover Dunkirk never returned. More than three hundred irreplaceable, highly trained, and experienced pilots were lost. Pilot Officer Allan Wright, who survived the battle but lost more than 30 percent of his squadron mates, had a difficult time reconciling the loss of so many skilled, clever men who had their lives still before them.

On May 31 an additional 68,000 men were evacuated, including Lord Gort. June 3 saw more than fifty ships risk the Dunkirk harbor and beaches to rescue 35,000 French soldiers. The British left behind more than 63,000 vehicles, 2,472 artillery pieces, and half a million tons of ammunition and supplies. They also left 68,111 men who were captured, missing, or killed. But the extraordinary ten-day operation had saved some 338,226 soldiers, and at 3:40 a.m. on June 4, HMS *Shikari* steamed from the shattered port—the final vessel to leave.* It was a tremendously successful rescue: lost equipment could be replaced, but it took twenty years to grow a soldier, and many had been saved to continue fighting. However, Churchill put it into perspective by reminding Parliament that "wars are not won by evacuations." By 2:23 p.m. that same day, Operation Dynamo had officially ended. The Royal Air Force had flown 4,822 combat sorties to cover the evacuation, adding another 106 fighter aircraft to the 329 Hurricanes lost during the Battle for France.† Altogether, 280 fighter pilots were lost to the RAF, leaving a mere 330 fighter aircraft and fewer than 800 pilots to defend Great Britain.

The day following the end of Dynamo, Generaloberst Erhard Milch took a flight over the beaches and Dunkirk harbor. Milch was second in command of the Luftwaffe and had long advo-

---

*According to the British War Office.

†Sixty-seven of these were Spitfires.

cated finishing Britain off immediately. Later that day he told Hermann Goering, "The British Army? I saw perhaps twenty or thirty corpses. The rest of the British Army has got clean away to the other side."

Milch wanted to do a Norway-style Luftwaffe attack using tactical bombers, with the German navy and paratroopers securing a beachhead in southeast England. If such a foothold could be seized, with the critical airfields intact, the British would be too weak to counterattack. After all, they'd left virtually all their heavy equipment and weapons on the beach. With the country reeling, it was time to strike—hard. Milch said, "If we leave the British in peace for four weeks it will be too late."

He was correct—and he was dead wrong.

He was correct in that there would never be a better time for conquering England. Britain was truly alone. Both Turkey and Egypt had failed to honor their promises for assistance, and from Norway to Spain the coasts were controlled by the Third Reich. Only tiny Gibraltar on the tip of the Spanish peninsula remained in British hands. Hulking darkly to the east was the Soviet Union—archfoe of England and utterly untrustworthy. Far to the west lay the great hope of the United States with its immense industrial might, resources, and manpower, but at least eighteen months away from waging war. There was no one else to fight off the Germans.

But he was wrong in assuming the British could be beaten that quickly. Invading England was no guarantee of victory—they weren't French, after all. The Germans would most likely find themselves with a protracted, nasty guerilla war on their hands. In any event, Nazi leadership hadn't decided yet whom to fight, and that was a *very* big problem. Indecision, "soft" objectives, and lack of a coherent strategy are ruinous to any military group.

There were those who wanted to stop and consolidate the immense territories gained by capturing Poland, Austria, Czechoslovakia, Norway, Denmark, Belgium, and France. They wanted Sweden to feed the growing German steel industry so that factories could produce more tanks and aircraft. Berlin persuaded a frightened Rumania to trade oil for arms, thus gaining a small but steady supply of the vital fluid. Reparations payments were mandated by the Germans and provided an infusion of hard cash from Luxembourg, Holland, and especially the French. Men needed rest, reorganization, new equipment, and replacements. There was also a crucial shortage of transport aircraft following heavy losses in the first days of the campaign. Pilots and aircrew of all types were in short supply.

Nor was the fighting over. When the Germans cut the Allied line during their dash for the coast, a large number of Allied troops were isolated west of the Somme. Most of these were support and communications troops from the huge BEF supply depots in Rouen and Le Havre. But the only British armored division (what was left of it) was also in the south, along with the 51st Highlanders. The 5th and 7th Panzer Divisions had broken through the Somme, and the British had no choice but to fall back to avoid entrapment. Operation Cycle, initiated on June 10, rescued 11,059 men of the British 51st Highlanders and First Armored Division from the little port of St. Valery in northern Normandy.

Sir Alan Brooke, who'd led II Corps during the retreat to Dunkirk, had been sent back in command and he immediately realized there was no hope of continuing a continental fight. Personally calling Churchill, he insisted on a withdrawal over the prime minister's objections. This was eventually approved, and Operation Ariel began on June 15, 1940, to gather up the remaining Allied soldiers. This included the 52nd (Lowland)

Infantry and 1st Canadian Divisions, which had fallen back on Cherbourg when Rommel's 7th Panzers severed the road to Le Havre. More than 30,000 men were evacuated between June 15 and 17, including the 5th Battalion of the Sherwood Foresters—Albert Ball's infantry unit from the Great War.

With the coast now closed from Normandy north to the Pas de Calais, 21,474 Canadians retreated to St. Malo in Brittany, from where they were evacuated. Another 32,000 men left from Brest, followed by RAF ground crew, Poles, and Czechs from St. Nazaire. Farther down the coast at La Rochelle, an English officer found no ships for the 14,000 Poles and British troops there, so he simply commandeered French merchant ships and sailed for home. Until June 25 evacuations continued along the Bordeaux coast for any stragglers; this included the last British and Polish diplomatic staff.

Though ships were attacked and some sunk, this second series of rescues brought back an additional 190,000 survivors—many of them able-bodied men who could continue fighting. The lack of an all-out effort by the Luftwaffe to prevent the escape is astounding. Again, one senses indecisiveness from Berlin and perhaps surprise from winning so quickly. Hitler basked in the glory of the French surrender, and Goering was so unconcerned that he went to Amsterdam to collect art. Dynamo and Ariel could not have been stopped, perhaps, but they certainly could've been more costly to the Allied forces. No doubt part of this underestimation stemmed from Hitler's belief that with no allies left, the British would have to sue for peace. Why wouldn't they? After all, the French had surrendered and become a puppet state, so why not Britain?

He quite obviously did not understand the English. Churchill's stirring, defiant words, delivered to Parliament, should've been a warning:

"We shall go on to the end, we shall fight in France, we shall fight on the seas and oceans, we shall fight with growing confidence and growing strength in the air, we shall defend our island, whatever the cost may be, we shall fight on the beaches, we shall fight on the landing grounds, we shall fight in the fields and in the streets, we shall fight in the hills—we shall never surrender!"

Dissent also came from Hitler's top military professionals, who did not want to invade. The heads of the Wehrmacht and Kriegsmarine (German navy) both expressed reluctance about Operation Lion, as it was initially known. However, Hitler's fundamental ambition was the conquest of the Soviet Union and the utter destruction of the perceived global Jewish Bolshevik threat. Without neutralizing the British, he couldn't deal with Stalin as he wished, or Germany would have another two-front conflict. Having endured this as a combat soldier during the Great War, Hitler was aware of the peril.

Besides, most of his military was poised along the Atlantic coast, so with Goering's unequivocal promise to sweep the skies clear, Hitler became convinced that finishing off England was expedient. There were big problems with this decision, and it caused considerable angst among the German generals. In the first place, the Wehrmacht was a land force designed around continental campaigns and had no marines, amphibious troops, or landing craft. The only specialty assault units were *Fallschirmjäger*—paratroops, and not many of them.

Also, the Luftwaffe was primarily a tactical air force built to support ground troops. There were no heavy bombers for strategic strikes, and airlift was limited by the shortage of Ju 52 transports. Hitler's belief, then, encouraged by Goering (who should've known better), was that the air force would bring Britain to her knees and the bargaining table. This delusion was infectious, and by late summer of 1940 millions of heavily armed and highly motivated Germans stared expectantly across a bare 25 miles of gray water at the faint white Dover cliffs. What remained of the Allies stared back, panting and bloody.

Control of the air was everything. It was the key to the survival of Britain and Western civilization against the threat of a Nazi-dominated Europe. Without German air superiority there could be no invasion, so Britain's hope could survive a while longer. Now, in the summer of 1940, fewer than a thousand fighter pilots stood between England and a German invasion.

They meant to prevail—or die trying.

CHAPTER 8

CLASH OF EAGLES

SUPERMARINE SPITFIRE MK I

THE MEN FACING each other in the air over the English Channel were very different, yet in many ways startlingly similar. The Luftwaffe certainly bears a closer look, as it produced the top 109 fighter pilots in history—all from World War II. These men accounted for a staggering 4,534 aerial victories, with 1,453 kills going to the top five alone. Erich "Bubi" Hartmann is the top-scoring ace of all time, with 352 kills over 1,404 combat missions. He survived the war and was held by the Russians for ten years before finally coming home in 1955.

As impressive as Hartmann was, the most-decorated pilot ever was Hans-Ulrich Rudel, king of close air support. Son of a Lutheran minister, Rudel was the only recipient of the Knight's Cross of the Iron Cross with Golden Oak Leaves,

Swords, and Diamonds.* Flying Stukas and Focke-Wulf 190s, Rudel survived an astonishing 2,530 combat missions while personally destroying 519 tanks, four trains, a battleship, two cruisers, and a destroyer. He accounted for 800 miscellaneous vehicles and more than 150 artillery pieces. During all this he was shot down, or forced down, on more than thirty missions and wounded five times.

So how were these men made into fighter pilots?

Once Germany began openly rearming and expanding her military, Hermann Goering set out to make his Luftwaffe the best air force in the world. Good pay and living conditions were big inducements, as were special uniforms. Before the war, he provided jobs with Lufthansa and civil aviation. Low-interest mortgages and government loans were also attractive incentives.

With fewer traditions to overcome, just as in the Great War, the Luftwaffe was relatively egalitarian. Officers were still definitely officers, but they all had a sense of belonging to a new, powerful, and elite organization. Pilots, especially *Jagdflieger* (fighter pilots), were special. The German air force was also home to the paratroopers, so these unique groups added to the attitude and mystique.

Prior to the war, new recruits endured a typical six-month basic training program focusing on time-honored military standards of discipline, marching, and rifle drill. Potential aircrew candidates were carefully selected and sent to *Flieger-Ausbildungsregiment* (aircrew development). Their performance here separated these men into potential pilots, potential aircrew, and washouts. Once war broke out, the process was combined into one basic training and screening program. This facilitated

---

*Roughly equivalent to four American Medals of Honor or four British Victoria Crosses.

the flow of replacements and eliminated superfluous nansense such as marching in formation.

So after six to nine months of screening, the pilot candidates finally arrived at flight school. *Flugzeugführerschule* A/B was initially divided into four sections. The "A" course was contact flying; takeoffs, landings, stalls, and other basic flight procedures needed to solo a student. Following this, the A2 section was mostly classroom instruction in navigation, aerodynamics, meteorology, and all the other diverse book knowledge that pilots need. The B1 part of the course was basic flying with more powerful single-engine aircraft. Following about 150 total hours, the student was advanced to the B2 section. This section introduced aerobatics, complex navigation, and multiengine aircraft. It was here that prospective fighter pilots were identified from the remaining students.

A/B *Schule* lasted a year, and upon completion each man had at least two hundred hours of flight time and wore his *Flugzeugführerabzeichen* pilot's badge. Those who failed the course but still had some aptitude were sent to navigator training. New pilots were then divided into single-engine or multi-engine categories. The multi-engine types, which included future Me 110 fighter pilots, were sent to C *Schule*, which added another fifty hours of Link simulators plus night and instrument flying. Dive-bomber pilots were also picked here after a grueling selection process. Anyone not picked for bombers went to the *Transportfliegerschulen* to fly cargo planes.

The very few selected to fly single-seat, single-engine aircraft went off to *Jagdfliegerschule* (JFS), fighter pilot school. A four-month course focusing on formation, air-to-air gunnery, and aerobatics, JFS was one more rite of passage. This was followed by intermediate flight school, which taught aerobatic maneuvers as they pertain to dogfighting. The instructors were combat veterans, if available, or highly experienced pilots who had been rotated back for a rest. In this fashion the latest knowledge, techniques, and tactics were passed along before the young pilot arrived at his fighter group for final polishing.

Waffensschule, fighting school, was just that. It was specific to each fighter group and was conducted by operational flyers to make the new pilot into an effective wingman. This was also the last bit of quality control before a man could enter the rarefied world of a line fighter squadron. All told, the process took over two years and produced a well-trained, disciplined wingman who flew extremely well *and* could shoot. The Luftwaffe never lost sight of a fighter pilot's true purpose, which was to kill.

Not so with the Royal Air Force.

During the 1920's and 1930's this extraordinary organization was emasculated by shortsighted politicians and budget cuts. Flying was once again a gentlemanly pursuit done in good weather with the sole aim of improving one's formation techniques. Those who disagreed with this were quietly sidelined or politely ignored.

But by 1936 Hitler's threat seemed real enough, so the RAF created a Volunteer Reserve. The goal of the RAFVR was to provide a pool of trained pilots who could be recalled during war. The regular RAF paid for their flight training, and in return they gave up weekends and periodic evenings for lectures.* The pilots were all sergeants, which enabled the RAF to lower the entry requirements somewhat and pay them less. The RAFVR was intended to supplement the Auxiliary Air Force (AAF) squadrons that had been formed back in 1925.

Auxiliary squadrons were truly flying clubs, recruited by district and initially composed of men with close personal or

*Identical in concept to the American National Guard system.

social ties. AAF units operated more or less independently of the RAF and added their sponsoring region to their squadron identification: for example, No. 603 (County of Edinburgh) Squadron, RAF, or No. 609 (West Riding) Squadron, RAF. These pilots were all officers and typically first-rate flyers who joined for the challenge, the danger, and patriotism, usually in that order. No. 601 (County of London) consisted of wealthy young men who generally owned their own aircraft. Called the "Millionaires Squadron," they cheerfully ignored RAF regulations that didn't pertain to flying. Known for their sports cars, playing polo, and lining their uniforms with red silk, they, like most RAF pilots, turned into raging tigers in the air.

Twenty fighter squadrons, one-fourth of the total RAF fighter strength, were formed by the Auxiliary Air Force by the summer of 1940. Regardless of the type of squadron or rank of the man, RAF pilot wings were earned through a process similar to the Luftwaffe's. One had to pass initial selection based on fitness and aptitude. Unavoidable military basic training followed unless the candidate was directly commissioned from a university. Basic flight training lasted seven weeks and got a "pupil pilot" to the solo stage. Advanced training followed, usually on a Tiger Moth, at a base such as Hadfield or Hartwell. After this the pilots were given a few weeks at RAF Depot Uxbridge to order uniforms and learn the etiquette required for the officers' mess.

Don't judge them by our mores and standards. Then as now, the military officer class was supposed to act differently and was held to other standards. In time of war they were expected to shoulder the responsibility that went with those privileges—and, if necessary, to die. The Millionaires' Squadron is again a good example. Those young men, by virtue of education and family connections, could have comfortably sat out the war in a safe position somewhere—yet they didn't. In fact, it wouldn't have occurred to them to do so.

One of the Americans in 601 Squadron, Billy Fiske, was the scion of a New England banking family. At St. Moritz in 1928, he became the youngest Olympic gold medalist in history at sixteen years of age. He repeated the feat four years later in Lake Placid before eventually completing his studies at Cambridge. Marrying the Countess of Warwick in 1938, Billy Fiske had it all, yet he never hesitated to join the RAF when war threatened. Carl Davis was another such American. With degrees from Cambridge and McGill University in Montreal, he worked as a mining engineer before joining the Royal Air Force. Davis would have nine confirmed victories before being killed in a dogfight south of London in 1940.

After Uxbridge, those going to fighters would spend the next nine months accumulating another hundred flight hours. Just before the war this meant flying Hawker Hinds, perfecting acrobatics and the "Six Fighter Attacks" (see Chapter 7, p. 194) beloved by the peacetime RAF. On the whole, the prewar Royal Air Force was built around a small cadre of regular professionals and augmented by well-meaning amateurs. War, however, turns all fighting men into professionals, even if only temporarily.

TWO ASSETS, ONE made by nature and the other by man, gave the British some desperately needed time during the summer of 1940. First was the Channel. Just as in the Great War, those 20-odd miles of water left the attackers staring impotently across at the Dover cliffs. Only now, in 1940, one could fly over the water to attack, and that was the problem. Since the Gotha strikes of 1916, the English had known that their island was vulnerable from the air. The sky, as any fighter pilot will tell you, is a big place. This is especially true when you have to find the enemy with only your eyeballs and fuel is always short. Knowing that if you miss the enemy the bombs fall on your families is a tremendous pressure. But what to do about it?

Heinrich Rudolf Hertz had changed electric sparks into waves in 1887, and in 1899 Marconi sent a wireless message across the Channel via wireless transmission. Both men, Hertz particularly, were aware that radio waves could be reflected from solid objects. Just as sound waves are used by bats and dolphins for ranging, might not radio waves be utilized for some similar military purpose? In 1934 this question was posed by Harry Wimperis, director of scientific research at the British Air Ministry. He actually had a sort of "death ray" in mind that would melt or disintegrated incoming aircraft.

Robert Watson-Watt of the National Physical Laboratory was a bit more pragmatic. Even if such a death ray could be constructed (and he doubted it), a threat would still need to be detected far enough away to use the thing. Could the detection mechanism be the solution to their problem? After all, destroying threats was exactly what fighter pilots were there for. Thus a system known as Radio Detection And Ranging (RADAR) was born—and it changed everything.

Calling it "radio direction finding" (RDF) as a cover, Watson-Watt proved his concept on a winter's morning in February 1935. Aligning his equipment to a railway line, he borrowed an RAF bomber and had it fly along the tracks 20 miles away. It was detected two out of three times, and Air Chief Marshal Hugh Dowding was satisfied enough to immediately provide funding.

A year later Watson-Watt was finding aircraft more than 60 miles away, and more stations had been built. This increased the total detection area and permitted not only range estimates but rough bearing calculations. By August 1937 a radar training school had been established and the Chain Home system, as it was called, was participating in Fighter Command exercises. With detection ranges over 100 miles now, Dowding could see the Belgian and French airfields that would inevitably be used by the Luftwaffe. Eventually there would be twenty such stations stretching from the Shetland Islands north of Scotland all the way south to Cornwall.

It certainly wasn't perfect. For one thing, the radar masts could be seen from France, and the Germans were well aware of their existence. It was also relatively primitive from a technical standpoint. Imagine radar as a flashlight shining about in the darkness. If it hits something that reflects light, then you have a target. Same thing with radio waves, except they'll bounce off anything metal and aren't affected by atmospheric conditions such as rain, fog, or darkness. So Dowding pointed these "spotlights" out over the English Channel and effectively blanketed the French coast. The huge antennas could either transmit and receive, but since they were stationary, no angle of arrival from an incoming signal could be measured. Without this, triangulation was an issue, so bearing and range estimates were problematic. Also, since the antennas couldn't really be directed or aimed, the coverage could be underflown by very low-flying aircraft.

Some of this was solved by the Chain Home Low (CHL) system. The Admiralty's research laboratory had been simultaneously developing a coastal defense radar of its own. Designed to aim guns, this radar had to be fairly accurate and utilized rotating instead of fixed antennas, with smaller wavelengths. These systems could measure the angle of arrival thus allowing higher-quality targeting data and the detection of low-altitude aircraft. CHL radars were like flashlights aimed into the low shadows under the massive stadium lights of Chain Home stations. Again, the biggest asset to the English was the Channel—there was no interference from ground clutter and no place for an attacker to hide.

Watson-Watt continuously improved the system and envisioned some of the critical advances required to make the most of it. These included alternating wavelengths in response to jamming and discriminating between friendly or hostile aircraft. He solved the latter problem by installing equipment that reflected incoming radar pulses with a coded "blip" to alert controllers. A derivative of this Interrogation, Friendly or Foe (IFF) system is used today on all military aircraft and remains the primary identification tool in the initial stages of air combat. Also, Dowding was well aware that fighters needed radios so that pilots could talk directly to controllers. Sounds simple nowadays, yet in the late 1930s this was a real technical challenge. But, he reasoned, what was the sense in having good targeting information with no way to act on it? Dowding was keenly aware of the tremendous advantage this technology provided, so he devised a unique system to exploit the information. It worked like this.

Responsibility for England was divided among three main fighter groups: 10 Group, west and southwest of London; 12 Group, which covered the Midlands north to Scotland; and 11 Group, which got London and the southeast coast closest to France. Far to the north was 13th Group, which was kept more or less as a ready reserve, training, and recovery area. Each group was further subdivided into sectors, like lanes on a highway. A sector would have its own CH stations and controllers responsible for the fighters in each area.

So when a gaggle of contacts was detected getting airborne from France, the various Chain Home radars would report the "plots" to their own sector's Central Operations Room. This would then be passed via telephone up to Group Operations and then to Fighter Command Headquarters at Bentley Priory. The nerve center for Fighter Command operations was the Filter Room, where all sector plots would be correlated with the radar displays from headquarters. Also, anything from the Observer Corps, noise detection stations, and civilian reports would all be analyzed and interpreted. Range determination, called "cutting," was accomplished here using lines of bearing from multiple stations. Enemy altitude was estimated and intercept bearings plotted. Each detected formation was given a wooden counter, black for friendlies and red for the Germans. Counters also showed the approximate number of aircraft, their altitude, and their direction.

A board called "the Tote" ran along one wall. Every squadron in a group was labeled, and colored lights indicated each unit's status, such as Airborne, Detailed to Raid, Enemy Sighted, and various forms of readiness based on rearming and refueling. The filtered plots were then passed back down to all the lower-echelon Operations Centers, which had matching maps, synchronized clocks, and identical tote displays. Group Operations would then decide which squadrons to commit from each sector based on the size of the raid and the friendly fighters available. Group Ops would also activate air-raid sirens and pass confirmed hostile targets to anti-aircraft batteries.

In effect, hundreds of men and women formed an interactive computer that provided a composite air threat picture, which could then be dealt with in the most lethal manner. Centralized information gave the best "big picture" possible. This, combined with Dowding's policy of decentralized execution and noninterference, ensured that the group commander, the man who knew his own situation, made tactical decisions.

This command style contrasted starkly to that utilized by the Luftwaffes. Goering spent much of the battle at his Carinhall estate, north of Berlin, routinely summoning his commanders away from the action for briefings and meetings.* Drawing on their experiences in Spain, Poland, and France, the Germans had organized their assets into three air fleets (*Luftflotten*). This was fine for tactical operations but didn't lend itself to a bigger, strategic type of front.

This battlefield mentality also showed in their own radar development. Called Dezimator-Telegraphie (DeTe), it was primarily the brainchild of Dr. Rudolph Kuhnold from the Navy Signals Research Department. A sonar expert, he'd realized that detection and ranging was possible over land or water using radio waves. The Freya and Seetakt early warning radars were adapted for use on ships. This led the German firm Telefunken to develop a compact, mobile system known as Wurzburg, which could locate aircraft about 30 miles away. Wurzburg was fairly sophisticated compared to the British systems: it rotated 360 degrees and mechanically scanned in azimuth.

Their own technical lead was one reason the Germans didn't think the British had such a system. Another reason was the two zeppelin missions that overflew the mysterious masts in the summer of 1939. The British were clever and the Chain Home operators said nothing about the airships, so the Germans heard nothing suspicious. Also, an English mobile system was recovered from the rubble of Dunkirk and the Germans were unimpressed with its primitive technology. Last, and probably most significant, the Luftwaffe of 1940 was an offensive

*One such commander's conference was mostly dedicated to showing off his new model train set.

force and had no need of a defensive network, so they didn't think in those terms . . . yet.

OBERST JOHANNES FINK was not a happy man. The colonel commanded KG 2 and was a battle-tested Stuka pilot. However, he'd just been made *Kanalkampfführer*—the Channel battle leader. Ironically, *Kanal* means either "channel" or "sewer drain," depending on the context, and Fink, along with many others, sardonically chose the latter meaning.

At this time, the operational air fleets, or *Luftflotten*, were roughly equivalent to an army corps and organized by geographical area. Luftflotte 2, for example, controlled all aviation-related issues within its territory of northern France, Holland and Belgium. Each air fleet's area was further subdivided and given to a *Fliegerkorps* depending on the type of aircraft (for example, II Fliegerkorps was composed of long-range bombers). Fighters belonged to Fighter Command and were parceled out as needed in the form of *Jagdfliegerführer* (*Jafu*) units—sort of a fighter corps within each air fleet. A *Korps* was then organized tactically into *Geschwader* (wings), each of which was usually composed of three *Gruppen* (groups). A group contained three to four *Staffeln* (squadrons) of nine to sixteen aircraft.

Launched on July 10, Kanalkampf was supposed to be the opening salvo for Operation Sealion, the invasion of Britain. Its main goal was to target convoys and ports along England's east coast, forcing the RAF to respond. The Germans believed if the RAF Fighter Command could be forced into combat, then it would surely be destroyed and air superiority achieved. To accomplish this, eight hundred Bf 109Es formed eight *Jagdgeschwader*, along with Me 110 Destroyers, Stukas, and bombers. From Norway to Spain, the Luftwaffe was poised to strike.

Once air superiority had been obtained, then Sealion could proceed. Actually, the interdiction of shipping would have been valid if there had been cooperation between the Luftwaffe and the U-boats prowling around Britain. There were about five hundred merchant ships using four main convoy routes at any one time. As it was, a dozen or so U-boats were sinking 300,000 to 500,000 tons of shipping each month—far beyond the capacity of British yards to replace.

Long-range Focke-Wulf 200s based in Brest or Bordeaux-Mérignac could reach Iceland, well beyond RAF fighter range. The British had never planned on defending their shipping lanes from the Luftwaffe because no one had foreseen a French collapse and rebasing of German aircraft along the Channel coast. It was a perfect strategic opportunity for Hitler to truly choke the life out of England. Merchant vessels that weren't destroyed could be damaged or at least located for the submarines to finish off. However, no such coordination existed between the Luftwaffe and the Kriegsmarine.

Trying to destroy airfields and ports was equally pointless. Most RAF fighter units used roughly prepared grass strips, and it was easy enough to fill craters or simply move to another location. Ports were just as difficult. Unless the entry can be blocked, the only other alternative is mining, and the Germans tried this. But the Royal Navy had hundreds of minesweepers and cleared mines as fast as they were dropped.

Looking back, the Channel Battle was an unfocused and costly affair. It was largely put into action because the German High Command simply didn't know what else to do while they waited and hoped for Churchill to capitulate. There is a tremendous advantage in keeping an enemy off balance and reactive, so if the Germans had immediately pressed across the Channel it's very likely that a foothold in southern England could've been secured. A limited assault with paratroopers might then have been able to seize key chokepoints and isolate the Norfolk and Surrey coasts. Though this would've taken several trips due to the shortage of Ju 52 transports, it was only a twenty-minute flight across the water. Done at night, with the reeling RAF at its least effective, airborne troops might have held out long enough for the infantry and a few tanks to arrive.

There would be no question of a large-scale, complex attack, or of conquering the entire island. But the shock of *Fallschirmjäger* combined with a small, hard-hitting ground force may have worked. There were no tanks in Britain—they'd all been left behind in France. Most of the million or so soldiers in England didn't have rifles, and if the southeast Chain Home stations had been captured then the RAF would be blinded. But this would all have to be done before the British could catch their breath and strengthen their defenses.

Which is precisely what happened.

During the spring of 1940, Spitfires and Hurricanes were being assembled at the catatonic rate of just two each per day. Controlled by the Air Ministry, aircraft production was in the same dire straits as pilot training, logistics, and maintenance. The ministry was a dysfunctional collection of politicos and career military officers long past their prime who were more concerned with turf battles than with saving England.

Churchill simply bypassed the whole mess by creating a new Ministry for Aircraft Production (MAP) and putting Max Aiken, Lord Beaverbrook, in charge. A Canadian by birth, Aiken was a brilliant businessman and newspaper mogul. Exactly as had happened with Harold Harmsworth during the Great War (see Chapter 4), someone who understood production was desperately needed to sort out the situation if Britain was to survive. Extremely competent and apolitical, Beaverbrook was indifferent to bureaucratic subtleties, personal feelings, and bruised egos. He had a job to do and he did it. Since the Air Ministry was of no use, he simply went around it altogether. Locks on hangar doors were replaced with his own, and the MAP took over all Air Ministry repair facilities and depots. He ignored labor regulations and shredded mountains of useless red tape. Using his own expertise, Beaverbrook streamlined production methods, cleaned up factories and distribution systems, and fired anyone who got in his way.

During his first week production increased by 130 new aircraft of all types, and by the end of May, after only two weeks, nearly 300 had been produced. While the Germans dithered, Beaverbrook worked, and six weeks later production had risen 60 percent, to 300 new planes per week. Nearly 450 new Hurricanes and Spitfires rolled off the lines in June, and Dowding ended the month with more fighters than he'd started with. By contrast, the Luftwaffe built just 220 new fighters and 340 bombers during the month of June.

But then the Germans didn't have Max Aiken—they had Ernst Udet. Though he was Germany's highest-scoring surviving ace from the Great War and a superb fighter pilot, Udet was totally out of his depth as the director of the Luftwaffe Technical Office. He'd told his old friend Hermann Goering, "I don't know anything about design and construction. I'm a flyer and nothing else."

Yet he remained in this crucial position, and his lack of vision would cost the Luftwaffe dearly. He was also a significant force in killing off the heavy bomber program, specifically the He 177. Heinkel had also produced the world's first jet-powered aircraft and flown it successfully back in 1939. However, Udet blocked future development because he'd promised the contract to Messerschmitt.* What might the skies over Europe have been like if the Luftwaffe had fielded jet fighters in time for the Battle of Britain?

Beaverbrook also streamlined and revamped the Civilian Repair Organization. This was a network of nearly a hundred civil companies that could repair damaged aircraft and return them to service. Britain was perennially short of raw materials, so anything that could be salvaged had to be. Beaverbrook reorganized the whole system and introduced three distinct types of damaged aircraft. Category 4 damage could be fixed, usually in place, within thirty-six hours. Category 5 was flyable to a repair facility, and if it could be fixed in a day, then the pilot waited. Category 6 was heavy damage that needed ground transport and would take longer than thirty-six hours to repair. By the end of the war the CRO would return some 79,000 aircraft to the sky.

Air Chief Marshal Dowding and Lord Beaverbrook saved Britain by saving RAF Fighter Command. Dowding provided modern fighters, backed by the entire Chain Home network, while the Ministry of Aircraft Production ensured a steady resupply of planes and engines. Both men knew that this was the very least they could do if brave young men were going to risk everything to defend their island—and by August it was clear that this was going to happen.

IF ONE SINGLE image had to symbolize the Battle of Britain, it would be the Spitfire. While fully acknowledging the contributions and sacrifices of the thousands of dedicated men and women performing countless unglamorous and essential jobs,

---

*An He 178 with a turbojet engine could reach a speed of 380 mph.

it was still the fighter pilot who took to the air. In this, too, England and the RAF owed a debt to Hugh Dowding. While serving in the Air Ministry as the Air Member for Research and Development in the 1930's, he'd vigorously promoted development of both the Hurricane and the Spitfire.

Reginald Mitchell, Supermarine's chief designer, created an open-cockpit, gull-winged monoplane that flew for the first time in 1933. With a top speed of just 235 mph, the new aircraft would never cut it as a fighter, so he started over. Then in 1935 the Air Ministry changed its requirement to include *eight* machine guns instead of the original four. Mitchell redesigned again and his new elliptical wing became the Spitfire's defining characteristic.* This prototype was powered by a Rolls-Royce engine and successfully flew during March 1936. The shape gave the wing more surface area, lowered the wing loading, and produced excellent slow-speed flight characteristics. Using a system of hollow girders, the Spitfire's wing was extremely strong near the wing root and very light at the wingtips. It was even thinner than the Messerschmitt and provided a 242-square-foot wing area versus 173.3 square feet on the Bf 109.

The fuselage had a monocoque center with removable forward and aft sections. The first seventy-seven Mark I aircraft used a fixed-pitch, two-bladed wooden propeller, giving the plane a takeoff roll of about 1,300 feet. Subsequent production aircraft were fitted with Rotol or de Havilland three-bladed, constant-speed props. This shortened a takeoff to 700 feet and made a tremendous difference in higher-altitude air combat.

Interestingly, the Spitfire also had two step rudder pedals.

---

*Mitchell was likely influenced by Heinkel's He 70 design. One such Heinkel was used to flight-test the Rolls-Royce Kestrel engine during the Spitfire's development period.

This was a second "stirrup" placed six inches above the first into which the pilot would slip his feet before combat. Changing the angle of his legs and raising them increased g-force tolerance by slowing the drain of blood from the head during a dogfight.*

Spitfire Mk I's first arrived in 19 Squadron during August 1938. The initial order of 310 aircraft was quite beyond Supermarine's ability to produce, and slow deliveries would continue until Beaverbrook's wartime methods took effect in 1940. Yet Supermarine listened to pilots and made other significant improvements, such as installing armor over the main fuel tank and around the seat. A thick, laminated windscreen was added to give further protection.

The belt-fed Brownings were an issue from the beginning. First, a .303 caliber was fine for rifle bullets, but even eight machine guns would only deliver 12 pounds of lethal metal during a three-second burst.† Just 30 percent of the rounds fired would reach a target at 200 yards, and even then only 6 percent would penetrate. This was exacerbated in the Spitfire's case because the guns were spread out along the wing. Second, ammunition was a problem, as the RAF essentially used British Army rifle shells, which contained cordite. This often caused breech explosions when the guns got hot, as they do in combat. The breeches also had a tendency to freeze up in the cold wet skies over Europe, but the peacetime RAF hadn't really caught on to that because gunnery wasn't practiced much. Eventually, hot engine bleed air was routed to heat the guns, but for many months a frozen breech was a real risk for pilots.

---

*Forty years later F-16 designers would angle the pilot's seat backward for the same reason.

†The Bf 109 combined armament put out 18 pounds for the same burst.

Supermarine then designed the Mark IB variant, which employed two Hispano-Suiza 20 mm cannons. But the muzzle velocity was much lower, so it only fired nine rounds per second per gun, versus seventeen rounds per second from the Brownings. In a dogfight, where a pilot usually had only two or three seconds to make a shot, you'd want as many shells as possible in the air. On the other hand, heavier projectiles meant a greater probability of kill if they actually hit the target.

The cannons also had to be installed on their sides to fit their top-mounted ammo drums within the wings. Under g-forces, shell casings often bounced back into the breech and frequently jammed. The Spitfire's flexible, thin wing didn't help, and there was also only room for 60 rounds per cannon—about five seconds' worth of fire, which was not nearly enough.* Some of these modified Spits would fight in the upcoming battle with Duxford's 19 Squadron, but they jammed so badly that the Brownings were reinstalled. A revised Mk Ib, with four Brownings and two cannons, wasn't fielded until after the Battle of Britain.

During the Great War, there were no wing-mounted guns, so everything fired through the propeller, over the wing, or from a rear cockpit. Wing mounts permitted more guns, which was good, and no synchronization gear was needed, since the weapons fired beyond the propeller arc. But now you have the problem of harmonization—aligning the weapons so the shells converge at a given range.

Prewar RAF regulations stipulated that 650 yards was the magic number, so all guns and sights were to be set for this. The logic, if it can be called that, was that a greater distance would produce a bigger pattern and a few bullets were likely to

---

*The Bf 109 carried enough ammunition for about fifty-five seconds of firing.

hit the target. This was flawed for several reasons. One is that at greater distances, aiming is much more difficult. Also, with a greater distance the target may move considerably while the rounds you've fired are on their way. Finally, bullets lose velocity rapidly, and at that distance they wouldn't pack much of punch even if you managed to hit something.

Veteran pilots like Sailor Malan scoffed at this nonsense and generally agreed that 250 yards was a good range, though they'd get much, much closer if the situation allowed. Unlike their German counterparts, early RAF fighters also didn't have rounds counters to display available ammunition remaining. So the British used Buckingham Mk IV tracer shells at the end of a belt; when the pilot saw these, he knew he was out of ammunition. Unfortunately, the Germans picked up on this too, and now knew when their Spitfire or Hurricane opponent had empty guns.

The type and mix of ammunition used was also very important. Each gun on the Spitfire, for example, could be loaded with different shells. By the spring of 1940 most squadrons loaded three guns with standard ball ammo, two with Mk IV incendiary, two with armor-piecing, and one with Mk VI incendiary. Also called a "de Wilde," the Mk VI contained barium nitrate, which would burn as it impacted, lighting anything flammable.* This also caused a small flash, or sparkle, which pilots immediately used for aiming.

The Luftwaffe had long decided that a mix of heavy and light armament was better. The Bf 109 was truly astounding for the punch it packed in relation to its small size. However, the German penchant for tinkering guaranteed that critical re-

*The de Wilde bullet used in combat had been completely redesigned by Major Dixon of the Woolworth Arsenal.

sources, especially time, were used up in experimentation when sticking with proven solutions was likely smarter. The 1940 vintage Bf 109 variants were all armed with at least two cowling-mounted MG 17 guns in addition to a mix of cannon and gun wing armament. Most common was the E-3 type, which had been retrofitted with seat and head armor.

Messerschmitt also removed the engine-mounted 20 mm cannon. It had always suffered from overheating issues so they added two new MG FF/M cannons in the wings of the Bf 109E-4. This would fire the newly developed *Minengeschoss* (mine shell), which was thinner and lighter than its predecessor. Because the casing was thinner, there was extra space for a larger explosive charge, and its lighter construction permitted a higher rate of fire.

Both fighter variants were powered by Daimler-Benz DB 601 twelve-cylinder liquid-cooled engines. One of the great virtues of this engine, which generated about 1,100 horsepower, was direct fuel injection. Essentially, this forces gas through a nozzle directly into the cylinder. Since the fuel is atomized into fine vapor by high pressure, the combustion sequence is more powerful, thus making the engine more efficient. Also, since the amount of fuel is mechanically controlled, changes in pressure don't really affect the engine operation.

Not so with the British Rolls-Royce engines, which used carburetors that metered fuel based on air pressure. So if the throttle was wide open, then a large volume of mixed air and fuel was sucked in for combustion. This was initially done with a float, like in a bathroom toilet, which operated a valve that kept fuel levels consistent. Based on throttle position, this permitted varying amounts of the fuel/air mix to pass into the chamber. But a carburetor is susceptible to pressure, so if you nosed over or "bunted" forward suddenly, then the negative g-forces would trap fuel at the top of the chamber and the engine would sputter due to lack of fuel. If this persisted, then the float would be pressed against the floor of the chamber, too much fuel would enter, and the carburetor would flood. The engine would then lose power immediately or often cut out altogether for a few seconds. But negative-g maneuvers are only used during very critical times, such as an attack or a last-ditch defensive action, which is hardly the time you want your engine to quit.

A young engineer named Beatrice "Tilly" Shilling temporarily solved the problem with a simple and brilliant answer. She placed a small disk with a hole in the center, just like a washer, in the float chamber. This way, if the float was forced away by negative g-forces, a small amount of fuel would still make it through the hole—enough to keep the engine running but not enough to flood it. Fighter pilots loved her for this device, which was officially labeled the RAE Restrictor, but with true RAF double meaning simply called it "Miss Shilling's Orifice."*

By late July 1940, the Channel battles were at their height and Sailor Malan was back as commander of 74 Squadron. He'd had his pilots practicing formation takeoffs up through the weather so that they could always get up after the Germans. On the twenty-eighth Malan had been forward deployed to Manston in southeast England at what was known as Hell's Corner. Scrambled to meet an inbound gaggle, Sailor and his twelve Spitfires ran into some thirty 109Es near Dover.

Angling in out of the sun, he pumped five quick bursts into one Emil and sent it spiraling down in flames. As the Germans

---

*Tilly held a doctorate in engineering, raced cars and motorcycles, and refused to marry her fiancé (George Naylor) until he had been awarded the Brooklands Gold Star racing award, just as she had. Incidentally, George was a bomber pilot and RAF wing commander during the war. Not surprisingly, Tilly was an outspoken advocate for women's rights.

broke apart to fight, Malan repositioned and squeezed off three more bursts at a 109 crossing in front of him. Thirty-six pounds of metal left the Spitfire's guns to hit the Emil and it staggered, losing pieces, before flipping over into a tight spiral. Out of ammunition, Sailor headed back to Manston, and the German limped across the Channel. Crash-landing at Wissant, Maj. Werner Mölders, the Luftwaffe's top ace and Condor Legion veteran, was an extremely lucky man. Wounded in the legs, the forty-victory ace and group commander of JG 51 would live to fly again.

"Vati" (Daddy) Mölders, as he was known, had left Spain with fourteen victories to his credit. Like Oswald Boelcke from the Great War, Mölders was a thinker and a great pilot. Largely responsible for refining the *Rotte* and *Schwarm* tactics, he, like most fighter pilots, was a nonconformist. Not intimidated by Berlin, he refused to compromise his principles for National Socialism. One of his best friends was half Jewish, and Mölders intervened to save him from a concentration camp. When his time came to marry, Mölders also insisted on a proper Catholic wedding and, despite Nazi disapproval, he did it anyway. Shot down by a Dewoitine 520 during the Battle for France, Mölders had been captured and beaten by a French soldier, and his Knight's Cross was stolen. A French officer discovered this and had the medal returned. The soldier who'd beaten him was later sentenced to death, but Vati personally asked Goering for leniency, and the man was spared.

As July ended it was obvious that the RAF was in no way defeated. Following the Luftwaffe's earlier victories in the war, this was somewhat of a shock to Hitler—and to Goering especially. Though both sides were relatively evenly matched, the Bf 109 was more heavily armed, was faster, and had a better engine than its opponents. The Luftwaffe was also on the offensive, which can be extremely important psychologically—depending on whom you're attacking. However, as Hitler would see, what worked against France would not work against the British. Operationally, being on the offense should allow better planning, since you're the one calling the shots. Rest and refitting can be scheduled, stores and spares stockpiled, and so on . . . it *should* make all the difference.

But the Germans were fighting over hostile territory and had the Channel to contend with. They could do nothing about a pilot who came down in England, but the Luftwaffe did have a highly developed air-sea rescue system and much better individual survival equipment—both of which the British lacked. However, when RAF pilots went down they often could get picked up, dry off, and climb back into another aircraft to fight again—and they frequently did just that.

AUGUST 1, 1940, was a busy day for the Luftwaffe.

In preparation for Operation Sealion, Hermann Goering finally asked for formal plans from his air fleet commanders to defeat the RAF. Inconceivably, nothing had been formalized during the six weeks following the fall of France and the Channel battles. Hitler's Directive 16 had been disseminated after July 6, but it provided only vague guidance for the destruction of the RAF and the economic strangulation of Britain through attacks on shipping and ports. Goering further complicated matters by forbidding any destruction of facilities and installations he felt Germany would need once England capitulated.

By August 6 a comprehensive strategy had been finalized, and Adlerangriff (Eagle Attack) was set to begin. The overall idea was to guarantee air superiority by destroying RAF Fighter Command. This would be done by attacking airfields, some industry and, above all, by luring the British pilots into the air and killing them. Goering's three great *Luftflotten* in Norway, Normandy, and France had 2,422 combat aircraft, including 868 Me 109s and 268 Me 110 destroyers, ready for action. German planners were well aware that the weather over the Channel would soon make a crossing impossible, but Goering reasoned that there was plenty of time, given the strength of the Luftwaffe. So he allowed himself and his pilots four days to destroy the Royal Air Force—actually, three days, with one extra for bad weather, just in case.

A large part of this bewildering overconfidence arose from German intelligence failures. Unlike the British system, there was no real cooperation among the various, and fiercely competitive, German intelligence organs. Within Luftwaffe Operations, the 5th Abteilung was responsible for collating information relating to enemy air forces. Goering had appointed a political crony and member of his personal staff to head this crucial department. Oberst Josef Schmid, known as "Beppo," spoke no foreign languages, had never visited England, and certainly was no pilot. As a Nazi party man, he delivered carefully sanitized information that portrayed the picture his superiors wished to see.

He'd reported over 350 RAF fighter aircraft destroyed and estimated that there were fewer than 500 of all types available to face the Luftwaffe. Not only that, but he projected that the monthly production of new fighters would not exceed 130 aircraft. In fact, Dowding had fifty-eight squadrons, with six more being formed, totaling about 700 fighters, with 350 new Spitfires and Hurricanes rolling off assembly lines every month. This didn't count those returned to service by the CRO, so the available numbers were actually much higher. Schmid also had no understanding of Fighter Command organization, nor did he grasp the Chain Home system. His overall conclusion, delivered to Goering, was that the Luftwaffe was far superior in equipment, pilots, and command over the Royal Air Force. It was to prove a colossal and costly underestimation.

Adlertag (Eagle Day) launched on August 13, 1940. Once again, Oberst Fink of KG 52 was not a happy man. He'd gotten airborne at 0700 and flown to Cap Gris Nez to rendezvous with the rest of the strike package set to attack England. Irritated by repeated close passes by Me 110s, he'd pressed off to the northwest at the appointed time only to find himself alone in the sky. Unbeknownst to Fink, the mission had been postponed until the afternoon, and without a common radio frequency the Destroyers had buzzed him to get his attention. He flew the mission anyway.

Over the Thames Estuary, east of London, he had the great misfortune to meet up with Sailor Malan's 74 Squadron. The South African ace picked out a three-ship "Vic" and opened fire 100 yards behind the leader. Raking all of them, he settled in on the last Do 17 and put four bursts into it, which sent it spinning down in pieces. Then one of his flight commanders took a hit in the engine's glycol coolant tank and couldn't see a thing in his vapor-filled cockpit. Leading him down for a formation approach, Malan didn't witness the results of his squadron's attack.

But Fink did. Having lost four of his aircraft, with four more heavily damaged, the colonel was apoplectic with fury when he landed. Eagle Day had gotten off to an inglorious start: the Luftwaffe would fly 1,485 sorties at a cost of forty German aircraft versus fourteen RAF fighters lost. The next two weeks were marked by some of the heaviest fighting in what became known as the Battle of Britain.

With no real targeting lists, or even firm priorities established, the Luftwaffe had not been able to accomplish much. Airfields, shipping, and nine manufacturing cities were attacked, with several Chain Home stations assessed as destroyed. In reality, though damaged and unable to receive signals, the British radar sites continued to transmit. This practice would eventually convince Goering that continued assaults against such targets were a waste of resources. Even though they were flying anywhere from 1,400 to 2,000 sorties per day, the Luftwaffe frittered away any real chance of victory by its lack of a coordinated, logical plan—that, and Beppo Schmid's useless, erroneous intelligence reports.

On August 18 Schmid reported that 770 RAF aircraft had been destroyed and less than 300 operational fighters remained. In reality, 214 had been lost, and Dowding still had 600 combat-ready Spitfires and Hurricanes. During the same period the Luftwaffe lost 400 aircraft, of which 181 were Bf 109 and Bf 110 fighters. Losses among the vaunted Stukas were heavy enough to necessitate a change of tactics. Much to the disgust of Adolf Galland and Werner Mölders, fighters were now to fly close escort for the vulnerable dive-bombers. A flawed idea from the beginning, this only handicapped them by having them close and slow instead of sweeping ahead to clear the skies. In a face-saving gesture the Stukas were eventually withdrawn from the battle, ostensibly to conserve them for the assault on England. The Luftwaffe High Command was finally learning what German fighter pilots already knew: that the British would not collapse like the Norwegians or surrender like the French.

Thanks to Beaverbrook's highly efficient organization, 300 new fighters had been built and 260 repaired and put back in the air over the same two weeks. In fact, during the Battle of Britain the RAF soon possessed more aircraft than it had at the beginning. But the Luftwaffe was also learning and fighting back hard. After a few days off for bad weather, the Germans were back with a vengeance and the attacks were beginning to make sense. Fighter Group airfields, particularly 11 Group in southeastern England, were the primary targets.

On August 24 alone, more than a thousand sorties were flown against Manston and Hornchurch. By month's end the Luftwaffe was hitting all the main airfields several times a day—nearly 1,500 sorties on August 31 alone—and it was working. Bombers, protected by swarms of fighters, were overwhelming the RAF, and because the Germans were constantly hitting the same targets the British rarely had time to repair the damage. Usually one *Gruppe* of fifty fighters would sweep ahead of the bombers and engage the RAF. If a Hurricane or Spitfire managed to get through, it would be short of fuel and ammo and then would have to contend with another *Gruppe* flying close escort. The strategy was also forcing the Spitfires and Hurricanes into combat with German fighters, and the RAF lost 273 aircraft from August 24 to September 6.

Flight Lt. James Nicholson came close to being a casualty on August 16, 1940, over Southampton. Scrambled with the rest of 249 (Gold Coast) Squadron to intercept a gaggle of bombers heading for Gosport, he ran straight into the escorting Emils and destroyers. As he tried to wriggle out of the way, 20 mm cannon shells from a Bf 110 shattered the Hurricane's cockpit, with fragments hitting him in the eye and foot. More hit his engine and the reserve fuel tank, which started a fire. Pulling his feet out of the flames, Nicholson yanked the burning fighter around and attacked another destroyer, sending it cartwheeling down in pieces. Badly burned, he finally managed to bail out, only to be shot in the buttocks by an excited Home Guardsman who thought he was German. Nicholson was the only member of Fighter Command to receive the Victoria Cross during the Battle of Britain.

The real issue was pilots. RAF loss rates of 120 pilots per week were horrendous by any standard.* A 30 percent loss rate was normal, and a few squadrons suffered 100 percent casualties in a single month. The intense concentration of flying is exhausting enough, but combat is on another level entirely. Stress, fear, and the sheer physical drain of flying three to five gut-wrenching missions per day added up quickly. Men aged perceptibly as close calls mounted and their friends died. Since Adlertag began some 385 pilots had been killed, were missing, or had been removed for severe injuries. Fewer than half the remaining 1,023 pilots were veterans, and the others often had less than 20 hours flying fighters. Some sources put the loss rate for fighter squadron commanders as high as 80 percent. The situation became so critical that one Hurricane commanding officer had no flying time in the plane—he managed a few overhead patterns, then led his squadron into combat.

Dowding had already shortened basic flight training by at least a week, and the operational training syllabus was cut from six months to mere weeks—many of the replacement pilots had never even fired their guns. By August more than 1,600 new pilots were in the pipeline, but this was part of the problem—there's a tremendous difference between a pilot and a combat-ready fighter pilot, and yet more difference between a combat-ready pilot and a proven veteran. Like Nicholson, many veterans were wounded and put out of action for weeks or months. A one-for-one swap with a "sprog" or "newbie" wasn't possible, as there was no replacement for experience except experience—and most young pilots didn't live long enough to learn. Dowding

*From all causes: killed, wounded, missing, and temporarily relieved.

was painfully, fearfully aware that under current conditions he had less than a one-month reserve of fighter pilots.

In early September Air Vice-Marshal Park had come up with a three-tier solution that would keep operational units effectively manned while giving inexperienced pilots a decent shot at survival. Class A squadrons had their full quota of aircraft and at least sixteen combat-ready pilots. This encompassed all 11 Group squadrons plus a few in 12 and 10 Groups. Class B units maintained between four and six combat-ready pilots, who usually were rotated out to form the nucleus of a new squadron. Class C units, usually part of 13 Group far to the north in Scotland, had about three combat-ready pilots. These men had usually been sent north to recover from prolonged combat, serious wounds, or both.

Park's counterpart, AVM Trafford Leigh-Mallory, took a dim view of this, since it cast his 12th Group into a supporting role. He'd been promoting what he called the "Big Wing" theory and was offended at the cool reaction from Dowding and Park. His idea was to employ multiple squadrons to meet German raids and then overwhelm them through sheer numbers. One problem was that the Chain Home network gave a maximum detection range of 80 miles, so even if Spitfires were scrambled immediately, which they were not, it would take a fighter twenty minutes to reach 25,000 feet. By that time the German bombers were past the point of interception. Another problem was coordination. Radios were fairly rudimentary, so getting several squadrons into position was very difficult and ate up precious fuel.

Long a political foe of both Dowding and Park, Leigh-Mallory desperately wanted to be Britain's savior during the battle, and he bitterly resented the geographical reality of his position. He even resorted to using Douglas Bader, the famous legless squadron commander, as his mouthpiece for the Big Wing. Bader, to his discredit, had a member of Parliament as his adjutant and frequently voiced his opinions through this man to the Air Ministry. So even in an incredibly desperate fight for survival, with the whole of Britain at stake, politics and jealousy reared their ugly heads. Park could've cared less; he was a warrior and fighter pilot engaged in the biggest air battle in history. As for Dowding, he had more important things to consider and was indifferent to the 12 Group commander's wounded pride and hurt feelings.

In the end, salvation for the British came in the unlikely form of Hermann Goering. On September 7, the same day Park put his plan into effect, Goering assumed personal, tactical command of the air war. He immediately discontinued attacks on radar stations and airfields, convinced that they were having no effect. If that wasn't bad enough, he switched priorities just when his assault was finally paying off. It was now the first duty of the fighters to protect bombers rather than killing Spitfires and Hurricanes. Flying at high altitude, moving at slower speeds, and being tied to a defensive role effectively negated the Luftwaffe's fighter advantage.

Even though Chain Home radar coverage was limited above 20,000 feet, without a heavy bomber any German strategic campaign was a moot point. This shift occurred exactly when Goering should have moved in for the kill. Instead, he gave the RAF a respite as the terror bombing of London, the "Blitz," began. London's Surrey docks were the first target, and the warehouses full of rum, paint, timber, and paper burned easily. Spices—pepper worst of all—caught fire and blew into the eyes of Civil Defensemen trying to contain the blaze.

As bad as the Blitz was, it signaled that by Friday, September 13, Goering had given up the war of fighter pilots. With a scant 130 flyers available to the British, it came just in time. Airfields and radars were repaired, spare aircraft were delivered, and pilots got a few precious days of rest, which they hadn't had since July. This would be a crucial factor over the next week, especially since the Germans had no such break. Astonishingly, the High Command didn't feel it was needed; indeed, Hitler said on September 14, "There is a great chance of totally defeating the British."

He'd initially set September 15 as the date for the invasion, and though the invasion didn't occur, the Luftwaffe sent more than 1,300 sorties against London that day. Fighter Command responded from both 11 and 12 Group with nearly two hundred Spitfires and Hurricanes accounting for fifty-eight Germans shot down, including twenty-six fighters. After what would be celebrated as Battle of Britain Day, it was clear even to Goering and Hitler that the Royal Air Force was not defeated. Adolf Galland got his fortieth kill that month but told Goering to his face, "In spite of heavy losses we are inflicting on the enemy fighters, no decisive decrease in their number or fighting efficiency was noticeable."

Generaloberst Alfred Jodl, chief of the Wehrmacht Operations Staff, would personally state to Hitler that "under no circumstances must the landing operation fail. The political consequences of a fiasco might be much more far reaching than the military . . . the landing must be considered a desperate venture, something which might have to be undertaken in a desperate situation but on which we have no necessity to embark at the moment." Jodl also indicated that "England can be brought to her knees by other methods," such as closing the Mediterranean to the British by taking Gibraltar or cutting England off from the Middle East by seizing the Suez Canal.

Faced with growing losses, bad weather over the Channel, and a worsening situation in North Africa, Hitler postponed Operation Sealion on September 17, 1940. British intelligence intercepted signals ordering that German air transport facilities be dismantled. The raids would continue for several months, with an increasing emphasis on night bombing, which neither primary British fighter was well equipped to meet. The Spitfire was particularly difficult due to its fiery exhaust plumes. Airfield lighting was haphazard, as was aircraft instrumentation for "blind," or instrument, flying. The Bristol Beaufighter was finally deemed a better choice, since it would have room for an airborne radar and an operator to employ it while the pilot flew. There was also no real interference with night vision, as the engines were on the wings, not in front of the pilot's face.

Fitted with a Mk IV Airborne Intercept radar by late September 1940, the Beaufighter was armed with four cannons and two machine guns. With a top speed of 320 mph, it wasn't a survivable fighter during the day, but at night, in the right hands, it was deadly. The most successful hands belonged to Flight Lt. John Cunningham of 604 Squadron. Cunningham learned the radar and night interception tactics to the point where he shot down twenty Germans—nineteen of them at night. He explained his nickname, "Cat's Eyes," like this:

> *I was given the nickname "Cat's Eyes" by the Air Ministry to cover up the fact that we were flying aircraft with radar because there was never any mention of radar at that period. So by the time I had had two or three successes, the Air Ministry felt they would have to explain that I had very good vision by night . . . it would have been easier had the carrots worked. In fact, it was a long, hard grind and very frustrating. It was a struggle to continue flying on instruments at night.*

On September 30 the final major daylight on London was launched. German losses that day totaled some forty-three aircraft destroyed against sixteen for the RAF, and the threat of invasion followed the myth of Luftwaffe superiority into history. The battle would continue for another two months, finally ending on December 18, as Hitler began preparations for the invasion of the Soviet Union.

Statistics relative to the battle are as varied as the number of agencies involved. The Luftwaffe started the fight in June with about 4,000 aircraft, of which 1,107 were Bf 109s and 357 were Bf 110s, for a total of 1,464 fighters. There were 1,450 fighter pilots to fly them, including highly experienced veterans of Spain, Poland, Norway, and France. Over the course of the battle, the Royal Air Force would claim 2,698 German planes (of all types) destroyed. The reality, according to postwar sources, was closer to 1,600, of which 762 were fighters. This tallies more closely with the known Luftwaffe record of more than 2,500 aircrew killed and 967 captured.

The Royal Air Force began the battle with 800 fighter aircraft, mostly Hurricane Mk Is and a few Spitfires. More than 400 fighter pilots had been lost during the Battle of France, so the RAF had about 1,000 remaining. This would be augmented by another 400 foreign pilots who'd escaped from the Germans and 600 more from the Dominions. The Luftwaffe would claim 3,198 kills during the battle, though the true losses were much less. Actually, 1,087 fighters were lost, plus bombers and Coastal Command aircraft, for a total of 1,600 aircraft. Of the fighter pilots, 900 would be killed, missing, or wounded—a 40 percent casualty rate.

The Battle of Britain is one of those pivots upon which history was decided. It marked Hitler's farthest western expansion and shattered the very real psychological advantage that the Germans had enjoyed. They *could* be beaten, and had been. On a more practical level, the battle bled the Luftwaffe of vital equipment and irreplaceable men at a time when it could ill afford the loss. This would make a crucial difference in the months to come as 1940 ended and Hitler's eyes turned south and east.

The British got a new lease on life. Not only had they stopped the most powerful air force in the world, but they had gained time to rebuild and replenish, time to get off the defensive and go offensive. Most important, the outcome signaled to the United States that victory was possible. But the two men who did so much to win the Battle of Britain were shamefully treated. Hugh Dowding was more or less forced to retire once the danger was over and "new ideas" were needed. He went quietly. Leigh-Mallory and his cronies also managed to remove Keith Park, who, unsurprisingly, did not go quietly. His disgust and contempt for political maneuvering at this dangerous juncture was very evident. As Lord Tedder, the chief of the Air Staff, would say of Park:

> *If any one man won the Battle of Britain, he did. I do not believe it is realized how much that one man, with his leadership, his calm judgment and his skill, did to save, not only this country, but the world.*

No one has ever said as much about Park's critics.*

It has been quite correctly pointed out that the fight was

---

*Leigh-Mallory's limited tactical depth would cause the deaths of more than five hundred RAF pilots in 1941 as they were forced into fruitless "sweeps" over France. He would die in a plane crash on his way to Burma in 1944. Douglas Bader was shot down in 1941, possibly by another Spitfire, and sat out the war in a POW camp.

won by *everyone* who took part, from the civilians who put out fires and repaired aircraft to the women who built more planes and ran Dowding's Chain Home system. There were bomber pilots who bravely attacked the Third Reich on lonely night missions and never returned. And credit must go to all on the island who refused to surrender when the world said it was impossible to stop Hitler.

However, it was the fighter pilots, alone in their cockpits, who lashed out against waves of enemy bombers and their escorts. These were men who fought within sight of those on the ground—even their own families. These were men who perished, screaming in burning cockpits or died lonely, freezing deaths bobbing helplessly in the Channel. As Winston Churchill expressed in his immortal speech:

> *The gratitude of every home in our Island, in our Empire, and indeed throughout the world, except in the abodes of the guilty, goes out to the British airmen who, undaunted by odds, unwearied in their constant challenge and mortal danger, are turning the tide of the World War by their prowess and by their devotion. Never in the field of human conflict was so much owed by so many to so few. All hearts go out to the fighter pilots.*

The Battle of Britain was over.

Now the battle for the rest of the world was about to begin.

CHAPTER 9

THE STAR AND THE ROSE

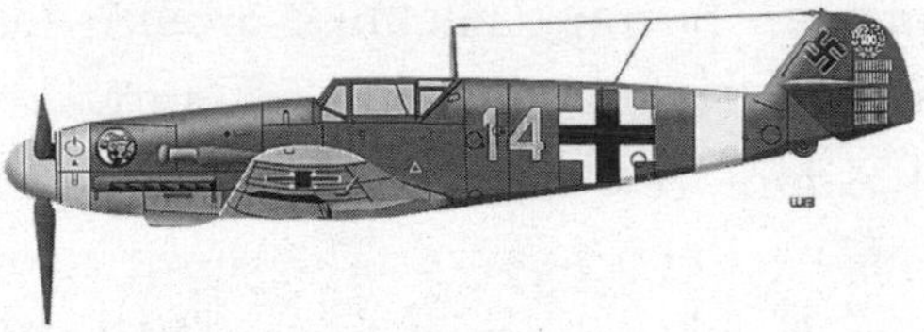

BF 109G

"PAUKE . . . PAUKE . . . Indianer . . . Zehn heur!"*

Three other helmeted and goggled heads swiveled to the ten o'clock low position and squinted through the glare. How their flight leader could see "Indians"—slang for the enemy—or anything against the bright sand was beyond them, but he always did. The lead Messerschmitt didn't wait for a reply but simply rolled inverted and pulled down toward the hard, tan Libyan earth.

"Horrido!"†

British Hurricanes were diving down toward the Stukas and

---

* *Pauke* means "tally-ho"—a visual sighting of an enemy.

†Battle cry of Luftwaffe fighter pilots. It roughly means "Fear me" or "I'm a horrible one and you're going to die."

their close escorts, but they hadn't seen the high group of Bf 109s dropping down on *them*. For Lieutenant. Hans-Joachim Marseille, it was a perfect situation. He jockeyed the throttle and stick to come screaming in behind the other fighter. Much, much faster than his target, Marseille had only a second or two to aim, fire, and reposition away. The Bf 109 Emil shuddered as he triggered off a short burst, paused a split second, then pulled hard away.

His twenty machine gun and cannon rounds went straight into the Hurricane's left wing, through the cockpit and into the engine. The fighter came apart smoking, and as Marseille rolled and the horizon spun, something hit the Emil—hard. Reacting instantly, Marseille pulled around to the northwest toward the German lines. Leveling off, he trimmed the 109 and quickly scanned his engine instruments. There—just to the right of the stick, the coolant temperature gauge was spiked in the red. Overheat. Whatever came off the Hurricane had hit his radiator, and the glycol was leaking out fast. With his right hand he opened the radiator flaps all the way.

Radioing his *schwarm* that his engine was hit, the twenty-three-year-old *experte* glanced at his altitude, his airspeed, and the endless wasteland stretching out beneath him. Plenty of altitude . . . he could make it back to Derna as long as his motor didn't quit.

Suddenly the engine knocked violently as the last of the coolant drained away. Reaching up with his left hand, Marseille cut off the fuel, then stared out to his left and realized he couldn't make Derna. But Matruba was 10 miles closer, and that would be no problem.

As he calmly radioed in his coordinates, something glinted below him. Sunlight on metal! He had excellent eyes, and as they narrowed against the glare he picked up another Hurricane. It was a good 5,000 feet lower and turning to attack, which was what had caused the wing flash. Never hesitating, Marseille instantly split-S'd down, converting the complex geometrical problem into stick and rudder movements. The planes rolled out nose to nose, with the German coming down. As the Hurricane's nose lifted Marseille opened fire, sending the other fighter diving into the ground.

Immediately zooming back up and turning toward Matruba, he bunted over to hold best glide speed. A few minutes later he coasted over the threshold, gear down, and made a superb deadstick landing. Rolling out, he unlatched the canopy, and the morning air dried his sweat. It was just past 0930 on February 13, 1942. Two Hurricanes shot down, thanks to another magnificent feat of flying, and his damaged Emil would fly again in three days. Locking the parking brake, the young pilot smiled, looking very boyish at the thought of his forty-fifth and forty-sixth kills. Pulling himself up and sitting on the canopy rail, he listened to the engine tick and watched the ground crews race toward him, the battered *Kübelwagens* stirring up the ever-present dust. This had been a good morning.

But it hadn't always been like this.

Hans-Joachim Marseille had been flying since he was eighteen. Born into a military family, son of a rigid German officer father, he was a rebel from his first step. Entering the Luftwaffe, he waltzed through flight school and was sent to fighters. A gifted natural pilot with a photographic memory, he was sent to the famous Jagdfliegerschule 5 in November 1939. As Marseille mastered aerobatics, navigation, and gunnery, his natural rebelliousness began to attract attention.

It must be appreciated that Nazi Germany in 1939 was *not* the place to be a nonconformist. There was no freedom of speech, much music (including American jazz) was banned, and undesirable people often just disappeared. Marseille simply didn't care. He drank, which was a serious offense, and fast became one of the most infamous womanizers in the Luftwaffe. He was in trouble so often that, according to one of his friends, "it was a noteworthy occasion when he was not on restriction."

He was late. He missed additional duties. One time on a cross-country training flight he landed on the Autobahn to relieve himself. Despite Germany's need for pilots and his obvious skill, everyone believed Marseille would wash out to the infantry. But he didn't. Whether it was luck or his father's good connections, he managed to graduate and was posted to Lehrgeschwader (LG) 2 in August 1940. Flying out of Calais-Marck at the height of the Battle of Britain, he was in combat within days. On August 24 he spotted a Hurricane over Kent in southern England and, without saying a word, deserted his flight and attacked.* The British fighter fell into the water, and Marseille was ecstatic—until he landed, to face his commander.

Herbert Ihlefeld was a veteran of the Condor Legion, Poland, France, and now Britain. A professional fighter pilot, he recognized the potential in Marseille but had no patience for a loose cannon who might get other pilots killed. Still, there's a fine line between teaching a spirited, aggressive pilot and crushing him. Ihlefeld would remember, "He was like a young boy who had just caught his first fish. I sat him down, broke out a bottle of cognac, and poured one for each of us. I told him the kill was visually confirmed, and I would credit him with it. I then told him that if he ever broke formation in my unit again, if I could not shoot him down myself, I would shoot him when he returned. . . . I smiled as I said it."

---

*Four days earlier Churchill had said, "Never in the field of human conflict was so much owed by so many to so few. All hearts go out to the fighter pilots."

It didn't really sink in. To Marseille, life must've seemed a big game, and the war was initially an extension of that, so why get bent out of shape over silly rules and regulations? In fact, most fighter pilots feel some of that, but most also are deadly serious about the business of fighting and killing. After Marseille's fifth victory in late September, Ihlefeld tore up the evaluation he'd just written and said, "Marseille, you must pull your head out of your ass. You are not alone; this is not the Hans Marseille show."

In the end Ihlefeld simply didn't have the time to reform one rogue pilot, so he transferred him to Jagdgeschwader 52 at Peuplingues on the Pas de Calais. For the next three and a half months Marseille flew, was grounded, flew some more, and generally got in trouble. Restricted to his quarters, he didn't take that to include the town, so he borrowed (stole) his commander's car and went barhopping. Coming back drunk with two French girls certainly did not endear him to his new commander, Johannes Steinhoff. One could forgive his utter lack of military bearing and even his rebelliousness up to a point, but not his seeming disregard for his fellow pilots. But in studying the man, I don't think that was truly his attitude. He was a warrior and a loner. The cold fact was that he really didn't need anyone's help in the air and was better alone.

Then in late January 1941 a very irate Gestapo major showed up looking for a fighter pilot who fit Marseille's description.* Apparently this man had a daughter just home from the university and Marseille "took advantage of her." It was the final straw.

Herbert Ihlefeld was no lightweight and would survive the war with 132 victories plus the Knight's Cross with Oak Leaves

---

*Gestapo (acronym for Geheime Staatspolizei), the state secret police.

and Swords. Steinhoff would also survive with 176 victories and he too wore the Knight's Cross with Oak Leaves and Swords. These men were true fighter pilots—they just couldn't afford to babysit an extremely troublesome albeit amazingly skilled aviator. With Operation Sealion postponed and Russia still in the future, North Africa seemed the perfect solution for getting rid of Hans Marseille. In a fit of overconfidence Mussolini, the Italian dictator, had ordered an invasion of Egypt in the fall of 1940. It was actually a shrewd tactical move to attempt to conquer North Africa, and especially the Suez Canal. Such a victory would cut Britain off from the vast resources and wealth of India while giving the Axis direct access to Middle Eastern oil. With control of the Mediterranean Basin, Europe's southern flank would be secure and a jab straight into the Soviet Union's belly through the Black Sea very possible. One wonders how different the world would be today if Hitler had turned south after the Battle of Britain instead of east. Fortunately for the Allies, neither Mussolini nor the Italian military was up to the task.

Under the very real threat of invasion in 1940, England was in no position to devote a great deal of resources to either the Mediterranean or North Africa. The Western Desert Force had been thrown together in June following Mussolini's declaration of war, but it consisted of only 36,000 men and about seventy tanks.* So when Marshal Rodolfo Graziani advanced east from Italian-controlled Cyrenaica in September, there was little to stop him.

Fearful of a large incursion into Egypt, the 200,000 Italians got just east of Tobruk to Sidi Barrani, and there they stopped

*Mussolini declared war on the Allies when the Wehrmacht marched into Paris on June 10, 1940.

on September 16, 1940.* Graziani then fortified open ground between the coastline and the Libyan Plateau to the south as the British forces withdrew to Mersa-Matruh, farther down the Egyptian coast. The British rightly concluded that success on the ground in North Africa would not be possible as long as the Regia Marina (Italian navy) dominated the Mediterranean Sea. With the German threat to their island somewhat diminished, the offensive-minded British commenced Operation Judgment.

At 10:58 p.m. on November 11 the first of two waves of obsolete Fairey Swordfish torpedo bombers attacked the Italian main battle fleet. Sheltered in the 2,600-year-old harbor of Taranto, the Italians had five serviceable battleships, seven heavy cruisers, and ten lighter warships. Nicknamed "Stringbag," the Swordfish was an open-cockpit biplane that could barely manage 135 mph under ideal conditions and carry a single torpedo or an assortment of bombs.

The Italians believed that the 39-foot-deep harbor was too shallow for aerial torpedoes and they were safe from that sort of attack.† This was despite the fact that Rear Admiral Bradley Fiske, USN, had proven the effectiveness of aerial torpedoes in 1915.‡ The Royal Navy had taken their standard Mark XII 18-inch torpedo and modified the fins so it could be dropped in water as shallow as 24 feet.

And that's precisely what they did.

By 1:22 a.m. three battleships were severely damaged, and nearly seven hundred Italian sailors were killed or wounded. Despite 15,000 anti-aircraft rounds fired, the British lost two

---

*The Battle of Britain Day had just ended the previous evening, September 15.

†Just as the Americans believed Pearl Harbor was too shallow for such a threat.

‡Fiske was an amazingly talented officer who designed more than 130 technical innovations, including naval telescopic gunsights, range finders, and the aerial torpedo.

aircraft, two killed, and two captured. The battleship *Conte di Cavour* later sank and although she was raised, she never fought again. In a tactically revolutionary move the British had pulled off the first naval attack conducted entirely by aircraft. The balance of seapower in the Mediterranean shifted, albeit temporarily, forcing the Italians to relocate to Naples. Control of the North African coast was still problematic, but the Royal Navy had shown quite clearly that it still had teeth and was prepared to use them.

Most important, it deprived the Axis of the initiative in this particular theater and permitted a British counteroffensive, which began on December 7, 1940. Italian forward positions east of Sidi Barrani were attacked from the air and shelled by the Royal Navy just off the coast. The 7th Armored Division, which became the legendary "Desert Rats," hit the Italians hard and shattered their lines. Supported by infantry, British armor made short work of the Maletti Group's Fiat tankettes and M11/39 battle tanks. Without any mechanized defense, most of the Italian infantry surrendered.

Sidi Barrani fell by December 10, and the Italians fled down the single coast road west toward the Libyan border. Twenty to 30 miles inland, most of the terrain was impassable for vehicles. Supply and support from the sea was vital, so this tug-of-war along the coast road would become normal for much of the desert campaign. Named for the former governor-general of Libya, the Via Balbo was the conduit by which North Africa would be controlled.* Capturing Fort Capruzzo, the British advance slowed for both supply and strategic reasons.

---

*Italo Balbo was made an honorary Sioux Indian in the 1930s and named Chief "Flying Eagle." He also opposed Mussolini's racial laws and thought Italy should side with Britain instead of Germany. While landing near Tobruk in June 1940, he was mistakenly killed by anti-aircraft fire from the cruiser *San Giorgio*.

But by late January, about the time Hans Marseille was involved with the Gestapo major's daughter, Tobruk surrendered. Derna followed, and on February 7, 1941, the Italian Tenth Army ceased to exist along the coast road south of Benghazi. In a parody of Churchill's famous Battle of Britain speech, Anthony Eden, the British foreign secretary, quipped, "Never has so much been surrendered by so many to so few."

In two months the British and Commonwealth forces had pushed the Italians out of Egypt and advanced 500 miles. They'd destroyed about 400 tanks and taken 130,000 prisoners at the cost of 1,600 dead and wounded. To be partially fair to the Italians, it must be remembered that the rank and file weren't totally committed to the war.

A motley collection of RAF aircraft called the Desert Air Force had been strung together under our old friend "Collie" Collishaw—now Air Commodore Collishaw. With an archaic collection of Gladiators, Lysanders, and Blenheims, his pilots attacked airstrips and strafed anything that moved. There was also a single Hurricane in theater, which Collie moved around, a ploy that convinced Italian intelligence he had a squadron of fighters.

Justifiably doubting the Italians' ability to fight the British, Hitler had at last intervened and sent one of his best tank commanders to the desert. Arriving four days after the Tenth Army surrendered, Erwin Rommel was to command the newly formed Deutsches Afrikakorps (DAK). He was to be supported by units of Jagdgeschwader 27, including a renegade young flyer who would become one of the greatest fighter pilots of all time, the future "Star of Africa," Hans-Joachim Marseille.

RECAPTURING TOBRUK WAS Rommel's immediate objective. It was far enough forward in Cyrenaica to be an ideal staging area, and its port was as vital to the British as to the Germans. A port meant replacement tanks, fresh troops, and fuel. Above all, it meant fuel, the lifeblood of any mechanized army, and especially so in the desert.

Rommel had retaken Benghazi and was in Derna by April 11. The advance contingent from JG 27 had arrived and by April 15 was setting up facilities in Gazala, about 50 miles up the coast from Tobruk. After fighting in the Battle of Britain, the wing was sent to the Balkans, then Greece. Already approaching their 1,000th victory, JG 27 was a solid mix of experienced and battle-hardened pilots.* The first *Staffel* of BF 109E's flew in on the eighteenth and began combat operations the following day.

Marseille reached Gazala on the evening of April 22 and was in combat the next day. Escorting Stukas in the vicinity of Tobruk, he spotted at least two Hurricanes and immediately attacked, sending one down in flames. However, as he turned to kill the wingman, four more enemy fighters swirled into the fur ball. Diving away, he returned to base, refueled and rearmed, and took off again for another mission over Tobruk. First to see targets, he dove into the middle of them without a radio call or a wingman and found three Hurricanes on his tail. This time he wasn't so lucky—the armored head plate behind him was hit, as were his engine and fuselage. Breaking away, he limped back to base, stinking of oil and glycol, and made a gear-up landing in his shot-up plane.

By this time the British Desert Air Force had been reorganized into the 204 Group under Collishaw's command. They'd also been reinforced with three squadrons of Hurricanes plus bombers and reconnaissance aircraft. Their main purpose was

---

*By 1945 twenty-three pilots from JG 27 would receive the Knight's Cross.

to prevent or disrupt German attacks on the Tobruk garrison and interdict Axis supply lines. Marseille's earlier kill, his eighth to date, was likely from No. 6 Squadron from Tobruk.* The Hurricanes that shot him up so badly later were from 73 Squadron, veterans of the Battle for France and the Battle of Britain. Due to the U-boat threat, the aircraft had been brought by ship to the Gold Coast, assembled, and flown to Egypt to oppose the German offensive.†

After three weeks, Rommel knew Tobruk would not be taken through a siege. The Australian 9th Division was too well dug in and too well protected by the RAF and Royal Navy. It was also commanded by Lt. Gen. Leslie Morshead, a schoolteacher turned infantry officer during the Great War. A veteran of Gallipoli and the Western Front, Morshead was nicknamed "Ming the Merciless," and the Germans discovered why. His stubborn defense forced Rommel into an encirclement that cut the Via Balbo on the Egyptian side but did nothing to prevent support from the sea.

The British launched several badly executed attempts to relieve Tobruk, but they all failed. If Rommel had been reinforced, he likely could've taken the harbor, pushed all the way to Cairo, and taken the Suez Canal. But German resources, and Hitler's priorities, lay thousands of miles to the north as Operation Barbarossa, the invasion of Russia, began on June 22, 1941. This left North Africa in the backwater, at least strategically, but to Hans Marseille it was a battle like any other.

All through that hot summer he worked on two things: per-

---

*No. 6 Squadron was made famous during the Great War by Major Lanoe Hawker (see page 42). Hugh Dowding was also a squadron pilot.

†One of her most famous Great War fighter pilots was William Stephenson, who was now Britain's top spymaster and would go down in history as the "Man Called Intrepid."

fecting his unique combat techniques and thoroughly pissing off his squadron commander. Asked by a visiting senior officer what he thought of Libya, Marseille answered, "They really should bring some girls here, sort of boring and all that, and not even a *pilstube* [bar] in the area."

The desert was taking its toll. As a result of dysentery, jaundice, poor food, and stress, Marseille dropped from 150 pounds to 110. Recurring malaria brought fever and chills to the point where he could barely climb into the cockpit. Sent home to recover, he regained his strength and returned at the end of August 1941.

During his absence, the Allies had been reinforced with additional tanks and an influx of Commonwealth fighter squadrons that had converted from Hurricanes to the Curtiss P-40. Called a Warhawk by the Americans, the early export version was known as the Tomahawk.

With no high-altitude bombers to protect, and short engagement distances, air combat in North Africa generally took place below 15,000 feet, and this favored the P-40. Horizontally, it could outturn both the Bf 109E and the Macchi C.202, and it could outdive either opponent. The Tomahawk was also a very stable gun platform, and the later 1942 variant, called a Kittyhawk, carried a lethal punch, with six .50-caliber wing-mounted machine guns. Engine and cockpit armor made it a favorite with pilots, though its roughly 8,000-pound weight and Allison engine gave it a slower rate of climb than the Emil.*

Like all great fighter pilots, Marseille knew his own aircraft intimately and understood exactly how to use its strengths to full advantage. Attacking out of the sun, from above if possi-

---

*About 2,100 feet per minute, vs. 2,600 feet per minute for the 5,800-pound Bf 109.

ble, and taking your enemy by surprise were all principles that hadn't changed since World War I. In this the Bf 109 was always its most lethal; to dive, fire at close range, and zoom away was to use it as its best. In the hands of experienced Luftwaffe pilots it could, and did, exact horrible tolls on Allied fighters.

One of the countertactics employed by Commonwealth pilots was a defensive circle—precisely like covered wagons circling against Indian attacks. In this move, also called a Lufbery, each plane in the circle was supposed to be protected because no enemy could get behind an aircraft without flying into the guns of another. Designed as a bomber defense, it was supremely ludicrous for anything else. One of the tremendous advantages of being a fighter pilot is an offensive mentality—that's why you're a fighter pilot. If your mind-set is to "circle the wagons" and go on the defense, you've thrown that advantage away.

And it absolutely did not work against Hans Marseille. He would roll over and dive, inverted, from above. Picking a target, he'd bore straight behind it, open fire at close range, then pull up into a chandelle (a climbing turn) away from the circle. As he never slowed down, he was never in one place long enough for the enemy fighters to shoot back. His marksmanship being what it was, he nearly always killed on each pass. Marseille was so accurate that he consistently brought planes down with a burst of fifteen 7.62 mm rounds and two from the cannon. After pulling up and away, he'd pick another victim, roll over again, and repeat the process; he often shot down multiple aircraft per mission. Sometimes he'd slash through a formation rather than zoom back up, and this worked fine before the P-40 came along.

In mid-October over Bir Sheferzan, southwest of Tobruk, he found a gaggle of South African P-40s. However, as he dove, two Australians from No. 3 Squadron attacked from overhead, following him down. Well aware that a Tomahawk could catch a 109 in a dive and chew it up with machine guns, he did something truly astounding: he chopped the power, dropped his flaps, and nearly stalled. Caught completely by surprise, and now traveling 200 mph faster than the 109, the two Aussies overshot before they could shoot.

Marseille retracted the flaps, pulled the stick into his lap, and firewalled the throttle. The Emil's nose staggered up, and Jochen opened fire as the P-40 flashed by overhead. As it spun away out of control, the other Tomahawk tried to zoom to safety, but the German fighter pirouetted on its tail, pulled 100 yards of lead, and opened fire again. The first P-40 made a forced landing; the second one managed to return to base but was a total write-off due to battle damage. A kill is a kill, though, and these were numbers twenty-four and twenty-five.

It shouldn't have worked. It should've made *him* an excellent target and gotten him killed. But it didn't. Marseille's fellow pilots were astounded. A "magnificent madman," one of them would say, but with the respect of someone watching a gifted man work his magic. Physically, this was tremendously punishing, as all air combat is. To the extent that g-forces were understood, people knew that too many would cause a blackout and almost certain death; how to counter the effects had not been worked out. Marseille had a self-imposed fitness routine of push-ups and sit-ups, and certainly his excellent physical condition made a difference, giving him the stamina needed to endure constant combat. Another of his friends said, "I can only attribute his great ability to recover to all the alcohol he drank. Thinning the blood probably allowed for a more fluid and flowing vascular condition."

But even the strongest wear out, and a few days after his twenty-fifth victory he was sent back to Germany for a rest and transition to the new Bf 109F. A major redesign, the "Friedrich" version was the pinnacle of the aircraft's evolution. The outboard cannons were removed, eliminating weight and permitting a redesigned wing. Semi-elliptical, the new wing was lighter, with less drag; thanks to its better leading-edge slats, the F model 109 could turn tighter than its predecessors. More power from the Daimler-Benz 1,159-horsepower engine also enabled the Friedrich to climb and turn quicker. All the armament was concentrated in the nose, which simplified feed mechanisms and reduced jamming. The cowling-mounted 7.62 mm guns remained, and a single *Motorkanone* was added, which fired through the propeller hub.

On November 18, while Jochen was still in Germany, the British launched Operation Crusader. Under abysmal conditions caused by a particularly nasty desert storm, the British Eighth Army began a buffalo-horned assault. A time-honored tactic, the idea was to attack in force with the center while two prongs flanked the enemy. While this was going on, the Tobruk garrison would break out in the German rear and cut their supply lines. Though initially successful, the British underestimated Rommel's genius for mobile, combined-arms warfare. Rapid, heavily concentrated armored counterattacks supported by the Luftwaffe threw the Allied plan into confusion.

By the time Marseille returned in early December, the fighting along the coast road was heavy and Rommel was forced to pull back from Tobruk. During an escort mission on the fifth he downed a South African Hurricane, though eighteen out of forty Stukas were lost. Two days later JG 27 relocated to Tmimi as the British pressed toward Tobruk and pushed Rommel to Gazala. Jochen shot down his twenty-ninth aircraft two days later but no one felt much like celebrating. It was December 7, 1941, and 8,700 miles to the east the U.S. Pacific Fleet was being attacked at Pearl Harbor, Hawaii. "Once we heard that America had been attacked and had declared war, everyone knew it was over. We may have been able to hold Europe," Bernhard Woldenga, the *Geschwaderkommodore* said, "but winning a total victory was out of the question."

Withdrawing west to the Gazala Line, Rommel hoped to hold there. Anchoring the Italians along the coast, the Afrikakorps then deployed southwest into the desert. JG 27 and the other Luftwaffe units bombed and strafed in a target-rich environment. On December 14, Hermann Forster bailed out during a dogfight against a flight of Tomahawks. Hanging in his parachute, he was strafed and killed by another P-40.* Enraged, some Germans wanted to respond in kind, but they were told that under no circumstances were helpless men to be killed. Hauptmann Eduard Neumann, Marseille's outstanding *Gruppenkommandeur*, was emphatic that the rules of war would not be violated by the men under his command regardless of what the enemy did. Luftwaffe pilots had a very high opinion of their British and Commonwealth foes as flyers and as men. Though not necessarily chivalrous, they believed, as most fighter pilots did (and still do), that those who fight in the sky are different from the others and should be treated as such. Woldenga agreed: "This is not Russia, it is not a war with animals."

Other than marksmanship and fearlessness, humanity was a defining characteristic of Hans Marseille. Like Hans-Ekkehard Bob, he showed a real compassion for the men he shot down, as well as their families. He personally took at least one wounded flyer to a field hospital and filled out another's Geneva Conventions card. On several occasions, and against orders, he dropped

*Heaton and Lewis believe the shooter was Flight Lieutenant Clive Caldwell, 250 Squadron RAF.

notes over Allied airfields concerning captured pilots. It was said that he brought some humanity back into the struggle in ways that had not been seen since the Great War. Marseille even escorted a damaged Hurricane back across the lines to a forced landing rather than simply shooting him out of the sky. He was still awarded a victory but saw no reason to kill the man. Such honest gallantry was definitely at odds with the popular image of murderous Nazi thugs. Marseille was none of that and steadfastly refused to ever join the National Socialist Party.

Mid-December also saw the British 4th Armored Division try to flank the Germans in the desert south of Tobruk. If they could get around behind the Afrikakorps, then it would be cut off and very likely defeated. With eight operational tanks remaining, Rommel made a fighting retreat due west back to Ajedabia on the Gulf of Sirte. Encamped in defensive positions here, he could rest over the winter and replenish his battered forces. Christmas Day found JG 27 scattered about the Marble Arch area and Hans Marseille leaving the next morning for Athens. Suffering from gastroenteritis, dysentery, jaundice, and malaria, he once again weighed a mere 110 pounds. Jochen would finish 1941 with thirty-six kills, just a few short of the forty victories now required to be awarded the Knight's Cross.

While he was gone, Rommel was reinforced with more tanks and men. Several merchant ships had slipped past the Royal Navy to dock in Tripoli and even into Benghazi before it fell. Nearly fifty tanks made it ashore, followed in January by a hundred more—including some of the new Mark IV panzers. Intelligence and reconnaissance showed a very thin Allied line. Numerous reports of British vehicular breakdowns and severe issues with the 1,000-mile supply line all pointed to an ideal time to counterattack. Rommel did just that. On January 21 his reinforced panzers smashed through and charged north for

Benghazi. He captured this, plus large Allied stockpiles of fuel and trucks, by the end of the month.

By February 3 he'd gotten all the way back to Tmimi but was stopped the next day at the Gazala Line. Stretching southward from the coast, this was a 50-mile line of fortified positions connected by minefields. Rommel had a plan to break through, but he needed his logistics to catch up, and he needed the Luftwaffe. Reconnaissance and tactical air support would be key to breaking through and resuming his drive into Egypt.

Hans Marseille returned to Libya two days later and was back in the air on February 8. After escorting a reconnaissance flight, he was coming in to land at about 0815 when five Hurricanes swept in over Matruba to attack the field. Slapping up the gear and flaps, he jammed the throttle forward and began to fight. What a sight . . . the Bf 109 a few feet off the ground and gaining speed fast as the Hurricanes dropped down, guns firing, to kill him. With tracers flashing past, he kicked the rudder back and forth, skidding the fighter sideways, and racked the 109 up into a spine-cracking left turn.

Unable to hit him and not willing to slow down over an enemy airfield, the first Hurricane overshot. The other four came streaking down the runway heading northwest as Marseille rolled out above them heading southeast. Two thousand feet of altitude isn't much for a dogfight, but everyone watching—and it was the entire fighter wing—saw him roll inverted and slice back to the north after the British fighters. All five Hurricanes cranked up in hard turns to head back over the field, then escape to the south. In an astounding feat of marksmanship—he was at low altitude with a high deflection angle—Jochen opened fire. Across the airfield, the farthest Hurricane burned and pancaked into the desert next to the runway. Without pausing, Marseille kicked the rudder, flicked the stick, and opened fire on a second fighter, which also crashed. Wheeling around, he fired again and hit a third aircraft as three more 109's showed up. The remaining Hurricanes raced south, one of them trailing smoke, toward their lines. And it was over, at least with that enemy on that mission.

But his conflict with his squadron commander was reaching new heights. Despite Marseille's skill in doing the only thing that really mattered at the time, his commander continued hounding him over haircuts, uniforms, and military bearing, in the middle of a war. Earlier in February, the normally good-natured pilot heard that he'd been passed over for promotion. A few weeks before, his sister had been murdered in Vienna, and this, plus the strain of eighteen months of combat, pushed him over the edge, albeit temporarily. Climbing into a plane, he took off, arced around the airfield, and proceeded to strafe the ground beside his commander's tent. Of course the man grounded him and insisted on a court-martial. Under peacetime circumstances he would've been quite correct to preserve order and discipline—but that wasn't the case here. I also don't believe that Marseille was trying to kill him; if he'd wanted the man dead, then he would have been dead. No, it was a warning and a reminder that men with weapons and the skill to use them will only be pushed so far. Marseille was saved again by Eduard Neumann, who knew he was too valuable a fighter pilot to waste.

Now, on February 8, Marseille had claimed his fortieth victim, and even saved his squadron commander's life in the process. This didn't ease the man's anger with Marseille, and he grounded him again after a thorough tongue-lashing. Jochen walked out of the tent, then sat down and talked with the Hurricane pilot who'd crashed on the field that morning. He got his name, Flight Sergeant Hargreaves, and unit location, then calmly took off alone to deliver a mercy message to the man's squadron. When he got back, his commander was speechless with rage, but Neumann intervened once again. He had a long, quiet talk with Marseille, who listened because he respected the man.

A few weeks later, Field Marshal Albert Kesselring landed at Matruba, and on February 24, 1942, Hans-Joachim Marseille received his nation's highest honor for bravery—the Knight's Cross of the Iron Cross. He flew one more mission that month, shooting down a pair of P-40's, then was sent back to Germany for medical treatment—dysentery again.

During March Rommel had been building up across from the Gazala Line. By mid-April, as JG 27 celebrated a year in the desert, he had about 550 tanks with 80,000 men on hand. This would have to suffice, since a great German summer offensive was under way in Russia.* Far away in the Pacific, the carrier USS *Hornet* turned into the wind to launch the Doolittle raid, and Hans Marseille was getting engaged in Berlin.

Rommel planned to launch Operation Venezia in late May with the aim of flanking the Gazala Line, taking Tobruk, and heading to Cairo. The line was anchored 50 miles south at the old Turkish fortress of Bir Hakeim, and it was here that Rommel's punch would hit the hardest. The Italian Ariete Division would assault the fortress while the 15th and 21st Panzers swung around Bir Hakeim to strike behind the line. Rommel knew that the British 1st and 7th Armored Divisions were held in reserve, and he anticipated a huge tank battle east of the Gazala emplacements. His ace in the hole was the 90th Light Afrika Division, which he would personally lead; the division would swing even farther around Bir Hakeim, avoid the tank battle, and head far into the British rear.

Throughout all of this the Luftwaffe would strike with

---

*Case Blue—Operation Fridericus. See page 295.

Stukas and strafing, hitting armored columns and fixed positions. On May 26 the middle of the line was struck hard with artillery and air attacks. This was supposed to decoy the British, and small Afrikakorps units were attached with Italian divisions to complete the illusion. The initial attack was devastating, and the German armored thrust penetrated over 20 miles north behind the British lines. Rommel led the Afrika Division all the way to El Adem, some 30 miles in the rear, by sweeping far to the south and using the Allied minefields to protect his flanks.

From the onset the British generals failed to react well. A defensive mind-set coupled with indecision and commanders who led from the rear compounded the problems. But Rommel had his, too. His supply and logistics situation, always severe, quickly became critical. Until Tobruk could be taken, everything needed to fight had to be brought overland from Benghazi and Tripoli.

Bir Hakeim, stubbornly and bravely defended by the 1st Free French Brigade, did not collapse. This left a fortified enemy position on his flank that could not be ignored. American-built Grant tanks had also arrived, and their 75 mm gun could penetrate German armor at greater range than his panzers' 57 mm weapon. The P-40E, called the Kittyhawk, had also made its appearance. Better armored, it had a slightly improved Allison engine to take the extra weight, but the real improvement was the six .50-caliber wing-mounted machine guns.

The Hurricane went through several upgrades and changes as well, completing its transformation to a primarily fighter bomber role. The Mk IIb variant carried two immense 40 mm cannons in gondola pods and was devastating to German armor. Supermarine had also fielded tropical versions of the Spitfire Mk V that included desert survival kits and better cooling systems.

None of this really slowed down the Luftwaffe, and despite

the lack of spare parts and fuel shortages they still controlled the skies during the Gazala battles. During the late morning of June 3, Marseille, now commanding 3 Staffel, took off with eight Messerschmitts to cover the Stukas attacking Bir Hakeim. The defending Free French brigade was defended by nine Tomahawks from No. 5 Squadron, including three aces. As the Stukas pulled off target the South Africans pounced, never seeing the 109's above them. Marseille dove straight into the middle, breaking up their attack and scattering them. One P-40 began a climbing defensive turn, and Marseille shot it down with a quick burst. Zooming up above the fur ball by a few thousand feet, he booted the plane over on its side and stared down at the fight.

The South Africans were forming into a right-turning defensive wheel, and no doubt Jochen shook his head slightly in disbelief. Immediately rolling over, he dove down and actually *entered* the Lufbery, shooting down a second Tomahawk. Because a 109 could turn tighter than a P-40, he simply cut across the circle a bit, pulled lead, and fired again. Doing this twice, he claimed two more South Africans. In less than eleven minutes he shot down six P-40's using only twelve rounds of 20 mm cannon shells and less than a third of his machine gun ammunition.

It was a new Luftwaffe record, and everyone was astounded. His friend Ludwig Franzisket said, "You really had to see Jochen in combat to really appreciate his gift. I have no idea how he managed the impossible angles, stalls and inverted over the top victories, but he always did this." The day's fighting brought his total kills to seventy-five and added Oak Leaves to his Knight's Cross.*

---

*The Knight's Cross was the German equivalent of the U.S. Medal of Honor or the British Victoria Cross. "Oak Leaves" denote a second award, "Swords" a third, and "Diamonds" a fourth.

Two days later the British Eighth Army finally counterattacked but was stopped by strong German defensive positions. Rommel sucked them into a trap by seemingly collapsing his center, then sending two pincers east and north. Armored units suffered losses of nearly 80 percent, with multiple infantry units overrun and captured. This made Bir Hakeim indefensible, and the French were ordered to evacuate.* In the north British units fell back as far as Tobruk, which surrendered on the twenty-first.

June 1942 was a momentous month. The Wehrmacht was advancing in southern Russia, taking hundreds of thousands of prisoners and closing in on Stalingrad. In the Pacific the Battle of Midway had begun, and it initially appeared to be a stunning Japanese victory over the American navy. For Hans Marseille it meant leaving Libya with 101 kills and orders back to Germany to receive the Swords to his Knight's Cross from Adolf Hitler himself—one of only twelve German officers to receive it.

Ten days later, during lunch at the Wolf's Lair in East Prussia, Goering asked the young hero, "So, you now have what, over a hundred conquests?"

He meant enemy aircraft, but Jochen, sincere or not, replied, "Herr Reichsmarschall, do you mean aircraft or women?"

Goering laughed so hard he nearly choked.

Marseille was then sent around Germany on a quick public relations tour to schools, hospitals, and various veterans' groups. He was also a gifted pianist, and at one of many parties he was asked to perform an impromptu recital for Hitler, Goering, Himmler, and the rest of the Nazi leadership. Mar-

---

*Very ably commanded by Marie-Pierre Kœnig, about 2,700 of the original 3,600 French soldiers slipped through the German lines at night to rejoin the British.

seille obligingly played Chopin and Beethoven for over an hour. Then, with a mischievous smile, he broke into a Scott Joplin jazz number—music specifically banned by Hitler himself! Finally overcoming his shock, the Führer stood and left.

Classic Hans Marseille.

On his way back to Libya he had a stopover in Rome to receive an Italian decoration from Mussolini himself—who apparently told Marseille he should get a haircut. After Jochen's fiancée left for home, he treated himself to a brief fling with a married Italian girl who apparently was one of Mussolini's nieces. The German High Command got a phone call from some very worried and angry Italian officers, but as Marseille was headed back into action, there wasn't much to be done. In any event, he made it to North Africa in late August, resumed command of his squadron, and found that during his eight-week absence Rommel had advanced 300 miles east into Egypt. The Allies had fought a series of delaying actions, wisely abandoning their indefensible positions at Mersa-Matruh. Claude Auchinleck, the British commander, had chosen to fall back on an obscure railway junction barely 60 miles away from the port of Alexandria.

El Alamein was a natural chokepoint between the coast and the Qattara Depression 40 miles to the south. There was no way into Egypt from the west but through here. The Allies constructed three heavily fortified "boxes" connected by minefields and protected by heavily emplaced troops. Two armored divisions were kept in the rear with air cover from the newly reorganized Western Desert Air Force (WDAF). Besides bomber and reconnaissance wings, there were two fighter groups with twenty-five squadrons between them: Hurricanes, Spitfires, and now three U.S. Army Air Forces (USAAF) P-40F squadrons.

The Afrikakorps arrived on June 30 and attacked in the

early morning of July 1, 1942. Using a classic mobile warfare plan, a hole was punched in the Allied line that was to allow pincers to sweep through the British rear. The 90th Light Afrika Division was supposed to swing north and cut the road/railway between El Alamein and Alexandria while the armored thrust cut off the British XIII Corps in the center. Artillery fire and heavy RAF interdiction attacks kept the 90th from reaching the coast. Some 800 to 900 sorties per day were flown and by some estimates cost the Germans 50 percent of their tanks. The battle broke apart into a series of running fights along the ridgelines, leaving both sides exhausted. Rommel, with his dwindling strength and receiving less than 15 percent of his required supplies, dug in and would stay there until the end of August. But Rommel knew he had to move quickly, as America's entry into the war and the increasing flow of Allied reinforcements meant he was on borrowed time.

Auchinleck had been replaced by Lt. Gen. Bernard Montgomery in mid-August, and this time the British were ready. Small, feisty, vain, and unpleasant, "Monty" had fought in the Great War and been shot through the lung by a sniper. He was also a fighting man and just what the confused and demoralized Eighth Army needed at the time. A memo sent out to his men read: "Everyone must be imbued with the desire to kill Germans, even the padres—one for weekdays and two on Sundays."

Under a full moon on August 30 the Germans moved across the minefields into a weakly defended section between Munassib and Himeimat. Rommel's plan was to then head north, behind the Allied positions, and again try to cut the road to Alexandria. But the "Desert Fox" had himself been outfoxed, as this was precisely what Montgomery wanted him to do. The moon made RAF night attacks possible, and they hit the Germans coming through the gap. Rommel lost two of his commanders, one dead and one wounded, but still pushed forward, then wheeled north as planned.

As they approached the Alam Halfa Ridge, Monty sprang his trap. With his tanks generally dug in and supported by artillery with air support, the Afrikakorps was stopped. On August 31, Marseille got airborne for the first time since June and promptly shot down two Hurricanes that were inbound to attack the 15th and 21st Panzer Divisions. Halted for a lack of fuel, most German armor didn't move much during the day. Neither did the British, as they were saving tanks for their forthcoming counteroffensive. During a late-afternoon mission, Jochen tangled with a Spitfire V just east of Alam Halfa and sent him down.

The next morning he was wheels up at 0756 with a total of thirty-five Bf 109's from both JG 27 and JG 53. Escorting Stukas again, they flew east past Ruweisat Ridge toward Alam Halfa. Thirty minutes after takeoff, Marseille found sixteen Hurricanes in a westerly climb, undoubtedly headed for the Afrikakorps panzers. Overflying them by a few thousand feet, he rolled inverted and pulled down hard, ending up heading west himself, below the British fighters and coming up fast.

Closing in from the six o'clock low blind spot, he opened fire from short range. As his target burned and fell away he fired another short burst, and a second Hurricane exploded. The others all broke away defensively, leaving the Germans to hunt at will. Marseille flashed through the sky, banking up hard in order to see behind and above. These were Mk IIc models of the Hurricane, and he must've grinned. The "Hurribomber," as it was called, had four 20 mm cannons plus bombs and was lethal for ground attack. But against a 109 it had no chance.

"Seille . . . break left . . . Indianer six o'clock low!"

Marseille heard the call, booted the rudder, yanked the power back, and dropped his flaps. As he pulled the stick back in his lap, the 109 went into a shuddering turn and nearly skidded to a stop. Unable to slow down or kill the 109 as it virtually stopped in space, a Spitfire streaked past, cranking up on one wing to keep the crazy German in sight. Reacting instantly, Jochen flipped up the flap lever, went to full power, and pulled his nose up. The mental 3-D geometry of lead angles, distance, and speed simply appeared in his mind, so he aimed and fired.

The Spitfire flew right through it. Kill number three for the morning . . . in nine minutes. Five minutes later he caught a straggler and sent another Spitfire into the desert.* When he landed back at Quotaifiya, his armorers found Marseille had used eighteen cannon shells and fewer than 250 machine gun rounds. About an hour later he was back in the air, eastbound toward the battlefield. It was plain to see, rising plumes of black smoke that thinned into gray fingers at altitude. There were yellow orange flashes followed by white puffs as tanks fired, and his eyes caught movement all over the desert floor as hundreds of vehicles scuttled about raising dust plumes.

This time it was eight P-40s that peeled away from the bombers they were protecting to attack the German fighters. Unable to climb to meet the 109s, the Allied fighters went into the standard but risky Wheel formation they loved so much. Not wanting a nose-to-nose pass against six .50-caliber guns, Jochen waited for the circle to form, then dove into the middle of it. He shot down three P-40's in as many minutes, which forced the Wheel apart. Twisting and diving with his head on

*The Hurricane Mk II's came from No. 1 and No. 3 Squadrons SAAF, while the Spitfire Mk VC's belonged to No. 92 Squadron RAF.

a swivel, Marseille accounted for five more P-40's in the next seven minutes. By the time the 109s turned for home, Jochen had sent eight fighters down in ten minutes. This brought his total for the day to twelve with no losses—and the day wasn't over.*

His *Geschwaderkommodore*, Eduard Neumann, was among the first to congratulate him—and also ordered him to sit out the next mission. Soaked with sweat, he drank at least a gallon of water, ate lunch, and fell asleep as only a man who is utterly physically, emotionally, and mentally exhausted can do. Nevertheless, he woke up and recovered for the wing's fourth mission of the day. Leading his eleven fighters over El Imayid, he waded straight into fifteen Hurricanes. Not worried about engaging them head-on, he flamed one before the pass, then did what would later be called a "no-respect lead turn"—basically starting a turn *before* you pass a threat because you know there's nothing he can do about it. This put Marseille directly off the wing of another Hurricane, and he immediately pulled lead, firing from at least a 90-degree deflection angle and sending it spinning down. He got another one after the pass by using his old power and flaps trick to turn inside and shoot. Nosing over with full throttle, Marseille then chased down two more and shot them both down from close range. It was 5:53 p.m., and he'd been fighting for just six minutes.

Hans-Joachim Marseille had just shot down seventeen aircraft in one day of combat.† And they were all fighters, not bombers, nor were they poorly trained Russians. They were British and South African, with at least three Americans. Truly

*The P-40's were from No. 2 and No. 5 Squadrons SAAF.

†This would be surpassed by only one other pilot: another Luftwaffe ace, Emil Lang, on the Eastern Front in 1943.

drained, he was still summoned to the phone to take a congratulatory call from Field Marshal Kesselring and was told that he'd been nominated to receive the Diamonds for his Knight's Cross.

The next day Rommel gave the order to withdraw, and the Afrikakorps fell back to their starting positions southwest of El Alamein. Alam Halfa had cost the Allies 1,800 dead and nearly seventy tanks against about 3,000 Axis casualties and forty-seven tanks. But the Germans had been stopped and Rommel would never again mount a major offensive in North Africa, so Egypt and the Suez Canal were safe.

Hans Marseille alone accounted for over a third of the sixty-eight Allied aircraft lost. For the rest of the month he'd fly another eight missions, and on four of them he'd shoot down anywhere from four to six fighters per mission. On September 7, a few days after the German withdrawal, his best friend, Hans-Arnold Stahlschmidt, was posted as missing and presumed dead. Jochen gave up drinking and became even more solitary, rarely leaving his tent when not flying. But he did come out on the sixteenth to meet with Field Marshal Erwin Rommel himself.

Recently promoted, Marseille at twenty-two was now the youngest *Hauptmann* in the German air force. He and Rommel talked about the war and how they could probably never win now that America had joined in. Marseille voiced his opinion that the Nazis were ridiculous and that captured pilots should be treated honorably. The Desert Fox agreed and said that they were all human beings and honor was a vital code for them to live by. It seemed that two kindred spirits, two gentleman warriors, had a few pleasant moments in each other's company. Rommel would fight on bravely for another few years in Africa, Italy, and France before dying by his own hand.

Hans Marseille would meet another fate.

Taking off in the late morning of September 30, 1942, he headed east toward El Imayid to intercept British fighters that had been spotted in the area. Unable to close with them, the Germans turned back west, and at 11:30 a.m. Marseille radioed in that he had engine trouble. Vapor was trailing from his plane and there was smoke in the cockpit. His flight closed in around him and guided him toward the German lines, which they crossed about six minutes later. Gasping on the radio, he said, "I have to get out now . . . can't stand it anymore . . ."

That was the last thing anyone ever heard him say.

A few minutes later, with less than 2,000 feet of altitude, his wingmen saw the canopy open, then blow off. The stricken Bf 109 pulled up slightly, then rolled over, with Marseille tumbling out through the heavy smoke.

No parachute opened, and he fell to the desert, dying on that last Wednesday morning in September. The 115th Panzergrenadier Regiment was just south of Sidi Rahman that day, and the regimental doctor happened to see the whole thing. He later stated, "The pilot lay on his stomach as if asleep. His arms were hidden beneath his body. As I came closer, I saw a pool of blood that had issued from the side of his crushed skull; brain matter was exposed. I turned the dead pilot over onto his back and opened the zipper of his flight jacket, saw the Knight's Cross with Oak Leaves and Swords [Marseille never actually received the Diamonds personally] and I knew immediately who this was."

The doctor had also found a horrible gash above the hip and across the chest that could've only been caused by striking the horizontal stabilizer. This had either killed Jochen or knocked him out. It was also later discovered that the reduction gear had come apart, severing a hydraulic line and dumping fluid back into the engine. This produced the intense heat and smoke that had forced Marseille to bail out.

His friends came and retrieved his body. They laid him out in a tent and said goodbye in their own ways. The next day he was taken to the German cemetery at Derna and laid to rest.* In a way it was fitting that Marseille died in the same desert where he'd sent so many others and that he, too, would remain there.

Hans-Joachim Marseille was a nonconformist in a police state who refused to surrender his individuality. A man who personally opposed everything the Nazis stood for, yet remained one of Germany's greatest warriors—and this is a distinction worth emphasizing. Most fighter pilots considered that they were fighting for their homes, their families, and the men with them, and in this Jochen was no exception. He fought for Germany, not for National Socialism or Hitler—a truly lethal man who never lost his humanity.

He certainly was an exception in that he flew 482 combat sorties and was credited with 158 victories. All but four of these were fighters, and all were flown by Western pilots. Erich Hartmann, the top ace of all time, and Adolf Galland both regarded Marseille as the very best. He was an extraordinarily gifted pilot, a very complex human being, and truly gallant—the very best word to describe this extraordinary lord of the sky.

The world was a grayer place without him.

PULL!

Back . . . just a bit more . . . a bit more. . .

His feet and hands moved almost at will. He pushed on the

*His remains were later reinterred at Memorial Gardens in Tobruk. There is a one-word epitaph: "Undefeated."

rudder pedals and pulled back on the stick to keep the twisting Yak-1 fighter in the center pane of his windscreen. It was an old trick: get the target in the window, then . . . *There!*

The Soviet fighter was waffling back and forth, out of airspeed. Flicking his wrist, the German pilot's mouth opened slightly and his breathing quickened as the stubby, thick wings filled up the REVI gunsight. Ignoring the dangling oxygen mask, he squinted at the faint orange glowing circle on the reflecting glass. Unconsciously holding his breath, the pilot jabbed down on the firing button atop the stick.

Two . . . three . . .

The Bf 109G, called a "Gustav," shuddered as ninety-six 13 mm shells left his guns. Even as his right thumb came up, the Yak skidded, and the German saw his rounds pass to the side and a little high of the dark green fighter.

"Scheiss!"

Instantly correcting, he watched for a moment, timing his next burst, then fired again. Pieces of wood flew off the Yak as his guns hit the wing and part of the tail. The Russian tried to roll away, but at least a part of the control surfaces was damaged. Jockeying the throttle to hold his range, Erwin Meier grinned and shot again, this time with the *Motorkanone*. Mounted with the engine and firing through the propeller hub, the cannon shook the whole aircraft. It had a slower rate of fire than the MG 131 guns and only coughed out about fifty rounds for the same three-second burst. But the 20 mm shells did horrible damage if they hit. Luftwaffe *experten* like Meier generally used the smaller guns for sighting and damaging a target, then finished up with the cannon, as he was doing now.

Roughly the size of a woman's forearm, the cannon shells nearly destroyed the Yak's rudder. *Not long now. . .*

Suddenly the Gustav rocked sideways like it had been violently kicked. Reacting instantly, he quit firing and slammed the stick left, booting the rudder at the same time. The kicking stopped, and he twisted sideways to look back over his tail.

Another Yak!

Swearing again, Meier flipped the fighter and reversed, trying to throw the Russian off his tail. He'd forgotten a cardinal rule and fixated on his target. In a dogfight you were most likely to get killed by the threat you never saw. *Not this time, Russian,* he thought, whipping his head around to watch the other fighter overshoot and fly past like all the others.

But it didn't.

Scheiss . . . shit! It was still there, hanging off his tail. Just then Erwin Meier, eleven-victory ace, felt his mouth go dry, his heartbeat quicken, and an unfamiliar pang of fear shoot up from his gut. The first Yak was completely forgotten as he fought for his life. He'd seen the Volga pass beneath and knew he was east of the great river running past Stalingrad—on the wrong side. Definitely on the wrong side!

Meier had to get away.

But he couldn't.

He flinched down behind the armor plate as more shells thudded into the 109. A horrible surging, clanking sound filled his ears, and even as the German jinked again, his eyes flickered to the tachometer and oil pressure gauge. Daimler-Benz made a superb engine, and the big DB 605 V-12 was the best he'd had, but it couldn't survive being holed by the Russian's ShVAK cannon. Running rough now, he couldn't see forward because of the smoke, which was rapidly filling the cockpit.

Yanking the throttle back, he groped for the engine instant-stop lever on the left bulkhead and pulled it. At least he wouldn't explode . . . or so he hoped. The controls were still responding, and he tried to turn back west, but the motor gave up. Bitter smoke filled his lungs and he coughed, eyes streaming. Grasping the red release handle on the left rail, he jettisoned the canopy. Blinking furiously against the cold wind, at least he could see to unfasten his belt. The Gustav was burning when he rolled left and tumbled out of the cockpit.

Unbeknownst to Erwin Meier, both Soviet pilots were women. The Yak he'd nearly shot down was flown by Raisa Beliaeva, who'd been on an aerobatics team before the war. The pilot of the other Yak he would meet later that same day.

After floating down east of the Volga with no chance of escape, the German was captured. He asked to meet the man who shot him down, and since they were fairly near the Yak airbase at Verkhnaia Akhtuba, his guards obliged. Much to his shock and dismay, the "man" was a tiny, gray-eyed female who proceeded to describe, in front of all the gathered pilots, how she'd shot down his Messerschmitt.

The girl was beautiful.

Lidiya Vladimirovna "Lilya" Litvyak was just twenty years old on that early fall day in the skies over Stalingrad. She'd been born in Moscow and raised during the dangerous, turbulent Russian Civil War that followed the Great War. In 1922, when she was a year old, the Bolsheviks became Communists and formed the Union of Soviet Socialist Republics (USSR)—the Soviet Union.* Despite the illusion that the new union was a workers' paradise ruled by the proletariat, it was, in fact, controlled by professional revolutionaries who'd never really done a day's work in their lives. With the exception of Lenin, the other prominent leaders weren't even ethnic Russians. Leon Trotsky, born Lev Bronshtein, was a Ukrainian Jew. Felix Dzierżyński was a Pole who would form the dreaded secret police,

*Initially from the Russian, Byelorussian, Transcaucasian, and Ukrainian republics.

the Cheka. Joseph Stalin, the man who would come to personify and symbolize the Soviet Union, was a Georgian.

By the time Lidiya turned six, Stalin had exiled or killed his competition and become the absolute ruler of the Soviet Union. Born Iosif Dzhugashvili, he Russianized his surname to Stalin, meaning "steel." Basically a thug with no trade and no skills, he was also a consummate plotter and politician. Ruthless and stubborn, Stalin had little regard for the lives of the common people under his control. In 1928 he unveiled his economic Five-Year Plan, which would elevate his empire, as he saw it, to its proper place in the world through industrialization. Certainly something was needed; many Russian families were crammed into 100-square-foot apartments in newly created "workers' cities." Literacy had declined to about 25 percent, bread was rationed, and factory output was 10 percent of prewar levels.* So much for paradise.

Agricultural output had fallen so far that famine ensued, adding another 10 million lives to the 9 million lost between 1914 and 1922. Land ownership passed from the nobility to the state, and millions of peasants were now homeless. Most made their way to the big cities, desperate for work. Suddenly the Five-Year Plan could become reality. The first task was to consolidate all resources under the state's (Stalin's) control. Farms became either collectives or directly run by the government. All businesses were nationalized and the middle class, such as it was, eradicated. Private enterprise died, and with it most forms of independent thinking and choices. This was the point—the Soviet Union could only tolerate one icon, and that wasn't a monarch, nobles, a free citizenry, or the church. It was Joseph Stalin.

*Literacy in the United States for the same time was 94 percent.

Liliya did it correctly. She became a Little Octobrist as a child and a member of the Communist Union of Youth (Komsomol) as a teenager. At fourteen she began hanging around the Moscow Flying Club, and she soloed in a U-2 biplane at fifteen. Female aviation legends were making news all over the world. In 1930 Amy Johnson was the first woman to fly solo from England to Australia, making the 11,000-mile flight in a Gipsy Moth. The next year she became the first pilot to fly from London to Moscow in a single day.

May 20, 1932, saw Amelia Earhart take off from Harbour Grace, Newfoundland, to land in Derry, Ireland, nearly fifteen hours later and become the first female to solo across the Atlantic. In 1938 three Soviet women, Valentina Grizodubova, Marina Raskova, and Polina Osipenko, made a 1,500-mile flight from Sevastopol in the Crimea to Arkhangelsk on the White Sea coast. Two months later, in September, the same three became national heroines by setting a 4,000-mile distance record.*

Stalin, who was rarely interested in women, showed considerable interest in Marina Raskova. He was seated next to her at a post-flight celebration banquet, and afterward the two stayed in touch. Raskova was a gorgeous, charismatic woman who'd trained for a career in opera, so perhaps Stalin's attraction isn't so hard to understand. She was frequently seen in his official car or at his country dacha outside Moscow. Sexually involved or not, they maintained a close friendship that would change many lives—Liliya Litvyak's among them.

The early 1930's marked an unprecedented growth in Soviet

---

*They'd planned to fly from Moscow to Komsomolsk on the Pacific Ocean side of the Soviet Union but ditched en route. They were all saved and became the first women decorated as Heroes of the Soviet Union.

military strength and capabilities. Stalin had finally realized that for the Soviet Union to be the world power he envisioned, the existing army of workers and peasants would have to be modernized. The absurd practice of democratically elected "officers" was abolished, military schools were reestablished, and training vastly improved. Modern equipment designs were purchased directly from Walter Christie, the famous American innovator, and would become the basis for the T-34 main battle tank. The Red Air Force had more than 15,000 highly experienced pilots and, just as the Germans had done, used Spain as a proving ground for better fighter designs.

Determined to consolidate his power, Stalin had long conducted political purges. Beginning in 1937, he introduced political commissars into military units. Essentially party hacks, commissars held a command status above that of the commanding officer and could veto any decision made. They also reported to a different chain of command, independent of the Red Army, and their assessments could, and did, prove fatal to many professional officers.

The Red Army alone lost thirteen of its fifteen army commanders, 88 percent of its corps commanders, and more than 80 percent of its divisional commanders to Stalin's paranoia. Some 36,000 officers were removed or executed, including 90 percent of the generals and more than 80 percent of the colonels. The air force in particular was hard hit, losing about 6,000 veteran officers and most of the top remaining aircraft designers. Andrei Tupolev's designs had won seventy-eight world records, yet he was arrested for treason and forced to continue designing from a prison cell. The results were unsurprising. Morale suffered, training often became a matter of form, and equipment obsolesced.

Nevertheless, in 1941 the Soviet military could still field

about 6 million men and more than 200 divisions. Nearly 3.3 million soldiers made up 132 divisions along the frontier with Germany alone. The air force had been organized into the Voenno-Vozdushnye Sily (VVS), which was the military air force of the Soviet Union, and the Protivo-Vozdushnoy Oborony (PVO), in charge of air defense. Though the VVS was committed to expansion, by mid-1941 nearly a quarter of its units were paper squadrons, and the majority of the 11,000 aircraft in the field were hopelessly outclassed. About 2,000 modern fighters such as the Yak-1, MiG-3, and LaGG-3 had been manufactured but had yet to be accepted and delivered to frontline squadrons in substantial numbers.

The aviation regiment (*aviatsionnyi polk*) was the basic element of the VVS. Similar to an RAF wing, it was usually formed by three squadrons (*eskadrilya*), each of which was in turn made up of three flights (*zveno*) of three aircraft each. Situations varied, of course, and by 1943 the Soviets would discard the three-ship group as a basic unit and fly four ships like everyone else.

Even if the aircraft were there, who was to fly them? The purge had taken most of the combat-experienced pilots and higher-ranking officers. Training was inconsistent and largely inadequate. Pilots in the Kiev Special Military District logged an average of four flying hours during the first quarter of 1941. And this wasn't unique—those in the Western Special Military District managed only three hours per pilot per month.

Many hard-core Nazis considered the German invasion of Russia as a true and proper cause, Western civilization against the godless Asiatic Communists. Others saw it as gaining *Lebensraum*—the "living space" of land, agriculture, and resources that the German nation was entitled to take. Others still were simply fighting whomever they were told to fight. Regardless, Hitler left no doubts as to his feelings in a March 30 speech to his generals:

> *The war against Russia will be such that it cannot be conducted in a knightly fashion; the struggle is one of ideologies and racial differences and will have to be conducted with unprecedented, unmerciful and unrelenting harshness. German soldiers guilty of breaking international law . . . will be excused. Russia has not participated in the Hague Convention and therefore has no rights under it.*

In the predawn darkness of Sunday, June 22, 1941, Lilya Litvyak was a carefree geology student in Moscow. Suddenly, hundreds of miles to the west, the sky along the Soviet frontier lit up from the flashes of 42,000 artillery pieces and mortars. While aircraft surged overhead and 3,400 tanks clanked forward, 3.8 million soldiers in three German army groups began their blitzkrieg to the east. More than 90 infantry divisions and motorized divisions, 17 panzer divisions, and some 3,200 combat aircraft slammed into the Red Army along an 1,800-mile front that stretched from the Baltic to the Black Sea.

Army Group Center, with 51 divisions and Luftflotte II, was to drive into the heart of the Soviet Union toward Moscow. Army Group North, with 20 divisions and Luftflotte I, was to capture Leningrad. And Army Group South, with 40 divisions and Luftflotte IV, was to roll over the Ukraine, capturing desperately needed agricultural land before driving east for the Volga River.

When the Germans invaded, Stalin froze. Initially he did nothing, convinced that the attacks were skirmishes designed to provoke him. Communications lines were down or disrupted, so any information Moscow received was likely bad information. Also, the overcentralized system that Stalin himself had insisted upon didn't function without direction from above, which wasn't happening. The result was chaos.

There were only a dozen or so airfields within 25 miles of the western border that could be used for air support, and many of these lacked ammunition, fuel, or adequate anti-aircraft guns. More than forty bases were in various stages of construction and, amazingly, hadn't been put on full war alert. Extensive German photoreconnaissance had revealed these weaknesses, and the hammer blows from the initial strike fully exploited them.

The Luftwaffe attacked in carefully planned waves, using 800 bombers and 500 fighters to strike more than 60 Soviet airfields. Warnings had been issued, troops were to be put on combat-readiness footings, blackouts were to be implemented and aircraft dispersed—but the orders weren't obeyed effectively. So hundreds of aircraft were caught on the ground, lined up in perfect peacetime rows and were summarily destroyed. First-day losses were approximately 1,200 Soviet planes to 63 Germans. By the end of the second day this had risen to 3,922 Red Air Force losses against 78 from the Luftwaffe.

The ground situation was equally unbalanced. The Soviets fell back nearly everywhere, and the Germans had advanced upward of 350 miles by the first week in July. Despite averaging 15 miles per day, with each soldier carrying 50 pounds of equipment, weapons, and supplies, infantry units were far behind the panzers—in some cases by hundreds of miles. The sheer size of the enemy's territory was staggering, and logistics were a nightmare. Despite the growing problems, the Wehrmacht overran Lithuania and Latvia then encircled the strategic linchpin of Minsk, which surrendered on July 9. The following day Army Group North assaulted Leningrad but was stopped two days later along the Luga River defensive belt. Soviet counterattacks also stopped Army Group South around Kiev and Odessa. One month into the war, Hitler changed his strategy and made Leningrad the priority due to its psychological and industrial importance. Generaloberst Hermann Hoth's 3rd Panzers and Guderian's 2nd Panzers were ordered away from Army Group South's push toward Moscow. Guderian was to be sent south toward the Pripet Marshes and Kiev, while Hoth was to drive north to Leningrad. Most German armor units were at half their starting operational strength by this time, and the field commanders knew that time was not on their side. Reminiscent of the confusion during the Battle of Britain, a nineteen-day delay followed, during which Hitler changed his mind, issued conflicting directives, and shifted priorities.

Despite having suffered more than 2 million casualties by this time, the Soviets held on, capitalized on Hitler's vacillation, and began to counterattack where they could. Yet, on August 8, more than 125 He 111 and Ju 88 bombers also attacked Moscow for the first time, dropping 104 tons of bombs and some 50,000 incendiaries on the Soviet capital. By the sixteenth, Stalin had issued his infamous Order 270, which stated that any Russian soldier who surrendered or was captured would be a deserter guilty of treason.* At the end of the month the Germans had cut the Leningrad–Moscow rail line, and the front had evened out except for the Soviet pocket around Kiev. During this time Lilya and others like her were relegated to conventional jobs for women within the Soviet system. More than 60 percent of the doctors in the USSR were women, and by this point almost half of the factory workers were as well.

---

*About 1.5 million former Soviet POWs were put into "filtration" camps after repatriation as a result of surrendering or being captured.

Though they stubbornly gave way, the Soviets were still falling back. In an amazing, though not always orderly, logistical feat, nearly 1,500 factories of all types were disassembled from threatened areas and moved east beyond the Ural Mountains. The vast railway network that moved millions of men west to fight returned east with entire steel, electrical, and chemical factories in pieces. Whole cities, like Tankograd, sprang up to build munitions, aircraft, and tanks.* Eighty percent of Soviet industry was taken out of harm's way in this fashion.

Aware that they were running out of time, the Germans fought on. The Kiev pocket shrank, and by September 16 three Soviet armies were cut off and surrounded. At month's end five entire Soviet armies, some fifty divisions, had been destroyed and more than 600,000 soldiers captured—the largest single amount taken together in history. As the Wehrmacht closed in on Moscow, 3 million Russians had been taken prisoner to date. Leningrad was besieged, Sevastopol cut off. And Lilya Litvyak joined the hundreds of thousands of Muscovites digging trenches.

As September changed to October, Hitler became more obsessed with the capture of Moscow. He felt, and many on the Army General Staff agreed, that if the city fell, then the Soviet Union would collapse. After all, it had worked with the French, so why not the Russians? In retrospect, it was another severe miscalculation—akin to believing that terror-bombing London would break British morale the year before. Operation Typhoon, the assault on Moscow, began on October 2 and was led by Field Marshal Fedor von Bock, Great War veteran and commander during both the Polish and French campaigns. A Prussian aristocrat who spoke French, Russian, and reasonable

* Chelyabinsk.

English, Bock had Army Group Center at his disposal. With three panzer groups and three armies, plus some 550 combat aircraft of Luftflotte II, he planned a double pincer movement to cut off and envelop the city.

But his army had suffered a half million casualties in the ten-week, 400-mile campaign. His remaining men were dirty, infested with lice, and slowly freezing. Newspapers, operations orders, and any other type of paper that could be had was stuffed into uniforms in a pathetic attempt to keep warm. This because Gen. Alfred Jodl, operations chief of the Oberkommando der Wehrmacht (OKW), forbade the issue of winter clothing because that conflicted with his guarantees that the Soviet Union would be subdued by winter. Supply wagons had long since broken down and had been replaced by Russian farm carts pulled by horses. Cold, sick, and short of supplies, the Germans attacked nevertheless.

But the snow began to fall on October 6, just as it had on Napoleon 129 years before. The *rasputitsa,* the "time of no roads," had come. When the snow melted, the hard-packed countryside, which was so ideal for tanks, turned into a muddy quagmire up to three feet deep that would not harden again until after the frosts. Low clouds and poor visibility made air support problematic. On October 8, as the panzers circled north and south of the city, a desperate People's Commissariat of Defense (under Stalin's direct order) established the 122nd Aviation Group—the first all-female combat aviation unit in history. It was to be commanded by Marina Raskova, and she was to choose her own pilots.

Three regiments would be formed: the 586th (Fighter), 587th (Bomber), and 588th (Night Bomber). But by the fifteenth, the lead German tank units were threatening Moscow and the 122nd was evacuated to Engels, about 400 miles southeast down the Volga River. Here they settled into military life and the world of combat aviation. Haircuts were given, uniforms were cut down to fit, but the women could do nothing about the huge winter boots. The reception from male Soviet officers was varied. Many didn't care—a body that could pull a trigger or fly a plane was welcome, no matter what the shape. Some were outwardly hostile and offended that a woman thought she could equal a man on a battlefield. Most were undecided, feeling that time would tell whether the girls, as they were called, could cut it.

The girls were educated, literate, and accomplished. They were musicians, poets, and generally graduates of an institute or university. Based on aptitude, prior records, and performance, they were divided into three categories: pilots, navigators, and administrative/other. Lilya, like Marina Raskova, was an accomplished aerobatic flyer, so she made the selection into fighters. Basic flying was taught to those with no previous experience, but there was no formation or gunnery training. This was all done in an open-cockpit Po-2 biplane during the Russian winter.

While the aviators froze, the Soviet defenders of Moscow fought. Guderian's 2nd Panzer Group swung southeast around Moscow toward Orel but ran into heavy resistance from the 1st Guards Rifle Corps. The "Guards" title had been resurrected from the old tsarist Imperial Army days by Stalin to denote those units who had fought with special tenacity and bravery. During the 1917 Revolution, Guards officers had the skin flayed from their hands by the vengeful masses in a mockery of the white gloves they wore. The irony was no doubt lost on Stalin.

Soviet army groups were organized into fronts and given geographic areas. Until now, VVS units were assigned to a front and placed under direct control of the army commander. The newly created Bryansk Front filled the gap between the Western Front around Moscow and the Southwestern Front east of Orel. Together all three fronts could muster seven hundred fighters from both frontal and PVO squadrons. Command-and-control being as spotty as it was, the Western Front VVS commander also concentrated all air assets in his region under his direct control.

The VVS was painfully aware that it needed a far more responsive and efficient system if they were to beat the Luftwaffe. Eliminating interference from the army commanders was a positive step, as was concentrating the several fighter regiments on the Central Aerodrome in Moscow. With hangars, maintenance facilities, and relatively easy access to spare parts and munitions, the field was only minutes away from the action. Pilots could, and did, fly four to five combat sorties per day. As Von Hardesty aptly observes in *Red Phoenix Rising*, "For three months the Soviets had traded geography for time. Time was now short."

The Mozhaisk Line was a rough defensive perimeter about 40 miles beyond the city, running from the Oka River in the south to the Sea of Moscow in the north. Covering this position, the Red Air Force was flying some four hundred sorties per day to stem the German advance. In contrast, the Luftwaffe was managing at least a thousand sorties per day, often more, and shooting down hundreds of Soviet aircraft. The Ilyushin IL-2, hopeless as a dogfighter, was proving itself a very capable ground attack aircraft. Called the Shturmovik (Storm Bird), the IL-2 was a 13,000-pound monster that actually had armor built into the structure in key places rather than plated over. It was so heavy that it carried relatively light bomb loads and could only manage 250 knots at best. But it was difficult to shoot down, and more than 43,000 of them would roll off the lines, making the IL-2 the most produced aircraft in history.*

Anna Yegorova was barely twenty-five years old during the Battle of Moscow. She'd been a prewar pilot and had been accepted to fly air transport aircraft and liaison aircraft. Shot down one day while carrying a message to the front, she evaded the strafing German fighter, then walked the rest of the way to deliver her message. Transferring to the Shturmovik, she became part of the all-male 805th Ground Attack Regiment and went on to fly more than 250 combat missions. Shot down again near Warsaw in 1944, Yegorova bailed out; she caught fire on the way, and her parachute didn't fully open. Barely alive, she was put in Stalag III-C, near Kustrin on the Polish border. She survived until liberation in 1945, when her immediate reward for her sacrifice and service was a Soviet filtration camp and interrogation. Eventually released, Anna Yegorova was invalided out of the military and permitted to remain a Hero of the Soviet Union.

Also surprisingly lethal were the Po-2 biplanes—if flown at night. One of the most successful units was the all-female 588th Night Bomber Regiment, flying some 23,000 combat sorties during the course of the war. They were nicknamed the "Nachthexen" (Night Witches), and the Germans hated them. In their miserable open-cockpit biplanes, the Witches would cut their engines and glide down silently on the enemy positions. Often the only warning given was the wind whistling through the struts or sudden, violent bomb blasts.

Some of these pilots were teenagers—the youngest was only seventeen—yet they often flew a dozen combat missions in a single night. One of the pilots would later recall, "You have to

*Including variants and its successor—the IL-10.

understand the German mentality . . . you are supposed to sleep at night; this is *Ordnung*, order, something sacred for the Germans. But we Russians didn't follow the rules. And suddenly in the middle of the night, we would disrupt their sleep with the sound of our propellers. The Germans went straight out of their minds."

But despite Marshal Zhukov's best efforts, the Germans still broke through the Mozhaisk Line, forcing the Soviets east across the Nara River. The situation in Moscow was desperate as food ran out, air attacks continued, and casualties mounted. There were fewer than 500,000 soldiers and 1,000 tanks, but the Germans were suffering horribly from hunger, a lack of winter clothing, and especially a shortage of fuel. Wehrmacht infantry divisions were fortunate if they had half their effective strength, and the German tanks were in worse shape—so bad that Guderian's Second Panzer Army finally lurched to a halt within sight of the city on October 29, 1941.

For two weeks both sides gasped for breath, bandaged their wounds, and tried to keep warm. While the Soviets hurriedly reinforced Moscow with anything possible, the Germans tried to straighten out their immense logistical mess. By November 15 the Wehrmacht was ready for one final assault, and the muddy ground had frozen hard enough to support tanks. In the center of the three-pronged attack, panzers captured a bridgehead over the Moscow–Volga canal and the Germans crossed. However, Kuznetsov's First Shock Army, consisting of some six rifles brigades, an infantry division, and several tank battalions, savagely countered and forced the Germans back across the bridgehead.

Guderian came up from the south and managed to get as far as Kashira by November 26. But Major General Nikolay Belov's 2nd Cavalry Corps countered with everything remaining and stopped the Germans. By December 9 the Orel–Tula railway was under threat, and Guderian stopped advancing to protect his principal source of supply. From the north the Third Panzer Army took Klin, and some units advanced to within 12 miles of Moscow before they halted. A reconnaissance unit seized the railway station at Khimki, five miles west of the city and the farthest advance of the Wehrmacht during the campaign.

With the temperature now below –30° F, there was no real hope of capturing Moscow. More than a hundred thousand cases of frostbite afflicted the exhausted Germans, and several thousand amputations were performed. Added to this, the Red Army had been reinforced by at least a dozen divisions, more than a thousand tanks, and nearly fifteen hundred aircraft from their Siberian forces. Stalin had delayed the transfer for six weeks, fearing a Japanese attack from Manchuria, but the top Soviet spy, Richard Sorge, informed the Kremlin that there would be no attack until Moscow was taken.* He also revealed that Tokyo had other intentions for immediate military action, and on December 7, 1941, this was proven true at Pearl Harbor. If the Japanese had attacked the Soviet Union instead of the United States, there would have been reinforcement possible, and Moscow likely would have been lost to the Germans.

Despite Hitler's insistence that they hold their ground, the Wehrmacht withdrew west of the Oka River by December 15 and began receiving the winter equipment long delayed in Poland. Several generals, including Guderian and the army commander in chief, were fired. Hitler ranted, but it didn't change the situation, and by Christmas 1941 the strengthened Red Army took back the majority of lost ground around Moscow. As the year

---

*Sorge had also warned Stalin that the Germans would invade on June 22. Ian Fleming called Sorge the Soviet James Bond.

turned, the front stabilized, with Army Group North dug in around Leningrad, Army Group South besieging Sevastopol and approaching Rostov, and Army Group Center holding west of Moscow.

That same month, January 1942, saw Lilya Litvyak among the first pilots (and the only female) to train on the new Yak-1 fighter. Capable of 400 mph, armed with a ShVAK 20 mm cannon and two machine guns, it was versatile, fast, and tough. The training base at Engels was just across the Volga from Saratov, and in April, following their conversion to the Yak, the 586th Fighter Regiment became part of the PVO at Saratov, now an important industrial city.*

Typical of fighter bases, there was much drinking, dancing, singing, and socializing. This was, and is, all common enough among those who have a very good chance of not living to see their next birthday. Lilya was especially welcome, as she was extremely pretty and apparently had a very pronounced effect on men. One of her stock answers to the hordes of smitten men was, "Let's get the fighting over with first, darling—then maybe we can think about love, eh?"

While Lilya was learning the tactics of Luftwaffe Messerschmitts and developing countertactics against her lovesick male comrades, Adolf Hitler issued Führer Directive 41, which stated bluntly: "Our aim is to wipe out the entire defense potential remaining to the Soviets, and to cut them off, as far as possible, from their most important centers of war industry . . . with the aim of destroying the enemy . . . in order to secure the Caucasian oilfields."

---

*Another ironic twist, as Engels had been the capital of the Volga German Republic—an autonomous concentration of German immigrants established in the 1920's to encourage agricultural development.

By early May, as the ground hardened, the panzers were moving east again. Operation Fridericus, the master stroke for finally dealing with the Soviet Union, was under way. It caught the Russians by surprise, as Stalin felt that Moscow would be the target of any German spring offensive. Hitler's plan was for Army Group South to thrust east toward the Volga, then south into the Caucasus Mountains between the Black and Caspian Seas. Fifty mixed divisions of Hungarians, Romanians, Italians, and even a Spanish unit combined with six German motorized infantry divisions and nine panzer divisions for the main thrust. The plan was to take advantage of the summer weather and make spectacular penetrations south and east through the richest areas of the Soviet Union. This would catch Stalin off balance and cripple him economically. Once the south was secure, then the necessary forces would redeploy in the north to finish off Moscow and Leningrad.

It was a perfectly plausible plan, except for the German habit of underestimation. First was the miscalculation of the immenseness of the Soviet Union. The sheer distances involved, and the corresponding logistical problems, were staggering. Army Group South was already some 1,500 miles from the Rhineland, and local supply lines were hundreds of miles long. Ammunition, spare parts, and especially fuel were all in short supply. The other critical underestimation concerned Soviet tenacity. Stalin had been persuaded to modify his illogical stand on surrender, and as a result, many Red Army units were able to withdraw to fight another day.

Nevertheless, the campaign started well, as most Wehrmacht actions did. When the Russians counterattacked from Kharkov, the First Panzer Army punched through and encircled the city. By early June more than 225,000 Soviet prisoners had been taken and some 1,200 tanks destroyed. Fearing a flank assault, the German High Command then made a momentous mistake and split the force. Army Group A continued south across the Don River into the Black Sea region. The goal was to destroy the four Soviet armies that were fleeing in that direction, seize the Maikop oil fields, and capture the port of Tuapse. Army Group B, composed of Generaloberst Freidrich Paulus's Sixth Army and Hoth's Fourth Panzer Army, would charge due east. They were to cross the great bend of the Don River and head for a city on the Volga that was the key to the whole region, an ancient city with a new name.

Stalingrad—and it would change history.

LILYA LITVYAK FLEW her Yak-1 into hell over the Volga on September 10, 1942. She and eight others were transferred from the PVO to the 437th Fighter Regiment out of Verkhnaia Akhtuba, south of the city. The reception from their male counterparts wasn't the best, as the battle hadn't become desperate—yet. Mechanics didn't want to service planes flown by women, and one male pilot even refused to fly a Yak that had been preflighted by "one of those girls." The regiment commander, Maj. M. S. Khostnikov, supposedly shook his head and said, "We're waiting for real pilots and they sent us a bunch of girls."

The attitude is understandable. Stalingrad was slowly being encircled on the west side of the river, no real help was in sight, and the odds were terrible. Since the German Sixth Army had arrived on August 23, more than two hundred VVS aircraft had been lost. Among other foes, the VVS was also facing the renowned Ace of Spades pilots (*Pik As*) from JG 53. The wing was part of the big assault, and Erwin Meier was flying with 2 Staffel when he met Lilya Litvyak over Stalingrad on September 13.

Veterans from Spain, the Battle for France, and the Battle

of Britain, the *Pik As* were hardened fighter pilots. During the Battle of Britain Goering discovered that the wife of the *Geschwaderkommodore,* Major Hans-Jürgen von Cramon-Taubadel, had distant Jewish ancestry. Goering made the entire wing remove their Ace of Spades emblem and replace it with a red band around the nose of each aircraft. After their commander was removed, the pilots retaliated by immediately painting over the swastikas on the tails. They were typically hard-fighting, irreverent, and unafraid of the Nazi hierarchy, or anything else, for that matter. One month into Barbarossa, the wing had shot down its one thousandth enemy aircraft.

But the Russians were fighting back—hard. As the German 16th Panzers crunched over the rubble on the outskirts of the city, they ran into the 1077th Anti-Aircraft Regiment. Though effective against aircraft, the 37 mm guns had a tough time with the extra armor plates carried on most Panzer III/IV tanks. After knocking out all the guns, the Germans were shocked to find they'd been fighting teenage girls. The twin thrusts were largely successful, and by mid-November Paulus had advanced to the Volga shore and controlled nine-tenths of Stalingrad.

It was over a year now since Barbarossa had ground to a halt, and once again winter threatened the Germans. Low clouds, fog, and killing temperatures made most flying difficult if not impossible. Luftflotte IV managed about 1,500 daily sorties but had lost at least 40 percent of its operational aircraft, and the strength of the Sixth Army had fallen by half. The VVS decided to form the 9th Guards Fighter Regiment, an elite unit composed solely of veterans and aces. Commanded by Lev Shestakov, the leading Soviet ace from Spain, the 9th was supposed to do battle with famous German units such as JG 52 and JG 53.

Apparently Shestakov wanted Lilya Litvyak and Katya Budanova in his regiment, given their blossoming reputations. "Watch out for the girls," he told his male pilots. "And don't offend them. They fly excellently and they have already killed some Fritzes." By this time prewar prejudices had disappeared and all that mattered was a pilot's ability to kill the enemy and not his (or her) comrades. This attitude was shared by most Russians, and in an eerie parallel to Hitler's Nazi ranting, the Russians were told, "If you have not killed at least one German a day you have wasted that day. If you leave a German alive, the German will hang a Russian and rape a Russian woman. Kill the German."*

By mid-November the snow was falling. The Volga had frozen, making transport of men and ammunition somewhat easier, and the Soviets did the unexpected—they counterattacked with Operation Uranus at 7:20 a.m. on November 19, 1942. Spearheaded by the 1st Guards Tank Army, the Soviet Southwest Front slammed into the Romanian forces on the German left following an eighty-minute artillery barrage.

As their northern flank collapsed, the German 48th Panzer Corps tried to stem the Russian armored assault, but with less than a hundred tanks, it just wasn't possible. The Stalingrad Front launched its southern attack at 8:00 a.m. the next morning. The Romanian 6th Cavalry Corps crumbled, and the 29th Panzer Grenadiers counterattacked. But with "allies" being routed on all sides, the Germans had to fall back to escape annihilation.

At the end of four days the northern pincer rolled through 90 miles to enter Kalach, due west of the city and *behind* the German lines. The southern arm of the trap closed nearby at Sovetskiy. It was November 23, and 300,000 Germans from the Sixth Army and 4th Panzers were cut off inside Stalingrad.

---

*Ilya Ehrenberg, a well-known war correspondent.

Hitler utterly refused to permit the Sixth Army to break out to the west. Stalingrad, though an important strategic objective, was a vital psychological one as well. Not only did it bear his archrival's name, but it had also been the launching point of Stalin's career. No, the Sixth Army would hold until a relief force could break the cordon around Stalingrad. Until von Manstein's Army Group Don arrived, they would be supplied by the Luftwaffe—after all, Goering promised it could be done. However, this was the same man who had sworn to conquer the RAF and stated in 1939 that "no enemy bomber can reach the Ruhr. If one reaches the Ruhr, my name is not Goering. You may call me Meyer."

Goering was in Bavaria on November 22 and, after assuring Hitler that the airlift could be done, left to visit Parisian art galleries. Von Richthofen was astounded. He had less than fifty Ju 52's on hand—not even a tenth of those required. An airlift would need to provide a bare minimum of 350 tons of supplies per day for the beleaguered Sixth Army to hold. A single Ju 52 transport was supposed to hold 2 tons of freight, but even that wasn't quite correct.

This was based on the "1,000 kg" labels fixed to standard Luftwaffe containers, which turned out to indicate only the bomb rack used to hold them. The actual load was about two-thirds of that, or 660 kilograms. So each Junker could manage about 2,600 pounds instead of the 2 tons used for planning. This meant that 270 flights delivering 350 tons would have to land *each* day to keep the army alive. Also, not every day was a flying day, due to the horrible winter weather. Generaloberst Kurt Zeitzler, the army chief of staff and an Eastern Front veteran himself, was aware of this and the flaws in Goering's math. A daily delivery of some 500 tons would be needed to take up the slack.

Under forward-area combat conditions, operational readiness for transports was 30 to 40 percent at best. Several hundred Ju 52's would be required to meet the need, but there were just forty-seven on hand. This was during a time when the German air force was heavily committed in North Africa and the yearly Ju 52 production was about five hundred aircraft. Even with available He 111's and Ju 88's, it wasn't enough, and every Luftwaffe officer from von Richthofen down knew the airlift was hopeless. Even when aircraft managed to land, sometimes it didn't help. One day 20 tons of vodka and bales of summer uniforms were delivered. Another aircraft arrived loaded with pepper and other spices.

On November 27 an angry Zeitzler had the courage to call Goering a liar to his face, and in front of Hitler. Yet despite the odds, they tried and managed about 80 tons per day even with a resurgent VVS prowling the skies. And the VVS was expanding and strengthening. More than 35,000 sorties would be flown during the battle for Stalingrad and, according to Soviet sources, 1,100 German aircraft would be shot down.*

The Red Air Force had successfully adapted to the situations they faced, taking from the Luftwaffe some tactics while inventing others themselves. Three-ship groupings were generally a thing of the past; like the British before them, the VVS now flew a four-ship *zveno* flight, which could be divided into the two-ship *para* if needed. They also utilized the *okhotniki,* or "free hunt," copied from the German *jagd frei,* or "roving fighters."

Others were uniquely Russian. The *taran,* or "ramming attack," was performed by VVS pilots on many occasions. The

---

*German sources admit to 488. As with most wartime figures the truth probably lies in between.

first recorded use was by a Russian named Nesterov in 1914 over the Ukraine—he didn't survive, and neither did his target.

There were different ways to do it. Ideally, you'd get close enough behind the other fighter to chew up its horizontal tail or rudder with your prop. If you were lucky, your plane was still flyable and you might make it back. Clipping the wing with your own was also possible. Some I-16's were modified with a beefed-up wing structure to make this more possible. Or, as a final option, you could simply dive straight into the other plane. The likelihood of living through that was next to nothing. It's estimated that more than five hundred *taran* attacks were made by the VVS during World War II.

Sokoliny udar, the "falcon blow," looked similar from the victim's point of view, but it wasn't a ram. It was a full-throttle, stick-in-the-lap move into the vertical. This very suddenly traded airspeed for altitude, and if the threat was close or didn't have the airspeed to follow, the idea was to roll back down and end up behind him as he flashed past.

So at this time, in late 1942 and early 1943, the ground situation gave the VVS enough of a breather to begin reconstitution. Though they'd suffered horrible losses, the Red air force didn't suffer from manpower potential nor from a crucial shortage of equipment. Logistics was easier in many respects given the local nature of the defense. Also, the factories that had moved to the Urals were beginning to produce again, and Lend-Lease deliveries, which would eventually total some 15,000 aircraft, were arriving in Russia.

So while Goering gathered art on the Seine, the last Axis soldiers limped over the Don River bridges into Stalingrad and blew up the bridges behind them. All through December men fought and died. And they starved. First they ate their transport horses. Then birds, dogs, and rats. Lastly they ate each other.

Soviet units recaptured all the airfields by the third week in January and the airlift, such as it was, ended.

On February 1, following 199 days of fighting and 2 million casualties on both sides, Paulus surrendered what remained of the Sixth Army. Just over 91,000 men and 22 generals were marched off to oblivion; fewer than 6,000 would return home ten years later. Hitler had promoted Paulus to *Generalfeldmarschall* on January 30 assuming that he would fight to the death or commit suicide, as no German officer of that rank had ever capitulated. Paulus chose life and said, "I have no intention of shooting myself for that Bavarian corporal."

TEN DAYS AFTER the Sixth Army surrendered, Lilya was back in action over the frozen earth west of Stalingrad. As Marshal Zhukov tried to push the Germans west, Stukas and fighter bombers continuously attacked his tanks. She shot down a Stuka on February 11, then, later that same day, ran into the newly fielded Focke-Wulf 190 fighter. February also brought Lilya an officer's commission, to *mladshii leitenant* (junior lieutenant), and a promotion to flight lead. So Litvyak now had a wingman of her own. With her recognition and acceptance from the male fighter pilots came a very distinctive self-confidence. She painted a white flower on the side of her Yak and through it became known as the "White Rose of Stalingrad."* By the end of March she'd added a bomber, another Fw 190, and an Me 109G to her tally. In one nasty fight on March 22, she was shot up by two Me 109G-6's from JG 3. These had 1,400-horsepower DB 605 engines, with even-numbered variants (such as the G-6) unpressurized and upgraded with a

*It was actually a lily, not a rose, from her nickname of "Lilya."

new 30 mm cannon. She shot one of them down and was saved by her wingmen from the other. Badly wounded, Lilya barely landed but had to be pulled from the cockpit.

Sent to Moscow to recover, she remained there until May. Promoted now to senior lieutenant, she returned to the 73rd Guards Fighter Aviation Regiment in early May. During an escort mission on May 5 she hammered a Messerschmitt to pieces, and a second one two days later. The time off had not dulled her reflexes or her marksmanship. Nor had it diminished another issue she had to deal with. Fighter pilots falling in love with each other had never been a problem, for obvious reasons, but when one of them happens to be a beautiful young girl, with long blond hair and gray eyes . . .

So it was for Alexei Solomatin. He'd flown with Lilya, and they'd become close, with a bond only combat can give. But he'd also fallen in love with her, and in all likelihood she felt the same. Yet with so much to overcome and so much to prove, she never openly allowed her feelings to show. Perhaps she gave in to the adoring young fighter pilot; perhaps not. She never revealed it, and Solomatin was killed three weeks after her return. She was never really the same again.

Her white-hot rage coincided perfectly with the beginning of the last great German offensive in Russia—Operation Citadel. Designed to eliminate the Kursk salient, straighten the German line, and improve the Wehrmacht's defensive positions, Citadel had been planned back in April 1943.

The VVS knew the attack would come on July 5, but not the precise time or location. So they boldly decided to attack preemptively and throw the Wehrmacht timeline into confusion. More than three hundred aircraft took part in the raid, but they were detected 80 miles out by German radar. Messerschmitts from JG 52 and JG 3 lifted off and hit the Soviets just as they were making their initial attacks, and more than a hundred VVS aircraft went down.

The Ninth Army began its pincer from Orel, north of the salient, as the 4th Panzer Army stabbed upward from the Kharkov area. More than 3,000 German tanks, including the new Panthers and Tigers, sliced into the Russian positions. Hitler had purposely delayed the offensive until his new tanks were ready, thinking they would be decisive. Unfortunately, the delay also gave the Soviets time to prepare 3,000 miles of trenches and lay nearly a half million mines. There were also over a million Russian troops with 3,600 tanks to oppose the Germans. The VVS could muster about 2,500 combat aircraft, of which half were fighters.

For a week both sides slugged it out. The Soviets, and in particular the VVS, took frightful losses. One estimate puts fighter losses at over 50 percent and ground attack aircraft down by a third. This again revealed Russian weaknesses in aircraft and especially in pilots. Numerically the VVS exceeded the Luftwaffe, by five to one in some cases, but pilot experience levels were vastly different, and it showed. JG 52 passed the 6,000-kill mark when Operation Citadel began. Bubi Hartmann, Gerd Barkhorn, and Günther Rall, the top three aces of all time, were part of this extraordinary fighter wing. Six of the fifteen top Luftwaffe aces flew with JG 52 and between them accounted for 1,580 aircraft.*

The Red Air Force had its ringers as well. Ivan Kozhedub ended the war as the top Allied ace, with sixty-four confirmed kills. Sasha Pokryshkin, a Siberian peasant who emerged as the top tactician of the VVS, was right behind him. Pokryshkin

---

*By the end of the war nearly 10,000 kills would be credited to JG 52—enough to fill 50 Allied squadrons.

pioneered a layered defense based on aircraft type. This type of "fighter stack" had been used by the Germans on the Western Front during the Great War and was adapted by both Mölders and Galland during the Battle of Britain. Pokryshkin's talent, other than killing, was defying conventional VVS and Russian dogma by thinking for himself. Just as the RAF's Hugh Dowding could see the value of radar, early warning, and radio-controlled intercepts, so too could Pokryshkin.

Three times a Hero of the Soviet Union, an honor he shared with Ivan Kozhedub, Sasha almost certainly had a higher number of actual kills than Kozhedub. At least a dozen of his earliest weren't credited to him, and he often gave his victories away to pilots who had been killed. This passed on the government-supplied bonus to the dead pilots' families and gave them some measure of support. Phenomenal aviator that he was, Sasha Pokryshkin was forbidden to fly after the summer of 1944 for fear that his death would devastate Soviet morale. Both Russian aces, like Hartmann, Barkhorn, and Rall, would survive the war.*

On July 12 Operation Citadel came to a head in an immense tank battle outside Prokhorovka, about 40 miles southeast of Kursk. The II SS Panzer Corps had been advancing north from the Belgorad area when several Soviet armies were thrown against them. More than a thousand tanks engaged, and at the end of the long, bloody day the German thrust had been halted. To be stopped in this, their last great offensive, meant time was running out for the Wehrmacht.

It was also running out for Lilya Litvyak. On July 16 she

*Pokryshkin was blunt, honest, and as apolitical as one could be in the Soviet Union. Despite his heroism and sacrifices he was largely passed over following the war because he had once stated that he preferred to fly non-Soviet aircraft.

ran up against a fifty-three-victory ace named Hans Grünberg. Pouncing on a formation of thirty Ju-88s near Luhansk, she'd shot one down when Grunberg jumped her. He'd already accounted for two Yaks that day and knew exactly who was flying this particular Russian fighter with the white flower painted on the side. Big 30 mm shells had ripped into her plane, but Lilya managed to slip and slide away from a lethal hit. Sometime during the joust the German overshot and Lilya repositioned, rolling around behind the Messerschmitt. Hosing off bursts from her own 20 mm cannon, she was able to watch him ditch the fighter.

Three days later she wasn't so lucky. Her wingman went down when they were attacked by at least eight 109s. Crashing, gear up, into a farmer's field behind enemy lines, Lilya thought her war was over. If she surrendered, she knew, she could never go home again due to Stalin's Order 270, and her family would also be thrown into prison. If she fought back against the approaching German infantry she would certainly die. But just then a dirty green Shturmovik dropped out of the sky and bounced in for a landing, and the pilot threw open the cockpit. Hobbling across the field, clutching her leg, Lilya made it to the plane. The pilot hauled her inside, goosed the power, and slammed the canopy shut as they staggered back into the air.

So many close calls normally means your bag of luck is empty. If possible, pilots go on leave or stay on the ground until the ominous signs pass. This couldn't be done when every experienced pilot was needed to fight the still very formidable Luftwaffe—not that Lilya would've done it anyway.

On August 1, 1943, Lilya Litvyak took off from her airfield near Krasny Luch in southeastern Ukraine. Her first two sorties involved escorting Shturmoviks to attack German positions to the west. The third time up, in late morning, she shot down a

109G and shared a second kill on another. Around noon, she took off on her fourth mission of the day, to intercept a large formation of Ju 88s crossing the lines heading east.

Weather had been building from the noonday heat; like a field of mushrooms, the big, puffy clouds reflected sunlight bounced from the edges. Yellow beams slanted into countless shifting canyons, as the dark green Russian fighter sliced down to line up on the bombers. The tired, wounded pilot never saw two of the escorting Messerschmitts roll inverted and dive at her.

Orange tracers arced across the sky as nearly fifty aircraft swirled, twisted, and killed each other. Lilya's wingman, Ivan Borisenko, was fighting for his own life, but he caught a glimpse of her turning back toward the Germans. As the three fighters clawed at each other they fell into the clouds and disappeared. As fast as it had begun it was over, and the survivors limped home, Borisenko among them.

But not Lilya.

Hours went by and the ground crews waited. Waited until night fell and the stars came out. Waited for word from somewhere that she'd bailed out or landed. But there was nothing. It was her 168th combat mission, and she never came back.

Thirty-six years later, in 1979, villagers near the town of Dmytrivka discovered the skeleton of a small woman. From the gold fillings in the teeth, the Soviet government identified the remains as those of Lidiya Vladirmirovna Litvyak. Eleven years later, during a celebration of the forty-fifth anniversary of World War II, the last premier of Stalin's Communist Russia awarded Lilya a medal—she was at last a Hero of the Soviet Union.

Many people, experts and friends alike, don't believe that she died that afternoon over the Ukraine. One very plausible theory is that she collided with, or rammed, one of the attacking Messerschmitts. Luftwaffe records confirm that Hans-Jorg Merkle, a twenty-nine-victory ace from JG 52, was credited with a kill against a Yak-1b on August 1, 1943, in the same area in which Lilya vanished. One of the surviving Germans also stated that Merkle had been rammed. In any event, he didn't survive. Whether she rammed the Messerschmitt or her plane was too badly damaged to make it back, Lilya very well could've survived only to find herself behind the German lines again, and this time she was captured. Dr. Kazimiera Cottam, an expert on Soviet female combat veterans, is certain Lilya survived. If she'd been captured, then knowing what awaited her in Russia after the war may have convinced her that there was no going back. She would've faced a filtration camp, or worse, as would her family. Maybe, she thought, it was better to have them think she was dead, her reputation untarnished and her family safe.

Cottam also wrote that "Russian television featured a broadcast from Switzerland during which a correspondent introduced a former Soviet woman World War II pilot, a mother of three children who was twice wounded during the war and resided abroad since the war." On a practical note, the village of Dmytrivka, where her remains were "discovered," is more than 50 miles northwest of where Lilya's final dogfight occurred. This was the wrong direction for a pilot trying to land a damaged plane, and she would have known that.

Lilya Litvyak may or may not have died that day in August 1943. Regardless of her end, in the end the White Rose of Stalingrad, and her legacy as an extraordinary fighter pilot, live on forever.

CHAPTER 10

MEATBALLS AND FLATTOPS

MITSUBISHI A6M ZERO

"WHUMP . . . WHUMP . . . whump . . . whump . . ."

The pilot's eyes opened, red and unfocused, as the explosions jarred his teeth together.

"What the . . . ?"

Rolling upright, he blinked against the light slanting in through a crack in the curtains. Dust particles hung suspended in space, and he swallowed, his tongue furry and thick.

"Whump . . . whump . . ."

A glass of water bounded off the nightstand and shattered on the floor. He blinked again, lids scraping painfully over his dry eyes. God, but his mouth tasted horrible!

"Tukka tukka tukka tukka . . ."

That got him moving. On a military base, explosions could have a number of different causes, but a machine-gun burst?

Groping for his pants, he tugged on a shirt and jammed on a pair of shoes.

There was screaming and yelling from outside now. Yanking open the door, Ken Taylor immediately shut one eye and held up a hand against the early-morning glare. The roar of aircraft engines floated over the trees, and a siren was wailing somewhere.

"Tukka tukka tukka . . ."

"Bastards actually did it!"

Taylor turned and saw his friend George Welch staring toward the plumes of smoke over the Wheeler Army Airfield flight line. Both men were wearing khaki uniform shirts over the tuxedo pants they'd had on the night before at the Officers' Club. Neither noticed or cared.

"Son of a bitch . . ."

Japs.

Welch meant the Japanese had really done it. They were attacking. Wheeler for sure, which had to mean Pearl Harbor. They wouldn't come all this way just to attack one base.

"Stay here," Taylor said, then turned and jogged down the big, open verandah. The bachelor officers' quarters had an enormous patio for impromptu barbecues and the occasional dance. It also had a telephone mounted on the wall.

"Tukka tukka tukka tukka . . ."

Much louder and much, much closer. He skidded to a stop and looked back long enough to see tufts of grass and dirt leap into the air. *Strafing . . . they're strafing us.* Taylor's brain processed it reluctantly. He knew exactly what it was because he'd done it, too. In practice, anyway. But Taylor had never expected to be on the receiving end. As he stared openmouthed, the wooden planks shredded when a long burst hit the verandah. Ducking around a corner, he waited till it passed, then made his way back to the phone to ring up his squadron.

Minutes later, he found Welch behind another corner, and the two fighter pilots looked long and hard at the parking lot. It seemed like every Jap over the field was strafing. Most of them were dive-bombers, Aichi D3s, which Americans called a "Val." Big and slow, with fixed landing gear, the Val was the main dive-bomber of the Imperial Japanese Navy. Not that the "meatball," the big red circle painted on the fuselage, left any room for doubt.

Welch punched him on the arm. "Well, let's wait till we hear the burst of machine guns, and then we'll run. That way the bullets are already behind us!"

It made sense at the time, so that's exactly what they did. Taylor's brand-new Buick sat in the "officers only" parking area, and they jumped in, peeling away amid a spray of gravel. Driving north off the base, both men watched enormous smoke clouds billow up to their left from the Schofield Barracks area.

After a moment, Taylor said, "George, we heard the ones that were by us, but we didn't hear the next volley that the guy fired at us. That was kind of silly."

Welch shrugged. "It worked."

Sometimes reaching 100 mph, they careened down the Oahu Central Valley for ten minutes, driving straight toward a beach on the north edge of Waialua Bay. Barely 200 feet off the beach, Haleiwa was a grass strip dispersal field that the 47th Pursuit Squadron used for gunnery training. Living there in tents since December 3, the pilots had welcomed the weekend to get back to the relative civilization that Wheeler offered. Poker, decent food, and nurses had kept them up all night, but now all was forgotten as Taylor swerved through the scrubby trees and skidded to a halt.

Two P-40s were up and running, their props spinning off tendrils of humid morning air. Ground crews swarmed over the six other fighters just in case they were needed. Several mechanics were pulling a dolly full of ammunition out of the way, and as the pilots appeared, the men squatting on the wings waved.

"Good to go, Lieutenant!" one of the ground guys shouted. "Fulla gas and thirty cal!"

There was no .50-caliber ammo at Haleiwa, so he'd have two empty guns. Taylor scrambled up along the wing root and jumped in. "I got it," he shouted over the engine to the crew chief, who was trying to buckle him in. "Pull the chocks." Pushing down hard to hold the brakes, he slapped the big yellow flap handle with his left hand, and with his right he opened the cowl flaps to keep the engine cool. Taylor eyeballed the fuel selector gauge and switched to the fuselage tank.

Running the red mixture knob to auto rich, he checked over the nose for the ground folks and smoothly eased the big throttle knob forward. As he taxied, Taylor quickly checked the magnetos, then cranked the canopy closed. For a tail dragger, the P-40 handled well enough on the ground. Eyes flickering around the cockpit, he scanned the fuel, oil pressure, coolant, and oil temperature, and ran a finger over the circuit breakers. Hesitating a moment while his right hand was there, Taylor flipped a switch and armed the guns—something he'd never done on the ground in peacetime.

Swinging around into the wind, both fighters wobbled forward, picked up speed, and lifted off tail first. As the rudder bit into the air Taylor gently pulled the stick right to keep the wings level. Coming away from the ground, he went through the normal routine of getting the gear and flaps up above 500 feet, the left wheel turning sideways and retracting back into the wing followed by the right. Constantly trimming the plane, he cross-checked his gauges while keeping sight of George Welch.

Holding 140 mph, they came around south toward Wheeler. The sun was shining over the eastern ridges of Oahu, surf was breaking white off Puaena Point, and there were only a few white clouds scattered against an amazing blue sky. Taylor's heart was thumping and he licked his dry lips, eyes darting upward and behind. The sky had to be full of Japs, but he couldn't see any yet. Taking a deep breath, he swallowed again and wished he'd brought a canteen. The pilot forced himself to slow down and scan correctly, just like he'd been taught. Aft quarter high . . . left then right. Then low . . . then ahead, left and right.

At Wheeler Field, smoke and fire were everywhere. What, he wondered, had happened to the sixty-odd fighter planes down there? Surely someone else would get airborne, too.

Surely.

Everything up till now had been pure reaction. But as they climbed he could plainly see stacks of oily black smoke rising above the southern edge of the island and what was obviously the main Japanese target: Pearl Harbor. It looked destroyed, and Taylor whistled softly, slowly shaking his head.

It was fifteen minutes past eight on the morning of December 7, 1941.

USAAF PILOTS LIKE Taylor and Welch went through a four-phase training program that lasted about a year, graduating them with more than two hundred hours of flight time. In the next four years of war, 191,654 students became pilots and 132,993 washed out, were medically disqualified, or died in training—a 40 percent loss rate. As in all air forces, some of those who washed out of pilot training were sent to navigator or bombardier schools. Formed in June 1941, the USAAF unified the Air Corps, which provided training and equipment, with the Air Force Combat Command, responsible for operational flying.

By early 1941 the Primary phase of pilot training was contracted through aviation schools of the Civilian Aeronautics Authority–War Training Service. In a course lasting anywhere from nine to twelve weeks, a student got about sixty hours in a variety of aircraft and learned takeoffs and landings, overhead patterns, and fundamental emergency procedures. If a student progressed to Basic, he'd acquire another seventy hours of formation, aerobatics, and cross-country navigation time. He'd also learn to fly at night and on instruments. More powerful aircraft such as the North American BT-14 or Vultee Valiant were used, exposing him to planes with a two-pitch prop and radio. The student's skills and grades in this section of the training determined his path in the Advanced phase.

The final nine weeks were spent in a Texan or Bobcat. Those destined for fighters perfected their formation flying and instrument procedures and were taught aerial gunnery against towed targets. If they survived all that and had high enough scores, then they were usually commissioned as second lieutenants upon graduation. Those who were not commissioned officers flew as sergeants. In either case, with their new silver wings the young pilots were sent on to Transition training with the specific aircraft they'd fly in combat. This lasted another two months, and besides aircraft familiarization, new pilots were taught the very latest tactics by experienced line pilots.

West Point graduates had a different process after the war began. Given the choice of the regular Army or the Air Corps, almost half of each class chose to fly, and primary training was conducted during the summer prior to their fourth year. This was done at a civilian school such as Spartan in Tulsa, Oklahoma, under the supervision of Army officers. A good student pilot would solo with about six hours and finish the summer with nearly sixty hours. Returning to the Point, cadets would finish Basic and Advanced training at nearby Stewart Field. Due to the officer shortage, academy classes were pushed up to graduate in three years, and this included the flight training. When a cadet graduated from West Point he had his wings and his officer's commission then went straight on to Transition training.

This was done at a field such as Williams, outside of Phoenix, Arizona, where he got more ground school, classroom instruction, and another seventy hours of flying over two months. Gunnery School was next, at someplace like Matagorda, Texas, or Las Vegas, Nevada. Fighter pilots flew AT-6 Texans with a single, fixed .30-caliber gun and used 16 mm cameras to evaluate their performance. As with the aviation cadets, the West Pointers finished with about two hundred hours and were as prepared as possible under the circumstances—certainly much better prepared than their fathers had been in 1917. Navy and Marine pilots followed a very similar path albeit on a smaller scale.

Twenty years before, in June of 1921, an Army pilot named Billy Mitchell shocked an audience of old-school admirals and generals by sinking the captured German battleship *Ostfriesland* with just eleven bombs.* A year later the American navy razed down USS *Jupiter,* a ten-year-old collier, gave her a flight deck, and recommissioned her as USS *Langley*—the first U.S. aircraft carrier.

During the early years only Naval Academy graduates could apply for flight training and then only after serving two years at sea, but as war approached this changed. Naval

---

*It certainly didn't hurt that Navy and Marine aircraft had pelted the *Ostfriesland* with over 50 bombs the day before—but the point was made that capital ships were not safe from air attack.

Academy cadets trained while in school and, just like West Pointers, graduated with wings and a commission. But neither service academy could meet the wartime needs of the expanding military, so the Naval Air Cadet program was established. With two years of college and ten hours of flying time, a man could apply for entry. If admitted as a cadet, he would start with Basic flight training at a civilian contracted field. Check rides were given at each twenty-hour mark, and if he passed, the student would advance to the Intermediate phase. This concentrated on formation flying, aerobatics, and navigation. It was here, again based on his performance, that he was selected for the type of aircraft he'd fly. There were VP (multi-engine), VO (surface ship reconnaissance), and VC (carrier) categories.

After a final check ride, a man chosen for fighters would go on to the Advanced phase. This was essentially a transition course that focused on instrument flying, gunnery, and tactics. A cadet who completed this wore the gold wings of a naval aviator and was a commissioned officer in either the Navy or the Marine Corps.

The last step in the process was a short assignment to the Advanced Carrier Training Group. This usually operated off Key West, where the new aviator had to make eight successful carrier landings (traps) and pass an evaluation from fleet pilots. He was now carrier qualified and on his way.

The Navy, like the USAAF, used limited numbers of enlisted pilots. Called naval air pilots (NAPs), these "bluejacket" pilots had to pass the standard entry exams and went through the same training. About 95 percent were eventually given temporary commissions as officers, and a very few retained their status after the war. The Marines, being perennially short of pilots, were less picky. Sergeant Ollie Michael was a good example of an enlisted aviator and sank three Japanese ships in late 1942.

So these were the men wearing wings in 1941 who stood up to fight the Germans, Italians, and Japanese in the air. In the Pacific they did it nearly single-handedly and against an implacable and often vicious enemy. Besides the expansion of its empire, Japan desperately needed the rice, rubber, and oil its conquests provided. Prewar Allied embargoes had left Tokyo with less than a twelve-month reserve of critical resources, so it was absolutely necessary that they resolve the diplomatic impasse or invade quickly. Any delay could have severe consequences, as Admiral Isoroku Yamamoto, commander of the Combined Fleet, was well aware. He had plainly stated to his prime minister, "If I am told to fight regardless of the consequences, I shall run wild for the first six months or a year, but I have utterly no confidence for the second or third year." Yamamoto very well knew that America was truly a sleeping giant that had now been thoroughly and angrily aroused.

At the root of most conflicts lies the quest for resources. It may be disguised as ideology, nationalism, or even religion, but without an economic motive there is no lasting impetus for war. The Japanese islands, totaling roughly the area of Montana, supported 73 million people and needed to import much of their rice from China. The islands produced no oil, no rubber, and less than 50 percent of the steel required. Nickel, essential for alloys, batteries, and magnets, was nonexistent and there was no bauxite for aluminum.

Japanese leaders, especially Army Minister (later Prime Minster) Hideki Tojo, were painfully aware of their situation. Though a Fascist and nationalist, Tojo was not a racist or a raving fanatic, as he is often portrayed. He was a product of the Imperial Japanese Military Academy and believed utterly in his nation's right to invade and subjugate others in order to survive.* He was as anti-Communist as he was anti-Western, and envisioned a Greater Asia controlled by Japan.

China, with her vast population and resources, was seen to be a solution, especially given Japan's control of the South Manchurian Railway. This was part of the Russian reparations package granted in 1905 and was patrolled by the Japanese Army. In September 1931 a section of track happened to blow up, giving a pretext for invasion.

However, the track had been blown by the Japanese themselves. When the Manchurian Incident, as it was called, was exposed, Japan withdrew from the League of Nations and joined Nazi Germany and Fascist Italy as diplomatic pariahs. Indifferent to world opinion, Tokyo had occupied most of littoral China by 1938, sparking protests and economic sanctions from Europe and the United States. In an effort to stall the Japanese, the British closed the Burma road, shutting off supplies to China. With the fall of France and Holland in 1940, imports to Japan were resumed from the Dutch East Indies, and the new Vichy French government quickly gave up basing rights in Indochina.

President Roosevelt countered by extending Lend-Lease to China in March 1941. In July the United States froze all Japanese assets and suspended critical exports of oil and aviation fuel. Washington also pressured the British and Dutch to embargo exports from their remaining Asian colonies, which they did, essentially throwing fuel on the fire. Japan retaliated

---

*After the war Tojo unsuccessfully attempted suicide and was incarcerated in Tokyo's Sugamo Prison. A new set of dentures was provided by an American dentist with the phrase "Remember Pearl Harbor" drilled into the teeth using Morse code. Tojo was hanged on December 23, 1948—still wearing the dentures.

by signing the Tripartite Act with Germany and Italy in September, thus joining the Axis. The Imperial Navy immediately began training carrier-based torpedo bombers in Sakurajima Bay, which bore remarkable similarities to Pearl Harbor, home of the U.S. Pacific Fleet.

Peace negotiations continued through October, but by the beginning of November Tokyo's decision had been made. Early on November 25, 1941, the Japanese Kido Butai (Carrier Strike Task Force) slipped quietly from Hitokappu Bay in the Kurile Islands and disappeared to the southeast. Detouring around commercial shipping lanes, the fleet avoided detection for twelve days before it suddenly reappeared 200 miles off the Hawaiian coast. Under the command of Vice Admiral Chuichi Nagumo, the task force consisted of the 1st Carrier Division (*Kaga, Akagi*), 2nd Carrier Division (*Soryu, Hiryu*), and 5th Carrier Division (*Zuikaku, Shokaku*). Between them they could put up more than four hundred dive-bombers, torpedo bombers, and fighters—the largest armada of naval aircraft in the world.

A typical Japanese fleet carrier was 740 to 840 feet long and contained anywhere from 1,100 to 1,700 men. Capable of about 30 knots, each ship was protected by 5-inch guns and an array of smaller anti-aircraft batteries, depending on the class of carrier. *Soryu* and *Hiryu* were the smallest and fastest, while *Shokaku* and *Zuikaku* were the newest—both completed just months before Pearl Harbor. Both *Akagi* and *Kaga* had been designed as capital ships but had been converted following the Washington Naval Treaty.*

Each carrier had its own air group, which usually comprised three squadrons: a fighter squadron of eighteen planes, plus two

*Capital ships are battlecruisers or battleships.

squadrons of dive-bombers and torpedo bombers, each containing twenty-seven aircraft. There were six additional aircraft of each type kept for spares. A typical *hikotai* (squadron) was based on flights of nine aircraft with a *shotai*, a three-ship Vic, serving as the normal fighting unit. Later in the war, as in nearly every air force, the Vic was replaced by basic fighting pairs.

There were several ways to become a Japanese naval pilot in the years before the war. Officer pilots came from the Imperial Naval Academy at Etajima and, after passing the additional required aptitude tests, could apply for flight school following a year at sea. Officers could also come through the reserves if they were university graduates and then similarly apply for flight school. Certain civilian pilots could seek a commission as well; if selected, they would enter military flight school through the reserves.

However, pilots were always in short supply, so exceptions had to be made in the rigid Japanese military caste system. Free public schooling was provided only through the elementary level and after that advancement to the comparatively few slots available was extremely selective. Much like the German *Gymnasium* system, it all hinged on aptitude test results. Private schooling was possible but very expensive, and quite beyond the financial ability of an average family. The Japanese navy was astute enough to recognize this waste of resources, so they created two alternative paths for young men of ability but limited finances.

A young man could simply enlist, spend a year at sea, then apply for permission to take the entrance exams for the *Soren*, a flight preparatory course. If a thousand men applied, then about 10 percent gained admission, and of those maybe fifteen graduated. *Yokaren* was another method by which the navy completed a teenage boy's education in return for military service. The men were taught standard military history, etiquette, and traditions, along with mathematics, navigation, and engineering, with English and Chinese grammar thrown in for good measure. Like a *Soren* graduate, a product of the *Yokaren* system would remain an enlisted man, although he'd be a naval aviator. Some five thousand boys applied for the first class, though only seventy-nine were selected—but it offered opportunities that would otherwise be unobtainable.

Basic flight school lasted a year and consisted of aircraft handling, takeoffs and landings, aerobatics, and some formation flying. Again, progression into the fighter pilot world was based on performance and instructor evaluations. If picked, the new pilot would then spend another six months in advanced training learning how to fly a fighter. All told, the program took a good two to three years depending on which pathway to wings the pilot took.

These, then, were the men staring down the decks as their carriers swung into the wind on December 7, 1941. They launched in two waves, one hour apart, and flew toward the north shore of Oahu. Led by Lt. Cmdr. Mitsuo Fuchida, a highly experienced veteran pilot from the *Akagi*, at 7:40 a.m. local time they reached the action point north of Kahuku Point and split into three attack groups.* The high-level bombers swung wide over the southwest shore, then headed into Pearl Harbor. Torpedo bombers, painted in ugly shades of green, brown, and black, came in over the trees just inland from the beach. They would hit the battleships and the three aircraft carriers believed to be present.† Another group would fly down the center of the island

*Fuchida was a Naval Academy graduate and the epitome of a pilot samurai. He would survive the war and eventually become a Christian evangelist in the United States.

†USS *Saratoga*, *Lexington* and *Enterprise*.

and attack the air bases at Wheeler Field and Ford Island. All told, 183 planes took part, including forty-three A6M2 Zero fighters to deal with any American resistance.

There wasn't any.

At least at the beginning.

Every Japanese pilot that morning believed he was at war with the United States, and most expected to die. They were unaware that diplomatic relations had not been formally broken and that the Americans were not on full war alert. Not that there was any doubt in Pearl Harbor that an attack was imminent. Secretary of the Navy Frank Knox had written: "If war eventuates with Japan it is believed easily possible that hostilities would be initiated by a surprise attack upon the Fleet or the Naval Base at Pearl Harbor."

Gen. Walter Short, commander of the Army's Department of Hawaii, had written his own analysis of the situation. In part, it read:

> *It appears that the most likely and dangerous form of attack on Oahu would be an air attack. It is believed that at present such an attack would most likely be launched from one or more carriers which would probably approach inside of 300 miles.*
>
> *In a dawn attack there is a high probability that it could be delivered as a complete surprise in spite of any patrols we might be using and that it would find us in a condition of readiness under which pursuit would be slow to start.*

The Japanese swept in, catching the defenders mostly by surprise. Four hours earlier a Navy minesweeper had sighted a periscope within two miles of the Pearl Harbor channel. The destroyer USS *Ward* then attacked it with depth charges and reported the incursion, which was ignored. The raiders had also been detected by radar but dismissed as a scheduled flight of B-17s due in from California. But by then it was too late.

Pearl Harbor was only about 40 feet deep, and despite the fate of the Italian battle fleet at Taranto in 1940, the American navy felt safe from aerial attack. But the Japanese had carefully studied the British methods at Taranto, adjusting their weapons and tactics accordingly. The same type of wooden-fin arrangement was utilized to prevent the torpedo from diving deep once released. The attack was also carried out at a 100-foot run in altitude instead of the normal 300 feet, with the weapon hung slightly nose low so it wouldn't skip across the water like a stone.

So as the Nakijima 97 "Kate" torpedo planes raced across the flat waters, there was literally nothing to stop them. Only a quarter of the eight hundred naval anti-aircraft guns were manned, and just four of the Army's thirty batteries. None of the various Navy, Marine, or Army Air Corps fighters were on alert—it was Sunday morning, after all. Worse, in an effort to counter local sabotage, the planes were all parked wingtip to wingtip for better ground security. From the air they made perfect targets.

Five battleships were sunk: the *Oklahoma*, *West Virginia*, *California*, *Utah*, and *Arizona*. The *Nevada* managed to get under way but was heavily damaged, so she was deliberately beached to avoid sinking in the channel. Both the *Maryland* and the *Pennsylvania* were damaged but serviceable. The Japanese second wave of 171 aircraft, all dive-bombers and fighters, hit the airfields again and reattacked the harbor area. The raid would destroy 18 ships and more than 160 aircraft, damaging 100 more. The Navy and Marines would lose 2,117 men, most from the *Arizona*, with another 779 wounded. Army casualties numbered 228 dead and 459 wounded. The Japanese lost 64 dead with one captured—and claimed a great victory.

But even surprised and unprepared, the Americans fought back ferociously, and despite the sneak attack, nearly 30 percent of the Japanese strike force sustained damage or didn't return. A few American fighter pilots managed to get airborne and hit back, so Welch and Taylor weren't completely alone that day.

After getting off the ground from Haleiwa, the two P-40s swung around the west coast of the island over the flight of B-17s coming in from the mainland. They then ambushed twelve Val dive-bombers attacking Ewa Field, a Marine air base on the southwest side of the island near the channel into Pearl Harbor. Taylor and Welch would go on to shoot down four enemy aircraft apiece, and both would survive the day—in fact, both would survive the war.*

Others weren't so fortunate. At least eight USAAF pilots got airborne, but one was killed by a Zero and another by friendly fire as he returned to land. Later that night five F4F Wildcats from VF-6 off the USS *Enterprise* flew into Ford Island. Lt. Cmdr. Howard Young, their carrier air group commander (CAG), had made it in earlier that day, informed the Navy of the flight's arrival, and was himself in the control tower as the fighters arrived. Perfectly illustrating a less discussed risk of combat flying, the Americans manning the airfield's anti-aircraft guns just saw planes and opened fire.

Lt. (j.g.) Fritz Hebel, the flight lead, was hit but evaded fire, got out of the harbor, and flew on to Wheeler, where the Army then shot him down. He fractured his skull against the gun-

---

*Taylor initially had two kills with two probables that were later confirmed based on Japanese records.

sight and would later die of his wounds. Hebel's wingman, Ens. Herbert Menges, was riddled with bullets and crashed into the Palms Hotel, dying on impact. Lt. (j.g.) Eric Allen bailed out over the harbor, and the gunners shot at him in his partially deployed parachute. Hit by a .50-caliber shell, Allen survived the impact and swam to a nearby minesweeper but died the next day.

Ens. Gayle Hermann's Wildcat was hit nearly twenty times, knocking the engine out. He came down in a cane field near Ford Island's seaplane base and, amazingly, was unhurt. That left Ens. James Daniels with the only airborne Wildcat. When the shooting started he promptly switched off his lights and dropped down low over the channel.* Lt. Cmdr. Young eventually got the trigger-happy sailors to cease firing and also managed to convince Daniels that the island was *not* in Japanese hands. Narrowly missing the beached *Nevada*, the ensign landed and taxied to the parking area in front of the control tower. As he rolled to a stop someone opened up with a machine gun. Gayle Hermann, the other surviving pilot, had just walked in from the cane field and was waiting for his friend. When the firing began he ran up and pistol-whipped the shooter, thus ending the stupidity for one night.

The infamous fourteen-point message from Tokyo that essentially declared war had finally been transcribed and presented to the Americans by Japan's diplomats in Washington. It was late, however, and the attack on Hawaii had already occurred. In fact, Japan's diplomatic code had been broken long before, so U.S. analysts had decoded and translated the message before the Japanese diplomats did so. The biggest difference that even

*The fact that these aircraft all had their lights on and were coming in to land, not attack, should have been a huge clue that they were friendly.

a one-hour warning would've made would have been fighter air cover over Oahu. If even a few squadrons had gotten airborne and caught the strike force by surprise, many lives could've been saved. Torpedo bombers and dive-bombers are extremely vulnerable to fighters, and their attack plan would've been thrown into confusion if they themselves were under attack. A much larger percentage of anti-aircraft guns would've been manned and ready as well.

Horrible as it was, the Pearl Harbor attack was not a complete military disaster. Depots, maintenance facilities, and dry docks were largely undamaged. The 140-million-gallon fuel farm was untouched. Both the *West Virginia* and the *California* were raised and returned to service by 1944, and *Utah*, though a battleship, had been demilitarized before December 7 and was only used for training. *Nevada*, *Tennessee*, *Maryland*, and *Pennsylvania* were all fully operational later in 1942. In any event, the Pacific naval theater would be controlled not by battleships but by aircraft carriers, and the U.S. carriers had all escaped the attack.

The Japanese slunk away to the north, then headed west for home. The fact that they missed the three Pacific fleet carriers negated, to a large degree, the effectiveness of their assault. This failure, combined with the rage produced in the United States, backfired badly on the Japanese. There was no hesitation now about full war mobilization and very little political opposition. In one stroke, the Japanese had provoked and irrevocably motivated the one enemy from which they had the most fear.

Steaming back west, Nagumo actually passed within a few hundred miles of the targets he most needed to destroy. On the morning of the attack Task Force 8, built around the USS *Enterprise*, was barely 200 miles west of Oahu. Commanded by Admiral Bill Halsey, she'd delivered Marine Fighting Squadron (VMF) 211 to Wake Island. The USS *Lexington* and Task Force 12 was returning from Midway Island and lay about 500 miles southeast of Hawaii, with the last carrier, USS *Saratoga*, was in San Diego completing a refit. All would return to Pearl Harbor, and the USS *Yorktown* would be transferred from the Atlantic Fleet within weeks.

Late in the afternoon on December 8, the U.S. Congress passed a joint resolution declaring war on the Empire of Japan. Winston Churchill couldn't help being relieved. Now America was in it openly. He would say to Congress later that month that the best war news of all was that "the United States, united as never before, has drawn the sword for freedom and cast away the scabbard." Churchill later wrote that he "went to bed and slept the sleep of the saved and thankful."

Across the world Hitler received the news happily and, thinking of Japan, said, "We can't lose the war at all. We now have an ally which has never been conquered in 3,000 years." Many of his fighting men, including Hans Marseille, had exactly the opposite reaction. Some even hoped that it would remain a conflict in the Pacific and that Germany would stay out of it. After all, the Tripartite Act stipulated German assistance only if Japan was attacked, not if it did the attacking.

But on December 10 both Germany and Italy declared war on the United States. Bogged down outside of Moscow, Hitler was certain that Japan would open a second front against the Soviet Union and relieve some of that pressure. The Japanese threat did initially keep Stalin from redeploying his Far Eastern forces, but by December he'd learned that as long as Moscow did not fall, then Japan would not attack. Tokyo had long experience with the Russians and had no intention of invading unless conditions were perfect. In any event, with the immediate threat from the American navy neutralized (or so they thought), the Japanese set the rest of their plan into motion.

On the American end of the Pacific this began with Wake Island, some 2,300 miles west of Oahu. The USS *Enterprise* wasn't at Pearl Harbor because on December 4 she'd delivered twelve Marine F4F Wildcats to the little atoll. Commanded by Major Paul Putnam, the group arrived with no real mechanics, no manuals, pilots who had very little experience in their new planes, and no radar. On December 8, thirty-six "Betty" bombers flew 650 miles from Kwajalein to attack the tiny American outpost. Nicknamed the "Hamaki" (Cigar) due to its tendency to burst into flame if hit, the Japanese planes nonetheless plastered Wake and destroyed seven of the twelve fighter aircraft.

Major James Devereux, the Marine commander, immediately repositioned his larger guns and erected dummy emplacements made from wood. His remaining pilots flew reconnaissance patrols and were airborne three days later when the Japanese arrived under Rear Adm. Sadamichi Kajioka and shelled the old gun positions. The defenders patiently held their fire. When the cruiser *Yubari*, the admiral's flagship, came within 4,500 yards of shore, the Marines opened up. Hit and trailing smoke, she limped back out of range. Then the destroyer *Hayati* was struck and blew up. The remaining four Wildcats had been circling overhead during all this and now attacked with bombs, machine guns, and a vengeance. A troop transport and second destroyer were damaged, and at 0815 the destroyer *Kisaragi* exploded. The last casualty that day was a Japanese submarine caught by Marine Lt. David Kliewer and his Wildcat.

Meanwhile, the USS *Saratoga,* accompanied by three heavy cruisers and nine destroyers, was charging west toward Wake Island. Task Force 14 also contained 300 Marine reinforcements, radar equipment, and 3 million rounds of machine-gun ammunition. However, the carriers *Soryu* and *Hiryu* were diverted from their homeward voyage to deal with Wake Island, and on December 21 they appeared offshore. With their arrival,

140 aircraft and some 1,000 Japanese marines faced off against the unsupported Americans.*

At this point, Task Force 14 was only 600 miles from the atoll, but the acting commander of the U.S. Pacific Fleet, Adm. William S. Pye, decided to recall the *Saratoga* and leave the Wake defenders to their fate.† Pye was the sort of officer who'd been awarded the Navy Cross for "exceptionally distinguished and valuable service on the staff of the commander in chief, U.S. Atlantic Fleet, in addition to excellent performance of his routine staff duties in preparing a series of orders for the conduct of battleship and fleet, based upon the best thought and experience of the United States fleet and British fleet during the late war."

The Marines were incensed. One wonders what might have happened if *Saratoga* had caught both Japanese carriers by surprise. There was a real tactical opportunity to make the Japanese bleed and prevent the fall of Wake Island. Of course, there was also a very real chance of losing a carrier, and given the catastrophe at Pearl Harbor two weeks before, most admirals were inclined to be cautious. However, it was all-out war at this point, Americans were in danger, and something other than a withdrawal should have been attempted.

Two days before Christmas 1941, Wake Island was surrendered by the ranking naval officer, Cmdr. Winfield Scott Cunningham—much to Major Devereux's disgust. The Marines had fought hard, giving the startled Japanese a taste of things to come. Capt. Henry Talmage Elrod became the first Marine aviator to be awarded the Medal of Honor for his ac-

---

*Japanese Special Naval Landing Force—Marines.

† Pye was relieved shortly thereafter and sat out most of his remaining years at the Naval War College—far from combat operations.

tions on Wake. He'd personally shot down two Zeros and was credited with sinking the *Kisaragi*. After VMF-211's planes were destroyed, he, like all the surviving pilots, continued fighting on the ground; he was killed by a Japanese soldier playing dead.* Cunningham didn't have much of a choice except fighting to the death, and with Pye's betrayal no one really considered that.

The end of 1941 saw Guam and Hong Kong fall into enemy hands. England, still reeling from the battles for France and Britain, was heavily committed in North Africa and in no real position to intervene effectively in the Pacific. The Royal Navy had also just lost the *Prince of Wales* and *Repulse* off the Malaysian coast to land-based Japanese aircraft. By January the British were in full retreat down the peninsula toward their great, supposedly impregnable fortress of Singapore—which fell on February 15, 1942.

Sweeping south and east, the Japanese then attacked the Philippine Islands, Dutch East Indies, and New Guinea in quick succession. The defenders were disorganized, surprised, and in many cases hindered by locals who believed the Japanese were liberating them from colonial oppression. They quickly learned otherwise after meeting the Japanese army: food was confiscated, men were pressed into labor gangs, and, following the Nanking pattern, women were raped.† For her part in the Great War, Japan had also been given the Marshall and Caroline Islands, Palau, Saipan, and Tinian (among others)—all former German colonies. These, plus the new conquests, were quickly turned into what were essentially unsinkable aircraft carriers.

The Allies were truly on their heels in the early spring of

---

*The fast frigate USS *Elrod* (FFG-55) was commissioned in his honor in 1985.

†The Japanese admitted to 140,000 deaths during the massacre of Nanking. The Chinese cited about 300,000 dead and 20,000 women raped. Again, the truth probably lies somewhere in between.

1942, and things looked bleak on all fronts. Rommel's Afrikakorps was sweeping toward Tobruk, and the Russians were about to face Operation Fridericus, the great German thrust into the Caucasian oil fields. America was mobilizing to meet wartime requirements with the remnants of a peacetime military, but relief would take time. With the country desperate for a victory of any kind, on April 2, 1942, the USS *Hornet* left Alameda, California. Rendezvousing with the USS *Enterprise*, four cruisers, and eight destroyers, the combined task force headed west, deep into the Pacific toward the Japanese home islands.

Hornet carried sixteen Mitchell B-25 bombers flown by Army pilots. Stripped down, the bombers each carried three 500-pound high-explosive bombs and one incendiary bomb. The Mitchell could cruise at about 230 mph with an 1,100-mile range. The idea was to hit targets in Tokyo, Yokohama, Kobe, and Nagoya, then dash across the Sea of Japan to land in China. The odds were terrible and no one really believed survival was possible, but with the indomitable spirit of Americans, they went anyway.

Lt. Col. Jimmy Doolittle had planned the mission and would lead it over the objections of his superior officers. Formerly a prizefighter and racing pilot, Doolittle also held degrees from UC Berkeley and a doctorate in aeronautics from the Massachusetts Institute of Technology. He pioneered many aspects of flight, but his most significant contribution was in the field of instrument flying. Doolittle was the first to really study relationships between our motion senses and visual cues and how these affected a pilot's ability to fly at night or in bad weather. After developing the technology, he became the first pilot to fly an entire flight, from takeoff to landing, solely on instruments.

Accomplished, independently wealthy and famous, Doolittle had earned the right to live as he pleased, but sitting in an office as a staff officer was not his idea of fighting a war. As he would later say:

> *The Japanese people had been told they were invulnerable. . . . An attack on the Japanese homeland would cause confusion in the minds of the Japanese people and sow doubt about the reliability of their leaders. There was a second, and equally important, psychological reason for this attack. . . . Americans badly needed a morale boost.*

At 7:38 a.m. on April 18, 1942, the task force was spotted by a Japanese picket ship, which was quickly sunk. The problem was that *Hornet* was still 170 miles beyond the planned launch point and at extreme range for the bombers. With the element of surprise lost, the decision was made and the raiders manned their planes. The carrier swung into the wind, surging forward at flank speed, and at 8:20 a.m. Colonel Doolittle's B-25 staggered off the bow with feet to spare and turned toward Japan.

Whiskey Pete, *Ruptured Duck*, *Hair-karier*, and the others followed. Last off was *Bat out of Hell* at 9:19, and the carriers immediately turned back to the east. More than five hours later the B-25s crossed the Japanese coast and headed inland, homing on a Tokyo radio station. Thirteen targets were hit, including the brand-new aircraft carrier *Ryuho*. Fifteen B-25s made it to China and one to the Soviet Union. Of the eighty men who flew off *Hornet* that morning, seventy, including Doolittle, survived and evaded capture. Two men were downed at sea, and eight more were caught by the Japanese.*

---

*Three were executed for "war crimes": Lieutenants Farrow and Hallmark with Corporal Spatz.

Doolittle had expected a court-martial for losing all his aircraft, but instead he was awarded the Medal of Honor as a national hero. Militarily the raid did little damage, but the psychological impact on both sides was immense. For the Americans it was a tremendous shot in the arm and gave everyone the confidence that the United States, even on the ropes, would fight back. On a practical level it again demonstrated the awesome potential of the aircraft carrier. Every major blow in the Pacific thus far had been dealt by aircraft, and "gun club" admirals commanding the battleship navy could no longer ignore the facts.

The raid had an equally significant effect on the Japanese. Those advocating peace were silenced by this assault on the homeland and its proximity to their emperor. Those who favored occupying an outlying, defensive ring of islands now had just cause. The attack was also an insult to the Japanese navy, which bore responsibility for protecting the islands, and to Admiral Yamamoto.

By May 1942, the fortress of Corregidor in the Philippine Islands had fallen. At the same time, as the Japanese pushed south from Rabaul, an invasion fleet was sent across the Coral Sea to Port Moresby, on the southern edge of Papua New Guinea. If they could capture it, then the northern shore of Australia would be in range of Japanese aircraft. Troop transports were escorted by cruisers and destroyers, with the carriers *Shokaku*, *Zuikaku*, and *Shoho* capable of putting up 120 combat aircraft.

Aware of the Japanese plans, Adm. Chester Nimitz, the new commander of the U.S. Pacific Fleet, dispatched two carrier groups to the Coral Sea: the USS *Yorktown*'s Task Force 17 and Task Force 11, centered on the USS *Lexington*. Nimitz knew the extreme risks, but he was no Admiral Pye and had commanded submarines, gunboats, and cruisers. Though never an aviator, he could think unconventionally and was well aware of the value of attack.*

Fought entirely by aircraft, the Battle of the Coral Sea was a milestone in military history. It was also a tactical draw in that the Americans scuttled the *Lexington* and sustained heavy damage to *Yorktown*. Nearly seventy planes were lost, along with 656 lives. The Japanese lost the light carrier *Shoho*, several smaller warships, and nearly a thousand men. Additionally, the fleet carrier *Shokaku* was heavily damaged and would spend the next two months out of action. *Zuikaku* was undamaged, but most of the ninety-two destroyed Japanese warplanes were from her, and she would be out of the fight until her aircraft were replaced.

Strategically, the battle was a decisive American victory. The invasion of Port Moresby had been stopped and the myth of Japanese invincibility shattered. Also, two front-line carriers had been put out of action—not permanently, but long enough. Neither would be a part of the fleet now sailing toward an obscure island and a battle that would turn the tide of the Pacific war.

THROUGH THE SEA breeze a mechanical bugle blared and the pilot looked up startled, a rice ball halfway to his mouth. Like angry ants, men poured from everywhere over the flight deck and ran toward waiting aircraft or anti-aircraft guns. *Air attack* . . . that was what the bugle was playing. Air attack. Jumping to his feet, Kaname Harada stared up and saw nothing. Then he squinted past the bow and saw little dark flecks appear against the lighter horizon band.

*He'd also remarked once that a "ship is always referred to as 'she' because it costs so much to keep her in paint and powder."

"Torpedo planes!" someone yelled over the noise. "Torpedo attack!"

Tossing his teacup overboard, the pilot sprinted to his waiting Reisen, clambered up the wing and plopped into the cockpit.* The ground crew already had the engine started and, ignoring the seat straps, he waved everyone back and held the brakes as the chocks were yanked out. Peering forward over the nose, Harada pushed the throttle up, and the fighter surged forward. His eyes were locked forward as his right hand checked the flaps down and switched on his guns.

Coming off the deck, the plane crabbed into the wind, and he held his takeoff pitch long enough to clear the carrier's bow, then retracted the gear. As the Zero sank toward the sea he felt the propeller really bite into the air, and the fighter slowly rose. Slapping up the flaps, he leveled off for a few seconds to gain more airspeed. Glancing toward the attackers, he was shocked to see how close they were. Escort ships were firing now, and he could see black and white puffs exploding over the Americans. Beginning a wide turn, Harada waited until his wingmen were loosely joined, then he began to climb. Eyes narrowed, he realized he wouldn't have to go too high—the Yankees were skimming the wave tops.

Hold it . . . hold it . . . He bunted slightly and began a gentle turn, gauging the intercept geometry from long experience. He could plainly see them now. They were the newer American torpedo bombers, big and ugly, like a bumblebee, with blue paint and bright white stars. The Avenger, made by Grumman, with a three-man crew.

Now . . .

Yanking back on the stick, Hamada flipped the nimble little

---

*Mitsubishi A6M Type 0 Model 21, known to the Allies as a "Zero."

fighter over and sliced down toward the lumbering planes. His two wingmen repositioned and floated into single file behind him. Leaving the throttle up, he lightly played the stick and rudder to swoop in from above. The Avenger had an enclosed ball turret, and as it started to swivel Harada opened fire with a three-second burst. His two cowling-mounted machine guns instantly spewed out a stream of fifty 7.7 mm shells, and the wings shuddered from the recoil of the bigger 20 mm cannons. Pieces flew off the other plane, but the American had banked up and his tail gunner was firing.

Yanking the stick back into his lap, Harada grunted and barrel-rolled the fighter up and over the torpedo bombers. Inverted, staring down at the blue water, he saw his second wingman firing and made a snap decision. Cutting in front of his third wingman, Genzo Nagazawa, Harada snap-rolled upright behind another Avenger. The other Zero immediately pulled straight up to avoid a collision, and as he did the American tail gunner fired a long, lethal burst into the fighter's belly. Horrified, Harada saw his wingman's plane burst into flames and smash into the sea.

Enraged, he screamed, pulled his nose to bear, and fired at point-blank range into the Avenger. The gunner's turret disappeared in a cloud of shredded metal, glass, and smoke. The big plane instantly nosed over and hit the waves, throwing up a tremendous fan-shaped spray of water. Blinking rapidly, Harada rolled up and over again, looking down as the rest of the Americans vanished in similar flaming splashes.

It was June 4, 1942, just past 7 a.m. on a clear, sunny morning. Admiral Yamamoto, commander of the Combined Fleet, was under tremendous pressure. The Doolittle raid had graphically demonstrated the home islands' vulnerability to air attack, and the Battle of the Coral Sea had shaken the Imperial Navy's cult of invincibility. Yamamoto also knew he was running out of time to achieve victory before America overwhelmed Japan. His plan was twofold. First was to take Midway Island as the key to an outer range of defense that would prevent another attack on Japan. Second, to complete the mission started at Pearl Harbor by luring the U.S. Navy into a final great sea battle, where it would be crushed. With no navy to protect the West Coast, Washington would be compelled to negotiate.

Yamamoto's complex plan involved three main prongs. First, an attack on the Aleutian Islands was intended to divert American attention and resources. Second, his main carrier strike group would hit Midway Island, destroying any chance of land-based U.S. air attacks against his fleet. The island would then be invaded and taken with its airfield intact for use by Japanese aircraft. By this time, Yamamoto calculated, the Americans would've sent their navy out to fight, and his Combined Fleet could trap and annihilate them.

There were several problems with this. Foremost was the broken Japanese JN-25 military code, which enabled Nimitz's intelligence section to read anywhere from 25 to 75 percent of any given message. They'd also figured a way to nail down Midway as the target by simply referencing it in a clear message, which the Japanese then repeated in their code.* Another problem was the Aleutian feint. It was so obviously a diversion that no one fell for it, least of all Nimitz, and the fact that it tied up Japanese Fifth Fleet resources (including the carriers *Ryujo* and *Junyo*) may well have turned the tide of the battle.

Last was the Japanese underestimation of American forces

---

* *MI* was "Midway Island," and the secondary target of the Aleutian Islands was referred to as *AL*—an astonishing oversight on someone's part. It was initially disregarded by U.S. intelligence as too obvious, yet turned out to be true.

and, perhaps most damning, of the Americans themselves. Pearl Harbor had convinced many of the Imperial Navy's superiority, and the lessons from Wake Island and Coral Sea hadn't been fully digested yet. They knew that the *Saratoga* was in California being repaired but also believed the *Yorktown* had been sunk in the Coral Sea. Limping back to Pearl Harbor, however, Nimitz put 3,000 workers onboard for seventy-two hours, and the big carrier was back at sea. In the meantime, Admiral Nagumo and the First Mobile Force sailed from Hiroshima Bay on May 26, 1942. The Japanese Fifth Fleet, called Mobile Force 2, had also steamed from the home islands heading northeast toward the Aleutians. As far as Yamamoto knew, only the *Enterprise* and *Hornet* were available and his intelligence placed them far down in the South Pacific.

Which they were not.

On the same day both carriers had returned to Pearl Harbor, followed by the damaged *Yorktown*. At noon on May 27 the *Enterprise* and *Hornet*, with fifty-four fighters, seventy dive-bombers, and twenty-nine torpedo planes, left Oahu. Commanded by Rear Adm. Ray Spruance, Task Force 16 was escorted by six cruisers and eleven destroyers. Midway was also reinforced by four USAAF B-26 bombers and eight additional Catalinas. By 1200 on May 30, Task Force 17 had sortied from Pearl Harbor. Escorted two cruisers and five destroyers, *Yorktown* was carrying twenty-seven fighters, thirty-seven dive-bombers, and fifteen torpedo bombers. By June 1 nine more B-17s from the 26th Bombardment Squadron had arrived, bringing the total to sixteen heavy bombers. Also, a third U.S. task force built around the *Saratoga* had sailed from San Diego heading west.

As the sun set during the afternoon of June 2, *Enterprise*, *Hornet*, and *Yorktown* rendezvoused 350 miles northeast of

Midway Island. The Japanese carriers of Mobile Force 1 had turned southeast and were about 700 miles when darkness fell. The invasion fleet was also 700 miles west and closing. Twelve American submarines were deployed in an early-warning screen along the northwestern approaches to Midway, and the Catalinas were still flying their patrols.

The island's airborne defenses now included twenty-one Marine fighters (Buffalo and Wildcats) and thirty-six dive-bombers (Dauntless and Vindicators). Ground forces included two companies of the 2nd Marine Raider Battalion, among whose officers was Maj. James Roosevelt, eldest son of the president of the United States.* The USAAF had deployed twenty-five bombers (B-17s and B-26s), and six new Grumman Avengers from VT-8 off the USS *Hornet* flew in on June 1. There were more than thirty long-range Catalinas; enormous planes with a wingspan over 100 feet, the PBYs were also used for interdiction and night attack. They could carry bombs, torpedoes, and four machine guns over their 2,500-mile range.

It was the Catalinas from VP-44 that discovered the Japanese on the morning of June 3, 1942. At 8:43 a.m. Ens. James Lyle discovered the Japanese minesweeping force about 600 miles southwest of Midway. Forty minutes later Ens. Jack Reid radioed his famous "Main body!" sighting followed up with a later report of eleven ships 700 miles west of the island, heading east. The pilot was convinced he'd found the strike force, but Nimitz was not; in fact, it was the invasion force. Still, nine B-17s from Midway launched at noon, and at 4:40 p.m. they attacked the Japanese Second Fleet Transport Group. Though no hits were scored, they did shake the Japanese up. If Midway

---

*Not something we'd see in present times. James Roosevelt later won the Navy Cross in combat.

was the point of an inverted triangle, Nagumo's carriers were at the top left corner, about 500 miles to the northwest of the island. Due east some 400 miles, on the top right corner of the triangle were the American carriers.

First blood was drawn early in the morning of June 4 when a flight of Catalinas hit the oiler *Akebono Maru* with a Mk 13 aerial torpedo. At 4:30 a.m., with the element of surprise lost, Admiral Nagumo's first strike against Midway came off the decks of *Akagi*, *Kaga*, *Hiryu*, and *Soryu*. Four squadrons of bombers with fighter escorts, the 108-plane package was picked up on radar at 5:35. By 6 a.m. everything on Midway that could fly was airborne—the bombers heading away to safety and the Marines from VMF-221 (Fighting Falcons) turning in to attack.

If the Grumman Wildcats were outclassed by the Japanese fighter, then the Brewster Buffalo was hopelessly overmatched. The Zero was at least 1,000 pounds lighter and could outclimb either American fighter by over 1,000 feet per minute. Though the Wildcat and Zero both spit out about 15 pounds of shells per three-second burst, they were outnumbered about five to one and quickly overwhelmed. Still, the Marines shot down four bombers and three fighters and put the attackers on the defensive as they approached Midway. Anti-aircraft fire took out another thirty or so aircraft and damaged most of the rest, so it was no wonder that the mission commander, Lt. Joichi Tomonaga, immediately called for a second strike.* At about 7:15 a.m. Nagumo ordered his reserve squadrons armed with contact fragmentation bombs for a final mission to neutralize the island's defenses.

As this was happening the USAAF B-26s and VT-8 Avenger

---

*The Air Group commander off the *Hiryu*.

While the Great War settled into a brutal stalemate on the ground, combat aviation evolved rapidly, developing from zeppelins and unarmed reconnaissance planes to increasingly sophisticated—and deadly—fighter aircraft. This poster celebrates the German Albatros, which the Allied Powers struggled to match.

Legendary English ace Albert Ball, VC. At the time of this death at age twenty, Ball was Britain's top ace—and a romantic hero back home.

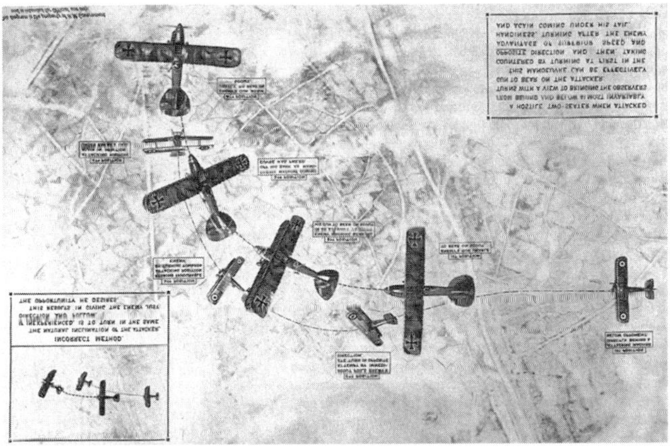

A diagram of proper World War I fighter attack maneuvers.

Edward "Mick" Mannock, Britain's leading ace, with 61 victories.

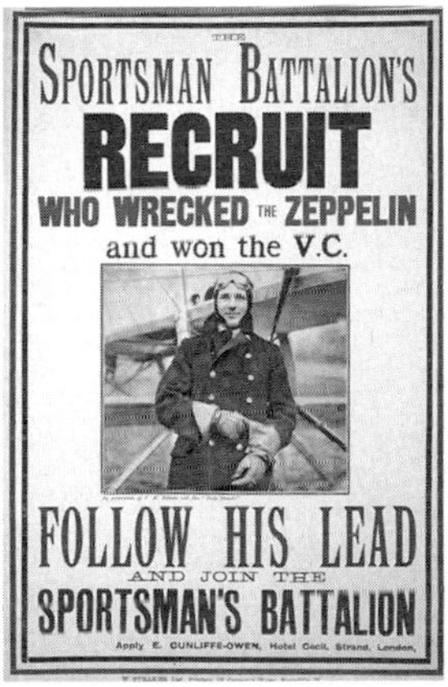

British recruiting posters.

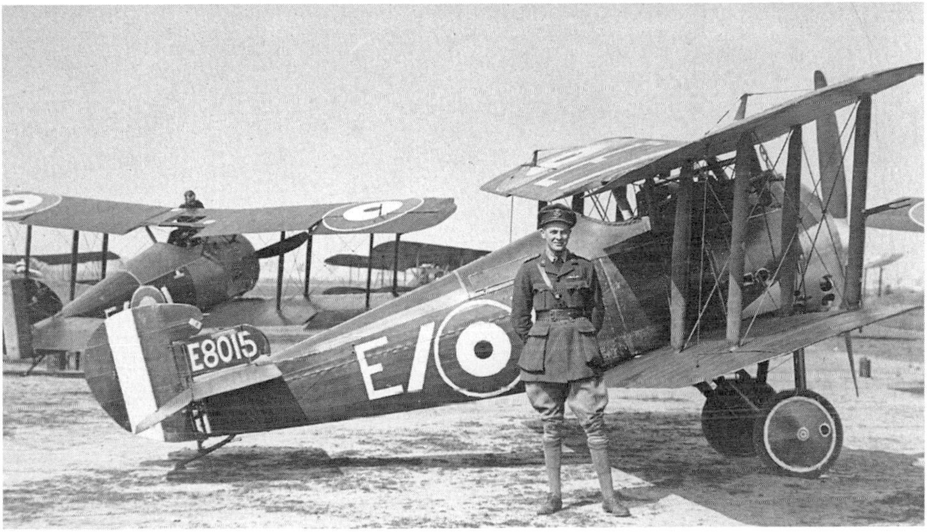

"The Eyes of the Army": the iconic Sopwith Camel.

A postcard celebrating the fortieth victory by German ace Oswald Boelcke, the father of combat aviation tactics.

Kaiser Wilhelm II "giving [the] Iron Cross to aviators." The Prussian military quickly incorporated pilots into their traditions.

A Fokker D-VII outfitted with duel Spandau guns and featuring the three interlocking rings of the Krupp corporation, the leading German armaments manufacturer during the war.

An Albatros D-III.

Manfred von Richthofen—the "Red Baron"—posing with his Blue Max, Prussia's highest order of merit.

The cover of Richtofen's ghostwritten memoirs, *Der rote Kampfflieger* (*The Red Fighterpilot*), published in 1917 though soon disowned by the baron.

A Fokker A1 triplane, made famous by the Red Baron.

A famous French aviator before the war, Roland Garros was the first pilot to mount a forward-firing machine gun and use it successfully in air-to-air combat.

A French Morane-Saulnier N monoplane.

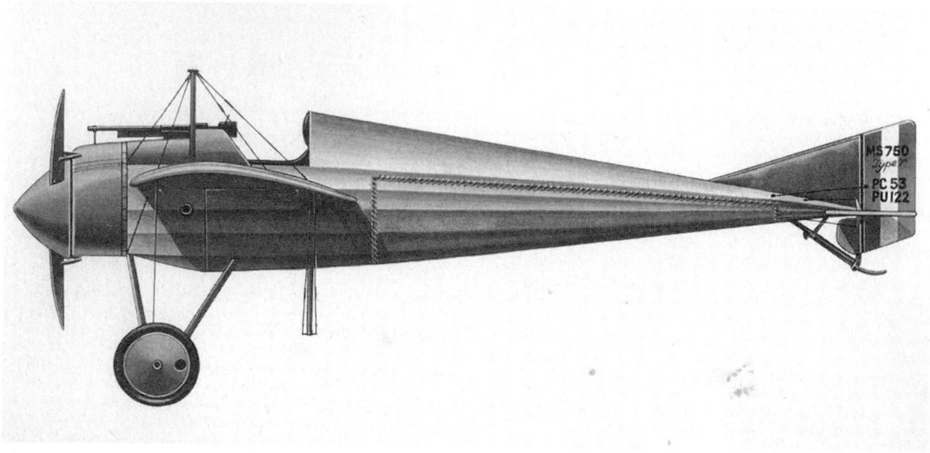

An excellent view of the deflector plates shielding the propellers of the Morane-Saulnier, first used by Garros in 1915.

Issues of the French magazine *La Guerre Aerienne Illustree* (top) and a popular biography of ace Georges Guynemer (left), all of which fed the tremendous popular appetite for stories about *les aviateurs.*

A SPAD XVI outfitted with both Vickers and Lewis guns.

An SE-5 with both fuselage- and over-wing-mounted Lewis guns.

The Lafayette Escadrille, July 1917. The squadron's two pet lions, Whiskey and Soda, share the front row.

Ceremonial flag celebrating the Escadrille's years of service.

A Nieuport 11 issued to the American volunteers of the Escadrille.

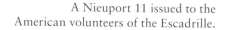

Eddie Rickenbacker, seated in his Nieuport 28 with offset machine guns. Captain Rickenbacker would become the top American ace of the war, with 26 victories.

An Army Air Service recruiting poster.

Members of the American 96th Aero Squadron stand before their Breguet 14 bomber. The dual machine guns mounted on the rotating Scarf ring were a vital defense against German fighter attack.

Billy Mitchell was the first American officer to fly into enemy territory during World War I and would end up commanding all U.S. air operations. After the war he became a visionary—if controversial—advocate for developing American air forces, particularly aircraft carriers.

A battlefield sketch of an injured Allied airman being helped from his plane.

An Allied aircraft's final descent.

German photograph of a "captured Russian aeroplane."

A German anti-aircraft gun.

Wreckage of a downed German Albatros.

"What England Wants!"—German propaganda poster from 1918 playing off fears of the devastating destructive capacity of air forces

Captured German planes are paraded as trophies through the streets of London.

Crowds gather for Boelcke's funeral. Upon learning of his death, the Royal Flying Corps dropped a wreath near his aerodrome that read, "To the memory of Captain Boelcke, a brave and chivalrous foe."

Albert Ball's temporary grave marker, erected by respectful Germans.

The monumental tombstone of France's Roland Garros.

Baron von Richthofen's funeral, attended to by the Australian Flying Corps.

December 1940; St. Paul's Cathedral, London, enveloped in smoke from the Luftwaffe's Blitz.

SEA TRAGEDIES
in Holderness
Village
SEE TO-DAY'S
HULL TIMES

Radio: Page 5

THE DAILY MAIL

FINAL CITY

Black-out: 8.56 to 5.17. Lighting-up: 9.26 to 4.47.

No. 17,097 TEL. 15100 (15 Lines) HULL, SATURDAY, AUGUST 17th 1940.

Curfew: 10 p.m. to 4.47

SOARING TOTALS OF NAZI LOSSES IN AIR BATTLE FOR BRITAIN

255 Raiders Down in Last Two Days

THE soaring enemy losses in Thursday's mighty air battles have now reached a total of 180.

This figure was officially announced to-day, when it was stated that 75 raiders were shot down yesterday. The R.A.F. lost 22 'planes, but 14 pilots are safe.

After these epic fights, enemy activity over this country during last night and early to-day was not on a heavy scale. Bombs were dropped in South Wales and

Nazi Losses Nearing 1,000

GERMAN air losses over and around Britain since the war began took another leap towards the 1,000 with the announced lost yesterday. They now total 830, and 819 of these are since mass raids began on June 18.

During this week Nazi 'planes have gone down at the rate of between 70—80 a day, and at a ratio of over 4—1 of the British losses—though many of the British pilots survive to fight again.

Comparative score-sheet

London newspaper coverage of the Battle of Britain.

RAF pilots sprint to their planes during the Blitz.

Spitfires in formation.

British ace Robert Sandford Tuck and twenty-three swastikas. He would add four more official kills before being shot down over occupied France and taken prisoner.

Hugh Dowding, the head of RAF Fighter Command who is widely credited with the successful defense of England in the Battle of Britain.

Nazi Stukas fly in formation, May 1940.

The fearsome Messerschmitt Bf 109.

A German Me 262, the first operational jet fighter. Though revolutionary, too few were produced, too late in the war, to make a measurable impact.

German ace Hans-Joachim Marseille, nicknamed "The Star of Africa" for his exploits in North Africa.

Marseille examines a British Hurricane he shot down, one of more than 150 total victories.

Marseille stands by as his fiftieth kill is recorded on his tail.

In Libya a British mechanic hooks up a bomb to the belly of an American-built P-40.

"German fighter planes attack Russian column" (Air Force Museum).

Soviet Air Force's LaGG-3 fighters head out to meet the Luftwaffe.

Lilya Lityvak, the world's first female fighter ace, earned fame for her performance in defense of Stalingrad.

Drastically outgunned at the start of World War II, the Soviets eventually closed the gap on the German Bf 109. Shown here is a Yak-9, brought into service in late 1942.

Japanese Zero pilots await the attack on Pearl Harbor aboard the aircraft carrier *Akagi*.

December 7, 1941: an aerial photograph taken by a Japanese pilot during the Pearl Harbor attack.

Mariana Islands, June 1944: "Japanese plane shot down as it attempted to attack USS *Kitkun Bay*" (National Archives).

"Japanese torpedo bomber explodes in air after direct hit by 5-inch shell from U.S. aircraft carrier attack on carrier" (NA).

Saburo Sakai: "With 62 victories, the Imperial Japanese Navy's second highest scoring pilot to survive World War II" (Air Force Museum).

A Mitsubishi A6M5 Model 52: the "Zero."

A land-based Kawanishi N1K2-Ja Shiden Kai: the "Violet Lightning."

U.S. Navy warplanes en route to avenge Pearl Harbor.

American F6F Hellcat pilots aboard the USS *Lexington.*

A battle-damaged F4F aboard the USS *Enterprise.*

"The crew of the USS *South Dakota* stands with bowed heads . . . in honor of fellow shipmates killed in the air action off Guam on June 19, 1944" (NA).

F4F Wildcats fly in "tactical formation," circa mid-1943.

Okinawa, June 1945: "Corsair fighter looses its load of rocket projectiles" (NA).

A Lockheed P-38J.

Chuck Yeager's P-51.

U.S. pilots star in posters aimed at increasing wartime industrial production.

"F4Us and F6Fs fly in formation during surrender ceremonies; Tokyo, Japan" (NA). September 2, 1945.

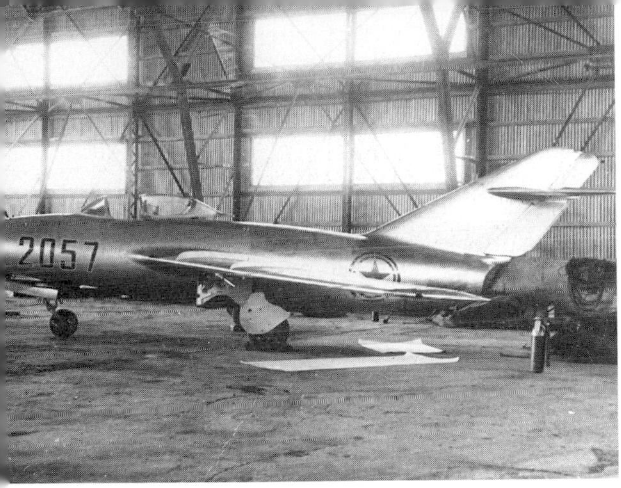

MiG-15s. The Soviet-designed jets gave the North Koreans an edge in the early stages of the Korean War.

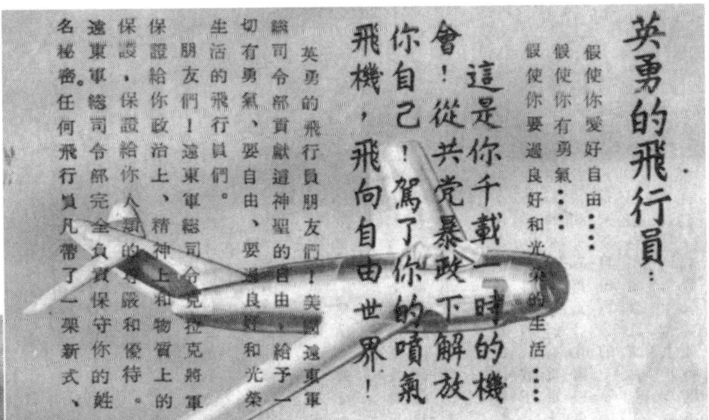

"Leaflet offering a $100,000 reward to any pilot who delivered a MiG" (AFM).

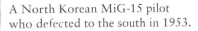

A North Korean MiG-15 pilot who defected to the south in 1953.

Rows of F-86Es being readied for a mission over Korea.

U.S. pilots headed to "MiG Alley," the nickname given to the enemy-controlled area on the North Korea–China border.

The F-86 Sabre, shown here with its full weapons load-out.

Gun camera photo of a MiG-15 being attacked by a USAF fighter.

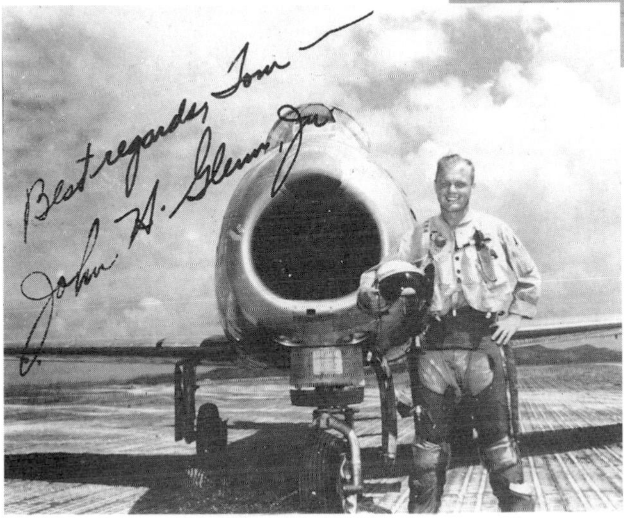

Medal of Honor recipient George A. Davis (above left), an ace in both WWII and Korea with 21 total victories; Ed Rock (above right), who would later go on to fame as a Wild Weasel in Vietnam; and future astronaut John Glenn (left) pose with their Sabres.

Thirty-nine USAF F-86 pilots (and one Marine Corps exchange pilot) became Korean War aces.

F-105 Thunderchiefs—nicknamed "Thuds"—in action over Vietnam during Rolling Thunder operations.

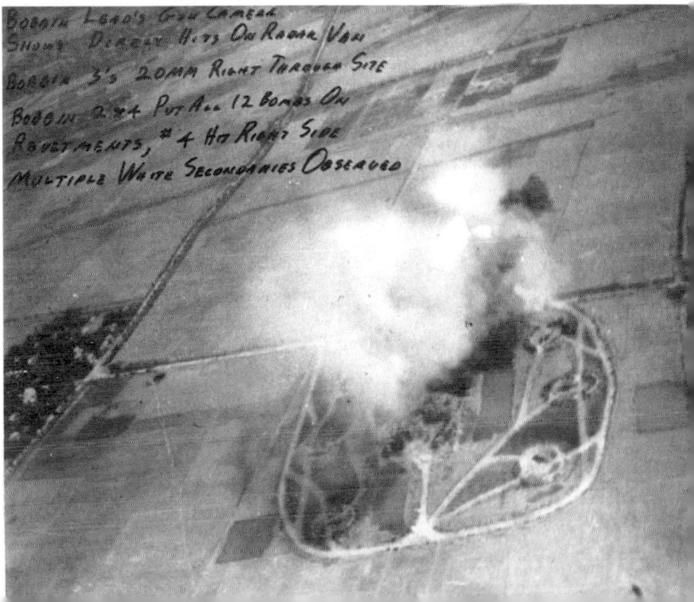

SA-2 surface-to-air-missile (SAM) site destroyed after an attack by Wild Weasels.

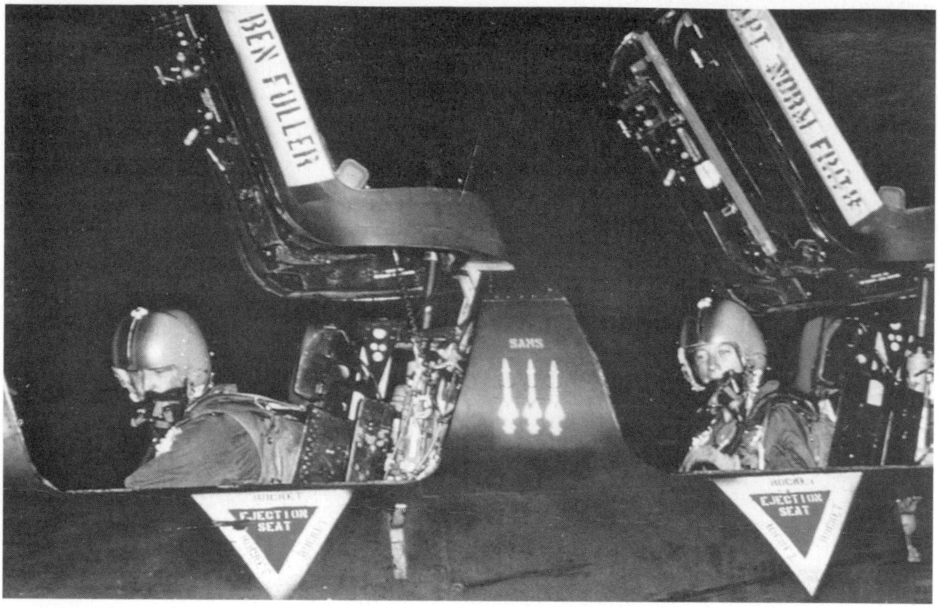

A Wild Weasel Thud team returns from a mission, April 1967. Note the three SAM kills stenciled between the cockpits.

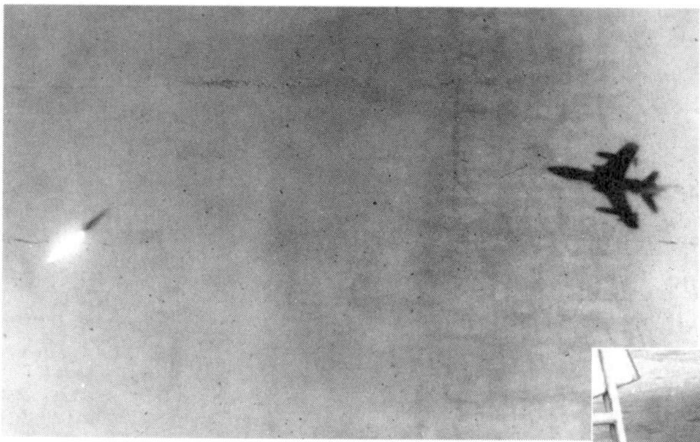

A Thud evades an SA-2 SAM.

Thud pilot (and Medal of Honor winner) Merlyn Hans Dethlefsen celebrates his 100th mission.

North Vietnamese MiG-17 pilots.

F-105 pilot Ralph Kuster shoots down a MiG-17.

MiG-21, the successor to the MiG-17.

An F-4G—the "Phantom"—flies over Vietnam.

A Phantom strike, April 1969.

Legendary F-100 Wild Weasel pilots Alan Lamb and Jack Donovan.

Wild Weasel patch.

An F-100F—the original Wild Weasel fighter—refuels over Vietnam.

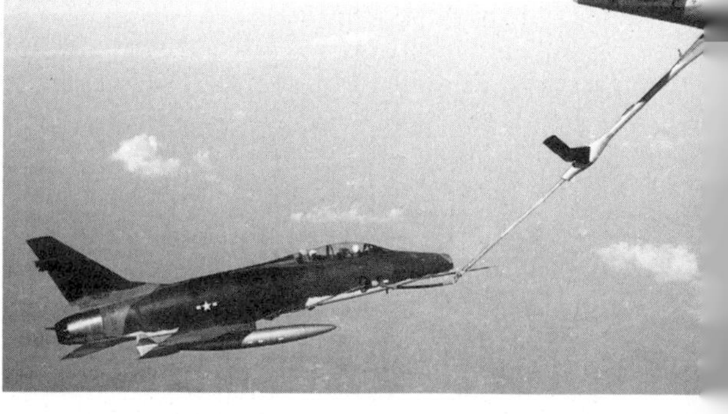

"Triple ace" Robin Olds, veteran of more than 250 combined combat missions in WWII and Vietnam.

An F-16 CJ patrols Iraq.

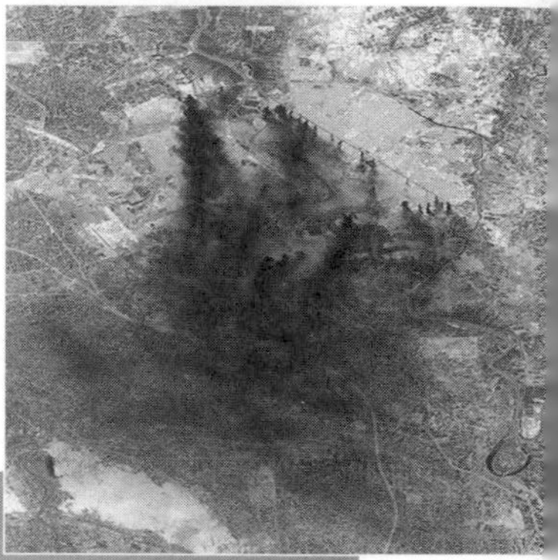

Baghdad reeling from Shock and Awe from an F-16 strike.

LTC Dave Moody ("Mooman") and his Viper—both from the 23rd TFS "Fighting Hawks"—during Desert Storm, 1991.

The author stands in front of his F-16 "CeeJay" after a mission over Iraq, March 24, 2003.

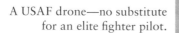

A USAF drone—no substitute for an elite fighter pilot.

detachment found the Japanese carriers. It was five of these six planes, led by Lt. Langdon K. Fieberling, that Harada and his combat air patrol of Zeros destroyed. Two of the four B-26 bombers were also shot down. Forty-five minutes later, Vindicator and Dauntless dive-bombers from VMSB-241 began their glide attacks from 8,000 feet and were cut to pieces by the Zeros. Nine of the twenty-seven didn't return. Shortly after 8:00 a.m. fifteen B-17s arrived overhead at 20,000 feet and added their bomb loads to the confusion.

The continued attacks by American shore-based aircraft had prevented Nagumo from launching the second strike. By this time his first strike force had arrived back at the fleet for refueling and rearming, and he chose to recover the first group before attacking Midway again. A cruiser scout plane had reported enemy ships, but it wasn't until 8:40 that an American carrier was confirmed. Once again the rearming was changed back to torpedoes and the hangar decks of all four carriers were chaotic as crews frantically worked. Stacks of bombs were everywhere, with high octane fuel hoses snaking between torpedoes and boxes of ammunition.

Unbeknownst to the Japanese, *Enterprise* and *Hornet* had launched their own attack at 7:02. Based on the timing for the Midway assault, Spruance's chief of air staff, Capt. Miles Browning, calculated that an American strike launched *now* would catch the Imperial Navy in the midst of recovery and refueling—and it happened exactly that way.

The *Hornet*'s strike group had arrived at the estimated target point and found empty sea. Figuring that Nagumo had headed to Midway, they turned southeast and flew toward the island—all except VT-8. Lt. Cmdr. John Waldron guessed that the Japanese might be lurking beneath a low cloud layer to the north, and that's where he found them. At 9:40, running low on fuel and without fighter escort, he attacked, followed by VT-6 off the *Enterprise* and VT-3 from the *Yorktown*. Thirty-five of forty-one torpedo planes were shot down by Zeros and anti-aircraft artillery with no hits on the ships.

But while the Japanese were taking evasive action, no launch was possible, so the flight decks were clogged with fully fueled, heavily armed aircraft. Most important, all fifty Zero fighters were down at low altitude chasing the surviving Americans. Kaname Harada later recalled, "The American aviators were exceptionally courageous. I was impressed at how bravely they pushed home their attacks."

Nagumo was vainly trying to reorganize, regroup, and launch the next strike when his luck finally ran out. Dive-bombers from the *Enterprise* had trailed the destroyer *Arashi* back to Mobile Force 1 and found four Japanese flattops ponderously turning into the wind. As fate would have it, Lt. Cmdr. Max Leslie arrived with seventeen more dive-bombers from the *Yorktown*.

At 10:22 Lt. Cmdr. Wade McClusky split his thirty-seven dive-bombers into two groups, rolling in from 14,000 feet on the *Kaga* and *Akagi*. Yorktown's VB-3 attacked the *Soryu*. Like lethal silver water droplets glinting in the sun, all fifty-four aircraft screamed down toward the Japanese. Harada and the other Zero pilots struggled to climb and engage, but they couldn't stop this attack.

At least one bomb went through *Akagi's* flight deck to detonate on the packed hangar deck below. Fuel and ammunition exploded, roasting flight crews in their planes and gutting the ship. *Kaga* went down three hours later, and *Soryu* would be torpedoed by a U.S. submarine and sink at sunset. The Japanese were shocked and shattered, while the exuberant Americans continued hunting for the last enemy carrier.

But the Imperial Navy still had a few teeth yet and immediately launched *Hiryu's* remaining aircraft. Following behind VB-3's returning strike force, they appeared on *Yorktown's* radar at 1:30 p.m. Eighteen dive-bombers were intercepted by Wildcats from Fighting Three (VF-3), which splashed ten of them, and two more were shot down by anti-aircraft fire. However, six got through and three scored hits on the carrier, one of them disabling eight of her nine boilers. Superb damage control had her steaming again within ninety minutes, and by 4 p.m. she could make 20 knots. At the same time, radar detected a second wave of Japanese planes inbound from the west. Four airborne Wildcats immediately committed out to intercept, while those on deck, some with only 20 gallons of fuel, also took off.

The protective combat air patrol (CAP) got six of the inbound Kate torpedo bombers, but at least four survived to drop their fish. Two missed, but two more hit the port side, eventually causing a 30-degree list. Though the ship was abandoned, *Yorktown*'s aircraft were recovered on the *Enterprise*. Ten of these dive-bombers, along with a full strike package from *Enterprise*, set off to find the last remaining Japanese carrier.

Kaname Harada had landed his fighter aboard the *Hiryu* after his own carrier was hit. The plane was so full of holes that a maintenance officer ordered it pushed over the side. He was wondering what to do when a spare Zero was brought up, and he hopped in. Getting airborne at 5 p.m., he'd just glanced back when a wave of hot air hit him, bouncing the lightweight plane sideways. The entire flight deck disappeared beneath a rolling wall of fire. Smoke poured up everywhere, and he whipped his head back around, staring upward. Dive-bombers were dropping like stones, little black bombs detaching as the aircraft pulled out with vapor streaming from the wings. It was a full package from the *Enterprise* plus ten from the *Yorktown*.

Harada fought back until he was out of ammunition and out of time—the sun was setting and he had no place to land. Locking the canopy open, he dropped flaps, pulled the power, and pancaked into the sea behind a destroyer. Even as it circled back to him, B-17s showed up overhead and dropped their bombs in Midway's final attack of the day. The destroyer fled and after floating all night, Harada was picked up the next morning by the *Makigumo*. In a strange twist of fate, the pilot who was first off the decks for the Pearl Harbor attack was the last one off at Midway. Harada was also rescued by the same destroyer that would scuttle the last Japanese carrier afloat—*Hiryu*.

Still refusing to sink, *Yorktown* remained afloat all night, and a second salvage operation got under way on June 5. By 3:30 p.m. that day, it actually appeared the ship might be saved. But then four torpedo wakes were spotted.* Two of them struck, and by early morning on June 7, the battered carrier finally rolled over and sank.

The Imperial Navy could not cover an invasion without aircraft carriers, so Admiral Yamamoto ordered a general withdrawal to the west. Spruance and Fletcher were later criticized for not pursuing the Japanese, but this is an unfounded judgment. They had no way of knowing if an invasion would occur, or even if something other than Midway might still be a target, so they remained where they could react if necessary. There was also a very real chance of running into Yamamoto's main battle fleet, and that would certainly have been disastrous for the few heavy American warships left.

The loss of four fleet carriers was a tremendous blow, as were the 3,000 Japanese lives lost. More than 240 aircraft went down, with nearly all their trained and experienced flight crews.

---

*Japanese submarine I-168.

It has also been estimated that 40 percent of the Imperial Navy's mechanics, armorers, and specialists were also lost in the battle. Though it would not stop the Japanese advance, Midway did cost them their ability to conduct unrestricted offensives. This means they lost the momentum that had carried them thus far, and they would never really regain it. Over the next two years the Japanese would produce just six fleet carriers.

The 307 American sailors, crews, and pilots lost were a bad blow to a sorely pressed navy. *Yorktown* was a heavy loss, but from 1942 to 1945 the Americans would launch twenty-six *Essex*-class carriers, 45,000-ton warships carrying 2,600 men that each supported a ninety-plane air group. Nine *Independence*-class carriers and more than a hundred light and escort carriers would also roll down the slipways into salt water. As Yamamoto had foreseen, time was running out for the Japanese. The giant was awake, angry, and out for blood.

After the Battle of Britain, Pearl Harbor, and the Pacific battles of Coral Sea and Midway, airpower no longer had any detractors. The startling results from those key conflicts demonstrated the influence of tactical aircraft, and the men who flew them, far beyond all expectations. *They* were the weapons, with potential and effects previously only imagined by a few visionaries. Conventional ground forces and naval vessels that had defined warfare for six hundred years stared up at the fight and watched, basically spectators, as a new era emerged.

CHAPTER 11

TOP OF THE FOOD CHAIN

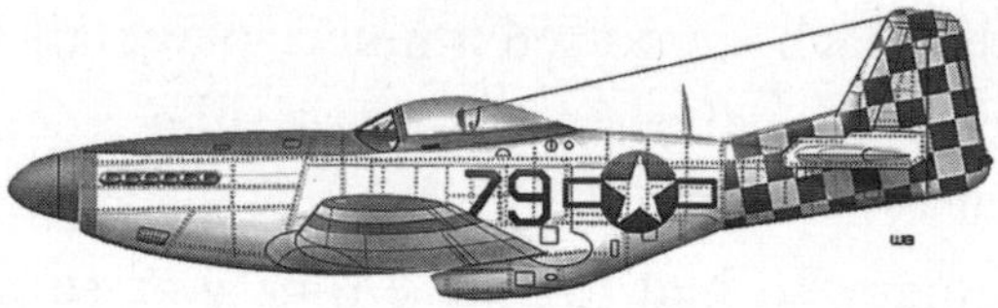

P-51D Mustang

September 18, 1944

SHUDDERING VIOLENTLY, THE P-51 bit into the thin air and continued to climb. The pilot winced; he knew that the vibration was from his supercharger, but he still didn't like the sound. The results were hard to beat, though, and he leaned forward a bit as the fighter passed 21,000 feet. As he bunted over a few seconds later, his butt came off the chute pack and mist spat out of the air-conditioning vents.

There!

Three distinct groups of dark flecks against the puffy clouds, about five miles away. Focke-Wulf 190 fighters. A little lower than him and not turning toward the flight of four Mustangs. He'd seen it before: they were going directly for the lumbering, slow-moving bombers. Unlike other escort missions he'd been on, these B-24s were loaded with supplies, not bombs. Operation Market Garden, an enormous Allied airborne assault, had begun the day before.

Forty thousand British and American paratroopers had been dropped along Highway 69 in Holland; the Americans were to take the bridges at Eindhoven and Nijmegen while the British 1st Airborne and the Polish Brigade would take Arnhem. Capt. Robin Olds shook his head, staring at the distant German fighters. Maybe it would work. He was a fighter pilot, not a ground pounder, but trying to move tens of thousands of troops along a single narrow road didn't seem a great idea. Then, of course, the poor Brits and Poles landed right on top of two SS panzer divisions that had been put in Arnhem for a rest. Talk about a bad break . . .

Which was why he was here right now. The lightly armed paratroopers were running out of food, medical supplies, and, above all, ammunition. So these B-24s *had* to get through. As the radio erupted with chatter, he shoved his goggles up and squinted up at the deep blue sky. That was where the threat would be—the new German jet. From higher up and incredibly, unbelievably fast.

Sunlight flashed off metal to his left as the P-51s closest to the bombers ramped over and dove at the Focke-Wulfs. The 190 was an awesome aircraft, tough, fast, and heavily armed with four 20 mm cannons plus two 12.7 mm machine guns. In the right hands it was a match for his Mustang below 20,000 feet. And one just never knew these days. It was either a novice who could barely fire his guns or one of the *experten*, aces with years of combat experience. His job this September morning was covering the high ground against any Messerschmitts that showed up. Again, you just never knew.

Glancing down, Olds reached around the stick and touched

a toggle switch on the console. It was up, where it should be, in the GUNS CAMERA & SIGHT position that armed his weapons and filmed whatever he shot. The glowing yellow dot on the combining glass could be activated with the camera for training, and it all looked the same. He wouldn't be the first pilot to squeeze the trigger and have nothing happen because the damn switch was in the wrong position.

Methodically scanning the sky, he then glanced at the line of fighters floating loosely nearly four miles above the earth. Most retained their silver paint on the top surfaces except for a dark strip along the cowling to the cockpit. Some had the rudders painted olive drab, and a few were solid green. The rudder bars and spinners were either red or yellow depending on the squadron, and most of the 18-inch alternating black and white invasion stripes had been removed by now. It didn't matter; they were beautiful planes. It always amazed him how motionless flying seemed to be unless you were passing a cloud or looking down at the ground.

Or in a dogfight.

Up ahead a deadly spiderweb of tracers began streaking over, into, and below the bomber formation. Darting black specks merged like a swarm of gnats and began twisting together. A bright flash popped from the mess and a fighter dropped away, burning and trailing black smoke. Then another . . . and another. His headset was alive with voices: excited yelling from the new guys and much calmer, terse directives from the veterans, who sometimes didn't say anything at all.

Suddenly the Mustang to his left sparkled brilliantly, and he flinched, surprised, as it staggered, pieces breaking loose and fluttering away. As he opened his mouth to call out, a mottled, torpedo-shaped plane flashed past overhead, heading for the bombers.

The jet!

Actually, there were two of them. He shoved the throttle forward and dumped his nose to follow, keying the mike at the same time.

"Roundtree Lead . . . Greenhouse Yellow One's got bandits . . . your seven o'clock level . . . inbound fast . . . jets!"

Like a thoroughbred out of the gate, the Mustang surged ahead as the Packard Merlin engine spun up. Jettisoning his own wing tanks, Olds looked left to see his wingmen do the same as the big 12-foot prop bit hard into the thin air.

"Gre—Yellow Two is hit! Hit . . . I'm . . ."

The pilot clicked his mike and shot a glance at the map on his kneeboard for an approximate position. Close to Maastricht . . . it was the best he could do. In a matter of seconds the P-51 accelerated past 400 knots, and he stared through the clear bubble canopy at the mess before him. The bombers had all turned north toward Arnhem, and he could see a few Mustangs in the vicinity. The rest were all below him, wrapped up with the Germans. Black smoke trails hung in the air, most curving straight down, but others streamed away east and west as wounded fighters tried to make it back home.

One of the B-24s was spinning in, and another looked like it had lost most of its right wing. The jets had slashed through the bomber formation then disappeared. Below to his right a dark, compact fighter turned wildly with three . . . no, four Mustangs. The yellow cowling on the Focke-Wulf was plain to see as the skillful pilot pirouetted away from the other planes. Kicking the rudder, Olds skidded his Mustang sideways and was about to jump in from above when he caught movement off to the east.

The jet again. This time he could only see one.

"Greenhouse Yellow One . . . tally bandit . . . three o'clock level . . . ah, three miles . . ."

Flipping the P-51 over, he sliced to the right as his two surviving wingmen rolled and maneuvered to stay with him. The Me 262 was about three miles away, sliding across the horizon like a cruising shark. As he watched, the thing cranked up on one wing and turned in toward the bombers.

"Yellow Three, tally one . . ."

The Liberators were heading due north. Racing in from the southeast was the jet, and the three Mustangs were right in the middle. With a combined closing velocity of 1,400 feet per second, there was less than ten seconds until firing range—no time for anything fancy.

Ten . . . nine. . .

And the German never hesitated.

Aiming straight at him, Robin Olds stared through the glass reflector of his gunsight. He'd already set the dial at 35 feet to account for the Focke-Wulf's wingspan and didn't bother to change it. The jet was a little bigger, but it wouldn't matter. His throttle was all the way forward, and Olds pushed it hard enough to feel the safety wire break. It moved another two inches, and five seconds of emergency power boosted the Merlin up to maximum power. This was only used in combat, since it could, and did, burn up engines.

Six . . . five. . .

He also twisted the throttle grip counterclockwise till the range indicator read 2,400 feet. The yellow aiming pipper stayed as it was, but the circle formed by the six surrounding diamonds shrank as the range setting was increased. The K-14 gyroscopic gunsight was a marvel that compensated for bullet drop *and* calculated the lead required for deflection shots. All the pilot had to do was put the pipper on the target, twist the grip until the diamonds matched the wingspan, and open fire.

Three . . . two . . .

Left hand rock steady on the throttle and his right hand on the stick, the pilot instinctively nudged the controls to keep the pipper on the deadly-looking fighter. *What a strange plane—no props.*

One . . .

Robin kept the pipper on the pointed nose and hammered down, the Mustang instantly vibrating against the recoil of six .50-caliber machine guns. Older P-51s had dangerous jamming problems because the guns were mounted sideways so they'd fit inside the wings. Not so with this Mustang; all six guns were electrically boosted to fire 1,200 rounds per minute per gun. The tracers streaked out, and even as Olds let up, the German's nose sparkled as he fired in return.

Olds quit firing, his two-second burst having sent more than 120 rounds at the other plane. Pushing over savagely, he kicked the left rudder and twitched the stick, skidding the P-51 down and right as the German's shells went exactly where he'd just been.

The 262 zipped past, and the Mustang pilot corkscrewed his fighter around, nose low, and pulled. Taking a deep breath against the g's, he felt the air bladders on his new Berger G suit inflate and for once was grateful to be wearing the damn thing. Both wingmen cross-turned above him, then sliced back to bring their noses to bear.

With the stick back in his lap, Olds brought the nose around in the direction of the bombers to cut off the jet, but he wasn't there! Blinking against the glare, he swallowed. *Not there.* Then he saw the smoke. A thin, dark gray trail that curved around to the south. Reversing the turn, he followed the smoke with his eyes and saw the jet. Two miles away already and arcing toward the ground, now heading southeast, back toward Germany.

"Ya got 'em, Yellow One . . ."

Well . . . a piece of him, anyway.

His number three man sounded relieved. Fighting something that different was disconcerting, especially after being told the Mustang was the best fighter in the world. And the men flying the jets were no novices; the Messerschmitts were too valuable for that.

Olds shook his head and watched a second longer before banking smoothly around to the north. Pulling the throttle back, he set a cruise speed of about 350 knots and glanced over the gauges: oil pressure, rpm, and especially coolant. All good. Exhaling, he checked his fuel and then the rounds counter to see how many shells were left. Everything was fine.

For a brief moment Robin Olds felt everything: heart thudding against his chest, the deep throb of the big Merlin engine, and his quick breathing slowly returning to normal. Cool air from the vents was drying the sweat on his neck, and the pilot sighed, shaking his head. He would've loved to send the German down in flames and watch that beautiful jet break apart under his guns. To fight and not kill was frustrating.

But if the Mustangs hadn't been there, then the Messerschmitt would've shredded those bombers and everything they carried would be lost. Squirming against the harness, he took a deep breath and shrugged. It was enough this time. And besides, Robin thought as he smiled under the mask, there would be other Germans on another day.

There always were.

FROM ITS BEGINNING, the Second World War appeared to be an unquestionable Axis success. Fortunately, Hitler's military decisions combined with the geography of the Soviet Union, the Pacific Ocean, and the English Channel to give the Allies a few desperately needed advantages. For the most part, these opportunities were seized and used with considerable fighting skill until overwhelming American war production took effect. The pivotal year was 1942, with the Japanese blunted in the Pacific and Hitler's Reich halted in Russia. Operation Torch brought Allied landings into North Africa that would threaten Europe's belly and eventually shatter the Axis.* Despite the Allied debacle at Kasserine Pass, May 1943 saw the remnants of the Afrikakorps with their backs to the sea and surrendering at Cap Bon, Tunisia. This came just five weeks after the German Sixth Army, surrounded and starving, capitulated at Stalingrad.

Italy's king Victor Emmanuel III dismissed Mussolini in July and eventually imprisoned his former prime minister at the Campo Imperatore ski resort in Gran Sasso. A daring raid by German paratroopers freed the dictator, and he promptly declared his own Italian Social Republic in northern Italy. Americans then crossed from Sicily, landing at Anzio and slugging their way up the Italian peninsula. They'd gotten off to a rough start during Torch, largely due to incompetent leadership, but learned very quickly.†

As many had foreseen, the entry of the United States into the war spelled doom for the Axis. Even without being bled white by four years of war, there was just no way to compete with the Americans. Once blooded, they rose to the occasion, as did their supporting economy, and it was an impossible combination to beat. In four years of war, shipbuilding had increased

* Confronted with Allied success, the French government switched sides—again. Mussolini was replaced as prime minister and Italy signed a separate armistice.

†The U.S. II Corps commander had been Lloyd Fredendall—a two-time washout from West Point who had never seen combat and stayed aboard his ship during the invasion. He was replaced by George Patton and the rest, as we say, was history.

elevenfold, munitions fifteenfold; aluminum manufacturing had quadrupled, and aircraft production was twelve times greater than it had been in 1940. The USAAF had begun the war with 354,161 men and 4,477 combat aircraft. By 1944 personnel exceeded 2.3 million and the USAAF could field some 35,000 combat aircraft. A standing Wehrmacht joke went, "When we see a silver plane, it's American. A black plane, it's British. When we see no plane, it's German."

The Allied bombing campaign was largely a result of the 1943 Casablanca conference where the British and Americans mapped out the Third Reich's destruction. Though the goal was identical, both sides were diametrically opposed on strategy. The RAF was committed to area bombing—basically the mass leveling of cities and industrial centers regardless of civilian casualties. Their firestorm method was calculated to destroy vast amounts of acreage (2,000 acres in Berlin alone) and sap German willpower. The first objective was arguably successful, but the second was not. In any event, Hamburg, Darmstadt, and a dozen other cities burned brightly under RAF bombs and eventually suffered 1.4 million civilian casualties. Of course, it also destroyed the submarine pens at Peenemunde and most of the industrial capability in the Ruhr Valley.

The Americans were convinced that only the annihilation of key military and economic chokepoints would force the Germans to their knees. To this end, they espoused the doctrine of daylight precision bombing, which would, in theory, focus immense tonnage in concentrated strikes to utterly wipe out a target. The idea had some merit in that the B-17 was the U.S. Eighth Air Force's primary heavy bomber. Extremely tough and well armed with ten guns, it also possessed the Norden sight, which made bombing deliveries within 135 yards from 15,000 possible. The actual CEP (circular error probable) was much higher—more than 50 percent of bombs were at least 2,000 yards off target. However, in terms of sheer volume, the damage was done.

Also, American production continued ramping up; bombers were pouring off the assembly line and there was no real shortage of planes. The concept was really put to the test on August 17, 1943, in a grand raid to destroy the German ball bearing manufacturing centers at Schweinfurt and Regensburg.

It was a disaster for the Americans. German fighter pilots obviously hadn't read the treatise on bomber theory and were unaware that the bomber would always get through—especially tight, heavily armed formations. Weather, timing, and complex plans aside, some 350 bombers of the 1st and 4th Bombardment Wings launched that morning, but only 290 returned. Sixty heavies and more than 550 men were lost that day, with more than eighty other bombers irreparably damaged—all for no appreciable strategic results. Ball bearing production did temporarily decrease by 30 percent, but losses were quickly made up by affiliated factories.

Bearings were essential as they were used for almost any military equipment with moving parts. Bombsights, engines, weapons, communication devices, and many others were all highly dependent on these tiny steel globes to reduce friction and support loads.* The giant Swedish firm SKF was the largest worldwide manufacturer of ball bearings. From Goteborg, Sweden, and Schweinfurt, Germany, it supplied 80 percent of the total European demand. There were also dozens of foreign affiliates, including the Hess-Bright Manufacturing Company in Pennsylvania, which had become SKF Philadelphia in 1919.

* A single Focke-Wulf 190 fighter contained over 4,000 ball bearings.

So when the Schweinfurt plant was bombed, the shortfall was largely covered from, of all places, the United States.

In a shameful footnote to the war, more than 600,000 ball bearings per year were shipped from American ports, via Central America, to Siemens, Diesel, and scores of other Axis companies. This was often to the detriment of U.S. companies that also needed the vital little globes. Curtiss-Wright, maker of the P-40, nearly shut down for want of bearings.* It was also very likely that the Swedes warned the Germans about the raid in order to protect their factory in Schweinfurt. The National City Bank of New York (later Citibank and Citicorp) funneled money back to Sweden, and business continued as usual while American boys died in the air over Germany.

The deep penetration raids produced two inescapable lessons. First, the bomber *does not* always get through against an intelligently defended target and a 17 percent loss rate was not sustainable, even by the United States.† The second lesson was the imperative need for a long-range escort fighter.

Enter the P-51 Mustang.

Arguably the finest fighter of the Second World War, the Mustang was the apex of piston-powered warplane development. Ironically, this iconic aircraft was created not by an initiative from the American government, but rather as a response to a Royal Air Force request. In fact, the entire design and initial production were a private venture between the British government and the North American Aircraft company.

Early in 1940 the British agreed to North American's proposal and in May signed a contract for 320 aircraft. The

---

*Among others, aircraft engine manufacturer Pratt & Whitney suffered a 150,000 shortfall from SKF. Sweden was hardly neutral, and more than 20 percent of the munitions fired at Allied troops came from Swedish iron ore.

†Actually a 41 percent loss rate if the irreparably damaged bombers are added.

company, headed by James "Dutch" Kindelberger and Edgar Schmued, was new and very small, and had previously fielded only one aircraft.* This meant there were no paradigms to overcome and no history of conventional solutions to fall back on.† This was very apparent when the first plane rolled out on September 9, 1940, barely 102 days after the contract was signed.

In addition to being a superb engineer, Kindelberger was also a very solid businessman. He realized that a plane that could be easily mass-produced would have a tremendous advantage once the United States began its wartime expansion. The P-51 was the first aircraft to incorporate an entirely mathematical design; all the contours were derivations of geometrical shapes and could therefore be expressed algebraically. This meant all the tooling and templates were extremely precise, yet easily duplicated for mass production.

Constructed in three main sections, the aircraft could be quickly disassembled if the need arose. Manufacturing of each section would be done separately, then the components shipped for final assembly. The engine mount only required four bolts, and the motor was easily removed by line mechanics with no special equipment. Unlike the Bf 109 or Spitfire, the Mustang's landing gear retracted inward toward the fuselage centerline. This kept more weight along the main axis and permitted nearly a 12-foot wheelbase for safe ground operations. The brakes were hydraulic and controlled via the rudder pedals.

Other significant improvements included the beautiful bubble canopy and the practical cockpit layout. Most of the vital elements, like trim tabs, coolant switches, landing gear

*NA-16 Harvard trainer.

†Ironically, Kindelberger was the son of German immigrants and Schmued was born in Germany.

lever, and engine controls, were located so the pilot could reach them with his left hand, since his right hand would be on the stick.

Another innovation was the deliberate design of a *laminar flow* wing. We know from basic aerodynamics that airflow divides over a wing, and as it splits, the change in velocity alters surface pressure to produce lift. If the flow separates past a critical point, more drag is produced than lift and the wing stalls. This can be delayed somewhat by keeping the thin boundary layer of air closest to the wing intact as long as possible. A laminar flow wing is symmetric, so the air divides evenly and flows over an extremely smooth finished surface. This considerably reduces drag while increasing lift.

One advantage to less drag is that the aircraft can be much heavier, yet still retain high performance. For the Mustang, the greater weight meant more weapons and fuel without a corresponding loss of speed or maneuverability. So high performance was preserved while range and firepower increased, thus giving the Allies a fighter capable of deep escort into the Reich. The U.S. Army had become aware of North American's aircraft and managed to keep the production line open by ordering a ground-attack version of the RAF fighter.* The USAAF purchased 310 of the newly designated P-51A fighters in August 1942, and the first one flew by early February 1943.

Though the Mustang promised to be an excellent aircraft, the Allison engine was a problem. Even with a supercharger and a larger prop, the V-1710-81 motor could only deliver 1,125 horsepower at 18,000 feet. The superb Rolls-Royce Merlin was the obvious choice for later Mustangs, but production was

*Called an A-36 "Apache," over 500 were built and they fought well in North Africa, Italy, and the Far East.

an issue. The British company was already heavily committed supplying the Spitfire, Hurricane, and Lancaster bombers, so an American company was needed to manufacture the engine under license. Back in 1940, Henry Ford offered to do the deal, but only for American defense—under no circumstances for Britain. Instead, Ford built five-ton trucks for the German army and his sixty-acre plant in Poissy, France, began turning out aircraft engines for the Luftwaffe.*

So Packard was selected to build the 1,500-horsepower Merlin V-1650. Capable of 400 knots at 30,000 feet, the new engine had a novel two-stage supercharger that would automatically kick in around 19,000 feet. This permitted a climb rate exceeding 3,000 feet per minute, with unmatched high-altitude maneuverability. Combined with the slick laminar flow design, the Allies had a fighter aircraft that could escort bombers all the way to Austria if needed.†

Previous hard-learned lessons regarding weapon systems were also heeded in the Mustang design. The RAF version carried four .50-caliber and four .303 caliber Brownings, while the Mk IA had four Hispano 20 mm cannons. American P-51A variants mounted four .50-caliber machine guns and could carry a pair of 500-pound general purpose bombs. Both versions were equipped with new gyroscopic gunsights that compensated for bullet drop and made accurate deflection aiming possible.‡

Correctly regarded as the culmination of Mustang development, the Merlin-powered P-51D model began appearing in March 1944. More than eight thousand of these magnificent

*Ford was mentioned in *Mein Kampf* and sent Hitler 50,000 Reichsmarks every year as a birthday gift.

†At 20,000 feet the Mustang's range was 950 miles at 350 knots.

‡RAF Mk II gunsight was manufactured by Sperry as the K-14.

machines were built, and they had a profound effect on the outcome of the war against the Third Reich. Bombers could now hit factories, laboratories, and key targets deep inside Germany. Steel production and electrical generating capacity fell by 30 and 20 percent, respectively. Hundreds of French locomotives were destroyed along with railyards and repair facilities. Bridges, depots, and rolling stock were attacked to the point where the entire French transportation system was operating at only 60 percent capacity. This made logistical support to the Atlantic Wall and any type of rapid German military response problematic. The Reich's already fragile economy steadily disintegrated.

It must've seemed like Germany of 1918 all over again for those unlucky enough to have experienced it. Rice was pressed into unappealing little cakes and flavored with animal fat. Flour was made from nuts and turned into something resembling bread while ersatz, vaguely resembling coffee, was once again brewed from roasted oats.

Oil production essentially halted, even from the dozen synthetic-oil plants that the Germans had constructed. Synthetic-oil manufacturing operations were particularly vulnerable due to their complex machinery and sheer size relative to conventional refineries. Fuel production eventually fell from 180,000 tons per month to less than 5,000 tons, with enormous tactical implications for the Luftwaffe. Combat units were throttled and training curtailed to the point where new pilots received just 120 hours of flight time before going into combat, barely half of the 1942 program.* And to alleviate the pilot shortfall, bomber pilots were transitioned into fighters. Both solutions produced disastrous results.

---

*By this time their RAF and USAAF counterparts had anywhere from 350 to 450 hours before facing the enemy.

By 1944 Luftwaffe losses were averaging 10 percent per mission, and dozens of Allied aces were created overnight. After its successes during the Battle of Britain and against the Soviet Union, the Luftwaffe was definitely seeing the other side of the coin. Only in this case there would be no geographical salvation from the English Channel or the Russian steppes.

Albert Speer, the Reich's minister of armaments, estimated that 98 percent of oil production had been destroyed by July 1944, which would leave Germany with less than a 400,000-ton reserve—not enough for six months. Combat aircraft were withdrawn from the Eastern Front to defend the Reich, and more than a thousand German fighter pilots were lost during the first four months of the year. Ironically, the man who created the Luftwaffe was also largely responsible for its destruction. Blame for the Allied bombings fell on Goering and his inability to prevent them; in turn, he blamed the fighter pilots. He fired Adolf Galland, Hannes Trautloft, and a score of other top officers. In an eerily Soviet manner, he also instituted a system of political officers who would report anyone failing to display a suitable commitment to National Socialism.

Perhaps the final nail in the Luftwaffe's coffin came from the blundering employment of a weapon that might have changed the air war. The Me 262 Schwalbe had actually been developed following Heinkel's successful flight of the He 178 in August 1939—six days before Germany invaded Poland.* Jet engine technology wasn't new, but neither was it well understood, and the technical difficulties were severe. The vexing issue of heat transference within the engine was exacerbated by Germany's shortage of metals for the alloys necessary to survive extreme temperatures. As it was, a normal engine would operate about twelve hours before needing an overhaul. The quick solution

* *Schwalbe*—"swallow."

was to fold the turbine blade, creating something like a metallic taco shell, which facilitated air cooling. This prevented rapid meltdowns, helping avoid the problem of an engine "throwing" a blade, which usually had catastrophic effects.

Messerschmitt's fighter flew its initial test flight in April of 1941, nearly two years before the British Gloster Meteor. Fortunately for the Allies, both Hitler and Goering were not supportive of the new program. In 1941 both men were convinced that victory was imminent and that Germany's resources would be better utilized manufacturing piston engine fighters. By the middle of 1943, Hitler mandated that the jet be developed as a *Schnellbomber* (fast bomber) that could be used to strike England with impunity. Professional fighter pilots like Adolf Galland wanted to use the jet against Allied bombers that were destroying Germany. With a speed at least 150 mph faster than the P-51's and four 30 mm Mk 108 cannons, it was an ideal bomber killer.

Or it would be if it was used correctly. The impressive speed advantage had a very real tactical downside: it was simply too fast for accurate aiming. Closing velocities for a head-on attack were over 1,000 feet per second, and the guns weren't accurate beyond 600 yards. The jet usually had to break off at 200 yards, about a second away, to avoid either a collision or debris. So under ideal conditions (which were rare), a pilot had a 400-yard window, about two seconds, to aim and fire. The big 30 mm cannons, though devastating, had a low rate of fire at only three hundred rounds a minute. So a two-second burst from all four guns delivered forty rounds, not much to bring down a Flying Fortress or a Liberator. Augmenting the guns were 55 mm Orkan rockets in underwing pods, and as their trajectory was similar to that of the cannons the REVI 16B gunsight could be used for aiming. Also, the rockets had a tactical range of about a half mile, far beyond the bomber's machine guns, and one Orkan hit was enough to bring down a Fortress.

Finally overcoming political opposition and most of the technical issues, the Me 262 went into action on July 26, 1944. Due to shortages, the test unit became an operational command under Maj. Walter Nowotny until his death in November. The influence of the Me 262 was profound and would be felt in future air wars, but for Germany it was too little and much too late.

Nowhere was this better illustrated than on D-Day, June 6, 1944. Operation Overlord was the Allied invasion of a 50-mile stretch of beach along the Normandy coast. The Germans were well aware that an invasion would occur; however, the location was hotly disputed. Conventional thinking anticipated an assault at the Pas de Calais, the narrowest point between England and France. It is here that a mere 21 miles of the Dover Strait separates continental Europe from the Kentish shoreline. It was the logical point to cross in a hurry due to an air or sea threat or if the attacker lacked sufficient transport. The Wehrmacht had faced all these issues in 1940, but the Allies had no such concerns in 1944. It was also too obvious. Plus there simply weren't enough ports along that section of the English coast to support an invasion fleet.

Shortly after midnight the attack began with airborne drops and glider assaults on the flank areas of the beaches. The British 6th Airborne was to seize bridges over the rivers Orne and Dives, while the U.S. 101st and 82nd Airborne took the neck of the Cotentin Peninsula. Unfortunately for the Americans, many of their glider pilots either panicked at the flak or landed their tows in the wrong drop zones. Despite high casualties, the survivors banded together where they could and created incredible confusion behind the German lines.

At 6:30 more than 150,000 Allied soldiers began coming ashore during the main amphibious assault. The western beaches belonged to 73,000 men of the U.S. First Army: Utah was hit by the U.S. 4th Infantry Division and Omaha by the 1st Infantry Division with two Ranger battalions. Three divisions of the British Second Army were given beaches code-named Gold, Juno, and Sword.

The 4th Infantry Division was landed on the wrong spot, prompting the assistant division commander, Brig. Gen. Teddy Roosevelt Jr., to say, "We'll start the war from here." And he did just that. As the 4th moved inland it linked up with the paratroopers and only suffered 197 casualties out of the 23,000 men put ashore. The 1st Division on Omaha was a combat-tested unit that had fought in North Africa and Sicily; however, accompanied by the inexperienced 29th Infantry Division, it was landed opposite the German 352nd Infantry Division. This was a well-supplied, well-emplaced unit mostly composed of Russian Front veterans. The beachhead was in serious doubt until a breakthrough was achieved and men began moving inland around nine o'clock. The majority of the 4,600 American casualties on D-Day occurred here.

The British XXX Corps, which would later lead the ground assault during Operation Market Garden, came ashore in the center at Gold. Juno went to the Canadians, who made it off the beaches to Bayeux by nightfall. The 3rd Infantry Division, accompanied by Royal Marines and French commandos, stormed Sword. Naval support included more than a hundred destroyers, a dozen cruisers, and two battleships. Four thousand landing craft brought men in to land, while the RAF and USAAF flew 14,000 combat missions. Against this, the Luftwaffe countered with 250 sorties. Nearly all the fighter units had been withdrawn for the defense of the Reich, and only a few forward detachments remained.

By the end of the day the great risk had abated somewhat. Taking nothing away from the unquestioned courage of those who battled their way ashore, the Allies didn't win the Normandy beachhead so much as it was lost by the Germans. Not by the soldiers on the ground who, despite their lack of supplies, fought tenaciously. No, the Allies were saved from worse consequences by the divided German High Command and, as always, Hitler himself. The 21st and 12th SS Panzers counterattacked on June 7 and nearly broke through to the beaches. What would've happened if all three complete panzer divisions had been released for combat on the morning of the invasion? Or if the Luftwaffe had been committed in strength against the extremely vulnerable beachheads and supporting naval units?

Much of the credit for this goes to a complex web of disinformation woven to deceive Hitler into believing the Pas de Calais was the true target. Or to the months of preparatory airstrikes that significantly crippled the French transportation network. In any event, the invasion succeeded and the continental foothold was established. Any plans the Germans had considered for a massive western redeployment were thrown out two weeks after D-Day.

On June 22, 1944 (the anniversary of Operation Barbarossa), the Soviet Union launched its own offensive from the east. When Operation Bagration commenced with 166 divisions, more than 2,500 tanks, and 4,500 combat aircraft, the days of Hitler's Reich were truly numbered. Minsk fell by July 3, followed by the encirclement of Warsaw. The Romanians overthrew their government, declaring war on Germany in late August, and by September Marshal Carl Gustaf Emil Mannerheim of Finland concluded a separate peace with Stalin.

By the end of January 1945 the Soviets had crossed into East Prussia for the final push, driving 2 million refugees before them. By January 16, the Red Army had crossed the Oder

River and was within 40 miles of Berlin. On that day, Hitler descended into his bunker beneath the Chancellery and would emerge only twice during the next three months. The city mobilized around him, some 330,000 defenders against 3 million vengeful Russians. As eight Allied armies swept across Europe from the west, they were ordered to advance no further than the Elbe River. Stalin was to get to Berlin first—this had been decided the previous year.

All through March the Russians built up 7 million artillery shells to feed their artillery around Berlin—300 guns to cover each half mile of city. More than 2,000 aircraft had been moved up for ground attack; as the Luftwaffe had effectively ceased to exist, there would be no air combat. Inside the capital, schoolchildren and Hitler Youth were armed and thrown into battle beside a motley collection of police, reservists, and a few fragmented veterans such as the 18th Panzergrenadiers. Others were hardened Waffen SS units who would never surrender to the Soviets and would fight to the death. Some of the SS units were made up of foreign volunteers who knew full well that they had nowhere else to die. Among these were the 11th SS Panzergrenadiers (Nordland) containing Spanish, Swedish, Danish, and Swiss volunteers. There was also the 33rd Grenadier (Charlemagne) Division of the SS—an entirely French unit.

On April 20, Hitler's fifty-sixth birthday, the guns opened fire and did not stop until Berlin fell. To the north, the Soviets broke through Hasso von Manteuffel's depleted panzers, the last real line of defense, and the encirclement of the capital was nearly complete. Russian tanks entered Berlin, and six days later the inner city was occupied by a half million Red Army soldiers with 13,000 heavy guns.

Early on April 27, Hitler wrote out his political statement justifying the war, expelled Himmler and Goering from the

Nazi Party, and then married Eva Braun. Three days later, on the afternoon of April 30, 1945, he killed his dog, Blondi, and supposedly shot himself. The 8th Guards Army under Gen. Vasily Chuikov (of Stalingrad fame) had every Soviet gun open fire on May 1 and destroy what remained of downtown Berlin. The next afternoon at 3:00 p.m. the firing stopped, and beneath the smoke of the ruined city cheers rang out from 500,000 Russian soldiers. German units in western Europe, Norway, and the Channel Islands began surrendering, and Victory in Europe Day was proclaimed on May 8, 1945.

On the other side of the world, while Berlin burned, the Americans had forced the Japanese back across the Pacific. Saipan had fallen nine months earlier, putting Japan within range of the new B-29 bombers. In March 1945, while the noose around Berlin tightened, the USAAF launched a 325-aircraft night strike against Tokyo. Upward of 250,000 buildings burned, with 89,000 Japanese casualties, and on April 1 the Americans stormed ashore at Okinawa. The nearly three-month battle cost the lives of 7,000 soldiers and Marines—more fatalities than D-Day.* It was a deadly harbinger of what an invasion of the Japanese home islands would cost.

The conviction that Tokyo would never surrender, that millions would fight to the death, led to a lonely bomber lifting off from the island of Tinian on August 6, 1945. Six hours later, flying under the call sign "Dimples 82," a B-29 named the *Enola Gay* made history as a single 10-foot-long bomb dropped from her belly.† Called "Little Boy," it fell for forty-five seconds before arming, and at 8:15 a.m. it detonated 1,968 feet above the Japanese city of Hiroshima. The atomic blast vaporized the city

*Japanese dead numbered more than 110,000.

†The pilot, Colonel Paul Tibbets, named the plane after his mother.

center, and the subsequent firestorm destroyed everything else within five miles. Three days later another B-29 called *Bockscar* also took off from Tinian's North Field and dropped "Fat Man" on Nagasaki. Between them the pair of bombs killed at least 150,000 Japanese and convinced Emperor Hirohito that immediate capitulation was his only option to end the war.

On September 2, 1945, representatives of the Japanese Empire stood on the deck of the battleship *Missouri* in Tokyo Bay. Rows of big, khaki-clad U.S. officers stood by and watched as the diminutive Japanese foreign minister, dressed in a black frock coat, meekly signed the surrender document. Senior officers representing the various Allied powers followed, the British in white shorts, the Americans grim and unsmiling. Even the Soviets showed up in dark uniforms and shoulder boards to claim a share of the spoils from their grueling twenty-five-day war against Japan.

As the short ceremony ended, aircraft roared overhead in a very visible display of U.S. military might. Flying one of the F6F fighters was James G. Daniels, the surviving wingman of the Wildcat flight shot down over Pearl Harbor on December 7, 1941—the only man known to be in the air at both the beginning and end of the war.

World War II cost at least 50 million lives and military casualties were less than half of those. The Soviet Union alone lost 18 million and, not counting Stalin's domestic butchery, at least 10 million of these were civilians. Poland's population was barely 80 percent of what it had been in 1939, and 4.5 million Germans didn't survive the war. The United States military suffered 292,000 dead, and of these, 45,520 were USAAF battle deaths—only Army ground forces sustained higher losses. Naval deaths from combat stood at 34,607, of whom 3,618 were aviators killed while fighting. The Marines lost 17,376 men in combat and 1,835 pilots.*

Combat aviation was certainly born during the Great War, and its potential was accepted during the intervening years that followed. However, World War II saw aviation advance to a level that would have been unimaginable just a decade before. Bombing theory was somewhat revised to coincide with reality, though this lesson would again be forgotten in later wars. Heavy air transport was vital for the Normandy invasion, just as the lack of it sealed Paulus's fate at Stalingrad. However, neither transport nor bombing success is feasible without the protection that can only come from fighters.

England's very existence after 1940, the Pacific theater after Midway, and the ultimate destruction of the Nazi Reich are perfect examples of what is possible with fighter air superiority—or the lack of it. Fighter pilots certainly can't win wars alone, but World War II absolutely proved that you cannot win a war without them.

*Twelve percent of Army deaths and 10 percent for the Navy and Marines, respectively, were aviators.

PART FOUR

DAWN OF THE JET AGE

I KNOW THAT SHALL MEET MY FATE
SOMEWHERE AMONG THE CLOUDS ABOVE;
THOSE THAT I FIGHT I DO NOT HATE,
THOSE THAT I GUARD I DO NOT LOVE
—W. B. YEATS

CHAPTER 12

MiGS AND MACHINE GUNS

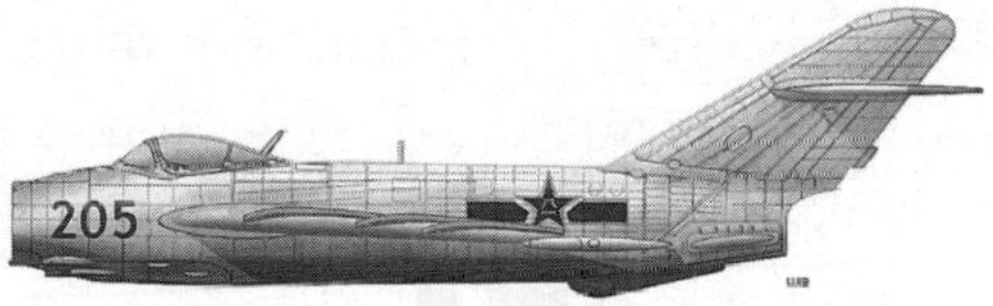

MiG-17

"CHEVY ONE . . . come left heading three zero-zero . . . bandits at your eleven o'clock, fifty miles . . . Angels Two Zero."

"Bromide, Chevy copies . . . left to three-zero-zero. Say numbers."

Thirty miles north of Kimpo Air Base, the eight F-86s were rejoined into two tight flights of four, Chevy and Buick, staggered slightly in altitude. Passing 25,000 feet, they were northbound for MiG Alley along the Korean-Chinese border. The leader turned left, heading northwest at 300 degrees, and the others followed.

"Chevy One . . . heavy group of bandits . . . estimate twenty contacts bearing three-two-zero, forty-five miles."

"Switches," someone said. Eight pairs of eyes swiveled around their cockpits taking in engine gauges, fuel, and armament switches. Seat straps were tightened, some men took off their gloves, and others loosened up their necks or fingers.

Major George Davis pulled his sunglasses off and dropped them in the leg pocket of his G suit. He also loosened his chin strap and wriggled the helmet a bit, his hand nearly covering the cartoony image of a boxing bird that was the emblem of the 334th "Fighting Eagles." Nicknamed "Curly" due to his straight hair, he was a thoughtful, quiet professional—until the fighting started, that is. Although he'd been in the Korean Theater of Operations for less than two months, he'd done this many times in the last war. As a P-47 Thunderbolt pilot with the 342nd Fighter Squadron, Davis had shot down seven Japanese planes over the Philippines and New Guinea. It was now November 30, 1951, and he'd opened his score in this war three days ago by flaming a pair of MiGs.

More than twenty-five of the little Russian fighters had been airborne the day before, but a backlog of squadron commander paperwork had kept him off the flight schedule, and he'd missed it. It had certainly been a prelude to something, and sure enough, this morning the Chinese invaded Taehwa-do Island in Yalu Bay off the North Korean coast.

Reaching 30,000 feet, his eight ship—eight jets flying in formation—was loafing along at 0.85 Mach, about 570 mph, when a distant flash of sunlight on metal caught his eye just above the horizon line. Leaning forward, Davis stared for a good minute till the black dots appeared.

There!

Big enough to be seen at 15 miles . . . bombers. Had to be. From long habit Curly checked above and behind them until the smaller dots showed up. He nodded. Escorts, at least a dozen. There were probably a few more mixed in with the bombers, but he couldn't see them. The Russians and their Chinese students were predictable if nothing else.

"Bromide . . . Chevy One is tally-ho, my nose . . . ten miles. Two groups . . . bombers low and fighters high."

They were coming right down the Yalu, heading toward the sea. Probably going to hit one of the islands again.

"Bromide copies . . . Chevy and Buick engaged at 1605 local. Green southwest."

Not me, Davis thought. "Green" was supposed to be the shortest direction back to friendly territory, and from a map in a controller's hut that's probably how it looked. But off to the west he could see the flat grayness of the Yellow Sea, and that was where he'd go. The Navy was out there somewhere with Task Force 77 and two carriers, *Essex* and *Antietam.* Davis knew a fighter pilot had a much better chance of living till his next birthday if he could ditch at sea, so "feet wet" over water was much better than "feet dry" anywhere north of the MLR—the Main Line of Resistance, current political-speak for the front lines.

"Buick One . . . fifteen right, ten miles . . . cleared off and cleared to climb."

"Buick wilco . . . in the climb."

Davis looked up over his right shoulder as the other four ship of Sabres arced up into the deeper blue sky. Within moments four white fingers streamed out behind them as the fighters passed through the contrail layer. Eyeballing the Chinese bombers, he angled a bit to the left and pushed up the throttle to hold 0.90 Mach, just below the speed of sound. If there were any MiG-15s up today, they'd be high, and he'd need all the airspeed, the "smash," he could get.

But as he did so, the smaller specks of Communist fighters peeled away and headed in his general direction. Still eight miles away, they'd immediately seen the cons from his other four ship and turned to intercept, just as he'd planned. Now the bombers were unprotected and even more vulnerable.

The Sabre was shuddering slightly, so Davis cracked the

throttle back a hair. Peering around the combining glass, he could clearly see the bombers now; twin-tailed, twin-engine Soviet Tu-2s left over from the last war. The Bat, as the Tupolev was called, could manage about 300 mph at 25,000 feet, and the Chinese People's Liberation Army Air Force (PLAAF) had imported a few hundred of them.

Nudging the stick, he angled even farther away and glanced at his wingmen. Chevy Two was about 100 yards down his left wing line and a little low. The other element of Sabres hung in space a mile off his right wing, with number four a good 500 feet higher than anyone else. It was a bit ironic, he knew, that the newly formed United States Air Force (USAF) exclusively used variations of the old Luftwaffe fighting tactics.

Glancing up to the right, he couldn't see Buick, so they were out of the cons and well above the escorting Chinese fighters. He could see *them* plain enough, though, about 10 miles away on a roughly opposite course and trying to climb. More Russian junk, La-11s. Piston powered, they could climb at 2,400 feet per minute and manage about 420 mph. Davis grinned under his mask; the Sabre climbed at 9,000 feet per minute and cruised along at 600 miles per hour. *No worries*.

At five miles he banked up smoothly and began a gentle pull to put the bombers on his nose. He'd chosen to attack head-on from above because the only forward-firing weapons the Tupolev carried were in the wings. His wingmen fanned out in the turn, and Davis keyed the mike.

"Chevy Three . . . you and Four take the Bats on the southern edge. Two . . . you take the far northern bomber and I've got the leader. We'll only get one pass 'cause of fuel . . . rejoin over Sahol at twenty K plus call sign."

Now they had a point at which they could rejoin if they got separated, with Two at 22,000 feet, Three at 23,000, and Four at 24,000. The sky was actually a small place when you'd lost sight of everyone.

The flight acknowledged, so he reached up and rolled the adjustment dial under the combining glass to 60 feet—the wingspan of the Tupolev—then keyed the mike again.

"Check wingspan set . . . check wingspan set . . ."

If the APG-30 radar worked, which it often did not, then the gunsight pipper would correct for maneuvering and show the bullet impact point. If he had to shoot manually, which he actually preferred, the range reticle gave an accurate prediction that he could use for aiming. Just like the old K-14 sight in the Thunderbolt. Smiling at the thought, Davis was unconsciously reacting to everything around him. His eyes and experience constantly adjusted the intercept geometry, which made his hands finesse the stick and throttle. Radio chatter was filtered, and he only processed the stuff that applied to his flight. His wingmen were in the right positions, and the Sabre was purring.

Sunlight gleamed through the bubble canopy, heating up the cockpit. He opened the air vent wider and stared out into clear space. It was like riding on the tip of a rocket. The adrenaline sharpened everything. His fingertips itched, and he felt like he could see everything: his jets, the enemy jets, his gauges . . . it all filtered in.

Davis wriggled in the seat and stretched his neck. Life was good.

"Buick's engaged . . . twelve bandits, south Sahol at two five thousand . . ."

"Bromide copies." Davis heard the GCI controller reply and added his own.

Three miles.

The nasty green paint job on the bombers was plain to see now, and so were the ugly little red stars. Leaning forward, he pulled the throttle back a knob's width to slow down a bit while keeping the enemy plane just below the combining glass and a little right. One last look around . . . Chevy Two had floated wider to the left, and the other element had split off altogether toward the south end of the bomber formation.

Then he saw them: close escorts directly behind the bombers.

"Head's up! Bandits close aboard, a mile past the bombers, slightly high."

"Chevy Three's tally-ho . . . we're still on the Bats."

Davis nodded. "Roger that . . . stick to the bombers and blow through."

He didn't like leaving enemy fighters alive, but there wasn't fuel for a fight and the bombers could kill Americans on the ground. *Besides,* he thought as he bunted forward and the bomber floated onto the combining glass, *a kill's a kill.* Reaching up, Curly spun the sight range dial all the way back. If he had to shoot manually, the ten-dot reticle would equal a fighter's 35-foot wingspan at minimum range to fire. He'd fudge it for the bombers, but aiming at them wasn't hard.

Two miles.

The slick F-86E didn't really slow down much, so he left the throttle alone and fanned the speed brakes out just a crack. The bombers still hadn't seen the Sabres swooping down, and so they flew on, docile and not maneuvering.

With about 9,000 feet and seven seconds to go, Davis pulled the bomber to the center of the glass, pushed down on the target reject switch on his stick, and held it. At a mile he released and stared at the Tupolev, waiting for the radar to lock. A half second later the light under the gunsight glowed red, indicating a radar solution.

But his smile disappeared when the pipper jumped. And jumped again. Closing at 800 feet per second, he had no time for analysis, so he immediately caged the gyro and nudged the stick to keep his pipper on the bomber.

Just then the Bat rolled up to the left and began nosing over. He'd been seen! Fanning the brakes wider, Davis yanked the throttle back and kept the pipper on the Tupolev's bulbous nose. The Sabre shuddered as it slowed, and for an instant time stood still, like a single frame during a movie.

Now!

Aiming squarely at the cockpit, he squeezed the trigger, and the fighter kicked as all six Browning machine guns opened up.

Two . . . three . . .

Releasing the trigger, he shoved forward on the stick, retracted the speed brakes, and shoved the throttle full forward to mil power. The pipper had disappeared when he fired, but it didn't matter. Flashing past underneath, Davis was barely 300 feet from the bomber and could see it was finished. His 350 bullets had pumped 50 pounds of lead into the nose and it had just vanished, leaving a mangled cave where the cockpit had been. The plane simply fluttered over and dove for the earth.

He wasn't nicknamed "One-Burst Davis" for nothing.

Processing this in the three seconds it took to close the distance, he avoided the wreckage and zipped under the other bombers. From down here their turret guns were ineffective, and the wing guns could only be brought to bear if they dove at him—which no bomber pilot was going to do. Grabbing the canopy rail with his left hand, Curly twisted sideways, looking up and right at the other blue-bellied bombers. At least one other Bat was on fire and the rest were scattering.

Snapping the Sabre up on its left wing, he pulled back and shot up into the rear group. They were breaking in all directions, but Davis picked one trying to head north. No time for fancy solutions, so in a split second he figured the geometry, pulled the nose into lead, bunted slightly, and opened fire.

Tracers shot forward in a converging stream, and he saw the bomber physically stagger under the impact of his burst. Rolling away hard right, Davis ignored the stricken Bat and charged straight into the escort fighters. Déjà vu hit him for a split second: the Lavochin was basically a Russian copy of the P-47 he'd flown in the Pacific six years ago. *Weird*.

Two of the fighters broke away, but the other was actually trying to bring his nose to bear and fire. Davis simply pulled back hard, and the Sabre zoomed up through the formation, hopelessly out of reach. As the G suit tightened around his legs, he corkscrewed around and with a single glance took in the scene around him. There were several dark trails leading down off to the northeast, and he hoped they weren't any of the Buicks. Three of the Bats were gone, one fluttering down like a bird with a broken wing and the others just black smears against the sky. Below him the surviving bombers were frantically trying to escape while their furious escorts thrashed around to face the Sabres. The La-11 could manage 375 mph at this altitude, and each carried three 23 mm cannons. Enough to kill a Sabre if you were careless enough to let one get close, which he had no intention of doing.

Seeing a flash of silver, Davis watched a Sabre arc clear of the fight and turn in his direction. Eyes flickering to the fuel gauge, he knew they had to leave. There was at least 150 miles of Indian country to cross, and who knew what they'd meet on the way.

"Chevy One . . . splash two . . . egress one eight zero."

Flipping the Sabre over, he banked around to the south, rolled out, and stared over his wings at the La-11s milling around below. Shame to leave them . . . but if his flight was out of fuel and then ran across some MiGs, they'd be up shit creek.

But a single Tupolev had turned all the way around and was now in front of him, maybe 1,000 feet lower and running the other way. *Too good to pass up* . . . Davis shook his head, pulled the throttle back to save gas, nosed over, and glided down for the attack. Ignoring the radar, he kept the pipper on the canopy and waited till it filled the dots. But the Chinaman must've seen him, because even as Davis fired, the bomber rolled up and away. Releasing the trigger and adding power, he saw some of his shells chew through the right wingtip, which came off.

Trading speed for altitude, Davis zoomed up to 25,000 feet and looked back. Two more Sabres were swinging in from the southwest, and his own wingman had rejoined on the right side about a half mile back. Suddenly a black dot fell from the maimed Tupolev . . . then another. White mushroom tops parachutes appeared and he grinned.

"Chevy One . . . Pistol One." A new voice.

"Go ahead."

"Pistols are south ten miles, inbound, and tally your fur ball."

Davis nodded. More Sabres . . . that was good. They could finish up.

"Pistol . . . probably six Bats remaining and a dozen LAs . . . you're cleared in below two five zero . . . we're southbound for the Emerald Palace."

Kimpo was hardly a palace, but compared to a rice paddy in North Korea it was positively opulent.

"Pistol copies all. Got your cons."

Davis twisted sideways and looked back over the tail at his thick white vapor trail. Didn't matter . . . they were on the way out.

"Chevy One . . . Buick Three . . ."

"Go!"

"Ah . . . Three is east Sahol by nine miles . . . wounded bird."

Davis frowned. Three was Ray Barton, and his jet was damaged. "Come southwest . . . we'll try and pick you up."

"Chevy One . . . ah, I'd love to, but I'm about to have some company up here . . . bandits inbound from the north . . . whole gaggle climbin' out over the river."

"Chevy Two say fuel."

"Bingo minus two."

Without being asked, the other element leader added, "We're both Bingo minus four."

Options flashed through his mind and were discarded. He'd already set a low combat Bingo of 1,200 pounds, and that was barely enough to get back to Kimpo from MiG Alley. Zippering the mike, he replied, "Three . . . you've got the lead. One's off to the north."

Banking back around toward the Alley, Davis spotted a thin gray trail against the blue sky. Following it to the source, he saw a silver Sabre heading south.

"Buick Three . . . where are the bandits from your position?" he asked, quickly glancing at the fuel totalizer and rounds counter. His kills had taken nine seconds' worth of bullets, about 1,100 rounds, and he had 520 remaining. Most pilots, himself included, didn't load the ammo up to full capacity because the guns could jam.

It was enough.

He smiled grimly. *Four seconds of ammo is two short bursts against* . . . He strained his eyes at the fast-moving black dots. *At least twenty MiGs.*

"Ah . . . Blue One . . . they're about five miles at my seven o'clock in a climb . . . looks like they're about twenty K . . ."

"Roger that . . . come right." He glanced at the compass

rose and did the geometry in his head. "Heading two two zero. I'll be on your nose for three miles high. Pass below and blow through to K-fourteen. I'll pick you up after."

"Copy all . . . in the turn."

Davis watched the other Sabre crank up and come right. As expected, the trailing dots immediately came harder right to cut off the American jet. They smelled blood.

So do I.

The turn plus the damaged Sabre's slower speed gave the MiGs cut-off angles for the intercept. This would happen fast. However, they were all fixated on the smoking F-86 in front of them, a classic combat mistake. Buick Three zipped past off Davis's left wing and nosed over slightly, trying to accelerate. The MiGs were badly spread out, but the leader and his wingman were out front and plain to see. Every time the leader's jet moved, all the others moved too. There must be two dozen of them, he realized.

Wish I had more ammo.

As the leader hit the ten o'clock position, Curly smoothly rolled and pulled, staying high through the turn. He didn't want to flash his wings or cross the horizon until it was necessary. Both would give him away.

The F-86 was slicing through the air, engine throbbing, and he felt the fighter's power straining against his hands. Leaving the throttle up, he held the jet on its left wing and paused.

Not yet . . . not yet . . .

Now!

Racking up to 6 g's, Davis grunted and pulled down hard, coming in right off the wing line. The fat MiG continued straight ahead, the Chinese pilot not seeing anything besides his target.

Gonna be close. His eyes flickered back and forth between Buick Three, the MiG, his wingman, and the gunsight. He couldn't slow down. He didn't dare, not with twenty other MiGs running up his tail.

A thousand feet . . .

Nine hundred . . .

Now!

He hammered down at 800 feet. *One . . . two . . .*

The Brownings spat again, and a stream of shells slammed into the Chinese fighter. Instantly bunting, rolling, and pulling right, Curly aimed in front of the MiG wingman and fired again. As the first jet blew up, the recoil from Davis's guns stopped abruptly, and the high-pitched whirring of the electric motors filled the cockpit. No bullets.

The other MiG panicked and rolled hard away to the right. Davis flashed through the smoke and rolled up to the left, hanging on a wingtip. If he had to, he'd draw the Chinese fighters off toward the south, where other Sabres would be coming from.

But they must've thought the same thing, and even as he watched unbelievingly, the entire gaggle broke away north toward the Yalu. Swallowing hard, he held his course away from the damaged F-86 for a few moments to make certain, then pulled the throttle back to hold 0.80 Mach. Leveling off, he unhooked the sweaty mask and exhaled, eyes bright and scanning for MiGs.

But they were gone . . . and the sky was empty.

WHAT WERE PLANES made in California and Texas doing in a river valley between Korea and Red China, in a place that few Americans had ever heard of and fewer cared about? Unlike the relatively black-and-white struggle during the world wars, this hard little peninsula had become a flashpoint between two diametrically opposed ideologies. It could have happened in other places, such as Eastern Europe, for instance, or even Indochina. But it was here.

With the end of World War II, even empires that didn't collapse immediately, namely the British and French, had to cope with millions of disaffected colonials in India, Asia, and the Middle East. These regions would become catalysts for many of the bitter conflicts that would dominate the world after 1945.

Japan's defeat had left much of Asia fragmented and rudderless. China's civil war had just ended, with the Communists under Mao Zedong in a state of exhausted victory. Chiang Kai-shek's Nationalists had retreated to the island of Formosa (later Taiwan), which the Communists vowed to conquer. Korea, like French Indochina, was suffering in a power vacuum. Ironically known as the "Land of the Morning Calm," it had been a Japanese protectorate since the turn of the century, though its difficulties went back much, much further. During the Cairo Conference in late 1943, Chiang Kai-shek of China, Franklin Roosevelt, and Winston Churchill had agreed in principle to future dismemberment of the Japanese Empire. China would get back Manchuria and Formosa, while "in due course Korea would become free and independent."

In August 1945, following the Soviet invasion of Manchuria, two young Americans pulled out a *National Geographic* map of Asia. One of the men was Dean Rusk, a State Department officer and future secretary of state. By the simple rationale that it lay in the center of the country, the 38th parallel was chosen as a demarcation line between the Soviet and American spheres of influence. Ignoring the practical demographics of population, industry, and agriculture the United Nations agreed.

Over the next five years Korea became a petri dish of discontent and suspicion. Added to this nasty mix were healthy doses of nationalism and corruption. Above the parallel the Korean

People's Republic (KPR) railed against the United States and their friendly treatment of the Japanese who'd brutalized Korea for so long. While not strictly correct, the American occupation forces had understood their former enemies much better than the subtle, scheming Koreans they'd encountered. Unfortunately, this meant using the National Police, who'd collaborated with the Japanese and brutalized their fellow Koreans. The Japanese were eventually sent home, but the locals were promoted and supported by the United States. To be fair, the American troops were not peacekeepers, but combat troops who just wanted to go home. So the quickest way for stabilization appeared to be utilizing those who'd ruled the country for so long.*

Below the parallel, Dr. Syngman Rhee and his Korean Democratic Party (KDP) offered an alternative. Urbane and charming, with degrees from Princeton and Harvard, Rhee told the Americans what they wanted to hear, which was primarily that he would resist the Communists and preserve a democratic state in the south—meaning a state centered around himself. Given the anti-Communist paranoia running wild in the West and the rise of McCarthyism in America, Washington took the path of least resistance and supported Rhee.

President Truman had promised to "contain" Communism while promoting liberalism and American-style democracy across the world. Admirable goals, however impractical, and diametrically opposed to the goals of the Soviet Union, which was attempting to promote its own system. In early 1948 the United Nations proposed supervised Korean elections, followed by independence and a joint withdrawal of the foreign military presence on the peninsula. Moscow and Pyongyang dismissed the whole idea and boycotted the elections. In effect, this failure

* Allied forces did the same thing in Europe with former Nazis.

by both sides ended any hope of unification because it officially recognized a divided Korea.

The inherent conflict between the Soviet Union and the United States had significantly worsened following World War II. Communist expansion into eastern Europe and Asia alarmed Washington, and when Stalin sealed off Berlin in 1948 the United States countered with the famous airlift that saved the city while humiliating Moscow—as did the $12 billion in American aid that the Marshall Plan provided to rebuild nations devastated by the war. The idea was that stable, productive countries would be less likely to fall prey to Communism—and in the long run this was correct. The Soviets could not compete with the West economically, but they believed they could do so militarily. On August 29, 1949, they demonstrated this by detonating an atomic bomb.

So at 4:00 a.m. on June 25, 1950, as four North Korean spearheads crossed the 38th parallel heading south, the United States paid attention. Ten divisions with 100,000 men, supported by T-34 heavy tanks and more than 130 aircraft, slammed into the South Korean defenses. With no armor or air force to speak of, the army of the Republic of Korea (ROK) collapsed almost immediately. Given that no one in Washington wanted a land war in Asia, Washington reacted with admirable speed and authorized action the very next day, perhaps to avoid escalation into another world war or maybe because this generation of leaders knew appeasement simply wouldn't work.

Non-Communist members of the United Nations were asked to contribute: Australians, Canadians, Turks, Greeks—even the French. The British immediately dispatched HMS *Triumph* with her forty aircraft and two cruisers to the Yellow Sea. The situation was correctly viewed as an opportunity to prove the UN concept and to act as a check on Communism.

Seoul fell to the northern Korean People's Army, on June 27, the same day that USAF Lt. William Hudson of the 68th Fighter Squadron opened air combat over Korea by shooting down a Yak-11. Two days later the USS *Juneau* shelled enemy shore positions, and on July 3, 180 miles off the coast, the USS *Valley Forge* turned into the wind and began launching aircraft. By noon they were over Pyongyang escorting interdiction and reconnaissance aircraft. Ens. E. W. Brown from the "Screaming Eagles" of VF-51 blew a Yak-9 out of the sky with a 20 mm burst from his F9F Panther. His flight lead, Lt. (j.g.) Leonard Plog, shot down another Yak, and U.S. naval aviation was officially in the air war.

But it wasn't enough to slow the North Korean advance, and the American 24th Infantry Division fought a delaying action south through Chonan, Chochiwon, and Taejeon. Most of the U.S. military was in deplorable shape by the summer of 1950, and it showed. Some of this was understandable given that World War II had only ended five years before and everyone wanted to get on with life. Many believed, as others had in 1918, that it had been the last war. After all, there were nuclear weapons in the mix now, so who would risk a fight?

The U.S. Navy had taken a particularly brutal hit in the postwar demilitarization mania. In 1945 there were thirty-eight fleet carriers on active service, and by the summer of 1950 just seven remained. Of these, only three were attached to the Pacific Fleet, and they were all *Essex*-class carriers left over from World War II.* At 35,000 tons and about 800 feet long, they could carry approximately a hundred aircraft. While the newer 60,000-ton *Midway*-class carriers were assigned to the Atlantic Fleet to counter the Soviet threat. With the Japanese

---

*USS *Boxer*, *Valley Forge* and *Philippine Sea*.

vanquished, there was no perceived naval threat in the Pacific, and this was part of the reason the Navy was losing the budget battle to the USAF. China had no navy, and the Soviet Union was occupied in Europe.

In fact, the Air Force was so enamored of its long-range bomber nuclear strike capability that it tried to eliminate the aircraft carrier altogether. After all, who would need sea-based airpower during a nuclear war? For that matter, who would need an army, either? In 1947 a lecture had actually been given way back behind the lines at Maxwell Air Force Base titled "Protesting the Need for a Ground Force."

The results of this mentality were all too obvious. One estimate put 80 percent of the U.S. Army reserves as effectively unusable. The fighting units in Korea lacked 60 percent of their assigned firepower, including support weapons and, most critically, ammunition. Almost all of it was World War II vintage, and men were lucky if it functioned half the time. Ironically, only five years after the surrender in Tokyo Bay, the U.S. government had to contract with a Japanese company to make land mines for the U.S. Army.

Even food was short. There wasn't a single C- or B-ration in all of Korea, and American troops had to make do with leftover K-rations from World War II until the newer types could be flown in. Fortunately, airlift was a skill and capability the United States possessed far beyond any other power in the world. Several years earlier the USAF flew 1,783,573 tons of supplies into Berlin over the heads of the incredulous, angry, and embarrassed Soviets. So the airlifters again rose to the occasion and averaged about 200 tons per day into Japan, or directly into Korea.

Mothballed Sherman tanks were hastily rebuilt and shipped to Korea along with many M24 Chaffee light tanks—neither was a match for the heavy, Russian-built T-34. This was another area where close air support would make a lifesaving difference to the beleaguered infantry. While the *Valley Forge* was turning around and heading back to the South China Sea, the Far Eastern Air Force (FEAF), based in Japan, responded immediately with its F-51s and F-80 Shooting Stars. With about four hundred aircraft available, the FEAF rapidly deployed the 8th and 18th Fighter Bomber Wings, the 35th Fighter Interceptor Group, and the 51st Fighter Wing, among others.

While this occurred, elements of the 1st Marines sailed from San Diego on July 12, followed two days later by the rest of the division. While America reacted, KPA forces advanced nearly 100 miles and forced the retreating South Koreans and U.S. forces into the southeastern corner of the peninsula. Centered around the port of Pusan, the defensive pocket was roughly defined by the Naktong River and the mountains near Pohang. The port was one of the most developed in Korea, with four piers to accommodate two dozen deepwater cargo vessels. There were heavy cranes, beaches, and a Japanese-built railhead. If the UN forces were to remain on the peninsula, then Pusan, sometimes likened to a Korean Dunkirk, must be held. But unlike the situation in France, there was no question of air superiority once the Americans committed.

Gen. Douglas MacArthur, in command of all UN forces on the peninsula, ordered a withdrawal southeast toward the coast. He planned to use natural barriers such as the Naktong River and the mountains near Pohang to halt the North Koreans. This would accomplish several objectives. First, reinforcements would land at Pusan. This would make it impossible for the Communists to capture it, while it would also consolidate American strength for a breakout offensive. Second, a stagnation would further stretch the already tenuous North Korean supply lines and weaken them further. Third, air support from the carriers and USAF would finish clearing the skies, interdict where possible, and then dismember whatever infrastructure remained. MacArthur's master stroke, which he'd seen from the beginning, was then to land an amphibious assault force at Inchon, near Seoul, some 200 miles behind the lines.

It was a good plan in many respects and, with hindsight, really the only way to quickly break up the Korean attack. Carrier-based Corsairs and land-based B-29s mauled enemy airfields while the Panthers, F-80C Shooting Stars, and Mustangs made short work of the Korean People's Air Force (KPAF). More than ninety Il-10 Shturmoviks and seventy-nine Yak-9P fighters began the war, and in two weeks the KPAF lost twenty-four planes. By mid-July there was one Yak-9 and fewer than twenty IL-10s remaining.

Dunkirk had possessed no natural defenses, nor did the Allies have reinforcements and air superiority in 1940. Pusan had all of these. On August 1 the U.S. 2nd Infantry Division landed at Pusan, with a brigade from the 1st Marines following the next day. Two more light carriers, the USS *Badoeng Strait* and the USS *Sicily*, had arrived carrying Marine attack squadrons for close air support. Across the Sea of Japan, the fleet carrier USS *Boxer* docked in Yokosuka with 145 F-51 Mustangs and 70 USAF pilots.*

By mid-July the B-29s no longer needed an escort and could roam about at will. August brought ninety-odd Corsairs, Panthers, and Skyraiders from the newly arrived USS *Philippine Sea* along with 141,000 UN troops and several hundred tanks.†

---

*With the formation of the USAF in 1947, all former "P" designations used by the USAAF were changed to "F" for fighter; e.g., P-51 became F-51.
†47,000 of these were U.S. troops.

Fighting had continued all around the Pusan Pocket, as it was called, with probing attacks and counterattacks. It's interesting that, despite the preoccupation with nuclear warfare and, in the case of the USAF, the absolute and unfounded belief in strategic bombing, two piston-engine legends from the Second World War proved more valuable on the tactical battlefields. One of these was the F-51 Mustang and the other was the F-4U Corsair.

A variant of the beautiful gull-winged fighter so deadly to the Japanese, the Corsair was built by Chance-Vought and first flown in 1940. The philosophy had been to cram the biggest engine and most firepower into the smallest, slickest airframe. The distinctive gull wing was a design solution permitting the immense Hamilton Hydromatic 13-foot 4-inch propeller to clear a carrier deck. The prop had to be huge to transfer power from the *eighteen-cylinder,* 1,850-horsepower air-cooled Pratt & Whitney radial engine. Featuring flush rivets, spot welding, and wing intakes (instead of air scoops), the Corsair could sustain 400 mph in level flight. Initially armed with six .50-caliber AN/M2 Browning machine guns, the F-4U also carried 150 pounds of armor plate and a bulletproof windscreen for the pilot. It was fast, tough, and the Japanese, somewhat prosaically, called it "Whispering Death."

But it was tough to land on a carrier. The nose protruded 14 feet in front of the pilot, so keeping sight of the landing signal officer (LSO) was difficult at best. Also, to land on a carrier a plane must be nearly at stall speed, and the Corsair had a nasty tendency to drop the left wing and stall when it got slow. So the Navy generally turned the plane over to the Marines for shore-based missions, during which it performed brilliantly.

By the time the Japanese surrendered, the F-4U had flown 64,051 combat sorties and claimed 2,140 air-to-air kills. Seventy percent of all bombs dropped from U.S. fighters during World War II came off the Corsairs—15,621 tons. All told, 189 were lost in air-to-air combat for a 11:1 kill ratio. Nearly twice that number, 349, were lost during close air support or anti-ship missions, graphically illustrating the dangers of surface attack.

The Corsairs that arrived in Korea were F4U-4 and F4U-5 models with four 20 mm cannons and an engine that was truly a monster, a 2,850-horsepower Pratt & Whitney. Flown by Marines, it provided close air support that initially was superior in quality to anything provided by the Navy or Air Force. Part of this came from concentrating on a single mission. The Air Force was concerned with air superiority and strategic bombing, while naval air's first priority was to protect the carrier. The Marines were different. They were amphibious experts, and their indigenous air support existed to protect the grunts. The pilots, like all Marines, went through the full gamut of infantry training before they went off to become aviators, and they generally understood the ground perspective better than their counterparts.

So by early August 1950, running out of supplies and time, all ten North Korean (NK) infantry divisions plus the 105th Armored Division were arrayed opposite the UN troops at Pusan. After building underwater bridges of rocks and trees, the NK 13th Division crossed the Naktong River 40 miles northwest of Taegu. Three F-51s from the 67th Fighter-Bomber Squadron had taken off from their forward base at Taegu. Flying north along the east side of the mountains, they circled over Andong at 10,000 feet with the morning sun behind them. The forward air controller passed a situation report, and it wasn't good.

The North Korean 8th and 13th Divisions were coming down out of the mountains and heading south along the river. One of the chokepoints was near Hamchang, northwest of

Taegu, and it was here that the Mustang's bombs, rockets, and guns were needed. Staying east, they coordinated the attack among themselves, then followed the lead F-51 west into the valley. They were lucky—the flight lead was Maj. Louis Sebille, a sixty-eight-mission combat veteran from World War II *and* their squadron commander.

The Mustangs found a heavy group of North Korean trucks, armored personnel carriers, and troops scrambling up along the riverbanks. When the soldiers ran for the trees, the F-51s went into a wheel over the area and began sorting out targets for each pilot to hit. Major Sebille rolled in first on a 30-degree bombing attack. His plan was to unload the flight's 500-pound bombs at the front and rear of the enemy concentration. Then, lighter and more maneuverable, they could reattack with rockets and guns.

But the World War II vintage equipment often malfunctioned, and this was one of those times. On his first pass only a single bomb came off, and the other one "hung." Feeding in trim to keep the fighter level, he pulled up away from the explosions and watched his wingmen, Capt. Martin Johnson and Lt. Charlie Morehouse, blow huge chunks from the narrow road. Mud, rocks, and body parts cascaded through the air as Sebille arced around for another attack.

Suddenly the plane rocked, like it had been kicked by a giant foot, and the major angled away from the river, eyes glued to his gauges. It was instantly obvious that the big Merlin engine had been hit and was overheating. A weakness of the F-51 was its engine placement and the liquid cooling system's vulnerability to ground fire. After all, the plane had been designed as a long-range escort and dogfighter, not to do close air support.

Johnson saw the damage to his leader's plane and gave a snap heading toward Taegu. He might make it back to land, or at least bail out over friendly territory instead of here. Anywhere but *here*. Yet the Mustang banked back toward the Korean position, trailing glycol mist and black smoke.

"No," Sebille replied calmly. "I'll never make it. I'm going back and get that bastard."

With that, the F-51 flipped over and dove down at the road. At 2,000 feet, six white smoke trails from the "Holy Moses" rockets snaked out from under the wings. These were immediately followed by bright ropes of tracers as he emptied the gun. Five-inch HVAR rockets plus several hundred pounds of .50-caliber bullets ate into the enemy column, shredding trucks and men. But the Mustang didn't pull off and recover. It went straight in, vanishing in a tumbling wave of fire from the remaining bomb and burning fuel. Most of the column disappeared, too, leaving the surviving North Koreans stunned and shocked by the attack.

Maj. Louis J. Sebille died that day in an ugly Korean valley, leaving behind a wife and a six-month-old son. The USAF, rather unbelievably, was reluctant to recognize this man's incredible sacrifice, as it resembled (they said) a kamikaze attack. That, of course, would send the wrong message to somebody. Appalled by that attitude, the 67th Squadron awards officer forwarded a mission write-up and proposed citation directly to the Pentagon.* A year later, in August 1951, Gen. Hoyt Vandenberg, the Air Force chief of staff, presented the Medal of Honor to Sebille's widow. Louis Sebille was the first member of the USAF to receive the award.

On the Pusan perimeter the fighting continued all through August. By the middle of the month the Navy had withdrawn to attack targets in the north, leaving South Korea to the FEAF. In response to intelligence reports, the USAF sent

---

*Lieutenant Don Bolt. He was killed in action shortly thereafter.

ninety-eight B-29s to carpet-bomb an area along the western bank of the Naktong. More than three thousand 500-pound bombs and a hundred fifty 1,000-pound bombs were dropped in a 27-square-mile area. Thousands of trees were turned into toothpicks, but no bodies were found, as the Koreans were already across the river.

A week later Chinese anti-aircraft artillery opened fire on a RB-29 flying south of the Yalu. Several days passed, then two Mustangs suddenly appeared and strafed the Chinese air base at Antung. A mistake, the USAF stated, the pilots had gotten lost—except the Yalu is impossible to miss, and since it roughly runs east–west, then a target *north* of the river is blindingly obvious. It was payback for the B-29 incident and a warning to the Chinese, courtesy of USAF fighter pilots. Nevertheless, the seesaw around Pusan continued until dawn on September 15, 1950.

On that morning 13,000 Marines and Army infantrymen came ashore at Inchon, 25 miles from Seoul and more than 100 miles *behind* the Korean lines. Operation Chromite was Douglas MacArthur's finest hour; and he knew it. Against the naysayers on the Joint Chiefs of Staff and over the objections of the Marines, he'd done it. Inchon had no beach; it had seawalls and a North Korean garrison on Moon Tip Island in the center of the harbor. Most problematic were the 30-foot tides and the time of day which the high and low tides would occur. A dawn landing on September 15 was chosen over an evening landing or waiting another month for the same conditions.

But MacArthur was right—this time.

He knew such an assault on the Communist rear would immediately throw Pyongyang into a tailspin. It would also cut the North Korean lines of communication, obliterate their fragile supply system, and permit the Eighth Army to break out from Pusan. It could then push north, driving the Communists straight into the waiting Marines and Army 10th Corps, which had landed behind them—a nutcracker.

Chinese intelligence had read the signs even if Kim Il Sung could not: hundreds of ships in Japanese harbors, practice amphibious assaults, and the well-known capabilities of the U.S. Marines. Yet despite ample warnings, Chromite caught Pyongyang completely by surprise.* Inchon was captured, followed by Kimpo airfield, and at the end of the day the Americans had suffered fewer than thirty casualties.

Attacking the South Korean capital of Seoul wasn't quite so simple. Finally aware of the danger to his army, Kim Il Sung sent 20,000 fresh troops south to reinforce the 25,000 NKA soldiers occupying the city. Had MacArthur given command of Chromite to a combat soldier, then the next few weeks might have gone very differently. Thousands of lives might have been saved, and the entire North Korean army might have been bagged as it retreated up the peninsula.

But Army Maj. Gen. Ned Almond wasn't that man. Primarily a staff officer, in World War II he'd blamed his division's combat failure on the fact that they were predominantly black troops. Relegated to the oblivion of personnel management in 1946, he'd eventually caught MacArthur's attention. Vain and aggressive, with no fighting skills whatsoever, Almond patronized the Marine commanders and, modeling himself after MacArthur, refused advice from anyone more experienced than himself. Only the token North Korean resistance had saved him from disaster at Inchon. In any event, the Eighth Army broke out of Pusan on September 16 and eventually linked up with

*On the streets of Tokyo the assault was called "Operation Common Knowledge."

10th Corps. Seoul was liberated by the end of the month, and a victorious MacArthur prepared for his real offensive, as he saw it.

On September 30 the South Korean 2nd Division headed north across the 38th parallel. A week later the U.S. 1st Cavalry Division crossed into North Korea and turned toward Pyongyang. MacArthur was jubilant, Truman and the Joint Chiefs were nervous, and American fighter pilots ruled the skies, looking for targets.

Two hundred miles to the north, across the Yalu River, the Chinese waited—and watched.

MORE THAN 60 percent of the American public favored going north across the 38th parallel and finishing off Kim Il Sung. Of course, these same people didn't have to eat C-rations, freeze at night, die in the air, or live without their loved ones. Most of the military hierarchy also wanted to continue, but that was expected. If a line was breached, you pressed through it; if an enemy was on the ropes, you kept hitting till he was down, out, and finished. The whole concept of a limited war hadn't caught on with the generation that fought and won the Second World War, least of all with MacArthur.

He never intended to stop at the 38th parallel once South Korea was liberated. His goal had always been reunification, and that meant destroying the North Korean Army—nothing less would satisfy his image of himself. You see, MacArthur saw himself as *the* man of this century, a truly pivotal figure destined for greatness, and someone that all lesser men should heed. Self-confidence and even arrogance are forgiven in winning generals, but obtuseness to the point of megalomania was frightening in one responsible for so many lives. MacArthur often referred to himself in the third person and insisted that photographs only be taken from a lower vantage so he'd appear taller, majestic—even his wife called him "the general." And rather than saluting the president of the United States, MacArthur merely shook his hand.

Without detracting from his judgment at Inchon and undoubted good fortune in bringing it off, Douglas MacArthur was not the general he believed himself to be. His pattern of career miscalculations included the Japanese, the North Koreans, and now the Chinese. He knew little or nothing about them; how they fought, their goals, and what their motivations might be. He didn't care, and to ask questions would imply that there was something he didn't know. Such contempt is dangerous in a commander and usually leads to disastrous underestimation.

And so it did.

The general flew to Wake Island to meet with President Truman in mid-October 1950 and not only did he tell Truman that the war was won, but he *believed* it. If it had been only Korea, then he would've been correct, but everyone else was worried about direct Chinese intervention. Everyone except Doug MacArthur. He told the president, "I believe that formal resistance will end throughout North and South Korea by Thanksgiving." He also planned to bring the Eighth Army back to Japan by Christmas.

"What are the chances for Chinese or Soviet interference?" Truman asked him directly.

MacArthur was dismissive, indicating that Beijing had had its chance at the beginning of the war but it was too late now. "They have no air force," he said. "Now that we have bases for our own Air Force in Korea, if the Chinese tried to get down to Pyongyang there would be the greatest slaughter."

Unfortunately, China had already made the decision.

Since August three army groups—more than twenty-seven divisions and half a million men—had moved into Manchuria. Chairman Mao Zedong had several very good motives for doing so, which MacArthur should have known about and considered. First, Mao wanted to send a sign to the world that he controlled the new China, a China free of foreign domination and taking its place in the world. Second, Chiang Kai-shek's establishment of the Republic of China on the island of Taiwan rankled Communist pride, especially as there was nothing Mao could do about it at the moment. There was just no way around the U.S. Navy and Air Force, nor did Red China have an amphibious capability. So Mao couldn't face the Americans across the Formosa Strait, but he could face them in a land war through Korea. If they could be defeated, it would send a very clear message to the Nationalists on Taiwan.

That he would achieve victory, he had no doubt; the Chinese soldier was, he knew, superior to the American. Revolutionary fervor and moral clarity ensured that, he believed. There was only one weakness in the plan—air cover. Without it his troops would fail in the face of overwhelming U.S. firepower. The North Korean air force had long since ceased to exist and his own PLAAF wasn't up to the task. There was only one military in the area that could possibly take on the Americans—the Soviet Union.

This was not as straightforward as it seemed to most Westerners, and it is a great mistake to think of Communist nations as a unified whole. They may espouse a similar surface ideology, but they were not, and are not, homogenous. Mao disliked Stalin personally and distrusted the Soviet Union because regardless of who sat in the Kremlin it was still Russia. On the other hand, Mao had no real choice because he needed the Red Air Force. For his part, Stalin was interested in a Communist

Korea to counterbalance Communist China and a resurgent, American-backed Japan. But he absolutely did not want open war with the United States. He remembered all too well that his Red Army had worn 11 million pairs of American boots during the last war and had driven into Berlin on two-and-a-half-ton trucks made in Detroit. There would be no Soviet troops actively fighting, but supplying aircraft and training fighter pilots was another matter altogether.

Despite the loss of overt Soviet support, the Chinese 13th Army Group secretly crossed the Yalu River on October 19, the same day UN troops entered Pyongyang. Marching only at night, the Chinese didn't use vehicles or radio communications. If any aircraft were spotted, the soldiers froze, knowing that movement attracts sight. Generally lacking heavy weapons, they were able to carry their supplies on their backs.* This would not be the last time a low-tech solution to American high technology plagued the U.S. military.

After the North Koreans destroyed the ROK II Corps at Onjong, their first combat with U.S. forces occurred on November 1, 1950, near Unsan. The Eighth U.S. Cavalry was surrounded, badly cut up, and had to fall back across the Ch'ongch'on River. Incredibly, MacArthur still didn't accept that the Chinese had invaded in earnest. Believing that it was simply harassment, he stuck to his "home by Christmas" plan, and by late November some units were actually cleaning equipment in preparation for the anticipated redeployment. To the utter amazement of other UN soldiers, the Americans actually managed to fly in a traditional Thanksgiving meal for their soldiers.

*The average Chinese soldier would need about 8 pounds of supplies per day versus 60 pounds per day for his UN opposition.

But the holiday ended the following day. The Chinese overran the South Koreans, and the U.S. 2nd Infantry Division was badly mauled to the west, creating an 80-mile gap in the UN lines. It was worse to the east, as the Chinese Ninth Army Group tried to encircle the Americans near the Chosin Reservoir. By December 1, with heavy Corsair air support, Regimental Combat Team 31 (RCT-31) of the U.S. 7th Infantry and the 1 Marine Division were able to fight their way clear.* The USAF dropped portable Treadway bridge spans that were hastily assembled by combat engineers. Consequently, the last U.S. Marines crossed the Funchilin Pass on December 11 heading for Hungnam on the east coast. Naval, Marine, and USAF aircraft provided nonstop close air support to slow the Chinese advance while 193 ships evacuated the soldiers. By Christmas Eve the port was empty and on Christmas Day 1951 the PVA 27th Corps entered the harbor; North Korea was effectively occupied by the People's Volunteer Army.

THE CHINESE CROSSED the Yalu into Korea over two main bridges. The North Korean 56th Guards Fighter Aviation Regiment was initially the only air cover available until it was thoroughly thrashed by the Mustangs. Air support then fell to Soviet Yak-9 fighters and three squadrons of the new MiG-15s.

The MiG had made its appearance two years earlier during the 1948 Tushino Air Show. Designed to counter a high-altitude threat posed by American bombers, the MiG was tough, simple, and easy to maintain. Self-sealing fuel tanks and cockpit armor

---

*Of the original 2,500 in RCT-31, over 1,000 were dead and less than 400 men were fit to fight after Chosin.

were good inclusions; however, there were problems with nearly everything else.

The weapons suite was powerful with one 37 mm cannon and two 23 mm cannons, but they were intended to knock down B-29s, not to dogfight. Left over from World War II, the ASP-1N gunsight was useless at speeds above 500 mph. The sight had been designed with .303-caliber ballistics in mind, not cannons. Bigger guns certainly packed a punch, but they fired relatively slowly and the MiG could only carry 11 seconds' worth of ammunition.*

Despite having captured thousands of German technicians, designs, and documents, the Soviets often had trouble turning theory into a workable jet. Over 80 percent of the Third Reich's aircraft production facilities were under postwar Soviet control so the Russians packed everything up and shipped it to Moscow. Jet engines were a real problem for the Soviets, until eventually the British Rolls-Royce Nene was reverse-engineered into the RD-45 and put into the MiG-15.† Installed in a relatively light aircraft, the powerful engine gave the MiG an exemplary thrust-to-weight ratio, allowing it to outperform any other fighter.

Thrust, as fighter pilots use it, is simply a measurement of a jet engine's power, similar to using horsepower as a piston engine rating. By 1950, jet propulsion was certainly not a new idea for fighter aircraft. Frank Whittle submitted designs for a patent in 1932 and, as mentioned, Heinkel had successfully flown the He 178 in August 1939. By the end of World War II, the Me 262 (see Chapter 12) and the RAF Gloster Meteor were

---

*A 23 mm shell weighs 6 ounces and a 37 mm shell weighs over 2 pounds. By comparison, a .50-caliber bullet weighs 1.5 ounces.

†The copied engine produced 5,000 pounds of thrust while the best indigenous Soviet engine was the RD-20 at about 1,800 pounds of thrust.

both viable jet fighters. The real attraction to jet propulsion was the power and potential speed such an engine produced.

Think of a squid sucking water in one end and expelling it from the other. The expulsion of fluid, in this case water, propels the creature through the sea. A jet works on exactly the same principle: air is sucked into an intake and compressed using a narrower chamber and series of spinning blades. It's then mixed with fuel and forced into a combustion chamber, where the mixture is ignited. The resulting high-pressure explosions are forced through turbine blades and expelled in the form of thrust. Once the process begins, the turbines continue to suck air to be compressed, mixed, exploded and expelled over and over until fuel is exhausted or the engine comes apart.

This was the real problem with early engines. The concept was simple, but putting it into practice was much more difficult until manufacturing techniques caught up with design. In conjunction with wing loading, the thrust-to-weight ratio, which is the engine's rated thrust divided by the aircraft weight, is vital in describing the performance capability of a modern jet fighter. The MiG-15 RD-45 produced 6,000 pounds of thrust and the fighter's loaded weight was about 10,000 pounds, giving a 0.60:1 thrust-to-weight ratio. A higher number means greater acceleration and climb performance but not necessarily a better fighter, and the MiG-15 is a perfect illustration of that discrepancy.

Poor metallurgical skills and extremely inconsistent manufacturing processes created astonishing problems with the wings. At higher airspeeds they would actually droop, and most of them weren't even the same length. This caused aerodynamic issues resulting in more than fifty-five documented (and truly spectacular) out-of-control situations during combat. The cockpit was a nightmare, cramped, badly organized, and with rearward visibility so poor that eventually a periscope was added!

Air combat technical capabilities, as we've seen so far, are about managing design trade offs to produce an effective aircraft. The MiG-15 was a point defense fighter meant to scramble off the ground and quickly zoom to altitude against a bomber threat. As long as the target was a heavy, nonmaneuvering aircraft, the MiG's one or two passes should bring it down.

Early in November a strike force of seventy-nine B-29s was sent to destroy both bridges over the Yalu, then level the North Korean city of Sinuiju. Though the bridges remained intact, the raid prompted the Soviet Far Eastern Military District air commander to ask the Kremlin to relax the restrictions on MiG combat. This was granted, and on November 10 a reconnaissance B-29 was ravaged by MiG-15s so badly that it crashed in Japan. During the next month another Superfortress was lost and five more were damaged.

This was a shock to the notion of UN air superiority and another blow to those advocates who still hadn't learned that bombers will not always get through. They did need protection, and though the F-80C was fine against Yaks, it was outclassed by the new Soviet fighter. There was really only one answer, and that was the F-86 Sabre.

Developed by North American, the XP-86 was first test-flown in October 1947 by none other than George Welch, of Pearl Harbor fame, and its defining characteristic was a swept wing adapted from the Messerschmitt 262 design.* When airflow over a wing approaches the sonic region, it compresses, and as this denser air increases drag, it generally precludes straight wings from achieving supersonic flight. Even if a straight-winged aircraft was able to break the sound barrier in a dive,

*German aerodynamicist Adolph Buseman introduced the concept in 1935 but was virtually ignored. Possibly because engine technology hadn't evolved to the point where a wing could be accelerated into the sonic region.

the thick, packed air would prevent control surfaces such as ailerons from functioning. Angling the wing back permits much greater speeds because the sonic shock waves form at the rear of the airfoil rather than at the front. This reduces drag, and with enough power an aircraft can transit the sound barrier.

But such a low-drag, thin wing also has much less area, so wing loading is greater, and the stall speed much higher. This is fine for an interceptor that never slows down, but in a high-g, turning dogfight a simple swept-wing design would be severely limited. To get the best of both worlds, North American adapted leading-edge slats (see page 165) that ran along 75 percent of the wingspan. As with the Bf 109, when the jet slowed down, the slats came out. This increased the wing area, lowered the stall speed, and allowed the ailerons to function.

In the fall of 1948, USAF Maj. Robert Johnson set a new world speed record of 671 mph with the F-86. The jet was delivered in February 1949 to the famous 94th Fighter Squadron, Eddie Rickenbacker's "Hat in the Ring" outfit from the Great War, and it was these flyers who chose to name it "Sabre." It was a fighter pilot's jet.

Powered by a J47-GE-13 engine, the Sabre had a 0.45:1 thrust-to-weight ratio. Visibility was excellent, and the layout of the pressurized cockpit was superb, unlike the MiG-15. The Sabre had speed brakes, a fuel totalizer, and a decent gunsight. The weapons were fairly light, but the six AN/M3 .50-caliber Browning machine guns had a magazine capacity of 1,800 rounds. Numerous solutions were attempted, but the heavier M39 20 mm cannons only allowed space for five seconds' worth of ammunition. The cannons also emitted large amounts of breech gases, and this sometimes flamed out the engine.* In the end it was discovered that at ranges less than 600 yards the

*This occurred six times in combat and resulted in the loss of two Sabres.

machine guns were a better answer. With superior gunsights and much better combat training, the Sabre pilots more than compensated for lighter armament.

The A1-C ranging gyroscopic sight was definitely more accurate than the optical system in the MiG-15. When the radar worked, it would lock at about 5,000 feet; the pilot put the pipper on the target, uncaged the gyros, and opened fire. Through the gyros the pipper compensated for g-forces and calculated lead for truly lethal aiming. The solution was more accurate with radar, as the ranging information was precise—again, when it worked. But even when it didn't work the pilot could use stadiametric ranging by entering a wingspan and firing when the enemy filled the ranging circle.* Radar, especially in a fighter, was still a relatively new technology, so many pilots simply caged the gyro and used it as a fixed sight. Col. Francis "Gabby" Gabreski, one of seven Americans to reach ace status in both World War II and Korea, didn't like the sight. He said, "I could do better with a piece of chewing gum on the windshield."

Maybe.

But technology advances, and fighter pilots have to advance with it. In the end with similar aircraft it was the pilot that made the difference, and despite the MiG's performance edge, the UN pilots were unquestionably more aggressive and better trained. Yet because of post–World War II demobilization and the shortsighted budget cuts, an acute pilot shortage was a problem in 1950. The U.S. armed forces had been so dramatically downsized that President Truman was forced to involuntarily recall reservists from all branches of the military.

The Air Force and National Guard brought back on active

*The AN/APG-5C radar was factory installed on the third production run of 333 F-86As and was eventually replaced by the APG-30.

duty 146,683 maintenance, support, medical, and flying personnel. These included twenty troop carrier (airlift) wings, five bomber wings, and fifteen various types of fighter wings. A positive aspect of this was that most of these men were veterans and required minimal refresher training to requalify. They also had skills you just can't acquire in peacetime, and in the case of the fighter pilots it more than balanced out the numerical inferiority. A tremendous negative was attitude and motivation, and who could blame them? These were men who'd already had their lives interrupted once and rightly considered that they'd done their duty. If Washington had been so shortsighted as to let this manpower crisis occur, then it was their problem. No one was certain where this war would lead, so the whole moldy organization creaked back to life in preparation for a larger conflict.

Even the recall wasn't sufficient, though, so pilot training was expanded and accelerated. Unfortunately, the American air force system was caught between two transitions: USAAF into the USAF, and piston power to the jet. The World War II aviation cadet program was still in place and in fact was expanded. In 1950 if a candidate was a high school graduate, was at least 20 years old, and could pass the entrance exams then he might be accepted.

Ed Rock was just such a man. Enlisting in July 1950 right out of high school, his first surprise was the Army uniforms that were left over, like everything else, from the Second World War. The Air Force actually had the recruits apply black dye over the brown shoes rather than just issue new footwear.*

*For the sake of appearances, today's USAF still has dirt painted green to look like grass and occasionally a tree trunk is spray-painted because it isn't "brown enough."

Not impressed with life as a radio repairman, Ed applied to the new and expanded aviation cadet program as soon as he heard about it. After successfully passing a review from a local officer's board, he was sent off for testing. There were standard academic tests, heavy on math, and a battery of specialized aptitude tests for flying. Sitting in a cockpit trainer, he had to manipulate the rudder pedals to keep a light centered. Among other things, there was also a turntable with a dot in the middle, and the idea was to keep a handheld wand on the dot while it spun. A flight physical was next. Eventually he was notified (by postcard) that he'd been accepted.

Basic flight training began with two weeks of academics on primary systems, local procedures, and meteorology. As before, this usually occurred at a civilian school that had been contracted to teach the course. Ed Rock was sent off to Bartow AFB in Florida to fly the T-6 Texan, taught by a former World War II Navy fighter pilot. This first phase hadn't changed much since 1940, and the emphasis was on takeoffs and landings, overhead patterns, and basic aerobatics. The washout rate was typically high, as always, but if a student could hack the program, he accumulated some eighty hours of dual instruction with about forty-five solo flying hours. Grades were pass/fail, and the check rides in combination with the all-important instructor evaluations determined who went on to fighters and who went elsewhere.

Primary flight for Ed was at Bryan AFB, Texas, in T-28 and T-33 trainers. This was later changed to advanced training, where the first two weeks were again academics concentrating on aircraft systems, instrument procedures, and emergencies. Student pilots spent two months on formation, aerobatics, and night flights in a more powerful version of the T-6. Surviving another seventy hours of this, they progressed into the T-33 or

F-80 phase. Learning now to handle a jet aircraft, they spent about sixty-five hours on complex aerobatics, cross-country flights, and, as always, formation.

Graduating from this first year got a student pilot his wings and a commission as a second lieutenant. Officer students arrived with their commissions from West Point or a four-year university, but both went through identical flight training programs. All told, if a pilot survived to get his wings, he'd log approximately 260 hours and be fully proficient at day and night operations, aerobatics, instrument flying, and, for the future fighter pilots, formation flying.

The USAF then sent the new pilot to a conversion course for his operational aircraft. The F-86 school was the "Home of the Fighter Pilot" at Nellis AFB in Nevada, just north of Las Vegas.* The course lasted ten weeks and was combat focused. Bombing, strafing, and air-to-air gunnery using towed targets were all perfected under top-notch instructor pilots. Many of them were combat veterans, and Lieutenant Rock was luckily assigned to the "Cadillac" Squadron under Maj. Willie Whisner. A double war ace, Whisner had flown P-47s and P-51s in Europe and had just returned from combat in Korea with the 334th and 25th Fighter Interceptor Squadrons (FIS). With twenty-one kills to his credit, he was an example of the Air Force doing it right—rotating superbly experienced veterans back to pass on tactics that might save a young pilot's life.† When the pilot departed for Korea, he'd been in the training pipeline for about eighteen

---

*Despite the base's illustrious history, apparently having "Home of the Fighter Pilot" on the main gate was deemed politically incorrect by the wife of General Norton Schwartz, transport pilot and former USAF Chief of Staff. Fortunately, his successor, General Mark Welsh, promptly had it put back where it belongs.
†Colonel Whisner also won the Bendix Trophy in 1953. He died from allergic complications following a wasp sting in 1989.

months and was now a fully qualified F-86 wingman with 350 flight hours.

His Communist Chinese opponent came from a much different environment and through a vastly different system. During the summer prior to the war, the PLAAF had one operational air "brigade." This consisted of four squadrons of thirty-eight MIG-15s and thirty-nine La-11s, plus Il-10s and Tu-2 bombers supplied by the Soviet Union. Moscow was anxious to use the Chinese as surrogates during the Korean conflict for a number of sound reasons. First, they could evaluate their own training and equipment without initially risking Russian lives. Second, a defeat of the Koreans or Chinese would not be a defeat of the Soviet Union, but a victory would be shared. Third, it was an intelligence windfall of information about their greatest enemy, the United States of America.

So the VVS sent the 106th IAD to Shanghai to train Chinese pilots. In June 1950, 126 of the best candidates began the Soviet flying course. This included much more theoretical instruction than the Americans endured, with at least seven hours of every day in a classroom learning academics by rote. This was partially due to the average ninth-grade educational level of the Chinese students and partially because it was a Russian course. The organization of the Red Air Force was heavily influenced by the army (hence the brigade and regiment system versus groups and wings), and this mentality permeated the syllabus. Elementary training consisted of very basic flying in a Yak-18 followed by basic training in a Yak-11. A Soviet candidate would do this in a year and log about 180 hours, but the Chinese program was shortened to six months, graduating 120 pilots with sixty flying hours.

They then entered a ten-week conversion course to learn the MiG-15. Again, the syllabus was heavy into theory, special equipment (like radios), and cockpit orientation. Unlike their American adversaries, most of these men had never driven a car, worked on engines, or been exposed to much modern technology. A Chinese pilot received about twenty hours in the jet, for a grand total of less than a hundred flight hours during the course. None of this included weapons or gunnery.

Then as now, the Soviet system conducted combat training in operational units. The advantage to this is a frontline mentality and an immediate absorption of the latest tactics from the men who developed them. A pilot would also get very quickly familiarized with the geography and weather around his combat duty station. However, this method cost jets, time, fuel, and, most important, experienced fighter pilots, who now had to be instructors. There was also a mentality issue, since the total focus of the unit wasn't on combat—it also had to deal with training.

The upshot was that at the "pointy end" of the conflict, you had limited numbers of exceptionally well-trained, often combat-experienced Americans. In the case of the Sabre pilots, they were flying a well-made and well-maintained jet designed to kill other fighters. It had lighter weapons, better aiming systems, more fuel, and could outfight the MiG-15 below 30,000 feet. The Americans were outnumbered ten to one by large numbers of hastily trained pilots flying a short-range jet that could outperform the F-86 but was notoriously hard to fly. The weapons were heavier, but the MiG wasn't designed to dogfight, and the aiming system was obsolete.

If war were an air show, then the MiG would've had the edge. As it was, the situation (politics notwithstanding) favored the better-trained and more aggressive UN pilots. Even after the Soviets began flying missions, the kill ratios reflected this. Much has been written about this, and the issue is hotly debated on both sides. The importance of realistic kill ratios and battle damage assessments for air-to-ground missions lies in the validation of weapon systems, tactics, and training. As discussed for other wars, most air forces made a concerted effort to confirm such claims through wreckage and/or eyewitnesses. Depending on the fight's location, this could be very difficult and, given the fast-paced nature of air combat, often incorrect. Add to it the fact that many aircraft that initially seemed mortally damaged were, in fact, flown back and landed.

In the jet age there was even less time for in-flight assessments, so reviewers relied extensively upon gun camera footage. There were several problems with this. First, the North Koreans simply didn't do it, and if a pilot actually survived to report, anything he said was believed. This explains the laughable figure of 5,729 UN aircraft claimed destroyed by the KPAF and provides ample justification for dismissing their figures. The Chinese weren't much better and claimed, by themselves, 211 Sabres destroyed. Soviet standards were theoretically higher but less so in practice. Their system filmed only when a trigger was depressed, so the shells were often not even at the target's range when the pilot quit firing and the camera stopped. Ground Control Interception (GCI) input was also used to assess a kill if the radar contact disappeared from a scope, which they often did when planes egressed at low altitude. It is also good to remember that both the VVS and PLAAF used political officers to grade combat film, and these men had a vested interest in creating high kill numbers, so it was hardly the most objective of systems.

U.S. jets typically used Fairchild gun cameras, which were plagued with problems. Additionally, the film was left over from the last war and, according to several pilots, functioned inconsistently.* Squadron intelligence officers usually did the

*This happened 10 to 60 percent of the time, according to Ed Rock, Dolph Overton, Charles Cleveland, and Glenn Carus.

reviewing and gave credit for a kill based on the number of camera frames showing bullet strikes. One source stated that if thirteen hits were observed, then a kill was assessed; however, considering the relative size of a .50-caliber round, this was optimistic unless a vital engine component or the pilot was hit. Maj. Sergei Kramarenko, a double-war Soviet ace, reported that MiGs often returned to base with "forty or fifty holes" from the Sabre "peashooters." In the end, hard evidence is limited to official admissions of loss or incontrovertible eyewitness accounts.

In examining just the Sabre combat, F-86 pilots claimed 800 MiG-15's destroyed. Sources from the post-Soviet era admit to 319 combat shoot-downs, with 309 to the Sabres. PLAAF archives acknowledge losing 224 MiGs, all to F-86 pilots. KPAF records don't exist, but a defector guessed that at least 100 MiGs had been shot down.* Allowing for his overestimation, 75 kills seems a reasonable approximation. This brings the total to a believable 608 MiG-15s lost in combat.

The USAF confirms that 78 Sabres were shot down in air-to-air fighting. Another 14 went down from battle damage or fuel starvation resulting from dogfighting. Twelve more are listed as "Unknown" but were somehow lost in combat. That brings the total F-86 count to 104. Yet 47 pilots were killed, 26 were captured, and a further 65 were reported missing in action. So if 138 pilots were casualties, it's valid to assume that the aircraft were lost too. Taking the two total numbers between Sabres and MiGs, we get a 4.4:1 kill ratio in favor of the F-86.

American B-29s flew 21,000 sorties and dropped 167,000 tons of ordnance over the course of the war, yet only seventeen of the big jets were lost to the MiGs. Given that bomber inter-

*Lieutenant No Kum-Sok, KPAF MiG-15 pilot.

ception was the primary mission of the MiG-15, the Sabres undeniably did their job.* Without detracting from the 224 USAF aircraft lost directly in air-to-air combat, it's definitely worth mentioning that more than twice that number went down during close air support, reconnaissance, and surface attack missions. A total of 579 USAF fighter, bomber, or attack planes were lost over 57,665 air-to-ground sorties. Marine air flew 32,190 close air support sorties, and in addition to thousands of trucks, tanks, and other targets destroyed, Marine pilots shot down 37.5 aircraft. Marine fighter pilots flying Sabres with USAF squadrons accounted for half of these. Maj. John Bolt, the sole USMC ace from Korea, got his five kills with the F-86 as part of the 39th Fighter Interceptor Squadron. Maj. John Glenn got three kills flying Sabres with the 25th FIS and Navy Panther pilots shot down five MiGs. All told, over one million combat sorties were flown.

Air superiority was never in doubt once the F-86 made its appearance, but the ground situation was entirely another matter. Eerily reminiscent of the Western Front thirty-five years earlier, the defensive positions had hardened and the armies were largely stagnant. Chinese emplacements included a fantastic network of tunnels, which generally negated UN air attacks. However bleak the ground situation was, General MacArthur never advocated the use of atomic weapons to deal with the Chinese. In fact, it was Gen. Omar Bradley, chairman of the Joint Chiefs, who first proposed placing nukes at MacArthur's disposal. President Truman agreed with that in the fall of 1950 but later retracted his statement.

Recapturing Seoul in mid-March, MacArthur then issued an astounding communiqué directly to the Chinese government.

---

*Sixteen MiGs were also destroyed by B-29 gunners.

In it, he proposed a cease-fire and openly discussed policy-level issues such as China's bid for a UN seat and the situation with Taiwan—all this from a military *theater* commander. Added to his continued arrogance and catastrophic misreading of China, this was the proverbial last straw, so he was finally relieved on April 11, 1951. Quoted a decade later in *Time* magazine, Truman said, "I fired him [MacArthur] because he wouldn't respect the authority of the President. I didn't fire him because he was a dumb son of a bitch, although he was, but that's not against the law for generals. If it was, half to three-quarters of them would be in jail."

Fortunately, MacArthur was replaced by Gen. Matt Ridgway, a true combat soldier and a much better commander.* Even by this point, both sides wanted out of the war, but they couldn't agree on how to do it, nor would either Korea recognize the other. So while the political wrangling continued, men died. The air war became a vast proving ground for improved variants of old aircraft and, more important at this point, tactical refinement. This was particularly true of ground attack and close air support.

The North Korean chief delegate for the initial cease-fire talks admitted that airpower had prevented defeat for the UN side. Lt. Gen. Nam Il said, "Without the support of the indiscriminate bombing and bombardment of your air and naval forces, your ground forces would have long ago been driven out of the Korean peninsula by our powerful and battle-skilled ground forces." The exaggeration of North Korea's military might aside, this admission revealed the profound effect that tactical airpower had upon the enemy. In fact, aircraft accounted for 72 percent of all artillery destroyed, as well as 75

---

*Nicknamed "Old Iron Tits," Ridgway wore two hand grenades on his chest.

percent of all tanks and nearly half of all enemy troop casualties, according to USAF statistics.

But by early 1953 several great events occurred that would end the stalemate in Korea: Joseph Stalin had finally died, and Dwight D. Eisenhower had become president of the United States. Even-tempered, worldly, and a tremendous compromiser, the former general had never been a combat soldier, but he thoroughly understood the military in a way impossible for Truman. Also, and perhaps most important, his credibility was unassailable. At this point in history he was precisely what the United States needed. In any event Eisenhower wanted America out of the war. By the time a truce was signed in July 1953, UN forces had suffered nearly 500,000 dead, wounded, or missing against 1.2 to 1.5 million Communist casualties.*

As the Korean War passed into history, it left the U.S. military struggling to deal with the complexities of a "limited" conflict and the notion of fighting for an ideology rather than an unambiguous cause. From an aviation perspective, Korea became a division between the past and the future. In barely three decades man had gone from flying fragile, fabric-covered, open-cockpit airplanes to a jet fighter capable of breaking the sound barrier. It was a gray area of old ideas, new realities, and rapidly emerging technologies. Indeed, technology is relative to time and, as we've seen, weapons, tactics, and aircraft all evolve to meet the situation.

By the early 1950s aircraft had achieved capabilities that meant guns and cannons would not remain the only weapon solutions. A new killer, the air-to-air missile (AAM), was being developed to answer the challenge of high-speed, high-g targets.

---

*The U.S. military suffered 33,686 battle deaths; 8,176 are still listed as missing in action.

Similarly, conventional anti-aircraft artillery guns were inadequate against fast jets at higher altitudes, though they were, and are, still remarkably lethal against anything fighting down low.

To counter the threat posed by advanced fighters, the surface-to-air missile (SAM) was also about to make its appearance. Radar development would go hand in hand with these new systems. Increased speeds and maneuverability necessitated better targeting solutions both in the air and on the ground. It was apparent to those who fought the war, and those beginning their fighter pilot careers, that aircraft had changed faster than the weapons. But had they also evolved faster than the men?

Throughout the first fifty years of fighter combat, men had always risen to the occasion and done what was needed. Would they continue to be able to do this in the future, in an aviation arena that demanded vast amounts of technical knowledge, previously unimagined physical demands, and sheer guts? No one knew . . . yet.

But, as always in this century, there would be more situations that, if handled badly, could lead to another war. In this case, it was an obscure Asian country known, in the 1950s, as French Indochina and an entire generation of American fighter pilots would soon come to know it by another name.

Vietnam.

CHAPTER 13

BOMBS, GUNS, AND GUTS

REPUBLIC F-105F "THUD"

"THERE THEY ARE."

The man leaned over the cheap metal chair and pointed at the rectangular display. "You see the radar picture? We call it a spike . . . a target return like that." Although wearing a plain, dark green uniform with no rank, he was obviously an officer. In fact, he was a Soviet colonel named Lubinitsky.

Behind him the two most senior students dutifully jotted that down in their little olive drab notebooks. The cheap paper tended to come apart in the humid air, so they wrote carefully. The younger one, whose Russian was better, spelled it out phonetically. Later he'd transpose it into his native Vietnamese, but now there wasn't time.

The radar operator, also a Russian like the other seated men, was twiddling a small dial under the screen with his left hand. With his right, he was slowly spinning a large black wheel next to his right knee, physically moving one of the antennas mounted on the van next to this one. All the men here were crammed into an eight-wheeled trailer called a UV. Inside were three big gray consoles along the left wall, with a chair for each operator, and on the right side was a smaller station facing the door. There was just enough space in the narrow aisle for the fire control officer to squeeze behind each chair. The FCO, who was also the missile battery commander, had responsibility for the tactical analysis and any launch decisions. There was a chair for him as well, but Lubinitsky liked to stand so that he could monitor the azimuth, range, and elevation search displays at each console. The Viets were clustered on both sides trying to watch this amazing new technology in action.

"You see, it's fairly easy to find a target in azimuth, and then we use this spike to steer the other antennas." Lubinitsky laid a hand on the back of the last chair. "Usually elevation is next. Then"—he gestured at the middle console—"range is fixed last."

The nodding Asians understood about every fifth word, but the concept was clear enough. All three operators had stopped using the coarse adjustment wheels and were fine-tuning their solutions. The elevation operator clicked his wafer knob to the right, then paused, staring at the display.

"Seven thousand meters . . ."

The first operator nodded and tapped the glowing rectangle on his console. ". . . and bearing two, six, zero degrees. There is more than one target. Maybe three or more." The SNR-75 radar could track six targets, though he'd never actually seen it hold more than four.

The FCO looked at the center station. "Range?"

"Thirty-five . . . thirty kilometers . . . closing."

Then the man straightened a bit and pointed at the scope. "No, wait . . . distance increasing. Thirty-three . . . now forty kilometers."

"They are aware of us?" the Viet lieutenant colonel asked. "Their detection gear, perhaps?"

Shaking his head, the Russian pointed at the azimuth console. "See . . . the angle has changed and now is steady, heading away." The officer was fairly certain about what was happening, and this was a good chance to impress these little monkeys. "Watch. It will reverse again."

And it did. The Viets murmured, nodded, and smiled as the target's aspect angle changed and the range once again decreased. They all stared for few moments until the Soviet colonel turned and explained. "It's an orbit. The Yankees call it a 'racetrack' and use it to keep their aircraft in one location."

"Why?" one of the officers asked tentatively. He'd been edging closer, trying to see and understand. The man understood the theory behind radar but had never seen it put to use. Once the Americans began arriving he, like the other North Vietnamese air defense officers, had eagerly anticipated the arrival of this missile system. They'd been briefed on its effectiveness and fervently hoped it could counter the threat of U.S. aircraft. After all, this same system had destroyed an American U-2 spy jet flying over the Soviet Union and another over Cuba. There were rumors that it had also shot down a Nationalist Chinese reconnaissance plane.

"They remain in one place until a threat is detected."

"Like one of our MiGs." A Viet grinned proudly.

You mean one of our *MiGs,* Lubinitsky thought sourly. *We just loan them to you and learn from your mistakes.* But he smiled. "Correct. Like a MiG. Then they will attack from their cap. This allows them to stay on station longer and save fuel."

"How do they have coverage for radar control way out there?" another asked, peering at the display.

The Russian colonel shook his head. "They don't use Ground-Controlled Intercepts the way we do. They use their own onboard radars."

That astounded them, and they chattered among themselves. Their own fighters were controlled from takeoff to landing.

"So we have several targets," the FCO continued, "and the speed with which range and aspect are changing means they're obviously fighter aircraft." The Russian colonel had been the guidance officer at the Cuban site that shot down Maj. Rudolf Anderson in October 1962. Because of his experience with the SNR-75 system and his assignment teaching Cubans, Lubinitsky had been sent here earlier in the year. After a lot of shit, that is. Months of delays to ship the equipment through China, then more shit once they were finally here. The Viets, he'd learned, were terrified of angering the Chinese and thought Beijing wanted to absorb their new country as another province.

He wiped his streaming face and wrinkled his nose slightly. As if anyone would want the fucking place. The colonel sighed. Cuba was so much better, with its sunshine, rum, and dark-haired, willing women. Personally, he thought the Americans were just posturing; after all, what would they do with this stinking shithole?

"How close did they approach this time?" he asked the range operator.

"About twenty-five kilometers, sir."

Nodding, Colonel Lubinitsky turned to the last station, the small one facing the door. "Status?"

"Ready, sir." The man was a captain and a highly experienced guidance officer. He'd been watching all three displays intently. The commander picked up a heavy black phone and repeated his question.

"As they begin the turn back northeast we will fire." The Viets understood that and perked up noticeably. "A salvo of three missiles."

"But the range, sir." One NVA (North Vietnamese Army) officer had been doing the math in his head. "Isn't it too far?" He'd been studying for months and was well aware that the tactical engagement zone for the system was twenty-eight kilometers.

"If they were receding, yes. Or beam on to us." That earned lots of blank stares, so the colonel held up his left hand perpendicular to his other. "Sideways." They understood that and bobbed their heads. "But if the target is flying at you, then his airspeed is helping to close the distance."

"Aspect shifting, sir," the first console operator reported. "They're turning in."

Glancing at the guidance officer, the commander got a nod, yet he hesitated a moment. There had been combat here before now with Russians involved, and after all, this was Vietnam. *Their* country, not his . . . and this equipment had been legally purchased for their use. It wasn't as if he was attacking the Americans. The Russian looked at the senior NVA officer and smiled.

"When you are ready, Colonel."

ONE MORE TIME.

The pilot tightened his grip on the canopy rail as the Phantom started a left turn. One more mission. He stared off the wing at North Vietnam, blanketed under a smooth carpet of clouds, and couldn't quite believe he'd done this fifty-four times before. For Ross Fobair, an F-4 Phantom pilot from the 45th Tactical Fighter Squadron, it was now almost routine. A newly arrived pilot, Capt. Richard "Pops" Keirn, was flying in the front seat and finishing his local checkout. No one in the 45th had been here that long, but you could get experienced real quick in combat and ninety days was a long time here.

They'd flown into Thailand from MacDill AFB in Florida on April 4, 1965, just three and a half months ago. With the first Phantoms in-country, the 45th Tactical Fighter Squadron was responsible for protecting striker aircraft and killing MiGs. Two weeks ago Tom Roberts and Ken Holcombe had bagged a pair of MiG-17s, chalking up the very first USAF air-to-air kills in this war. Maybe they'd come up and fight today. *Now* that *would be something to go out on,* Fobair thought, and grinned under his mask.

"Leopard Two . . . tighten it up." The flight lead, Lt. Colonel Bill Alden, didn't bark, but his voice was terse. *Second time he's said that.* Fobair watched the back of the other man's head as he fidgeted in the front cockpit, staring left. *He's trying too hard . . . gotta loosen up when you fly formation. This must've been how the RAF guys thought when they flew over Britain at first with their silly air-show formations. Combat isn't the place for it, but that's what was briefed this morning. Probably because the flight lead was hoping for a commit against some MiGs and wanted his guys close together.* The Vietnamese fighters didn't stay up very long, so there was never much time.

The Phantom bobbled as Keirn corrected his formation. Overcorrected, actually, but flying loose route at 23,000 feet in an F-4 wasn't that easy. *Wasn't that hard, either*, he thought, and closed his eyes. Keirn was a retread; he'd been a bomber pilot during World War II before being shot down and spending nine months as a prisoner in Stalag Luft 1. This was his fifth mission in Vietnam, and he'd be a fully checked-out wingman if all went well today.

The whole notion of using bomber pilots to fly fighters was

absurd, Fobair thought. A few of them had come through before and never really gotten it. Something about all those years of non-maneuvering flying with a crew riding along got to a guy. Fobair sighed. *Damn, I hate the pit.* He wiped his face. No pilot liked riding in the backseat and letting someone else fly. He sighed again. It didn't matter . . . not today of all days.

The twenty-nine-year-old captain was packed up to leave as soon as they got back to Ubon. It was July 24, 1965, and later that night the "Freedom Bird," a transport aircraft to the States, was heading home. So was he—back to California and a well-deserved rest with his wife, Anita. His sister was there, too, and his young nephew, Bruce. The 45th would be returning to MacDill later in the summer to teach other pilots on their way to Southeast Asia, and Fobair was leaving early to set it up.

Squirming down into the seat, he tried to get comfortable, but that wasn't really possible in a Martin-Baker ejection seat. *Ah,* he thought with a yawn, *the life of a fighter pilot.* They'd taken off from Ubon, hit a refueling track over Laos, and were now 40 miles west of Hanoi in Route Pack V—and he'd be back in California in seventy-two hours. Weird world. That made him smile, so he shut his eyes again. At least it was quiet. The flight lead had told them all to switch off the noisy safety frequency, called "guard," used for emergencies, a SAM launch, or a downed pilot. If Leopard had to get into action quick, the last thing they needed to hear was a bunch of Navy pukes trying to find their carrier. Those guys used guard like a private telephone and completely garbaged it up.

Ross yawned.

Today was pretty straightforward, Fobair thought, so none of that should be needed. Leopard was a four-ship combat air patrol, called a MiGCAP, covering a strike of F-105 Thunderchiefs. The Thuds were whacking a factory near Hanoi, so a sweep was necessary this close to the capital, and that was the good part. They got to roam around and look for trouble, forcing enemy fighters to fight *them* and let the Thuds drop their bombs.

It didn't work out that way this time, though.

West of Hanoi three SAMs shot up through a soggy cloud deck, and one hit Leopard Two. The orbiting EB-66 had seen the launch electronically and called out on the guard frequency, but the Phantoms couldn't hear it. No one in the flight had seen the missile, and even if they had, there wasn't time to react. They also didn't carry the threat detection gear that would become standard equipment on later jets. Unfortunately for Keirn and Fobair, the previous SA-2 shoot-downs had involved spy planes, so the CIA and Air Force hadn't released much useful information. Nothing was really known about this new SAM, and the pilots hadn't been trained yet to defeat it. The missile was the same radar-guided SA-2 that had knocked down Gary Powers and killed Major Anderson—it left little margin for error.

Following a spine-jarring impact the Phantom immediately went out of control. In the front seat Pops Keirn struggled to assess the flashing lights and aural warnings as acrid smoke filled the cockpit, making his eyes water. Getting no response from the pit, he twisted around against the mounting g-forces and saw the other pilot slumped over, blood streaming from his nose. As the F-4 spun into the clouds, Keirn ejected and would spend the next seven and a half years as a prisoner of war in the infamous "Hanoi Hilton."

But Ross Fobair disappeared.

"POWER COMES FROM the barrel of a gun."

Mao Zedong of China said it, and Nguyen Sinh Cung—better known as Ho Chi Minh, "He Who Enlightens"—believed it. Though he had lived in France, Britain, the Soviet Union, and the United States, Ho first and foremost saw himself as a Vietnamese patriot.* He was an ardent Communist, but more as a pure revolutionary rather than an adherent to an economic system. His concern was an independent Vietnam, not Communist regional or global domination, so he returned home in 1941 to fight the Japanese and Vichy French.

With Ho's leadership and the generalship of Vo Nguyen Giap, they formed the Viet Minh (VM), a coalition of all Vietnamese Communists. Operating from the forests of Tonkin and Annam, they carried out a small-scale guerilla war until the Japanese surrendered in 1945. The very next day, on September 2, Ho Chi Minh declared independence for the Democratic Republic of Vietnam. Unknown to Ho and Giap, however, Vietnam's fate had already been decided by the Potsdam Agreement of 1945. This stipulated, in part, that all Japanese troops north of the 16th parallel would be disarmed by the Nationalist Chinese and those to the south, in the area known as Cochinchina, would be disarmed by the British.

Despite initial U.S. support for Ho Chi Minh, when World War II ended, Washington chose ideology over practicality and refused to deal with a Communist leader. In all fairness, China was in the middle of her revolution, the Soviet Union was emerging as *the* threat to America, and the situation on the Korean Peninsula was unstable. Following the war, decolonization had become a global momentum and was occurring in Egypt, Italian North Africa, British India, and Malaysia. Exhausted by the past five years, most former colonial powers accepted the inevitable and did what they could to somewhat peacefully transfer power.

France did not.

Conservative leaders in Paris decided that one way to erase

---

*Among other things, he was a cook at the Parker House Hotel in Boston in 1913.

her wartime humiliation was to reassert French power (whatever that was) and regain control of the colonies that had constituted her prewar empire. Indochina, composed of Laos, Cambodia, Tonkin, Annam, and Cochinchina, was the cornerstone of France's Far Eastern possessions. The first French soldiers were brought in by C-47 transport on September 12, 1945, and with Chiang Kai-shek's approval, French troops landed in the Red River Delta during March 1946. Later that year, following the withdrawal of Nationalist Chinese forces, the French Expeditionary Force increased to 30,000 men. By now, confrontation was a foregone conclusion, and in November 1946, war erupted between the Viet Minh and France.

Most of the French soldiers were colonials from North and West Africa, but there were also paratroopers and Foreign Legionnaires, the latter a group of soldiers of every nationality who agreed to fight under French officers in return for eventual citizenship. They were essentially government-sponsored mercenaries and were very tough, very ruthless men. Those who did come from Europe were all volunteers; France never sent conscripts to fight in Indochina.

For several years there were no major operations, just insurgent attacks and counterinsurgency ripostes. The French aircraft carrier *Dixmude,* a former merchant ship built in Pennsylvania, arrived on station in 1947 to conduct limited operations using Dauntless dive-bombers. Originally commissioned into the Royal Navy as HMS *Biter,* the ship had a 400-foot deck with a single catapult. Loaned to the French Navy in 1945, she carried about twenty aircraft.* After the Chinese Commu-

---

*Named for the World War I battlefield of Dixmude. It was just to the south of this city that Roland Garros scored the first air-to-air kill with his forward-firing machine gun in April 1915. See Chapter 1.

nist victory over Chiang Kai-shek's Nationalists in September 1949, Beijing began supplying the Viet Minh.

In the fall of 1950, as Americans advanced into North Korea, the French were pulling in their Tonkin garrisons. Gen. Marcel Carpentier, commander in chief of French Indochina, had decided that the forts were too vulnerable in the face of a Chinese-reinforced Viet Minh. The subsequent withdrawal down Route Coloniale 4 northeast of Hanoi was a disaster, as the French had no helicopters and were repeatedly ambushed all along the miserable little road. Of the 6,000 soldiers involved, fewer than 700 finally reached safety. Citizens in Hanoi panicked as the backwoods threat of Ho Chi Minh suddenly materialized on their doorstep. As a result, everything north of Hanoi in the Tonkin Highlands became undisputed Viet Minh territory. The French arsenal in Lang Son was also captured and contained enough weapons to equip an entire VM division.

A defeat of a modern, European-trained army by a ragged peasant militia, as they were seen, shocked the world. Of all the interested powers, the United States should've been the least surprised. The whole scenario was strikingly similar to the Revolutionary War: irregulars fighting a guerilla war against a technically superior, infinitely better organized modern army. The parallel didn't escape everyone, and there were those in both the French and American military who recognized the fight for what it was. Unfortunately, they were not the policy makers, and the war continued.

Giap became overconfident with his victories and made the mistake of fighting in open country against the French. Through June 1951 he attacked around the Red River Delta and was handily defeated, losing more than 20,000 of his soldiers. But he *learned*. More significant, he didn't repeat his mistakes. This ability to adapt was missed by French and American politicians and was one of the greatest strengths the VM possessed. Following these victories, the French formed mobile brigades and committed armor with additional paratroops. Despite this, without real airlift and helicopters, their mobility was still tied to the vulnerable road network and therefore under constant attack.

Air support consisted of the Far East Forward Group, composed of U.S.-supplied C-47s and initially Spitfire F-IXs from 273 Squadron, RAF, out of Tan Son Nhut. Though jets were available, the French air force preferred fast, powerful piston-engine aircraft like the American F-9F Bearcat. They were aware that a very survivable attack aircraft with a long loiter time and a relatively quiet engine might be of more use than the more glamorous jets. *Groupes aériens tactiques* (GATACs), aerial tactical groups, were formed: GATAC North in Hanoi, GATAC Center in Hue, and GATAC South in Saigon.

Bases Aero-Terrestres, called BATs, were essentially fortified airstrips in remote locations. Like a castle or a fort in Indian country, it was a striker base intended—at least in theory—to dominate a specific geographic area. One of these was constructed near a remote town ringed by low hills near the Laotian border. Deep in Tonkin Province, Dien Bien Phu was an ideal location from the French standpoint, and its fortification was a nasty shock for the Viet Minh. By March 1954 there were 10,133 French soldiers in the little valley accompanied by ten Chaffee light tanks with several F8F-1's on the old Japanese airstrip west of the village. Col. Christian de Castries, the French commander, had eight pillboxes built on the surrounding hills and emplaced twenty-nine pieces of artillery covering his position.*

*The pillboxes all had female names: Gabrielle, Anne-Marie, Huguette, Béatrice, Françoise, Éliane, Claudine, and Isabelle—supposedly for de Castries's local mistresses.

Determined to wipe out the BAT and send an unmistakable signal to the French, Viet Minh soldiers hand-carried 144 field guns and mortars, together with over 100,000 rounds of ammunition, through the jungle. These were dug into the jungle hillsides and concealed along with 130,000 troops. On March 13, 1954, the siege began and "Béatrice" fell. Despite having 107 combat aircraft available from GATAC North near Hanoi, bad weather and lack of coordination usually prevented any real close air support. The Viets also had nearly two hundred anti-aircraft guns carefully placed around the airstrip and the approaches into the valley. Six F8Fs with one F6F-5 fighter, plus at least three transports, had been lost by March 15 when "Gabrielle" fell. Dismayed by his failure to halt the enemy, the French artillery commander, Lt. Col. Charles Piroth, promptly rose to the occasion and committed suicide with a hand grenade.

By early April two parachute battalions had been dropped into the perimeter, but with little success. The Pentagon came up with a plan code-named "Vulture" that included massive B-29 strikes on Viet Minh positions around the valley, and even the nuclear option was briefly considered. Both were discarded, either for fear of provoking the Chinese or because of the belief that enough American boys had already died for France. In any event, Dien Bien Phu fell on May 7 with a French surrender that cost 2,293 dead, 5,134 wounded, and nearly 9,000 men taken prisoner. GATAC North flew 3,700 combat sorties, losing forty-eight aircraft with 167 damaged.

The next day peace talks began in Geneva, and a formal cease-fire took effect on July 21, 1954. Vietnam would be divided at the 17th parallel, while Cambodia and Laos were granted outright independence. More than 1.6 million Vietnamese, including most of the remaining educated professionals, relocated into what was now the Republic of South Vietnam. To the rest of the world it seemed that the conflict was over, or had at least abated somewhat. After all, partitioning had worked on the Korean peninsula, so why not in Vietnam?

The real tragedy wasn't that France lost another war, but rather that Washington didn't learn from it—even with the recent Korean experience. American politicians didn't understand that, with or without Communist assistance, the Viet Minh were determined to finish their civil war and forcibly unite their new country. Even if that meant fighting the United States.

THERE IS NO one answer, nor any easy answers, for the escalation of U.S. involvement in Vietnam. Like Korea, the initial response was represented as ideological. Simply a struggle between communism and capitalism, freedom and oppression—a proxy war between the United States and the Soviet Union or China. Trying to explain it in these terms, the politicians believed, put the impending conflict on the same moral level as World War II. Not understanding Korea was one thing, but failing to grasp the causes and significance of involving America in Vietnam *after* fighting in Korea was something else. This decision is especially baffling following the French experience at Dien Bien Phu.

It must be said up front that none of America's experience in Vietnam reflects poorly on the military. As always, fighting men are instruments of policy, not the creators of it and this is best. Yet it is also hoped that those in Washington use good sense and are responsible with the priceless resources they possess, but if not, there isn't much the military can do about it.

Though training and advisory groups had been present in Saigon since the 1950s, the first ground deployment of any consequence took place in 1961 with the insertion of Army Green Berets. This was augmented in 1962 by air commandos from the USAF flying a strange collection of low-tech World War II leftovers like the B-26. These units were part of Operation Farm Gate, a training mission that very rapidly involved Americans conducting combat missions against the Viet Cong. Ranch Hand, the official defoliation project, came next.*

Various others followed, including Water Glass and Candy Machine, both created as part of Washington's strategy of "gradual response." This grew, in part, from Secretary of Defense Robert McNamara's statement that Vietnam was to be "a laboratory for the development of organizations and procedures for the conduct of sub-limited war." With statements like that becoming foreign policy, it was inevitable that the military situation would become confused.

At this point the conflict in Vietnam was almost exclusively fought south of the 17th parallel. In 1959 the North Vietnamese Communist Central Committee passed Resolution 15, essentially justifying war. Hanoi condemned the United States as an imperialistic replacement for France and denounced the South Vietnamese Republic as lackeys. Disputing the 17th parallel and the Republic of Vietnam as irrelevant, Ho Chi Minh and Giap saw nothing wrong in invading what they regarded as their own country. They never viewed the conflict as anything other than a civil war, and this also was never understood in Washington until it was much too late.

Since the mid-1950s Hanoi had recruited southerners and brought them north. They were formed into three divisions for weapons training, then split up into small units and sent

*Trichlorophenoxyacetic acid mixed with dichlorophenoxyacetic acid, better known as Agent Orange.

back south. These native southerners became the National Liberation Front—better known as the Viet Cong (VC). The VC conducted a fairly disruptive guerilla war in response to the growing American presence. On May 2, 1964, the former escort carrier USS *Card* was sunk alongside the Saigon docks by a Communist frogman.*

Two months later the Navy lost an RF-8 and an F-8 Crusader to anti-aircraft fire over the Plaine des Jarres in Laos. The RF-8 was flown by Lt. Charles Klusmann of VFP-63, from the USS *Kitty Hawk* in the Gulf of Tonkin.† The problem was that the time over target was specified by the secretary of defense himself, and the missions were mandated to occur every other day at 1300 Laotian time. *Any* type of pattern in combat is dangerous, but McNamara was adamant in his belief that he knew best. The result was an ambush.

When Klusmann went down Cmdr. Glenn Tierney was on the air operations staff for Adm. Harry Felt, commander in chief, Pacific (CinCPac). Word filtered down that no rescue attempt was to be made, so Tierney, appalled, confirmed this with the Joint Chiefs of Staff duty officer. Bypassing his entire chain of command, Tierney then called Admiral Felt directly and they talked face-to-face. CinCPac heard the brief, then had the commander pick up a second secure telephone and listen as Felt called McNamara directly. Tierney wrote down the conversation.

"Mr. Secretary, I have been told that you are aware that we just had a Navy photo pilot shot down in the Plain of Jars and that an order had been issued by your office that there was to

*The water was only 20 feet deep and the *Card* was patched up, repaired, and returned to service in December.

†The first USN combat jet loss in Southeast Asia.

be no 'round-eye' [American] effort to rescue the pilot. Is that correct?"

"That is correct, Admiral," McNamara replied.

"May I ask by whose authority this order was issued?"

"The recommendation came from State and the Secretary of State and I discussed it and agreed that this is the best course of action."*

Admiral Felt concealed his disgust, looked at Commander Tierney, then said, "Mr. Secretary, that is not a decision that can be made by the Secretary of State or the Secretary of Defense. This decision to rescue this pilot or not to rescue him can be made only by the commander in chief of the United States Armed Forces, and I am asking you to put me through to the commander in chief—now."

McNamara hemmed a bit about the hour and that it had been such a long day in Washington, but Felt was unimpressed. The downed pilot, all alone on the Plain of Jars, had had a much longer day. His bluff called, the secretary had no choice but to call Lyndon Johnson. Felt explained the situation to the president, including the complicity of McNamara and Rusk. To his credit, Johnson immediately replied, "I'll be damned. Of course, go in and get him—and let me know how it comes out."

Two helicopters from Air America (an airline covertly owned and run by the Central Intelligence Agency) tried to pick up the pilot but were badly damaged. Klusmann was captured by the Pathet Lao but managed to escape in August, eventually making it to safety on his own. In response to the shoot-down, the USAF deployed eight F-100Ds from the 615th Tactical Fighter Squadron out of Clark AB, Philippines, to Da Nang AB,

---

*Secretary of State Dean Rusk—see Chapter 12. This is the same man who drew the arbitrary line separating Korea at the 38th parallel.

South Vietnam. On June 9, 1964, with no maps, coordinates, or photo reconnaissance, the Super Sabres were sent to the Plain of Jars in Laos after the Triple-A (anti-aircraft artillery) site that got Klusmann. One flight bombed the wrong site, the other damaged the primary target, and one of the pilots, Capt. Lloyd Houchin, later said, "The first F-100 combat mission was a disaster—what we used to call a 'group grope.' "

It didn't matter. For all intents, America was once again at war.

On August 2, 1964, three North Vietnamese P-4 motor torpedo boats attacked the USS *Maddox* in the Tonkin Gulf. The destroyer was carrying out a DESOTO signals intelligence mission gathering information from radar and shore installations.* Four F-8 Crusaders from the USS *Ticonderoga* were called in and they attacked the boats, damaging two and leaving one dead in the water.† Three days later President Johnson authorized *Constellation* and *Ticonderoga* to launch retaliatory airstrikes against the oil facilities at Vinh, which they did. This chain of events led to the Gulf of Tonkin Resolution (formally the Southeast Asia Resolution) granting the president authority to use conventional military force without congressional approval.‡

The Navy supplied most of the early muscle, and by Christmas eight carriers had been deployed to the Pacific. About half were 36,000-ton *Essex*-class carriers left over from World War II and Korea. The USS *Coral Sea* was a 60,000-ton *Midway*-class

---

*DEHAVEN Special Operations off TsingtaO. The USS *DeHaven* made the first such patrol in 1962.

†In 1962 the USS *Ticonderoga* had been commanded by Captain James G. Daniels, formerly Ensign Daniels of Pearl Harbor fame. See Chapter 10.

‡Senator Ernest Gruening (D-AK) objected to "sending our American boys into combat in a war in which we have no business, which is not our war, into which we have been misguidedly drawn, which is steadily being escalated."

carrier, but three of the new "supercarriers" were also deployed. The USS *Ranger*, *Constellation*, and *Kitty Hawk* were 80,000-ton, 1,000-foot-long warships capable of 30 knot speeds and carrying eighty aircraft. Carriers patrolled the Tonkin Gulf on Yankee Station, or off the South Vietnamese coast on Dixie Station in the South China Sea.*

During the fall of 1964 the USAF was also building up its presence. Pacific Air Force (PACAF) had the regional responsibility for Southeast Asia, but then as now, air assets were transferred in from around the world if needed. These included F-105 Thunderchiefs from the 4th Tactical Fighter Wing and 18th Tactical Fighter Wing to Korat, Royal Thai Air Force Base (RTAB), Thailand; and the 6441st Tactical Fighter Wing to Takhli, RTAB. F-100 Super Sabres from the 405th Tactical Fighter Wing and 35th Tactical Fighter Wing also went into Takhli. Of course, there were also the essential KC-135 air tankers, reconnaissance planes, and assorted command-control aircraft.

Armed reconnaissance flights of Laos began in December, but early in 1965 the war changed. A VC mortar attack in February against Pleiku destroyed twenty-five aircraft and a Special Forces team was overrun at Camp Holloway in the Central Highlands. The Air Force was now in theater, in strength and ready to attack anything in Vietnam with heavy-hitting force. Gen. Curtis LeMay, the USAF chief of staff, and Adm. Harry Felt both believed that the war was in the north. Anything less than an all-out air campaign against Hanoi's industry, harbors, and infrastructure would be ineffective. Unfortunately, that was exactly what the president, through McNamara, had in mind.

Operation Rolling Thunder began on March 2, 1965, with

*Until 1966 when Dixie Station was discontinued and all the carriers went north.

a hundred-plus aircraft assault on Quang Khe naval base and the Xom Bang ammunition depot, losing four strikers to anti-aircraft fire. Lt. Hayden Lockhart of the 613th Tactical Fighter Squadron was flying an F-100D (#55-2857) when he was shot down by Triple-A near the ammo dump. He was the first recognized, official USAF combat loss of the Vietnam War and would spend the next seven and a half years as a POW. Later that month 3,500 Marines came ashore at Da Nang, marking the first employment of regular U.S. combat troops and an unmistakable escalation of the war.

The fledgling air campaign was only permitted targets near the demilitarized zone close to the 19th parallel, and these were selected in Washington, not by the field commanders. Of primary concern was the Truong Son strategic supply route—which the Americans called the Trail. Far from primitive, the Trail was highly organized, containing its own engineers to repair damage, anti-aircraft units, and thousands of porters to move equipment. It was also not one trail but hundreds of narrow pathways cut through the jungle with no chokepoints or open terrain. Unpaved, it was impossible to destroy with bombs, as the craters were simply refilled with dirt. So the notion of interdiction, especially in the south, where the Trail spread out, was like fighting a jellyfish tentacle by tentacle, rather than just stomping on its head.

McNamara would later state that this conflict wasn't about toppling the Communist government in Hanoi but about curbing its aggression toward the South. It was, he said, "a very, very limited political objective." This raises the question, then, of why the United States should be fighting there at all. Washington was adamant, though, convinced that the North would back down once they experienced a taste of U.S. military force. In keeping with this strategy (a word used rather loosely), airfields were also not on the approved target list. If, McNamara reasoned, the North Vietnamese Air Force (NVAF) was destroyed, then mightn't the Chinese assume the air defense role as they had done in Korea? Well, what if they did? the fighter pilots asked. The same thing that happened over the Yalu would happen over the Red River.

In any event, the restricted operation was to continue initially for eight weeks, and there were issues right from the beginning. Though PACAF was the coordinating authority for Rolling Thunder, this did not include operational control of naval air. The Navy had been forming "Alpha" strikes based on a package of about thirty aircraft. With limited assets, naval tactical employment was generally on a smaller, more efficient scale out of necessity. Early advocates of electronic combat, the Navy embedded their Alpha packages with SAM suppression aircraft and jammers. Using the A-6A variant of the Intruder, the Navy was more interested in the suppression of air defenses for a given strike rather than the destruction of a SAM. Steven Coonts, who wrote the novel *Flight of the Intruder* based on his experiences in Vietnam, agreed with this: "We'd arrive in the area a few minutes ahead of the package and just try to keep their heads down while the bombs were dropped . . . then we'd get the hell outa there. No point in hanging around."

Geography had much to do with this. Navy packages generally had to transit about 25 miles of hostile territory, while packages inbound from Route Pack V had more than 100 miles of hostile territory with which to contend. It made sense to destroy SAMs whenever possible so they wouldn't have to face them another day. The Navy was also steadfast in maintaining that their aircraft were an inseparable component of the Seventh Fleet and would not be placed under USAF control. However, with hundreds of aircraft involved in an area the size of Arizona or New Mexico, a deconfliction plan was needed.

This came in February 1966 with the division of Vietnam

into route packages that started at the DMZ and moved north. Route Pack (RP) I went north to the 18th parallel and belonged to the Air Force, though most operations were conducted by the Military Assistance Command, Vietnam. RP II extended to the 19th parallel and was controlled by the Navy, as was RP III. This was the largest of the packages but contained the fewest targets. Thanh Hoa Bridge was in the Navy's Route Pack IV, as was the Bai Thuong air base and the railyards at Nam Dinh. The biggest zone was Route Pack V, in the northwest part of the country. With China on the north and Laos to the south and west, it was controlled by the USAF. All the lines of communications and railroads leading into northern Laos ran through Pack V.

Route Pack VI held the prizes of Hanoi and Haiphong. A rail line running northeast divided it into an eastern USAF zone and a coastal Navy zone. This area contained the Paul Doumer Bridge, most of the main irrigation dikes, and a majority of the original targets designated by the Joint Chiefs.

Then in early April a pair of F-105s attacking the Thanh Hoa rail bridge were brought down by NVAF MiG-17 fighters. The USAF responded by deploying the F-4, its newest multirole fighter, into theater. Based out of Ubon, Thailand, the 45th Tactical Fighter Squadron was attached to the 12th Tactical Fighter Wing and immediately began trolling for MiGs. Against military objections, the first of several bombing "pauses" occurred on May 13, 1965, courtesy of Washington sensitivities, as that date corresponded with the Buddha's birthday. The idea was to give Hanoi a chance to digest the effects of the air campaign and to realize the futility of opposing the United States.

All the pause accomplished was to give the North Vietnamese time to rebuild railroads and fill in craters along the Ho Chi Minh Trail. Time also to strengthen the air defenses around

Hanoi—including making the newly built SA-2 sites fully operational. Losing Gary Powers and Rudy Anderson in the early 1960s had made the SAM threat very real, but little had been done about it. Aware that the missiles had been deployed to North Vietnam, the 2nd Air Division commander, Major General Joe Moore, sought permission to attack the sites while they were under construction. The assistant secretary of defense, an academic with no military qualifications at all named John T. McNaughton, openly ridiculed the request.

"You don't think the North Vietnamese are going to use them!" His scorn was obvious. "Putting them in is just a political ploy by the Russians to appease Hanoi."

Unfortunately, it was no political ploy that attacked Leopard Two on July 24, 1965.*

"CEDAR ONE . . . offload was 12,100 pounds."

Major Ed Rock could see the boom operator through the plastic blister on the KC-135's belly. The boomer had a mustache and headphones and was wearing glasses. Not taking his eyes off the tanker's director lights, Rock lifted his left hand, waved, then dropped it back on the throttle. Disconnecting from the boom, he pulled the power back slightly, and the F-105F Thunderchief dropped back until the whole tanker was in sight. Closing the air refueling door, he glanced right, then slid beneath his wingman over to the tanker's right wing. Rock was the last to top off and simply kept turning, with Number Two falling in behind him. He didn't have to look to know the other element, Cedar Three and Four, would cross under the KC-135 and follow. There were four other tankers stacked up in the

*Ironically, McNaughton himself died in a plane crash two years later.

track, separated by 1,000 feet, so he stayed in his altitude block until they cleared to the west.

"Red One One . . . thanks for the gas . . . Cedar's off to the north at fourteen K."

"Cedar . . . Red One One copies. Good huntin'."

Rock zippered the mike and continued turning. They'd been southbound in the Red Track and were now over the Plaine des Jarres, heading for the North Vietnamese border. He looked down at the desolate, cratered landscape, then eyeballed his tactical air navigation system, leaving it set to Udorn. It was the closest piece of friendly concrete to their target, way up in Route Pack 6. He took a deep breath, hoping it wouldn't come to that. As a former F-86 pilot, Rock was certainly no stranger to danger, but some things never got easier. You just never knew . . .

Switching frequencies again, he checked in with Cricket and passed his flight's call sign and mission number. Cricket was a converted C-130, a sort of airborne command post that kept up with every flight going in and out of Vietnam. The controller passed him a weather update for Hanoi and wished them good luck.

"Cedar, go strike prime."

He switched the radio to a preset frequency that the whole striker package would monitor. Tactical changes, updates, and emergency information could all be passed if necessary. After waiting a few seconds, he keyed the mike.

"Cedars . . . clean it up, green it up, music on."

The other three Thuds all acknowledged, checked their switches, armed their systems, and turned the ECM pods to transmit.

"Gotta few Fire Cans up," his backseater, Capt. Curt Hartzell, the electronic warfare officer (EWO), finally chimed in over the intercom, and Rock glanced at the little round scope to the right of his glare shield. The APR-25 radar homing and warning (RHAW) system was a fairly new addition. It would see incoming radar signals, then display them along the detected azimuth. Stronger signals were displayed as a long line from the center of the scope. A Fire Can was a Triple-A radar, and that meant guns—but there were always guns. These only flickered at the center or were displayed as short solid lines. The signal was weak and likely not a threat, so Rock relaxed a bit, nothing to worry about.

Yet.

Dialing up the next turnpoint, he smoothly banked right and headed northeast toward Yen Bai on the Red River. Strike Prime was garbage, as usual. Teal, the EB-66 jammer flight, was talking to Cadillac and Buick, eight F-4s in a MiGCAP. Then there was the Navy yakking away on the guard frequency again. Cracking the power back to hold 480 knots, he kicked the rudder several times, fishtailing the jet, and his wingmen immediately spread out. The others were all in single-seat D models and would have no problem keeping up with his heavier, two-seat F-105F.

Ramping down, he leveled off at 11,000 feet and looked at the ground. Like gray warts, karst mounds poked up through the dark jungle, and fog crept through the valleys. Rock glanced at his watch as the strikers checked in five minutes behind him and right on time. Elm, Maple, Redwood, and Pine: sixteen F-105Ds, each with six 750-pound bombs. They'd make quite a mess if the SAMs and guns didn't get them—but that was what he was here to deal with. It was December 2, 1966, and his flight of Wild Weasels was fragged to protect the strikers by fighting SAMs. Weasels had two mottos: "First in, last out" and "You gotta be shittin' me."

Both applied today.

Intelligence estimated twenty to thirty SAM batteries around Hanoi—the "Golden Circle," as the fighter pilots called it. A safe haven for the North Vietnamese, mandated by American politicians. He snorted. What a crock of shit.

"Fan Song now," Hartzell added, referring to the radar used for SA-2 fire control. "Multiple emitters."

"Where?"

A dry chuckle came out of the pit. "Anywhere in front of us."

Well, that's the whole idea. Rock shook his head slightly. *We're the targets, not the bomb droppers.* Eyes flickering over the cockpit, the pilot was glad to be in a Thud. The initial Wild Weasel aircraft had been the F-100F Super Sabre, and it just wasn't made for the job. The 105 was bigger, heavier, and it carried much more ordnance. Designed for low-altitude nuclear strikes against a Communist threat, the Thud could *move*. The big Pratt & Whitney J-75 would put out an astounding 24,500 pounds of thrust in full afterburner and would keep the 105 supersonic on the deck.

"Pushin' it up," he replied, nudging the throttle forward. Off to his left, the Hoang Lien range twisted its way north past the Fansipan massif into the Himalayas. Up ahead the mountains suddenly opened onto a wide valley in Phu Tho Province. Through the middle of it snaked the Red River, all the way to the dark blue waters of the Tonkin Gulf. About halfway down to the sea, on the river's western bank, lay Hanoi. Rock looked left and right. The other jets were right where they should be, so he dropped to 10,000 feet and held 540 knots.

As he headed for the little town, which was just south of a lake that was off his nose, the hills broke apart in a deep pass called the Western Gates. That made him smile, since the Weasels were here to kick the gates in. Racing down over the valley, the four 105s crossed the Red River just south of Yen Bai. A green, slug-shaped hill rose up past the river and pointed southeast like a long, knobby finger. At the end of it, on the plain, was the MiG base at Phuc Yen. To the locals the hill was Tam Dao. The Americans called it Thud Ridge.

Rock pushed the throttle up to mil power and saw the airspeed Mach indicator tape on his console jump to 580 knots. Second rule of combat . . . speed is life! Switches, fuel, engine . . . he ran his eyes over them all, flipping the oxygen to 100 percent and keeping the stick steady against his leg. It always thrilled him to hold such power in his right hand, and the combat rush welled up in his chest. Sitting in a solid hunk of metal thundering his way across the valley, he could see everything, *feel* everything, and he grinned, despite the situation. First rule of combat . . . keep your head out of your ass. The sheer power of the F-105 was amazing, quivering to be let loose, to turn and burn. To fight and kill. Dialing up the RHAW volume, he looked out at the smaller hills at the tip of the ridge. It was time.

"Comin' right," he said, giving the EWO a warning. He paused, then rolled the big fighter up on its wingtip and pulled hard. Through the top of the canopy he watched Cedar Two float overhead and disappear behind his left wing. Three and Four would play the turn to end up about three miles behind him in an offset box formation. Rock heard Hartzell grunt against the g's, then he popped the jet upright, staring far off the node at the Gulf with Thud Ridge on his left. The Red River was off his right wing as they roared down the valley toward Phuc Yen and Hanoi. Visibility off the nose wasn't the best, so he bunted forward slightly and rolled a little left. Sometimes the gomers put guns on the hilltops, and—

"Shee-it!"

The sky was suddenly alive with expanding little puffy clouds . . . like someone threw a thousand pieces of popcorn in his face. Rock slammed the stick forward and Hartzell's head thunked against the canopy. The pilot instantly reversed, pulling back hard right.

"Cedars, Triple-A over the ridge . . . ten K, heads up!"

Bunting again, the streams of fire curved away behind him and then the sky was clear.

"What the *fuck* . . . ?"

"Not over yet." The EWO was breathing hard. "Multiple Fan Songs . . . nose, close!"

No shit. Hanoi was right there. There were at least a hundred radars in this part of the country, so it was a wonder the RHAW worked at all. Rock swallowed and craned his neck to see out the front. Banking left, back toward the ridge, he booted the left rudder and skidded the jet sideways. Fan Songs could be at Phuc Yen or Hanoi.

"BEEP . . . BEEP . . . BEEP . . ."

"Missile launch!" Hartzell really was breathing hard now. "Twelve o'clock . . ."

"I got it." Rock rolled up, then pulled back to the right. A big white cloud was boiling up south of the Red River near Son Tay. Then another. Keying the strike freq, he broke in over the chatter. "Missiles off the ground . . . twenty northwest of Bull!"*

Immediately slamming the throttle into afterburner, Rock flipped over, hanging in the straps a moment, then buried the stick in his crotch. Dirt, a tiny screw, and even a cigarette butt floated into his face as he pulled for the valley floor.

**Bull's-eye* is a common reference point used to describe threat locations or your own position. Hanoi, often called "Dodge City," was commonly used.

"Cedars . . . take it down!"

"BEEP . . . BEEP . . . BEEP . . ."

Missile launch warnings were screeching in his helmet, and he stared wide-eyed straight down at the cluster of hills. Slapping the throttle back to midrange, he twisted in the seat and watched the SAMs. The big smoke trails had bent over, and both missiles looked like they'd corrected to stay on him. The SA-2 was a command-guided system, so the Fan Song had to have line-of-sight to the target. Quickest way to defeat them was to put something between himself and the radar—like hills.

"Cedar Three, tally two missiles . . . right three o'clock!"

"One . . . One's defendin . . . ah, tally three missiles!"

Rock just picked up the third one off to the southwest. It hadn't pitched as high as the others and was already curving back across the Red River at him. With the ground rushing up, he smoothly pulled the stick back, and as the jet's nose lifted he shoved the throttle intoafterburner again.

"Umpf . . ." Curt Hartzell grunted from the pit. "Still locked . . . still on us."

Scattered clouds left black shadows against the dark green mass of Thud Ridge, and little roads ran off in all directions, like white spiderwebs. Flying instinctively, Rock bumped down to 500 feet, his eyes on the nearest SAM. He didn't dare look away, so the terrain to his left was just a green smudge, and the fighter was muscling through the air at 600 miles per hour. He had to be supersonic, or close to it. Water zipped past on the left side. Another little crappy river . . . which one? . . . his eyes never left the incoming SAM.

The missile's booster had burned out, but the sustainer left a thin gray trail that was still visible. Unbelievably, both had stayed with him, even down at 500 feet. *Not supposed to do that!* Intel bozos got it wrong. Chay . . . that was the river.

The Chay River. Mind racing, he knew he'd have to do a "last-ditch" maneuver in a few seconds.

Half a mile . . .

Rock's hands were firm on the stick and throttle, his head back, watching,

Almost . . .

A brilliant orange and black flash made him blink. It blew up! The missile had exploded maybe 2,000 feet away.

"Ya see *that*?"

"Uh-huh." The pilot's eyes were locked on the second missile. His right hand moved by itself to keep the jet steady as Vietnam blurred past. Then the other SAM detonated, leaving a dark stain against the pale blue sky.

"Gone!" Hartzell exhaled loudly. "We've got—"

"Third missile," Rock interrupted him. "Right three o'clock, just below the ridgeline." He was staring west and watched the thing correct its aim. Bumping the stick, the 105 instantly climbed a few hundred feet, then he bunted over, paused, and yanked the stick back.

Two hundred feet . . . so low that Thud Ridge looked enormous.

"It's still on us!"

Sonovabitch . . .

A SAM break meant pulling straight up and blending in a barrel roll to create guidance problems the incoming missile couldn't solve. Do it too soon and you were a sitting duck; do it too late and you were dead.

Three . . .

A stubby hill flashed past on the right side.

"Whaddya gonna *do*?"

Two . . .

"Rock . . . " Hartzell sounded like he was being strangled.

One . . .

Rock flinched as the hilltop to his right erupted in a magnificent, violent explosion. Dirt, flame, trees, and debris flew up everywhere. A tumbling mass of orange fire, black smoke, and bits of Vietnam shot out in all directions.

Immediately easing back on the stick, Rock lifted the Thud away from the ground and he realized he'd been holding his breath. Still, zipping along at 1,000 feet per second just north of Hanoi was no place to relax. Whistling lightly, he pulled harder, and the fighter rocketed up, Thud Ridge and the valley falling off under the wings. Beginning an easy turn to the west, he saw wispy gray smoke from the missiles drifting over the Red River, but couldn't make out the site.

"You gotta be shittin' me," the EWO muttered from the backseat, and the fighter pilot managed a slow smile. *All in a day's work*. Quickly looking over the gauges, he exhaled—nothing wrong, nothing hit. Glancing at the fuel, Rock knew there wasn't much time. Now they had to do what the Weasels were there to do.

Go kill the little bastards.

CHAPTER 14

CHANGING OF THE GUARD

A-4H SKYHAWK

WILD WEASELS HAD been created to counter the threat posed by Leopard Two's shoot-down in the summer of 1965. Triple-A had been around since World War I and attacks from enemy fighters were just facts of life. SAM systems, on the other hand, with their 5,000-pound, 35-foot-long guided missiles, were a new threat, but they had weaknesses. One was that the SA-2 missile had to be completely guided by the controlling radar, and these sites were huge. Though they weren't mobile, critical components such as the radar and missiles could be relocated relatively easily to another prepared site, and this was done often to keep the Americans guessing. When the site that shot down Leopard Two was attacked, there was nothing there but dummy equipment—and lots of Triple-A.

Another weakness of early SAMs was the *command guidance*

required for the missile intercept. Visualize the radar signal as a flashlight beam locked onto a shiny metal target. The reflection from this is seen by the ground radar, and then guidance corrections are sent via radio signal to the missile. This meant that the radar had to have line-of-sight to its target and continue illuminating that target all the way through the detonation. If a radar is emitting, then it can be found; it is also vulnerable to anti-radiation missiles that home in on those emissions.

The SA-2 could be detonated either by a signal from the fire control officer or by actually hitting the aircraft. Radar fusing was also used, so if the missile passed within a preset distance from the target, then it would explode. The 480-pound high-explosive warhead would spray out a blast pattern up to 800 feet, depending on the altitude. Bombers had warning gear, jammers, and electronic warfare officers, but a fighter initially had no way to detect the presence of the Fan Song.

The actual missile launch was fairly easy to see if a pilot was looking that way, but sites were well camouflaged and weather could obscure a launch. Cloud decks mean nothing to radar, so aircraft above them could be tracked with no visual indication whatsoever, and this is precisely what happened to Leopard Two. If launches were seen, they could be defeated by special maneuvers, such as the "last ditch," that gave a Fan Song too many guidance problems to solve and the missile went stupid and missed. Fighters could do this easily if they saw the missile, but bombers could not, so another solution was needed.

Electronic countermeasures (ECM), like radars, were also developed during the Second World War from the principle that if a radar detects targets through reflected energy, then it would also be possible to deceive such a system by creating false reflections. The notion of using semi-rigid strips, initially coated with aluminum, was proposed in 1942 by a Welsh-born physicist named Joan Curran.* These strips (called "Window") would reflect radar waves and generate clutter. With enough clutter, real targets could not be discerned. (In future years, missiles that did their own tracking would be decoyed onto the chaff.) Primarily used to interfere with German 88 mm flak guns, chaff was extensively employed on D-Day to simulate huge numbers of ships in the Dover Strait.

Jamming equipment was standard on bombers, but it was quickly adapted to attack jets following the Keirn/Fobair shootdown. The basic idea is to generate signals that interfere with a radar's picture and a variety of techniques can be used. Spot jamming is like a narrow stream of water from a hose; it works against a single frequency and can be very effective as the power is concentrated, but the difficulty is knowing which frequency to jam. Barrage jamming clutters up multiple frequencies, like a sprayed stream of water, but the range is limited. This means that "burning through" the jamming with the radar is easier and a clear picture can be regained faster.

Countertactics develop against any new technology, and electronics was certainly no exception. To negate jamming effectiveness, some method of switching frequencies was needed, and a hopping algorithm (based on the mechanisms of a player piano) was patented in 1942. Out of eighty-eight frequencies, one is randomly selected and used for guidance. The system will automatically switch, or hop, to another frequency at preset times or when jamming is detected.†

---

*A pioneer like Beatrice Shilling (see Chapter 8), Joan Curran and her husband, Sir Samuel Curran, also developed the proximity fuse and were later members of the Manhattan Project. Joan rowed crew at Cambridge, where she earned a degree in physics, but was not awarded this in 1935 because she was a woman.

†Patent #2,292,387. To Hedy Lamarr, the gorgeous American actress famous for playing Delilah. Born in Vienna during the Great War, she was fiercely pro-American and had a magnificent brain to complement her terrific legs. Her technique is the basis for many forms of modern communications, including Bluetooth.

In tandem with these efforts, a company called Applied Technologies, Inc. (ATI) modified a series of receivers into a system that would detect, identify, and roughly locate an emitter radar. A threat like the Fan Song must emit a radar signal, called a beam, to track a target, so with beams bouncing all around, it was simple enough to install antennas that detected them. Once a signal hit an antenna, its strength could be measured, giving an approximate distance. The angle at which the beam struck the antenna also provided a direction of arrival, thus giving a rough bearing to the radar. The frequency was also detected, and in the early days, before the proliferation of radars, it was fairly easy to positively identify which system was looking at you.

This wasn't a new idea. The Ferret I program had been fielded in 1943 using modified B-24D Liberators. They initially flew radar countermeasure (RCM) missions against Japanese Mk I radars in the Aleutian Islands, while the Ferret III and VI programs flew B-17Fs from Foch Field in Tunisia until late 1944. Ravens, the first jamming aircraft, were B-24s, B-25s, and B-29s that carried receivers to find radars, pulse analyzers to identify the systems, and jammers to disrupt signals.

Hunter-Killer teams appeared during the Korean War, with TB-25Js locating radars and B-26s, then killing them. After the war the 9th Tactical Recon Squadron was formed, and there was subjective agreement that electronic combat was indeed useful. However, it wasn't considered extremely urgent until the surface-to-air missile became operational and planes began going down. Then suddenly jamming, signals analysis, and countermeasures weren't science fiction anymore; they were survival.

ATI called their system the Vector IV. It was composed of the APR-25 radar homing and warning system, APR-26 launch warning receiver, and IR-133 panoramic receiver/signal-analysis set. The government ordered five hundred sets and the USAF immediately began installing them into the F-100F. Called a "Hun," this was a two-seat version of the F-100 Super Sabre and, combined with Vector IV, it became the Wild Weasel I program. Flying from Korat, Thailand, four modified Huns of the 6234th Tactical Fighter Wing commenced Weasel "Iron Hand" missions on December 1, 1965. Three weeks later Capt. Allen Lamb and Capt. Jack Donovan killed the first SA-2 near Phu Tho on the Red River, northwest of Hanoi.* Allen Lamb would later say:

> *Our flight that December morning was call sign Spruce, and our F-100F was Spruce 5. The F-105s, Spruce 1 through 4, took off right after we did. Everything was standard through form-up and refueling with a tanker over Laos. We took the lead at our pre-briefed initial point, and with two Thuds on each wing, we headed for the Red River Valley, a flood plain that was home to some of the best air defense systems in North Vietnam. The mission parameters were fairly fluid after that. We didn't have a specific objective or a series of known targets. Our job was to probe the enemy's air defenses until they warmed up to take a shot at us.*
>
> *There was complete radio silence after going to the strike frequency. A little after noontime, Jack*

*Donovan was a former B-52 EWO. When the new, fighter-based program was explained to him he replied, "You want me to fly in the back of a little tiny fighter aircraft with a crazy fighter pilot who thinks he's invincible, home in on a SAM site in North Vietnam, and shoot it before it shoots me, You Gotta Be Shittin' Me!" The abbreviated version of this, "YGBSM," has been a Weasel motto ever since. Thanks, Jack!

told me that the Vector IV had picked up a Fan Song radar in search mode about 100+ nautical miles out. I pushed the engine up to 98 percent and locked the throttle. This gave us 595 knots airspeed, just under max while carrying ordnance. After I started homing in, I transmitted "Tallyho." That was it. I kept the SAM at ten to eleven o'clock so he wouldn't get the idea I was going after him. When I could, I dropped into shallow valleys to mask our approach. Every now and again, I'd pop up for Jack to get a cut. This went on for about ten to fifteen minutes.

After breaking out into the Red River Valley, I followed the strobes on the Vector and turned up with the river alongside. The IR-133 had receiver antennas located on either side of the fuselage in line with the cockpit for homing on a target. The strobes started curling off at twelve o'clock, both to the right and left. And I knew we were right on top of him. I started climbing for altitude and Jack kept calling out SAM positions literally left and right. The right one turned out to be a second site. I was passing through 3,000 feet, nose high, and I rolled inverted while still climbing to look.

Jack started calling the first site to the right. I said it was to the left, because I could see it below. "Right!" he said. "Left!" I said. "Right!" he said. "Look outside!" I said. Jack did and saw that we were inverted, so the signals from the left and right antennas were reversed. "OK, left," he agreed.

I rolled in to line up the site but came in way too low. Later, some of the Thud drivers told me they thought I was going to mark the target with my air-

craft. My rockets hit short, but as I pulled off there was a bright flash. I figured I must have hit the oxidizer van for the SA-2's liquid-fuel motors. I called out the site, and the F-105 lead, Don Langwell, said that he had it. He went in, and Spruce 2, Van Heywood, came after him, firing rockets on the site.

We all broke the cardinal rule of "one pass, haul ass" to ensure the kill. I came back around for a second pass in front of Spruce 4, Art Brattkus (the F-100s were agile birds!), and went down in beside Spruce 3, Bob Bush, who was hitting AAA alongside of the Red River (Bob Bush would be KIA on a subsequent mission). On this pass I strafed the control van, and he went off the air. Each of the Thuds came around again, expending all their 20 mm ammunition. Jack was now calling out the second SAM site, but we had nothing left to hit it with. But we really blew away the site that we did hit.

We got out of there, rejoined, and refueled. There was a USO show with Bob Hope that day at Korat, and we made a flyover with the F-100 leading and two F-105s on each wing. A number of people down there knew that meant we had made a SAM kill and left the show early to celebrate.

After landing, we debriefed and went to the club. What a party! Jack drank martinis. After a while, he started holding them by the rim with his thumb and finger and began dropping them. The more he drank the more he dropped. The club was raising Cain as they were running out of glasses, so we taped a glass in his hand. After dinner he drank crème de menthe and went around sticking out his green tongue.

All six of us in Spruce Flight received the Distinguished Flying Cross for killing the first SAM site. Jack would fly twelve more missions with me before going stateside in February 1966 to get the ball rolling on what would become the Wild Weasel School at Nellis AFB. I stayed in Southeast Asia for a total of six months and received credit for two more SAM kills.

Unfortunately, on December 20, two days before Allen's flight, the Weasels lost an F-100F. John Pitchford became a POW for seven years and Bob Trier went down fighting against North Vietnamese soldiers. Though it was agile and quick, serving well as a fast forward air control aircraft (FAC), the F-100F simply didn't have the survivability or enough weapons carriage capability to duel with SAMs. More space was also required for the specialized SAM hunting equipment, so a replacement aircraft was needed.

Big, tough, and fast, the F-105 Thunderchief was the obvious choice. The Thud had also been involved in the killing side of Weaseling from the beginning, so the tactics were understood and could be easily adapted to the new airframe.

Designed by Alex Kartveli, who had the P-47 Thunderbolt and F-84 Thunderjet to his credit, the first YF-105 flew in 1955. Intended for low-altitude nuclear attack against the Soviet Union, the F-105 reflected the Air Force's love affair with nuclear weapons. Utterly convinced that the next war would be in Europe and be nuclear, the USAF put most of its yearly budgets toward that scenario.

Required to air-refuel and reach Mach 2.0 with a nuclear bomb in the internal bay, the Thud incorporated several innovations. The distinctive, forward-swept intakes contained movable plugs, which altered the cross section and matched airflow to meet engine requirements. This meant developing a central air data computer (CADC) that automatically monitored the system and adjusted components accordingly. Contrary to the current philosophy of high-altitude interceptors and nonconventional warfare, Republic wisely retained a M-61 20 mm cannon and the four underwing hard points.

Aerodynamically, it was basically an engine with little wings attached. The 385-square-foot area gave a wing loading of about 130 pounds per square foot.* Full-span leading-edge slats helped maneuverability at slower speeds, as did the Fowler trailing edge flaps. Another innovation was the precise milling of airframe sections to reduce gross weight, rather than the past practice of overengineering all the panels.

The cockpit represented ongoing American efforts to reduce the pilot's workload, thereby leaving him free to concentrate on fighting. This was in marked contrast to Soviet cockpit designs that were indifferent to the pilot, to say the least.† Arranged in a T-shaped console, the Airspeed Mach Indicator (AMI) and vertical velocity indicator (VVI) were placed alongside an attitude indicator. The radar scope and weapons panel were just below it, centrally located and easily accessible.

Nonconventional ordnance included B28, B43-1, and B61 nuclear weapons. All conventional general-purpose bombs, air-to-ground missiles like the radio-controlled Bullpup, and cluster bombs were in the arsenal. The M61 Vulcan cannon had a 1,100-round magazine allowing ten seconds of firing, and air-to-air Sidewinders could be carried on dual launchers. Special-

*By comparison, the F-86 wing area was 313 sf for a 50 lb/sf wing load. Sopwith's triplane carried 6.5 lbs/sf over a 201 foot wing area.

†The author has been in the MiG-29 and flown the MiG-21—both are ergonomic disasters.

ized anti-radiation missiles, such as the AGM-45 Shrike and the AGM-78 Standard ARM, combined with CBU-24s or rockets, were used for Wild Weasel work.

With the introduction of the APR-25 and the inclusion of a highly skilled EWO, five modified F-105Fs landed at Korat air base in May 1966 to fight the SAMs. The early Weasels went out as hunter-killers, paired with the single-seat F-105D. Their presence was felt immediately: in 1965 it took eighteen SAMs to bring down an aircraft, while by 1968 more than a hundred were needed. The USAF ordered eighty-six additional F-105 conversions, putting the Wild Weasel III program in full swing.

As Hanoi began losing the air war and sent the NVAF into China to reconstitute, the air defense system grew proportionately. This would become a trend in future conflicts as American airpower surpassed all others, forcing enemy reliance on anti-aircraft artillery and surface-to-air missiles for defense. But for now, armed with a mix of conventional bombs, anti-radiation missiles, and a surplus of guts, the Weasels were part of every Air Force package that struck North Vietnam.

WHILE ROCK WAS racing around the Red River killing SAMs, the newly arrived 8th Tactical Fighter Wing Commander had a problem. Colonel Robin Olds had arrived at Ubon air base in September 1966. The "Wolfpack," as it was known, had lost eighteen jets and twenty-two pilots during the last year. Renowned for his tactical ability, greatly respected for loyalty to his men and his utter intolerance for rear echelon sensitivities, Olds was exactly what the wing needed. His problem, besides the combat losses, was the increasing threat of MiG-21 fighters over North Vietnam.

Derived from lessons learned during the Korean War,

Mikoyan-Gurevich designed a new single-seat, single-engine point defense fighter. Like most Soviet designs, the Fishbed was a copy of something else; in this case, it was the American Convair YF-102. Built to counter B-47 and B-52 bombers, the prototype flew in February 1955. Of note were the distinctive delta wings and bottle-shaped fuselage. Aerodynamically, this was an *area-ruled* design, an approach that reduced the aircraft cross section where the wing met the body. The wasplike shape that this produced decreased transonic drag, so the jet could sustain supersonic flight. This was a prime concern for a point defense fighter needing to get high and fast very quickly.

By the Vietnam War it was powered by a R-13-300 afterburning engine rated at 14,300 pounds of thrust. Weighing only 19,000 pounds fully loaded, the jet could climb at 21,000 to 40,000 feet per minute, depending on the variant. For comparison, the F-105D was about 35,000 pounds fully loaded, yet could climb at 38,000 feet per minute in full afterburner. But the MiG had definite advantages: it had lower wing loading than the American jets and, being unburdened with bombs or ECM pods, it had a lower thrust-to-weight ratio. Due to its small size the MiG was also extremely difficult to see. Its engine didn't smoke much, and it was armed with AA-2 Atoll missiles.

The Soviet missile was copied from a Navy AIM-9B Sidewinder acquired by the Chinese during the first Taiwan Strait crisis.* Both were infrared homing missiles, known as "heat seekers," that tracked hot carbon dioxide emitted from a jet's exhaust. Later improvements would lock onto hot metal engine parts and even heat caused by skin friction at high speeds. But for now, using a combination of detectors that provided steer-

*The Sidewinder snake moves forward by rapid side-to-side movements as does the missile as it corrects, and zigzags to its target.

ing guidance to the fins, the missile was best fired straight up the tailpipe into hot exhaust.*

The first cadre of VPAF MiG pilots were well-educated, regular serving officers, and most had some experience fighting the French. Hanoi trained its own pilots on MiG-15s and YAK-8s, then sent them off to China or the Soviet Union for a MiG conversion course. The physical standards were high due to the unaugmented flight controls on Soviet aircraft, but the Vietnamese, like the Chinese and Koreans before them, suffered from the lack of a technical background. The syllabus was still very Russian and taught by rote; independent action and creative thinking were not encouraged, and ideological devotion was the single most important factor in picking a pilot candidate.

The program could take as long as five years and was generally accomplished on MiG-21U and L-29 trainers. VPAF pilots, like the Soviets, were heavily dependent on ground-controlled intercept (GCI) control, and it was used from takeoff to landing. A controller would dictate airspeeds, headings, weapons to be used, and even how many dogfights a pilot was allowed. Again, this did not leave room for tactical innovation and initiative. Still, when cornered and forced to fight on their own, most MiG pilots gave a good account of themselves.

They typically flew in flights of four, like the Americans, but only had eight to ten aircraft per squadron and maintained typical operational readiness rates below 30 percent.† This was alleviated somewhat by the advantage of fighting over their own

---

*Colonel Ed Rock's first experience with the AIM-9 was in 1957 at Nellis AFB. The tech rep stood on the other side of the hangar waving a lit cigarette so everyone could watch the missile fins move accordingly.

† U.S. fighter squadrons typically maintained at least a 70 percent readiness rate.

country. Like the British during the Battle of Britain, the MiGs could wait until the most favorable time to launch and attack any incoming strike packages. English-speakers monitored radio chatter, thus forcing U.S. pilots to construct elaborate code words, which the Vietnamese also mostly deciphered. A favored tactic was to wait until a "Bingo" call was heard (meaning an aircraft had reached a fuel level requiring it to return to base), then launch the MiGs knowing the Americans didn't have much gas left for fighting.

Hanoi had also worked out the basics of an integrated air defense system. This overlapping network used SAMs to keep attackers at a distance and disrupt strike packages that got too close. While defending themselves against the missiles, aircraft were often forced lower and could then be engaged by Triple-A. Whatever lived through this was then attacked by MiGs and then reattacked by SAMs on the way back out. Such a defense system was hardly invulnerable: fighter cover by F-4s could handle the VPAF, while jamming was tremendously useful in blinding the early-warning and GCI radars. But it turned out that jamming had unintended consequences. The QRC-160 pod carried by the F-105 was a noise jammer that cluttered up a radar scope to the point where information was flawed and, one hoped, the targets were obscured. Unfortunately the North Vietnamese figured this out and used the noise strobes to locate the jamming aircraft, and the strike aircraft, for the MiGs.

Killing MiGs was the objective behind Operation Bolo, which was Colonel Olds's plan. He would simply emulate the call signs, formations, predictable routes, and times of a Thud strike package with his Phantoms. When the MiGs appeared, *they* would be the ones ambushed. The McDonnell-Douglas F-4C was ideal for the mission: powerful and versatile, it could easily outperform the MiG when only configured for air-to-air combat. Like the Sidewinder, the Phantom began as a Navy project and was originally designated the F-110A Specter. The enormous tail was partially constructed using a unique, lightweight honeycomb structure, while the upward-canting tips and downward-drooping stabilators compensated for instability. A distinctive "dogtooth" notch was added on each side of the fuselage to improve high-angle-of-attack maneuvering. Installing a stability augmentation system also made the F-4 very maneuverable for its time.

The Phantom I was the McDonnell FH-1, so the new fighter was called the Phantom II.* The USAF began ordering them but called it the F-4C; the folding wings remained, but wider wheels were added and an Air Force air refueling receptacle replaced the Navy probe. Despite its strengths, there were problems, mainly with armament. Intended as a long-range interceptor for fleet defense, the Phantom's air-to-air missiles reflected this. They would do fine if launched from straight and level flight against non-maneuvering bombers but were severely degraded in any type of turning fight. A cannon could've nicely covered this gap, but due to the Pentagon's certainty that dogfighting was passé, the F-4 was fielded without one, since it was conceived in the bomber-centric, nuclear-obsessed decade before Vietnam.

The AIM-7 Sparrow was envisioned as the principal ordnance to be carried by the Phantom. Unlike the within-visual-range, heat-seeking Sidewinder, the Sparrow was a beyond-visual-range (BVR) missile. It could be fired at targets up to 20 miles away because it was guided by radar, in this

*James McDonnell named it himself, though his designers wanted to call it the "Ghost." The Phantom I had been the first jet aircraft to fly from a U.S. carrier—the *Franklin D. Roosevelt* in 1946.

case the APG-50 fire control system. Using semi-active radar homing (SARH), the aircraft's radar illuminates the target, and then the missile seeker receives the reflected signal and makes steering corrections. The biggest drawback to SARH is that the fire control radar must provide guidance throughout the entire missile time of flight and this can place significant maneuvering limits on the attacking aircraft.

In the F-4 an allowable steering error (ASE) circle and a "death dot" pipper were used. The circle would "breathe" depending on the target's range and grow larger as the distance decreased. A pilot put the pipper inside the circle, and when geometry and range were within parameters for a launch, the death dot changed from white to green. If the launching aircraft could be forced to defend itself or the radar lock was broken by target maneuvering, then the missile went "stupid" and missed.

Called the "pit," the rear cockpit was designed for a naval radar intercept officer who worked the fire control systems. He wasn't a pilot and couldn't land the jet, so there was no reason for good visibility. This caused problems when the USAF inexplicably decided to make the Phantom a two-pilot aircraft yet changed none of the unfriendly rear-seat features. This practice also meant that when one plane went down you lost two pilots.* Needless to say, the USAF policy was eventually changed and a weapons system officer (WSO) or EWO rode in the back instead depending on the type of fuel. By the 1964 Tonkin Gulf incident, thirteen of thirty-one Navy squadrons were flying the F-4B, and the USAF 555th TFS (Triple Nickel) had F-4Cs. Ross Fobair and the 45th TFS deployed to Ubon in 1965, and the Marines of VMFA-542 and 531 deployed to Da Nang.

So when Gen. William "Spike" Momyer gave Olds approval

*This was conceived to provide a pool of trained pilots for rapid USAF expansion.

for his plan, it was with the F-4C, each loaded with four AIM-7E radar guided missiles and four AIM-9B Sidewinders. They also jury-rigged a QRC-160 ECM pod to each jet and took off on January 2, 1967. Well aware that their communications were monitored, they used F-105 call signs for the administrative parts of the flight, such as takeoff and air refueling.*

After leaving the Red refueling track, normally used by Thuds, they flew the tighter F-105 formation up into North Vietnam. Crossing the Black River, the seven flights of Phantoms headed east toward Dog Pecker, just like strikers would on their way to Thud Ridge. Turning southeast down the ridge, the first three flights of four, led by Robin Olds of course, spread out for their sweep down the Red River Valley. The timing was all built around the sweep. It was hoped that everything they'd done up to that point would get the North Vietnamese airborne to intercept what appeared to be F-105s. While the MiGs got their nasty shock, three of the other flights would arrive and cap over the enemy bases so any survivors couldn't land. The last flight would take up position between Thud Ridge and the Chinese border to intercept any MiGs running north to hide. It was a good plan, simple and easy to execute like all good battle plans.

Except the MiGs didn't take the bait.

Olds got to the southern end of the ridge over Phuc Yen and had to turn around back to the north. This complicated things, as there were now friendlies, the other incoming F-4 flights, out in front coming south. This meant no BVR shots were possible, so a visual ID would have to be made. In other words, a dogfight. And that's what happened.

The MiGs were late getting off the ground because of bad

---

*Once the battle began, they would revert to their own flight call signs: Olds, Ford, Rambler, Lincoln, Tempest, Plymouth, and Vespa.

weather so they came shooting up through the overcast, drooling with anticipation, and ran straight into the first twelve Phantoms. In the blink of an eye *they* became the targets, and seven of them went down in flaming pieces. Nguyen Van Coc, future commander of the Vietnamese National Air Force, was one of those shot down that day. He later recounted:

> *The MiG-21s were taking off one by one, and each of the first four was shot down by Phantom IIs. The same fate was waiting for the leader of the second formation. This serious loss was due to . . . indecisiveness in the Central Command Post and a faulty concept—we expected F-105s.*

Not one American fighter was lost.

Robin Olds was the quintessential combat fighter pilot commander. Whereas Albert Ball and Hans-Joachim Marseille were great warriors, Olds took it a step further. Undeniably a first-class flyer, he was something more. Like Boelcke, Hawker, or George Davis, Olds was a thinker and a *leader.* A few months later, while attacking industrial targets in Thai Nguyen, two F-4s were badly hit by ground fire. The first one, flown by Capt. Bob Aman, was losing fuel so quickly he'd never make the Laotian border. Capt. Bob Pardo was flying the second damaged jet and had Aman lower his tailhook, then used his own F-4 to push his buddy toward safety.* With one engine on fire, Pardo got the pair as close to Laos as possible, then both crews ejected. They were all picked up, and four irreplaceable lives were saved. But someone sitting safely behind a desk at Seventh Air Force

---

*Incidentally, Pardo and Aman were both wingmen. Their flight leads had already gotten separated and were on their way home when all this occurred.

Headquarters decided that it was all just showboating by some cowboy fighter pilot; what's more, it was a direct violation of USAF regulations. Never mind that four Americans were alive and well, fit to continue the fight and not dead on a hillside or in the Hanoi Hilton. Believe it or not, an investigation was started.

Olds flew directly to Saigon and without regard to his own career personally intervened with Spike Momyer. The whole ridiculous investigation disappeared and Pardo earned a well-deserved Silver Star.

Two months later Colonel Olds came off a strike west of Thud Ridge critically low on fuel and barely managed to rendezvous with Orange 56, a KC-135 out of Clark AB in the Philippines. Normal practice is to take a few thousand pounds of fuel (enough to decrease the pucker factor), then go back for more when everyone was breathing easier. When all the Phantoms cycled through, Olds moved back in to top off. To his astonishment, he found the refueling boom that passed gas from the tanker raised and stowed.

"Hey," Robin yelled, "wait a minute . . . give me my fuel."

"We're Bingo. Returning to base."

"Bingo, hell! You don't know what Bingo is! Give me some fuel!"

The tanker guy wasn't budging. "No, we're Bingo, headed home."

Fuming and with less than 300 pounds of gas left (about two minutes of flying time), Colonel Olds replied, "OK, I have a couple of Sidewinders left. I'm going to drop back behind you, and before I punch out, I'm going to pull the trigger. Put your parachutes on." The boom immediately came down.

His willingness to defy bureaucracy in the name of common sense, to lead from the front, and to get the mission done regardless of the imposed constraints made Olds a legend. Of course, none of this endeared him to PACAF and the Pentagon, so they began scheming to get him out of Southeast Asia. Olds was nowhere near the 100-mission limit, but he had bagged a few MiGs and was famous enough for the North Vietnamese to put a $25,000 bounty on his head.* All good reasons, the Pentagon decided, to relieve him as soon as he got five kills and bring him home. So rather than leaving his wing by becoming an ace again, at least a dozen times Robin set up kills and let his wingmen shoot the MiGs. Keeping his men alive by being there and leading combat missions was more important than kills or careerism. One of his pilots, another MiG killer, said it like this: "The Robin Oldses of this world are born for combat, not the Pentagon, and I would have flown as his wingman over Hanoi in 1967 even if we had been armed with .45-caliber pistols!"

A lord of the sky, indeed.

BY LATE 1967 the North Vietnamese economy was in tatters. American airpower had severely damaged or destroyed bridges, power plants, roads, and petroleum facilities. There was bitter division within the Hanoi government as well; one faction believed in reunification through political means, while the other held that only through force could Vietnam be joined. This latter group was supported by Red China, which feared that a drawn-out conventional war would pull them in as it had in Korea. The political, negotiating faction was backed by the Soviet Union and, in either case, Vietnam was wholly dependent on the big Communist powers to continue the war. Both sides also knew that the North could not win a conventional conflict against the United States.

---

*$171,500 in 2012 U.S. dollars.

A protracted guerilla war was the only type of fight that made sense. It would wear down the political will in Washington and further erode any remaining popular support among the American people. Going offensive, Hanoi ultimately decided, was the best way to accomplish this. If surprise was achieved and a great victory won, then it would show the United States that the North would continue at any price, that there was no point in more Americans dying, and that the South Vietnamese were not worth fighting for. It would also demonstrate to both China and the Soviet Union that the war could be won if they continued providing weapons and aircraft.

This offensive began early on the morning of January 21, 1968, when the Marine Combat Base at Khe Sanh was attacked. Thanks to effective reconnaissance and information from a defecting North Vietnamese officer, the Americans were quite ready. However, there were three NVA regular divisions of about 20,000 men arrayed against three battalions of the 26th Marines. The base was geographically important, as it lay south of the DMZ along Route Nine—a perfect location for long-range patrols and interdicting nearby sections of the Ho Chi Minh Trail. Like Dien Bien Phu, Khe Sanh was surrounded by low hills and suffered from bad weather. The overland paths to the base were constantly harassed by the Viet Cong, so resupply by air was crucial.

The North Vietnamese intended on using Khe Sanh to pull in U.S. and ARVN (Army of the Republic of South Vietnam) resources to divert attention from what was coming next. On January 30, the Tet Offensive erupted, overrunning everything in its path *except* Khe Sanh. NVA and Viet Cong forces attacked most of the provincial and district capitals, plus Hue and Saigon, where the U.S. embassy was captured for eight hours. Caught by surprise, American and ARVN forces nevertheless fought back ferociously, and the assault rapidly lost momentum. Even so, it took nearly two weeks to liberate Saigon and over a month to recapture Hue.

All through this the Marines held on, but there's no doubt Khe Sanh would've fallen without air support. Possibly emboldened by their similar success against the French, the Vietnamese seemed to have forgotten whom they were fighting and badly underestimated the American response, both militarily and politically. Lyndon Johnson, rather surprisingly, had decided that Khe Sanh would be no Dien Bien Phu and ordered it held at all costs. Operation Niagara was the all-out air support operation for the beleaguered base. For the first time, all Navy, Marines and Air Force air units involved were unified under the Seventh Air Force commander, General Momyer.

A controversial figure, Momyer was nevertheless a frontline aviator with two hundred missions, eight kills, and three Silver Stars to his credit. By this time in his career he was a fine general, though not necessarily a good commander—and there is a difference. Nevertheless, he *knew* tactical airpower, and the results bore that out. Some 450 combat aircraft per day were flying coordinated missions into the Khe Sanh area. When the siege finally broke the USAF had flown 9,691 sorties, with 7,098 from the Marines, and the Navy finished with 5,337 combat missions. More than 39,000 tons of bombs had been dropped, sometimes within 1,000 yards of the defensive perimeter. Ground-directed bombing (GDB) was used by the Marine Air Support Squadrons (MASS) with great success via their TPQ-10 close air support system.

Fielded during World War II, this system was employed with A-26 bombers, and command guidance was sent directly to the pilot direction indicator. Ever the pioneers with close air support, the Marines enthusiastically used GDB with their

Corsair night fighting squadrons in Korea.* Skyspot was the USAF equivalent and was used for night and bad-weather deliveries of B-52s and usually F-100 fighters. Skyspot had a slightly better accuracy, 11 yards versus 50 yards, but both computed a weapon release point based on inbound course, friendly locations, and winds.

Yet despite this unequivocal demonstration of properly used tactical airpower, a halt of offensive operations above the 20th parallel was called in March 1968. It was a test, Washington believed, to ascertain Hanoi's intentions and their willingness to negotiate. During the monsoon shift, springtime weather was atrocious anyway, and air operations would be minimally affected. Senior military commanders had all watched the Korean War drag on as a result of the "fighting and talking" strategy and had no wish to repeat it now. The North Vietnamese immediately began rebuilding their rail network and repairing the marshaling yards at Kep and Thai Nguyen. Air Defense networks were expanded, fresh ammunition was brought in by sea, and the NVAF continued to rebuild.†

A permanent halt was called on October 31, 1968 (incidentally, three days prior to the U.S. presidential elections), and all bombing stopped. Escorted reconnaissance missions into North Vietnam, known as "protective reactive" flights, were permitted, as was the continued interdiction of the Ho Chi Minh Trail. American domestic support for the war had fallen from 70 percent in 1966 to 42 percent by the fall of 1968. Incoming U.S. president Richard Nixon announced that he would begin a

*900 of the 2,584 GDB sorties were flown by Marines. USAF B-29 missions made up the remainder.

†Mining of the ports to prevent seaborne resupply still wasn't permitted by Washington.

withdrawal of ground forces, so as always, Hanoi took advantage of the lull to rebuild and, in this case, to expand.

Well aware that the existence of South Vietnam depended on American air support, the North Vietnamese air defense system was considerably strengthened, and much of it, including three SAM regiments, moved toward the DMZ. Seven antiaircraft regiments deployed below the line, meaning that South Vietnamese airspace was no longer a safe haven. The numbers of MiG-21s increased from thirty-eight remaining in 1968 to nearly a hundred in 1971.

By this time the protective reactive flights more resembled Navy Alpha strike packages rather than reconnaissance missions. But their efforts weren't on a scale large enough to really slow the southward Communist flood, and on March 30, 1972, Hanoi launched what become known as the Easter Offensive. More than 40,000 NVA regulars crossed the DMZ supported by field artillery and tanks. The new SA-7 man-portable surface-to-air missile (MANPAD) was also deployed. Called a Grail, the SA-7 was a simple, rugged, and cheap infrared system. Though it had a very short range, because it was a heat seeker it gave no warning unless the launch was seen visually, so it took a fearsome toll of slow-moving U.S. helicopters and FAC aircraft. The ARVN 3rd Division collapsed, and to Hanoi's surprise, the Americans began redeploying tactical assets. Seventh Air Force had been down to less than five hundred aircraft but quickly built up to the thousand-plane mark. Five aircraft carriers were put back on Yankee station, and on May 8 Washington allowed the war to be fought as it should have been in 1965. More than three hundred sorties per day were flown, including massive B-52 raids, and all six North Vietnamese ports were mined. With no seaborne resupply, the NVA ran out of ammunition in just ten days.

Operation Linebacker gave U.S. airpower a free hand to deal with virtually all targets in the North and they did so, using a new generation of precision guided munitions, Wild Weasels, and all-weather Navy attack aircraft. More than 265 tanks were destroyed and the enemy halted. Stunned by the reaction, with the ground offensive stalled and North Vietnam on fire, Hanoi sought to reopen peace talks. Under a decisive president, with clear military objectives and no operational interference, Linebacker achieved more in four months than Rolling Thunder managed in three years.

Hanoi claimed the rather ludicrous figure of 651 aircraft destroyed and 80 U.S. warships sunk; however, no ships sank, and of the 104 combat aircraft lost only 18 were from SAMs. The operation was paused in October, and peace talks began again in Paris. Intrigue, outright deception, and mistrust temporarily derailed the process, leading Secretary of State Henry Kissinger to conclude that Hanoi was stalling again. Unwilling to accept this, Nixon turned the military loose for Linebacker II, a final operation designed to end the war.

During what was also called the "11-Day War," 15,237 tons of bombs were dropped on military and industrial targets, most near Hanoi. By the end of it, 80 percent of North Vietnam's electrical grid was destroyed, as were over 3 million gallons of petroleum and some 300 pieces of rolling stock—not to mention roads, bridges, railroads, and SAM sites. Though the operation was condemned by some, it did what was intended, bringing Hanoi back to the table.* Though with the benefit of hindsight, the North Vietnamese were well aware the Americans wanted

---

*Olof Palme, prime minister of Sweden, likened the bombings to other international crimes like Guernica and the Katyn Forest. Apparently he'd forgotten his own nation's involvement with Hitler and SKF. See Chapter 11.

to withdraw and decided to continue talking to preserve what was left of their infrastructure. Hanoi likely would've made any agreement to get the carriers, fighters, and bombers out, but they'd been fighting for twenty years and could continue if necessary. But it wasn't. Presented with a way to pull back, both sides took a breath and signed a cease-fire on January 23, 1973.

The war in Vietnam—at least for the Americans—was over.

"THREE'S UP!"

Uri Bina's voice was calm, and his wingmate Tulip Four, piloted by Lt. Col. Giora Rom, took a deep breath. Eyes fastened on his section leader, he watched the A-4N Skyhawk suddenly roll up on one wing and pull hard away from him, vapor streaming from the wingtips. Instantly the Israeli Air Force (IAF) pilot followed, grunting against the g's and blinking rapidly to keep the other jet in sight. Bina popped upright, and Rom followed through the first pull, the unfamiliar jet wobbling slightly as the desert raced by.

He took a breath and counted.

Alef . . .

Rom glanced at the combining glass and saw the pipper for the continuously computed impact point jiggling slightly. It was on, set, and ready. His eyes darted around the cockpit. He was forgetting something . . . had to be forgetting something.

Bet . . .

His leader's A-4 suddenly stopped moving forward and shot upward from the desert, dust clouds peeling away from the jet wash. It was Giora's first flight in an Ayit—an "Eagle," as the Israelis called the A-4—*and* it was a combat mission. But there'd been no choice. Ami Gadish, No. 115 Squadron's commanding officer, had been killed accidentally three days earlier, and Rom had only made it to Tel Nof Air Base last night to take over. The IAF commander, Benny Peled, had told him point-blank: "The squadron is in a state of shock. Do whatever it takes tomorrow and on Friday—and next week you will take a A-4 conversion course."

Gimel . . .

He tensed his stomach muscles. Second pull. Yanking the stick straight back to his lap, the fighter soared upward, the milky blue Mediterranean Sea filled his right eye and the vast, tan wasteland of Sinai was to the left. The Skyhawk was throbbing with power, and he held the stick lightly in his hand. Bunting forward to freeze a 60-degree climb angle, he watched the altimeter spin crazily.

Three thousand feet.

Straining forward against his shoulder straps to see over the canopy rail, he peered out at Port Said and the battle. As always, the contrast was striking; the perfect north-south cut of the Suez Canal separating dirty brown desert to the east from the startlingly green Nile Delta of Egypt to the west.

Four thousand feet.

Maybe only ninety minutes had passed since the Egyptian Second Army had attacked along the canal from Port Said south to the Great Bitter Lake. It was 3:30 p.m. on October 6, 1973. He could see dust everywhere, columns of black smoke and hundreds of vehicles darting about like angry beetles. Attacking the Bar Lev Line was considered suicidal—truly crazy. It was impregnable, but then again, the French had believed the same about the Maginot Line thirty-three years earlier.*

Five thousand feet.

---

*Moshe Dayan, the one-eyed defense minister, called the canal the best antitank ditch in the world. He lost his eye to a Vichy French sniper in 1941.

There. He could see the army outpost quite clearly right beside the north-south-running infantry road; Lexicon, the track was called. His eyes flickered back and forth between the altimeter and the terrain. Up from the outpost . . . white flashes of weapon fire . . . 5,500 feet . . . more smoke . . . *there!* A line of dark armored vehicles inching along the tan sand toward the road. If the Arabs could get around the northern edge of the line . . . It couldn't happen.

Six thousand feet.

The third pull was a roll inverted, leaving him hanging in the straps. Giora stared down through the clear canopy at the appalling panorama below. Tens of thousands of Egyptian troops were massed as far south as he could see. Tracer fire arced over the turquoise-colored canal and white puffy explosions from anti-aircraft fire dotted the sky around him.

Snapping upright, he rolled out with the nose about 50 degrees low. *Too much* . . . he struggled to assess the unfamiliar bombing symbology, but it seemed straightforward enough unlike the French Mirage III he had flown. Bumping the stick up to hold 45 degrees nose low, Giora was trying to line up the pipper on the Egyptian vehicles when he caught a flash from the corner of his right eye.

SAM! From Port Said.

His breathing quickened but he ignored it. The missile was at least twenty seconds away, and he had to get his eight bombs off. Israelis were dying down there. Feeling the jet accelerate at such a steep angle, Giora pulled the power back. The ground fire worsened, and the fighter buffeted from something exploding nearby.

Almost there . . .

The SAM had curved up and over, leaving a thick white trail against the blue sky, but the pilot ignored it all. Nudging the trim button forward, Giora twitched the stick back and forth slightly to keep the pipper below the target. He held his thumb poised over the pickle button on the left side of the stick.

Almost . . .

Egyptian anti-aircraft fire was streaming up in all directions, and the SAM was gone. That meant the sustainer had burned out and it was only seconds away from impact. Mouth dry, chest heaving, he felt time slow as the pipper touched the lead armored vehicle in the Egyptian column.

Now!

Mashing down hard, he paused, then pulled straight up, g's pressing him back into the seat and sweat pouring from under his helmet. As the Skyhawk's nose came level with the horizon, he had a split second to decide which way to egress.

It didn't matter—there were Arabs everywhere. Shoving the throttle forward, Giora rolled right toward the water, then flipped the jet over and dove for the beach. No Triple-A over the ocean, he thought. Turning back east, he remembered the SAM and whipped his head around, then chuckled. It was way too late; he would've been dead if the SAM had guided. A dark shape flashed by overhead, and his heart thudded against his chest. There could be MiGs anywhere . . . but then he saw the lizard-colored paint around the bright blue Star of David and smiled. It was one of his jets. *His jets* . . . that sounded good.

"Four . . . your bombs didn't release." Uri Bina's voice broke in through the radio chatter.

What?

Giora's eyes swiveled down to the weapons panel, then out to the wings. The eight big, green Mk-82 1,000-pounders were still hanging there. Then he saw it. The master arm switch was still in the centered safe position.

As the two fighters raced east, he took a deep breath and

keyed the mike. "Four copies . . . I'll go back to reattack." Releasing the switch, Giora Rom pounded his knee. He shouldn't be here; it was madness to fly a combat mission in an unknown aircraft. The pilot flipped the master arm toggle switch to arm. But he didn't have a choice. Giora Rom was a professional, a fighter pilot. He'd do what he had to do. Pushing his visor up, he looked west toward the canal, then sliced back, picked up speed, and headed to the initial point for his attack.

He could do it . . . he *had* to do it.

And he did.

Giora Rom got his bombs off the second time and went on to command No. 115 Squadron for the duration of the short war. But the Bar-Lev Line did not hold. Constructed after the 1969–1970 War of Attrition, the fortification was essentially an Israeli version of the Hindenburg or Maginot Line. At a cost of $300 million in 1973, its first defense was a 60- to 80-foot wall of sand, inclined at least 45 degrees, sitting atop a massive concrete retaining wall. Interspersed down the line, twenty-two forts and thirty-five strong points dominated likely canal crossing areas. Protected by minefields and barbed wire, these were air-conditioned and reinforced to withstand a 1,000-pound bomb.

Lexicon Road was immediately behind the line and permitted rapid reinforcement of any position. Six miles past this, the Artillery road connected armor staging areas and various air defense positions. About 20 miles farther back the Lateral road allowed Israeli reserves to move and assemble without the threat of artillery attack. Other arteries ran east-west at various points to expedite movement and the concentration of forces. The Israelis also built a system of pipes that would pump crude oil into the canal and ignite if necessary. This entire system was predicated on holding the Egyptians at bay for forty-eight hours while the Israeli Air Force (IAF) gained air superiority, activated its reserves, and brought them forward where needed. In many ways, the plan made sense, but in other ways it was a copy of the French disaster of 1940.

Assuming that your enemy will do as you expect is always dangerous, and the Egyptians did not cooperate. They'd been conducting large-scale military exercises along the canal zone for months to desensitize Aman, Israeli military intelligence. Cairo had also ordered all officer cadets back to class by October 9 and made a very public point of releasing reservists prior to October 6. Late on the evening of October 5, Egyptian divers plugged up the crude oil vents along the canal. A bright young engineer named Baki Yousef also came up with the idea of using water cannons to breach the sand walls. After all, the canal was full of water and when the sand poured off under a high-pressure water deluge, then pontoon or Bailey bridges could be quickly erected.*

That was what happened. At 2 p.m. on October 6, 1973, several thousand guns opened up from the Egyptian side of the Suez Canal. During the first minute 10,500 shells fell on the startled Israeli Defense Force (IDF) positions. More than two hundred MiG-21s, MiG-19s, and MiG-17s then attacked key Israeli bases, followed by commando raids behind the lines. Behind this carefully planned wave the Egyptian Second and Third Armies charged the Bar-Lev Line. On Israel's northern border, the Syrians also attacked, moving south to seize the Golan Heights. This two-pronged, coordinated assault wasn't part of the Israeli defensive plan, but it should've been. Egypt,

---

*Bailey bridges were prefabricated and could be assembled without using heavy equipment. They were used extensively in World War II, and due to the modular design, combat field repairs were easy to make.

Jordan, and Syria had all attacked Israel in 1967 during the Six-Day War.*

Fortunately, in the early morning hours of October 6, the Israelis had finally chosen to believe that an assault was imminent. They began full mobilization, calling up reservists and moving men and equipment. Yom Kippur, the holiest day of the Jewish year, had begun. The Egyptians correctly reasoned that Israelis on active duty would be spread paper-thin and the rest of the military would be at home. This actually helped, to some degree, because the fighting men were easy to round up and the normally congested roads were empty.

Egypt and Syria could put up 750 combat aircraft against Israel's 340 fighters. Additionally, and very nearly decisively, both Arab armies possessed new SAMs like the SA-3 and SA-6 systems (the latter called a "Kub" by the Soviets, "Gainful" by NATO). Fielded in 1966, it was smaller, lighter, and infinitely more lethal than anything that had come before. Three of the 20-foot-long, 1,300-pound missiles were carried on a transporter erector launcher (TEL). The basic SA-6 used a separate but also mobile Straight Flush radar system, and the whole battery could be on the road in fifteen minutes.

Like radar-guided air-to-air missiles, the SA-6 used semiactive homing. This permitted very fast reactions so the system was deadly against fighter aircraft. It could see out to 40 miles and began tracking at 20 miles, depending on the target's parameters. Once locked by the Straight Flush, the TEL would fire a salvo, usually of three missiles, beginning at 10 miles. Radar tracking was possible down to 300 feet and under 200 feet

*Interestingly, though the United Arab Republic, the union between Egypt and Syria, formally ended in 1971, UAR stamps were still being used by Egyptian customs agents in 1992.

using TV optics. The missile topped out at 2.8 Mach (nearly three times the speed of sound) with a 130-pound warhead that used contact or proximity fusing. During the nineteen-day Yom Kippur War, Egyptian and Syrian SA-6s would bring down sixty-four Israeli aircraft from ninety-five missiles fired. This is partly because it was a deadly system, but also because countertactics and equipment hadn't evolved yet to fight it.

A key component of any defense of Israel was, and is, air force. From 1948 onward, realizing that they would be continually attacked by their Arab neighbors, Tel Aviv knew that control of the air meant survival for the nation. Flying P-51s and Spitfires immediately after independence in 1948, the IAF quickly upgraded to Gloster Meteors and F-86s during the 1950s. These gave way exclusively to French Mystères and Mirage IIIs in the next decade, but during this time the IAF switched back to American combat aircraft.

There were several reasons for this. Coming out of Korea and into Vietnam, the United States was regarded as much more combat savvy than the French, and their designs reflected this. Additionally, Tel Aviv was wary of depending on a single source, and Paris had proved unreliable in the past. French aircraft were also complicated: maintenance was difficult, and they weren't easy to fly. This was especially critical for an air force that relied heavily upon reservists and emergency postings, if needed, for their defense. Both the reserves and emergency postings were fully trained pilots who had already served their commitments and now held civilian jobs. They maintained lower levels of qualifications than the regulars but the idea was that, like the old British Volunteer Reserves and Auxiliary Air Force pilots, in a crisis they could be rapidly brought up to speed.

Pilots were selected a bit differently in Israel than in most countries. In advance of compulsory national service at eighteen years of age, if a boy had high grades from secondary school, was in excellent physical shape, and scored well on the aptitude tests, he could apply. Those considered were asked to a *gibush*, a second round of selection that included additional aptitude tests and unique problem-solving scenarios presented to the candidate. This was to weed out those who looked good on paper but couldn't think on their feet. Other air forces, including the USAAF and Luftwaffe, had used a similar system prior to World War II.

Once selected, a cadet would enter a six-month preparatory phase that introduced basic academics with rudimentary infantry and officers' training. The Basic phase came next, and for five months the cadet studied more infantry tactics, underwent survival training, and learned to parachute. He also continued elementary flying in a Grob trainer. Many were eliminated during this first year and sent back to the army for their national service. At the end of Basic, cadets were rank-ordered by flying skill, grades, and instructor evaluations. Those who had some aptitude but hadn't qualified as pilot candidates were sent to navigator training. The others were divided into combat pilots, helicopter pilots, and transport pilots and from here would go to Primary.

This course took another six months and taught regular contact flying skills, takeoffs and landings, patterns, and elementary aerobatics. Whoever remained after this was sent to college for a year, courtesy of Ben-Gurion University, and permitted to choose one of four areas of study. Following this academic phase, the cadet had six more months of advanced training: formation flying, aerobatics, instrument flying, and of course, there were continuous evaluations. The abbreviated academic coursework was also completed, and the cadet had to endure a final committee review of all he'd done in the past three years. If he passed and graduated, the young man was given a B.A. or B.S. degree along with his lieutenant's commission and wings.* After this came a year of operational training in whichever aircraft the pilot had been selected to fly before a posting to a line squadron.

The men who fought the Yom Kippur War were aware that they were Israel's first and best line of defense. Each squadron was a unit of precisely placed, mobile high explosives—aggressive, highly motivated men who would do what they had to do for the safety of their country. After the Bar-Lev Line was breached, the IAF went into crisis mode and began scrambling aircraft, like Tulip flight, to plug the gaps. There were F-4 squadrons, but they were primarily engaged in air-to-air combat and heavy bombing missions, so the majority of close air support and defense suppression missions fell to the A-4 Skyhawks.

Developed from a U.S. Navy requirement for a light attack jet aircraft, McDonnell-Douglas flew the prototype in June 1954, and it went out to the fleet in 1956. The design was relatively conventional: a low-delta-wing, single-seat fighter with one engine. The leading-edge flaps were aerodynamically activated, like those on the Bf 109s had been, so there was no extra mechanical weight. Also, the stubby little 26-foot wings were small enough that no folding mechanism was required—all of which meant that McDonnell was able to deliver a plane at 50 percent of specified gross weight.

The diminutive fighter was hard to see, which is good in any kind of fight. It was quick, simple, tough, and, as Giora Rom proved, easy to fly. Small though it was, the Skyhawk could carry a 9,900-pound weapons payload plus two 20 mm can-

*They were all men until 1994. In 2001, Roni Zuckerman, granddaughter of two leaders from the Warsaw Ghetto uprising, became the first Israeli woman to earn pilot's wings.

nons. Capable of 650 mph, the A-4 climbed out at 8,400 feet per minute with a combat range around 600 miles, depending on its load. It was ideal for close air support. Equally important, the unit cost was about 25 percent of the Phantom's—and it carried more bombs.

When the United States decided to sell F-104 Starfighters to the Royal Jordanian Air Force in the mid-1960s, the IAF saw an opportunity. Wanting an alternative to the French, Tel Aviv agreed not to object to the Jordanian sale if Washington would offer the IAF something just as good, and by 1966 Operation Rugby—delivery of Skyhawks to Israel—was under way. In the summer of 1967, while Robin Olds and the Wolfpack were killing MiGs, Israeli pilots were in Florida learning to fly their new jet. Though the Israelis were all qualified combat pilots, the Americans had weapons and techniques that the IAF hadn't yet mastered such as air-to-air radar, catapult launches, and air refueling.

The first Skyhawks arrived by boat in Haifa a few days after Christmas 1967, and were immediately assembled. The IAF version, called the A-4H, had some modifications, including a different engine, the J52-P-8A. The Israelis had also replaced the 20 mm cannons with twin DEFA 30 mm guns and added a tailpipe extension to shield the engine from heat-seeking missiles. Though it performed well during the War of Attrition, the A-4 was hard hit during the Yom Kippur War.

Israel's continuous struggle since independence had been overwhelmingly successful from a military standpoint, and though always outnumbered, superior training combined with good equipment had kept the edge. After all, it was no ideological struggle for Israel—it was survival. However, this string of victories led to some degree of overconfidence, and it caught up to the IDF in October 1973. Had it not been for the geography of Sinai and the Golan Heights *and* the skill of her fighter pilots, Israel would very likely have ceased to exist; or at least been driven to the point of using nuclear weapons.

There was another lesson here as well. Namely, that close air support without air superiority is a costly business, and this no longer applied to just enemy fighters. Air superiority now included operating in a SAM-free environment. Anti-aircraft artillery and MANPADs would always be present, but they were a risk that had to be taken. Larger fixed SAMs could be avoided or destroyed, but the new mobile SAMs had changed the battlefield. They had to be dealt with before close air support aircraft and helicopters could roam about with impunity. Altitude, either high or low, was no longer an exclusion zone, at least not without jamming. Medium altitude was untenable against SAMs, and low altitude without countermeasures was equally dangerous.

Therefore, in any future battle all the elements had to come together. Jamming—the stand-off type against early warning and search radars, plus tactical systems that kept fighters alive in battle—was essential. Countermeasures such as chaff and flares had to be fully integrated. Automatic options were needed if certain types of guidance were sensed, along with a manual capability the pilot could use at will. Most of all, fighter pilots had to go into future conflicts prepared to be flexible, as always. Those who planned such wars needed the creative willingness to realize that there is no one solution to a tactical problem. Hard lessons need to be remembered, but tactics should be derived against the next threat, not for the last one.

Vietnam and the Arab-Israeli wars should have been a warning, but they were not immediately regarded that way by Washington. In all fairness, the Soviet Union was still the main threat for the West, and the U.S. military had learned from their experience and those of others. Air-to-air combat would always be a critical fighter pilot skill, but American primacy in that area nearly eliminated such a threat from enemy pilots. The real danger, far more extensive and far more lethal, came from air defense systems. Vast networks of SAMs, plus radars and all the weapons that could be guided from them, had replaced most of the air threats. The guard was changing from the glory days of mass dogfights to a new age of supersonic missiles and radar-guided anti-aircraft fire.

Electronic and passive countermeasures were now constantly being developed and refined, much as better engines and guns had been a few decades earlier. Aircraft development was generally veering away from single-mission aircraft, and the age of the multirole fighter was at hand. Advances in ergonomics, microtechnology, and computers had improved designs to the point where vast amounts of information could be processed by one pilot. This rapidly brought an end to the need for two-seat tactical aircraft.

As the threat from the East diminished and the Soviet Union careened toward a bloodless economic collapse, many believed that the time of danger was over. It was a fond wish but a wish nonetheless—flawed and as dangerous as those that emerged in 1918, 1945, and 1953. Proxy fights would continue, but the new wars were increasingly fought between violently opposed ideologies rather than socioeconomic systems. In less than two decades, the West would face an unexpected threat that would shape the world of the fighter pilot for decades to come.

CHAPTER 15

THE CIRCLE CLOSES

USN F/A-18 HORNET

FEBRUARY 6, 1991
NORTHERN IRAQ

"SAM IN THE air! SA-6 . . . *two* SAMs . . . over Ally's Twat . . . northbound!"

The F-16 flipped over and pulled sideways to put the incoming missiles off its left wing. Popping upright, the pilot gasped, rolled slightly to see over his canopy rail, then stared down at the mottled brown landscape. Twenty miles farther east, next to the gray-green Tigris River, it was darker, but here the tan plumes were easy to see, hanging in the air over the launch sites. The missiles were plain enough; dirty white fingers reaching up through a light blue sky, at three times the speed of sound. He had only seconds to react.

Lt. Col. Dave "Mooman" Moody slapped the chaff dispense button on the left bulkhead, then keyed the mike.

"Satan Two . . . Slapshot Six . . . bearing two, zero, zero . . ."

He banked a bit harder, nudged the throttle against the mil power stop, and punched out a few more chaff bundles. *Question marks,* he thought. *They look like fucking question marks.* Both of the smoke trails were bending around to the north at his two-ship. He'd split his flight of four, and the other pair, called an element, had gone east of the Al Sharqat target area. Called "Ally's Twat," of course, it lay off Highway One just west of the Tigris River. South of Mosul and due west of Kirkuk, Sharqat was the site of a major military complex. Intel also said it was a possible chemical weapons depot, or maybe even a nuclear research facility.

The colonel shrugged; either way, it was just a target. What made it suspicious, though, were the defenses. It had been ringed by SA-2 and SA-3 batteries, but over the past two days his squadron had destroyed them and their early-warning radars. The remaining SAMs were nasty. Short-ranged, very fast, and tough to jam, the SA-8s had to go before strikers could get in and flatten the place—and they'd be here in fifteen minutes. Bareta, Hodja, and Phaser—twelve more of his Viper brothers.

"Satan Two . . . Magnum Six . . . Ally's Twat."

Mooman glanced back to his left seven o'clock position. The big, dark F-4G was plain to see about 9,000 feet behind him, and so was the immense bright white cloud erupting beneath its wing. The trail detached itself from the fighter, and the high-speed anti-radiation missile in front of the smoke wobbled a moment. Then it turned and abruptly pitched down at the crappy little village to the south.

". . . and another raghead on a cell phone bites the dust," the colonel muttered.

From the corner of his eye he saw the Phantom crank back

toward him, digging down hard to get the nose around. As it disappeared past his tail Mooman stared at the SAMs. They'd finished the turn and both were pointing northwest of the village—at him. Holding the F-16 rock steady, he eyeballed the ALR-69 radar warning receiver (RWR), then popped the chaff button two more times. The RWR soaked up radar beams of all types, then compared them to a library in its memory. It also measured the signal's angle of arrival and put a matching symbol on the display.

In this case it was a Straight Flush fire control radar that was tracking him. The signal would bounce off his jet, and a smaller antenna within the missile's seeker head would "see" it. In fractions of a second, angular differences were measured and the missile fins moved accordingly. Semi-active radar homing gave quicker corrections and was much, much more difficult to defeat than the older command-guided SA-2 system.

"Satan Three, tally a third missile off the ground at Ally's Twat!"

Mooman risked a glance away and saw the rolling dust plume of a third launch. Before he could say anything, the other element lead did. "Satan Four . . . Slapshot Six bearing three, one, zero . . ."

Good kid, he thought.

The "Fighting Hawks" of the 23rd Tactical Fighter Squadron were a class act, and being the squadron commander was the high point of his career. Detached from the 52nd Tactical Fighter Wing out of Spangdahlem Air Base, West Germany, they flew F-16Cs and F-4Gs together as mixed pairs. It was a continuation of the Hunter-Killer concept that came out of Vietnam; the Phantom had the APR-47 for hunting SAMs and the Viper carried GP bombs, air-to-ground missiles, or cluster bombs to kill the thing.

He bunted, rolled inverted and hung upside down as

dirt floated through the cockpit. A gum wrapper too . . . *sonavabitch* . . . Staring down at Iraq, he slapped the button four times then pulled directly for the earth. The floating crap disappeared with g's and in an instant the Viper was 90 degrees to the ground. Mooman corkscrewed the jet, yanked the throttle back to idle, and looked for smoke trails.

One. Only one . . .

"Shit!"

Still pointed straight down at 13,000 feet, he pirouetted the Viper, putting its tail on Al Sharqat. Tensing his stomach muscles, Mooman immediately pulled back hard with his right hand and mashed the chaff button again with his left. The digital readout in his heads-up display (HUD) went to 7.1 g's, and as the jet's nose came up he rotated the throttle out, then shoved it into full afterburner.

"Satan Three's tally the site . . . in from the southeast."

The burner kicked, and the F-16 rocketed up as Mooman strained against the g-forces, watching. His ECM jamming pod was on automatic, so all he could do now was put out more chaff and fly better than a shot of scotch. Bunting to hold 60 degrees nose high, his eyes flickered to the HUD again as the fighter rolled off to the right: 19,200 feet and 360 knots.

Tugging the throttle back to mil power, the colonel braced his left hand on the rack running along the bottom of the canopy. He could twist against the g's easier now, and did just that, looking back high over his tail. *That's where the first missile should be . . .*

Suddenly a flash of movement caught his eye, and Mooman felt ice shoot through him. *Mother of God . . .*

"Satan One, break!" His F-4 wingman saw it, too, and was trying to warn him.

"SAM . . . close aboard, break now!"

Reacting instantly, he threw the jet into a wild, descending corkscrew and groped for the chaff button. Heart in his throat, he gasped at the g's and reefed back on the stick with all his might. As his helmet hit the seat, Mooman's eyes grayed out and his skin itched, but he kept pulling back up through the horizon. Shaking his head to clear it, he swallowed hard and savagely bunted the Viper over.

"Satan Two . . . attacking Six . . . Ally's Twat!"

The F-4G was trying to help by turning in as well. Flying reflexively, he barrel-rolled back to the right, his vision narrowing. The faint green symbology in his HUD went to gray. *Should be dead* . . . his mind processed that thought, along with the faint noise on the radio. *Talking* . . . Satan Three had come off the target, and there were secondary explosions . . . someone was asking about fuel.

"Satan One . . . ah, both SAMs missed aft. Third went ballistic . . . status?"

Ears ringing, Mooman rolled upright and stared straight ahead. Color returned to his vision and the HUD was green again. He took a deep breath and answered on the interflight VHF radio. "Mr. Toad's Wild Ride . . . I'm good."

"Satan One . . . Satan Three."

"Go." Colonel Moody began arcing back west to keep the target area in sight.

"Looks like two launchers destroyed. Tally on the Straight Flush . . . can you hit it?"

Mooman blinked and craned his neck over the canopy rail. A cloud of dust had risen over the desert and was drifting south with the wind. Blacker smoke on the edges . . . He squinted and saw two distinct burning areas: revetments. Even from 15,000 feet they were plain enough now that he knew where to look. Running his eyes over the cockpit, he moved the fuel select knob back to NORM and checked the totalizer. His wing tanks were empty.

"Roger that . . . Satan One's got about ten mikes on station."

The rest of them came back with fuel and weapons remaining. There was one HARM left on Satan Four, and Moody's two cans of CBU-58. Zippering the mike, he swung the Viper back around to the east and pulled the power back to hold 400 knots.

"One is contact the two burning launchers."

It was a start point for a visual talk-on. Three was a brand-new captain called Scorch, but he was already a combat flight lead. "Rog . . . take the distance between the burning targets as one unit . . . go one unit southeast under the smoke to a small hill . . ."

Mooman did it and found the hill. There was something on top of it, something big enough to cast a shadow. "Contact . . . and vehicles on top."

"Straight Flush. Third launcher is due east one unit."

From long habit, Colonel Moody's fingers danced over the cockpit just to make sure. Master Arm . . . camera . . . A/G master mode . . . He looked up through the HUD and flicked the drift cutout switch off so that his bombing symbology would show the winds. Twisting around again, he found the Phantom hanging back two miles at his seven o'clock. Attacking with the wind was better, but there wasn't enough time. He held the two-way mike switch aft. "Satan Four . . . Slapshot Six, Ally's Twat. One's in from the northwest."

The reply was immediate. "Satan Four, attacking Six."

Mooman had already flown the Viper to a decent offset position, so he pulled sideways, then rolled inverted, slid the throttle back, and sliced toward the ground. At the top of the HUD was a little bore sight cross and he played the roll-in to put this cross above the hill.

"Satan Four . . . Magnum Six, Ally's Twat!"

Snapping the jet upright, Moody leveled his wings and pulled the throttle all the way to idle. If he didn't, he'd be supersonic, and that would spoil his aim. The long continuously computed impact point (CCIP) line hung down the HUD like a pendulum, and at the base was a little circle with a pipper. He kept this frozen in place as the altitude unwound.

13,500 feet.

He saw another big white smoke trail, but this one was going down, not coming up. It was a HARM from the other Phantom, Satan Four.

12,000 feet.

Fanning open the speed brakes, Mooman kept the Viper at 450 knots, hoping the HARM would keep the little fuckers' heads down. As soon as he thought it, another dirty brown mushroom cloud bloomed next to the hill. *Shit* . . .

"Satan, head's up! SAM in the air from Ally's Twat."

Twitching the stick, he kept the CCIP line running through the target and ignored the missile. Best way to beat that thing was to kill the Straight Flush.

10,500 feet. Almost there . . . *almost*. The pipper was just under the hill.

"Triple-A . . . ten thousand . . . head's up, One!"

Several flashes . . . but as time slowed down, he saw nothing except the pipper. *There!* It was on the base of the hill. Bunting slightly, Mooman froze the tiny dot on the cluster of vehicles and mashed down on the red pickle button.

The SAM began its climbing turn. Some Eagle flight named Scoff was talking about airborne MiGs, and the AWACS was asking for Satan's position. The jet rocked as the cans of CBU fell free, so Mooman closed the speed brakes, shoved the throttle to mil, and pulled back on the stick. Slapping out a few more chaff bundles, he cranked over sideways to look for Triple-A, then abruptly banked up hard to the right . . . then to the left. Being predictable during a fight was stupid. Proving the point, a cluster of white puffies suddenly appeared exactly where he'd been.

Triple-A, probably 57 mm. Twitching his tail again, he pumped some chaff, but didn't put out any flares. Lots of SAMs could launch optically, and they would if they saw flares. Passing 13,000 feet, Mooman shoved the burner in and began an easy turn back to the north. The RWR scope was hopelessly cluttered with symbols.

"Satan Three . . . tied . . . visual." Meaning he had a radar lock and could see his leader. *Kid's got great eyes* . . .

"Posit?" he snapped back.

"Ten south of Key West . . . over the highway, northbound . . . four point two."

Moody pictured it in his head and glanced down at his multifunction display (MFD)—sort of a god's-eye electronic map in this case. Scorch was farther south than he was and had 4,200 pounds of gas remaining. The kid had already proven he could take care of himself. "Satan Three, cleared to the Gates above thirty K . . . we'll meet up with Arco 54 . . . remain this Victor."

"Three copies all. Good hit with secondarys . . . stick a fork in 'im, he's done."

The colonel threw his head back and laughed. Cocky bastard. Still, why not? The captain was, what, twenty-five years old and leading around $100 million worth of aircraft in combat and killing gomers? Leveling off, he unhooked the sweaty mask and stared out at Mosul. They'd blown the SAMs there to bits during the first two weeks of the war, but there were still MiGs, so most fighters returning north gave the place a wide berth.

Nudging the stick, he headed directly for the air base south of town. After all, it was on the way home. Maybe the Rags would be stupid enough to scramble a few of their shitty jets and make his day complete. Mooman chuckled and adjusted his air-to-air radar to search low. Fuck 'em in the heart . . . then there'd be a few that wouldn't be coming back.

Three hundred and sixty miles to the south, a pair of U.S. Navy Hornets wheeled over the plains northwest of Basra. Powerful twin-engine fighters, these F/A-18s belonged to the "Dambusters" of VFA-195, and today they were out hunting. The city sprawled out from the west bank of the Tigris River like a gray ink blot and beyond its muddy banks lay Iran; a huge spiderweb of deserted revetments, roads, and cantonments covered the ground there like some grotesque tattoo. West of the city the north-south-running airfield was plain to see, as were the mounds and revetments of several SA-3 sites. The river area was dark brown with green edges that rapidly vanished a mile or so from water.

"What a shithole," Lt. Cmdr. Jeff Ashby muttered into his sweaty mask as he stared out over the canopy rail. Leading Hobo flight, he'd been launched off the USS *Midway* in the Persian Gulf to find an enemy helicopter. Specifically, an Iraqi Super Frelon loaded with Exocet anti-ship missiles. Ashby, known as "Bones," was well aware that the 1,500-pound missile could reach 100 miles into the Gulf. One just like it had hit the destroyer USS *Stark* three years ago and killed nearly forty Americans. *And that was when Saddam was our buddy.* He shook his head disgustedly.

"Hobo Two's Joker."

He zippered the mike and looked at his own fuel. Ten more minutes, maybe. Pulling the jet around to the west, he twisted the RWR volume up a tad. It had been relatively quiet so far, but you just never knew. Cranking up again, Bones rolled out heading southeast and stared through his HUD. A little green diamond showed the location of coordinates he'd been given before the mission. It was sitting nicely over empty ground. No helo. He sighed and eyeballed the SAM sites off to the southeast. A few white puffy blotches appeared, then some black ones a bit higher.

"Triple-A over Basra," his wingman chimed in on the interflight UHF frequency.

"Got it . . . not a factor."

For the third time he began a quick, methodical scan around the diamond. Each time he'd run in from another angle, knowing very well the differences that sun and terrain could make. Still, at 450 knots there was never much time. Pushing his visor up, Jeff rubbed his eyes and sighed again. One more, then he'd—

A shadow on the ground.

Using his left index finger, Jeff slewed a little knob on the right throttle and moved the diamond over the dark asterisk shape on the desert floor. Glancing down to his right MFD, he squinted at the grainy TV picture and slowly smiled.

"Gotcha."

The ugly six-bladed copter squatted on the ground, partially covered by netting. *That's why I didn't see it.* It was the shadow of the rotor blades that had caught his eye. "Hobo Two . . . One's tally the target . . . off the nose, ah . . . four miles."

"Ah . . . Hobo Two's blind."

Perfect. Fucking perfect. Jeff looked up and around but couldn't see him. Eyeballing the radar, there was nothing there either. *Must be behind me.* At least they wouldn't hit each other.

The pilot's hands moved around the cockpit, touching the master arm switch, flipping the wafer knob to check his wing tanks, and turning up the intensity of his HUD. There wasn't fuel enough for anything fancy. "Hobo One's attacking."

Everything was set, and for once the Walleye's picture was fairly clear. Pulling the throttles back a knob width, he eased the nose over to set up a long, shallow dive. The AGM-42 had no rocket motor; it was essentially a guided glide munition that used the dropping jet's speed to get to a target. Through a TV camera mounted on the front of the bomb, the pilot designated, or "locked," the weapon. Once released, the Hornet could maneuver as needed, since the fins steered the Walleye directly to the designated point. This one was a Fat Albert, a 2,000-pound Walleye II that could drop a bridge and would make a mess out of this crappy little helicopter. Bones grinned at that and checked the aiming cross. It was steady on the intakes above the cockpit.

He pushed up the throttles and the Hornet lunged forward. Ashby glanced at the HUD; nearly 500 knots. Then back to the MFD and saw the pointing cross was steady. Then back to the HUD—range to the diamond was 8.7 nautical miles. He paused, then jabbed down on the red pickle button. The fighter immediately lurched as the big Walleye dropped free.

Watching a moment, Bones saw the fins pop out. The bomb wobbled, then nosed over slightly. It was guiding. Pulling the power back a bit, he pulled up and away to the left, away from Basra and Iran, scanning the ground for Triple-A or the dirty tails of SAM launches.

It took longer than he thought. Bones stretched his tired neck and craned over the rail to look but saw nothing. Glancing inside at the fuel, he knew they'd have to leave now.

"Whoa!"

Jeff's head snapped up at his wingman's voice. Then he saw it. A tremendous black cloud spreading out across the ground. Dirt and something light gray had been flung up higher than the rest of the mess. Other bits of the helo were spinning off in all directions. Fuel had ignited, throwing an orange fan out to the northwest. Even as he watched, it was swallowed up by the dust and oily smoke.

Chuckling, he zippered the mike and banked back to the right. Hobo Two flushed out in a wide tactical formation and both fighters began a slow climb, away from Basra and the dead helicopter toward the greenish blue waters of the Gulf.

SADDAM HUSSEIN'S INVASION of Kuwait on August 2, 1990, caught the U.S. military by surprise. Washington made the assumption, as it had so often in the past, that the mere threat of armed American intervention would discourage any aggression. Baghdad gambled that whatever it did to Kuwait would not meet America's threshold for war. So both sides underestimated the other, and the result was a massive buildup of military force throughout the fall of 1990. President George H. W. Bush continued to threaten, and Hussein continued to believe that it was simply rhetoric. Any action against Iraq, he dearly hoped, would trigger a massive, pan-Arab reaction. As with Korea and Vietnam, it was colossal miscalculation—on both sides.

A coalition of more than fifty nations had formed to deal with Saddam. The United Nations got involved, passing UN Security Council Resolution 678 warning Hussein to leave Kuwait by January 15, 1991. If he did not, there would be consequences.* Publicly Iraq was defiant, but privately Saddam was extremely worried. It was one thing to thumb one's nose at Washington, but quite another to face the American armed

* Saddam wasn't concerned about the United Nations. After all, Israel had defied the UN since 1947 with no consequences—even for 45 condemnations by the UN Human Rights Council.

forces. This military was unchallenged in the world, especially in their ability to power project across the globe. Both the Navy and the USAF were masters at this, as they'd proved for decades. Pilots, in particular, were weapons that could suddenly and lethally appear from a carrier deck or some remote air base—anytime and anywhere. Where did they come from, these men?

Unlike the Israelis, American fighter pilots had to be commissioned officers *before* they could be considered for pilot training, and there were several paths to achieving this status. An exceptionally qualified high school graduate could procure an appointment to either the Air Force Academy in Colorado Springs or the Naval Academy in Annapolis.* After four years of training and study, usually in an engineering or technical field, a graduate earned an accredited bachelor's degree and was commissioned into the Navy, Air Force, or Marine Corps.

Another method was to receive a four-year degree from a civilian university and then apply for officer candidate school where, after completing a 90-day crash course, the graduate was commissioned. The last way was to participate in a Reserve Officers' Training Course (ROTC) while attending a university. Upon graduation, commissioning would usually follow within the year.

In parallel with obtaining a commission, the potential pilot could apply for a flying training slot. This involved an entirely separate battery of physical, psychological, and aptitude tests. A series of interviews combined with multiple selection committees resulted in further eliminations. In this fashion, the military was able to send only the best-qualified candidates off to flight school. Jets and weapon systems had evolved to the point

*The U.S. Military Academy at West Point trains officers, but the U.S. Army doesn't fly fixed-wing combat aircraft.

where the ability to absorb vast amounts of technical information was a necessity, so the criteria were exceptionally demanding. Although there was no immediate war, everyone expected it, and a young officer's entrance to flight school was just the beginning. A chance to get up to bat, nothing more. Success past this point was a combination of natural ability and perseverance. Each service had similarities in their training programs but approached the process somewhat differently.

Jeff Ashby, former NASA astronaut, Navy captain (O-6), and F/A-18 fighter pilot, began flight training during the late 1970s. Basic, as it was called, lasted about five months and earned a student 40 hours in the T-28 piston-engine trainer. Elementary contact flying focused on takeoffs, landings, and emergencies, and despite the intense selection process, student pilots began dropping out like flies. As in past programs, skill and scores determined which follow-on track came next: jets, helicopters, or prop aircraft. For Jeff, primary jet training took place in the T-2 Buckeye at Kingsville, Texas. A few like him progressed to the TA-4J, flying formation, advanced aerobatics, and learning carrier operations. He came away from the next six months as a fully qualified (day) naval aviator with gold wings.

Navy and Marine pilots then went through a two-month instrument course on their way to the yearlong Replacement Air Group (RAG) on the East or West Coast. Here they were introduced to the jet they'd fly operationally; in Jeff's case, the F/A-18 Hornet. After a year of emergency procedures (EPs), basic fighter maneuvers, air combat maneuvers, and surface attack, he made ten more day traps on a carrier, plus six night traps. The whole program lasted from twenty-four to twenty-six months and the new pilot arrived at his fleet squadron with about 250 flying hours.

The Air Force began its program with undergraduate pilot training (UPT). Student pilots spent their first two weeks in academics and another complete round of physical exams. Classwork focused on aircraft systems, EPs, ground procedures, and local area familiarization. Critical EPs, called "boldface," were memorized verbatim. These were problems that would kill you in the air: engine fires and failures, out-of-control situations, ejections, et cetera. There were daily exams. During this time a stud, as he was called, was fitted with life support gear and given a parachuting refresher class.

After about ten days of this, he went to his squadron and began flying. There were usually three squadrons per aircraft type, and each was subdivided into flights. A flight contained about twenty students, four to each instructor pilot (IP). This man was responsible for scheduling, flying, and supervising each student's overall training. Good ones, like Capt. Russell Greer, *the* Daddy Rabbit, was a screen for his young officers. Isolating them from the inevitable bureaucratic nonsense in any organization, he encouraged, cajoled, and, when he had to, threatened his students to get results. The Daddy Rabbit was an expert at cutting to the chase on any given subject and a magnificent pagan bastard of a pilot.

He was the man with the plan and cared little about Training Command sensitivities, etiquette, or egos. Of the other instructors, the most numerous were the FAIPs (first assignment instructor pilots). A new pilot right out of UPT himself, a FAIP had scored fairly high in the program but was not selected as a potential fighter pilot. Sometimes there just weren't enough fighters to go around, but more often the IPs came to a subjective conclusion, supported by performance, that a particular lieutenant just wouldn't cut it in a fighter cockpit. Instead, he became a mighty pissed-off T-37 or T-38 pilot for three years till he grew up and might be able to try again. Some turned out very well, others not so well.

Then there were those who were brought back from operational flying units. Most of these came from tankers or transports, with some BUFF drivers, like the Daddy Rabbit, and a sprinkling of fighter pilots. These men and women knew about life beyond the Training Command, had wide experience all around the world, and usually were excellent at instructing. They were there to keep an eye on the FAIPs, provide some mature decisions, and keep things in line. And Rus Greer did. Fiercely loyal to his varmints, as his students were called, he went to the wall for several of them. He won most of the battles, and in a jet that man could play a cockpit like a virtuoso.

USAF students began flying in a T-37 jet trainer named the "Tweet" after the high-pitched whistle its tiny engines produced, or maybe because it was small and had a rounded nose like Tweety Bird.* As with most training programs, this was basic contact work: patterns, spins and stalls, aerobatics, and of course emergency procedures—everything needed to solo a jet. As in all other first-class flying training, people started washing out immediately. Many were around on Monday and gone by Friday—it didn't take long. And for good reason, as too much was at stake to pull punches.

Each morning during the mass briefing, a situation was described by an instructor pilot, then handed off to a student to finish. He had to stand up, with only his in-flight publications, and finish the scenario in real time. Every flight and simulator session was graded, plus academics covering every aircraft system, meteorology, and other subjects. After six months of

*The USAF *finally* got rid of the T-37 in favor of the T-6 Texan II, a slick turbo-prop aircraft with a glass cockpit.

this and three check ride evaluations, anyone left standing was allowed to go across the street to the T-38 Talon.

By this time some of the stud's abilities were known and he'd begun to prove himself somewhat. The T-38 handled like a little, underpowered fighter, and some who'd done very well with the docile, forgiving Tweet had problems in the Talon—landing particularly. The interminable coursework aside, this phase focused on advanced aerobatics, instruments, night flying, and, above all, formation. Not because it was tactical but because being calm enough and skilled enough to fly three feet from another maneuvering jet said a great deal about potential. Check rides, daily grades, and instructor evaluations all went into a class rating. In any group about 5 percent of a class (maybe four pilots) emerged above what was then called the fighter attack reconnaissance (FAR) line. Fighters were assigned based on Air Force needs, but personal preference was considered, and most pilots above the FAR line got one of their top three choices.

After graduating from UPT, the stud was now a rated pilot with silver wings and about two hundred hours of flight time. In addition to aerobatics, formation, and low-level flights, he walked away with ninety hours of instrument time, perhaps ten hours at night. Next were a few months going through land and water survival, escape, evasion, and resistance training on his way to lead-in fighter training (LIFT). Conducted at Holloman Air Force Base in Alamogordo, New Mexico, this lasted about two months and utilized the AT-38, an armed version of the T-38.

A thoroughly useful course that has now been eliminated, LIFT introduced the pilot to air-to-air and air-to-ground combat. Basic surface attack (see appendix B) and basic fighter maneuvers (BFM) were taught—and something more. These were squadrons composed entirely of line fighter pilots brought back to transition a new flyer from the training command environment to a tactical mentality. They taught attitude. They made you understand how different the fighter world really was and your part in it. All LIFT students went through the Advanced Physiological Course at Holloman, which added g-induced loss of consciousness (GLOC) through centrifuge training—essential for those going into high-performance jets that could sustain nine times the force of gravity. For the first time, a pilot began to realize that flying was just something you did so you could fight. A fighter pilot was someone who killed things. Taking off, landing, navigating, instruments . . . all were incidental to that single purpose.

Leaving Holloman with about thirty-five more flying hours, the pilot arrived at a Replacement Training Unit (RTU) base and began learning his operational jet. For new F-16 Viper pilots this meant either MacDill AFB in Tampa, Florida, or Luke AFB in Phoenix, Arizona. Those going to F-15 Eagles also went to Luke or to Tyndall AFB in Florida, and A-10 Warthog pilots got Davis-Montham AFB down in Tucson, Arizona. At nine months, Viper RTU was the longest, as it covered both air-to-air and air-to-ground combat to graduate a pilot with about eighty hours of fighter time. As always, there was extensive ground school for the complex systems of a modern jet fighter, plus all the weapons, tactical employment, and emergency procedures.

While at RTU an aviator also became instrument rated for the third time and qualified to air-refuel. So at the end of two years, a fully qualified USAF pilot headed off to a line squadron with an excellent mix of skills, tactical qualifications, and more than three hundred total flying hours. Once there, he'd start over at the bottom of the totem pole and go through a mission qualification course lasting several months. Taught by a variety of instructors, this covered the local area, instrument and night work, and theater-specific threats, plus a verification of all the air and ground combat training skills the pilot had been taught. Finally, after another tactical check ride, he was at last considered a fighter pilot. Training had come a long, long way since the 1915 five-hour flying program.

The 52nd Tactical Fighter Wing from Spangdahlem AB, West Germany, was typical in many ways, yet also unique. Home to the only three mixed Hunter-Killer squadrons in existence, it was heir to the Wild Weasels and their mission of dueling with SAMs. Following Vietnam, the USAF end of killing SAMs passed entirely into the F-4 community, this time with the Advanced Wild Weasel V pairing of the F-4E and F-4G. The G model, called a "Gzel," was essentially the F-4E with the gun removed, a modified backseat, and the addition of the APR-38 system. This was later replaced with an APR-47, which located emitters and identified them through an internal library. An EWO could also listen to audio signals and tell exactly what type of radar was up. Once the location was known, the G model would typically provide cover with anti-radiation missiles while the Killer attacked. But by the early 1980s it was apparent that some changes were needed. The F-4G, with its backseater and specialized equipment, would remain as the Hunter, but a Killer was needed that could duel with the next generation of mobile SAMs.

Enter the F-16.

Initially conceived as a lightweight, ultra-maneuverable daytime fighter, the first production model of the Viper, as it was known, first flew in August 1978. With a satisfying irony, European production of the F-16 would be accomplished in the Fokker Aircraft facility at Schiphol-Oost—exactly where Anthony Fokker had first demonstrated his Eindecker monoplane's synchronized gun during the Great War. Truly revolutionary, the F-16 was the first fighter fielded with RSS—relaxed static stability. Inherently unstable, the plane could fly only if equipped with a digital flight control computer that performed thousands of calculations per second and kept the jet under control. The advantage of this design was unbelievable maneuverability: a jet that could turn all the way around in a few thousand feet while maintaining over 400 miles per hour.

Composite materials were used, and a unique bonded honeycomb structure made the Viper extremely light but very strong. The cockpit combined all the previous ergonomic lessons into a pilot's dream and was contained under a beautiful bubble canopy. At the heart of this was the HOTAS (hands on throttle and stick) system. Every weapon and every system needed to fight could be controlled by switches on the stick and throttle; a pilot never need take his fingers away. A pair of multifunction displays would give a pilot his air-to-air and air-to-ground radars, display his weapons, and let him navigate anywhere in any type of weather, day or night. All of this was repeated in the heads-up display, so the net effect was the ability to fly and fight with perfect visibility while never looking away from the action.

Powered by a variety of Pratt & Whitney or General Electric engines, the maximum thrust available could exceed 32,000 pounds in full afterburner.* Capable of carrying all types of precision guided munitions (PGMs), conventional or nuclear bombs, the F-16 was also equipped with a 20 mm internal cannon. Air-to-air ordnance was initially just the AIM-9, but the AIM-120 BVR missile was added in the 1990s. Small, smokeless, nearly impossible to see, and capable of flexible weaponeering, the Viper was an excellent choice as a follow-on Weasel.

*There is no direct comparison but this is approximately 55,000 horsepower. A long way indeed from Roland Garros's little 80-horsepower Gnome engine.

However, this decision wasn't greeted with universal enthusiasm, particularly (and understandably) in the EWO community. The USAF also didn't help matters with its typical ham-handed approach to personnel issues. About five experienced F-4 pilots from each of Spang's three squadrons were chosen to convert to the F-16, and the rest were really given no options. Neither were the EWOs. They knew their jet was going away, and they were, too—at least out of the cockpit, which is the same as going away. There were also bad rumors that all the leadership positions would be assumed by the incoming F-16 pilots. According to Capt. Dale Shoupe, a highly experienced EWO and flight commander, there was much angst (quite understandably) accompanying all of this.

Well, the rumors weren't true, and the wing compromised by generally alternating leadership positions within a squadron between F-4 crews and F-16 pilots. A half dozen EWOs were also chosen to become F-16 simulator evaluators. They were taught the basics of Viper systems and how the checklists worked, and they were given as many familiarization flights in the few available two-seat F-16s as possible. The result was a cadre of men who knew the electronic warfare mission back to front and now could tailor what they knew to the F-16's capabilities.

They could tailor it to the new pilots as well. Again, this wasn't something smart that the USAF did; it was a group of professional aviators like Dale Shoupe who knew the mission had to continue and were willing to do whatever was needed to ensure that it did. This included extraordinary patience with brash, young single-seat fighter pilots who'd never seen an EWO, along with a talent for formulating new tactics based on those pilots and their new jet. This was especially true in the air-to-air environment. No longer did the F-4 have to retrograde away in the presence of MiGs; it could stay on station, hunting and killing because of the F-16. By the same token, the Viper was unable to locate enemy radars on its own, but by working with the Phantom, SAMs could be found and destroyed. It was a good match, as Mooman and the 23rd Tactical Fighter Squadron would soon prove.

The Korean War decade saw a shift from piston-driven warplanes with guns to jets and missiles in Vietnam. It was a technological leap, to be sure, but the short time between the two wars meant that many Korea veterans had to make the jump into advanced jets. However, eighteen years passed from Vietnam to the Persian Gulf War, and it was in many ways an uneasy transition. With no combat, everyone just flew harder, applying the lessons of the Arab-Israeli wars and Southeast Asia to the Cold War as best they could.

The Navy, Marines, and Air Force all trained to fight a low-altitude European war. Vast, complex war plans were formulated, revised, and recolored all through the 1970s and 1980s. Unlike in most previous conflicts, the forces that would fight got to fly over the terrain every day and practice—for two decades. Every hill and every valley were known, and endless training scenarios were played out on daily missions and tactical evaluations. Operational peacetime flying (overseas especially) was the best there was.

In an age before abject political correctness, men (still only men) flew hard, trained hard, and drank hard. Officers' and Enlisted Clubs remained as they had been; there were no cost-cutting measures and no combined clubs, no mission statements framed on squadron walls or little printed pamphlets enumerating roles, duties, and responsibilities.* Everyone *knew* why they were there. The Soviet horde loomed just across the border,

---

* *United States Air Force Core Values,* also known as "The Little Blue Book," published by the tens of thousands in 1997, when line fighter squadrons were running out of paper for their copy machines.

ready to pour through the Fulda Gap into Western Europe. You could see them, especially at night when they shut off their electrical grids to save money and Eastern Europe got dark while the West was lit up like Las Vegas.

Once a flight took off and got clear of its base defense zone, it was fair game for any NATO aircraft. Rules of engagement had been prearranged, so you could be attacked anywhere, anytime, and at nearly any altitude by any fighter jet in the inventory. Germans, Dutch, Belgians, Canadians . . . they were all there. It was terrific training and as close to combat as one could get without actually being shot—though you could die, and many did.

Because of the development of the low-altitude SA-3, SA-6, SA-8, and other man-portable killer SAMs, the training attacks were low and fast. *Very* low. There were immense swaths of Germany designated as 250-foot low-fly areas, but it often got done below 100 feet at 500 knots. Looking at the threat maps, it was obvious there was simply no way to survive in Central Europe at medium altitude. This was not the Sinai, or the Mekong Delta; as bad as those places had been, they were limited geographically and logistically. There were no such constraints here. This fight would be against the Soviet Union and Warsaw Pact countries, which had built the weapons used by the Vietnamese, Syrians, and Egyptians.

It was this superb training that made what happened next possible.

DOWN THE TIGRIS River, 225 miles to the southeast of Baghdad, the city of Basra sprawled along the dusty floodplain of the Shatt al Arab marshes. Less than 50 miles from the port of Um Qasr on the Persian Gulf and 20 miles from the Iranian border, Basra had always been the strategic key of the region.

Just before dawn on August 2, 1990, six Iraqi divisions moved out of the Rumaila oil fields south along Highway One. Special teams had been inserted after midnight by helicopter and had seized border posts and bridges, so the invasion was unopposed. Crossing the Kuwaiti border, the main force drove straight into the capital, and Kuwait City fell quickly.

Anyone with money, which was most Kuwaitis, fled the country for Cairo, Geneva, and New York. Saudi Arabia immediately began screaming for help because despite the billions spent on their military, they were utterly incapable of stopping the Iraqi army. With the potential for sixty divisions and a million men under arms, the Iraqis under their leader, Saddam Hussein, had more than five thousand tanks and five hundred combat aircraft. The Iraqis were a formidable foe for the Iranians, Kuwaitis, or Saudis. But much of this was paper strength. Poorly trained and unmotivated conscripts made up at least half of the Iraqi army, while most of the Iraqi air force flew MiG-21s and MiG-23s, hardly a threat to modern warplanes. There were, however, Mirage F-1s and the MiG-29.

Called a Fulcrum, the MiG-29 was another Soviet copy of several American designs, yet remained a capable, well-armed point defense fighter. But enemy aircraft weren't really a concern, in fact. Coalition fighter pilots were practically salivating at the chance to destroy the Iraqi air force. No, like other combatants before them, the Iraqis had already lost the battle of fighter pilots to the West. Air defense in the form of Triple-A and SAMs was the biggest threat, and in this Baghdad had invested heavily. Eight thousand pieces of anti-aircraft artillery included the smaller 37 mm and 57 mm varieties, plus bigger 85 mm to 130 mm guns, and many of these were radar-guided. The extremely dangerous ZSU-23-4P system was everywhere and could be effectively fired using optics with no warning given.

There were larger SA-2 and SA-3 systems protecting Baghdad, Basra, Mosul, and Kirkuk, but the Iraqis also had several hundred mobile SAMs. Soviet-made SA-6 and SA-8 batteries were camouflaged around train stations, oil refineries, power plants, and dams. The Roland was a Franco-German creation with a better radar and higher-quality optics than Soviet SAMs. Particularly nasty was the SA-9/13 mobile missile system. It could use a Gun Dish Triple-A radar for initial pointing, then its own infrared tracking would take over after launch. Small and quick, it smoked very little and also gave no warning.

The Iraqis also learned a lesson from the Vietnamese and built a first-class integrated air defense system. Designed and constructed by Thomsen, a French company, the network was called KARI and it worked like this.* Outlying EW and search radars were connected to a central tactical operations center. From here, the air defense commander could assign targets to SAM sites and scramble fighters to intercept incoming aircraft. Communications were redundant; there were landlines, HF radios, and fiber-optic cables. It was a compact, very centralized system and worked well—against the Iranians and their thirty-aircraft strike packages.

Iraq had battled Iran from 1980 to 1988, ostensibly over the Shatt al Arab coastal region. The reality was somewhat more complicated. Always fearful of the large resident Shi'ia minority in Iraq, Hussein was convinced that predominantly Shi'ia Iran was encouraging a rebellion. Even after Hussein used mustard gas against the Iranians in 1983, Washington supported him and continued government subsidies of grain, weapons, and technology. Emerging from the war with another 500 square miles of territory, Baghdad was also deeply in debt: over $65

---

*KARI—*Irak*, the French word for "Iraq," spelled backward.

million was owed to the Soviet Union and Europe, with another $80 billion to Saudi Arabia, the United Arab Emirates, and Kuwait. Desperately needing revenue, Saddam counted on increasing his oil production while his neighbors voluntarily reduced their own.

On July 25, 1990, over the objections of President Bush, the U.S. Senate passed the Iraq International Law Compliance Act. This stipulated Baghdad's observance of the Genocide Protocols and Nuclear Non-Proliferation Treaty in return for continued American aid. Bush opposed any action against Iraq, despite the gassings and mass murders, as Washington's notion of *realpolitik* meant supporting Iraq against Iran. April Glaspie, the U.S. ambassador in Baghdad, spoke at length with Hussein at the end of July, reassuring him over the Senate vote and passing along President Bush's wish for continued good relations. She left for her summer holiday on August 1, 1990, after telling Hussein, "We [the United States] have no opinion on inter-Arab disputes, like your border dispute with Kuwait."

Saddam read into that exactly what you'd expect, and invaded the next day. But this wasn't his mistake. His mistake was stopping at the Saudi border.

With 130,000 men, 1,200 tanks, and a numerically impressive air force, Hussein should've continued straight into the Port of Dhahran and seized the Ghawar oil fields. These are the largest in the world and account for at least 65 percent of total Saudi production. As fast as the United States could move, effective intervention within forty-eight hours would've been difficult, if not impossible. With northern Arabia and Kuwait in his possession, Saddam's bargaining position would've been virtually unassailable.

Fortunately, he stopped. Perhaps he believed that the point had been made; he'd again proven Iraq's willingness to attack, so further aggression wasn't necessary. Besides, he now occupied Kuwait. Hussein may have also judged that an invasion of Saudi Arabia, home to the holiest sites in the Islamic world, would provoke a reaction among his Muslim neighbors or give Iran a pretext for thrusting into his exposed flank. Whatever his reasons, he certainly believed from his communications with Bush and Glaspie that he had nothing to fear from the United States or Europe.

At 2:10 a.m. (Baghdad time) on January 17, 1991, even Saddam Hussein understood his colossal miscalculation, as the largest air attack since Vietnam was unleashed against him. It opened with Operation Normandy, a helicopter assault on Iraqi early warning radars along the Saudi border. This was followed by a USAF strike against Iraq's western airfields, primarily MiG-25 bases that could target Coalition command and control aircraft or air refueling tankers. The first bombs fell on Baghdad at 3:00 a.m. as F-117 fighters hit command posts and palaces.

Out in the Persian Gulf the USS *Saratoga*, *John F. Kennedy*, *Theodore Roosevelt*, *Ranger*, and *Midway* shot A-6s, A-7s, F-14s, and F/A-18s into the night toward Iraq. Hundreds of Tomahawk missiles flashed over the dark water, then headed north to destroy power plants, communications nodes, and TV and radio stations. In exactly the way Vietnam should've been fought (and could have been fought), airpower delivered a disorienting and crushing first blow from which Iraq never recovered. In denial and thuggishly defiant, Saddam took to a surviving radio station to rave, "The great duel, the mother of all battles, has begun! The dawn of victory nears as the great showdown begins."

Dawn actually brought something very different, and not at all what he had in mind. More than 2,700 coalition sorties would be flown during those first twenty-four hours. KARI was overwhelmed and destroyed, leaving the centralized Iraqi High Command blind and deaf. After the next few days they'd be toothless as well. With the first priorities of early warning and command control obliterated, airstrikes now began a systematic rollback campaign against critical infrastructure and military targets.

Anytime an Iraqi fighter got airborne, it was shot down. One U.S. strike package in northern Iraq was eleven minutes late to their target because the entire bunch of F-16s, F-4s, and F-15s found two hapless MiG-23s running for Iran. All forty jets wheeled east and gave chase while the panicked Iraqis fled across the border. It was the same for SAMs; if one came up, it was immediately targeted and all efforts were made to destroy it.

But the air war had some glitches. The strikers generally attacked their targets from vast, unwieldy packages called "Gorillas." A remnant from Vietnam and reinforced through two decades of peacetime exercises, a Gorilla was a long train of four-ship flights that stretched for miles. If everyone was on time, the weather cooperated, and there were no threat reactions then it worked well enough.

But that was a lot of ifs.

It was also done at medium altitudes above 20,000 feet. There were some Navy and British Tornado flights that went in low and got hammered from Triple-A and SAMs. Bottom line, there really wasn't a reason to do it. If there had been, all right, but the use of precision guided munitions generally precluded this. Besides the Walleye, Maverick missiles came in both infrared and electro-optical (TV) versions and were rocket-powered. Primarily designed for anti-armor, in 1991 the TV Maverick had a range of only a few miles. The IR D-model Maverick had a much better stand-off capability but suffered from normal infrared problems like temperature changes and dust.

Laser-guided bombs (LGBs) were glide weapons, old MK-82 and MK-84 bombs that were retrofitted to permit guidance on a laser "spot" from the launching aircraft. LGBs were slow, but they were cheap and very accurate. Still, the overwhelming tonnage of bombs dropped in 1991 were "dumb," in that they had no guidance once dropped, and so they went where they'd been aimed. However, the accuracy of weapons delivery systems by this point obviated much of the error. Pilots could use radar-assisted deliveries for night or bad-weather attacks and a variety of computed options under better conditions.

The CCIP pipper used by the Israelis in 1973 had been improved to where a skilled pilot could put a dumb bomb within three feet of where he wanted it. Air-to-ground radar burst ranging was directed through the pipper, giving precise angles and distances to the target. The pilot had to fly the correct parameters (see appendix B) for his chosen weapon, but if he did that and pickled on the desired impact point, then that's where the bombs would go. Every weapon, or "store," in the U.S. inventory was preloaded in the aircraft's stores management system (SMS) with its associated ballistics. It was then selected from an electronic menu with all the fusing options and timing.

The continuously computed release point (CCRP) was another method that used a known target location to calculate a release point for a selected weapon. This had been developed for the old GDB blind delivery system and adapted for nuclear bombing deliveries. However, it would work for any target with a known latitude and longitude, such as buildings, bridges, and oil refineries. By the Gulf War, space-based global positioning system coordinates were available, and this permitted exact bombing, even from medium altitudes.

Air-to-air fire control radars permitted a lethality that would've been unimaginable a generation earlier. Earlier systems had severe limits when looking down over land due to "clutter" caused by the ground. Pulses from airborne radars couldn't distinguish the small return of a target against the big return from the earth. One reason why the British Chain Home stations were so effective was that incoming German aircraft had no clutter to hide in over the English Channel. This clutter problem had been solved by measuring the velocity shift of a target return as well as its range. Think of an ambulance siren; as it draws closer, the sound becomes louder, and as it moves away the sound recedes. Caused by sound waves bunching up and then spreading out, this Doppler shift can be precisely measured.* So velocity information is now combined with exact ranging from pulsed signals thus giving a very precise targeting solution. Better solutions mean much more effective radar missiles are possible and an enemy fighter is killed long before he can engage.

Superb and realistic prewar training plus the technology gap ensured that if an Iraqi got into the air, he would never land—at least not in a single piece or in his own country. Thirty-eight fighters were shot down, and the cost was (maybe) one F/A-18.† After a monthlong air campaign Saddam Hussein was reeling. His vaunted air force had been mauled, and his air defense system, so effective against Iran, had been shut down. Surface-to-air missiles and thousands of anti-aircraft guns still operated, but without any centralized control. When radars turned on to fight, usually a Maverick missile or a Walleye

---

*This is happening to you next time a police radar gun is pointed your way.

†LCDR Scott Speicher from VFA-81 off the USS *Saratoga*. It has never been satisfactorily proven what shot him down on January 17, 1991.

came through the roof. Understandably, many of the SAM battery commanders decided to wait out the conflict rather than die from a threat they couldn't see. After all, they reasoned, the coalition wouldn't invade Iraq—that would be madness against the world's fourth-largest army.

But that is precisely what happened on February 24, 1991.

Crossing the Saudi-Kuwaiti border, the U.S. Marine 1st and 2nd Divisions with the 1st Light Armored Infantry Battalion headed toward Kuwait City. The main thrust came from the U.S. VII Corps, with the French 6th Light Armored on its left and British 1st Armored on the right. Ground operations into Iraq had actually begun at the end of January with several eight-man patrols from B Squadron of the British Special Air Service. They'd gathered targeting information, destroyed fiber-optic communications links, and eliminated SCUD missile launchers aimed at Israel.

If Israel was attacked (and Saddam had sworn to do just that), then Tel Aviv would retaliate. If this happened, Washington feared that the Saudis would withdraw their support, including basing for the hundreds of thousands of soldiers on their soil. This political handwringing was unfounded because if the British and Americans left, then who would defend the Ghawar oil fields? Certainly not the Saudis. Nevertheless, Israeli involvement would complicate an already complex situation.

The ground war lasted 100 hours, forcing the Iraqi army out of Kuwait. The retreat up Highway One toward Baghdad was an abject humiliation for Hussein and should've been a warning of things to come. In any event, the Coalition's objective had been achieved and, unlike Vietnam, there was nothing vague about it. Sources vary on Coalition combat deaths, but about 300 lost their lives. Initial Iraqi casualties of 100,000 dead were grossly overestimated by the Defense Intelligence Agency; a more realistic postwar assessment was 8,000 to 10,000 combat casualties. Still, the disparity in numbers is quite revealing; as Lt. Gen. Tom Kelly said, "Iraq went from the fourth-largest army in the world to the second-largest army in Iraq in 100 hours."

Over 109,000 combat sorties were flown, with 88,000 tons of ordnance delivered on Iraqi targets*; the Allied coalition lost thirty-nine fixed-wing aircraft in combat, of which twenty-two were U.S. fighter/attack jets. One Specter gunship went down near Kuwait, and six RAF Tornados were lost. The completeness of the military victory lay in personnel quality and technical superiority with a sound plan and limited political interference. This was, and is, an unbeatable combination. Valuable lessons were learned that would impact how wars, and particularly American wars, would be fought for the foreseeable future. It was not an ideological quagmire managed by amateurs; it was a purely military operation, at least in the field.

The amazing variety of aircraft that emerged from Vietnam weren't needed, but a house cleaning was. Older aircraft such as the F-111 and the venerable F-4 simply were not survivable on a modern battlefield, and their maintenance costs were prohibitive considering the aircraft's value. Technological advances dictated that true multimission platforms were the future, though this wouldn't always be remembered.† Jamming, for instance, is essential, but why use a separate jet for it if a fighter can carry its own effective pod? Tactically, the war began as a mix of aircraft and tactics that had worked in peacetime and during the last shooting war. It was a struggle to figure out how best to employ a new generation of jets and weapons using older mentalities.

Fortunately, the Gorilla package was largely abandoned

---

*By way of comparison, an entire year of the Vietnam Rolling Thunder campaign (1966) flew 79,000 sorties and dropped 136,000 tons of bombs.

†The Raptor's brief, incredibly expensive debacle as the F/A-22, for example. It is now, once again, simply the F-22.

(except during certain exercises) in favor of compact, flexible smaller flights. Improvements such as data link and GPS obviated the need for flights to operate within sight of each other. Advances in weapons turned selective targeting into reality and generally achieved the desired results without dropping tons of bombs. This meant the ongoing refinement of PGMs and the systems required to get them on target. The advantages of night combat had always been known, but the practice of it was limited. This also changed following the Gulf War with better forward-looking infrared systems (FLIR) and, above all, the widespread use of night vision goggles (NVGs).

Tactical flexibility, always discussed but often ignored in favor of the tried and true, was brought to the forefront again. A low-altitude air force was suddenly forced to fight much higher, and this resulted in very different types of attacks than those previously perfected. Middle Eastern geography was also vastly different from the jungles of Southeast Asia or the forests of Europe. There were mountains, wide-open plains, and a deceptive morass of wadis, or gullies, offering shelter or camouflage. Wind and dust could kick up with no warning, rendering infrared weapons useless and interfering with electronics. Combat jets and their pilots needed to be able to fight anywhere, because no one knew where the next war would occur. Iraq clearly showed the danger in assuming too much.

Military lessons from the Gulf War were significant and had far-reaching consequences. Yet perhaps the greatest value lay in *how* America viewed war rather than in the methods of fighting one. It seemed that in the mistakes of the past had been rectified and never again would Americans be forced to fight blind and one-armed as they had 18 years before. Never again, it was hoped, would lives be risked for political rather than national security objectives.

Of course, it hasn't worked out that way.

Lessons are forgotten and politics never really change. However, one very important specter has been laid to rest, at least for the United States. Protests against war, right or wrong, are directed at the source of the conflict and not at those who do the fighting. In this lies the true value of the Gulf War—the ghosts of Vietnam were finally laid to rest.

APRIL 1, 2003

NEAR BAGHDAD, IRAQ

"Where're ya hiding, ya little bastard?" the fighter pilot muttered, leaning forward and staring out over the canopy rail. Lizard skin. It looks like lizard skin, he thought. Dark brown and green splotches over a tan background. Except for the rivers. The Tigris, off to the east, was almost a steel gray color, meandering southeast like a broken snake. Beyond his other wing the Euphrates was a lighter green, almost an emerald tinged with milk.

He saw all this but didn't process it. Not that way, at least. Rivers meant no air threats. The pilot saw roads and bridges; moving vehicles and, above all, popcorn bursts of anti-aircraft fire. Not for the first time he found being back here in combat slightly unreal. Twelve years earlier he'd been in these same skies fighting the same enemy.

"Toxic 03, this is Luger."

"Go."

"Toxic . . . I have Ozark One One inbound for Killbox 87 and 88 Alpha Bravo."

The pilot, known to his friends as Scorch, squinted at the line-up card on his kneeboard. The arriving fighters were Hornets—F/A-18s from one of the carriers in the Gulf. He whistled softly. Fifteen miles from Baghdad was a long way for them to come. Gas would be tight. "Copy all. Ozark is cleared to both boxes above two zero zero. Have him come up Zinc 76."

Beginning a wide, left turn away from Baghdad, he rolled out every few seconds looking for smoke trails. Often it was the only way to know a SAM had been fired. He also had an ALR-56 Radar Warning Receiver, ALE-50 towed decoys, plus chaff and flares. On the Viper's center station the big ALQ-131 jamming pod was doing its thing. It could be programmed to cover five entire frequency bands with a variety of nose or deception programs.

Coming wings level heading west, Scorch looked down the wing at the big, U-shaped bend of the Tigris in the middle of Saddam's capital. There were three . . . no, four SAM launches, all toward the north. He knew three other Weasel flights from his squadron were up there so they were dealing with it. He was directly south of Baghdad International Airport; the tan-colored parallel runways were plain against darker suburbs.

"Toxic Three . . . Ozark One One . . . checkin' in."

Scorch swung the fighter around in a left turn, dipped down to 18,000 feet and slung the dogfighting mode of his radar out to the southeast.

"LOCK . . . LOCK . . ." Sure enough, the system grabbed something and he glanced at the HUD they rolled out. The target designator (TD) box was firmly around something 9.1 miles away and a little higher.

The RWR chirped and he saw the symbol for the F/A-18's own air-to-air radar. So the Navy pilot could see him too, which definitely helps. Scorch liked Hornets; they could do lots of missions and the pilots were flexible. *Just like us.*

"Toxic Three is contact . . . Bull's-eye one four five for sixty-nine." Good number, he smiled.

"That's Ozark." He didn't need to say more because he knew Toxic locked him. There were two Hornets at 21,000 feet heading northwest at 425 knots. "We're Joker plus one so not much time."

The Viper pilot nodded. Joker fuel usually gave about five minutes of tactical flying before Bingo was reached and that meant leaving. "Copy that . . . we'll skip the Five Line. Call contact on the north-south hardball road off your nose."

He pulled the power back to hold 400 knots and continued turning left. The Navy fighters were visible just above the horizon, about five miles off his nose.

"Ozark's visual on the Vipers . . . contact on the road."

Good. The Hornet lead saw Toxic and the target. He zippered the mike, rolling out heading north on the east side of the highway. "Look north toward the city till you see a cloverleaf intersection with an east-west hardball road."

"Contact."

Scorch watched the two F/A-18s pass off his nose about a mile heading west. He continued northbound across their tails, then angled off eastward toward the air base at Salman Pak. "Ozark . . . there's a green east-west canal south of the cloverleaf that cuts the road."

"Contact."

"Between that canal and the cloverleaf is a line of ten APCs . . . that's your target."

Scorch flipped his fuel switch to check the wing tanks then eyeballed his HTS pod. It was cluttered with radars, all off to his right toward Baghdad. Expanding the view didn't help, it was still full of threats. His RWR sounded like a nest of angry birds chirping away. He took a breath. There was no way to tell with all these electrons flying back and forth. Back to using eyeball, he chuckled grimly. The SAMs were out there . . . but so was he.

"Contact the APCs." The Hornet driver was good. Calm and precise. He'd obviously done this a few times before. He was running out of gas, though, so this had to be quick. That's why they'd dispensed with the whole elaborate Five or Nine Line procedure normally used for this sort of thing. That and there were no friendly troops down there.

Yet.

But that was the point of all this. The Army was moving up from the south and the Marines were coming in from the east in a big pincer around Baghdad. Any Iraqis that showed their faces had to die. That went doubly for SAMs and Triple-A of any kind. Ground forces depended on helicopters for movement, reconnaissance and supplies. With any type of SAM or gun threat the helos would die wholesale.

And we can't have that.

"Ozark, vehicles are your target. No friendlies in the vicinity."

"Ozark copies, no friendlies."

Fighters were always very careful about this. It was too easy to mistake vehicles at 450 knots—especially when they were shooting at you. Scorch nodded. "You're cleared hot, your discretion . . . any altitude . . . stay west and south of the roads and call off. Toxic is north and east of the roads fifteen to nineteen."

Five miles away the Marine pilot nodded. Major Mark Larsen had done this many times before and obviously so had this Viper driver. He was putting himself between the Hornets and Baghdad . . . bait. Larsen glanced at his card and started a wide, left turn. Toxic . . . two F-16CJs. He nodded again—Wild Weasels. That would explain why they were sitting up there looking pretty for the SAMs. Well, that was their problem. His was killing Iraqis. Pushing up the throttles, Larsen keyed his interflight UHF radio.

"Two . . . the wind is from the south so you hit the southern edge of the line. I'll get the north."

That way the smoke and dust from his bombs wouldn't ruin his wingman's picture. The radio clicked and he began an easy slice to center up his symbology. "Ozarks are in from the south."

"Cleared hot," Scorch immediately replied and began a left-hand turn, into Baghdad, from the east side of the highway. "Head's up," he said on the common frequency. "Flares."

He wasn't watching the F-18s, he was watching the ground. Hopefully, anything down there would see him, not the Hornets. To help them out, he popped out a few flares.

Fifteen miles southwest, the Marines saw the string of flares and Larsen smiled. He knew exactly what the Viper pilot was doing. Gutsy. Then he concentrated on his attack . . . there'd only be one shot at this.

Scorch didn't have data link with the Hornets but he listened to the radio calls and saw the attack in his head. The Marines had called in from southwest and were probably just over the Euphrates, heading northeast. Toxic just crossed the Tigris and was headed west toward the cloverleaf.

Flashes. All up and down the road. Big stuff, no tracers. He pumped over, paused, then slid sideways. "Triple-A . . . along the road north of the cloverleaf." Repeating the maneuver every five seconds or so, Scorch continuously looked between his HTS pod and the ground. Popcorn clouds appeared, pretty close to his altitude but farther back. They couldn't see him so it had to be radar guided.

Dropping his eyes to the radar, he saw the little white squares off to his left some seven miles away. That's about right, he did the math, not wanting to lock them up. Dozens of fires were burning in Baghdad and more SAMs came up to the east side.

None turned, though, so they were busy with someone else. Dora Farms was plain to see just below the big donkey dick bend of the river. That's where it all started this time, what . . . five weeks ago?

"Ozarks are off target . . . east. Twenty Kay."

Zipping over the Tigris just north of the cloverleaf. Scorch stared to the south and caught one of the F/A-18s in the pull-off. Then the other, probably five miles from him. Banking up slightly, he craned his neck over the canopy rail at the city, looking for SAMs. If they were coming it would be now.

Nothing.

Risking a glance back at the target, he was keying the mike when he saw it. The unmistakable brownish white plume of a SAM . . . from the cloverleaf! The Hornet pilot saw it too, judging by the stream of flares.

"Toxic Two, attacking . . . south Bull fifty."

Outstanding. Kid didn't have to be told. Scorch keyed the mike, "Missile launch! Bull one eight five for fifty-five." Slamming the throttle forward, he cranked over and pulled six g's to get the Viper moving.

"Ozark's defending . . . SA-6." The Marine sounded very calm considering he had a SAM up his ass.

"Toxic Two, Magnum Six . . ."

Just then the road south of the intersection blew up. A brown cloud shot upward with thicker, black edges mushrooming out on all sides. Something heavier that was square on one end went flipping off into the desert. Looked like the Hornet's scored.

Scorch's butt lifted off the seat as he bunted forward, slapped the throttle back and pointed directly at the cloverleaf. The huge white smoke trail from the HARM came off his wingman's jet two miles away, porpoised, then nosed over at the ground. Suddenly another SAM shot up, moving incredibly fast.

Not like the older stuff. Scorch leaned forward, staring down at the road intersection. With his left thumb he slewed the little diamond in the HUD down the smoke to the ground where it came from, then jabbed the Target Management Switch forward with his right thumb. The diamond jumped and stayed right on the spot.

"Toxic One's attacking, south Bull fifty."

His eye flickered to the MASTER ARM switch, selected Air-to-Ground and then checked the HUD . . . 490 knots, passing 15,200 feet. Pulling the throttle back to IDLE, he streamed out a decoy and punched out a few bundles of chaff. The right MFD glowed gray but the darker black on white Maverick symbology was plain to see. He had two of the big guided missiles; one infrared heat tracker and one that used electro-optical tracking. It looked like a black-and-white TV screen.

"Ozarks are clear to the east . . . thanks Toxic," the Marine added.

"Ya got a good hit," Scorch replied. "I'll pass the BDA."

Battle Damage Assessment was vital so other flights weren't risked hitting the same targets. Never taking his eyes off the cloverleaf, he stared through the Maverick seeker head and flew by feel. The whole area was cluttered with wrecked vehicles and garbage.

Then suddenly one of them moved.

He saw the pointed ends of the missiles and smiled as the thing slid back into the shadows. That's where the little fucker is . . . *under* the overpass. No wonder nobody saw him. He'd hide in the shadows, radar off, taking information feeds from the hundred other radars up. Probably visual sightings too. Every gomer down there had binoculars. Then he'd dart out like a crab, turn on, lock, shoot, and scuttle back. Bet that's how they got the Hog a few days ago.

With his right forefinger he switched to the IR Maverick and changed the missile's polarity to hot on cold . . . and there it was. The metal was fairly cool but the engine was running, giving a nice hot smudge to track.

He did the rough calculations in his head: 5.2 miles, 6,900 pounds of gas, passing 12,000 feet, and 510 knots . . . too fast. He fanned open the speed brakes, then closed them. The Viper immediately shuddered and slowed to 480 knots. He did it again and keyed the mike. "Toxic Two . . . Slapshot Six."

Closing the brakes, he pushed the throttle up and held 450 knots. Delicately moving the little cross, he kept it over the hot engine and released the switch.

"Toxic Two . . . Magnum Six."

Not bothering to look up, he saw the symbology yaw over to one side, away from the vehicle. *Shit* . . . didn't lock.

4.1 miles.

He pressed and slewed again. 9,000 feet and 460 knots. Nudging the throttle back slightly, he released the TMS then slapped out more chaff. The tiny orange indicator lights counted down but he never saw them. This time the cross hairs "bounded" the target. They wavered a bit but held steady as the Maverick calculated microns, contrasted heat differences and whatever else it did.

Angling down through 6,000 feet at 3.8 miles he pushed and held the red pickle button on the stick. A long half second passed, then the Viper lurched sideways like it had been kicked. The AGM-65 slid off the rail, spewing smoke, then instantly arced over and raced toward the shadows under the overpass.

"BEEP . . . BEEP . . . BEEP . . ."

Shit.

Gun Dish fire control radar. Close!

Scorch shoved the throttle into MIL power, popped chaff

and pulled up in a hard, rolling turn back to the west, away from the road, the ground troops, and Baghdad. As the nose came up through the horizon, he bunted forward, grunted as his helmet whacked the canopy, then snapped the jet left.

It was a good thing he did.

Colored whips of tracer fire passed behind and below him. Twitching his tail the other way, Scorch pulled straight up, then rolled back to the southwest, sweating. Crossing the Euphrates at 10,000 feet, he began a left turn and looked at his fuel: 6,100 pounds.

Thumbing the transmit switch outboard, the data link crinkled in his headset and Toxic Two appeared on the MFD. He was on the other side of highway, off to the east by ten miles.

"Two, did you see the last burst of Triple-A?"

"Rog . . . came from the cloverleaf."

It was a Zoose, he knew—a ZSU-23-4 anti-aircraft weapon system, radar guided, with high-rate-of-fire anti-aircraft guns mounted on an all-terrain vehicle. Very mobile and very nasty. Scorch took a deep breath. If it could threaten him in a Viper, what would it do to an A-10? Or an Apache helicopter?

"Say fuel."

"Five-point-nine."

"Confirm you're clean?"

"Two's clean." Scorch stared at the glowing Gun Dish symbol on his RWR. The thing was only looking at him. Of course, there could be another one, but he had to go with what he could see.

"Listen up . . . arc northeast of the road four miles from the cloverleaf. Turn in when I clear you and empty your gun under the overpass. Come off to your right."

"Two copies." Four miles. Thirty seconds at this speed.

Scorch punched up the GUN symbology and checked his decoy. Still there. Racking the fighter up, he popped out chaff and stared sideways out at the road before slicing back. He was about five miles from the cloverleaf, passing through 9,000 feet and angling in from the southwest. He'd rather attack straight up the road, but that meant overflying the Iraqi shooters on the highway.

Pulling the power back to midrange, he held the speed steady at 450 knots. Dumping the nose a bit, Scorch knew he have to shallow the dive out to shoot under the overpass. Crossing some canals, the corners of the pilot's eyes picked up the terrain changes from mottled darks to a shade of moldy green.

Three miles. 3,000 feet.

Popping more chaff, he put the bigger gun pipper between another canal and the cloverleaf. The chatter on the radio faded to a dull hum as Iraq slid up to meet him. At two miles and 3,000 feet he keyed the mike.

"Toxic Two . . . cleared in!"

The radio zippered. He stopped bunting forward and let the pipper slowly rise. Passing 1,000 feet the Viper was a mile from the overpass. He could see vehicles in the ditches on both sides of the highway, men running as the American fighter roared in above them. Scorch flashed over the last canal at 300 feet as the pipper rose into the darkness under the overpass. Bunting, pausing and holding his breath, he squeezed the trigger. The roaring whine of the 20 mm M61 cannon filled his ears and he held the jet rock steady.

It clattered on empty as he zipped over an orchard, so low he could see the irrigation pipes. Yanking the nose up, he rolled right, jammed the throttle up to MIL, popped chaff with flares, and pulled eight g's to the right toward the road. Snapping upright, Scorch kept the Viper at 300 feet and thundered across the highway. From the corner of his eye he saw dust and chunks of concrete fly off the cloverleaf as five hundred 20 mm cannon shells smashed into it.

"BEEP . . . BEEP . . . BEEP."

The RWR was frantic, still the Gun Dish. But no SA-6, he realized, twitching his tail right, then left. Right over another canal . . . great way out. No Triple-A. Cranking up to the left, he followed the greenish water due east away from the road.

"Two's off," his wingman sounded close. "Secondary's!"

The Gun Dish symbol had disappeared. A mile from the highway, Scorch curved around to the south and sent a data link. Toxic Two was five miles away, also southbound on the other side of the road.

"Hold One Nine Zero . . . climb."

Zooming upward, the pair of F-16s shot into the powder blue sky. Scorch leveled off, blinked and trimmed the fighter. Exhaling loudly, he looked back toward dozens of comma-shaped black clouds rising over the burning city. White flashes sparkled along the roads south and east of the capital while below him thousands of American tanks and APCs crawled north. Baghdad would fall. Not today or tomorrow, he knew. But soon.

Pulling a half-empty water bottle from the ankle pocket of his G suit, he put it on the glare shield next to the HUD. Dropping his mask from the right side, Scorch wiped his sweaty face and rubbed his bloodshot eyes. Glancing left, he saw his wingman hanging in space about two miles away, seemingly motionless against the sky. You only saw movement if you looked down . . . or flew past a cloud. Flicking his left wing, Scorch watched the other F-16 pull up in an immense, lazy half barrel roll. As he floated overhead, upside down, the other pilot's visored head was plainly visible and he lifted a hand.

Cocky little bastard.

Wouldn't have it any other way, he chuckled, then raised his mask and keyed the mike.

"Luger . . . Toxic Three."

"Go ahead, Toxic."

"Toxic Zero Three, mission number Six Five Four Five . . . one by Roland destroyed, one Zoose probable. Estimate three APCs destroyed at north three, three . . . zero, four . . . seven, zero; east four, four . . . two, two. Relay for Ozark One One . . . cloverleaf destroyed at Mahmudiya. How copy?"

There was a pause and he dropped the mask to take a swig of warm, plastic-flavored water. The TWITCH air refueling track was on the nose for 226 miles so he pulled the power back to hold 400 knots. Fast enough. They'd hit the tanker, top off then beat feet for PeeSab.

"Toxic . . . Luger copies all. What type mission? CAS, SEAD or Killer Scout?"

The pilot swallowed the horrible warm water, then looked around the cockpit at the radar, the HUD, and all the displays and panels that let him do everything he'd done today. Chuckling again, he raised the mask to his face.

"That's right, Luger . . . guess you could say that."

EPILOGUE

IN JUST NINE decades spinning propeller blades, fabric and machine guns gave way to advanced composites, amazingly powerful afterburning jet engines, and weapons that stagger the imagination. Technological spin-offs from conquering the air have given us Wi-Fi, space travel and cable television, to name just a few. Today every corner of the world is linked together, open to us in a way those first aviators could certainly appreciate, if not fully understand.

And what of aviators?

True, they've had to evolve from the first daredevil adventurers who replaced their cavalry horses with a flying machine. The nearly overwhelming amounts of information to be absorbed has necessitated technical aptitude and education far exceeding those early days of armed flight. Yet flying a fighter is still, as it ever was, an extremely physical profession. Muscles tear, joints come apart, and vertebrae crack; this is above the inherent risks and normal physiological strain of flying. No, a modern combat pilot fights with the mind as much as the muscles and would not survive without equal parts of both. But still there is something more. Something that has not changed, nor will it as long as there are fighter pilots.

Fighting spirit.

This elusive quality goes all the way back to the beginning, to Rippon and Manuel's 1918 study of *The Essential Character-*

*istics of Successful and Unsuccessful Aviators.** Has that spirit been altered with the rise of technology? Has it been diluted or slowly bred out by those who don't possess it themselves? In 1918, combat aviators were usually under twenty-five years of age, enjoyed "motoring, sports and women," and valued "good hands" and a "controlled" nature. A 2013 survey conducted for this book revealed that 98 percent of the American fighter pilots had a technical degree, they engaged in sports of some type, and over 50 percent of them played a musical instrument. They were all fond of the fighter pilot lifestyle; taking risks, flying hard and being part of a truly elite group. Nearly all of them admitted to enjoying the opposite sex, yet somewhat surprisingly, unlike 51 percent of 1918 fighter pilots, the modern group held no grudge against marriage—only the *wrong* marriage!

They unanimously valued "good hands" and universally agreed, as did their forefathers, that this cannot be taught; you either have it or you don't. Asked to identify the defining characteristics of successful fighter pilots, the answers included discipline (in the air at least), resourcefulness, physical and mental agility with the ability to "stay calm but become instantly aggressive" when needed.

As Rippon and Manuel concluded, "Anyone who has lived with pilots for any length of time cannot fail to notice that they possess in a very high degree a fund of animal spirits and excessive vitality." So fortunately there have been no alterations in the essentials. The spirit of attack, aggressiveness, and absolute self-confidence remain most important whether the year is 1918 or today.

Eighty-eight years passed between Roland Garros shivering in an open cockpit as he fired his machine gun and the fighter

---

*See Chapter 1.

pilots over Iraq cursing supersonic missiles and radar-guided anti-aircraft fire. It's certainly fair to ask what has changed in that time.

Everything.

Afterburners and nine g's; fighting faster than the speed of sound with weapons that can level nations. Dark nights, low fuel, and the coldness that only a fighter pilot can know as he's isolated in a tiny, glowing cockpit hundreds of miles deep behind enemy lines. A pilot who can fly across the world without stopping and put a thousand pounds of high explosive within six inches of a target. Fighter pilots who are proud; these lords of the sky who fight and die for those they love and that which they hold dear.

Indeed, everything has changed.

And nothing has changed.

LEST WE FORGET.

ACKNOWLEDGMENTS

MY PERSONAL THANKS to fellow pilots and authors Walter Boyne, Steven Coonts, Gen. Don Shepperd, Col. Jack Broughton, and Col. Ed Rock for volunteering not only their aviation expertise, but also their literary skills. So many other outstanding people contributed their time and experiences to this book that merely mentioning their names doesn't seem quite enough. I wholeheartedly acknowledge the debt owed to each of you for giving up time and energy to push me in the right direction—a work of this magnitude would not have been possible without them. My profound gratitude to:

Capt. Jeff Ashby, USN; Dr. Stein Bronsky; Bob Dorrough; Col. Jim Good, USMC; Col. Dan Hampton, USMC; Biddie Hampton; Phillip Handleman; Gen. Paul Kattu, USAF; Lt. Col. Mark Larsen, USMC; Col. Scott Manning, USAF; Diane Manning; Gen. David Moody, USAF; Marion Moody; Christina Olds; Dolphin Overton Jr.; Gen. Bill "Kanga" Rew, USAF; Christy Rew; Buddy Sims; DeEtte Star; Dr. Philip Steeves; Stacey Strock; Ken and Jennifer Wyatt. And always to Beth, Tiffany, Dana, and Jaime Hampton for their forbearance and patience.

Several organizations have been invaluable in gathering the immense volume of material required to write this book. My sincere appreciation to the Pritzker Military Library in Chicago, the Library of the U.S. Military Academy at West Point, the National Museum of the Air Force, the United States Naval Academy, the River Rats, the Society of Wild Weasels, and the Vintage Aero Museum. My admiration and gratitude also to Mr. Will Boucher, for his painstaking research and beautiful artwork and to Mr. Michael Aten, for the stories about Marion Aten, a nearly forgotten warrior.

Special respects to Col. Tom Kirk and Col. Jack Broughton for both their personal sacrifices and their willingness to share memories of Vietnam and the mighty Thud. To Col. Ed Rock, Sabre jock and Thud pilot, for his patience and corrections with the Korean and Vietnam War chapters, and to Buddy Sims, former Forward Air Controller, who introduced me to both men. Fighter pilots like you were a true inspiration to all who followed, especially me.

Humble thanks to Allen Lamb, fighter pilot extraordinaire, not only for his memories and flying skill but for helping to create the Wild Weasels. To Rus Greer, the "Daddy Rabbit," and Dale Shoupe, voices from my past who made it possible for me to be part of all this. Last, and always, my deepest appreciation to my editor, Peter Hubbard, and everyone at HarperCollins who worked so hard to make this idea a reality.

APPENDIX A

ANATOMY OF A DOGFIGHT

MIDWAY THROUGH THE Great War many of the basic principles of aerial combat had been worked out. Interestingly, most of them would never change and survive, in one form or another, to this day. Others, most notably aircraft performance and weapons capabilities, would evolve dramatically over the years. New technology would permit new tactics. Methods of fighting would vary with all this but the underlying rationale would be as familiar to Edward Mannock or Oswald Boelcke as they are to a modern fighter pilot.

BASIC FIGHTER MANEUVERS

The notion of the *Turn Circle*—the radius made by a turning aircraft—is a prime example. Visualize a plane leaving a wake in the air as a boat does in the water, a wake you could see if you were sitting on a cloud looking down at the moving fighters. Not truly a circle, it's more like a series of expanding and contracting ellipses created by a maneuvering aircraft.

The Turn Circle grows or shrinks as the conditions in a dogfight change—airspeed, altitude, and aircraft performance all influence this as do the pilot's maneuvers. Now, understanding this concept was vital because it meant getting into an ideal firing position. Single-seat fighters, originally with forward-firing guns, were aimed like a rifle by physically pointing the plane at the target. If you got behind your single-seat enemy, then he couldn't shoot back *and* by attacking from back there he might not see you until it was too late. So to get behind and stay there long enough to fire, you had to "enter" his circle by fitting your turning aircraft inside his turn long enough to kill him.

Where a clear technical advantage existed this wasn't a problem, like Hawker's fight against the Red Baron. But if two similarly capable planes meet on equal terms then something else has to be done to get the edge.

Turn Circles can also be exploited by other things. By maneuvering in the vertical (using altitude), an aircraft with a bigger circle can fit inside a smaller circle by using that altitude as room to turn. Known as Turning Room, this is the physical distance (in feet) required to rotate the aircraft and point where you want to shoot. In World War I this meant turning enough to bring your forward guns to bear. An aircraft with better maneuverability will normally require less distance to turn and fire.

A Turn Circle also changes because of an engine's capability to sustain or increase power. During the Great War there was really none of the fine throttle control, called power management, found in later conflicts. Most pilots just went to full throttle during a fight and left it there. Power, along with performance, dictated how fast you could move the nose of the aircraft around to where you wanted it. This was especially critical in the first air war since the principal single-seat weapon was a forward-fixed machine gun.

Airspeed, your engine's power to sustain that airspeed, and the altitude you have available to exchange for Turning Room or speed all make a difference. There is no such thing as a "standard" dogfight because the parameters are always different. This is one reason why a pilot must thoroughly understand what his plane can do so he can instantly apply these capabilities to any situation.

Adapting aerobatics to achieve a weapon's parameters in a dogfight was a very natural progression. To *loop*, the pilot continuously pulls straight back on the stick bringing the plane straight up, over the top and back down the other side of a big ellipse, like an egg viewed in profile. The narrowest point is the top of the egg where the aircraft is slow and the turn is the smallest. Looping is a very basic maneuver nowadays but was quite daring in 1914. Aircraft were fragile, wing loading wasn't really understood nor were the stresses caused by g-forces, so motors could quit or wings could come off. The *Immelmann turn* is a variation of this maneuver except the pilot rolls out at the top of the loop heading in the opposite direction from which he started. This exchanges airspeed for altitude so the pilot comes out of it much higher but slower. A *split S* is the descending version of this, where the pilot rolls out at the bottom of the loop. He's now exchanged altitude for airspeed and will emerge much lower but faster. Most maneuvering at this stage was a variation of these basic aerobatics. *Spinning* was usually fatal until mid-1916, when a recovery procedure was devised, and from then on it was taught as a last-ditch maneuver to defeat gunshots.

GUNNERY

You could be the greatest natural aviator in the world but if you can't hit anything you've failed as a fighter pilot. As opposed to other types of flying, here you actually, physically *fight* and you need weapons for this—anything else is just an air show. Now, you certainly don't have to shoot an enemy down from behind but it is easier this way since he may not see you and there are few angles involved. Firing from higher angles, called *deflection* shooting, takes a great deal of practice and natural skill. Think of standing in a field watching a flock of ducks fly by perpendicular to where you are. Shooting directly at the duck won't work because as the bullet travels so does the bird, and your shot will miss behind. So you have to guess where the bullet and bird will come together and aim at this point.

Keep in mind that in addition to the hand-eye coordination and mental processing that goes into this, if you're in a dogfight you're not standing still on the ground. So this visualizing and maneuvering has to be done in three dimensions, against a twisting, turning target while you yourself are twisting and turning in three dimensions. And you still must physically fly the plane, keep track of fuel, your location, and a few dozen other essential details.

As illogical as it sounds, flying is secondary to *fighting* in air combat. A man could be a great natural pilot but an abysmal marksman, which meant he'd be noneffective as a warrior. Conversely, there were men like Mannock and Richthofen who were average flyers but became great fighter pilots by virtue of their exemplary shooting and fighting spirit.

Many pilots in the Great War simply solved all the math by eliminating range from the equation. They figured if they got close enough, then complex angles, and even marksmanship, didn't really matter. This is correct—up to a point. First of all, getting that close to another aircraft, even at the comparatively slow speeds of 1917, isn't easy. Also, he's trying to avoid getting shot so he's wildly turning, twisting, and spinning all over the sky. Lastly, if you do hit him and are that close, pieces of him are likely to hit you too. So pilots would perfect their own techniques. Some would race in and fire at the last second, never slowing down to "saddle up" behind a target. Others, like Albert Ball, would try for belly shots. Some were outstanding natural marksmen and had mastered deflection shooting. However it had to be done, successful fighter pilots found a method which worked for them and stuck to it.

Unlike many theoretical ground situations for which countertactics can be taught with a "cookbook" approach, air combat is wildly unpredictable. The fast-developing repertoire of basic fighter maneuvers could be mastered, but applying them when needed was something else entirely.

HUNTING

So you're out on a lone patrol and you see the enemy. Throttle goes forward; you adjust your goggles and check your guns. The plane vibrates and it's cold. You're instinctively taking in the sun position, clouds, and your location relative to the lines. How many fighters do you see and what type are they? One is a two-seater, probably a reconnaissance aircraft. The other is much smaller and flying above and behind the larger one. They're about three miles from you at the ten o'clock position on a watch face, heading west with the late-morning sun behind them.

You angle away slightly to the right and climb, careful not to make any big movements that might attract a watchful eye. You think about your fuel and figure you've got about 15 minutes to fight. The winds are behind you, from the west, and will push you deeper into enemy territory. They could also slow you down if you need to escape. If you can get a few thousand feet higher, you can slice down on their vulnerable rear quarter, partially shielded by the sun and catch them by surprise. If they don't change position or get separated, then you'll attack the fighter first.

But suddenly the enemy scout begins rocking his wings and the bigger plane slowly peels away and dives toward a scattered cloud deck. You instantly nose over to gain speed and turn to point at the other fighter as he turns toward you. Scanning the sky above and behind him, then above and behind you, you're fairly certain that this is a one-on-one fight—but that can always change in a flash. There was about three miles between aircraft as the turns began, and the combined airspeed of both planes, called closing velocity, is about 200 mph. This is 300 feet per second so you'll meet head-on in less than a minute.

Both planes slice down a thousand feet and level off, gaining speed. Your enemy is on your left side and is growing bigger by the second. You hold the stick lightly in your hand, the entire plane is throbbing. The engine roars and wind screams past the little screen and over your ears. You hunch forward, squinting. He's a biplane, like yours, and now less than a half mile in front of you. You roll suddenly left, drop your nose toward the empty space in front of him, and open fire for a count of two, then release.

Shoving the stick forward, you roll back right and see the tracers streak toward the other aircraft. He pulls up and banks hard away. You caught him off guard and the burst of lead took him by surprise.

And that was the point. For a critical second as the two planes come together, he's not looking at you, he's avoiding the bullets. It's a hard shot to make but your enemy flinched and maybe one golden bullet hit him or his engine or a spar.

Doesn't matter.

As you meet, you're already turning and he's late. As you pull across his tail, he reverses back into you in what's called a *One Circle* fight. But the second delay cost him some distance and you're farther around your turn than he is. You also dipped a little low as you turned and he stayed level. Descending as you are, your airspeed stays up while he gets slower. This makes his circle bigger and you're turning inside of it. The front view of his plane becomes the side view as you come through about 180 degrees of the turn.

You spare a quick glance over your shoulders on both sides, then deepen your slice. Your plane is now cutting across his turn circle and the profile picture changes to his back quarter and tail. He realizes this and reacts by flipping over in the direction of the turn and pulling down toward the earth. It's not a spin so you follow, floating behind and above him as he comes out of the bottom in a sloppy split S.

He's gotten his speed back in the dive, which is good for him, but he rolls out momentarily. His tail is slipping back and forth and you realize that he's kicking the rudder and looking for you. Vertical down often does that—it's hard to keep sight of the enemy. Going up is better but much more difficult given current engine technology. Piston motors of the Great War didn't produce the excess power needed for lots of sustained vertical maneuvering. Besides, getting "anchored" in a fur ball, a dogfight, is an excellent way to get killed. No matter how good your situational awareness is or how experienced you are, there's just no way to keep track of everyone. More than likely, the one you don't see is the one who gets you.

Like now.

The enemy biplane is weaving back and forth as the pilot tries to find you. He should've gone straight down and dashed back to his lines. Or gone the opposite direction from the reconnaissance plane he'd been protecting. Anything but roll out and look around.

You've flushed out of your own split S below and behind him. Now, about 50 yards back, you pull the nose up and stare through the Aldis scope. Your plane has been modified with the machine-gun trigger on the stick and you wriggle your fingers to loosen them up. The other biplane begins a right turn back toward the east and the wings fill up your aiming circle.

Suddenly a white flash catches your eye. And another and another!

From long-ingrained habit, you kick the rudder hard and flip over into a falling leaf maneuver as the tracers zip past. Twisting around, you grunt against the force and stare nearly straight up as your plane tumbles down.

There!

Another fighter. No . . . two!

Your brain takes in the details in a second. Not torpedo shaped like the Albatros, these are boxy-looking planes but very, very fast. The closest one rolls once to try for another shot but can't do it and pulls away to avoid a collision. The fuselage is painted with the mottled purples, blues, and yellow lozenges that the Germans use. The other one, circling the fight maybe a thousand feet overhead, is darker with a green nose and blurry camouflage behind.

Fokker D-VIIs.

Coming through the leaf, like a spinning top, you grope for the throttle and pull it back. If you're too fast the fabric will tear off your wings. The first D-VII streaks overhead, big black crosses on the wings and fuselage. His ailerons are painted black on one side and white on the other. The second Fokker has circled around to the east and the Pfalz is nowhere to be seen. Swallowing hard, you pull back on the stick, careful not to yank too hard, and as the nose comes up through the horizon you fly by feel, keeping your eyes padlocked on the enemy fighters. As you come around, you get a face full of sun and the other planes vanish. Adding power, you bunt forward, then hold one hand up as a shield. Heart thumping, you stare a second, then realize *you're* not the hunter at the moment . . . you're the target. Booting a rudder, you glance back left, high and low, then forward. Nothing. Then back to the right, high and low. Nothing.

The sky is empty.

Immediately slicing back to the left, you drop down a few thousand feet and head west toward friendly territory. As your breathing slows somewhat, you unconsciously continue scanning the sky and realize your mouth is bone dry. Fumbling for the canteen you carry, you remember the black and white ailerons. The markings of Jasta 2—the Boelcke Squadron. Taking a deep breath, you shake your head.

Next time.

APPENDIX B

ANATOMY OF A SURFACE ATTACK

THE WHOLE IDEA is to hit something on the ground from the air. Sounds basic, right? But how many people standing still on the ground can throw a ball and hit a target? Now add constant movement in multiple dimensions, several hundred feet per second of velocity and add in people shooting at you. And in combat you have to hit what you aim at or the entire risk of life is wasted.

Surface Attack is a component of basic bombing—putting airborne weapons on generally unlocated targets in the middle of some type of ground battle. Troops in contact, it's called. This differs from high-altitude bombing against fixed, high-priority objectives whose locations are well known and unmoving. Static targets may not move, but if they're important enough to attack, then they're very likely heavily defended. Ground attack is very fluid and dynamic, since there's no such thing as a predictable battle.

BOMB AIMING THEORY

When a bomb comes off an aircraft it immediately begins to slow down from the effects of gravity, drag, and wind. This change in the bomb's velocity, called drift, must be compensated for in order to get close to the target. In aerial gunnery, unless you were shooting from a position directly ahead or behind a target, then angles (deflection) had to be considered. However, unlike in dogfighting where you can squeeze off multiple bursts, once a bomb was off the aircraft, then it was gone, so any compensation for all those variables had to be done before the weapon left the rack. Again, from a known release altitude and airspeed, at a given dive angle, these factors could be combined into an *aim off distance*. This is a physical, measurable distance that represents the sum of all the variables—just like aiming ahead of a moving target.

In the beginning, the pilot did this all with his eyes and a great deal of trial, error, and experience. The relative inaccuracy of bombing attacks, and their effectiveness, reflected this, so a better solution had to be found. Basic attacks are built around the target: what is it made of, is it stationary or moving, and how is it defended? These factors (and many more) dictate the weapon to be used. Once the weapon is known, the type of *delivery,* or attack, is decided. This is based on tactical considerations including the time of day, air-to-air and ground-to-air threats, weather, and time needed over the target.

For instance, if a target is heavily defended by enemy fighters, then the attacking aircraft might want to sneak in at low altitude, using terrain to mask their presence. If the target is defended by lots of anti-aircraft artillery (in the pre-missile world), then the attacker might be able to stay above the ground fire and attack with impunity. In any event, once the type of weapon and attack has been chosen, this determines the altitude above the ground required, the dive angle, release altitudes, and in some cases a minimum or maximum airspeed. These fixed numbers are known as *parameters* and together form the *bombing triangle.*

Now, dropping a weapon from a bomber flying relatively straight and level at a preplanned altitude is a straightforward trigonometry problem. Except for wind, early bombsights like the Number Seven and Gortz could solve the math. However, they all assumed that the dropping aircraft would fly into the wind and that the wind would remain constant. This, of course, just doesn't happen for a bomber three miles above the earth. Nor would any kind of solution which depended upon fixed, stable parameters work for a fighter, especially one engaged in the wild maneuvering of close air support.

There was a long way to go with this and fully grasping the principles was occurring simultaneously with the evolving technology. This made efforts like the school at Lipetsk all the more important because theory could meet practice face to face. Again, the Germans led the field here because the Luftwaffe was conceived as a primarily ground support arm. As we'll see, this would have dire consequences for hundreds of thousands of men.

WEAPONS

Early general purpose (GP) bombs like the 20-pound British Cooper bomb used during the Great War were quite simple. There would be an amount of high explosive encased in a heavy body that would fragment after detonation. This explosive, usually TNT or Tritonal, constituted about 50 percent of the weight for a given bomb and GP bombs are labeled by gross weight. Detonation was caused by a contact fuse—an initiating device—that would function when the bomb decelerated by hitting the target. Other types of fuses would eventually be developed in conjunction with rises in technology; proximity fuses which used electronics, and radar fuses to detonate bombs at specific distances above the ground. Timed fuses could be set for delayed detonations against to achieve greater penetration of hardened (reinforced) targets.

The ingenious mind of man quickly devised other ways to improve the destructive power of these weapons. There were firebombs, predecessor of the incendiary type, made of kerosene and dropped in finned containers.* Cluster bombs, which contain a number of smaller, individual bombs inside the casing, would be developed to produce a shotgun blast effect.

All bombs produce blast effects—that's the point. The severity of this depends on the type of weapon, the fuse and whatever pieces of the target are flying through the air. Aside from destroying the objective, the attacker doesn't want to be killed by its own weapons so minimum release altitudes allow the aircraft to get clear of its own blast effects.

During the 1930's the Luftwaffe had developed the Stachelbombe specifically for close air support work. The Strabo, as it was called, had a long spike attached to the nose which would keep the bomb from ricocheting at low graze angles and give the attacking aircraft time to get away. Others were also developed like the British Mark 1 and the German Butterfly bomb.

---

*The first recorded modern use was by German zeppelins during the night of January 18 or 19, 1915.

MAPS

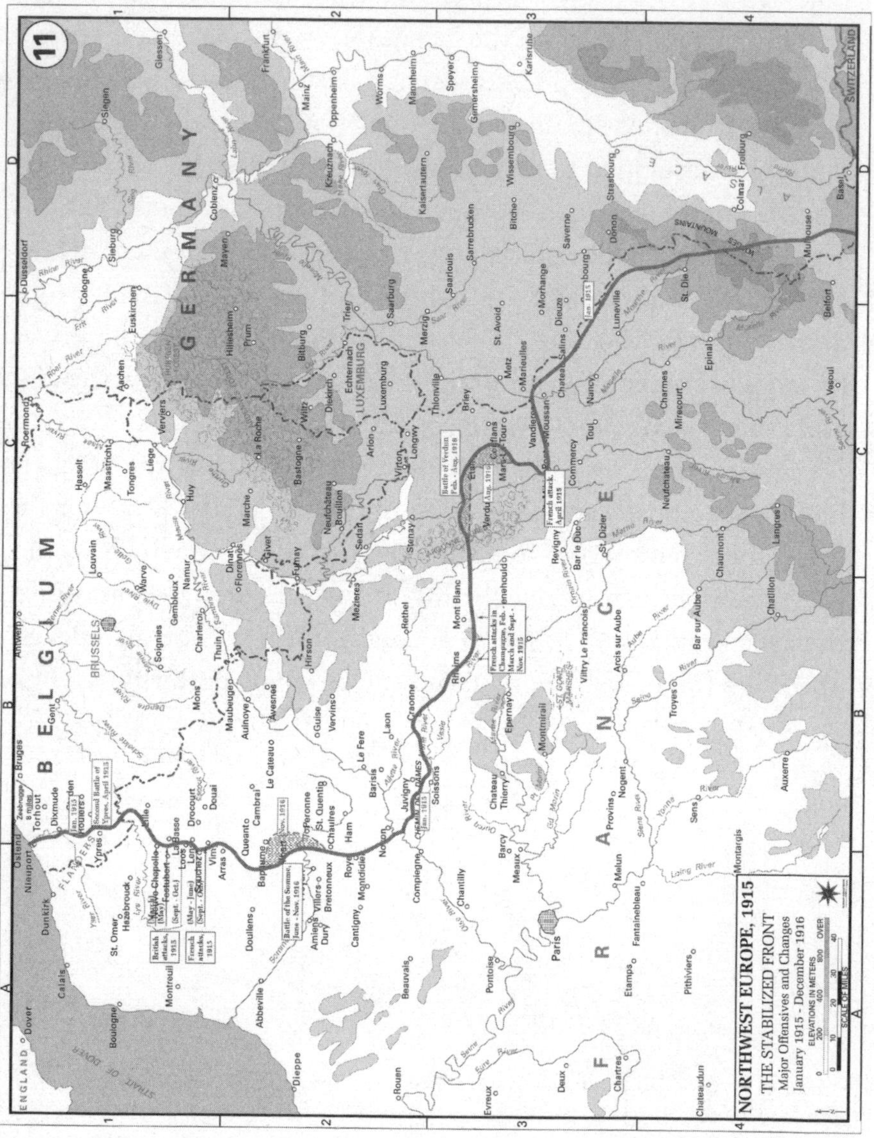
11
NORTHWEST EUROPE, 1915
THE STABILIZED FRONT
Major Offensives and Changes
January 1915 - December 1916
ELEVATIONS IN METERS
0 200 400 800 OVER
SCALE OF MILES
0 10 20 30 40
ENGLAND
Dover
STRAIT OF DOVER
BELGIUM
GERMANY
LUXEMBURG
FRANCE
ALSACE
VOSGES MOUNTAINS
SWITZERLAND
FLANDERS
BRUSSELS
Paris
Ostend
Nieuport
Dunkirk
Calais
Boulogne
Dieppe
Rouen
Evreux
Chartres
Chateaudun
Zeebrugge
Bruges
Gent
Antwerp
Dixmude
Roulers
Torhout
Ypres
Second Battle of Ypres, April 1915
Lille
Jan. 1915
Hazebrouck
St. Omer
Montreuil
British attacks, 1915
French attacks, 1915
Neuve Chapelle
Festubert
(May)
(Sept. - Oct.)
(May - June)
La Basse
Loos
Lens
Douai
Drocourt
Arras
Vimy
Queant
Cambrai
Le Cateau
Doullens
Abbeville
Amiens
Villers-Bretonneux
Battle of the Somme, June - Nov. 1916
Bapaume
Peronne
St. Quentin
Chaulnes
Ham
Roye
Montdidier
Noyon
Cantigny
Compiegne
Beauvais
Pontoise
Chantilly
Soissons
Juvigny
Barisis
Le Fere
Laon
Craonne
CHEMIN DES DAMES
Guise
Vervins
Avesnes
Aulnoye
Maubeuge
Mons
Charleroi
Thuin
Namur
Dinant
Florennes
Givet
Fumay
Mezieres
Rethel
Rheims
Epernay
Chateau Thierry
Meaux
Barcy
Montmirail
ST. GOND MARSHES
Provins
Nogent
Melun
Fontainebleau
Etamps
Pithiviers
Montargis
Sens
Auxerre
Troyes
Bar sur Aube
Arcis sur Aube
Vitry Le Francois
St. Dizier
Bar le Duc
Revigny
Mont Blanc
French attacks in Champagne, Feb. - March and Sept. - Nov. 1915
Sedan
Stenay
Verdun
Battle of Verdun Feb. - Aug. 1916
French attack, April 1915
Commercy
Toul
Nancy
Luneville
Chateau Salins
Dieuze
Metz
Thionville
Briey
Longwy
Virton
Arlon
Luxemburg
Bastogne
Neufchateau
Bouillon
Marche
Huy
Liege
Tongres
Maastricht
Hasselt
Louvain
Wavre
Gembloux
Soignies
Roermond
Aachen
Verviers
Euskirchen
Cologne
Dusseldorf
Siegburg
Siegen
Giessen
Frankfurt
Mainz
Worms
Mannheim
Speyer
Karlsruhe
Coblenz
Mayen
Trier
Saarburg
Saarlouis
Merzig
Sarrebrucken
St. Avold
Morhange
Kaiserlautern
Bitche
Wissembourg
Saverne
Strasbourg
Donon
St. Die
Epinal
Charmes
Mirecourt
Neufchateau
Chaumont
Langres
Chatillon
Vesoul
Belfort
Mulhouse
Basel
Colmar
Freiburg
Rhine River
Meuse River
Marne River
Seine River
Aisne River
Somme River
Oise River
Loing River
Aube River
Moselle River

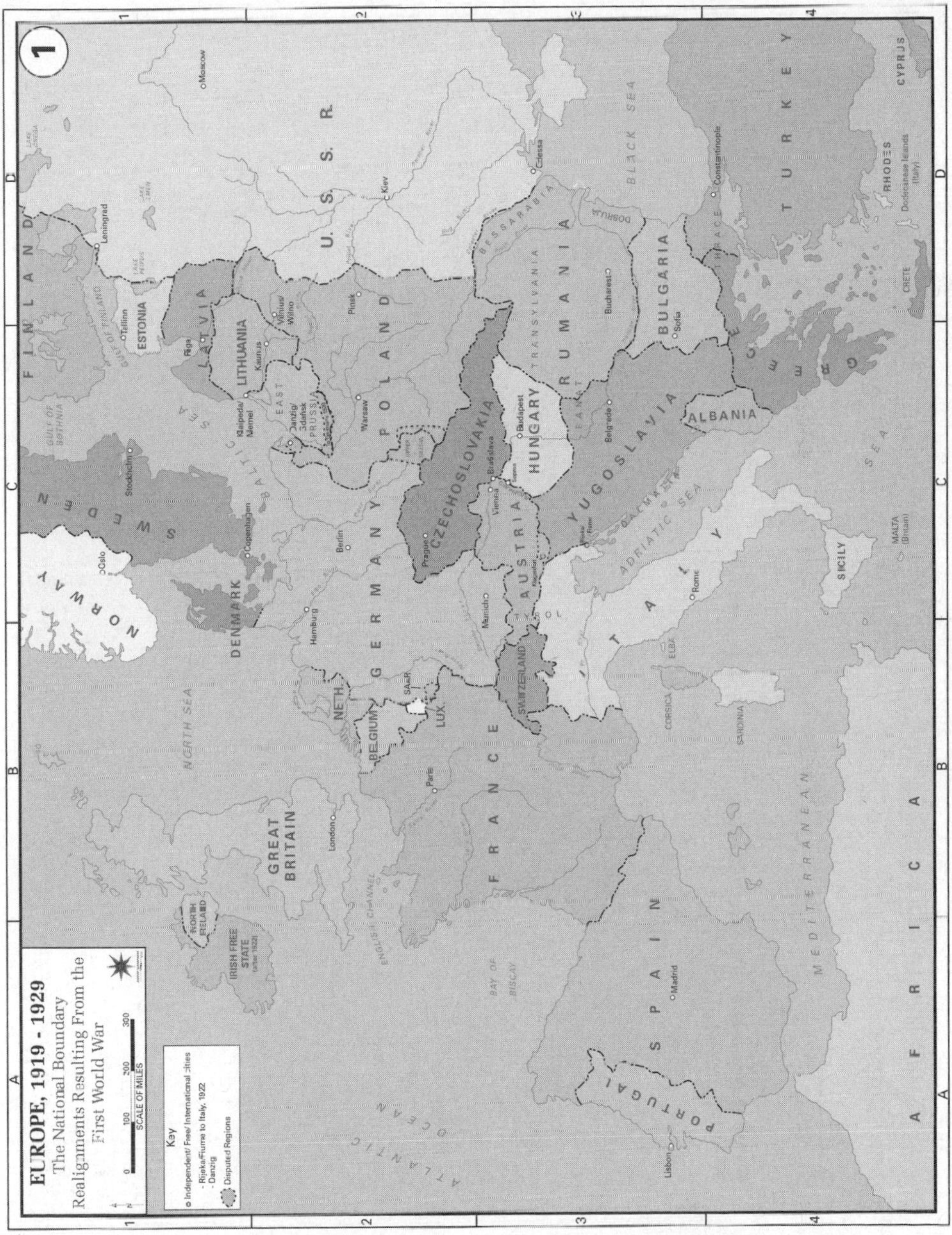
1
EUROPE, 1919 - 1929
The National Boundary Realignments Resulting From the First World War
SCALE OF MILES
0 100 200 300
Key
Independent/ Free/ International cities
- Rijeka/Fiume to Italy, 1922
- Danzig
Disputed Regions
NORWAY
SWEDEN
FINLAND
ESTONIA
LATVIA
LITHUANIA
EAST PRUSSIA
U. S. S. R.
POLAND
GERMANY
DENMARK
NETH.
BELGIUM
LUX.
SAAR
FRANCE
SWITZERLAND
AUSTRIA
CZECHOSLOVAKIA
HUNGARY
RUMANIA
TRANSYLVANIA
BESSARABIA
YUGOSLAVIA
BULGARIA
ALBANIA
GREECE
TURKEY
ITALY
SPAIN
PORTUGAL
GREAT BRITAIN
NORTH IRELAND
IRISH FREE STATE
AFRICA
NORTH SEA
BALTIC SEA
BLACK SEA
ADRIATIC SEA
MEDITERRANEAN SEA
ATLANTIC OCEAN
BAY OF BISCAY
ENGLISH CHANNEL
GULF OF BOTHNIA
GULF OF FINLAND
CORSICA
SARDINIA
SICILY
CRETE
RHODES
CYPRUS
MALTA (Britain)
Dodecanese Islands (Italy)
Moscow
Leningrad
Kiev
Odessa
Tallinn
Riga
Kaunas
Vilnius/ Wilno
Pinsk
Warsaw
Danzig/ Gdańsk
Klaipeda/ Memel
Stockholm
Oslo
Copenhagen
Berlin
Hamburg
Prague
Vienna
Bratislava
Budapest
Bucharest
Belgrade
Sofia
Constantinople
Munich
Paris
London
Madrid
Lisbon
Rome

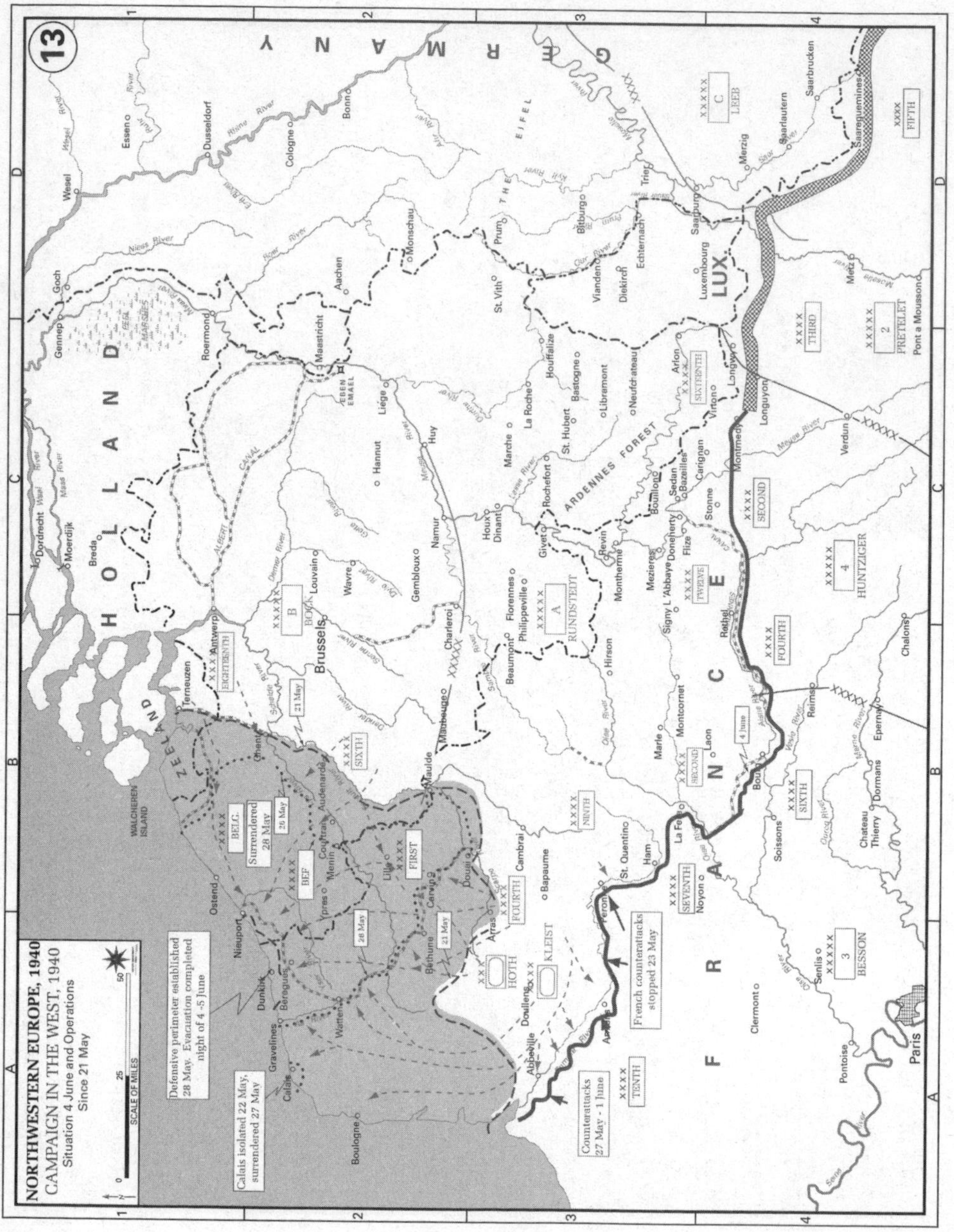
13
NORTHWESTERN EUROPE, 1940
CAMPAIGN IN THE WEST, 1940
Situation 4 June and Operations
Since 21 May
SCALE OF MILES
0
25
50
Defensive perimeter established
28 May. Evacuation completed
night of 4 -5 June
Calais isolated 22 May,
surrendered 27 May
Counterattacks
27 May - 1 June
French counterattacks
stopped 23 May
Surrendered
28 May
BELG.
BEF
FIRST
SIXTH
EIGHTEENTH
NINTH
FOURTH
HOTH
KLEIST
TENTH
SEVENTH
SECOND
SIXTH
BESSON
TWELVE
FOURTH
HUNTZIGER
SECOND
SIXTEENTH
THIRD
PRETELET
FIFTH
LEEB
RUNDSTEDT
BOCK
21 May
26 May
28 May
21 May
4 June
HOLLAND
ZEELAND
WALCHEREN ISLAND
GERMANY
LUX
FRANCE
ARDENNES FOREST
THE EIFEL
ALBERT CANAL
EBEN EMAEL
PEEL MARSHES
Paris
Brussels
Dunkirk
Calais
Boulogne
Ostend
Nieuport
Gravelines
Bergues
Watten
Ypres
Menin
Courtrai
Lille
Douai
Arras
Cambrai
Bapaume
Bethune
Carvin
Abbeville
Doullens
Amiens
Peronne
St. Quentin
Ham
La Fere
Noyon
Laon
Marle
Montcornet
Rethel
Reims
Epernay
Soissons
Chateau Thierry
Dormans
Chalons
Clermont
Senlis
Pontoise
Hirson
Signy L'Abbaye
Mezieres
Flize
Donchery
Sedan
Bazeilles
Carignan
Stonne
Bouillon
Montherme
Revin
Givet
Dinant
Houx
Rochefort
Marche
St. Hubert
Bastogne
La Roche
Houffalize
Libramont
Neufchateau
Arlon
Virton
Longwy
Longuyon
Montmedy
Verdun
Metz
Pont a Mousson
Luxembourg
Echternach
Diekirch
Vianden
St. Vith
Prum
Bitburg
Trier
Saarburg
Merzig
Saarlautern
Saarbrucken
Saareguemines
Monschau
Aachen
Maastricht
Roermond
Gennep
Goch
Wesel
Essen
Dusseldorf
Cologne
Bonn
Liege
Huy
Hannut
Namur
Gembloux
Wavre
Louvain
Charleroi
Maubeuge
Beaumont
Philippeville
Florennes
Maulde
Audenarde
Ghent
Antwerp
Terneuzen
Breda
Dordrecht
Moerdijk
Meuse River
Moselle River
Rhine River
Oise River
Aisne River
Somme River
Marne River
Seine River
Schelde River
Lys River
Dyle River
Sambre River
Ourthe River
Niers River
Roer River
Our River
Saar River

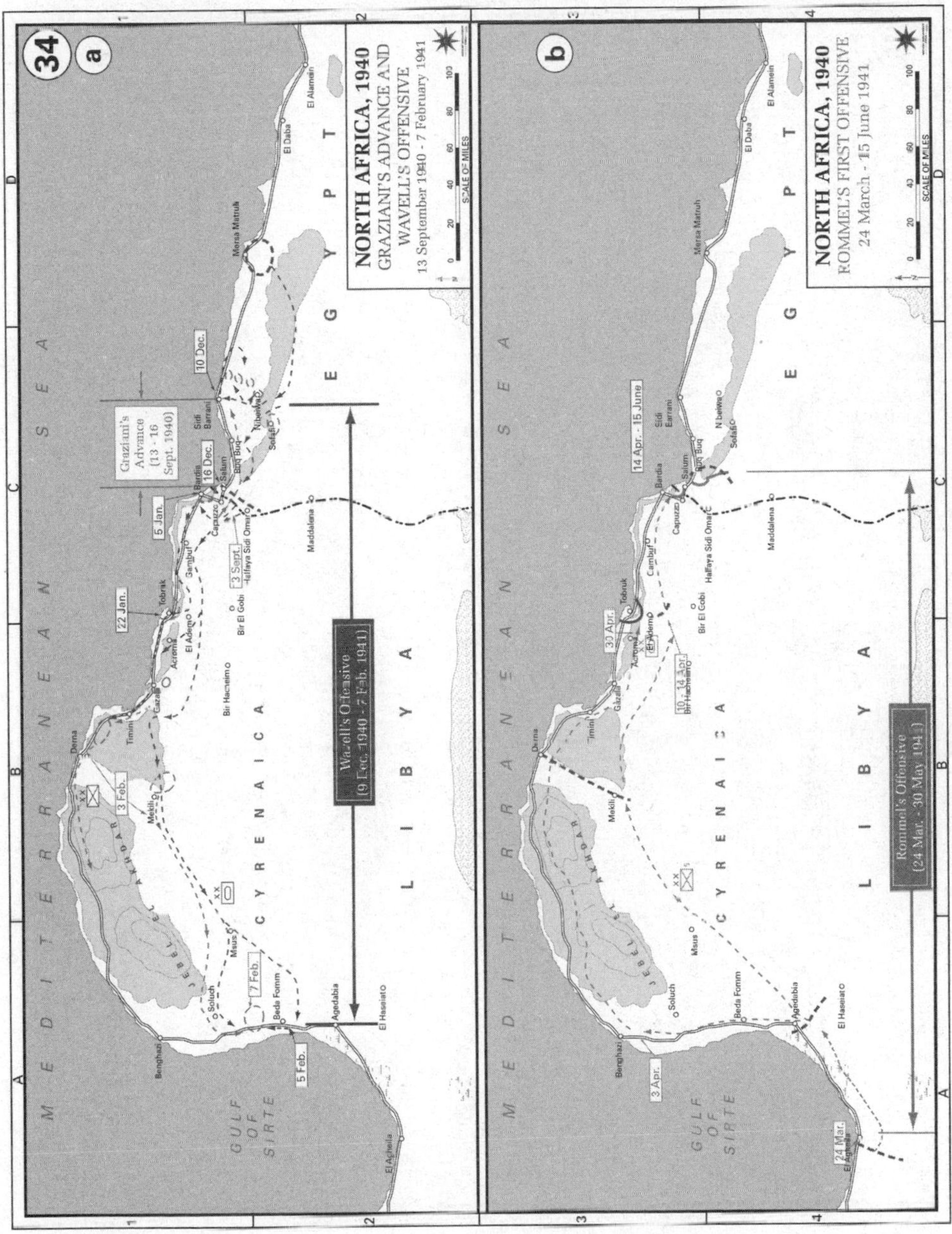
34
a
NORTH AFRICA, 1940
GRAZIANI'S ADVANCE AND WAVELL'S OFFENSIVE
13 September 1940 - 7 February 1941
Graziani's Advance (13 - 16 Sept. 1940)
Wavell's Offensive (9 Dec. 1940 - 7 Feb. 1941)
MEDITERRANEAN SEA
GULF OF SIRTE
CYRENAICA
LIBYA
EGYPT
JEBEL EL AKHDAR
Benghazi
Soluch
Beda Fomm
Agedabia
El Haseiat
El Agheila
Msus
Mekili
Derna
Timini
Gazala
Acroma
El Adem
Tobruk
Bir Hacheim
Bir El Gobi
Gambut
Capuzzo
Bardia
Salum
Halfaya
Sidi Omar
Maddalena
Buq Buq
Sidi Barrani
Nibeiwa
Sofafi
Mersa Matruh
El Daba
El Alamein
3 Sept.
10 Dec.
16 Dec.
5 Jan.
22 Jan.
3 Feb.
5 Feb.
7 Feb.
SCALE OF MILES
b
NORTH AFRICA, 1940
ROMMEL'S FIRST OFFENSIVE
24 March - 15 June 1941
Rommel's Offensive (24 Mar. - 30 May 1941)
24 Mar.
3 Apr.
10 - 14 Apr.
30 Apr.
14 Apr. - 15 June

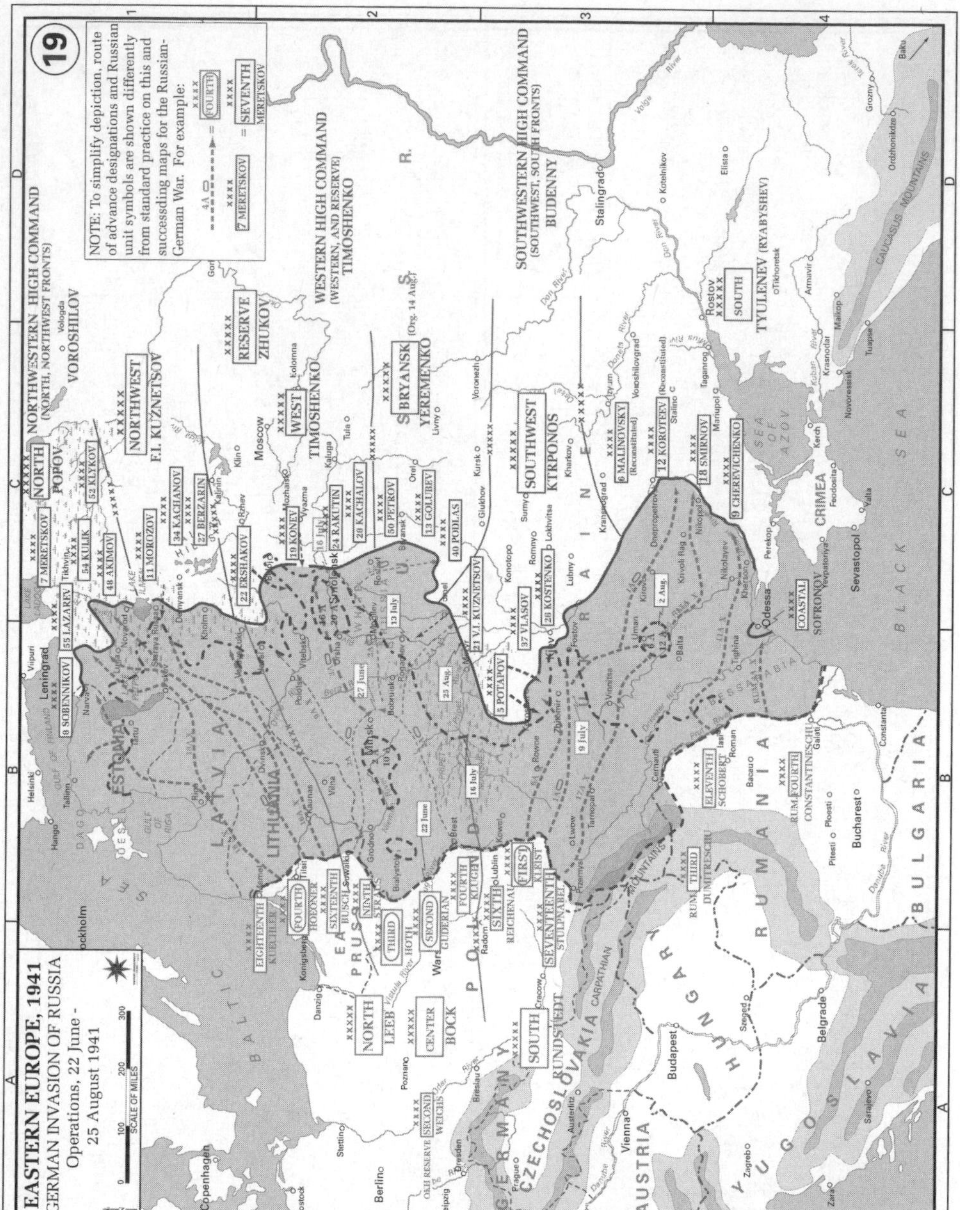
19
EASTERN EUROPE, 1941
GERMAN INVASION OF RUSSIA
Operations, 22 June - 25 August 1941
SCALE OF MILES
NOTE: To simplify depiction, route of advance designations and Russian unit symbols are shown differently from standard practice on this and successding maps for the Russian-German War. For example:
NORTHWESTERN HIGH COMMAND
(NORTH, NORTHWEST FRONTS)
VOROSHILOV
WESTERN HIGH COMMAND
(WESTERN, AND RESERVE)
TIMOSHENKO
SOUTHWESTERN HIGH COMMAND
(SOUTHWEST, SOUTH FRONTS)
BUDENNY
NORTH LEEB
CENTER BOCK
SOUTH RUNDSTEDT
NORTH POPOV
NORTHWEST F.I. KUZNETSOV
RESERVE ZHUKOV
WEST TIMOSHENKO
BRYANSK YEREMENKO
SOUTHWEST KIRPONOS
SOUTH TYULENEV
COASTAL SOFRONOV
ESTONIA
LATVIA
LITHUANIA
EAST PRUSSIA
POLAND
UKRAINE
CRIMEA
RUMANIA
HUNGARY
CZECHOSLOVAKIA
GERMANY
AUSTRIA
YUGOSLAVIA
BULGARIA
BALTIC SEA
BLACK SEA
SEA OF AZOV
CAUCASUS MOUNTAINS
CARPATHIAN MOUNTAINS
Leningrad
Moscow
Smolensk
Kiev
Odessa
Stalingrad
Rostov
Sevastopol
Warsaw
Berlin
Budapest
Bucharest
Belgrade
Vienna

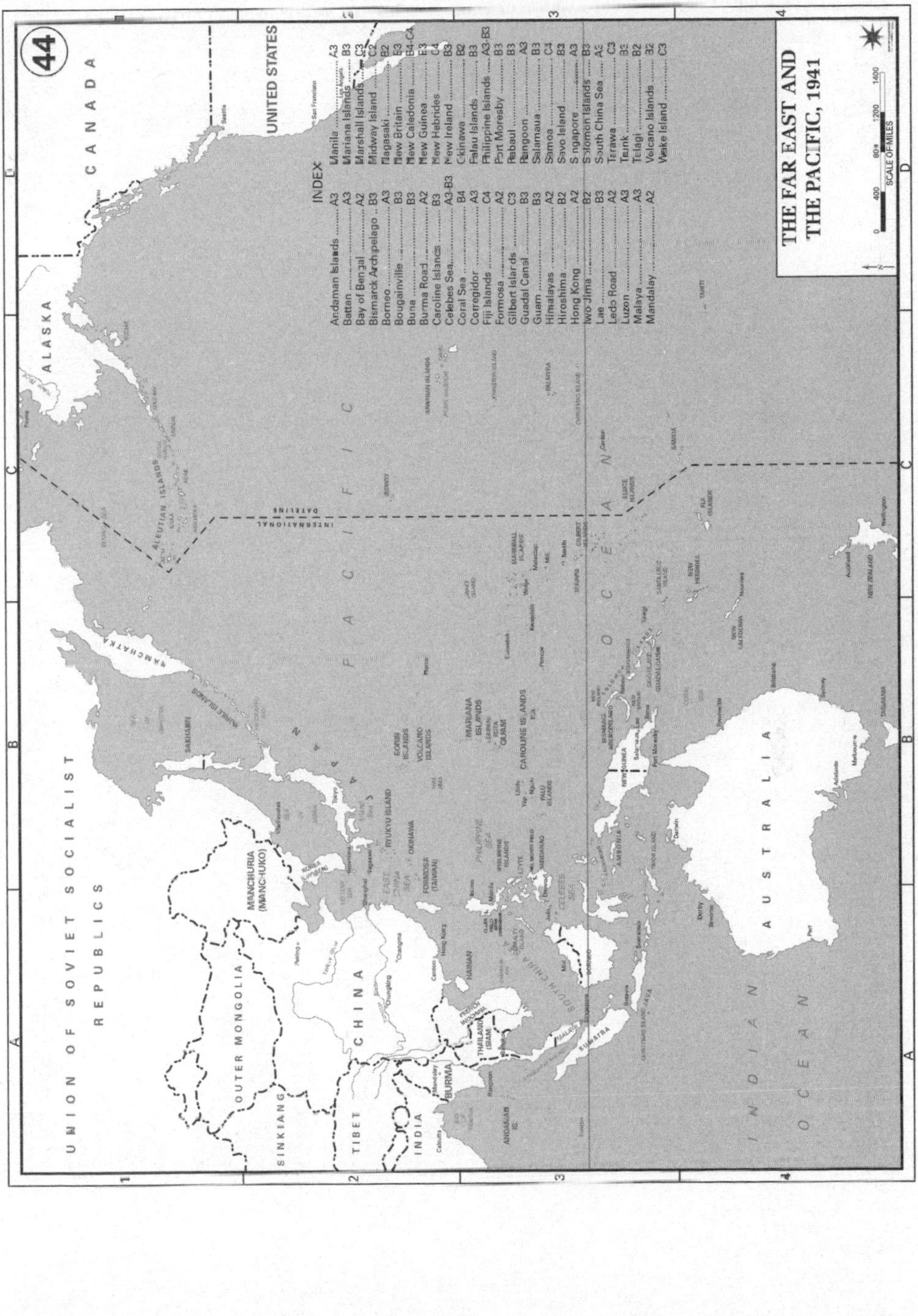
44
THE FAR EAST AND THE PACIFIC, 1941
SCALE OF MILES
0 400 800 1200 1400
A B C D
1 2 3 4
UNION OF SOVIET SOCIALIST REPUBLICS
OUTER MONGOLIA
MANCHURIA (MANCHUKO)
SINKIANG
TIBET
CHINA
INDIA
BURMA
THAILAND (SIAM)
HAINAN
FORMOSA (TAIWAN)
RYUKYU ISLAND
OKINAWA
VOLCANO ISLANDS
MARIANA ISLANDS
GUAM
CAROLINE ISLANDS
PALAU ISLANDS
SAKHALIN
KAMCHATKA
KURILE ISLANDS
ALEUTIAN ISLANDS
ALASKA
CANADA
UNITED STATES
INTERNATIONAL DATELINE
PACIFIC OCEAN
INDIAN OCEAN
SOUTH CHINA SEA
CELEBES SEA
PHILIPPINE SEA
EAST CHINA SEA
AUSTRALIA
NEW GUINEA
BISMARCK ARCHIPELAGO
AMBONIA
BORNEO
SUMATRA
JAVA
NEW ZEALAND
INDEX
Andaman Islands A3
Battan A3
Bay of Bengal A2
Bismarck Archipelago .. B3
Borneo A3
Bougainville B3
Buna B3
Burma Road A2
Caroline Islands B3
Celebes Sea A3-B3
Coral Sea B4
Corregidor A3
Fiji Islands C4
Formosa A2
Gilbert Islands C3
Guadal Canal B3
Guam B3
Himalayas A2
Hiroshima B2
Hong Kong A2
Iwo Jima B2
Lae B3
Ledo Road A2
Luzon A3
Malaya A3
Mandalay A2
Manila A3
Mariana Islands B3
Marshall Islands C3
Midway Island C2
Nagasaki B2
New Britain B3
New Caledonia B4-C4
New Guinea B3
New Hebrides C4
New Ireland B3
Ckinawa B2
Palau Islands B3
Philippine Islands A3-B3
Port Moresby B3
Rabaul B3
Rangoon A3
Salamaua B3
Samoa C4
Savo Island B3
Singapore A3
Solomon Islands B3
South China Sea A3
Tarawa C3
Truk B3
Telagi B2
Velcano Islands B2
Wake Island C3

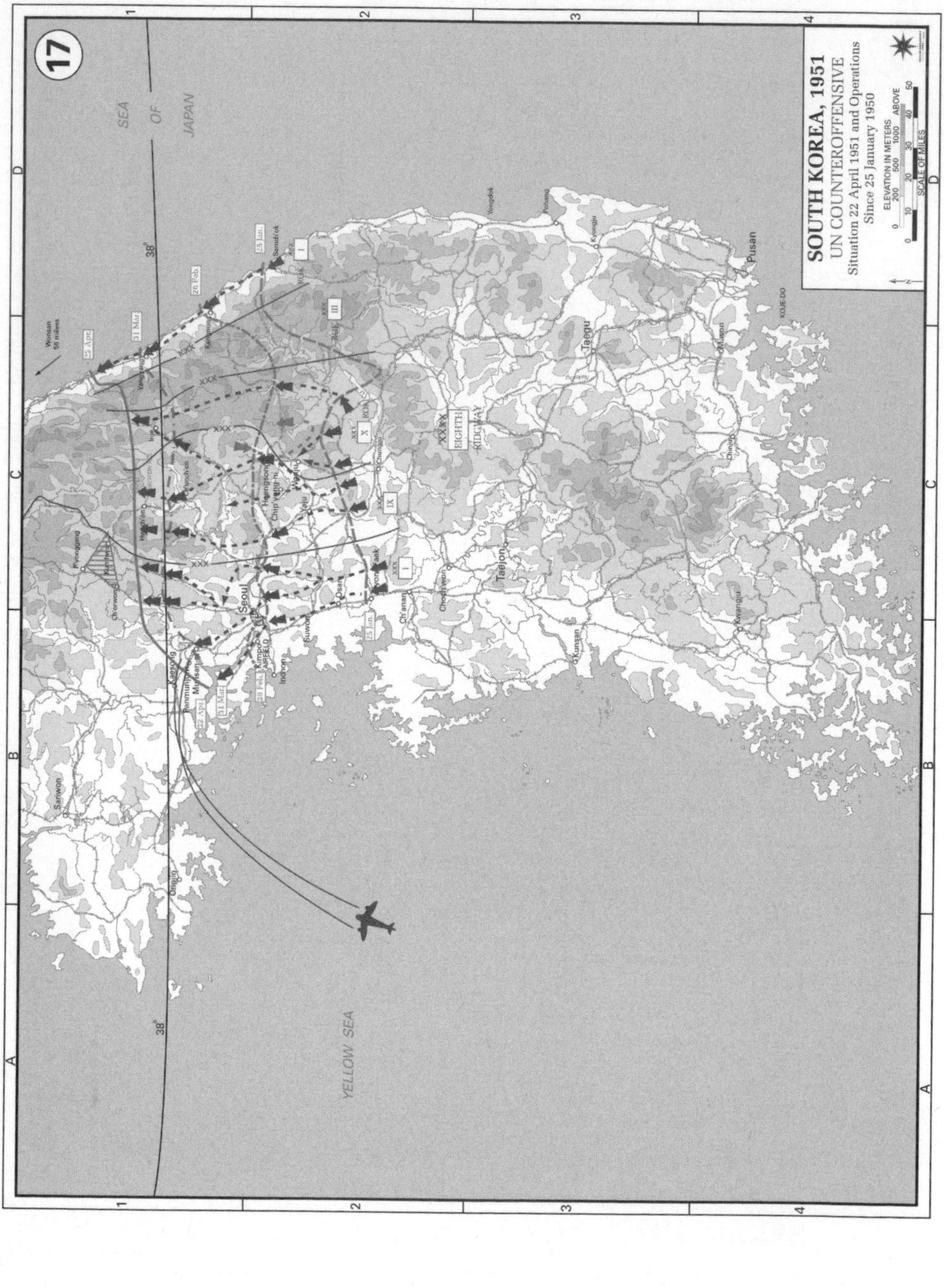
17
SOUTH KOREA, 1951
UN COUNTEROFFENSIVE
Situation 22 April 1951 and Operations
Since 25 January 1950
ELEVATION IN METERS
0 200 500 1000 ABOVE
0 10 20 30 40 50
SCALE OF MILES
SEA OF JAPAN
YELLOW SEA
38°
Wonsan 50 miles
Seoul
Taejon
Taegu
Pusan
Kwangju
Kunsan
Suwon
Inchon
Osan
Wonju
Hoengsong
Chipyong-ni
Chunchon
Hwachon
Chorwon
Pyonggang
Kaesong
Panmunjom
Munsan-ni
Ongjin
Sariwon
Kyongju
Pohang
Yongdok
Masan
KOJE DO
EIGHTH
RIDGWAY
25 Jan.
26 Feb.
31 Mar.
22 Apr.
A B C D
1 2 3 4

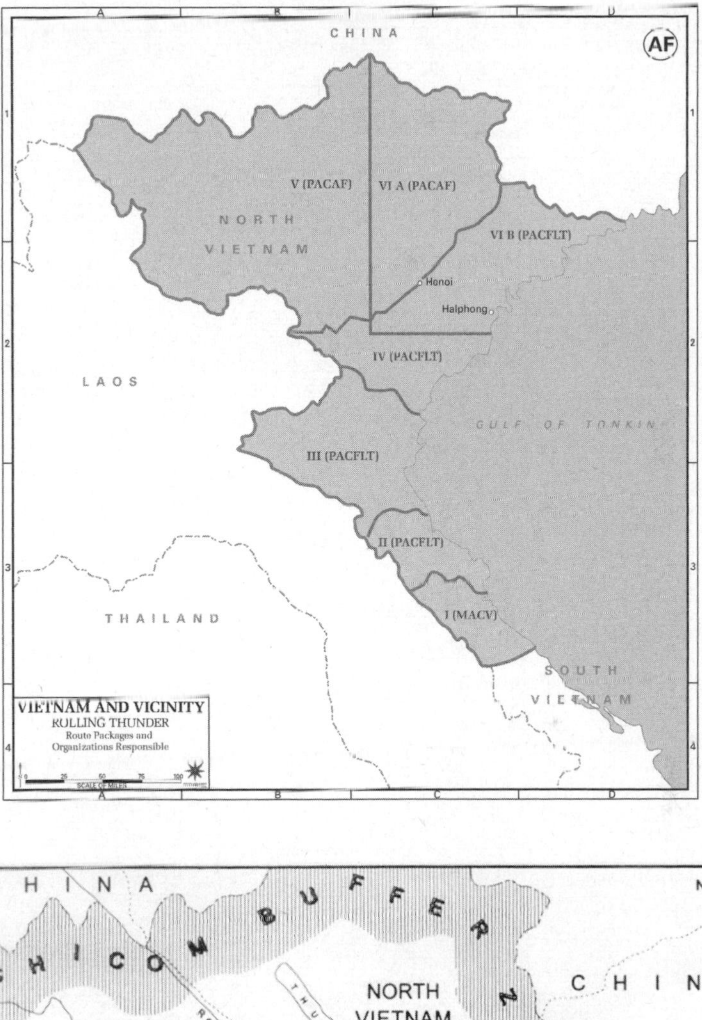
CHINA
AF
V (PACAF)
VI A (PACAF)
VI B (PACFLT)
NORTH
VIETNAM
Hanoi
Halphong
IV (PACFLT)
LAOS
GULF OF TONKIN
III (PACFLT)
II (PACFLT)
I (MACV)
THAILAND
SOUTH
VIETNAM
VIETNAM AND VICINITY
ROLLING THUNDER
Route Packages and
Organizations Responsible
SCALE OF MILES

CHINA
CHICOM BUFFER ZONE
Nanning
NORTH
VIETNAM
CHINA
THUD RIDGE
Red River
Yen Bai
Phu
Tho
Thai Nguyen
(steel works)
Black River
Dien Bien Phu
Son La
Viet
Tri
Kep (Mig base)
Phuc Yen (Mig base)
Hoa Lac
Hanoi
LAOS
THUD RIDGE
AND THE HANOI AREA
Hoa Binh
Ile Ba Mun
Haiphong
Scale of Miles
0 25 50
Border
Railroad
River
Nam Dinh
Gulf of Tonkin

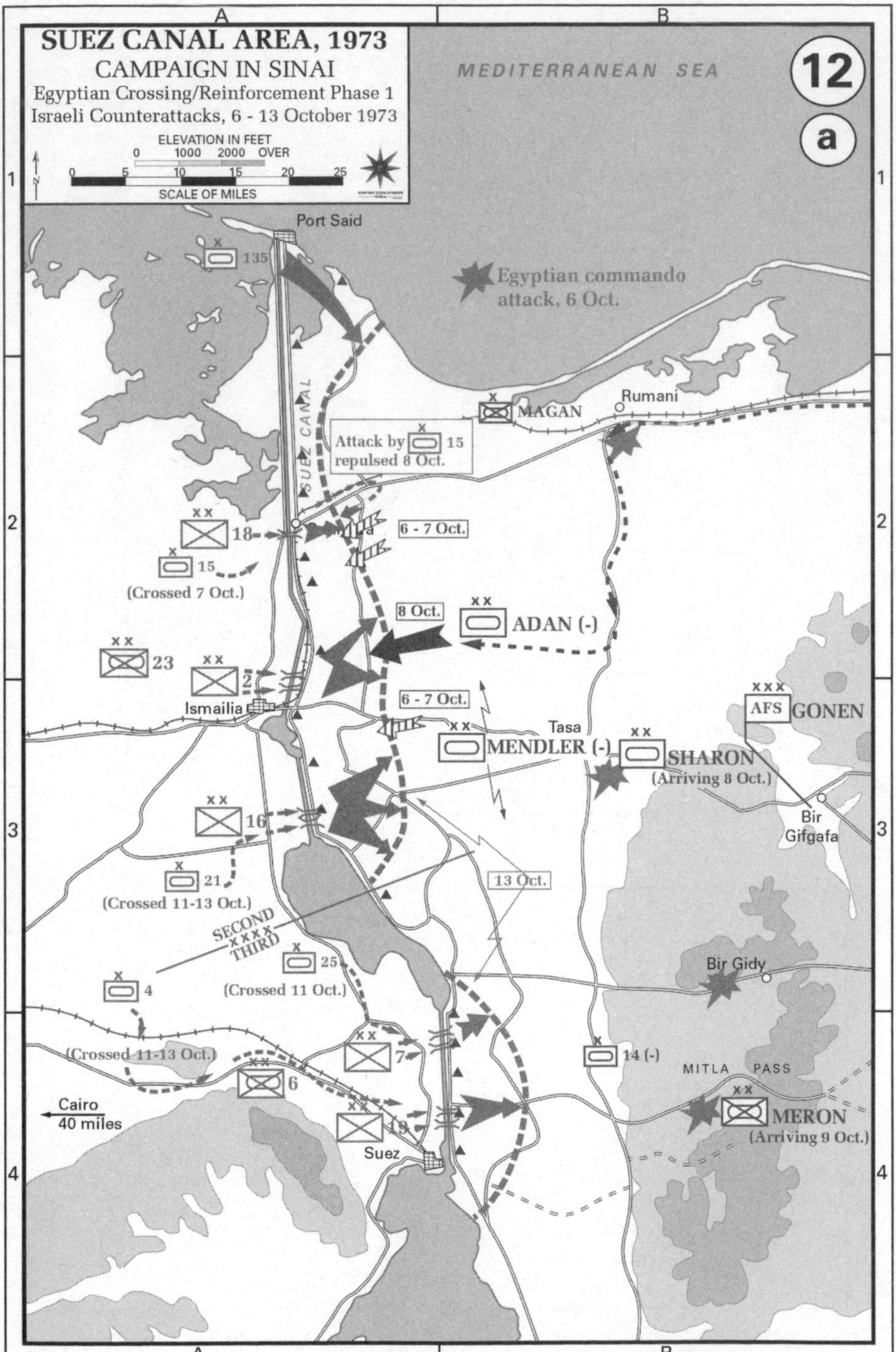
SUEZ CANAL AREA, 1973
CAMPAIGN IN SINAI
Egyptian Crossing/Reinforcement Phase 1
Israeli Counterattacks, 6 - 13 October 1973
ELEVATION IN FEET
0 1000 2000 OVER
0 5 10 15 20 25
SCALE OF MILES
12
a
MEDITERRANEAN SEA
Port Said
135
Egyptian commando attack, 6 Oct.
SUEZ CANAL
MAGAN
Rumani
Attack by 15 repulsed 8 Oct.
18
15
(Crossed 7 Oct.)
6 - 7 Oct.
8 Oct.
ADAN (-)
23
2
Ismailia
6 - 7 Oct.
Tasa
MENDLER (-)
SHARON
(Arriving 8 Oct.)
AFS
GONEN
Bir Gifgafa
16
21
(Crossed 11-13 Oct.)
SECOND THIRD
13 Oct.
25
(Crossed 11 Oct.)
4
Bir Gidy
7
(Crossed 11-13 Oct.)
6
14 (-)
MITLA PASS
Cairo 40 miles
19
Suez
MERON
(Arriving 9 Oct.)
A
B
1
2
3
4

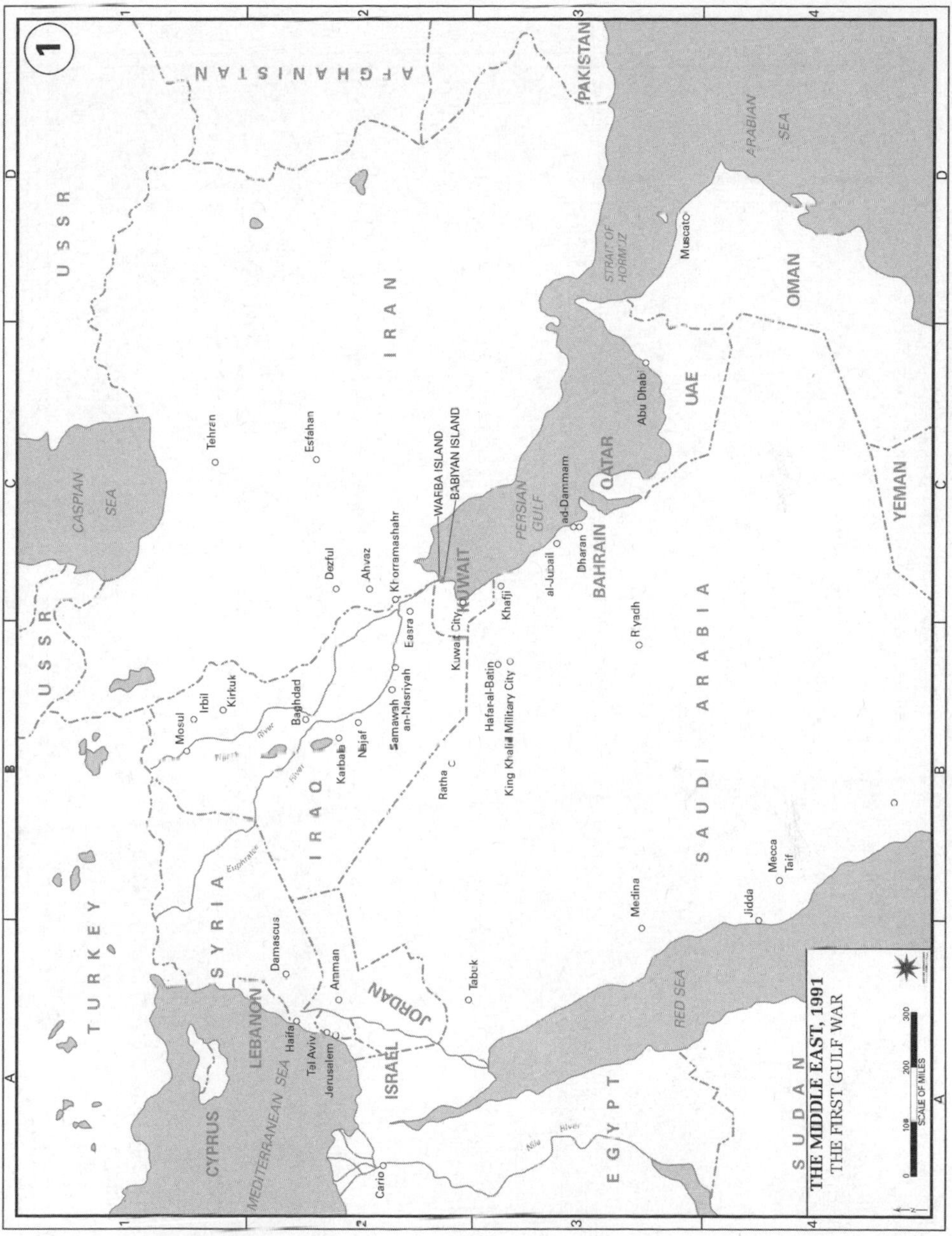
1
TURKEY
USSR
AFGHANISTAN
PAKISTAN
IRAN
IRAQ
SYRIA
LEBANON
ISRAEL
JORDAN
KUWAIT
SAUDI ARABIA
BAHRAIN
QATAR
UAE
OMAN
YEMEN
EGYPT
SUDAN
CYPRUS
CASPIAN SEA
MEDITERRANEAN SEA
RED SEA
PERSIAN GULF
ARABIAN SEA
STRAIT OF HORMUZ
Tehran
Esfahan
Dezful
Ahvaz
Khorramashahr
WARBA ISLAND
BABIYAN ISLAND
Mosul
Irbil
Kirkuk
Baghdad
Karbala
Najaf
Samawah
an-Nasriyah
Basra
Kuwait City
Khafji
Hafar-al-Batin
King Khalid Military City
Ratha
al-Jubail
ad-Dammam
Dharan
Riyadh
Abu Dhabi
Muscat
Medina
Mecca
Taif
Jidda
Tabuk
Damascus
Amman
Haifa
Tel Aviv
Jerusalem
Cario
Tigris River
Euphrates River
Nile River
THE MIDDLE EAST, 1991
THE FIRST GULF WAR
SCALE OF MILES
0
100
200
300

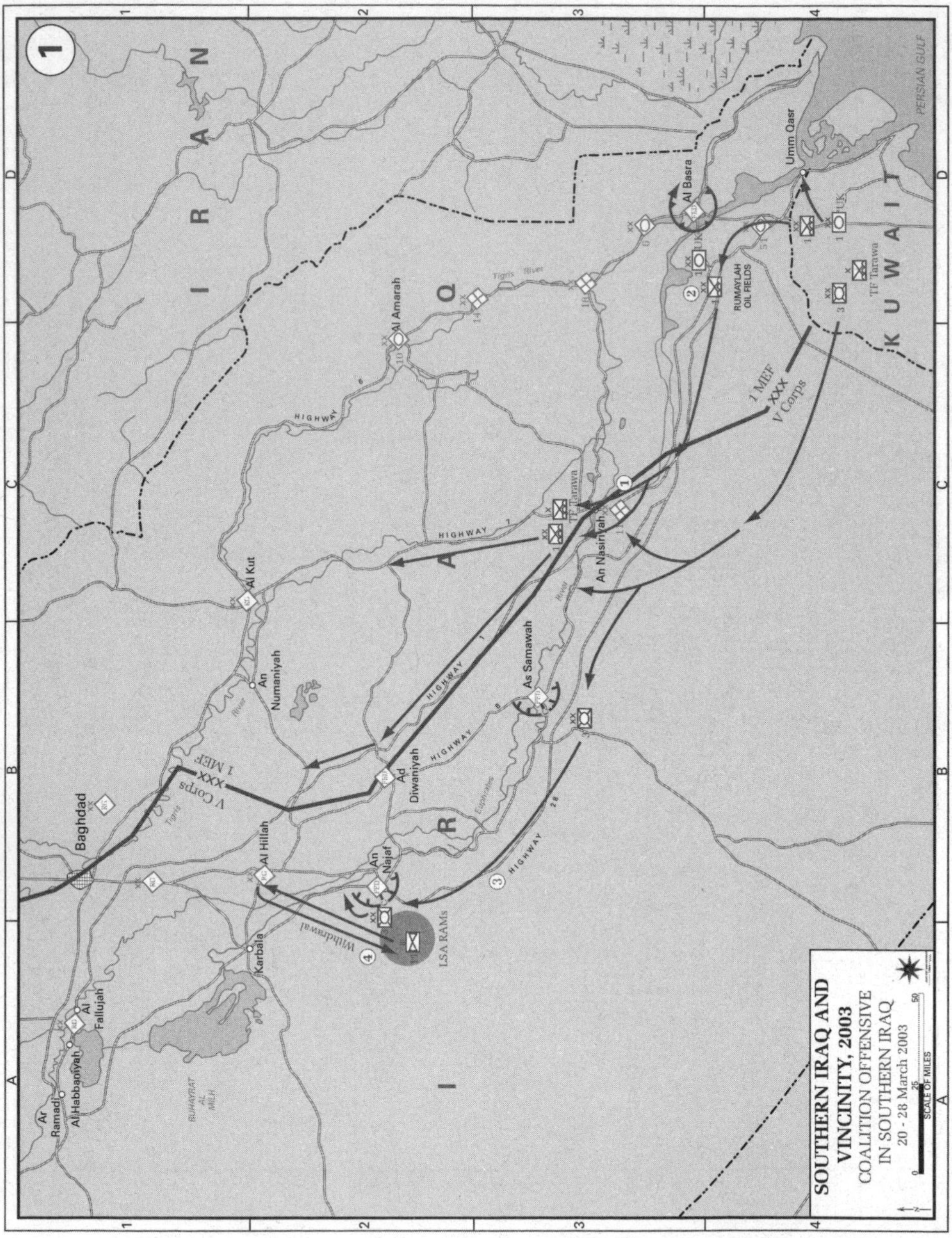
1
SOUTHERN IRAQ AND
VINCINITY, 2003
COALITION OFFENSIVE
IN SOUTHERN IRAQ
20 - 28 March 2003
SCALE OF MILES
0
25
50
I R A N
I R A Q
K U W A I T
PERSIAN GULF
Baghdad
Ar Ramadi
Al Habbaniyah
Al Fallujah
BUHAYRAT AL MILH
Karbala
Al Hillah
An Najaf
Ad Diwaniyah
As Samawah
An Numaniyah
Al Kut
Al Amarah
An Nasiriyah
Al Basra
Umm Qasr
RUMAYLAH OIL FIELDS
TF Tarawa
LSA RAMs
Withdrawal
1 MEF
XXX
V Corps
HIGHWAY 1
HIGHWAY 6
HIGHWAY 8
HIGHWAY 28
Tigris River
Euphrates
A
B
C
D
1
2
3
4

GLOSSARY OF TERMS

AAM: Air-to-air missile. Can be either radar guided or heat seeking.

ACC: Air Combat Command. The major command containing all stateside fighter units.

ACM: Air combat maneuvers.

ACT: Air combat training. Generally as one or two pairs against an unknown number of adversaries.

AGM: Air-to-ground missile.

AIRFOIL: Cross-sectional view of a wing or propeller blade. The overall shape determines the airfoil's efficiency relative to aerodynamic forces such as lift and drag.

ANGELS: Altitude in thousands of feet. Technically only used for friendly aircraft.

AOR: Area of responsibility. Places like Iraq, Afghanistan, et cetera.

ARVN: Army of the Republic of Vietnam.

ATC/AETC: USAF Air Training Command.

AWACS: Airborne Warning and Control System and aircraft.

BFM: Basic fighter maneuvers. Dogfighting.

BLIND: Lost visual on a friendly flight member.

BLOCK 50: A type of F-16. Block designations are for different specific capabilities. Block 50 includes the HARM Targeting System pod and associated avionics.

BOARDS: Slang for speed brakes.

BURNER: Afterburner.
BVR: Beyond visual range.
CAMBER: The measured difference between the top and bottom of an airfoil; in this case a wing.
CBU: Cluster bomb unit.
CEEJAY: F-16CJ. Also a Block 50.
CHANDELLE: An aerobatic/dogfighting maneuver resembling an oblique, climbing turn that trades airspeed for altitude. The aircraft ends on a reciprocal heading from where it began.
CHORD LENGTH: A notional line drawn from the trailing edge to the leading edge of a wing. Also used to measure the width of an airfoil section.

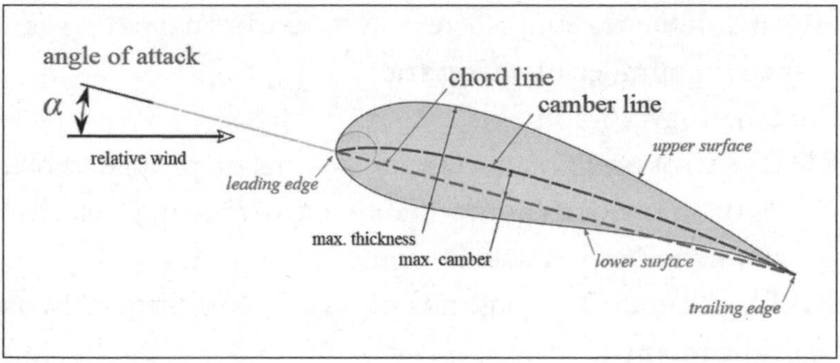

COMPANY GRADE OFFICER: Junior officers. A Second Lieutenant, First Lieutenant, or Captain.
DEFENDING: Technically a defensive reaction against a SAM or anti-aircraft artillery. Usually accompanied by the type of threat, if known, and a direction for the maneuver.
DMZ: Demilitarized zone.
EAGLE: F-15C.
EMPENNAGE: All the parts which comprise the tail assembly of an aircraft.
EOR: End of runway. This area is directly to the side of the runway and used for arming/de-arming.

EW: Early warning radar.
EWO: Electronic warfare officer. A specialist in signals analysis.
FALLSCHIRMJÄGER: German paratroopers belonging to the Luftwaffe.
FEAF: Far Eastern Air Force.
FIELD GRADE OFFICER: A Major, Lieutenant Colonel, and Colonel.
FIGHTING WING: A fluid, loose formation that puts a wingman on about a one-mile string behind his leader. Think of a water skier behind a boat.
FINGERTIP: Close formation. Usually about three feet from wingtip to wingtip.
FOX ONE/TWO/THREE: Air-to-air-missile shots. "Fox One" refers to an older radar-guided AIM-7 Sparrow. "Fox Two" is a close-range infrared Sidewinder, and "Fox Three" is the advanced medium-range air-to-air missile (AMRAAM).
FRAG: Fragments from an explosion. Also a Fragmentary Order, a squadron's piece of the larger Air Tasking Order detailing missions, targets, and weapons.
FUSELAGE: The central core of an aircraft to which the wings and empennage are attached. From the French *fuselé,* meaning "spindle-shaped."
FWIC: Fighter Weapons Instructor Course.
G-FORCE: Actually an acceleration against gravity producing stress on the human body that is felt as weight. This can be positive (the force acts downward) or negative (the force acts upward). A 200-pound man would feel 1,800 pounds of force acting in the opposite direction from his acceleration.
GOMER: Slang for an enemy.
GRUNT: Slang for an infantryman. Friendly ground forces.
HARAH: Hebrew for "shit."
HARM: High-speed anti-radiation missile.
HOG: Slang for A-10 Thunderbolt II.

HORNET: Slang for the F/A-18 multi-role fighter.
HOTAS: Hands on throttle and stick. Technology that permits the activation of weapons, aircraft systems, and cockpit displays from multifunction switches on the control stick and throttle.
HTS: HARM Targeting System pod.
HUD: Heads-up display. A transparent plastic rectangle mounted on the glare shield with superimposed flying symbology and weapon attack cues.
HUN: Slang for the F-100 Super Sabre.
IFF: Identification Friend or Foe. An electronic code which can be read by other friendly aircraft.
ILS: Instrument landing system.
IMMELMANN TURN: A purely vertical dogfighting maneuver that produces a half-loop. The aircraft rolls out at the top of the loop, much slower and much higher than where it began.
INLINE ENGINE: A piston engine with the cylinders arranged alongside the crankshaft; can be in a block, straight-up, or inverted alignment.
JINK: Usually a quick, violent, three-dimensional defensive maneuver.
KILL BOX: A 30-mile-square piece of airspace. Given an alphanumeric identifier, kill boxes are used for deconfliction between flights of fighters.
KLICK: A kilometer. A little over half a mile.
LANTIRN: Low-Altitude Navigation Targeting Infrared Night. An older, specialized system used on Block 40 F-16s for low-level night-strike missions.
LOOP: A vertical turn. Resembles an egg if viewed in profile.
LOOSE DEUCE: A wider, more flexible form of fighting wing. A two-mile string.
LUFTSTREITKRAFTE: German Imperial Air Service of World War I.
LUFTWAFFE: German Air Force of the Second World War.

MAGNUM: Warning call made to indicate a HARM firing.
MFD: Multi-function display.
MiG: An abbreviation for Mikoyan and Gurevich, a prominent Soviet/Russian aircraft manufacturer. Sometimes generically applied to any enemy fighter.
MiGCAP: A flight of fighters dedicated to counter-air operations.
MIKE: Short for microphone. Also denotes millimeter, as in "twenty mike mike" (20 mm cannon).
MIL POWER: Full non-afterburning power.
NO JOY: Lost visual. Should be used only for enemy aircraft. Often used in place of "Blind."
NVAF (VPAF): North Vietnamese Air Force, or Vietnamese People's Air Force.
NVG: Night vision goggles.
OFFSET BOX: A four-jet tactical formation. Two pairs separated by three to five miles.
PADLOCKED: Brevity communication for "my eyes are locked and if I look away I'll lose sight."
PATCHWEARER: Graduate of the USAF Fighter Weapons School. Also called "Target Arm."
PAVN: People's Army of Vietnam (Communists).
PDJ: Plaine des Jarres (Plain of Jars) in Laos.
PGM: Precision guided munition.
POW: Prisoner of war.
QRC: Quick reaction capability. Used mainly for jamming pods; the forerunner of the ALQ series pods.
QUARTER PLANE: An aggressive diagonal move made by an attacker to reposition behind a defender. Used when closure is too high and airspeed (energy) needs to bleed off.
RADIAL ENGINE: Internal combustion, piston engine with the cylinders aligned in a radial star shape around the crankshaft.
RAF: Royal Air Force. Formed from the RFC in April 1917.

RFC: Royal Flying Corps. Britain's air force during World War I.
RHAW: Radar homing and warning. Systems to detect radar tracking and missile guidance.
RIFLE: Brevity communications for a Maverick missile shot. Used commonly for any guided munition.
RNAS: Royal Naval Air Service. Merged with the RFC to form the RAF.
ROTARY ENGINE: Internal combustion engine which rotates around a crankshaft.
ROUTE: A wider, more relaxed version of fingertip formation.
ROUTE PACK: One of six aviation zones of responsibility for operations conducted by the USAF and USN/USMC in North Vietnam.
RTB: Return to base.
RTU: Replacement training unit.
RWR: Radar warning receiver. Tells the pilot which radar system has locked him.
SAM: Surface-to-air missile. Can be radar guided or infrared heat seeking.
SIDEWINDER: U.S. made AIM-9 heat-seeking, air-to-air missile.
SLAMMER: Slang for the U.S.-built AIM-120 advanced medium-range air-to-air missile.
SLAPSHOT: A quick-reaction HARM shot along a line of bearing to a threat.
SLICEBACK: An aggressive vertical maneuver from a higher to a lower altitude, at the end of which an aircraft is heading the opposite direction.
SMS: Stores management system. Onboard computer that accounts for all weapons ballistics and aiming symbology.
SPLIT S: A purely vertical "down" maneuver used in aerobatics and dogfighting. Opposite of an Immelmann.
TACAN: Tactical air navigation system. Provides bearing and

range to a selected channel that can be located at a ground station or between other aircraft.

TALLY-HO: Visual sighting of an enemy aircraft. Sometimes used to indicate sighting any aircraft.

TARGETARM: A graduate of the USAF Fighter Weapons School. Also called a "Patchwearer."

TD BOX: Target designator box. Put around anything locked onto by the F-16 radar.

THRUST-TO-WEIGHT RATIO: Expressed by dividing the available thrust by the overall weight of an aircraft. Both variables can change constantly; thrust varies by throttle position and air density, while weight changes in-flight due to fuel consumption and the release of weapons.

THUD: Common nickname for the Republic F-105 Thunderchief.

TOT: Time over target.

TRIPLE-A: Anti-Aircraft artillery. Gunfire directed at aircraft visually or by radar.

UNIFORM: UHF radio.

USAAF: United States Army Air Forces.

USAF: United States Air Force. Formed from the USAAF on September 18, 1947.

VICTOR: VHF radio.

VIPER: Slang for the F-16 multi-role fighter.

VISUAL: Sighting of a friendly aircraft.

VNAF: Vietnamese Air Force. Republic of South Vietnam.

VUL: Short for "vulnerability" time. This is the fragged, or allotted, time that a fighter is given in a target area.

WALKING THE DOG: Streaming an activated towed decoy.

WEHRMACHT: German armed forces of the Second World War.

WILCO: Will comply. A military way of saying "I'll do it!"

WING LOADING: The loaded weight of the aircraft divided by the area of the wing. The faster an aircraft flies, the more lift is produced by each unit area of wing, so a smaller wing can carry the same weight in level flight, operating at a higher wing loading. Correspondingly, the landing and takeoff speeds will be higher. The high wing loading also decreases maneuverability. The same constraints apply to winged biological organisms.

WSO/RIO: Weapons system officer/radar intercept officer. Controlled the radar in older fighters like the F-14 and F-4. Though a flying officer, the WSO/RIO is not a pilot.

WVR: Within visual range.

ZAP: A data link.

ZIPPER: Clicking the mike several times by way of an affirmative reply.

BIBLIOGRAPHY

NOTES ON SOURCES

Literature covering the past century, in particular the wartime conflicts between 1914 and 2003, is overwhelming; each period could be, and often is, the work of a lifetime. My purpose is to create a window, if you will, into each of these times rather than an encyclopedia. Through this, hopefully a better understanding is possible and a desire for deeper reading is stimulated. In all cases, every effort has been made to give proper credit for the vast amounts of information contained within and if any have been inadvertently left out, please accept my profound apologies.

Perhaps the best overall source for World War I, the issues leading up to it, and the evolving phases of this evocative conflict is *A World Undone: The Story of The Great War,* by G. W. Meyer. I found it extremely readable with a great deal of background beyond military operations that described the economic, social, and political issues that determined the eventual outcome.

For the little-known and often-confusing period between the world wars, Margaret MacMillan's *Paris, 1919* is an excellent place to begin. *Udet: A Man's Life,* by Hans Herlin shows one former officer's struggle in postwar Germany. The best work on the Polish-Soviet War of 1919–20 was Norman Davies's superb *White Eagle, Red Star.* I have long admired the underdog spirit of the Poles and their willingness to fight, and this book has become a favorite of mine.

Mountains of books have been written covering the period of 1939–45, as well they should. It was the defining time of the last century and its consequences still resound in our world today. Michael Korda's magnificent *With Wings Like Eagles* rests prominently beneath a Spitfire portrait on my library wall. His ability to condense vast amounts of information into readable phrases is astounding. Similarly, James Holland's *Battle of Britain* is a must for the serious student of these terrible few months in world history. Chris McNab's *Hitler's Eagles* is packed with details, technical data, and wonderful artwork, while Winston Groom's *1942* offers a superb analysis of the most critical year of this pivotal conflict.

Absolutely essential for the fifty years following World War II is Victor Flintham's *Air Wars and Aircraft.* His unit tables, deployment histories, and commentaries were extremely useful for the accuracy necessary in a book such as this. Of similar weight and importance is General William "Spike" Momyer's *Air Power in Three Wars.* Though the layout is sometimes tough to follow, the depth of his personal knowledge of each conflict more than compensates. Kenneth Werrell wrote two books that were indispensable: *Sabres over MiG Alley* and *Archie to SAM: A Short Operational History of Ground Based Air-Defense*. Both are very enjoyable to read and contain hard-to-find technical details.

Korea and Vietnam are both complex regional wars that had (and have) global ramifications. Max Hastings's *The Korean War* and John Prados's *Vietnam: The History of an Unwinnable War, 1945–1975* offer the best overall picture of both conflicts. Finally, John Anderson's *A History of Aerodynamics* remains my favorite work on a highly technical subject. These and the other works gratefully used are listed below. Also, a Notes section has been added with amplifying remarks.

Abrams, Richard. *F4U Corsair at War*. London: Ian Allen Ltd., 1977.

Adams, Briggs Kilburn. *The American Spirit*. Boston: Atlantic Monthly Press, 1918.

Adams, Michael C. C. *The Best War Ever: America and World War II*. Baltimore: Johns Hopkins University Press, 1994.

"Air War over Vietnam and Lessons Learned." n.d. http://forums.navalwarfare.net. July 20, 2013.

Aloni, Shlomo. *Israeli A-4 Skyhawk Units in Combat*. Oxford: Osprey Publishing, 2009.

———. *Israeli Mirage and Nesher Aces*. Oxford: Osprey Publishing, 2004.

"AN/ALR-69 Radar Warning Receiver." April 22, 2000. http://www.fas.org. September 1, 2013.

Anderson, John D. *A History of Aerodynamics*. Cambridge: Cambridge University Press, 1997.

Anonymous. "Giving Them More Hell." *Time Magazine*. December 3, 1973.

———. *History of the Medical Department of the United States Navy in World War II*. Washington, D.C.: U.S. Government Printing Office, 1950.

———. *Substance of Statements Made at Wake Island Conference on October 15*. Declassified on March 29, 1977. Washington, D.C.: U.S. Government Printing Office, 1950.

———. *Utah Beach to Cherbourg*. After Action Report. Washington, D.C.: Department of the Army, 1947.

Appleman, Roy E. *South to Nanking, North to the Yalu: United States Army in the Korean War*. Washington, D.C.: Department of the Army, 1998.

Argyle, Christopher. *Chronology of World War II*. London: Marshall-Cavendish, 1980.

Army, Department of the. *Army Battle Casualties and Nonbattle Deaths in World War II—Final Report*. Washington, D.C.: Department of the Army, GPO, 1953.

Army, Department of the. *USAAF Casualties in European, North African and Mediterranean Theaters of Operations, 1942–1946*. Army Battle Casualties in World War II—Final Report. Washington, D.C.: Department of the Army, GPO, 1953.

Ashby, Jeff. *Astronaut and Navy F/A-18 Fighter Pilot Dan Hampton*. August 27, 2013.

———. *F/A-18 Training and Operations*. Dan Hampton. August 29, 2013.

Astor, Gerald. *Wings of Gold: The U.S.Naval Air Campaign in World War II*. New York: Random House, 2005.

Aten, Marion, and Arthur Orrmont. *Last Train Over Rostov Bridge*. California: Messner, 1961.

Aten, Michael. *Marion Aten*. Dan Hampton. March 2013.

Atkinson, Rick. "The Road to D-Day." *Foreign Affairs*, July/August 2013, pp. 55–75.

The Aviation History Online Museum. n.d. http://www.aviation-history.com. February–July 2013.

Bader, Douglas. *Fight for the Sky: The Story of the Spitfire and Hurricane*. London: Cassell Military Books, 2004.

Bailey, F. W., and Christopher Cony. *The French Air Service War Chronology 1914–1918*. London: Grub Street, 2001.

Barber, Mark. *RAF Command Pilot: The Western Front 1939–42*. Oxford: Osprey Publishing, 2012.

Barber, S. B. *Naval Aviation Combat Statistics: World War II, OPNAV-P-23V No. A129*. Washington, D.C.: Air Branch, Office of Naval Intelligence, 1946.

Barr, Niall. *Pendulum of War: The Three Battles of El Alamein*. London: Pimlico, 2005.

Bates, Peter. *Dance of War: The Story of the Battle of Egypt*. London: Leo Cooper, 1992.

Beechy, Robert. "Ferrets, Ravens & Weasels." February 3, 2013. http://hud607.fire.prohosting.com/uncommon/reference/usa/sead.html. August 2013.

Beavis, L. E. *Baron von Richtofen's Death*. Letter (Courtesy of the Park's Collection). London: Army Quarterly, 1931.

Beckman, Allan. *The Nihau Incident*. Honolulu: Heritage Press of the Pacific, 1982.

Bekker, Cajus. *The Luftwaffe War Diaries in World War II*. Cambridge: Da Capo Press, 1994.

Belyakov, R. A., and J. Marmain. *MiG: Fifty Years of Secret Aircraft Design*. Annapolis: Naval Institute Press, 1993.

Bergstrom, Chriter. *Barbarossa—The Air Battle: July–December 1941*. London: Classic Publications, 2007.

Bharucha, P. C., and B. Prasad. *The North African Campaign, 1940–43*. Delhi: Combined Inter-Services Historical Section, India & Pakistan, 1956.

Biddle, Wayne. *Barons of the Sky*. New York: Simon & Schuster, 1991.

Board, Major A. G., RFC. "Combats in the Air." Combat report. June 20, 1918.

Bob, Hans-Ekkehard. *Betrayed Ideals: Memoirs of a Luftwaffe Fighter Ace*. Cerberus Publishing Ltd., 2003.

Bodansky, Yossef. *The Secret History of the Iraq War*. New York: HarperCollins, 2004.

Boniface. *MIGs over North Vietnam: The Vietnam People's Air Force in Combat, 1965–75*. Mechanicsburg: Stackpole Books, 2008.

Borch, F., and D. Martinez. *Kimmel, Short and Pearl Harbor: The Final Report Revealed*. Annapolis: Naval Institute Press, 2005.

Bowman, Martin. *P-51D vs Fw 190: Europe 1943–45*. Oxford: Osprey, 2007.

Bowyer, Chaz. *Men of the Desert Air Force, 1940–43*. London: William Kimber, 1984.

Boyne, Walter and Philip Handleman. *Brassey's Air Combat Reader*. London: Batsford Brassey, Inc., 1999.

Boyne, Walter. *Aircraft of the Korean War*. http://www.airforcemag.com/MagazineArchive. n.d. *Air Force*, June 10, 2013.

Boyne, Walter J. "Goering's Big Bungle." *Air Force Magazine* 91 (2008).

Bradley, James. *Flyboys*. Boston: Little, Brown and Company, 2013.

Broughton, Jack. *Going Downtown*. New York: Pocket, 1990.

———. *Thud Ridge*. Manchester: Crecy, 2006.

Bruce, J. M. *The Aeroplanes of the Royal Flying Corps (Military Wing)*. London: Putnam, 1982.

Brune, Lester H. *The Korean War: Handbook of the Literature and Research*. Westport: Greenwood Publishing Group, 1996.

Budiansky, Stephen. *Air Power*. New York: Penguin, 2004.

Bureau of Naval Weapons. *Navy Model A4D-2N Aircraft*. United States Navy, 1962.

Caccia-Dominioni, Paolo. *Alamein 1933–1962: An Italian Story*. Crows Nest, New South Wales: Allen & Unwin, 1966.

Cacutt, Len. *Great Aircraft of the World: Hawker Hurricane*. London: Marshall Cavendish, 1989.

Caldwell, Donald, and Richard Muller. "The Oil Campaign May–August 1944." In *The Luftwaffe Over Germany: Defense of the Reich*. St. Paul: MBI Publishing Company, 2007.

Callander, Bruce D. "The Aviation Cadets." *Air Force Magazine* 73 (1990).

"Carriers: Airpower at Sea." n.d. http://www.sandcastlevi.com/sea/carriers. May 15, 2013.

Chorlton, Martyn. *Allison-Engined P-51 Mustang*. Oxford: Osprey Publishing, 2012.

Church, Francis Conover. *Diary of a WWI Pilot*. Spokane: Conover-Patterson Publishers, 2004.

Churchill, Winston S. *The Second World War*. Vol 3. London: Cassell, 1948–1954.

———. *The Second World War: Closing the Ring*. Boston: Houghton-Mifflin, 1951.

Clarke, Ron Wallace. *British Aircraft Armament: RAF Guns and Gunsights from 1914 to the Present Day*. London: Haynes, 1995.

Clifford, Alexander. *Three Against Rommel: The Campaigns of Wavell, Auchinleck and Alexander*. London: George G. Harrap & Co., 1943.

Cohen, S. *The Forgotten War*. Altona: D. W. Friesen & Sons, 1981.

Connor, Roger, and Christopher Moore. *In the Cockpit*. New York: HarperCollins, 2010.

Coombes, David. *Morshead: Hero of Tobruk and El Alamein*. South Melbourne: Oxford University Press, 2001.

Coonts, Steven. *USN SAM Suppression During Vietnam*. September 6, 2013.

Correll, John. "Daylight Precision Bombing." *Air Force Magazine,* October 2008, pp. 60–63.

Correll, John T. "MIG Alley." *Air Force Magazine,* April 2010, pp. 61–64.

Corrigan, Paul. *Last of the Aerial Gunfighters.* Naples: First Books, 2003.

Cottam, Dr. Janina Kazimiera. *The Golden Tressed Soldier.* Manhattan: Military Affairs/Aerospace Historian Publishing, 1983.

Courtois, Stephanie. *The Black Book of Communism: Crimes, Terror, Repression.* Cambridge: Harvard University Press, 1999.

Cowin, Hugh. *Allied Aviation of World War I.* London: Osprey Publishing, 2000.

Craven, W. F., and J. L. Cate. *The Army Air Forces in World War II. Volume Six: Men and Planes.* Washington, D.C.: Office of Air Force History, 1983.

Cull, Brian, and Dennis Newton. *With the Yanks in Korea. Volume One: The First Definitive Account of British and Commonwealth Participation in the Air War, June 1950–December 1951.* London: Grub Street, 2000.

Cynk, Jerzy B. *History of the Polish Air Force 1918–1968.* Reading: Osprey Publishing, 1972.

———. *Polish Aircraft 1893–1939.* London: Putnam & Company, 1973.

Davies, Norman. *White Eagle, Red Star: The Polish-Soviet War 1919–1920.* London: Macdonald & Co., 1972.

Davies, Peter. *F-4 Phantom II vs MiG-21.* London: Osprey Publishing, 2008.

———. *Republic F-105 Thunderchief.* Oxford: Osprey Publishing, 2012.

Davies, Peter E., and David W. Menard. *F-100 Super Sabre Units of the Vietnam War.* Oxford: Osprey Publishing, 2011.

Deighton, Len. *Fighter.* London: Random House UK, 2000.

Diggens, Barry. *September Evening: The Life and Final Combat of the German Ace Werner Voss.* London: Grub Street, 2003.

Dildy, D. C., and W. E. Thompson. *F-86 Sabre vs MiG-15.* London: Osprey Publshing, 2013.

Doolittle, James H., and Carroll V. Glines. *I Could Never Be So Lucky Again.* New York: Bantam Books, 2001.

Dorr, Robert F. *Phantoms Forever.* London: Osprey Publishing, 1987.

Dorr, Robert F., and Warren Thompson. *Korean Air War.* Osceola Zenith, 2003.

Dunn, Walter S. *Hitler's Nemesis: The Red Army, 1930–1945.* Westport: Praeger Publishers, 1994.

———. *The Soviet Economy and the Red Army, 1930–1945.* Westport: Praeger Publishers, 1995.

Eberspacher, Warren A., and Jan P. Koniarek. "PZL Fighters part Two—P.11 Variants." *Historical Aircraft Digest 00–5,* 2001.

Ellis, L. F. *War in France and Flanders.* London: H. M. Stationery Office, 1953.

Elward, Brad. *McDonnell Douglas A-4 Skyhawk.* Ramsbury, Wiltshire: Crowood Press, 2000.

Endicott, Judy G. *The USAF in Korea Campaigns, Units and Stations, 1950–1953.* Washington, D.C.: U.S. Government Printing Office, 2001.

Everett, Susan. *The Two World Wars, Vol I.* Bison Books, 1980.
Fenby, J. *Chiang Kai-Shek: China's Generalissimo and the Nation He Lost.* New York: Carroll & Graf Publishers, 2005.
Field, Alexander J. "The Most Technologically Progressive Decade of the Century." *American Economic Review,* September 2003, 399–413.
Fiske, Rear Admiral Bradley. *New York Times* quote. 1924.
———. "The Admiral's Chair." *The New Yorker.* February 10–11, 1942.
Fitch, Willis. *Wings in the Night.* Nashville: Battery Press, 1989.
Flack, Ronald. *Fundamentals of Jet Propulsion with Applications.* New York: Cambridge University Press, 2005.
Fleming, Nicholas. *August 1939: The Last Days of Peace.* Pasadena: Davies Publishing, 1979.
Flintham, Victor. *Air Wars and Aircraft: A Detailed Record of Air Combat, 1945 to the Present.* New York: Facts on File, 1990.
Ford, Daniel. *Flying Tigers.* New York: HarperCollins, 1991.
Forsyth, Robert. *Aces of the Condor Legion.* Oxford: Osprey Publishing, 2011.
Foss, Joe, and Matthew Brennan. *Top Guns.* New York: Simon & Schuster, 1991.
Fozard, John W. *Sydney Camm and the Hurricane: Perspectives on the Master Fighter Designer and His Finest Achievement.* London: Airlife, 1991.
Franks, Norman. *Sky Tiger: The Story of Sailor Malan.* London: William Kimber & Co., 1980.
Franks, Norman, and Frank W. Bailey. *Above the Lines: The Aces and Fighter Units of the German Air Service, Naval Air Service and Flanders Marine Corps, 1914–1918.* London: Grub Street, 1993.
———. *Over the Front: A Complete Record of the Fighter Aces and Units of the United States and French Air Services, 1914–1918.* London: Grub Street, 1992.
Franks, Norman, Frank W. Bailey, and Rick Duiven. *The Jasta Pilots.* London: Grub Street, 1996.
Franks, Norman, Russell Guest, and Christopher F. Shores. *Above the Trenches: A Complete Record of the Fighter Aces and Units of the British Empire Air Forces 1915–1920.* London: Grub Street, 1990.
Franks, N., and G. Van Wyngarden. *Fokker D.VII Aces of World War I.* London: Osprey, 2003.
Freudenberg, Matthew. *Negative Gravity: The Life of Beatrice Shilling.* Derby: Charlton Publications, 2003.
Frisbee, John L. "Epitaph for a Valiant Airman." *Air Force Magazine* 73 (April 1990).
Galbraith, Peter W. *The End of Iraq.* New York: Simon & Schuster, 2006.
Gannon, James. *Stealing Secrets, Telling Lies: How Spies and Codebreakers Helped Shape the Twentieth Century.* Washington, D.C.: Brassey, 2002.
Gibbons, Floyd. *Red Knight of Germany.* New York: Garden City Publishing Co., 1927.
Good, William, Major USMC (ret). *Marine Combat Aviation in Vietnam.* August 25, 2013.

Gordon, Dennis. *The Lafayette Flying Corps*. Atglen: Schiffer Publishing, Ltd., 2000.

Gordon, Yefim, and Keith Dexter. *Polikarpov's I-16 Fighter: Its Forerunners and Progeny*. Leicester: Midland Publishing Ltd., 2002.

Gough, Terrence, J. *U.S. Army Mobilization and Logistics in the Korean War*. Washington, D.C.: Center of Military History, 1987.

Gregor, Neil. *Daimler-Benz in the Third Reich*. New Haven: Yale University Press, 1998.

Groom, Winston. *1942: The Year That Tried Men's Souls*. New York: Grove Press, 2005.

Grossnick, Roy, and William J. Armstrong. *United States Naval Aviation, 1910–1995*. Annapolis: Naval Historical Center, 1997.

Gunn, Roger. *Raymond Collishaw and the Black Flight*. Toronto: Dundurn, 2013.

Guttman, Jon. *Fighting Firsts*. London: Cassell & Co., 2000.

———. *The Origin of Fighter Aircraft*. Yardley: Westholme Publishing, Inc., 2009.

———. *Spad VII vs. Albatros DIII*. New York: Osprey Publishing, 2011.

Gyorgy, N. I. "Albert Fono: A Pioneer of Jet Propulsion." International Astronautical Congress (1977).

Halberstam, David. *The Coldest Winter: America and the Korean War*. New York: Hyperion, 2007.

Hallion, Richard P. *Rise of Fighter Aircraft 1914–1918*. Annapolis: Nautical & Aviation Publishing Company of America, 1984.

Hampton, Dan Colonel (ret) USMC. *A-4 Skyhawk Combat Operations*. August 30, 2013.

———. *Viper Pilot*. New York: HarperCollins, 2013.

Hannig, Norbert. *Luftwaffe Fighter Ace*. London: Grub Street, 2004.

Hardesty, Von, and Ilya Grinberg. *Red Phoenix Rising: The Soviet Air Force in World War II*. Lawrence: University Press of Kansas, 2012.

Harrison, Gordon. *Cross Channel Attack*. After Action Report. Washington, D.C.: Department of the Army, 1951.

Harrison, Mark, ed. *The Economics of World War II: Six Great Powers in International Comparison*. Cambridge: Cambridge University Press, 1998.

Hart, Peter. *Aces Falling*. London: Orion Books Ltd., 2007.

———. *Bloody April*. London: Cassell, 2005.

Hastings, Max. *Armageddon: The Battle for Germany, 1944–1945*. London: Pan, 2005.

———. *The Korean War*. New York: Simon & Schuster, 1987.

Hata, I., Y. Izawa, and C. Shores. *Japanese Army Fighter Aces*. London: Grub Street, 2002.

Hata, Ikuhiko, and Yasuho Izawa. *Japanese Naval Aces and Fighter Units in World War II*. Annapolis: Naval Institute Press, 1975.

Hay, William. *Cheerful Sacrifice*. J. Nicholls. n.d., 92.

Heaton, Colin D., and Anne-Marie Lewis. *The Star of Africa*. Minneapolis: Zenith, 2012.

Henshaw, Trevor. *The Sky Their Battlefield*. London: Grub Street, 1995.

Herlin, Hans. *Udet: A Man's Life*. Hamburg: Macdonald & Co. Ltd., 1958.
Herris, Jack, and Bob Pearson. *Aircraft of World War I, 1914–1918*. London: Amber Books, 2010.
Higham, Charles. *Trading with the Enemy*. New York: Barnes & Noble, 1983.
Higham, Robin, and Carol Williams. *Flying Combat Aircraft of USAAF-USAF (Vol. 2)*. Manhattan: Sunflower University Press, 1978.
Higham, Robin, John Greenwood, and Von Hardesty. *Russian Aviation and Airpower in the Twentieth Century*. London: Frank Cass, 1998.
Historian, USAF. "Development of Airborne Armament 1910–1961." Historical. Vol. III, Fighter Fire Control.
Hoeppner, General Ernest Von. *Germany's War in the Air*. Nashville: Battery Press, 1921.
Holland, James. *The Battle of Britain*. New York: St. Martin's Press, 2010.
Holmes, Tony. "Saga of Billy Fiske: Part One." *Air Classics* 39 (2003).
———. "Saga of Billy Fiske: Part Two." *Air Classics* 40 (2004).
———. *Spitfire vs Bf-109: Battle of Britain*. Oxford: Osprey Publishing, 2007.
Hubbers, Reinout. *De Fliegende Huzaar*. 2007.
Hynes, Samuel. *Flights of Passage*. Annapolis: Naval Institute Press, 1988.
Jackson, Robert. *Fighter Pilots of World War I*. New York: St. Martin's Press, 1977.
———. *Fighter Pilots of World War II*. New York: Barnes & Noble, 1976.
Jane's. *Jane's Fighting Aircraft of World War I*. New York: Military Press, 1990.
Jefford, C. G. *The Flying Camels; History of No. 45 Squadron*. London: Privately published, 1995.
Jerez-Faran, C., and S. Amago. *Unearthing Franco's Legacy*. South Bend: University of Notre Dame Press, 2010.
Johnson, J. E., Air Vice Marshal. *Full Circle—The Story of Air Fighting*. London: Cassell Military Paperbacks, 1964.
Johnston, Mark. *Fighting the Enemy: Australian Soldiers and Their Adversaries in World War II*. Cambridge: Cambridge University Press, 2000.
Kaplan, Philip. *Fighter Aces of the Luftwaffe in World War II*. Auldgirth: Pen & Sword Aviation, 2007.
Karnow, Stanley. *Vietnam: A History*. New York: Penguin Group, 1983.
Karolevitz, R. F., and R. S. Fenn. *Flight of Eagles: The Story of the American Kosciuszko Squadron*. Sioux Falls: Brevet Press, Inc., 1974.
Katz, Samuel M. *Israel's Air Force*. Osceola: Motorbooks International, 1991.
Keegan, John. *The Second World War*. New York: Penguin, 1989.
———. *Six Armies in Normandy*. New York: Penguin Books, 1982.
Keeney, D. *The War Against the Luftwaffe, 1943–1944*. Campbell: FastPencil, Inc., 2011.
Kennett, Lee. *The First Air War 1914–1918*. New York: Macmillan, 1991.
Kilduff, Peter. *Douglas A-4 Skyhawk*. London: Osprey Publishing, 1983.
King, Dan. *The Last Zero Fighter*. Irvine: Pacific Press, 2012.
King, O. H. P. "Air Force Probe Is Ordered After Major Davis Shot Down In Korea." *Lubbock Avalanche-Journal,* February 12, 1952.
Kitchen, Martin. *The German Officer Corps 1890–1914*. Oxford: Clarendon Press, 1968.

Kitchens, James H. III and John R. Beaman. *Hans-Joachim Marseille: The Luftwaffe Ritterkreuztager, 1939–1945*. East Sussex: AirPower Editions, 2007.

"Klusmann Report." *Homecoming II Project*. POW Network, May 15, 1990.

Knott, Richard C. *A Heritage of Wings: An Illustrated History of Navy Aviation*. Annapolis: Naval Institute Press, 1997.

Kopp, Dr. Carlo. "SNR-75M3 Fan Song E Engagement Radar." March 29, 2013. http://www.ausairpower.net. Technical Report APA-TR-2009–0702-A. July 2013.

Korda, Michael. *With Wings Like Eagles*. New York: HarperCollins, 2009.

Krylov, L., and Y. Tepsurkaev. *Soviet MiG-15 Aces of the Korean War*. Oxford: Osprey Publishing, 2008.

Kurowski, Franz. *German Fighter Ace: Hans-Joachim Marseille: Star of Africa*. Atglen: Schiffer Military History, 1994.

Laffin, Jon. *British VCs of World War 2: A Study in Heroism*. Stroud: Budding Books, 1997.

Lamb, Allen. *The First Wild Weasels*. September 9, 2013.

Lanza, Colonel Conrad H. "Perimeters in Paragraphs: The Axis Invades Egypt." *Field Artillery Journal* (1942).

Latham, Colin, and Anne Stobbs. *Pioneers of Radar*. Tharp: Sutton Publishing Ltd., 1999.

Lewis, Cecil. *Sagittarius Rising*. London: Greenhill Books, 1936.

Libby, Frederick. *Horses Don't Fly*. New York: Arcade Publishing, 2012.

Linder, Rear Admiral James B., USN, and Dr. A. James Gregor. "The Chinese Communist Air Force in the Punitive War Against Vietnam." 1981. http://www.airpower.maxwell.af.mil/airchronicles. July 5, 2013.

Longstreet, Stephen. *The Canvas Falcons*. New York: Barnes & Noble, 1970.

Lucas, Laddie, ed. *Wings of War: Airmen of All Nations Tell Their Stories*. London: Hutchinson, 1983.

Lumsden, Alec. *British Piston Engines and Their Aircraft*. Marlborough: Airlife, 2003.

Lund, Lt. Colonel Earle, USAF. "The Battle of Britain: A German Perspective." Campaign Analysis Study. 1996.

Macklin, Graham D. "Major Hugh Pollard, MI6, and the Spanish Civil War." *Historical Journal* (2006): 277–80.

MacMillan, Margaret. *Paris 1919: Six Months That Changed The World*. New York: Random House, 2001.

Makos, Adam. *A Higher Call*. New York: Penguin, 2012.

Manning, Thomas A. *History of Air Education and Training Command, 1942–2002*. San Antonio: Office of History and Research, 2005.

Marshall, Chester. *Warbird History: B-29 Superfortress*. Osceola: Motorbooks International, 1993.

Maurer, M. *Air Force Combat Units of World War II*. Washington, D.C.: Office of Air Force History, 1983.

———. *Combat Squadrons of the Air Force, World War II*. Washington, D.C.: Office of Air Force History, 1982.

McCarthy, Brig. Gen. James R., and Lt. Col. George B. Allison. Montgomery: *Linebacker II: A View from the Rock*. Air University Press, 1979.

McCudden, James T. B. Major. *Flying Fury: Five Years in the Royal Flying Corps*. Havertown: Casemate, 2009.

McCutcheon, Kimble D. "Aero Engines." n.d. http://www.pilotfriend.com. January 2013.

McNab, Chris. *Hitler's Eagles: The Luftwaffe 1933–45*. Oxford: Osprey Publishing, 2012.

Meyer, G. W. *A World Undone: The Story of the Great War 1914 to 1918*. New York: Random House, 2006.

Mindell, David A. *Between Human and Machine: Feedback, Control and Computing Before Cybernetics*. Baltimore: Johns Hopkins University Press, 2002.

Ministry of Munitions. "Handbook of 'C.C.' Interrupter Gear, SECRET." *Production, Department of Aircraft*. March 1918.

Mitcham, Samuel W. *Rommel's Desert War: The Life and Death of the Afrika Korps*. Mechanicsburg: Stackpole Books, 1982.

Molesworth, Carl. *P-40 Warhawk vs Bf-109*. Oxford: Osprey Publishing, 2011.

Momyer, General William W. *Air Power in Three Wars*. Washington, D.C.: Department of the Air Force, 1978.

Moore, J. *The Wrong Stuff*. Stillwater: Voyageur Press, 1997.

Murray, W. *Strategy for Defeat: The Luftwaffe 1935–1945*. Honolulu: University Press of the Pacific, 2002.

Myles, Bruce. *Night Witches: The Amazing Story of Russia's Women Pilots in World War II*. Chicago: Academy Chicago Publishers, 1997.

Nagel, F. *Fritz: The World War I Memoirs of a German Lieutenant*. Huntington: Dre Angriff Publications, 1981.

Naval History and Heritage Command, "Logistics and Support Activities, 1950–53." n.d. http://www.history.navy.mil. August 2013.

Neil, Gregor. *Daimler-Benz in the Third Reich*. New Haven: Yale University Press, 1998.

Nelson, Craig. *The First Heroes: The Extraordinary Story of the Doolittle Raid—America's First World War II Victory*. London: Penguin Press, 2002.

Newman, Rick, and Don Shepperd. *Bury Us Upside Down*. New York: Random House Publishing Group, 2007.

Nimitz, Chester, and E. B. Potter. *Sea Power*. New York: Prentice Hall, 1960.

Nordhoff, Charles, and James Norman Hall. *Falcons of France*. Read Books Design, 2011.

Northrop Grumman Defensive Systems Division. "The Radar Warning Story." n.d.

Norton, Bill. *Air War on the Edge: A History of the Israel Air Force Since 1948*. Hinckley: Midland Pub. Ltd., 2002.

Obermaier, E., and W. Held. *Jagdflieger Oberst Werner Molders*. Stuttgart: Motorbuch Verlag, 1996.

O'Connell, Dan. *Messerschmitt Me 262: The Production Log 1941–1945*. Hersham: Classic Publications, 2006.

O'Connell, Major William J., USMC. "Marine GCI: Past, Present and Future." 1988. http://www.globalsecurity.org. June 20, 2013.

Olds, Christina, and Ed Rasimus. *Fighter Pilot*. New York: St. Martin's Press, 2010.

Oliver, W. E., and D. L. Lorenz. *The Inner Seven*. Paducah: Turner Publishing, 1999.

Parshall, J., and A. Tully. *Shattered Sword: The Untold Story of the Battle of Midway*. Dulles: Potomac Books, 2005.

Peczkowski, Robert. *North American P-51D Mustang*. Krakow: Stratus, 2009.

Pennington, Reina. *Wings, Women, and War: Soviet Airwomen in World War II Combat*. Lawrence: University Press of Kansas, 2007.

Plunkett, W. Howard. "Part II: Combat Lancer and Commando Club." n.d. http://www.thefreelibrary.com. July 9, 2013.

Postan, M. M. *History of the Second World War—British War Production*. London: H.M. Stationer's Office, 1952.

Potter, Lt. Colonel Joseph. "A Handful of Pilots." *Journal of the American Aviation Historical Society* (1982): 282–85.

Prados, John. "The '65 Decision: Bombing Soviet SAM Sites in North Vietnam." January/February 2006. http://www.vva.org. August 2013.

———. *Vietnam*. Lawrence: University Press of Kansas, 2009.

Price, Alfred. *The Last Year of the Luftwaffe: May 1944–May 1945*. London: Greenhill Books, 1993.

Prien, Jochen. *Jagdgeschwader 53: A History of the "Pik As". March 1937–May 1942*. Atglen: Schiffer Military History, 1997.

Rakobolskaya, I. V., and N. F. Kracova. *We Were Called the Night Witches*. Moscow: MGU. Izdatelstvo, 2005.

Rasimus, Ed. *When Thunder Rolled*. New York: Random House, 2003.

Reda, Helmut H. *Because I Fly*. New York: McGraw-Hill, 2002.

Rew, William Lt. General, USAF (ret). *Gulf War Air Operations*. July 2013.

Rikhye, Ravi. May 28, 2003. *Task Force 77: U.S. Navy Fleet Carriers in the Korean War 1950–1953, an Overview*. http://orbat.com. July 2013.

Rimell, Raymond Laurence. *The Royal Flying Corps in World War One*. London: Arms & Armour Press, 1985.

Rippon, Manuel. *The Essential Characteristics of Aviators*. London: Lancet, 1918.

Risner, General Robinson. *The Passing of the Night*. Old Saybrook: Konecky & Konecky, 1973.

"Robert Smith-Barry." Editorial. *Flight*, May 5, 1949.

Roberts, E. M. *A Flying Fighter*. Leonaur, 2012.

Robertson, Bruce. *Sopwith: The Man and His Aircraft*. Letchworth: Air Review, 1970.

Robinson, Anthony. *Flying the World's Great Aircraft*. London: Orbis Publishing, 1979.

Rock, Ed. *First In, Last Out: Stories by the Wild Weasels*. AuthorHouse, 2005.

———. "Korean War Fighter Pilots." August 7, 2013.

———. "Training a Fighter Pilot in the 1950s." August 8, 2013. Interview.

———. "Vietnam SAM engagement, Dec. 1965." August 8, 2013. Interview.

———. "Vietnam Wild Weasels." August 8, 2013.
Rommel, Erwin, and John Pimlott. *Rommel: In His Own Words.* London: Greenhill Books, 1994.
Rosenberg, B., and C. Macaulay. *Mavericks of the Sky.* New York: HarperCollins, 2006.
Rossano, Geoffrey. *Hero of the Angry Sky.* Athens: Ohio University Press, 2013.
Rottman, G. L. *US Marine Corps Pacific Theater of Operations.* London: Osprey Publishing, 2004.
Sakaida, H. *Aces of the Rising Sun, 1937–1945.* London: Osprey Publishing, 2002.
Sassaman, Richard. "Pilots with Stripes." *Americans in WWII: The Magazine of a People at War* 7, No. 2 (2011).
Schnitzer, George. *Panthers over Korea.* Baltimore: Publish America, 2007.
Schroer, Werner. Interview. 1984.
Schuck, Walter. *Luftwaffe Eagle.* Aachen: Helios, 2007.
Seeger, Eric H. *A Century of Manned Powered Flight.* Tampa: Faircount LLC, 2003.
"Selected Equipment Loss Statistics World War II (1937–1945)." n.d. http://www.taphilo.com/history/WWII/Loss-Figures-WWII. May 30, 2013.
Shaw, Albert. "The Lafayette Flying Corps." *The American Review of Reviews; An International Magazine,* July–December 1917, p.192.
Shaw, Robert L. *Fighter Combat: Tactics and Maneuvering.* Annapolis: Naval Institute Press, 1985.
Shepperd, Major General Don, USAF (ret). *Vietnam.* August 6, 2013.
Sherrod, Robert. *History of Marine Corps Aviation in World War II.* Washington, D.C.: Combat Forces Press, 1952.
Shore, Moyers S. *The Battle for Khe Sanh.* Military Bookshop, 2012.
Short, Lt. General Walter C., USAAF. *Pearl Harbor Attack, Part 39.* Military After Action Report. Washington, D.C.: USAAF, 1942.
Shoupe, Dale. F-4G—F16 Hunter Killer pair notes. August 30, 2013. Interview.
Sims, Buddy. *Vietnam FAC and Close Air Support.* May 2013.
Sims, Edward H. *The Fighter Pilots.* London: Cassell & Co. Ltd., 1967.
607th AC&W Squadron, Korea, "Tadpoles." http://www.607acw.org/tadpoles.html. n.d. August 15, 2013.
Smith, Colin. *England's Last War Against France: Fighting Vichy 1940–1942.* London: Orion, 2009.
Smith, R. K., and R. C. Hall. *Five Down, No Glory: Frank G. Tinker, Mercenary Ace in the Spanish Civil War.* Annapolis: Naval Institute Press, 2011.
Sparks, Billy R. *Takhli Tales.* CreateSpace, 2013.
Spick, Mike. *The Ace Factor.* Annapolis: Naval Institue Press, 1988.
Steinhilper, U., and P. Osborne. *Spitfire on My Tail.* Keston, Bromely: Independent books, 1990.
Stepanov, Evgeny. Interview. *Aviation History Magazine.* n.d.
Steven, Lt. Colonel G. R. *The Fourth Indian Division.* London: Naval & Military Press Ltd, 2011.
Stevenson, William. *A Man Called Intrepid.* Guilford: Globe Pequot Press, 1976.

Stille, Mark. *USN Carriers vs IJN Carriers: The Pacific 1942*. New York: Osprey Publishing, 2007.

Stimson, G. W. *Introduction to Airborne Radar*. El Segundo: Hughes Aircraft Co., 1983.

Stokesbury, James. *A Short History of the Korean War*. New York: Harper Perennial, 1990.

"The Story of World War 1 Aviation." n.d. http://www.wwiaviation.com/. November–December 2012.

Sturtivant, Ray, and John Hamlin. *RAF Flying Training and Support Units*. London: Air-Britain, 2007.

Swanborough, Gordon, and Peter M. Bowers. *United States Navy Aircraft Since 1911*. Annapolis: Naval Institute Press, 1990.

Tassava, Christopher J. "The American Economy during World War II." 2010.

Taylor, Jay. *The Generalissimo: Chiang Kai-Shek and the Struggle for Modern China*. Cambridge: Belknap Press, 2009.

Taylor, Ken, interview. "47th Pursuit Squadron." December 4, 1986.

Taylor, Ken, interview. "December 7th, 1941." Chris Conybeare and Daniel Martinez. December 4, 1986.

Taylor, Stewart K. "Just Watch Me." *Over the Front* 27 (2012): 44–71.

Thomas, Andrew, and Warren Thompson. *American Nightfighter Aces of World War 2*. Oxford: Osprey Publishing, 2008.

Tillman, Barrett. *Above and Beyond: The Aviation Medals of Honor*. Washington, D.C.: Smithsonian Institution, 2002.

Tine, Major Gregory C. "Berlin Airlift: Logistics, Humanitarian Aid and Strategic Success." n.d.

Toll, Ian. *Pacific Crucible, War in the Pacific, 1941–1942*. New York: W. W. Norton & Co., 2012.

Townsend, Peter. *Duel of Eagles*. London: Cassell Publishers Ltd., 1970.

Treadwell, T. C., and A. C. Wood. *German Knights of the Air, 1914–1918*. New York: Barnes & Noble, 1998.

"Up From Kitty Hawk." *Air Force Magazine*. 1903–Present. http://www.airforcemag.com. January–May 2013.

USAAF. "K-14 Gyroscopic Gunsight." *Pilot Training Manual for the Thunderbolt P-47N*. Headquarters, Army Air Forces, September 1945.

Van Creveld, Martin. *The Age of Airpower*. New York: PublicAffairs, 2011.

Velocci, Anthony L., Jr. "Naval Aviation: 100 Years Strong." *Aviation Week and Space Technology*, April 4, 2011, pp. 56–80.

Vines, Mike. *Wind in the Wires*. Osceola: Motorbooks International, 1995.

Von Hoeppner, Ernest General. *Germany's War in the Air*. Nashville: Battery Press, 1921.

Werner, Johannes Professor. *Knight of Germany*. Havertown: Casemate, 2009.

Werrell, Kenneth P. *Archie to SAM: A Short Operational History of Ground Based Air-Defense*. Montgomery: Air University Press, 2005.

———. *Sabres over MiG Alley*. Annapolis: Naval Institute Press, 2005.

White, Rowland. *The Big Book of Flight*. London: Bantam Press, 2013.

Whitehouse, Arch. *Decisive Air Battles of the First World War*. New York: Meredith Press, 1963.

Wiest, Andrew. *Rolling Thunder in a Gentle Land: The Vietnam War Revisted.* London: Osprey Publishing, 2006.

Williamson, Gordon. *Knight's Cross with Diamonds Recipients 1941–45.* London: Osprey Publishing, 2006.

Willmott, H. P. *World War I.* London: DK Publishing, 2009.

Wise, S. F. *Canadian Airmen and the First World War: The Official History of the Royal Canadian Air Force.* Toronto: University of Toronto Press, 1980.

Withington, Thomas. *Wild Weasel Fighter Attack.* Barnsley: Pen & Sword, 2008.

Wood, D., and D. Dempster. *The Narrow Margin: The Battle of Britain and the Rise of Air Power.* Washington, D.C.: Smithsonian Institution Press, 1990.

"World Carrier Lists." n.d. http://www.hazegray.org/navhist/carriers/. June 5, 2013.

Wright, Peter. "From Scraps to Scrap." *Aeromilitaria,* December 2010.

Wubbe, Walter. *Hauptmann Hans Joachim Marseille Ein Jagdfligerschicksal in Daten, Bildern und Dokumenten.* Schnellbach: Verlag Siegfried Bublies, 2001.

Yenne, Bill. *Aces High.* New York: Berkley Publishing Group, 2009.

———. *The American Aircraft Factory in WWII.* Minneapolis: Zenith, 2006.

———. *The White Rose of Stalingrad.* n.d.

NOTES

PROLOGUE

A detailed account of Roland Garros and his machine gun is found in Arch Whitehouse's *Decisive Air Battles of the First World War* (New York: Meredith Press, 1963). Records of Great War dogfights were usually fairly sketchy and the best references are either personal diaries or, when available, combat reports, though the latter tend toward extreme brevity. My account of his dogfight, and the specific workings of the Hotchkiss gun, was a compilation of all available sources in addition to the information provided in Trevor Howard's excellent book, *The Sky Their Battlefield* (Grub Street, 1995), pp. 31–32.

F. W. Bailey and Christopher Cony's compilation *The French Air Service War Chronology 1914–1918* (Grub Street, 2001) contains every known and documented engagement by French aircraft during the war. Due to the paucity of accurate information from the early years of combat aviation I cross-checked battles, facts, and personal information from as many sources as possible.

Will Boucher's superb website, An Illustrated History of WWI (www.wwiaviation.com), provides well-written summaries and excellent color line drawings of every combatant aircraft used by all sides in the conflict.

CHAPTER ONE

I found the origins of World War I fascinating. Viewed through modern eyes it is an extremely complicated, yet vital part of our history as a bridge between the old and new worlds, the fall and rise of empires, and the birthplace of modern technology. See H. P. Willmott's *World War I* (DK Publishing, 2003) and chapter 4 of G. W. Meyer's *A World Undone* (Bantam Dell, 2006) for very readable accounts of the backgrounds, causes, and opening moves of this complex conflict.

Lee Kennett's *The First Air War: 1914–1918* (Simon & Schuster, 1991), pp. 24–40, traces the early period when aircraft take over scouting from the cavalry and the military potential of the aircraft is first seriously considered. I particularly liked this book as he logically discusses details of World War I aircraft, their evolution into warplanes, and the men who flew them.

Stephen Longstreet does much the same in *The Canvas Falcons: The Men and Planes of WWI* (Barnes & Noble: 1970). Chapter 3 is especially relevant in revealing the early days of the war, each side's reactions, and how the ground situation created the air war.

Arch Whitehouse's *Decisive Air Battles of the First World War* (Meredith Press, 1963), pp. 41–43, also describes the new aluminum link system, which replaced canvas ammo belts.

In the spring of 1915 Anthony Fokker built his Eindecker, armed with a Parabellum machine gun. This was detailed in Trevor Howard's *The Sky Their Battlefield* (Grub Street, 1995), p. 33. The interrupter gear, which permitted the firing of bullets through the propeller arc, was the first true technological advance that fundamentally changed aircraft into warplanes. I found the original *Handbook of "C.C." Interrupter Gear, SECRET* (Ministry of Munitions, Department of Aircraft Production, March 1918). This permitted men like Oswald Boelke to quantify, direct, and lead the first true fighter pilots. His story is told in *Knight of Germany,* by Professor Johannes Werner (Casemate, 2009).

CHAPTER TWO

One of the more interesting avenues I researched concerned the men who became fighter pilots. I was fortunate enough to find several very good, albeit slightly obscure, sources on the subject. These included Robert Jackson's *Fighter Pilots of World War I* (St. Martin's Press, 1997) and Martin Kitchen's *The German Officer Corps, 1890–1914* (Oxford University Press, 1998). Both provided insight not only into training, but the relative social backgrounds of specific pilots. An excellent article by James A. Shaw titled "Officer and Gentlemen: Gentlemanly Mystique and Military Effectiveness in the Nineteenth Century British Army," provided some spectacular insights.

Rippon and Manuel's *The Essential Characteristics of Aviators* (Lancet, 1918), was an amazing find, as it contained the first known medically sponsored survey of men who flew.

J. Herris and B. Pearson, *Aircraft of World War I* (Amber Books, 2010), along with F. Hugh W. Cowin, *Allied Aviation of World War I* (Osprey Publishing, 2000), provided very good technical data on the early Avros, Nieuports, and Fokkers.

Another surprising discovery was the Vintage Aero Museum in Fort Lupton, Colorado. Mr. Andy Hall was kind enough to donate time, historical material, and expertise—including Leutnant Josef Jacob's Blue Max and his actual wartime logbooks.

Richard P. Hallion's *Rise of Fighter Aircraft 1914–1918* (Nautical & Aviation Publishing, 1984) and Jon Guttman's *The Origin of Fighter Aircraft,* (Westholme Publishing, 2009) were invaluable guides to the minute, yet often significant, aerodynamic and weapons advances made in the turbulent months of 1916.

Germany's War in the Air: The Development and Operations of German Military Aviation in the World War (Battery Press, 1921) by General Ernest von Hoeppner, is an authoritative look at German pilot selection, training, development, and operations.

CHAPTER THREE

H. P. Willmott's *World War I* (DK Publishing, 2003), pp. 154–55, describes living conditions in the trenches and how the front lines were built. G. W. Meyer's *A World Undone* (Bantam Dell, 2006) goes into considerable detail about German fortifications.

Aviators usually live a bit differently, simply because they have to remain near their aircraft. Both Werner's *Knight of Germany*, pp. 121–22, and Longstreet's *The Canvas Falcons*, p. 13, provide good descriptions of aerodrome life, food, and personnel sketches.

Frederick Libby, *Horses Don't Fly* (Arcade Publishing, 2000), and Francis Conover Church, *Diary of a World War I Pilot* (Conover-Patterson Publishers, 2004), reveal the personal thoughts of the young men flying and fighting through their letters and diaries. As Libby states, "Girls weren't expensive. . . . what more could a fellow ask?"

This chapter also explores and illustrates some of the changes that had taken place in formal flight training between 1914 and 1917. This was important not only as a sign that aviation was growing up, but also as a basis for the next seven decades of air combat. Kennett's *The First Air War*, pp. 119–30, and particularly Conover's *Diary*, pp. 200–205, were very helpful in telling it like it was.

Other necessary background includes some very basic aerodynamic principles and a limited discussion of engines, fuels, and how weapons are used in the air. Jane's *Fighting Aircraft of World War I* (Military Press, 1990) and John D. Anderson's superb *History of Aerodynamics* (Cambridge: Cambridge University Press, 1997) contain a great deal of supplementary information, as does Alec Lumsden's *British Piston Engines and Their Aircraft* (Marlborough, Wiltshire: Airlife Publishing, 2003).

Evolution of aiming systems and description of the gate, ring and bead, and Aldis gunsights can be found in Wallace Clarke's *British Aircraft Armament Vol 2: Guns and Gunsights* (Haynes Publications, 1995).

Whenever applicable, I felt that direct quotes from the pilots themselves were highly valuable. Among the very good sources for these are C. G. Jefford's *The Flying Camels: The History of No. 45 Squadron* (Privately published, 1995), p. 25. See also the accounts of Major James McCudden, VC, *Flying Fury* (Casemate, 2009).

Spring of 1917 saw the pace of the air war build toward a crescendo; many new designs were fielded that incorporated the lessons learned the previous years. Tommy Sopwith led the way here, and Bruce Robertson's *Sopwith: The Man and His Aircraft* (Air Review, 1970) describes not only the man but the manufacturing.

Jasta Pilots (London: Grub Street, 1996) by Norman Franks and Frank Bailey is one of many sources I used for a look at the "other side." To me, it is essential in any historical text to view the situation or conflict from as many sides as possible. Among others are Barry Diggens's *September Evening: The Life and Final Combat of the German Ace Werner Voss* (Grub Street, 2003), E. D. Crundall's *Fighter Pilot on the Western Front* (William Kimber, 1975), pp. 56–64, and Floyd Gibbons's *Red Knight of Germany* (Doubleday, Page & Co., 1927).

As always, the personal stories concerning pilots on both sides reveal much of who they really were. Descriptions of Mick Mannock and Albert Ball in Robert Jackson's *Fighter Pilots of World War I* (St. Martin's Press, 1997) were very helpful, as was *Above the Lines: The Aces and Fighter Units of the German Air Service, Naval Air Service and Flanders Marine Corps, 1914–1918* (Grub Street, 1993) by Norman Franks, Frank W. Bailey, and Russell Guest.

Bloody April (Orion Books, 2005) by Peter Hart is a magnificently detailed description of the men, machines, weapons, and politics of this crucial stage in the war. Particularly intriguing are the accounts of Albert Ball, pp. 333–44.

CHAPTER FOUR

Comments about Robert Smith-Barry and details concerning his training methods can be found in Vincent Orange's "Robert Raymond Smith-Barry (1886–1949)" in the *Oxford Dictionary of National Biography* (Oxford University Press, 2004).

The events of Werner Voss's death are well recorded by James McCudden in his own *Fighting Fury*, pp. 198–201, Howard's *The Sky Their Battlefield*, p. 230, and *Fighter Pilots of World War I*, pp. 31–38.

Norman Franks, Frank W. Bailey and Russell Guest compiled a splendid collection that I utilized throughout the first section of this book. See their *Over the Front: A Complete Record of the Fighter Aces and Units of the United States and French Air Services, 1914–1918* (Grub Street, 1992).

Mr. Andy Hall of the Vintage Aero Museum has a wealth of knowledge, much of it from his own family, concerning the Lafayette Escadrille. Multiple interviews and visits were conducted in February 2013.

An extensive reference is *The Lafayette Flying Corps* (Atglen: Schiffer Publishing, 2000) by Dennis Gordon. Recommended reading are pp. 25–32, concerning wartime Paris, and pp. 368–72, which sketch the life of Norman Prince.

A few of Raymond Collishaw's "Black Flight" adventures with Sopwith Triplanes are chronicled in *Decisive Air Battles*, pp. 300–304, *The Sky Their Battlefield*, pp. 191–206, and Roger Gunn's *Raymond Collishaw and the Black Flight* (Dundurn, 2013).

For an excellent summary of the war's toll by early 1918 read chapter 1, pp. 8–20, of Peter Hart's *Aces Falling* (Orion Books Ltd., 2007).

The death of Manfred von Richthofen has been a century-long enigma. Very good details of the circumstances, as far as they are known, can be found in Gibbon's *Red Knight of Germany*, pp. 353–60, and Hart's *Aces Falling*, pp. 166–70. My own conclusions are described in chapter 4 and take into account all of these, plus my own experience as a fighter pilot and—most importantly—the Beavis Letter. This was originally a letter to the editor of the *Army Quarterly* (British) in 1931. Courtesy of Andy Hall, I've examined the actual document, which resides in the Vintage Aero Museum.

CHAPTER FIVE

Willmott's *World War I,* pp. 252–58, describes final German offensives as they try to end the war prior to large-scale American involvement, as does all of Part Six of Meyer's *A World Undone.*

Accounts of the deaths of many of the great aces can be read in Terry C. Treadwell and Alan C. Wood's *German Knights of the Air, 1914–1918* (Brasseys, 1997), Franks, Bailey, and Guest's *Above the Lines,* and Shores, Franks, and Guest's *Above the Trenches.* As always, Peter Hart's unique perspectives are well worth reading in *Aces Falling,* pp. 200–204.

Major Billy Barker's astounding final dogfight is described in several sources, among them Howard's *The Sky Their Battlefield,* pp. 444, and Jackson's *Fighter Pilots of World War One,* pp. 82–90.

Germany in 1918 is poignantly illustrated in Willmott's *World War I,* p. 285.

CHAPTER SIX

As President Woodrow Wilson remarked, ". . . it is finished, and, as no one is satisfied, it makes me hope we have made a just peace; but it is all in the lap of the gods." The final chapter of Meyer's *The Great War,* pp. 705–715, gives a solid understanding of the post-1918 world, as does the first two chapters of *Paris 1919: Six Months That Changed The World* (Random House, 2001) by Magaret MacMillan.

A truly seminal event, the Polish-Soviet war of 1919–21, had lasting, if largely unappreciated, results for Western Europe. See Jerzy B. Cynk's *History of the Polish Air Force 1918–1968* (Osprey Publishing Ltd., 1972) and the 1st edition of *Polish Aircraft 1893–1939* (Putnam & Company Ltd.). I also personally visited the Muzeum Narodowe (Polish National Museum) in Warsaw, as well as several of the battlefields to gain a better perspective on this period.

White Eagle, Red Star (MacDonald & Company, 1972), by Norman Davies, is irreplaceable for the serious historian of this conflict. Of particular note is chapter 2, "A Winter of Disillusionment," pp. 62–104.

Marion Aten and Arthur Orrmont's memoir, *Last Train Over Rostov Bridge* (Messner, 1961), is a jewel. Aten was a mercenary fighting for the White Russians and gives an invaluable, firsthand account of life, war, and flying.

"I was high-spirited, loved excitement, took chances and got caught too many times." Such was the self-assessment of a young American named Merian Cooper upon his resignation from the U.S. Naval Academy at Annapolis in 1915. *Flight of Eagles* (Brevet International, 1974), by Robert F. Karolevitz and Ross Fenn, reveals much of the Polish side of the conflict as well as the Kosciusko Squadron of American volunteers.

Feeling "no moral aloofness" about the war in Spain, another former American naval officer turned mercenary's story is related by Richard K. Smith and R. Cargill Hall in *Five Down, No Glory: Frank G. Tinker, Mercenary Ace in the Spanish Civil War* (Naval Institute Press, 2011). This book is also a highly readable source on the causes and results of the Spanish Civil War.

See Graham D. Macklin, "Major Hugh Pollard, MI6, and the Spanish Civil War." *Historical Journal* (2006): pp. 277–80.

See also Robert Forsyth's *Aces of the Legion Condor* (Oxford: Osprey, 2011).

The situation and Germany's involvement are well summarized on pp. 6–14, the Legion Condor organization between pp. 40–50, and Messerschmitt's progress with tactical lessons learned on pp. 51–84.

CHAPTER SEVEN

The Jericho-Trompete dive siren was initially an effective addition to the Stuka, especially in dealing with soldiers unused to technology. John Keegan's *The Second World War* (Penguin, 1989), pp. 11–50, gives a very compact, informative look at the starting conditions.

The Battle of Britain (St. Martin's Press, 2010) by James Holland provides a magnificent, multifaceted look at the politics, people, and aircraft in the initial stages of the war. See pp. 32–38 for some intriguing German details. Information on the the Battle for France can be found on pp. 52-69.

Voluminous writings exist covering aircraft development of the period. I would suggest Len Cacutt's *Great Aircraft of the World: Hawker Hurricane* (Marshall Cavendish, 1989), Walter Boyne and Philip Handleman's *Brassey's Air Combat Reader* (Batsford Brassey, Inc., 1999), and Douglas Bader's *Fight for the Sky: The Story of the Spitfire and Hurricane* (Cassell Military Books, 2004) as good places to start. Production and design notes for the Hurricane largely came from John W. Fozard's *Sydney Camm and the Hurricane: Perspectives on the Master Fighter Designer and his Finest Achievement* (Airlife, 1991).

Details about the French collapse and inner workings of their system can be found in Holland's *Battle of Britain,* pp. 67–68, 112–19, and p. 154.

German ace Hans-Ekkard Bob is a true lord of the sky. His book *Betrayed Ideals: Memoirs of a Luftwaffe Fighter Ace* (Cerberus Publishing Ltd., 2003) is a fascinating look into the war and a German fighter cockpit.

Once again I owe a debt to James Holland's *Battle of Britain* for the outline of Dunkirk, pp. 240–43 and 188–92).

CHAPTER EIGHT

As in the Great War, a detailed look into pilot background and training explains much about the conduct of air battles. My initial notes for the Luftwaffe came from *Hitler's Eagles: The Luftwaffe 1933–45* (Osprey Publishing, 2012) by Chris McNab. There is excellent information on the structure, selection processes, unit designations, and even uniforms on pp. 56–118.

Michael Korda's exceptional work, *With Wings Like Eagles* (New York: HarperCollins, 2009), similarly explains much of the origins, both political and technical, of the Royal Air Force and the Luftwaffe. I found the comparisons between the two organizations, pp. 60–66, particularly revealing.

Len Deighton's *Fighter* (Random House UK, 2000), pp. 61–85, has a very clear summary of the Hurricane, Spitfire, and Bf 109 in terms of development, engineering, and weapons. It's always interesting that so many valid solutions to the same problem (frontline fighter effectiveness) could be discovered by different designers.

For detailed looks at the German system see also *Jagdgeschwader 53 A History of the "Pik As" Geschwader March 1937– May 1942* (Schiffer Military

History, 1997) by Jochen Prien and Ulrich Steinhilper's *Spitfire on my Tail* (Independent Books, 1990).

Cockpit views of dogfighting and ground attacks are possible since I've been there—but for help with the World War II vintage aircraft, J. E. "Johnny" Johnson's *Full Circle: The Story of Air Fighting* (Cassell Military Paperbacks, 1964) was invaluable. Also, Norman Frank's *Sky Tiger: The Story of Sailor Malan* (William Kimber & Company, 1980), pp. 28–43, was very useful in cross checking switches, radio communications, and procedures.

The importance of radar cannot be overstated for either side during the Battle of Britain, as a disaster for the Luftwaffe and as salvation for the Royal Air Force. Korda's *With Wings Like Eagles,* pp. 31–42, and Holland's *Battle of Britain,* pp. 327–31, both contain descriptions of development and the Chain Home network, which was so effective. What I found very useful in Deighton's *Fighter,* pp. 84–101, were the comparisons between the German and British systems and details concerning how the British integrated Chain Home into their air defense system.

Max Aiken, Lord Beaverbrook, was, with Hugh Dowding, largely responsible for saving England in the spring of 1940. Both men's commitment to salvage, production, and putting wartime needs ahead of ego and politics kept aircraft available for the fight. Much of this is detailed in *History of the Second World War: British War Production* (HMSO, 1952) by M. M. Postan, and again in Holland's *Battle of Britain,* pp. 167–70 and 322–24.

Engine development on both sides is worth reading about in Matthew Freudenberg's *Negative Gravity: The Life of Beatrice Shilling* (Charlton Publications, 2003), Neil Gregor's *Daimler-Benz in the Third Reich* (Yale University Press, 1998), and Alec Lumsden's *British Piston Engines and Their Aircraft* (Airlife Publishing, 2003). Like most fighter pilots, I gave scant thought to how my aircraft systems came to be; I only wanted them to work as advertised. Learning a bit about everything that goes into putting a pilot in the right place at the right time was humbling.

CHAPTER NINE

Winston Groom's *1942: The Year That Tried Men's Souls* (Grove Press, 2005), pp. 1–16, is a very good introduction to the second year of the war, as is Keegan's *The Second World War,* pp. 127–220.

Hans Joachim Marseille, known as "Jochen" to his friends, is one of the most intriguing pilots of the war. *Star of Africa,* by Colin D. Heaton and Anne-Marie Lewis (Zenith, 2012), is the seminal work on his life and times. This is also a well-witten account of the North Africa campaign from the German point of view. See also Groom's *1942,* pp. 377–91.

Luftwaffe Eagle (Helios, 2007), pp. 16–18, discusses ongoing changes in the Luftwaffe.

Messerschmitt's continued improvement to the 109 fighter are accessible through several sources, though I found Carl Molesworth's *P-40 Warhawk vs Bf-109* (Osprey Publishing, 2011) and Tony Holmes's *Spitfire vs Bf-109: Battle of Britain* (Osprey Publishing, 2007) to be among the best.

For a good look at the Soviet Union, see *The Black Book of Communism:*

Crimes, Terror, Repression (Harvard University Press, 1999) by Stephanie Courtois. See also Keegan's *The Second World War,* pp. 450–516.

See *Red Phoenix Rising: The Soviet Air Force in World War II* (University Press of Kansas, 2012) by Von Hardesty and Ilya Grinberg, pp. 5–20. This book provides extraordinary detail into a sparsely known area. Soviet records are notorious for being poorly kept and difficult to access, yet the authors managed admirably.

"I am completely absorbed by combat life. I can't seem to think of anything but the fighting." Hardly the sentiments associated with a normal young girl, but Lidiya Litvyak was anything but that. Bill Yenne's *The White Rose of Stalingrad* (Osprey Publishing, 2013) is a superb look at Soviet pilots and aircraft during the ugly days following the German invasion.

First-day losses are quoted from Hardesty and Grinberg, *Red Phoenix Rising,* pp. 9–12.

Figures and the situation in December 1941 are from Keegan's *The Second World War,* pp. 196–208. Also of considerable interest is the chapter on war production, which begins on p. 209.

Soviet technical information is found throughout the following books, but of particular note is *Red Phoenix Rising,* pp. 108–113 and 229–231, and pp. 173–75 from *The White Rose of Stalingrad.*

Dr. Janina Kazimiera Cottam's *The Golden Tressed Soldier* (Military Affairs/Aerospace Historian Publishing, 1983) is another excellent source of information regarding Lilya Litvyak.

"Let's get the fighting over first, darling—then maybe we can talk about love, eh?" A great quote from Lilya that she used innumerable times to counter bad pickup attempts from her male contemporaries. See *The White Rose of Stalingrad,* p. 179.

An excellent firsthand source for German training, squadron life, and the war after the invasion of Russia is *Luftwaffe Fighter Ace* (Grub Street, 2004) by Norbert Hannig. The book doesn't begin its examination of the military until 1941, and makes a very good comparison to the earlier programs and war prior to Hitler's great mistake. Of special note is the "Conduct in War of the German Soldier," p. 186.

Edward H. Sims, *The Fighter Pilots* (Cassell, 1967), pp. 123–30.

CHAPTER TEN

The opening attack on Pearl Harbor was largely extrapolated from the transcript of an oral interview of Ken Taylor on December 4, 1986 (Chris Conybeare and Daniel Martinez).

Background for the events leading up to Pearl Harbor were largely taken from Keegan's *The Second World War,* pp. 251–90, and John Costello's *The Pacific War: 1941–1945* (HarperCollins, 1981).

P-40 Warhawk specifications were generally taken from Molesworth's *P-40 Warhawk,* pp. 10–16 and 23–27.

Information for pilot selection and training was taken largely from Richard Sassaman's "Pilots With Stripes," *America in WWII,* August 2011, Wesley Frank Craven and James Lea Cate's *The Army Air Forces in World War II, Volume Six: Men and Planes* (Office of Air Force History, 1983), and

"The Aviation Cadets," *Air Force Magazine,* November 1990, by Bruce D. Callendar. An invaluable source for Navy and Marine flyers was Roy Grossnick and William J. Armstrong's *United States Naval Aviation, 1919–1995* (Naval Historical Center, 1997).

Christina Olds and Ed Rasimus's *Fighter Pilot: The Memoirs of Legendary Ace Robin Olds* (St. Martin's Griffin, 2010) was instrumental in detailing USAAF training for West Point officers. See specifically pp. 7–11 and 18–23.

As always, the other point of view is vital in providing a complete picture, and Dan King's *The Last Zero Fighter* (Pacific Press, 2012) is replete with facts on Japanese pilot selection, training, and wartime perceptions. Kaname Harada's firsthand account, pp. 15–68, was particularly revealing, as he fought through the entire war—and survived.

See *The History of Marine Corps Aviation in World War II* (Combat Forces Press, 1952) by Robert Sherrod, pp. 39–40, for the Wake Island details.

See James H. Doolittle and Carroll V. Glines's *I Could Never Be So Lucky Again* (Bantam Books, 2001) for descriptions and details of the Doolittle Raid.

Battle of Midway references were drawn primarily from Mark Stille's *USN Carriers vs IJN Carriers: The Pacific 1942* (Osprey, 2007), Ian Toll's *Pacific Crucible, War in the Pacific* (W. W. Norton & Co., 2012), Douglas V. Smith's *Carrier Battles: Command Decision in Harm's Way* (U.S. Naval Institute Press, 2006), Robert Cressman's *That Gallant Ship: U.S.S. Yorktown (CV-5)* (Pictorial Histories Publishing Company, 1985), and Jonathan Parshall and Anthony Tully's *Shattered Sword: The Untold Story of the Battle of Midway* (Potomac Books, 2005).

CHAPTER ELEVEN

See Olds and Rasimus's *Fighter Pilot*, pp. 96–100, for much of the switches and cockpit layout. The combat mission description is expanded from the one mentioned on pp. 101–115.

The pinnacle of piston-engined fighter development, the Mustang changed the course of the air war. Robert Peczkowski's *North American P-51D Mustang* (Stratus, 2009) provided text from the pilot's manual and cockpit photographs of every lever, button, and switch.

See also Martin Bowman's *P-51 vs Fw 190: Europe 1943–45* (Osprey, 2007), pp. 8–14, for development and pp. 39–52 for combatants and tactics.

The early North American program, especially as it related to the RAF, is discussed in Martyn Chorlton's *Allison-Engined P-51 Mustang* (Oxford: Osprey, 2012), specifically pp. 4–36.

Squadrons and call signs are courtesy of Maurer's *Air Force Combat Units of World War Two* (1983) and *Combat Squadrons of the Air Force: World War Two* (1982), both published by the Albert F. Simpson Historical Research Center, Office of Air Force History, Headquarters United States Air Force.

See Keegan's *The Second World War*, pp. 425–33, for the European situation in 1944.

The ball bearing story is told best in Charles Higham's *Trading with the Enemy* (Barnes & Noble, 1983), pp. 118–22. It was a truly shameful commentary on war and business, and I was happy to have an opportunity to reveal it again.

Bill Yenne's informative *The American Aircraft Factory in WWII* (Zenith Press, 2006) is a good source for those curious about the support and manufacturing side of combat aircraft. Chapter 2, "Backing into World War II," pp. 28–47, was particularly interesting.

Keegan's *The Second World War* was used extensively for D-Day, pp. 369–95, and for the end of the war in the Pacific, pp. 561–95.

Statistics were primarily derived from *Army Battle Casualties and Nonbattle Deaths in World War II—Final Report* (Department of the Army, 1951) and the US Navy Bureau of Medicine and Surgery's *History of the Medical Department of the United States Navy in World War II: The Statistics of Diseases and Injuries,* vol. 3 (Government Printing Office, 1950).

CHAPTER TWELVE

Air Wars and Aircraft: A Detailed Record of Air Combat, 1945 to the Present (Facts on File, 1990) by Victor Flintham is a superb compilation of facts, figures, units, and photographs. The Korean War section is on pp. 219–44.

Major George Davis's dogfight ws derived from several sources, among them *The Inner Seven* (Turner Publishing, 1999) by William E. Oliver and Dwight L. Lorenz, pp. 25–35, and Paul Corrigan's *Last of the Aerial Gunfighters* (First Books, 2003). I had the flying scenes reviewed by several ex-Sabre pilots, including Colonel Ed Rock, USAF (ret).

Max Hastings's *The Korean War* (Simon & Schuster, 1987) is a splendid reference, specifically the "Origins of a Tragedy," pp. 23–45.

See *The Coldest Winter: America and the Korean War* (Hyperion, 2007) by David Halberstam, pp. 293–319 and 599–617, for a fascinating portrait of Douglas MacArthur.

General William W. Momyer's *Air Power in Three Wars* (Department of the Air Force, 1978) is quoted throughout the next three chapters. As he was intimately involved in each conflict, it's a very detailed, though somewhat dry, reference.

For further technical data on the combatants see D. C. Dildy and W. E. Thompson's *F-86 Sabre vs MiG-15* (Osprey Publishing, 2013) and L. Krylov and Y. Tepsurkaev's *Soviet MiG-15 Aces of the Korean War* (Osprey Publishing, 2008).

Kenneth Werrell's *Sabres over MiG Alley* (Naval Institute Press, 2005), pp. 3–44, is a wonderful source for development, maintenance issues, and armament. Also see his "Air War Overview," pp. 75–93.

CHAPTER THIRTEEN

As a former Wild Weasel, I'm fortunately well aware of how surface-to-air missiles operate. I'd also researched the Leopard Two shootdown for a previous book, *Viper Pilot* (HarperCollins, 2012).

Pulitzer Prize winner Stanley Karnow's *Vietnam: A History* (Penguin Group, 1983) is referenced throughout the description of this complex and emotional struggle. I found "The War with the French," pp. 139–75, extremely interesting in shedding light on a few of the roots of this conflict.

John Prados's *Vietnam* (University Press of Kansas, 2009) was often referenced, not only because of its style, but also as it covered the conflict from its origins in 1945 through the American withdrawal.

Rolling Thunder in a Gentle Land: The Vietnam War Revisited (Osprey Publishing, 2006) by Andrew Wiest, specifically chapter 11, "Swatting Flies with a Sledgehammer," pp. 191–206, describes some of the air war.

Personal interviews with men who fought the MiGs and SAMs are irreplaceable; among them were Steven Coonts, USN (September 6, 2013), Major William Good, USMC (August 25, 2013), Buddy Sims (September 9, 2013), Colonel Ed Rock, USAF, August 8th 2013, Colonel Jack Broughton, USAF (July 2013), and Major General Don Shepperd, USAF (August 6, 2013).

See Flintham's *Air Wars and Aircraft* section on Indo-China and the French involvement, pp. 253–65; pp. 265–310 supplied units, deployment dates, losses, and general information.

General William W. Momyer's *Air Power in Three Wars* was referenced for interdiction missions, pp. 163–242, and for details concerning the ground war, pp. 247–87. See also *Bury Us Upside Down* (Random House, 2007) by Don Shepperd and Rick Newman for a detailed and truthful look at the FAC/Misty mission.

Books written by several other true lords of the sky were well-referenced: *Fighter Pilot,* as previously mentioned, specifically pp. 247–70 for the F-4 Phantom and pp. 271–312 for Operations Bolo and Rolling Thunder; *Passing of the Night: My Seven Years as a Prisoner of the North Vietnamese* (Konecky & Konecky, 1973) by General Robby Risner—an American hero. See also Jack Broughton's *Going Downtown* (Pocket, 1990) and *Thud Ridge* (Crecy, 2006). Colonel Ed Rock's *First In, Last Out: Stories by the Wild Weasels* (AuthorHouse, 2005) is a wonderful anthology of personal accounts.

CHAPTER FOURTEEN

See Thomas Withington's *Wild Weasel Fighter Attack* (Pen & Sword, 2008), pp. 1–65.

Karnow's *Vietnam: A History,* pp. 582–628, and Wiest's *Rolling Thunder in a Gentle Land,* pp. 59–274, take a look at the conclusion of the Vietnam War.

Technical data was largely taken from personal interviews and also from Peter Davies, *F-4 Phantom II vs MiG-21* (Osprey Publishing, 2008), pp. 53–64, and *Republic F-105 Thunderchief* (Osprey Publishing, 2012), pp. 5–31.

See Shlomo Aloni's *Israeli A-4 Skyhawk Units in Combat* (Osprey Publishing, 2009), pp. 6–62, for an in-depth look at the Israeli Air Force. See also *Israeli Mirage and Nesher Aces* (Osprey Publishing, 2004), pp. 62–79.

A-4 cockpit switches and flying scene particulars were derived from *Flight Manual: A-4 Skyhawk,* Bureau of Naval Operations Handbook, and from interviews with Skyhawk pilot and Marine aviator Colonel Dan Hampton, USMC (ret).

Prado's *Vietnam* contains very readable conclusions about the war, pp. 488–550. Especially poignant is the commentary on how misunderstood Americans were by the South Vietnamese.

CHAPTER FIFTEEN

Yossef Bodansky's *The Secret History of the Iraq War* (HarperCollins, 2004) is a very good place to start for basic background and politics leading up to the second Gulf War. I recommend chapter 2, "The Gathering Storm," pp. 34–50.

Having fought in both Gulf Wars, I was again fortunate enough to have much firsthand knowledge, at least from an operational point of view, of these conflicts. My personal logbooks, diaries, and combat mission materials were used to reconstruct the flying scenes. I was aided by an interview with Dave "Mooman" Moody, Brig. Gen., USAF (ret).

Also utilized was the F-16CJ-1CL-1 checklist, Operation Iraqi Freedom Intelligence MisReps (Mission Reports), the 77th Fighter Squadron Air Tasking Orders covering March 22–April 13, 2003, and the USCENTAF "Operation Iraqi Freedom—By the Numbers" report, generated by the Assessment and Analysis Division, April 30, 2003.

See also Stephen Budiansky's *Air Power* (Penguin, 2004), pp. 406–41, and Marin Van Creveld's *The Age of Airpower* (PublicAffairs, 2011), pp. 438–31.

INDEX

C

D

слава героям
отечественной
войны! слава
сталинским
соколам!